I SAMUEL

VOLUME 8

The ANCHOR BIBLE is a fresh approach to the world's greatest classic. Its object is to make the Bible accessible to the modern reader; its method is to arrive at the meaning of biblical literature through exact translation and extended exposition, and to reconstruct the ancient setting of the biblical story, as well as the circumstances of its transcription and the characteristics of its transcribers.

THE ANCHOR BIBLE is a project of international and interfaith scope: Protestant, Catholic, and Jewish scholars from many countries contribute individual volumes. The project is not sponsored by any ecclesiastical organization and is not intended to reflect any particular theological doctrine. Prepared under our joint supervision, THE ANCHOR BIBLE is an effort to make available all the significant historical and linguistic knowledge which bears on the interpretation of the biblical record.

THE ANCHOR BIBLE is aimed at the general reader with no special formal training in biblical studies; yet, it is written with the most exacting standards of scholarship, reflecting the highest technical accomplishment.

This project marks the beginning of a new era of co-operation among scholars in biblical research, thus forming a common body of knowledge to be shared by all.

William Foxwell Albright
David Noel Freedman
GENERAL EDITORS

THE ANCHOR BIBLE

I SAMUEL

A NEW TRANSLATION
WITH INTRODUCTION, NOTES AND COMMENTARY
BY

P. KYLE McCARTER, JR.

THE ANCHOR BIBLE
DOUBLEDAY
NEW YORK LONDON TORONTO SYDNEY AUCKLAND

An Anchor Bible
PUBLISHED BY DOUBLEDAY
a division of Bantam Doubleday Dell Publishing Group, Inc.
1540 Broadway, New York, New York 10036

Library of Congress Cataloging-in-Publication Data
Bible. O.T. I Samuel. English. McCarter. 1980.
I Samuel.
(The Anchor Bible; v. 8)
Bibliography: p.
Includes index.
1. Bible. O.T. I Samuel—Commentaries.
I. McCarter, Pete Kyle, Jr. 1945- . II Title.
III. Series: Anchor Bible; v. 8.
BS192.2.A1 1964.G3 vol. 8 [BS1325.3] 220.7'7s
[222'.43'077] 79-7201
ISBN 0-385-50909-X

PRINTED IN THE UNITED STATES OF AMERICA

BVG 01

To Sherry Ann, Robert Kyle
and David Kyle McCarter

PREFACE

This commentary is written for two audiences. It is intended first of all for those readers of the Bible who, though they have no special training in its history and philology, wish to approach their task informed about the ancient context of the stories and alerted to the special qualities of the language. With this audience in mind I have identified in the NOTES all references in the narrative which might not be familiar to the non-specialist, I have tried to introduce technical discussions in an intelligible way, and I have designed the COMMENTS to serve as an ongoing interpretation of the story, providing continuity where the transitions are abrupt and highlighting features which seem especially important to the literary development of the story. I hope above all that I have done nothing to detract from the excellence of the Hebrew original, which needs little help from a commentator to tell its tale. The other audience addressed here is the community of biblical scholars. Because I hoped that they might find something useful in the book, I have not avoided technical discussions. I have grappled with the ponderous literary-critical issues and have attempted new solutions to a number of old problems of interpretation and translation.

The segregation of the *Textual Notes* from the other NOTES is meant to assist both audiences. It would be discourteous and presumptuous to ask every user of the NOTES to wade through great quantities of Hebrew and Greek in order to reach the general information located there, and the present arrangement will permit the reader who is not concerned with textual matters to ignore them. On the other hand I believed the text to be of such great importance in the study of Samuel that it could not be given less than a full treatment. The special apparatus is also intended, therefore, to enable scholars to isolate textual problems and focus attention on them.

This volume and its author are indebted in so many ways to Frank Moore Cross of Harvard University that it is not possible to list them all, but a few must be mentioned. It was Professor Cross who opened the door through which I entered upon this project in the first place. He provided me with photographs of all the unpublished Qumran materials, so that I might use them in establishing the text. He read portions of the completed manuscript and offered many suggestions for its improvement in his characteristically insightful and authoritative way. I am at a loss to find an adequate way to express my appreciation of his generosity.

Series editor David Noel Freedman and his assistant Michael O'Connor read the manuscript with thoroughness and patience and improved it immeasurably by their extensive comments. I have found it impossible to cite every contribution of theirs. It might suffice for me to confess that the first *Textual Note* was inspired by Freedman, that the last COMMENT was corrected by O'Connor's vigilance, and that there is more of their work in between than I am willing to admit in print.

I wish to thank David Baily Harned and my other colleagues at the University of Virginia for support and encouragement without which the completion of this volume would still lie in the future. Much of the work was done under the auspices of summer research grants awarded me by the University.

Previous Anchor Bible authors have spoken of the expertise and professionality of Ms. Eve F. Roshevsky and Mr. Robert W. Hewetson of Doubleday. I now know that, at least in their prefaces, those authors were telling the truth.

This book was written too quickly. I have tried to disguise this fact by both honest and dishonest means. But since the reviewers will probably discover it anyway, I wish to admit it in order to evoke sympathy for the family who have had to put up with a husband and father who wrote day and night for two years. To them I SAMUEL is dedicated.

P.K.Mc., Jr.
Christmas, 1978

CONTENTS

LIST OF MAPS

Maps by Rafael Palacios

PRINCIPAL ABBREVIATIONS

ANET^3	*Ancient Near Eastern Texts,* ed. J. B. Pritchard, 3d ed. Princeton University Press, 1969
AOTS	*Archaeology and Old Testament Study,* ed. D. Winton Thomas. Oxford University Press, 1967
BAR^1	*The Biblical Archaeologist Reader, 1,* eds. G. Ernest Wright and David Noel Freedman. Anchor Books. Garden City, N.Y.: Doubleday, 1961
BAR^2	*The Biblical Archaeologist Reader, 2,* eds. Edward F. Campbell, Jr., and David Noel Freedman. Anchor Books. Garden City, N.Y.: Doubleday, 1964
BAR^3	*The Biblical Archaeologist Reader, 3,* eds. Edward F. Campbell, Jr., and David Noel Freedman. Anchor Books. Garden City, N.Y.: Doubleday, 1970
BDB	F. Brown, S. R. Driver, and C. A. Briggs, eds. of W. Gesenius' *Hebrew and English Lexicon of the Old Testament.* Oxford University Press, 1907
(*bis*), (*tris*)	two occurrences, three occurrences
Bright, *History*	John Bright, *A History of Israel.* 2d ed. Philadelphia: Westminster, 1972
Budde	K. Budde, *Die Bücher Samuel**
c, cc	chapter, chapters
CAD	*The Assyrian Dictionary of the Oriental Institute of the University of Chicago,* 1965-
Caird	G. B. Caird, *The First and Second Books of Samuel**
Cross, *CMHE*	F. M. Cross, *Canaanite Myth and Hebrew Epic**
CTCA	*Corpus des tablettes en cunéiformes alphabét-*

* For the full citation, see the bibliography.

	iques, ed. Andrée Herdner. Mission de Ras Shamra, Tome X. Paris: Imprimerie Nationale, 1963†
CTH	*Catalogue des textes hittites,* ed. Emmanuel Laroche. 1956-58
Dhorme	E. P. Dhorme, *Les livres de Samuel**
DJD	Discoveries in the Judaean Desert (of Jordan)
Driver	S. R. Driver, *Notes on the Hebrew Text of the Books of Samuel**
EA	*Die El-Amarna-Tafeln,* ed. J. A. Knudtzon (= *Vorderasiatische Bibliothek* 2)
Fisher, *Ras Shamra Parallels*	*Ras Shamra Parallels,* ed. Loren R. Fisher. Analecta Orientalia 49, 50. Rome: PBI, 1972 (vol. 1), 1975 (vol. 2)
GK	*Gesenius' Hebrew Grammar,* ed. E. Kautzsch, tr. A. E. Cowley. 2d English ed. Oxford University Press, 1910
Gordon, *UT*	C. H. Gordon, *Ugaritic Textbook.* 4th ed. Rome: PBI, 1965
Hertzberg	H. W. Hertzberg, *I and II Samuel**
IB	*The Interpreter's Bible*
IDB	*The Interpreter's Dictionary of the Bible,* eds. G. A. Buttrick et al. 4 vols. Nashville: Abingdon, 1962
IDBSup	*The Interpreter's Dictionary of the Bible,* Supplementary Volume. 1976
Jastrow	M. Jastrow, *A Dictionary of the Targumim, the Talmud Babli and Yerushalmi, etc.* Brooklyn, N.Y.: Traditional Press, [1903]
Josephus *Ant.*	Josephus' *Jewish Antiquities*
KAI	*Kanaanäische und aramäische Inschriften,* by H. Donner and W. Röllig. Wiesbaden: Harrassowitz, 1962–64
KB	*Lexicon in Veteris Testamenti libros,* eds. L. Koehler and W. Baumgartner. Leiden: E. J. Brill, 1953
KJV	*The King James,* or *Authorized Version,* 1611
LXX	The Septuagint
LXX^{A}	The Codex Alexandrinus, a major uncial manuscript of the Septuagint

† Ugaritic passages are cited by the *CTCA* number followed in parentheses by the corresponding number in Gordon, *UT*.

* For the full citation, see the bibliography.

LXX[B]	The Codex Vaticanus, a major uncial manuscript of the Septuagint
LXX[L]	The so-called Lucianic manuscripts of the Septuagint
Moore, *Judges*	G. F. Moore, *A Critical and Exegetical Commentary on Judges*. ICC. New York: Charles Scribner's Sons, 1900
MS, MSS	manuscript, manuscripts
MT	The Masoretic Text
Noth, *History*	M. Noth, *The History of Israel,* tr. Peter R. Ackroyd. New York: Harper, 1960
Noth, *Israelitischen Personennamen*	M. Noth, *Die israelitischen Personennamen im Rahmen der gemeinsemitischen Namengebung*. BWANT 10. Stuttgart: W. Kohlhammer, 1928
Noth, *US*	M. Noth, *Überlieferungsgeschichtliche Studien**
OG	The Old Greek translation
OL	The Old Latin translations
Pedersen, *Israel*	Johannes Peder Ejler Pedersen, *Israel.* 4 vols. London: Oxford, 1940
PN	proper name
RS	Ras Shamra
RSV	*The Revised Standard Version,* 1946, 1952
Smith	H. P. Smith, *Samuel**
Stoebe	H. J. Stoebe, *Das erste Buch Samuelis**
Syr.	The Syriac translation or Peshitta
Targ.	The Targum (Jonathan)
TDOT	*Theological Dictionary of the Old Testament*
TWAT	*Theologisches Wörterbuch zum Alten Testament*
de Vaux, *Ancient Israel*	R. de Vaux, *Ancient Israel: Its Life and Institutions,* tr. John McHugh. 2 vols. New York: McGraw-Hill, 1961
v, vv	verse, verses
Vulg.	The Vulgate (Jerome's Latin translation)
Wellhausen	Julius Wellhausen, *Der Text der Bücher Samuelis**
(1), (2), etc.	first occurrence, second occurrence, etc.
4QSam[a,b,c]	Samuel manuscripts from Qumran Cave IV
[ ]	Words or phrases enclosed in brackets in the

* For the full citation, see the bibliography.

translation do not appear in the reconstructed Hebrew text. In most cases a proper name has been replaced by a pronoun or a pronoun by a proper name for the sake of the English translation.

JOURNALS AND SERIES

AASOR	Annual of the American Schools of Oriental Research
AB	The Anchor Bible, 1964–
AfO	*Archiv für Orientforschung*
AJSL	*American Journal of Semitic Languages and Literatures*
BA	*Biblical Archaeologist*
BASOR	*Bulletin of the American Schools of Oriental Research*
BBB	Bonner biblische Beiträge
BeO	*Bibbia e Oriente*
BJRL	*Bulletin of the John Rylands University Library of Manchester*
BO	*Bibliotheca orientalis*
BR	*Biblical Research*
BS	*Bibliotheca sacra* (Dallas)
BT	*The Bible Translator*
BWANT	Beiträge zur Wissenschaft vom alten und neuen Testament
BZAW	Beihefte zur *ZAW*
CBQ	*Catholic Biblical Quarterly*
ConB	Coniectanea biblica
CQR	*Church Quarterly Review*
CTM	*Concordia Theological Monthly*
DTT	*Dansk teologisk Tidsskrift*
EH	Exegetisches Handbuch zum alten Testament
EvT	*Evangelische Theologie*
ExpT	*Expository Times*
FRLANT	Forschungen zur Religion und Literatur des alten und neuen Testaments
HSM	Harvard Semitic Monographs
HTR	*Harvard Theological Review*
HUCA	*Hebrew Union College Annual*
ICC	International Critical Commentary
IEJ	*Israel Exploration Journal*
JANES	*Journal of the Ancient Near Eastern Society of Columbia University*
JAOS	*Journal of the American Oriental Society*

JBL	*Journal of Biblical Literature*
JBR	*Journal of Bible and Religion*
JCS	*Journal of Cuneiform Studies*
JNES	*Journal of Near Eastern Studies*
JQR	*Jewish Quarterly Review*
JRAS	*Journal of the Royal Asiatic Society*
JSS	*Journal of Semitic Studies*
JTS	*Journal of Theological Studies*
KAT	Kommentar zum alten Testament (Leipzig, Gütersloh)
MUSJ	*Mélanges de l'université Saint-Joseph*
NedTTs	*Nederlands theologisch Tijdschrift*
OLZ	*Orientalistische Literaturzeitung*
OTS	*Oudtestamentische Studien*
PEQ	*Palestine Exploration Quarterly*
RB	*Revue biblique*
RHPR	*Revue d'histoire et de philosophie religieuses*
RSO	*Rivista degli studi orientali*
SBLDS	Society of Biblical Literature Dissertation Series
SBT	Studies in Biblical Theology
SOTSMS	Society for Old Testament Study Monograph Series
ST	*Studia Theologica*
TBl	*Theologische Blätter*
TLZ	*Theologische Literaturzeitung*
TS	*Theological Studies*
TZ	*Theologische Zeitschrift*
UF	*Ugarit-Forschungen*
VT	*Vetus Testamentum*
VTSup	*VT* Supplements
WMANT	Wissenschaftliche Monographien zum alten und neuen Testament
WZ	*Wissenschaftliche Zeitschrift der Martin-Luther-Universität* (Halle-Wittenberg)
ZAW	*Zeitschrift für die alttestamentliche Wissenschaft*
ZDMGSup	*Zeitschrift der deutschen morgenländischen Gesellschaft* Supplements
ZKWL	*Zeitschrift für kirchliche Wissenschaft und kirchliches Leben*
ZTK	*Zeitschrift für Theologie und Kirche*

INTRODUCTION

I. THE TITLE OF THE BOOK

Originally the Books of Samuel were one book. The division into two derives from the Greek and Latin traditions of the text, not the Hebrew. In classical antiquity books were written on scrolls of more or less fixed length, and because the Book of Samuel, like that of Kings or Chronicles, was twice too long, it was divided into two in early MSS of the Septuagint (LXX) or Greek Bible. The rationale behind the choice of a place to separate the books seems clear enough: it was chosen to conform to the custom of concluding a book with the death of a major figure—of Jacob and Joseph at the end of Genesis, of Moses at the end of Deuteronomy, of Joshua at the end of Joshua, and thus of Saul at the end of I Samuel. The new arrangement was perpetuated in the Vulgate and so into modern times.[1] But the two books were originally one in the Jewish canon. The great Samuel scroll from Qumran (4QSam[a]) includes both, the Talmud regularly refers to a single Book of Samuel, and the marginal notes of the Masoretes assume a one-book arrangement.[2] The division into two books of a Hebrew text of Samuel is first attested in a handwritten MS of the fifteenth century, and the earliest printed edition with such an arrangement was the so-called first Rabbinic Bible of 1516/17, edited by Felix Pratensis and published in Venice by Daniel Bomberg. The division gained a kind of ongoing sanction from its use in Bomberg's authoritative second Rabbinic Bible of 1524/25, edited by Jacob ben Chayyim, which enjoyed currency until the present century.

In the LXX the title of our book is *basileiōn a'*, that is, 1 Kingdoms, since the Books of Samuel and Kings are grouped together in the Greek tradition as 1-4 Kingdoms or Reigns (*basileiōn a'-d'*). Doubtless the ancient Hebrew title, Samuel, arose from the fact that the great prophet was the leading figure at the beginning of the book, but the two-book arrangement created the curious circumstance that Samuel is not even mentioned in the second book that bears his name. It seems to have been assumed in antiquity that the title was assigned because Samuel actually *wrote* all or

[1] The church fathers were aware of the originality of the one-book arrangement. Cf. Eusebius of Caesarea, *Ecclesiastical History* 6.25.2, and Jerome's preface to the Books of Samuel in the Vulgate.

[2] I Sam 28:24 is annotated as *ḥṣy hspr bpswqym*, "half of the book in verses," and at the end of II Samuel appears the notice *skwm hpswqym šlspr 'lp whmš m'wt wššh*, "the sum total of the verses in the book: 1506."

part of the book(s). In particular, Talmudic tradition (Babylonian Baba Batra 14b) held that Samuel was the author of the book that was named for him and also of Judges, at least of the narratives concerning events that occurred before his death (I Sam 25:1), the rest having been supplied by the prophets Nathan and Gad. But scholars have long agreed that this notion, which was based at least in part on an interpretation of the reference in I Chron 29:29 to "the Chronicles of Samuel, the seer . . . Nathan, the prophet . . . [and] Gad, the visionary" (*dibrê šĕmû'ēl hārō'eh . . . nātān hannābî' . . . gād haḥōzeh*), has little to recommend it and that Samuel's participation in the story is enough to account for the traditional attachment of his name to it.

II. TEXT AND VERSIONS

The received Hebrew text of Samuel in its Masoretic dress (MT) is in poor repair. It is a short text, but its shortness is not the wholesome shortness of a text free of expansion and interpolation; rather it is the result of countless copying errors and omissions, some of them extensive, scattered throughout the book. This unfortunate situation was recognized centuries ago,[3] but the first systematic attempt to correct it did not come until 1842 in Otto Thenius' commentary in the Kurzgefasstes exegetisches Handbuch zum alten Testament (KeH) series. Thenius believed the text of the Greek Bible or Septuagint (LXX), which is much fuller than that of the MT and often widely divergent from it, could be used to recover original readings at many points where the MT was corrupt, and he set out to do this on a grand scale. But Thenius' textual decisions often seemed arbitrary and subjective to his readers, and for this he was severely criticized, especially by Max Löhr, who succeeded him in responsibility for the KeH Samuel volume.

So it was not Thenius who put the study of the text of Samuel on a fully scientific footing. This task remained for Julius Wellhausen, whose monograph *Der Text der Bücher Samuelis untersucht,* published in 1871, is generally acknowledged to be a major landmark in the development of the textual criticism of the Bible. By expert and judicious comparison of the evidence of the MT, the LXX, and the other versions, Wellhausen established the outline of an eclectic text of Samuel which better than any other reconstruction has withstood the influx of new data brought about by subsequent research and discovery. The influence of Wellhausen's work was widespread, and the major studies of Samuel from the late nineteenth and early twentieth centuries—those of H. P. Smith, Budde, Dhorme, and others—all show its impact. Of these the most important textually was S. R. Driver's *Notes on the Hebrew Text of the Books of Samuel* (1890); though Driver fell short of Wellhausen in the latter's keen sense of the independent importance of the LXX, his *Notes* drew heavily and successfully upon the conclusions of the earlier work and went beyond it in attention to the details of Hebrew grammar and syntax.

[3] The Huguenot Hebraist Louis Cappel (Ludovicus Cappellus) in his *Critica sacra* (1634) came to this conclusion on the basis of his study of the ancient versions. One still finds a number of the suggestions from his *Commentarii* (1689) for the emendation of the MT of Samuel cited in the apparatus of modern commentaries.

To critics like Wellhausen, Driver, and their followers the comparative use of the LXX and the other ancient versions seemed to go a long way toward clearing up the problems in the MT of Samuel. Difficulties remained, but these were no more extensive than those encountered in other books. Not everyone, however, was convinced. Certain questions stood in the way of full confidence in the results achieved by the comparative method. Was it safe to assume that the distinctive readings of the LXX reflected the details of a divergent Hebrew original, as Wellhausen and the rest took for granted, or had the Greek translators artificially "corrected" a text that was close to that of the MT? After all, even Wellhausen and Driver assumed that the LXX often paraphrased its Hebrew *Vorlage* and thus that many discrepancies in the texts of the MT and the LXX were not due to differences in the Hebrew MSS that stood behind the two traditions. Was it not then possible, some skeptics asked, that *every* apparently superior reading in the LXX was a product of the translation process?[4] There was no incontrovertible reply to such questions, and in the twentieth century confidence in the usefulness of the LXX of Samuel eroded steadily in many circles. Thus, for example, when the meticulous textual studies of P. A. H. de Boer appeared in 1938 and 1949, they reflected a completely negative attitude toward the LXX.

The recovery, beginning in 1952, of ancient Hebrew MSS of Samuel from Cave IV at Qumran[5] began a revolution in the study of the text. Three MSS were found: (1) 4QSam^a, a large, fairly well preserved scroll dating from 50-25 B.C. and containing in fragmentary form parts of much of I and II Samuel;[6] (2) 4QSam^b, a poorly preserved MS of the mid-third century B.C. containing fragments of a small part of 1 Samuel;[7] and (3) 4QSam^c, a MS of the early first century B.C. preserving small fragments of I Samuel 25 and II Samuel 14-15.[8] In these ancient docu-

[4] The issue, then, was the very nature of the Greek Bible. Moreover, the debate over LXX origins was being carried on along other lines. The generally accepted thesis of Paul Anton de Lagarde that behind the multiplicity of surviving recensions of the LXX lay one original Greek translation was challenged beginning in 1915 in a series of studies by Paul E. Kahle, who contended that there had never been one original Greek translation but that a variety of vulgar and "unofficial" translations, which arose locally in Greek-speaking Jewish communities (in similar fashion to the Targums among Aramaic speakers), were eventually assembled into a kind of "official" version (analogous to the Targums Onkelos and Jonathan). For bibliography and a full discussion, see Jellicoe, *Septuagint*, 1-73 and esp. 5-9, 59-63.

[5] On the discovery and archaeology of Cave IV, see the discussion of de Vaux in *Qumrân Grotte 4*, 3-22.

[6] The MS is unpublished. Cf. Cross, "New Qumrân Biblical Fragment" and Oldest Manuscripts," 165, n. 40. On the date, see Cross, "Development of the Jewish Scripts," 16-18 and fig. 2, line 3.

[7] Partially published in Cross, "Oldest Manuscripts," 165-172. On the date, see most recently Cross, "Theory of Local Texts," 311.

[8] To be published by Eugene C. Ulrich in *BASOR*. On the date, cf. Cross, "Contribution of the Qumran Discoveries," 285.

ments, older by a millennium than any extant exemplar of the Masoretic tradition, F. M. Cross recognized a textual type widely at variance with that of the MT but consistently close to the one reflected by the LXX.[9] This observation seriously undermined the position of those who had depreciated the usefulness of the LXX for textual reconstruction. It was no longer possible to suppose that the peculiarities of the LXX were translational in origin now that ancient Hebrew MSS closely aligned with the reconstructed *Vorlage* of the LXX had appeared. At this point the older textual studies, especially those of Wellhausen, deserved and gained renewed respect.

Further work on the scrolls showed that the situation was somewhat more complex. Throughout I Samuel the text of the original Greek translation of the Bible, the so-called Old Greek (OG), is readily accessible through the Codex Vaticanus (LXX^B), a major uncial MS of the LXX.[10] But the text type of the Qumran Samuel MSS proved to stand less close in detail to the text of the LXX^B than to that of the so-called Lucianic MSS of the LXX (LXX^L), the independent importance of which Wellhausen had recognized already in 1871.[11] Now the text of the LXX^L has three distinct layers or strata. The basic stratum is the OG. The latest stratum is a series of additions made (at least according to tradition)[12] by the church father Lucian (fl. A.D. 300) with the intention of bringing an older Greek text into closer conformity with the currently established Hebrew text, a forerunner of the MT. An intermediate, "proto-Lucianic" stratum is assumed to exist because distinctive Lucianic readings, differing from those of the OG, are sometimes reflected in pre-Lucianic witnesses, notably in the writings of the Jewish historian Josephus (first century A.D.) and in the Old Latin translation (OL; second century A.D.);[13] nevertheless, this stratum, apart from the distinctive readings it shares with Josephus, the OL, etc., stands so close to the OG that it cannot be supposed to have been an independent translation. Reckoning from these data Cross concluded that the proto-Lucianic text represents a revision of the OG toward a Hebrew text type from Palestine (and thus known to Josephus), of which the Qumran Samuel scrolls are exemplars.[14] Cross took this Palestinian text type to be a third tradition, inde-

[9] Cross, "New Qumrân Biblical Fragment," 15-26; "Oldest Manuscripts," 165-172.

[10] See Shenkel, *Greek Text of Kings,* 7-8 and bibliography cited there.

[11] *Der Text der Bücher Samuelis,* 221-224. On the Lucianic MSS in general, see below, p. 9.

[12] Cf. Jellicoe, *Septuagint,* 157-158.

[13] For a complete list of sources of Lucianic readings, see Tov, "Lucian," 104-105.

[14] See most recently Cross, "Theory of Local Texts," 306-320, especially his reply to the criticisms of Tov, 314-315.

pendent of the traditions of both the MT and the OG, though ultimately related to the latter.[15]

For these reasons there are several ancient witnesses that compete for the attention of the modern text critic, each with a claim to originality at any given point in Samuel. It is no longer possible to defend a textual reconstruction that relies exclusively on the MT or turns to the versions only when the MT is unintelligible. Wherever alternative readings exist—that is, wherever two or more of the principal ancient witnesses differ from each other and the Hebrew original of each can be determined—the critic must weigh the merits of each reading according to the accepted rules of textual analysis. As the *Textual Notes* in this volume show, none of the ancient witnesses to the text of Samuel has a monopoly on primitive readings. At times the MT must be followed, at other times the LXX^B; often both must be rejected in favor of the evidence of the LXX^L and/or the scrolls. Only an eclectic reconstruction can bypass the haplographic defectiveness of the received Hebrew text on the one hand and the expansionistic conflateness of the Old Palestinian tradition on the other, and arrive at an approximation, however rough, of the primitive text of Samuel.

The chief characteristics of the most important ancient witnesses to the text of I Samuel are listed below:

1. *The Masoretic Text* (*MT*). The MT of Samuel is a defective text. It has suffered extensively from haplography, that is, from scribal omission triggered by repeated sequences of letters, most often at the ends of words or phrases (*homoioteleuton*). As the *Textual Notes* show, some of the haplographies are of extraordinary length. On the positive side it should be noted that the MT, however riddled with holes in its present form, harks back to a legitimately short textual tradition that was generally free

[15] With the goal of imposing order on the great mass of data Cross developed a theory of local texts in an effort to describe the history of the Hebrew text of the Bible. It may be summarized as follows, insofar as it pertains to the text of Samuel (cf. esp. Cross, "Contribution of the Qumran Discoveries," 93-95; "Theory of Local Texts," 306-320). Distinct local traditions began to develop in the Jewish communities in Babylon and Palestine during the Persian Period. It was a Palestinian text that was drawn upon by the Chronicler early in the fourth century for his historiographical work. It was also a Palestinian text that, perhaps a century later, was carried to Egypt and, after undergoing an independent development there, was used as the basis for the translation of the OG in the third or second centuries B.C.; thus the Egyptian and Palestinian texts are ultimately related. The latter continued to hold sway in Palestine—it is reflected in the Qumran Samuel scrolls, in the proto-Lucianic revision of the OG, and in Josephus—until the reintroduction of the Babylonian text sometime before the beginning of the Christian era. During the centuries of isolation since its removal from Palestine the Babylonian text had suffered extensive haplography; nevertheless it was chosen as the text of Samuel in the first recensional efforts that eventually led to the MT. So it is that a local Babylonian text type is now reflected in the MT, an Egyptian type in the OG (LXX^B), and a Palestinian type in a substratum of the Lucianic MSS of the LXX (LXX^L).

of the kinds of expansion displayed by some of the versions; thus it often provides us with a corrective to the fuller text of the LXX$^{(BL)}$.

2. *The Codex Vaticanus* (*LXX*^{B}). The LXX^{B} in I Samuel represents a Greek tradition, which, because it seems to have escaped the systematic revisions to which other Greek MSS were subjected, provides a direct link with the OG. The OG proves to have been a fuller text than the ancestral text of the MT or, for example, the text of 4QSam^{b} (see below), but it was generally superior to the MT in the latter's present, defective condition. A point that has not received sufficient stress is that the LXX^{B} has itself suffered from frequent haplography, though not nearly to the extent of the MT. It serves as the basic text of the Larger Cambridge edition of the LXX, from which citations in the present volume are drawn.[16]

3. *The Codex Alexandrinus* (*LXX*^{A}). The LXX^{A}, the second major uncial MS witnessing to the Greek text of Samuel (missing in I Sam 12:20-14:9),[17] is of considerably less value than the LXX^{B} since (in Samuel) it shows systematic revision toward the developing tradition of the MT.[18]

4. *The Lucianic Manuscripts* (*LXX*^{L}). We considered above the three strata of the LXX^{L}. The latest of these, since it is basically a series of revisions toward the established ancestral text of the MT, is (like LXX^{A}) of limited usefulness. The proto-Lucianic stratum, however, provides a valuable witness to the Old Palestinian tradition described by Cross, insofar as (if Cross is correct) it represents a revision of the OG toward this tradition. The independent evidence of the LXX^{L}, therefore, especially when supported by one or more of the other witnesses to the Palestinian text (4QSam^{a,b,c}, Josephus, the OL), may be set beside the readings of the MT and the OG for comparative evaluation. The chief witnesses to the LXX^{L} in Samuel are the minuscules boc_2e_2.[19] The three strata in these MSS—the OG, the proto-Lucianic stratum with its revisions toward the expansionistic Palestinian tradition, and the Lucianic additions—give them an extraordinarily full, conflate appearance. The user of the *Textual Notes* will observe that time and again the reading of the LXX^{L} conflates the readings of the MT and the LXX^{B}.

[16] *The Old Testament in Greek . . .*, eds. A. E. Brooke, N. McLean, and H. St. J. Thackeray. Volume II. *The Later Historical Books*. Part I. *I and II Samuel*. London: Cambridge University Press, 1927.

[17] See Jellicoe, *Septuagint*, 183-188.

[18] That is, it is heavily influenced by Origen's revision of the Greek text toward the established ancestral text of the MT in the fifth column of the Hexapla. Thus the LXX^{A} is the best witness to the hexaplaric text of Samuel. Cf. Johnson, *Hexaplarische Rezension*.

[19] These are the sigla of the Larger Cambridge LXX. In other editions (Göttingen, Holmes and Parsons) these MSS are identified as 19+108, 82, 127, and 93 respectively.

5. *The Old Latin* (*OL*). The OL translations—plural because there was probably no single parent text but rather a number of originally independent translations—arose in the second and third centuries A.D.[20] As translations of the LXX they do not offer independent witness to the Hebrew text, but they do seem frequently to reflect original readings of the OG and so are of considerable importance to the text critic. As the *Textual Notes* in the present volume will show, the OL in Samuel regularly sides with the LXX against the MT but frequently diverges from the LXX^B on the side of the LXX^L and other witnesses to the proto-Lucianic tradition. "Whether the Itala [= the OL] was translated from the proto-Lucianic recension or translated from the Old Greek," writes Cross, "is not certain and must be determined in future studies. I am inclined to assign its base provisionally to the proto-Lucianic tradition."[21]

6. *The Targum Jonathan* (*Targ.*). The standard Jewish Aramaic version of Samuel (and the Former and Latter Prophets as a whole) is the Targum Jonathan. Because it has been reworked to conform to the developing MT, the Targ. is of little independent value to the text critic except occasionally where it reflects a different interpretation of the consonantal text from that of the Masoretic punctators.

7. *The Syriac* (*Syr.*). In general the Syr. or Peshiṭta stands close to the MT, though, as Driver observes, not as close as the Targ. Driver also (lxxi, n. 2) provides a short list of passages in which the Syr. sides with the LXX^L against the MT. It seems likely that behind the Peshiṭta in its standardized form lies an old Syriac translation of some utility in recovering the primitive text, though the older readings are often difficult to perceive because of the subsequent correction toward the developing text of the MT. Doubtless there was also some late contamination by the readings of the LXX, but (contrary to the assumption of many critics) agreement between the Syr. and the LXX often reflects shared readings in the Hebrew *Vorlagen* of the OG and Old Syriac translations.

8. *The Vulgate* (*Vulg.*). Jerome's translation, because it was based on the established proto-Masoretic text, infrequently diverges from the MT; and where it *is* different, it usually reflects no more than Jerome's acquaintance with the LXX or the work of a later Greek translator and so is of little independent value to the critic.

9. *The Archaic Samuel Scroll* (*4QSam^b*). The older of the two principal MSS from Qumran Cave IV that witness to the text of I Samuel (see above) is an early exemplar of a textual tradition of high quality. In the *editio princeps* of one group of its fragments Cross characterized it as follows:

[20] See Jellicoe, *Septuagint*, 249-251.
[21] "Theory of Local Texts," 312-313; cf. also Driver, lxxvii-lxxxii.

> Its affinities with the tradition to which the *Vorlage* of the Old Greek belongs is most important, and cannot be neglected in developing new methods and evaluations in future critical studies of the text of Samuel. Nevertheless, the most extraordinary characteristic of the text of 4QSam^b is the high proportion of original readings which it preserves, whether it be in agreement with the Greek, or in agreement with MT, or against both in its several unique readings.[22]

As the *Textual Notes* in the present volume show, analysis of the rest of the fragments of the scroll lends further weight to this conclusion.

10. *The Larger Samuel Scroll* (*4QSam^a*). 4QSam^a is a later exemplar of the textual tradition represented by 4QSam^b and shares many of the merits of the older MS. It is a fuller text, however, and its fullness betokens an expansionistic tendency in the developing Palestinian tradition. We have already noted its special affinity with the proto-Lucianic stratum of the LXX^L, with the OL, and with Josephus—in short, with the various witnesses to the Old Palestinian text.

11. *Josephus'* Jewish Antiquities (Ant.). References in the *Ant.* to the events in I Samuel imply a textual tradition in close agreement with 4QSam^a and the earlier stratum of the LXX^L and seem, therefore, to reflect Josephus' use of a developed Palestinian text in a Greek form.[23]

22 "Oldest Manuscripts," 172.
23 This is the conclusion of Ulrich, "Qumran Text."

III. LITERARY HISTORY

The necessary preoccupation of Samuel scholarship with textual studies may have retarded somewhat the higher criticism of the book. The great scholars of the nineteenth and early twentieth centuries diverted to the investigation of the text considerable energy that might otherwise have been spent in source-critical analysis, and more than one recent student of Samuel, whose ambition it was to advance our understanding of the literary history of the book, has found himself engaged largely or wholly in textual work. This situation is probably one of the reasons that so little agreement exists today about the original formation of the Samuel materials. The higher criticism of Samuel has not been neglected, however; the literature is replete with longer and shorter studies reflecting the perspective of every school of biblical scholarship. Enough has been done, at any rate, that we might reasonably expect Samuel research to have kept pace with the work on most other books, were it not for the fact that the source-critical problems encountered in Samuel are so complex within the book itself and so subtle in their relations to other parts of the Bible as to have defied generally accepted solutions in most cases.

The narratives about Samuel, Saul, and David that make up our book have a heterogeneous appearance even to the untrained eye. Numerous internal thematic tensions, duplications, and contradictions stand in the way of a straightforward reading of the story. The figure of Samuel dominates the first three chapters, then vanishes suddenly and completely in cc 4-6, only to return again in c 7. In c 8 kingship is depicted as wholly offensive to Yahweh, while in cc 9-10 the first king is anointed at Yahweh's command. Saul becomes king by lottery in 10:17-27 but, apparently, by popular proclamation in c 11. He seems to be rejected by Yahweh not once but twice (in cc 13 and 15), and he acquires the services of David not once but twice (in cc 16 and 17). There are two accounts of David's betrothal to a daughter of Saul (c 18), two of his defection to the Philistine king of Gath (cc 21 and 27), and two of his refusal to take Saul's life (cc 24 and 26).

The pioneering scholars of the early nineteenth century (Eichhorn, Thenius), aware of these inconsistencies and mindful of the successes of parallel source theories in dealing with similar problems in other books of the Bible, posited the existence of discrete strands within the Samuel narratives. Their successors (Stade, Kuenen, and especially Wellhausen) identified two such strands in particular: (i) an early stratum (including I Sam 9:1-10:16; 11; 13-14), which despite its romantic atmosphere was believed to preserve information of considerable historical value and which presents a generally favorable view of the institution of monarchy; (ii) a late stratum (including I Sam 7-8; 10:17-27; 12; 15), which was assumed to derive from a time so far removed from the events it describes as to be generally devoid of historical value and which views the institution of monarchy with grave suspicion in keeping, it was supposed, with the theocratic ideal of the post-Exilic (and thus post-monarchical) community; it was also said to exhibit the particular influences of an ongoing Deuteronomic (hence Deuteronomistic) theology. Still other scholars (Cornill, Budde) specifically associated the two strata with the Pentateuchal sources J and E (thus requiring a considerable upward adjustment of the date of the late stratum) and distinguished from the latter the Deuteronomistic elements, which they believed to have come in still later, a contribution of the redactor of the older sources. The work of Budde in particular seems to have led to an orthodoxy of sorts at the beginning of the twentieth century: while some scholars clung to positions close to that of Wellhausen (e.g. Smith), more (e.g. Driver) seem to have been persuaded first that the late or "anti-monarchical" stratum could be equated loosely or closely with the Elohistic source of the Pentateuch and second that the whole had been subjected to a late, more or less extensive, Deuteronomistic revision.

In light of subsequent developments it seems fair to say that in this early period Samuel scholarship was not yet free of the dominating influence of Pentateuchal criticism. It remained for the next generation of scholars to break away from this influence and reevaluate the problems on their own terms. While a few (Eissfeldt, Hölscher) continued to maintain the existence of continuous narrative strands in some form, many others came under the influence of a kind of fragmentary hypothesis, associated especially with Hugo Gressmann, according to which the book grew from a variety of independent narrative units of larger and smaller size, which were combined editorially at a late date. There was an increasing tendency to view the strata, whether taken as early (Lods, cf. Eissfeldt) or late (Pfeiffer, Press, Weiser), as composite; the older material that formed the basic narrative was thought to derive from several discrete sources and the later material to represent a series of progressive redactions that gave the book its present shape and import. The early stratum was no longer assumed to be of uniformly high historical value, and estimates of the historical value of the late stratum were revised upward (Weiser; see below).

An early and highly influential advocate of the composite nature of the older materials was Leonhard Rost, who used stylistic and thematic arguments to isolate distinct and originally independent narrative sources within the early stratum. In particular he identified an old history of the succession to David in II Sam 9-20 + I Kings 1-2 and an even more ancient "ark narrative" in I Sam 4:1b-7:1 + II Sam 6 (see below, "The Ark Narrative"). Though modified in many details, Rost's *Thronnachfolge Davids* has remained the starting point in the discussion of the sources of Samuel, and while there is still wide disagreement about the nature of the later materials, contemporary scholarship, with rare exceptions (Schulte), is close to consensus in sustaining Rost's view of the early materials in the book as originally unrelated narratives of diverse origin and point of view.

Martin Noth's *Überlieferungsgeschichtliche Studien* (1943) with its hypothesis of an Exilic, Deuteronomistic history extending from Deuteronomy through II Kings has had an important effect on the discussion of the late stratum of Samuel, which Noth does not distinguish from the Deuteronomistic redaction. It was the Deuteronomistic editor, he says, who brought the older materials together for the first time and incorporated them into his history by a series of redactional links and editorial expansions, the so-called "anti-monarchical" stratum of the book, all of which is from his hand (I Sam 7:2-8:22; 10:17-27a; 12:1-25). Noth's work, therefore, represents a kind of renewal of Wellhausen's two-layer analysis, though with due adjustment of many details. Among the voices dissenting from this conclusion the most influential has been that of Artur Weiser, who has repeatedly denied the unity of the anti-monarchical stratum. While not ruling out the possibility of a final Deuteronomistic version of the whole, Weiser argues that behind the stories in the late stratum lies a variety of tradition, by no means uniformly devoid of historical value, which has as its common denominator a prophetic interpretation of history. At the present time Weiser's insistence upon a pre-Deuteronomistic prophetic layer within the late stratum enjoys wide acceptance (Fohrer, Kaiser, Birch), though whether the older layer itself represents a literary unit (contrary to Weiser's arguments) or not remains an open question. Nor, as we are about to see, can the unity of the Deuteronomistic layer itself be taken for granted; a number of scholars now prefer to describe it as dual (Cross) or plural (Smend, Dietrich, Veijola), positing two or more successive revisions of the ancient materials from a Deuteronomistic point of view.

The critical positions adopted in the present volume are reviewed below.

THE DEUTERONOMISTIC HISTORY

Deuteronomism was a style of theology that drew its major tenets from the teachings of the Book of Deuteronomy. It stressed centralization of worship in Jerusalem, obedience to Deuteronomic law, and the avoidance of any kind of apostasy, all according to a rigid system of reward and punishment. That the entire history recorded in Deuteronomy through II Kings is the work of a single Deuteronomistic theologian (Dtr) was, as we have already seen, the thesis of Martin Noth. According to Noth this writer was looking backward from the Exile at the experience of Israel, which he saw as an unmitigated disaster, a long history of sin and punishment culminating in the fall of the state, in the aftermath of which his own generation was living, and he collected, organized, and annotated his sources into an extended historical work reflecting this perspective. Noth's critics, however, have had difficulty accepting his analysis of the Deuteronomist's view of Israel's past as wholly negative, and some (von Rad, Cross) have pointed out at least one clearly positive theme in the Deuteronomistic presentation of the history, viz. that which is founded in the divine promises of dynasty to David. The presence of such a theme offers a note of hope and suggests that the Deuteronomistic history might have had a constructive function in an age when the house of David could still be appealed to as a source of confidence and an impetus to reform. Such considerations and others have led Cross to posit in the Deuteronomistic redaction of the larger history two editions, one from Josianic times (Dtr_1), the other Exilic (Dtr_2). It was a Josianic writer, he says, who gave the material in Deuteronomy through II Kings its primary shape, a history written to support the reform of Josiah with its emphasis upon the priority of the Jerusalem temple and allegiance to the Davidic king; the denunciation of idolatry is to be understood not as bitter reflection on a hopeless situation but as reinforcement of the call to reform. The smaller task that remained for the Exilic Deuteronomist, then, was to bring the earlier work up to date and provide an explanation for the failure of the Josianic reform (this explanation he found principally in the sins of Manasseh, Josiah's grandfather).

The most striking aspect of the Deuteronomistic redaction of Samuel, whether Josianic or Exilic, is its sparseness. The hand or hands that imposed such a rigid structure on the sources of Judges on the one hand and those of Kings on the other seem(s) to have found little to do here. Our discussion below will suggest that this was because the sources of Samuel most often came into Deuteronomic circles as narratives of considerable length, already arranged in accordance with a "proto-Deuteronomic" viewpoint. It is sufficient to state at this point that the characteristic editorial touch of the school is light here. For this reason if we follow Cross's description of the larger history, we shall have to distinguish only one verse (12:25) from the rest as a contribution of the Exilic writer.[24] Wherever

[24] See Cross, *CMHE*, 178, n. 17, and 287.

else thematic or stylistic considerations enable us to recognize Deuteronomistic materials we may regard them as from the hand of the Josianic historian, and so we can treat the Deuteronomistic redaction of the book almost as if it were a monolithic whole.

The following is a tabulation of the Deuteronomistic additions to I Samuel, identifiable either because they display the peculiar concerns and devices of the Josianic historian (nos. 1, 6-9) or because they contain characteristically Deuteronomistic clichés (nos. 2-5); for details the corresponding NOTES and COMMENTS should be consulted.

1) The oracle against the house of Eli: 2:27-36 (+3:11-14). This passage, which is replete with the phrases and devices of the Josianic historian, is intended to associate the death of Eli and his sons (4:12-22) with the massacre of the priests of Nob (22:6-23) and the rejection of Abiathar in favor of Zadok, the primogenitor of the dominant priestly family of Jerusalem (cf. I Kings 2:26-27,35b). In this way the old stories are made to express the Deuteronomistic polemic against the non-Jerusalemite priesthood—the priests of the "high places."

2) Additions to the stories of Eli and Samuel: 4:18b; 7:2aβ-4,6b (and the summaries in vv 13-14,15-17). The editor's purpose was to incorporate the stories of Eli and Samuel into the Deuteronomistic theology of history as found in the Book of Judges (see below).

3) An interpolation in Yahweh's reply to the people's demand for a king: 8:8. The insertion was meant to associate the people's behavior with the pattern of repeated apostasy that Deuteronomistic theology found throughout the history of Israel.

4) Additions to Samuel's farewell address: 12:6-15,19b(?),20b-22, 24-25. The expansion of Samuel's speech prepares it to serve in the series of addresses by major figures (Moses, Joshua, Solomon) that structure the larger history (see below).

5) The notices about Saul's kingship: 13:1-2; 14:47-51. The inclusion of such archival material is characteristic of the Deuteronomistic treatment of the period of the kings.

6) Revision of the account of the battle in the Valley of the Terebinth: c 17 *passim*. The popular Jerusalemite story of David's victory over a Philistine champion overlies the old battle report that originally stood at this point in the history of David's rise to power. Though the precise extent of the secondary material cannot be determined and the time of its incorporation cannot be said with certainty to have been Josianic, it does share some features with the kind of Deuteronomistic expansion found in subsequent passages.

7) Additions to the story of David and Jonathan: 20:11-17,23,40-42. The expansion points ahead to events in the succession narrative (especially II Samuel 9), the next great narrative complex included in the

larger (Deuteronomistic) history, and puts explicit statements about David's future kingship in the mouth of Jonathan.

8) The first account of David's refusal to take Saul's life: 23:14-24:23. Though partially constructed of older materials this passage is fundamentally a tendentious retelling of the old story in c 26, putting Saul in a most unfavorable light and showing him openly acknowledging David's future kingship. As in the additions to c 20 (see above) there are also explicit connections made with subsequent parts of the Deuteronomistic history.

9) An interpolation in Abigail's speech: 25:28-31. The insertion transforms David's future wife into a kind of prophetess, who foresees the dynastic promise to the house of David in phrases that explicitly anticipate the Josianic rhetoric of the oracle of Nathan, which now stands at the end of the history of David's rise in II Samuel 7.

It seems clear from this tabulation that the Deuteronomist's purpose in reworking these materials was first of all to impose a structure on them whereby they could be incorporated into his larger history.[25] The additions to c 7, especially the summarizing formulae in vv 13-17, mark the passage as the end of the story of a judge. The notice in 13:1, on the other hand, is the formula by which a king's reign is introduced. The unit embraced by these verses (cc 8-12) is thus marked off as transitional between the period of the judges and the age of the kings according to the larger divisions of the history. This great turning point is reflected upon in the expansions of Samuel's farewell address in c 12, which, like Joshua's long speech at the end of the conquest and the beginning of the period of the judges (Joshua 23), provides Deuteronomistic commentary on the transition.

It follows that the stories of Samuel, Saul, and the young David stand at mid-career in the Deuteronomistic history. The annotations of the historian are both retrospective and prospective. On the one hand the life and work of Samuel are incorporated into the Deuteronomistic theology of history as it pertains particularly to the preceding period, that described in the Book of Judges, with its fourfold pattern of apostasy, punishment, repentance, and deliverance through the agency of a "judge" (cf. the NOTE at 7:2b-4 and the COMMENT on 7:2-17). On the other hand the Deuteronomistic theology of the Books of Kings is anticipated in the additions to the stories of the young David, insofar as these additions associate events in David's early career with his later actions as king and foreshadow, sometimes explicitly, the dynastic promise made in II Samuel 7, the Deuteronomistic capstone of the history of David's rise to power (see further below, "The History of David's Rise").

[25] See esp. Miller, "Saul's Rise to Power."

THE PROPHETIC HISTORY

The middle stage in the growth of the First Book of Samuel has received less than its share of scholarly attention, which has gone instead to investigation of the ancient sources or discussion of the Deuteronomistic overlay. Once the limited scope of the latter is recognized, however, it becomes apparent that it was at some pre-Deuteronomistic stage that the stories were set in their basic order, and the middle stage takes on considerable importance. Indeed the chapter by chapter analysis in the body of the present volume shows it to have been at this penultimate point in the development of the book that the chief ideas the stories now convey—whatever their earliest import or purpose and however modified by later annotation—were introduced.

A number of scholars have offered descriptions of the developmental stage in question. Almost all agree with Weiser that it is prophetic in perspective and suspicious of the institution of monarchy; most also agree against earlier views that it reflects an authentic and ancient stream of tradition that existed alongside other traditions more favorable to kingship. Weiser's resistance to interpreting this middle stage as any kind of literary unit, however, has met with less agreement. Fohrer speaks of a supplementary *stratum,* and Birch goes further to describe a complete pre-Deuteronomistic *edition* (of at least cc 7-15) stemming from early prophetic circles.

The detailed analysis in the NOTES and COMMENTS that follow tends to confirm the argument for a connected stratum at this intermediate stage. Indeed it appears that throughout the first half of the book (cc 1-15) and to a lesser extent the second half as well (cc 16-31) the older sources were systematically reworked to produce a continuous prophetic history of the origins of monarchy in Israel. At least three major sources, all containing what was probably well-known information, were involved: (1) an account of the capture and return of the ark; (2) an old complex of stories about Saul's early career; and (3) a discursive narrative usually designated "the history of David's rise." These are discussed separately below. The prophetic writer who incorporated them into his history amplified them and reworked parts of them, sometimes with considerable license, to reflect his particular *Tendenz.* Everywhere he introduced the dominant figure of the prophet Samuel, whose activity became the organizing feature of his work. The result was a systematic narrative in three sections, each structurally complete within itself but pointedly interconnected with the others.

The three sections are:

1) The story of Samuel: cc 1-7. This first section teaches a lesson in the effectiveness and sufficiency of prophetic leadership. Samuel is born under the most propitious circumstances and grows up in Yahweh's service to become a prophet whose word guides all Israel. When the consequences of the battle of Ebenezer threaten Israelite society with complete dissolution, he leads the people in a second great battle, in which the enemy is crushed and Israel is left in complete security and harmony. The positive function of this section is to portray the ideal of prophetic leadership to which the prophetic writer subscribed; its negative function is to demonstrate in advance the gross impropriety and senselessness of the people's demand for a king that introduces the next section. All this was achieved by a series of literary devices that are, as we shall see, characteristic of this writer. First he has incorporated into his account of Samuel's nativity (c 1) certain spectacular elements drawn from a story about Saul's birth (see the NOTES on 1:20 and 1:27,28), which probably belonged originally to the old Saul complex that especially underlies the second section of his work. Next he interpolated a series of favorable remarks about the boy Samuel into the condemnatory report on the behavior of the sons of Eli that stood among his sources (2:11-26; see below, "The Ark Narrative"). The tension set up by this invidious juxtaposition he resolved in a long passage from his own hand, in which Samuel, having received a vision condemning the house of Eli, is identified as Yahweh's prophet to all Israel (c 3). At this point he included the bulk of the old ark narrative without interruption (4:1-7:1), evidently finding in it the most dramatic demonstration possible of a threat to Israelite society, a threat he then showed to have been completely overcome by the good offices of the prophet in a final passage of his own design (7:2-17).

2) The story of Saul: cc 8-15. The second section shows the scandalous beginning of the monarchy and the establishment of the ongoing role of the prophet. Despite the success of Samuel's leadership the people wantonly demand a king, and when a warning about the evils of kingship fails to dissuade them, Yahweh instructs his prophet to give them a king. The young Saul is Yahweh's choice, and having been secretly anointed by Samuel, he is elected by lot at Mizpah, after which he leads Israel in a brilliant victory over the Ammonites, and his kingship is reaffirmed at Gilgal. Then in a solemn speech Samuel declares the new institution to be official and reminds the people of his own past services. After a fresh demonstration of his prophetic power, they entreat him to continue to act on their behalf even under the changed circumstances. At this point Israel seems well served by both king and prophet. Saul, however, quickly falls out of favor with Yahweh. Twice he disobeys the prophetically mediated divine word. In punishment he is first deprived of his dynastic prospects and then, in a final, tumultuous interview with Samuel, of his kingship it-

self. We are told that Yahweh will replace him with "a man of his own choosing." The function of this section is not only to present the origin of monarchy from a prophetic perspective, but also to introduce paradigmatically the relationship between king and prophet and, as we have seen, to establish the ongoing role of the prophet. The writer's chief source was a complex of stories about Israel's first king. He prefaced this with his own description of the people's demand for a king (c 8), which was to operate under the impact of the first section of the book, especially the account of Samuel's judgeship in 7:2-17, thus setting the prospect of monarchy in a negative light from the beginning. The old folktale in which Saul went looking for lost asses and found a kingdom (9:1-10:16) the writer then included with certain revisions that introduced Samuel into the story and with him the concept of the prophetic anointing of the king. The report of Saul's election by lot is also prophetic, at least in its final form (10:17-27a), but the story of Saul's victory over Nahash the Ammonite (10:27b-11:15) was drawn from the old Saul complex with only slight revision. Samuel's address in c 12 was intended as a key passage in the prophetic history, showing the people's belated acknowledgment of the authority of the prophet and implying his ongoing role as an intercessor between Yahweh and his people (cf. vv 16-20a,23). The old Saul materials underlying cc 13-14 were then taken over more or less intact into the prophetic history, except that the initial confrontation with the Philistines was used as an occasion for introducing the prophetic passage in 13:7b-15, in which Saul's dynasty is condemned for his failure to keep an appointment with Samuel as he had been instructed. The prophetic writer then concluded the section as he had begun it, with an episode from his own hand (15:1-34): Samuel condemns Saul's kingship once and for all, again for disobedience to the prophetically mediated word of Yahweh.

3) The story of David's rise: cc 16*ff*. The final section gives expression to a theme already implicit in the story of Saul, viz. that Yahweh will have a man of his own choosing as king. Samuel is sent to Bethlehem to anoint David in Saul's place. The stories that follow show a continual rise in David's fortunes and a corresponding decline in those of Saul, until finally the old king hears the shade of the deceased Samuel confirm the grim warnings of c 15 and falls in battle on Mount Gilboa, while David, in material that lies beyond the scope of the present volume (II Samuel 1-5), becomes king. The function of this third section, then, is to look beyond the negative appraisal of monarchy presented previously. Once the institution has been given divine sanction, however reluctantly, it may be described as acceptable to Yahweh; and this is the condition upon which Yahweh will accept it: that he choose the king for himself. To make this final point the prophetic writer took an extended narrative that already presented David as the divinely chosen successor to Saul and prefaced it with a characteristic passage of his own in which he showed Samuel ex-

ercising the prophetic prerogative of anointing the future king. No other signs of prophetic reworking may be discovered in cc 16-31, except in the brief episode near Ramah in 19:18-24 (which, however, does not seem to be pre-Deuteronomistic in origin; see the COMMENT), in the notice of Samuel's death in 25:1, and in the weird account of the seance at En-dor (28:3-25). In the last case our prophetic writer revised an old story, in which an anonymous ghost predicted Saul's death in the ensuing battle, by identifying the ghost with Samuel himself and expanding the divined message to include a recapitulation of the charges leveled against Saul in c 15, thus offering the reader a final reminder of the prophetic involvement in the course of events.

In summary we may conclude that the First Book of Samuel derives its basic shape from a prophetic history of the origin of the monarchy that was intended to present the advent of kingship in Israel as a concession to a wanton demand of the people. Beyond this purely negative purpose, however, the history was written to set forth according to a prophetic perspective the essential elements of the new system by which Israel would be governed. The prophet, whom the example of Samuel showed to be capable of ruling alone, would continue to be the people's intercessor with Yahweh. The king would now be head of the government, but he would be subject not only to the instruction and admonition of the prophet acting in his capacity as Yahweh's spokesman but even to prophetic election and rejection according to the pleasure of Yahweh. Anyone who would become king, therefore, would have to be (like David) a man of Yahweh's own choosing.

What conclusions can we draw about the provenance of this history? Its view of kingship as an office limited by prophetic authority is, as has been long recognized, distinctively northern, especially with regard to the practice of prophetic election and rejection, which is often mentioned in connection with northern kings (I Kings 11:29-39; 14:1-16; 16:1-4; II Kings 9:1-10) but out of place in the south where the dynastic principle was in constant operation. The geography of the prophetic history, which is focused on Benjamin and especially the cities of Ramah and Mizpah, is also northern. And when we recall the inclination of Budde and others to identify this middle layer of the book with the northern, Elohistic source of the Pentateuch, and the long-recognized affinity of the anti-monarchical parts of Samuel with Hosea's so-called "anti-royalism,"[26] we arrive at a rather strong presumption in favor of a northern origin. With regard to date we can say immediately that it is pre-Deuteronomistic and yet, especially if our interpretation of "the way of the king" passage in 8:11-18 is

[26] Cf. Hosea 8:4a: "They made kings, but not through me! They made princes, but I did not recognize them!" and Hosea 13:11: "I give you a king in my wrath, and I take him away in my anger!" See, for example, Astour, "Amarna Age Forerunners," 6-7.

correct, late enough to have inherited a legacy of bitter experience with the institution of monarchy. Our sources suggest that the prophetic perspective flourished in some circles throughout the independent history of the northern kingdom, but in seeking to understand this particular prophetic writer we must also account for a certain *southern* orientation as exhibited in his explicit acknowledgment of David's right to succeed Saul. This is a northern writer who is prepared to acknowledge the legitimacy of the Davidic throne, at least insofar as he finds in the transfer of kingship from Saul to David a paradigm for the prophetic rejection and election of kings. Moreover, he preserves and nowhere attempts to modify the plain assertion of the history of David's rise to power that David was Yahweh's chosen king (see below, "The History of David's Rise"). To account for such an attitude in a northern writer it is best to assume that he was writing during or shortly after the collapse of the northern kingdom, thus near the end of the eighth century B.C.[27] His background was northern, and he drew the fundamental principles upon which he based his interpretation of history from the teachings of the prophetic circles of the north; but his orientation was to the south, to which he looked for hope and in which he knew the future of Israel to be. It was also in the south that his work wound up, and there a Deuteronomistic writer incorporated it into his larger history.

It is worth remembering at this point that a number of scholars have sought the origin of Deuteronomic law and theology in northern prophetic circles.[28] Those who dissent from this view have usually conceded at least that pre-Deuteronomic and northern prophetic tradition, if traced back far enough, will eventually dovetail at some point. On the basis of what we have just said about the provenance of our prophetic history and in view of its manifest affinities with Deuteronomic tradition (illustrated especially well by the relationship of the details of I Samuel 8 to the tradition preserved in Deut 17:14-20 or by the holy war ideology shared by I Samuel 15 and Deuteronomy 20) it does not seem overly precise to describe it as "proto-Deuteronomic" in character. It stood alongside the Deuteronomic legislation itself among the received resources of the Deuteronomistic school, having arisen originally in circles of thought that were to some degree ancestral to the school's theology. It was for these reasons that the Deuteronomistic historian found it necessary to revise it only slightly, annotating it as needed to smooth its incorporation into his

[27] So already Birch, *Rise of the Israelite Monarchy*, 152-154; cf. also Mildenberger's hypothesis of a "nebiistic" redaction of cc 9*ff* from the same period in "Saul-Davidüberlieferung," 12 and *passim*.

[28] See the convenient discussion of Nicholson (*Deuteronomy*, 58-82), who sustains the hypothesis of a northern prophetic provenance after considering the objections of H. W. Wolff, G. von Rad, and others.

larger history or to introduce specifically southern concepts, such as that of the dynastic promise to David, into the whole.

THE OLDEST NARRATIVE SOURCES

As we have seen, the writer of the prophetic history just described drew extensively upon at least three older narratives or narrative complexes in the course of his work. Each of these—the ark narrative, the Saul cycle, and the history of David's rise—requires independent introduction.

The Ark Narrative

The isolation of an independent "ark narrative" (AN) within the Books of Samuel was, as noted earlier, the achievement of Leonhard Rost, who in 1926 identified an originally separate compositional unit comprising I Sam 4:1b-7:1 + II Sam 6 as among the blocks of traditional material he believed to have been available to the author of the succession history of David (II Sam [6] 9-20 + I Kings 1-2).[29] Rost recognized a distinctive character in the AN in that within it interest is focused on no human being, as it is on Samuel in cc 1-3, but on the ark of Yahweh itself. The sequence of events in the story shows, according to Rost, how this old Shilonite cult symbol came to Jerusalem, and the narrative as a whole, therefore, must have originated at the Jerusalem sanctuary, where it served to inform visitors about the ark and its significance; it served, in other words, as a kind of *hieros logos* for the shrine of the ark itself. The author, said Rost, should be sought in Jerusalem, probably among the priests charged with the care of the ark in Davidic or very early Solomonic times and in any case before the erection of the temple.

This hypothesis has been among the most durable of modern scholarship. The emphasis of earlier scholars (especially Budde) upon the search for parallel strands within the chapters treated by Rost has been generally though not universally (Eissfeldt, Hölscher), replaced by a preference for study of the unit as a whole. Only a few recent writers have found it necessary to describe the growth and interrelatedness of I Samuel 4-6 + II Samuel 6 in terms differing radically from those of Rost's analysis (Stoebe, Schicklberger), and even these are willing to acknowledge at least a general commonality of theme within the larger unit. Otherwise dissent has been confined largely to Rost's analysis of the narrator's purpose—cult legend seems too narrow a category for a composition that portrays the rejection of Shiloh and the house of Eli in favor of Jerusalem and its priesthood (Campbell)—and to his definition of the pericope—some scholars have found reason to include parts of the old material about Eli that now

[29] *Thronnachfolge Davids,* 119-253.

stands in c 2 (Caspari, Press, Segal), others to exclude II Samuel 6 (Hylander, Vriezen, Schunck).

Patrick D. Miller, Jr., and J. J. M. Roberts in their 1977 monograph *The Hand of the Lord* have redefined the terms in which the AN must be discussed. Their analysis brings us back to the simple fact, almost obscured by Rost's emphasis on II Samuel 6 as the climactic scene, that the most urgent theme in the bulk of the story, however its boundaries are determined, is the Philistine captivity of the ark. Once this is recognized the AN can be seen to find its place within a considerable literature from the ancient Near East concerned with the capture in battle and return of an enemy's "gods," and the light shed by the comparative materials makes a fresh evaluation possible.

The practice of carrying off divine images as spoils of war was widespread and is well documented, and the documents show that the practice gave rise to considerable theological reflection on the part of both victor and vanquished. The materials assembled by Miller and Roberts suggest that a victorious army regarded the capture of its enemy's gods as a demonstration of the superior power of its own gods. Accordingly the captured images would be placed in the temples of the victor's gods as spoils of war, a gesture that evinced the inferiority of the enemy's gods. Moreover, the images might be returned home in an act of magnanimity that showed the superiority of the victor's gods even more pointedly than the original capture itself. In the reports of the defeated army, however, the same events were described from a different theological viewpoint. The capture of the images and the defeat itself were seen as consequent upon deeds of the conquered army's own gods acting most often out of anger and in any case of their own free will. Similarly the return of the images was understood as a result not of the generosity of the enemy but of the gods' own decision to come home. The power of the gods of the defeated army was thus affirmed in every detail.[30]

[30] Illustrative of the abundant materials of this kind is a Babylonian account, preserved in two fragments, of the capture of Marduk's image during the Elamite conquest of Babylon and its return during the reign of Nebuchadnezzar I (for fragment 2 see Miller and Roberts, 79-81; fragment 1 is published in W. G. Lambert, "Enmeduṛanki and Related Matters," *JCS* 21 [1967] 126-138, text [i]). Miller and Roberts (13-14) summarize the account as follows: "At the time of a former king, there was disorder in the land, good departed, evil became regular, and, as a result, Marduk grew angry and commanded the gods to desert Babylon. The wicked Elamites took advantage of the ensuing helplessness of the country to carry off the divine images and ruin the shrines, but Marduk observed everything and was displeased. At this point the first fragment ends. The second, which may be a later continuation of the same text, begins with what appears to be the end of an account of Marduk's devastation of Elam. Then, in response to the king's constant prayer, Marduk became merciful, left the wickedness of Elam, and took a joyous road back to Babylon. The people of the land stared in joyous admiration of his lofty stature as the jubilant procession led to Marduk's lofty cella, where sacrifices were then offered in great abundance."

There can be little doubt that in the AN we have an Israelite example of this type of literature, specifically of the latter category—an account by a vanquished army of its defeat and the capture of its "gods" (of which the ark was the Israelite equivalent; cf. 4:7). As pointed out in detail in the NOTES and COMMENTS on 4:1-7:1, the reported events provide a reaffirmation of the power of Yahweh in a time of apparent defeat. The woeful implications of the battle and capture of the ark are faced forthrightly, and the questions thus raised are put to the test. The crucial moment is that of the battle of the gods, Yahweh and Dagon, in the temple in Ashdod (5:2-4), where Yahweh's superiority is demonstrated unambiguously, but the narrative makes it clear at every stage of the journey—the capture of the ark, the sojourn in Philistia, the return of the ark—that Yahweh is in complete control of every event.

It is with this affirmation that the narrator is chiefly concerned, and it follows, according to Miller and Roberts, that his audience was one for whom the theological problem raised by the Philistine victory described in the narrative was still a burning issue. Indeed the ancient parallels show that the searching questions and pronounced affirmation were most characteristic of accounts composed relatively soon after the fact and in any case before subsequent events had removed the doubts to which they were addressed. This implies that the AN was written before David's defeat of the Philistines reported in II Sam 5:17-25, in which the former situation was reversed, the Philistines' own idols captured (v 21), and the issue resolved. "In other words," write Miller and Roberts (74), "the formulation of this narrative belongs to the period of religious crisis between the disastrous defeat at Ebenezer and the much later victories of David."

The comparative materials also provide help in determining the extent of the AN. The ancient texts usually make the reason for a god's departure clear, but if the AN begins in 4:1b, as Rost supposed, it is an exception to the rule. For this reason it seems necessary to side with those scholars mentioned above, among whom we may now include Miller and Roberts, who find the beginning of the narrative in the report of the wickedness of the sons of Eli that stands in I Samuel 2. Only with this material in place does the AN disclose the reason for Yahweh's departure, viz. his displeasure with the priests of Shiloh. On the other hand we must exclude II Samuel 6 from the original narrative not only because it describes events that took place after David's Philistine wars (see above) but also because it corresponds to a related but different genre of ancient literature, viz. "the historical chronicles that record the return of despoiled images by victorious monarchs" (Miller and Roberts, 23). So those scholars who have denied the connection Rost made between I Samuel 4-6 and II Samuel 6 seem to have been correct, though as Miller and Roberts concede (24), the author of the latter was probably working with the former before him. The original narrative found its conclusion in the return of the ark to Kiriath-jearim, where it was still located in the time of the narrator.

For these reasons we conclude that the AN was an independent composition including the materials now found in I Sam 2:12-17,22-25 + 4:1b - 7:1.[31] But we should not forget that it has come down to us in a secondary setting that modifies its force significantly. All of it now functions within the story of Samuel, and it is in this context that its tensions are resolved. The wickedness of Eli's sons is set in relief by the contrasting example of the boy Samuel, and the violent disruption of Israelite society represented by the battle of Ebenezer and its consequences is completely mended by the exploits of the man Samuel, insofar as in "judging" Israel after the return of the ark he reconciles the people to Yahweh and eliminates the Philistine threat (see the COMMENTS on 2:11-26 and 7:2-17). The present location of the AN, therefore, has the effect of emphasizing the achievement of the great prophet in the spirit of the larger prophetic story of Samuel (I Sam 1-7) in which it stands (see above, "The Prophetic History").

The Saul Cycle

A loose collection of materials about Saul's early career was among the resources of the author of the prophetic history of the rise of the monarchy. Included in this collection were:

1) An account of Saul's birth: [c 1]. Most of this has been lost. We know of its existence only because, as I. Hylander has shown,[32] elements of it were incorporated into the account of Samuel's birth (see the COMMENT on 1:1-28). The formal similarity between 1:1 and 9:1, in which the fathers—not the sons—are introduced as in Judg 13:2 (see the NOTE at 9:1), suggests that Saul's birth story may have stood originally before the story in 9:3 - 10:16.

2) The tale of the lost asses of Kish: 9:1 - 10:16. Here again there has been substantial prophetic reworking: the role of Samuel, the prophetic anointing of the future king, and other elements are secondary (see the COMMENT [§ XII]). But in this case the basic story, an old folktale, is preserved. In unrevised form it told how Saul went to look for the asses and met a seer who revealed to him that he would become king of Israel.

3) The report of Saul's victory over the Ammonites: 10:27b - 11:15. Except for light retouching (see the NOTES at 11:7,14) this account survives in its original form. It describes in a manner reminiscent of the

[31] Miller and Roberts (30-31) also include 2:27-36, the oracle of the anonymous man of God, in which they find evidence of no more than light Deuteronomistic retouching. Our NOTES and COMMENTS on 2:27-36 give reasons for regarding the passage as thoroughly Deuteronomistic.

[32] *Samuel-Saul-Komplex*, 11-39.

exploits of the heroes of the Book of Judges Saul's deliverance of Jabesh-gilead, in consequence of which he is proclaimed king.

4) Anecdotes from Saul's Philistine wars: 13:2-7a,15b-23; 14:1-46. This material portrays events from Saul's maturity, focusing especially on the heroism of his son Jonathan.

Within this collection we may designate item (4), the anecdotes about Saul's Philistine wars, as miscellaneous. It exhibits no organic relationship to the rest, being an independent complex of stories probably deriving from early northern tradition. Items (1), (2), and (3), however, seem to belong together in a unified Saul cycle that is similar in some ways to the Samson cycle in Judges 13-16 and in others to the stories of the so-called "major judges" of the earlier chapters of Judges. As pointed out in the NOTES and COMMENTS, the cycle serves to establish a continuity between the stories of Saul's rise to power and the old northern tradition of "saviors" that Wolfgang Richter has discerned underlying the Deuteronomistic redaction of Judges 3-9.[33] The story of Saul's liberation of Jabesh, while based largely on historical memory (see the COMMENT on 10:27b-11:15), has nevertheless been surcharged with this "savior" theology and now stands as the climactic episode in the cycle. The cycle as a whole, when viewed from this perspective, serves to present a peculiarly northern, though not prophetic or "anti-monarchical," explanation of the rise of kingship as having evolved out of the "savior" tradition.

The provenance of the Saul cycle is certainly to be sought in the northern kingdom, perhaps at the time to which Richter assigns his pre-Deuteronomistic "savior"-book, viz. the latter part of the ninth century; but the ultimate origin of both the tale of the lost asses of Kish and the report of Saul's liberation of Jabesh was still earlier.

The History of David's Rise

As in the case of the ark narrative it was Leonhard Rost who put the study of the history of David's rise (HDR) on an independent footing. He identified a unified account of David's early career extending from I Sam 16:14 to II Samuel 5, and thus, though he offered no precise statement of its character of the sort he had provided for the AN, initiated a movement away from the attempt to isolate parallel strands within these chapters and running beyond them into adjacent materials in favor of treating them together as one of several discrete narrative units that had been combined into the larger story. Rost's original insight has been substantially sustained by subsequent research. Scholars influenced by the work of Gressmann and his successors have found it necessary to emphasize the fact that the HDR, even apart from Deuteronomistic expansion, has a

[33] See Richter, *Richterbuch,* 319-343, and *"Retterbuches," passim.*

strikingly heterogeneous appearance betraying, in their judgment, a diverse traditional background (Weiser, Ward, Grønbaek), but the same scholars (unlike Gressmann himself) have also stressed the creative role of the author who brought the bits of material together and imposed upon them their present unity. It is now widely agreed that the HDR must be viewed as a composition with a purpose beyond the antiquarian impulse of its author.

What was this purpose? Generally speaking it was to show the legitimacy of David's succession to Saul as rightful king of all Israel, north as well as south (Weiser). Within the narrative, therefore, David is presented as a favored courtier from Judah, who marries the daughter of the Benjaminite king of Israel and earns by deeds of martial valor the allegiance of all Israel and Judah; his rise to power, moreover, is shown to have been completely lawful, and any suspicion of wrongdoing on his part is gainsaid by the events themselves as depicted in the story. A number of recent scholars, however, have emphasized one neglected nuance of this theme, viz. that David's legitimation is worked out against a theological background in which David is envisioned as Yahweh's chosen king and Saul as the king abandoned by Yahweh. That is, the concept of the divine election and rejection of kings, generally thought of as northern, seems to be at work here. Some have taken this as evidence that an early, Jerusalemite version of the history of David's rise was later revised in the north (Nübel), perhaps in prophetic circles (Mildenberger). Others have insisted that this nuance was a component of the original author's point of view (Grønbaek, Mettinger). The analysis in the NOTES and COMMENTS below generally sustains the latter viewpoint. The prophetic writer of the larger history seems to have revised the HDR only slightly (see above, "The Prophetic History"), and where source-critical considerations do oblige us to bracket a block of material as secondary, it proves most often to have been added to link a certain passage with events in other parts of the Deuteronomistic history or to give explicit statement to a particular Deuteronomistic theme and thus to derive from a Deuteronomistic hand (see above, "The Deuteronomistic History"). This is not to say that the HDR in its original form did not address itself to northern ideas. The nuance noted by Nübel and others is certainly there and must be reckoned with in determining the provenance of the original composition. Though it seems almost certain that we must assume its author to have been a Jerusalemite or at least an individual sympathetic with the Jerusalemite point of view, it seems equally certain that his audience did not necessarily share his sympathies. His style, as we shall see, is defensive and apologetic; he is not schooled in (or at least avoids explicit use of) the high royal theology of Jerusalem—the only certain allusions to the dynastic promise are, as we have seen, in Deuteronomistic additions to the story (I Sam

25:28-31; II Samuel 7 *passim*). In short, he was a Jerusalemite with a non-Jerusalemite audience. We might, therefore, agree with several recent scholars (Ward, Grønbaek, Mettinger) that he was working in the early years of the divided kingdom, addressing himself to the issue of the secession and offering his defense of the Davidic throne. But because of his work's support of the free divine election of a new king it might seem actually to undergird the usurpation of Jeroboam rather than to oppose it. A defense of the Davidic *dynasty* is conspicuously lacking. It seems more likely, then, that the HDR is a document from the time of David himself, written before the development of the theology of dynastic promise under Solomon and directed toward those conservative elements in the north, especially in Benjamin, who were suspicious of the new king; that is, it was written in the atmosphere illustrated by the accounts of the Shimei incident in II Sam 16:5-14 and Sheba's revolt in II Sam 20:1-22. Its purpose was to justify the succession as a reflection of Yahweh's will and offer rebuttal to charges made against David.

When seen in this light the HDR finds its place within a special category of ancient Near Eastern literature in which the accession of a ruler whose right to the throne is somehow suspect is shown to have been in accordance with the will of the gods and therefore lawful. The best example is the so-called "Apology of Ḫattušiliš" (*CTH* 81), in which the thirteenth-century B.C. Hittite king, who usurped the throne of a less than able kinsman, justifies his actions.[34] Ḫattušiliš declares that he complied fully with his predecessor until he began to seek to destroy him, at which time he had no recourse but revolt. His victory was the result of the help of the goddess Ishtar, the patroness of kingship, who had long before deserted his predecessor and promised him the throne. Moreover, the divine assembly itself had debated the issue, and the gods' verdict had been in favor of Ḫattušiliš. After his victory, he concludes, he disposed of his enemies without vindictiveness. The HDR shares this apologetic tone, taking note of specific historical developments, justifying David's part in them, and attributing everything finally to the divine will. We are shown that David, like Ḫattušiliš, was quite willing to comply with Saul's will until absolutely forced to flee the court to save his life. To the objection that he became the leader of a band of outlaws, the narrator replies that David never sought thereby to harm or in any way threaten Saul but simply to ensure the safety of himself and others in like circumstances (22:2); indeed he refused to lay violent hands on Saul when the opportunity presented itself (c 26). To the objection that David served in the Philistine army, the narrator replies that again David took this course of action only when forced

[34] Cf. provisionally Wolf, "Apology of Ḫattušiliš," who finds this composition to be the only real example of the same genre as the HDR, which he therefore (dubiously) supposes to have been somehow dependent upon it.

to by Saul (27:1); moreover he never led his troops against an Israelite city but, on the contrary, used the position to harass the enemies of Israel (27:8) and finally even to enrich the people of Judah (30:26-31). All of this, we are told, was in accordance with Yahweh's will. Yahweh had abandoned Saul, whose madness made him unfit to rule, but he made David successful in everything he did, and indeed the theological leitmotiv of the story is "Yahweh was with him" (I Sam 16:18; 17:37; 18:14; 18:28; II Sam 5:10). In consequence of this special favor David, though consistently unassuming and loyal to his king, spontaneously commands the love and loyalty of the people (18:16; cf. II Sam 5:2), and not only the people but even Saul himself (16:21), his daughter (18:20), and especially his son Jonathan (19:1 and *passim*). Thus David was caught up in events that were beyond his control as surely as they were beyond Saul's. In short, says our narrator, David was Yahweh's choice as king of Israel and his assumption of that role, as described at the end of the HDR in II Samuel 5, was fully legitimate in the eyes of the highest authority.

The HDR begins in I Sam 16:14. Some scholars have preferred to include 16:1-13 (Weiser) and others add c 15 as well (Grønbaek, Mettinger), but we have taken these passages to be secondary with respect to the earliest sources, wholly from the hand of the prophetic writer who incorporated the HDR into his larger history (see above, "The Prophetic History"). The end of the HDR is found in II Sam 5:10, where a conclusion is reached with a final reiteration of what we have just described as the theological leitmotiv of the entire story; thus we read, "David continued to become greater and greater, because Yahweh Sabaoth[35] was with him." There follows a collection of supplementary materials, including the Deuteronomistic capstone of the HDR, Nathan's oracle in II Samuel 7, in which the dynastic promise to David, already foreshadowed in the Deuteronomistic expansion of the speech of Abigail in I Sam 25:28-31, is given its definitive expression.

[35] Reading *yhwh ṣb'wt* with 4QSam^a, LXX^{BL}. MT has *yhwh 'lhy ṣb'wt*, "Yahweh, *god of* hosts."

BIBLIOGRAPHY

I. COMMENTARIES*

Ackroyd, Peter R. *The First Book of Samuel.* The Cambridge Bible Commentary. Cambridge, 1971.

van den Born, Adrianus. *Samuel.* BOuT IV/1. Roermond en Maaseik, 1956.

Bressan, Gino. *Samuele.* Bibbia di Garofalo. Turin, 1954.

Brockington, L. H. "I and II Samuel," in *Peake's Commentary on the Bible,* eds. Matthew Black and H. H. Rowley. Rev. ed. New York: Nelson, 1962. Pages 318-337.

Budde, Karl. *Die Bücher Samuel.* KHC VIII. Tübingen: J. C. B. Mohr, 1902.

Caird, George B. *The First and Second Books of Samuel.* IB. Nashville: Abingdon, 1953. 2. 853-1176.

Caspari, Wilhelm. *Die Samuelbücher.* KAT VII. Leipzig: A. Deichter, 1926.

Dhorme, Édouard Paul. *Les livres de Samuel.* EB. Paris: J. Gabalda, 1910.

Gehrke, Ralph David. *1 and 2 Samuel.* Concordia Commentary. St. Louis: Concordia, 1968.

Goldman, Solomon. *The Books of Samuel.* The Soncino Books of the Bible. Bournemouth: Soncino, 1951.

Goslinga, C. J. *Het eerste Boek Samuël.* COuT. Kampen: J. H. Kok, 1968.

Gressmann, Hugo. *Die älteste Geschichtsschreibung und Prophetie Israels.* SAT II, 1. Göttingen: Vandenhoeck und Ruprecht, 1910; 2d ed., 1921.

de Groot, Johan. *I. Samuël.* Tekst en Uitleg. Den Haag, 1934.

Gutbrod, Karl. *Das Buch vom König: Das erste Buch Samuel.* Die Botschaft des alten Testaments. XI/1. Stuttgart: Calwer, 1956.

Hertzberg, Hans Wilhelm. *I and II Samuel. A Commentary,* tr. J. S. Bowden. The Old Testament Library. Philadelphia: Westminster, n.d.

Keil, Carl Friedrich. *Die Bücher Samuel.* Biblischer Commentar über das alte Testament. II/2. Leipzig: Dörffling und Franke, 1864; 2d ed., 1875.

* Commentaries are cited by author's name.—Ed.

Kennedy, A. R. S. *Samuel.* The New Century Bible. New York: Henry Frowde, 1904.

Kirkpatrick, Alexander Francis. *The First and Second Books of Samuel.* The Cambridge Bible for Schools and Colleges. Cambridge, 1930.

Kittel, Rudolf. "Das erste Buch Samuel," in *Die Heilige Schrift des alten Testaments.* 3d ed. (E. Kautsch). 4th ed. (A. Bertholet). Tübingen: J. C. B. Mohr, 1922. 1. 407-451.

Klostermann, August. *Die Bücher Samuelis.* SZ III. Nördlingen, 1887.

Leimbach, K. A. *Die Bücher Samuel.* HSAT III/1. Bonn, 1936.

Löhr, Max. *See* Otto Thenius.

Mauchline, John. *1 and 2 Samuel.* New Century Bible. London: Oliphants, 1971.

McKane, William. *I and II Samuel: The Way to the Throne.* Torch Paperback. London: SCM, 1963.

Nowack, Wilhelm. *Richter, Ruth und Bücher Samuelis.* HK I/4. Göttingen: Vandenhoeck und Ruprecht, 1902.

Oesterley, William Oscar Emil. *The First Book of Samuel.* Cambridge, 1931.

Rehm, Martin. *Die Bücher Samuel,* in *Die Heilige Schrift in deutschen Übersetzung* (Echter-Bibel), vol. II. Würzburg: Echter, 1956.

Schlögl, Nivard. *Die Bücher Samuel oder erstes und zweites Buch der Könige.* Kurzefasster wissenschaftlichen Kommentar zu den Schriften des alte Testaments. I/3,1. Vienna, 1904.

Schulz, Alfons. *Die Bücher Samuel.* EH VIII/1. Münster: Aschendorff, 1919 (I), 1920 (II).

Segal, Moses Hirsch. *spry šmw'l.* Jerusalem: Kiriath Sepher, 1964.

Smith, Henry Preserved. *A Critical and Exegetical Commentary on the Books of Samuel.* ICC. Edinburgh: T. and T. Clark, 1899.

Stoebe, Hans Joachim. *Das erste Buch Samuelis.* KAT VIII/1. Gütersloh: Gerd Mohn, 1973.

Thenius, Otto. *Die Bücher Samuels.* KeH 4. Leipzig: S. Hirzel, 1842; 2d ed., 1864; 3d ed. (Max Löhr), 1898.

de Vaux, Roland. *Les livres de Samuel.* Paris: Les Editions du Cerf, 1943; 2d ed., 1961.

II. TEXT AND VERSIONS

Aberbach, D. "*mnh 'ḥt 'pym* (1 Sam. I 5): A New Interpretation," *VT* 24 (1974) 350-353.

Bewer, Julius A. "Notes on 1 Sam 13_{21}; 2 Sam 23_{1}; Psalm 48_{8}," *JBL* 61 (1942) 45-50.

——— "The Original Reading of 1 Sam 6:19a," *JBL* 57 (1938) 89-91.

de Boer, P. A. H. *Research into the Text of I Samuel i-xvi.* Amsterdam: H. J. Paris, 1938.

——— "Research into the Text of I Samuel xviii-xxxi," *OTS* 6 (1949) 1-100.

——— "I Samuel xvii. Notes on the Text and the Ancient Versions," *OTS* 1 (1942) 79-104.

Cappellus, Ludovicus. *Commentarii et notae criticae in Vetus Testamentum.* Amsterdam: Jacobus Cappellus, 1689.

Cross, Frank Moore. *The Ancient Library of Qumran.* 2d ed. Garden City, N.Y.: Doubleday, 1961.

——— "The Contribution of the Qumran Discoveries to the Study of the Biblical Text," *IEJ* 16 (1966) 81-95.

——— "The Development of the Jewish Scripts," in *The Bible and the Ancient Near East: Essays in Honor of William Foxwell Albright,* ed. G. Ernest Wright. Garden City, N.Y.: Doubleday, 1961. Pages 170-264.

——— "The Evolution of a Theory of Local Texts," in *Qumran and the History of the Biblical Text,* eds. F. M. Cross and Shemaryahu Talmon. Cambridge, Mass.: Harvard, 1975. Pages 306-320.

——— "The History of the Biblical Text in the Light of Discoveries in the Judaean Desert," *HTR* 57 (1964) 281-299.

——— "A New Qumrân Biblical Fragment Related to the Original Hebrew Underlying the Septuagint," *BASOR* 132 (1953) 15-26.

——— "The Oldest Manuscripts from Qumran," *JBL* 74 (1955) 147-172.

Deist, Ferdinand. "*'APPAYIM* (1 Sam. I 5) < **PYM?*" *VT* 27 (1977) 205-209.

Driver, Godfrey R. "Old Problems Re-examined," *ZAW* 80 (1968) 174.

——— "On the Hebrew *pĕṣîrâ* (1 SAM XIII 21)," *AfO* 15 (1945/51) 68.

Driver, Samuel Rolles. *Notes on the Hebrew Text of the Books of Samuel.* Oxford: Clarendon, 1890. *Cited as* Driver.

Finkelstein, Emunah. "An Ignored Haplography in I Sam. 20:23," *JSS* 4 (1959) 356-357.

Gordis, Robert. "A Note on 1 Sam 13_{21}," *JBL* 61 (1942) 209-211.

Jellicoe, Sidney. *The Septuagint and Modern Study.* Oxford: Clarendon, 1968; reprint: Ann Arbor, Mich.: Eisenbrauns, 1978.

Johnson, Bo. *Die hexaplarische Rezension des 1. Samuelbuches der LXX.* ST 22. Lund, 1963.

Noort, Edward. "Eine weitere Kurzbemerkung zu I Samuel XIV 41," *VT* 21 (1971) 112-116.

Seebass, Horst. "Zum Text von 1 Sam. XIV 23b-25a und II 29, 31-33," *VT* 16 (1966) 74-82.

Shenkel, J. D. *Chronology and Recensional Development in the Greek Text of Kings*. HSM 1. Cambridge, Mass.: Harvard, 1968.

Speiser, E. A. "Of Shoes and Shekels," *BASOR* 77 (1940) 15-20; reprinted in *Oriental and Biblical Studies,* eds. J. J. Finkelstein and M. Greenberg. Philadelphia: University of Pennsylvania, 1967. Pages 151-159.

Stoebe, Hans Joachim. "Anmerkungen zu 1 Sam. VIII 16 und XVI 20," *VT* 4 (1954) 177-184.

——— "Die Goliathperikope 1 Sam. XVII 1–XVIII 5 und die Textform der Septuaginta," *VT* 6 (1956) 397-413.

Talmon, Shemaryahu. "The Old Testament Text," in *The Cambridge History of the Bible*. Volume 1: *From the Beginnings to Jerome,* eds. P. R. Ackroyd and C. F. Evans. Cambridge, 1970.

——— "1 Sam. XV 32b—A Case of Conflated Readings?" *VT* 11 (1961) 456-457.

Thomas, David Winton. "A Note on *wĕnôda' lākem* in I Samuel VI 3," *JTS* 11 (1960) 52.

Thornhill, R. "A Note on *'l-nkwn* in 1 Sam XXVI. 4," *VT* 14 (1964) 462-466.

Toeg, A. "A Textual Note on 1 Sam XIV 41," *VT* 19 (1969) 493-498.

Tov, Emanuel. "Lucian and Proto-Lucian," *RB* 79 (1972) 101-113.

Ulrich, Eugene C. "The Qumran Text of Samuel and Josephus." Unpublished Ph.D. dissertation. Harvard University, 1975.

de Vaux, Roland. *Qumrân Grotte 4*. DJD 6. Oxford: Clarendon, 1977.

Weingreen, J. "A Rabbinic-Type Gloss in the LXX Version of 1 Samuel i 18," *VT* 14 (1964) 225-228.

Weiss, R. " 'La main du Seigneur sera contre vous et contre vos pères' (1 Samuel, XII, 15)," *RB* 83 (1976) 51-54.

Wellhausen, Julius. *Der Text der Bücher Samuelis untersucht*. Göttingen: Vandenhoeck und Ruprecht, 1871. *Cited as* Wellhausen.

Zakovitch, Y. *"bdn=ypth,"* *VT* 22 (1972) 123-125.

III. LITERARY HISTORY

General Studies

Albright, W. F. *Samuel and the Beginnings of the Prophetic Movement*. Cincinnati: Hebrew Union College, 1961.

Alt, Albrecht. *Essays in Old Testament History and Religion,* tr. R. A. Wilson. Garden City, N.Y.: Doubleday, 1968.

Bentzen, Aage. *Introduction to the Old Testament.* 3 vols. Copenhagen: G. E. C. Gad, 1952.

Blenkinsopp, Joseph. *Gibeon and Israel: The Role of Gibeon and the Gibeonites in the Political and Religious History of Early Israel.* SOTSMS 2. Cambridge, 1972.

Budde, Karl. *Die Bücher Richter und Samuel: Ihre Quellen und ihr Aufbau.* Giessen: J. Ricker, 1890.

Cornill, Carl Heinrich. *Einleitung in die kanonischen Bücher des alten Testaments.* Tübingen, 1891; 7th ed., 1913.

——— "Ein elohistischer Bericht über die Entstehung des israelitischen Königtums in I. Samuelis 1-15 aufgezeigt," *ZKWL* 6 (1885) 113-141.

Cross, Frank Moore. *Canaanite Myth and Hebrew Epic.* Cambridge, Mass.: Harvard, 1975.

Dietrich, Walter. *Prophetie und Geschichte. Eine redaktionsgeschictliche Untersuchung zum deuteronomistischen Geschichtswerk.* FRLANT 108. Göttingen: Vandenhoeck und Ruprecht, 1972.

Eichhorn, J. G. *Einleitung in das alte Testament.* Göttingen, 1780-83; 4th ed., 1823-24.

Eissfeldt, Otto. *Die Komposition der Samuelisbücher.* Leipzig: J. C. Hinrichs, 1931.

——— "Noch einmal: Text-, Stil-, und Literarkritik in den Samuelisbüchern," *OLZ* 31 (1928) col. 801-812.

——— *The Old Testament. An Introduction,* tr. P. R. Ackroyd. New York: Harper and Row, 1965. *Cited as* Eissfeldt, *Introduction.*

——— "Text-, Stil- und Literarkritik in den Samuelisbüchern," *OLZ* 30 (1927) col. 657-664.

Fohrer, Georg. *Introduction to the Old Testament.* Initiated by Ernst Sellin; tr. David E. Green. Nashville: Abingdon, 1968.

Gunn, D. M. "Narrative Patterns and Oral Tradition in Judges and Samuel," *VT* 24 (1974) 286-317.

Hölscher, Gustav. *Geschichtsschreibung in Israel.* Lund: C. W. K. Gleerup, 1952.

Hylander, Ivar. *Der literarische Samuel-Saul-Komplex* (*I. Sam. 1–15*) *traditionsgeschichtlich untersucht.* Uppsala: Almqvist & Wiksell, 1932.

Kaiser, Otto. *Introduction to the Old Testament,* tr. John Sturdy. Oxford: Basil Blackwell, 1975.

Knierim, Rolf. "The Messianic Concept of the First Book of Samuel," in *Jesus and the Historian,* ed. F. T. Trotter. Philadelphia: Westminster, 1968. Pages 20-51.

Kuenen, Abraham. *Historisch-kritische Einleitung in die Bücher des alten Testaments.* Volume 1, part 2. *Die historischen Bücher des alten Testaments.* German tr. from the Dutch by T. Weber. Leipzig, 1890.

Macholz, Georg Christian. "Untersuchungen zur Geschichte der Samuelüberlieferungen." Unpublished dissertation. Heidelberg, 1966.

McCarthy, Dennis J. "II Samuel 7 and the Structure of the Deuteronomic History," *JBL* 84 (1965) 131-138.

McKenzie, John L. "The Four Samuels," *BR* 7 (1962) 3-18.

Mendenhall, George E. *The Tenth Generation: The Origins of the Biblical Tradition.* Baltimore: Johns Hopkins, 1973.

Mettinger, Tryggve N. D. *King and Messiah: The Civil and Sacral Legitimation of the Israelite Kings.* CB: Old Testament Series 8. Lund: C. W. K. Gleerup, 1976.

Nicholson, Ernest W. *Deuteronomy and Tradition.* Philadelphia: Fortress, 1967.

Noth, Martin. *Überlieferungsgeschichtliche Studien. Die sammelnden und bearbeitenden Geschichtswerke im alten Testament.* Tübingen: Max Niemeyer, 1943; 2d ed., 1957.

Pfeiffer, Robert H. *Introduction to the Old Testament.* Rev. ed. New York: Harper and Brothers, 1941.

——— "Midrash in the Books of Samuel," in *Quantulacumque. Studies Presented to Kirsopp Lake,* eds. R. P. Casey et al. London, 1937.

von Rad, Gerhard. *Old Testament Theology,* tr. D. N. G. Stalker. 2 vols. New York: Harper and Row, 1962.

——— *Studies in Deuteronomy.* SBT 9. London: SCM, 1953.

Richter, Wolfgang. *Die Bearbeitungen des "Retterbuches" in der deuteronomischen Epoche.* BBB 21. Bonn: Peter Hanstein, 1964.

——— *Traditionsgeschichtliche Untersuchungen zum Richterbuch.* BBB 18. Bonn: Peter Hanstein, 1963.

Rost, Leonhard. *Die Überlieferung von der Thronnachfolge Davids.* BWANT III, 6. Stuttgart: W. Kohlhammer, 1926. Reprinted in *Das kleine Credo und andere Studien zum alten Testament.* Heidelberg: Quelle und Meyer, 1965. Pages 119-253.

Schmidt, Ludwig. *Menschlicher Erfolg und Jahwes Initiative. Studien zu Tradition, Interpretation und Historie in Überlieferungen von Gideon, Saul, und David.* WMANT 38. Neukirchen-Vluyn, 1970.

Schulte, H. *Die Entstehung der Geschichtsschreibung im alten Israel.* BZAW 128. Berlin/New York: de Gruyter, 1972.

Schunck, Klaus-Dietrich. *Benjamin. Untersuchungen zur Entstehung und Geschichte eines israelitischen Stammes.* BZAW 86. Berlin: A. Töpelmann, 1963.

Segal, Moses Hirsch. "The Composition of the Books of Samuel," *JQR* 55 (1964) 318-339; 56 (1965) 32-50.

——— *mbw' hmqr'*. Jerusalem: Kiriath Sepher, 1964.

Smend, Rudolf. "Das Gesetz und die Völker: Ein Beitrag zur deuteronomistischen Redaktionsgeschichte," in *Probleme biblischer Theologie* (Gerhard von Rad Volume), ed. H. W. Wolff. Munich, 1971. Pages 494-509.

Soggin, J. Alberto. *Introduction to the Old Testament,* tr. John Bowden. London: SCM, 1976.

Stade, Bernhard. *Geschichte des Volkes Israel.* Volume 1. 2d ed. Berlin, 1889.

Szikszai, S. "I and II Samuel." *IDB* 4. New York: Abingdon, 1962. Pages 202-209.

Thornton, T. C. G. "Charismatic Kingship in Israel and Judah," *JTS* 14 (1963) 1-11.

——— "Solomonic Apologetic in Samuel and Kings," *CQR* 169 (1968) 159-166.

——— "Studies in Samuel. I. Davidic Propaganda in the Books of Samuel," *CQR* 168 (1967) 413-423.

Tiktin, H. *Kritische Untersuchungen zu den Büchern Samuelis.* FRLANT 16. Göttingen: Vandenhoeck und Ruprecht, 1922.

Tsevat, Matitiahu. "I and II Samuel." *IDBSup*. New York: Abingdon, 1976. Pages 777-781.

Veijola, Timo. *Die ewige Dynastie. David und die Entstehung seiner Dynastie nach der deuteronomistischen Darstellung.* Annales academiae scientiarum Fennicae. Series B 193. Helsinki, 1975.

Vriezen, Th. C. "Die Compositie van de Samuël-Boeken," in *Orientalia Neerlandica.* Leiden: A. W. Sithoff, 1948. Pages 167-189.

Weinfeld, Moshe. *Deuteronomy and the Deuteronomic School.* Oxford: Clarendon, 1972.

Weiser, Artur. *The Old Testament: Its Formation and Development,* tr. B. M. Barton. New York: Association Press, 1961.

Wellhausen, Julius. *Die Composition des Hexateuchs und der historischen Bücher des alten Testaments.* 3d ed. Berlin: B. Reimar, 1899.

——— *Prolegomena to the History of Ancient Israel,* trs. Munzies and Black. Cleveland: World, 1961; original German edition, 1878.

The Story of Samuel
(I Samuel 1-7)

Bentzen, Aage. "The Cultic Use of the Story of the Ark in Samuel," *JBL* 67 (1948) 37-53.

Birch, Bruce C. *The Rise of the Israelite Monarchy: The Growth and Development of 1 Samuel 7-15*. SBLDS 27. Missoula, Mont.: Scholars Press, 1976.

Blenkinsopp, Joseph. "Kiriath-jearim and the Ark," *JBL* 88 (1969) 143-156.

Bourke, Joseph. "Samuel and the Ark: A Study in Contrasts," *Dominican Studies* 7 (1954) 73-103.

Brentjes, B. "Zur 'Beulen'-Epidemie bei den Philistern in 1. Samuel 5-6," *Altertum* 15 (1969) 67-74.

Bressan, G. "Il cantico di Anna," *Biblica* 32 (1951) 503-521; 33 (1952) 67-89.

Campbell, Anthony F. *The Ark Narrative (1 Sam 4-6; 2 Sam 6). A Form-Critical and Traditio-Historical Study*. SBLDS 16. Missoula, Mont.: Scholars Press, 1975.

Delcor, Matthias. "Jahweh et Dagon ou le Jahwisme face à la religion des Philistins, d'après 1 Sam. V," *VT* 14 (1964) 136-154.

Driver, Godfrey R. "The Plague of the Philistines (1 Samuel v,6-vi,16)," *JRAS* (1950) 50-51.

Dus, Jan. "Der Brauch der Laderwanderung im alten Israel," *TZ* 17 (1961) 1-16.

——— "Die Erzählung über den Verlust der Lade," *VT* 13 (1963) 333-337.

——— "Die Geburtslegende Samuels, I. Sam. 1: Eine traditionsgeschichtliche Untersuchung zu 1 Sam 1-3," *RSO* 43 (1968) 163-194.

——— "Die Länge der Gefangenschaft der Lade im Philisterland," *NedTTs* 18 (1963/64) 440-452.

——— "Noch zum Brauch der 'Laderwanderung'," *VT* 13 (1963) 126-132.

Eissfeldt, Otto. "Die Lade Jahwes in Geschichtserzählung, Sage und Lied," *Altertum* 14 (1968) 131-145.

Flower, H. J. "I Sam I, 1," *ExpT* 70 (1955) 273.

Fohrer, Georg. "Die alttestamentliche Ladeerzählung," *Journal of Northwest Semitic Languages* 1 (1971) 23–31.

Garbini, Giovanni. "Osservazioni linguistiche a I Sam cap. 1-3," *BeO* 5 (1963) 47-52.

Haran, Menachem. "The Disappearance of the Ark," *IEJ* 13 (1963) 46-58.

Hillers, Delbert R. "Ritual Procession of the Ark and Ps 132," *CBQ* 30 (1968) 48-55.

Houtman, C. "Zu I Samuel 2:25," *ZAW* 89 (1977) 412-417.

Jackson, Jared Judd. "The Ark Narratives. An Historical, Textual, and Form-Critical Study of I Samuel 4-6 and II Samuel 6." Unpublished Th.D. dissertation. Union Theological Seminary, New York, 1962.

Klein, Ralph W. "The Song of Hannah," *CTM* 41 (1970) 674-684.

Maier, Johann. *Das altisraelitische Ladeheiligtum.* BZAW 93. Berlin: A. Töpelmann, 1965.

Miller, Patrick D., Jr., and J. J. M. Roberts. *The Hand of the Lord: A Reassessment of the "Ark Narrative" of 1 Samuel.* The Johns Hopkins Near Eastern Studies. Baltimore: Johns Hopkins, 1977.

Newman, Murray. "The Prophetic Call of Samuel," in *Israel's Prophetic Heritage. Essays in Honor of James Muilenburg,* eds. B. W. Anderson and W. Harrelson. New York: Harper and Row, 1962. Pages 86-97.

Noth, Martin. "Samuel und Silo," *VT* 13 (1963) 390-400.

Richter, Wolfgang. *Die Bearbeitungen des "Retterbuches" in der deuteronomischen Epoche.* BBB 21. Bonn: Peter Hanstein, 1964.

Roberts, J. J. M. *See* Patrick D. Miller, Jr.

Schicklberger, Franz. *Die Ladeerzählung des ersten Samuel-Buches. Eine literaturwissenschaftliche und theologiegeschichtliche Untersuchung.* Forschung zur Bibel 7. Würzburg: Echter, 1973.

Schmitt, Rainer. *Zelt und Lade as Thema alttestamentlicher Wissenschaft. Eine kritische forschungsgeschichtliche Darstellung.* Gütersloh: Gerd Mohn, 1972.

Timm, Hermann. "Die Ladeerzählung (1. Sam. 4-6; 2. Sam. 6) und das Kerygma des deuteronomistischen Geschichtswerks," *EvT* 29 (1966) 509-526.

Tsevat, Matitiahu. "The Death of the Sons of Eli," *JBR* 32 (1964) 355–358.

——— "Studies in the Book of Samuel. I. Interpretation of I Sam. 2:27-36. The Narrative of *kareth,*" *HUCA* 32 (1961) 191-216.

Tur-Sinai, N. H. "The Ark of God at Beit Shemesh (1 Sam. VI) and Peres 'Uzza (2 Sam. VI; 1 Chron. XIII)," *VT* 1 (1951) 275-286.

de Ward, E. F. "Superstition and Judgment: Archaic Methods of Finding a Verdict," *ZAW* 89 (1977) 1-19.

Weiser, Artur. *Samuel: seine geschichtliche Aufgabe und religiöse Bedeutung. Traditionsgeschichtliche Untersuchungen zu 1. Samuel 7-12.* FRLANT 81. Göttingen: Vandenhoeck und Ruprecht, 1962.

——— "Samuels 'Philister-Sieg': die Überlieferung in 1. Samuel 7," *ZTK* 56 (1959) 253-272.

Wilkinson, John. "The Philistine Epidemic of I Samuel 5 and 6," *ExpT* 88 (1977) 137-141.

Willis, John T. "An Anti-Elide Narrative Tradition from a Prophetic Circle at the Ramah Sanctuary," *JBL* 90 (1971) 288-308.

——— "Cultic Elements in the Story of Samuel's Birth and Dedication," *ST* 26 (1972) 33-61.

——— "The Song of Hannah and Psalm 113," *CBQ* 35 (1973) 139-154.

The Advent of Kingship
(I Samuel 8-15)

Ap-Thomas, D. R. "Saul's Uncle," *VT* 11 (1961) 241-245.

Astour, Michael C. "The Amarna Age Forerunners of Biblical Anti-royalism," in *For Max Weinreich on His Seventieth Birthday: Studies in Jewish Language, Literature, and Society*. The Hague: Mouton, 1964. Pages 6-17.

Bardtke, H. "Samuel und Saul. Gedanken zur Entstehung des Königtums in Israel," *BO* 25 (1968) 289-302.

Beyerlin, Walter. "Das Königscharisma bei Saul," *ZAW* 73 (1961) 186-201.

Bič, Miloš. "Saul sucht die Eselinnen (I Sam. IX)," *VT* 7 (1957) 92-97.

Birch, Bruce C. "The Choosing of Saul at Mizpah," *CBQ* 37 (1975) 447-457.

——— "The Development of the Tradition of the Anointing of Saul in I Sam 9:1 - 10:16," *JBL* 90 (1971) 55–68.

——— *The Rise of the Israelite Monarchy: The Growth and Development of 1 Samuel 7-15*. SBLDS 27. Missoula, Mont.: Scholars Press, 1976.

Blenkinsopp, Joseph. "Did Saul Make Gibeon His Capital?" *VT* 24 (1974) 1-7.

——— "Jonathan's Sacrilege. 1 Sam 14, 1-46," *CBQ* 26 (1964) 423-449.

Boecker, Hans Jochen. *Die Beurteilung der Anfänge des Königtums in den deuteronomistischen Abschnitten des I. Samuelbuches*. WMANT 31. Neukirchen-Vluyn, 1969.

Bratcher, R. G. "How Did Agag Meet Samuel? (1 Sam 15:32)," *BT* 22 (1971) 167.

Brauner, Ronald A. " 'To Grasp the Hem,' and 1 Samuel 15:27," *JANES* 6 (1974) 35-38.

Buber, Martin. "Die Erzählung von Sauls Königswahl," *VT* 6 (1956) 113–173.

Clements, R. E. "The Deuteronomistic Interpretation of the Founding of the Monarchy in 1 Sam. VIII," *VT* 24 (1974) 398-410.

Conrad, D. "Samuel und die Mari-'Propheten.' Bemerkungen zu 1 Sam. 15:27," ZDMGSup 1 (1969) 273-280.

Davies, P. R. "Ark or Ephod in 1 Sam xiv. 18?" *JTS* 26 (1975) 82-87.

Dornseiff, Franz. "Archilochos von Paros und Saul von Gibea," *TLZ* 80 (1955) 499.

Eppstein, Victor. "Was Saul among the Prophets?" *ZAW* 81 (1969) 287-303.

Fritz, V. "Die Deutungen des Königtums Sauls in den Überlieferungen von seiner Entstehung," *ZAW* 88 (1976) 346-362.

Hauer, Christian E., Jr. "Does I Samuel 9:1-11:15 Reflect the Extension of Saul's Dominions?" *JBL* 86 (1967) 306-310.

——— "The Shape of the Saulide Strategy," *CBQ* 31 (1969) 153-167.

Irwin, W. A. "Samuel and the Rise of the Monarchy," *AJSL* 58 (1941) 113-134.

Jobling, David. "Saul's Fall and Jonathan's Rise: Tradition and Redaction in 1 Sam 14:1-46," *JBL* 95 (1976) 367-376.

Langlamet, F. "Les récits de l'institution de la royauté (I Sam., VIII-XII)," *RB* 77 (1970) 161-200.

Lods, Adolphe. *Les sources des récits du premier livre de Samuel sur l'institution de la royauté israélite.* Etudes de théologie et d'histoire . . . en homage à la faculté de théologie de Montauban. . . . Paris, 1901.

Luck, G. C. "The First Glimpse of the First King of Israel," *BS* 123 (1966) 60-66.

——— "The First Meeting of Saul and Samuel (1 Sam 9)," *BS* 124 (1967) 254–261.

McCarthy, Dennis. "The Inauguration of Monarchy in Israel: A Form-Critical Study of I Samuel 8-12," *Interpretation* 27 (1973) 401-412.

——— *Treaty and Covenant: A Study in Form in the Ancient Oriental Documents and in the Old Testament.* Rome: Pontifical Biblical Institute, 1963.

McKane, William. "A Note on Esther IX and I Sam XV," *JTS* 12 (1961) 260-261.

Mendelsohn, Isaac. "Samuel's Denunciation of Kingship in Light of Akkadian Documents from Ugarit," *BASOR* 143 (1956) 17-22.

Miller, J. Maxwell. "Saul's Rise to Power: Some Observations Concerning 1 Sam 9:1-10:16; 10:26-11:15 and 13:2-14:46," *CBQ* 36 (1974) 157-174.

Möhlenbrink, Kurt. "Sauls Ammoniterfeldzug und Samuels Beitrag zum Königtum des Saul," *ZAW* 58 (1940/41) 57-70.

Muilenburg, James. "Mizpah of Benjamin," *ST* 8 (1954) 25-43.

Press, Richard. "Der Prophet Samuel. Eine traditionsgeschichtliche Untersuchung," *ZAW* 56 (1938) 177-225.

——— "Sauls Königswahl," *TBl* 12 (1933) 243-248.

von Rad, Gerhard. "The Early History of the Form-Category of *I Corinthians* XIII. 4-7," in *The Problem of the Hexateuch and Other Essays.* New York: McGraw-Hill, 1966. Pages 301-317.

Richter, Wolfgang. *Die sogenannten vorprophetischen Berufungsberichte. Eine literaturwissenschaftliche Studie zu 1 Sam 9,1-10,16, Ex. 3f. und Ri 6,11b-17.* FRLANT 101. Göttingen: Vandenhoeck und Ruprecht, 1970.

Robertson, Edward. "Samuel and Saul," *BJRL* 28 (1944) 175-206.

Schicklberger, Franz. "Jonatans Heldentat: Textlinguistische Beobachtungen zu 1 Sam XIV 1-23a," *VT* 24 (1974) 324-333.

Seebass, Horst. "1 Sam 15 als Schlüssel für das Verstandnis der sogenannten königsfreundlichen Reihe 1 Sam 9_1-10_{16} 11_{1-15} und 13_2-14_{52}," *ZAW* 78 (1966) 148-179.

——— "Traditionsgeschichte von I Sam 8, 10,17ff. und 12," *ZAW* 77 (1965) 286-296.

——— "Die Vorgeschichte der Königserhebung Sauls," *ZAW* 79 (1967) 155-171.

Soggin, J. Alberto. "Charisma und Institution im Königtum Sauls," *ZAW* 75 (1963) 54-65.

——— *Das Königtum in Israel: Ursprünge, Spannungen, Entwicklung.* BZAW 104. Berlin: A. Töpelmann, 1967.

Stoebe, Hans Joachim. "Noch einmal die Eselinnen des Kiš," *VT* 7 (1957) 362-370.

——— "Zur Topographie und Überlieferung der Schlacht von Mikmas, 1 Sam. 13 und 14," *TZ* 21 (1965) 269-280.

Sturdy, John. "The Original Meaning of 'Is Saul Also among the Prophets?' (I Samuel X 11,12; XIX 24)," *VT* 20 (1970) 206-213.

Tsevat, Matitiahu. "The Biblical Narrative of the Foundation of Kingship in Israel" [Hebrew], *Tarbiz* 36 (1966/67) 99-109.

——— "Studies in the Book of Samuel. II. Interpretation of I Samuel 10:2. Saul at Rachel's Tomb," *HUCA* 33 (1962) 107-118.

Wallis, Gerhard. "Die Anfänge des Königtums in Israel," *WZ* (1963) 239-247.

——— "Eine Parallele zu Richter 19:29ff. und I Sam. 11:5ff. aus dem Briefarchiv von Mari," *ZAW* 64 (1952) 57-61.

Weingreen, J. "Saul and the Ḫabirû," in *Fourth World Congress of Jewish Studies.* Volume I. Jerusalem: World Union of Jewish Studies, 1967. Pages 63-66.

Weiser, Artur. "I Samuel 15," *ZAW* 54 (1936) 1-28.

——— *Samuel: seine geschichtliche Aufgabe und religiöse Bedeutung. Traditionsgeschichtliche Untersuchungen zu 1. Samuel 7-12.* FRLANT 81. Göttingen: Vandenhoeck und Ruprecht, 1962.

——— "Samuel und die Vorgeschichte des israelitischen Königtums (1. Samuel 8)," *ZTK* 57 (1960) 141-161.

Wildberger, Hans. "Samuel und die Entstehung des israelitischen Königtums," *TZ* 13 (1957) 442-469.

The Rise of David
(I Samuel 16-31)

Ackroyd, Peter R. "The Verb Love—*'āhēb* in the David-Jonathan Narratives—a Footnote," *VT* 25 (1975) 213-214.

Bič, Miloš. "La folie de David. Quelques remarques en marge de 1 Samuel 21," *RHPR* 37 (1957) 156–162.

Buccellati, Giorgio. "I Sam 13,1," *BeO* 5 (1963) 29.

——— "Da Saul a David," *BeO* 1 (1959) 99-128.

Conrad, J. "Zur geschichtlichen Hintergrund der Darstellung von Davids Aufstieg," *TLZ* 97 (1972) 321-332.

Gehman, H. S. "A Note on I Samuel 21, 13(14)," *JBL* 67 (1948) 241-243.

Glück, J. J. "Merab or Michal?" *ZAW* 77 (1965) 72-81.

Gottlieb, H. "Die Tradition von David als Hirten," *VT* 17 (1967) 190-200.

Grønbaek, Jakob H. *Die Geschichte vom Aufstieg Davids (1. Sam. 15-2. Sam. 5). Tradition und Composition.* Acta Theologica Danica X. Copenhagen: Munksgaard, 1971.

Hoffner, Harry A., Jr. "A Hittite Analogue to the David and Goliath Contest of Champions?" *CBQ* 30 (1968) 220-225.

Honeyman, A. M. "The Evidence for Regnal Names among the Hebrews," *JBL* 67 (1948) 13-25.

Kessler, Martin. "Narrative Technique in 1 Sam 16:1-13," *CBQ* 32 (1972) 543-554.

Lemche, N. P. "*ḥpšy* in 1 Sam. xvii 25," *VT* 24 (1974) 373-374.

Levenson, Jon D. "1 Samuel 25 as Literature and History," *CBQ* 40 (1978) 11-28.

Mildenberger, F. "Die vordeuteronomistische Saul-Davidüberlieferung." Unpublished dissertation. Tübingen, 1962.

Morgenstern, Julian. "David and Jonathan," *JBL* 78 (1959) 322-325.

Nübel, H.-U. *Davids Aufstieg in der frühe israelitischer Geschichtsschreibung.* Bonn: Rheinische Friedrich-Wilhelms Universität, 1959.

von Pákozdy, L. M. "'Elhånån—der frühere Name Davids?" *ZAW* 68 (1956) 257-259.

Rendtorff, Rolf. "Beobachtungen zur altisraelitischen Geschichtsschreibung anhand der Geschichte vom Aufstieg Davids," in *Probleme biblischer Theologie,* ed. Hans Walter Wolff. Munich: Chr. Kaiser, 1971. Pages 428-439.

Rinaldi, G. "Golia e David (1 Sam 17:1-18:8)," *BeO* 8 (1966), 11-29, tab. I-II.

Smith, Morton. "The So-Called 'Biography of David' (I Sam 16-II Sam 5-9. 21-24)," *HTR* 44 (1951) 167-169.

Stoebe, Hans Joachim. "David und Mikal: Überlegungen zur Jugendgeschichte Davids," in *Von Ugarit nach Qumran* (Otto Eissfeldt Volume), eds. J. Hempel et al. BZAW 77. Berlin: A. Töpelmann, 1958. Pages 224-243.

——— "Gedanken zur Heldensage in den Samuelbüchern," in *Das ferne und nahe Wort* (Leonhard Rost Volume). BZAW 105. Berlin: A. Töpelmann, 1967. Pages 208-218.

Thompson, J. A. "The Significance of the Verb *Love* in the David-Jonathan Narratives in I Samuel," *VT* 24 (1974) 34-38.

de Vaux, Roland. "Single Combat in the Old Testament," in *The Bible and the Ancient Near East,* tr. Damian McHugh. Garden City, N.Y.: Doubleday, 1971. Pages 122-135.

de Vries, Simon J. "David's Victory over the Philistine as Saga and as Legend," *JBL* 92 (1973) 23-36.

Ward, Roger Lemuel. "The Story of David's Rise. A Tradition-historical Study of I Samuel xvi 14 - II Samuel v." Unpublished Ph.D. dissertation. Vanderbilt University, 1967.

Weiser, Artur. "Die Legitimation des Königs David. Zur Eigenart und Entstehung der sogen. Geschichte von Davids Aufstieg," *VT* 16 (1966) 325-354.

Wolf, Herbert M. "The *Apology of Ḫattušiliš* Compared with Other Political Self-Justifications of the Ancient Near East." Unpublished Ph.D. dissertation. Brandeis University, 1967.

I SAMUEL

Translation

Textual Notes

Notes

&

Comments

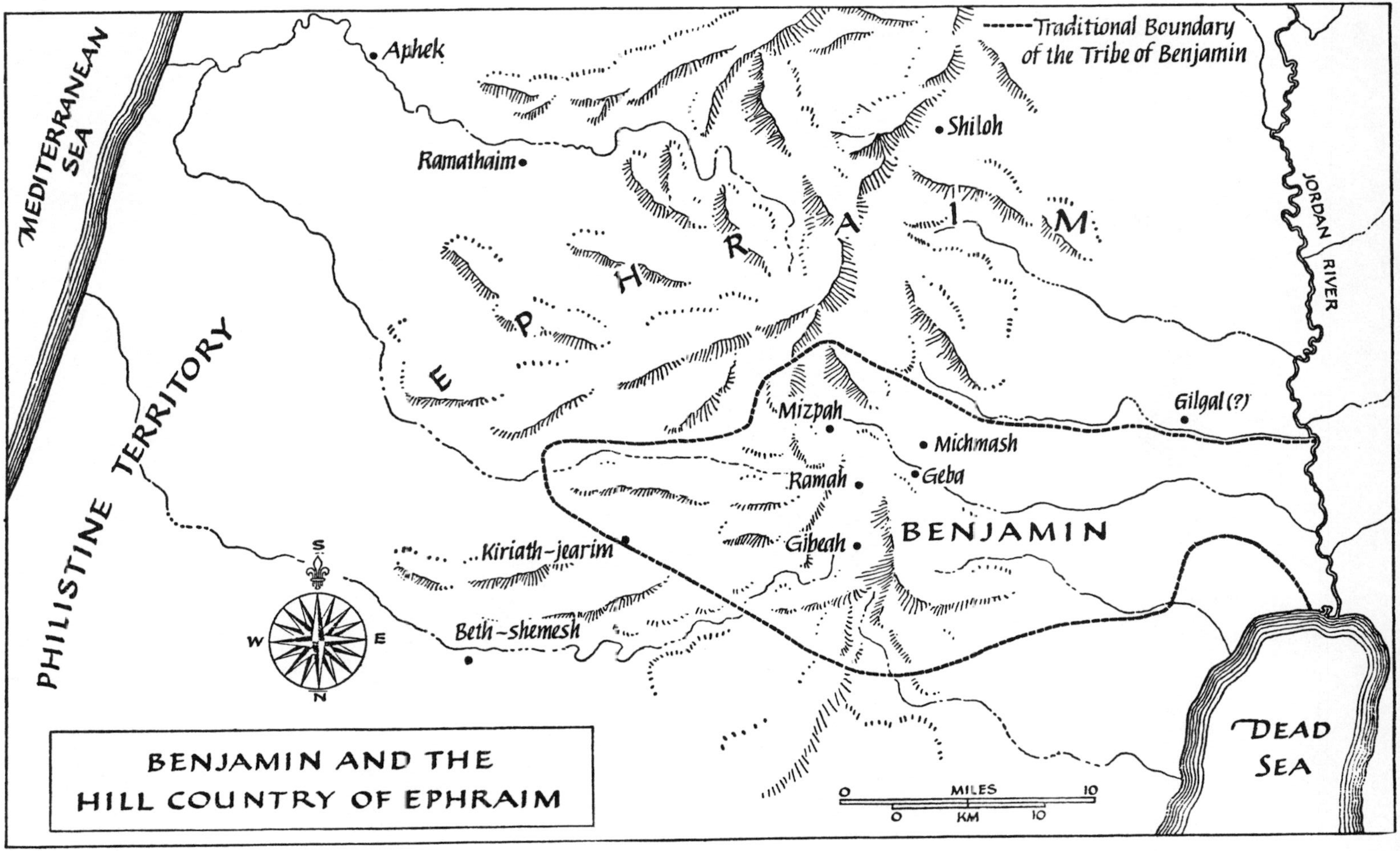

BENJAMIN AND THE HILL COUNTRY OF EPHRAIM

THE STORY OF SAMUEL

I. THE BIRTH OF SAMUEL
(1:1-28)

1 1 There was a man from Ramathaim, a Zuphite from the hill
country of Ephraim. His name was Elkanah, the son of Jerahmeel,
the son of Elihu, the son of Toah, the son of Zuph, an Ephraimite.
2 He had two wives: the name of the first was Hannah, and the name
of the second was Peninnah; Peninnah had children, but Hannah had
no children.

3 This man used to go up regularly from his city to worship and
sacrifice to Yahweh Sabaoth at Shiloh. There Hophni and Phinehas,
the two sons of Eli, were priests of Yahweh. 4 One day when Elkanah
was sacrificing— (Now when he gave portions to Peninnah and her
sons, 5 he would give Hannah a single portion equal to theirs; for
Hannah was the one he loved, though Yahweh had closed her womb.
6 Moreover her rival used to provoke her to anger, so that she would
complain aloud that Yahweh had closed her womb. 7 Year after year,
as often as she went up to the house of Yahweh, [Elkanah] would do
this and [Peninnah] would provoke her this way.) One day when
Elkanah was sacrificing, [Hannah] began to weep and would not eat.
8 Elkanah, her husband, said to her, "Hannah, why are you weeping?
Why do you not eat? Why are you so resentful? Am I not better to
you than ten sons?"

9 After she had eaten, Hannah arose privately and presented herself
before Yahweh. (Now Eli, the priest, was sitting in a chair beside the
doorpost of the temple of Yahweh.) 10 From the bitterness of her
heart she invoked Yahweh and, weeping greatly, 11 made the following vow:

O Yahweh Sabaoth,
If you will take notice of your maidservant's affliction,
If you will remember me and not forget your maidservant,
If you will grant your maidservant offspring,
Then I shall set him before you all the days of his life:
Wine or strong drink he will not drink,
And no razor will touch his head.

[12] As she continued to pray before Yahweh, Eli watched her
mouth. [13] She was speaking within her heart: only her lips quivered;
her voice could not be heard. Eli, assuming that she was drunk,
[14] said to her, "How long will you be drunk? Put aside your wine!"

[15] "No, my lord!" said Hannah in reply. "I am an unfortunate
woman. I have drunk neither wine nor strong drink. I was only pour-
ing out my soul to Yahweh. [16] Do not think your maidservant a
worthless woman! It is because my complaint and my vexation are so
great that I have tarried this long."

[17] "Go in peace," replied Eli, "and may the god of Israel grant the
request you have made of him!"

[18] Then saying, "Let your maidservant find favor in your eyes!" the
woman went her way, and when she came to the chamber, she ate and
no longer wore her [disconsolate] expression. [19] Early in the morning, having bowed down before Yahweh, they started back and came
to their home in Ramah. Then Elkanah knew Hannah, his wife, and
Yahweh remembered her.

[20] So when a year had passed, [Hannah] was pregnant and bore a
son. She named him Samuel, "because," [she said,] "it was from Yahweh that I requested him." [21] And when the man Elkanah went up
with the rest of his family to make the seasonal sacrifice to Yahweh,
[22] Hannah did not go, for she said to her husband, "[I shall stay] until
the child goes, when I have weaned him. Then he will appear before
Yahweh and remain there forever, for I shall present him as a
Nazirite forever."

[23] Elkanah, her husband, told her, "Do what seems best to you.
Stay until you have weaned him. May Yahweh confirm what you have
said!"

So the woman stayed to nurse her son until she had weaned him.
[24] Then she went up with him to Shiloh when her husband went up to
sacrifice to Yahweh at Shiloh with a three-year-old bull, an ephah of
flour, and a skin of wine.

After they had gone before Yahweh [25] and slaughtered the bull,
Hannah took the child to Eli. [26] "Pardon me, my lord!" she said. "As
surely as you live, I am the woman who stood here with you praying
to Yahweh! [27] It was for this child that I prayed, and Yahweh has
granted me the request I asked of him; [28] so I in turn have dedicated
him to Yahweh. For as long as he lives, he is dedicated to Yahweh!"
Then she left him there and worshiped Yahweh.

TEXTUAL NOTES

1 1. *There was a man* So LXX^B: *anthrōpos ēn* = *'yš hyh,* which has been replaced in MT (cf. LXX^A) by the more common sequence *wyhy 'yš,* to which MT adds *'ḥd*—thus, "And there was a certain man. . . ." In light of the last detail we should probably conclude that the text of MT at this point is not simply the result of the substitution of a more common reading for a less common one, but of the influence of Judg 13:2, especially in view of the influence of the text of Samson's birth narrative on our story elsewhere (cf. the second *Textual Note* at v 11 below). The disjunctive sequence *'yš hyh* marks the inauguration of an entirely new narrative (cf., for example, Job 1:1) in contrast to the much more common sequence *wyhy 'yš,* which regularly marks the introduction of one narrative in a chain of similar narratives, most notably in the immediately preceding material (Judg 13:2; 17:1; 19:1). This then is a textual hint of the original independence of the prophetic history of the rise of kingship that begins here with the story of Samuel (see pp. 18-23 in the Introduction).

a Zuphite Reading *ṣûpî* on the basis of LXX *seipha* (reflecting *ṣypy,* understood as *ṣêpay*) and the names of Elkanah's ancestor (*ṣûp,* "Zuph," below) and the district in which Samuel lived (*'ereṣ ṣûp,* "the land of Zuph"; see the NOTE at 9:5). MT gives *hārāmātaylm ṣôpîm,* "Ramathaim-zophim," as the name of Elkanah's city; but such a name is grammatically impossible (Driver) and corrupt, arising from dittography of the following *m.* Read *mn-hrmtym ṣwpy mhr 'prym* with most critics.

Jerahmeel LXX *Ieremeēl,* reflecting *yrḥm'l* = *yĕraḥmĕ'ēl.* MT elsewhere (I Chron 5:12,19) reads *yĕrōḥām,* "Jeroham," and this has influenced the present passage. The variants are simply longer and shorter forms of the same name.

Elihu MT *'ĕlîhû';* LXX *ēleiou.* Cf. I Chron 6:12, *'ĕlî'āb, eliab;* I Chron 6:19, *'ĕlî'ēl, eliēl.*

Toah With LXX^B *thoke,* LXX^L *thōe,* and MT of I Chron 6:19 *tôaḥ,* against MT *tōḥû.*

Zuph Reading *ṣûp* with MT. LXX^B *en naseib* reflects a corruption of *bn ṣwp* to *bnṣyb.*

an Ephraimite MT *'eprātî.* LXX substitutes the more familiar *ephraim.*

2. *the first* MT *'aḥat.* The expected reading *hā'aḥat* has some manuscript support and probably ought to be restored.

children (2) So MT: *yĕlādîm.* LXX has *paidion,* "child."

3. *the two sons of Eli* LXX *ēlei kai hoi duo huioi autou,* "Eli and his two sons," is an understandable expansion. Smith argues for its originality.

4. *and her sons* LXX^B *kai tois huiois autēs.* MT *wlkl bnyh wbnwtyh,* "and to all her sons and daughters," is expansive.

5. *a single portion equal to theirs* Conjectural. MT reads *mānâ 'aḥat 'ap-*

pâyim, for which there is no acceptable translation. The difficulty is *'appayim,* which normally means "face" (cf. LXX^L *kata prosōpon*). Hertzberg surmises "portion of the face," but whatever this might mean, it is grammatically awkward, supposing, presumably, some kind of apposition ("one portion, namely, the face"). LXX^B has *plēn hoti,* pointing to *'epes kî,* "except that, but that." This reading, since it relieves the immediate difficulty of *'pym* by assuming that it is a mistake of *'ps,* has enjoyed the support of many critics. So, for example, Driver translates: "But unto Ḥannah he used to give one portion . . . *Howbeit* he loved Ḥannah; but Jehovah had shut up her womb." This interpretation, assuming as it does that the narrator's point is that Elkanah gave Hannah only one portion despite the fact that he loved her, leaves Peninnah's rancor unexplained, unless by simple displeasure at sharing her husband's affections. We expect some evidence of preferential treatment of Hannah (thus Targ. *ḥwlq ḥd bḥyr,* "a choice portion"). On purely textual grounds, moreover, the more difficult reading is to be preferred. It is unlikely that a straightforward conjunction like *'epes* (*kî*) could become altered to the obscure expression extant in MT. LXX^B, then, probably reflects a corruption of a text identical to MT, after which the explanatory plus, *hoti ouk ēn autē paidion = ky 'yn lh yld,* "for she had no child," arose. We are obliged, therefore, to account for *'appayim,* or rather *'pym,* as an obscure term or an early corruption. One attractive possibility is that the word means "double," comparable somehow to *py šnym* (cf. esp. Deut 21:17) if not in fact a corruption of *kplym* (Isa 40:2). This solution was favored by many early critics, though it leaves the grammatical relationship of *mānâ 'aḥat* in some doubt. Another possibility is that *'pym* bears some relationship to *pîmâ,* "fat" (Job 15:27), which has itself been related to Arabic *fa'ama,* I "fill, gorge," IV "make wide, fill with fat, fatten." Thus we might read "one fat portion, one rich portion," although we should then find it necessary to restore some acceptable adjectival form. A third possibility is adopted here as grammatically most defensible. Restoring *kpym* on the assumption of an early confusion of *k* and *'*, and read *kĕpîm,* "proportionate to them, equal to them." The expression is not common but well attested. It usually refers to a distribution according to size or another criterion. In Num 35:8, for example, the cession of Levitical cities by the various tribal groups is to be "proportionate to" (*kĕpî*) the size of the grants of land they have received. Therefore in the present passage, thus understood, Hannah is receiving preferential treatment insofar as, despite her childlessness, her single portion is equivalent to the several portions of her rival's family. Recently D. Aberbach, *"mnh 'ḥt 'pym,"* has attempted to relate *'pym* to *pym,* "paim," the unit of weight mentioned in 13:21 (see the NOTE there), with prosthetic *'alep*—thus, "one portion, *a paim in value.*" Contrast F. Deist, *"'APPAYIM."*

6. *used to provoke her to anger* Reading *wĕkî'ăsattâ . . . gam-kā'ēs* (MT *ka'as*) with most commentators. The force of *gam* is to suggest that this is an additional hardship (cf. Gen 31:15; 46:4; Num 16:13). We might paraphrase colloquially, "Yahweh had closed her womb, and, to make matters worse, her rival used to provoke her spitefully. . . ."

so that she would complain aloud Hebrew *ba'ăbûr harrĕ'îmāh* (*sic;* on the anomalous form, see GK §§20h,22s). There is no reason to doubt the text.

This meaning of *hir'îm*, lit. "thunder" and hence "complain aloud," is unique to this passage in the Hebrew Bible but attested for the Aramaic equivalent.

8. *Hannah* LXX adds *kai eipen autō idou egō kurie kai eipen autē*, "and she said to him, 'Here am I, lord!' And he said to her . . ." (reflecting an original with the common formula *wt'mr lw hnny 'dny wy'mr lh*. We read the shorter text of MT.

why MT *lāmeh;* LXX *ti estin soi hoti*, reflecting *mh lk ky*. There is no basis for choosing between these variants.

are you so resentful MT *yēra' lĕbābēk*, which might mean simply, "(Why) are you so wretched?" But cf. Deut 15:10, where a begrudging attitude is implied. LXX *typtei se hē kardia sou*, "(Why) does your heart smite you?" reflects *ykk lbbk*, an expression that elsewhere (24:6) implies remorse and self-reproach, which seem inappropriate here (so Driver, but cf. Smith).

9. *After she had eaten* Repointing MT *'aḥărê 'oklâ*, "After eating," as *'aḥărê 'oklāh*. LXX reflects "After *they* had eaten." Subsequently MT (cf. LXX[AL]) adds (after *bšlh*, see below) *wĕ'aḥărê šātōh*, "and after drinking"; omit with LXX[B].

privately MT has *bšlh*, "at Shiloh," and the versions offer nothing substantially different. The mention of Shiloh seems oddly repetitious here, and Smith, based upon a suggestion by Wellhausen and followed by Hertzberg and others, proposes to redivide MT *'ḥry 'klh bšlh*, "after eating at Shiloh," as *'ḥry 'kl hbšlh*, "after eating *the boiled meat* (*habbĕšēlâ*, cf. 2:13)." But a better solution is at hand. In the present passage the original reading was *bšly* "privately, quietly," exactly as in II Sam 3:27. This was misread as *bšlw*, "at Shiloh," *w* and *y* being easily confused in the scripts of many periods. "Shiloh" is written variously in MT as *šlh* (1:3; 2:14; 3:21; 4:3,4,12) and *šlw* (1:24; 3:21; 14:3), reflecting different periods in the orthographic history of the text, so that the final change from *bšlw* (< **bšly*) to *bšlh* was purely orthographic.

and presented herself before Yahweh LXX *kai katestē enōpion kyriou*, reflecting *wttyṣb lpny yhwh*. The phrase was omitted in MT through haplography after *šth*, "drinking" (*homoioteleuton*).

11. *and not forget your maidservant* MT *wl' tškḥ 't 'mtk* (also LXX[L], Syr., Vulg., Targ.); missing in LXX[B]. Though some have thought it suspiciously redundant, the rhetorical symmetry of the vow suggests that the phrase is original.

Then I shall set him before you . . . his head Though there is much confusion in the text at this point and MT is defective, a reconstruction is possible with the help of LXX and 4QSam[a]. Especial caution is required by the tendency of this verse and v 22 below to conflate. MT reads *wnttyw lyhwh kl ymy ḥyyw wmwrh l' y'lh 'l r'šw*, "Then I shall present him to Yahweh all the days of his life, and a razor will not touch his head." The mention of the razor is isolated and too abrupt. Something has fallen out here. LXX[(B)] has a fuller text: *kai dōsō auton enōpion sou doton heōs hēmeras thanatou autou kai oinon kai methysma ou pietai kai sidēros ouk anabēsetai epi tēn kephalēn autou*, reflecting *wnttyw lpnyk nzyr 'd ywm mwtw wyyn wškr l' yšth wmwrh l' y'lh 'l r'šw*, "Then I shall set him before you as a Nazirite until the day of his death, and wine and strong drink he will not drink, and a razor will not touch his head."

4QSam^a, though quite fragmentary at this point, requires a text of similar length. We reconstruct: . . . *wnttyhw l*[*pnyk nzyr ʿd ywm mwtw wyyn wškr lʾ yšth w*]*mwrh lʾ yʿbwr* ʿ[*l rʾšw*]. This differs from LXX only in reading *yʿbwr* for *yʿlh* in conflict with the unanimous witness of the versions and the stereotyped usage of *ʿālâ* with *môrâ* (Judg 13:5; 16:17; contrast Num 6:5). The words *wyyn wškr lʾ yšth,* attested by LXX and necessary to fill the space in 4QSam^a, alleviate the abruptness of MT and are probably original. This leaves to be settled only the question of the variants *wnttyw lyhwh kl ymy ḥyyw* (MT) and *wnttyhw lpnyk nzyr ʿd ywm mwtw* (LXX, 4QSam^a). The variation in the spelling of the verbal suffix is not significant. The insertion of *nzyr,* though entirely appropriate, is probably secondary, under the influence of v 22 (see there the second *Textual Note*). The reading *lpnyk* is better than *lyhwh* insofar as the deity is directly addressed in this passage. Finally we regard *kl ymy ḥyyw* (echoed in an expansion to v 22 in 4QSam^a) as original; *ʿd ywm mwtw* shows the influence of Judg 13:7 Thus we reconstruct: *wnttyw lpnyk kl ymy ḥyyw wyyn wškr lʾ yšth wmwrh lʾ yʿlh ʿl rʾšw.*

12. Reading *wayhî* for MT *wĕhāyâ;* GK §112uu.

13. *She* With LXX^BL, 4QSam^a; against MT, which has *wĕḥannâ hîʾ*, "And as for Hannah, she . . ."—an explicating expansion.

15. *unfortunate* Reading LXX *hē sklēra hēmera,* reflecting *qšt ywm,* lit. "hard of day" (cf. Job 30:25), with most commentators, against MT *qĕšat-rûaḥ,* which is unparalleled but seems to mean (inappropriately) "hard-spirited, obstinate."

16. *Do not think* All witnesses are unintelligible. MT has *ʾl ttn . . . lpny, "Do not set* your maidservant *before* a worthless woman," or perhaps, *"Do not make* your maidservant *into* a worthless woman." Comparison with Job 3:24 and 4:19 is hardly sufficient to establish that *nātan lipnê* can mean "regard as, treat as" (so many commentators). Smith's suggestion to read *kbt* for *lpny bt* is without textual warrant; nor is it clear by any means that *nātan kĕ-* can mean "reckon to be" (in Gen 42:30, read *wayyittēn ʾōtānû bammišmār kimraggĕlîm,* "and he put us in prison like spies" with LXX). Nevertheless, as all critics recognize, the meaning "Do not think your maidservant a worthless woman" is required here. Perhaps read *ʾl ttn ʾt mtk lpnyk lbt blyʿl* (cf. I Kings 8:50; etc.), lit. "Do not set your maidservant before you as a worthless woman," that is, "Do not reckon your maidservant a worthless woman."

my complaint and my vexation So MT: *śyḥy wkʿsy* (cf. LXX^AL, Syr., Vulg.). LXX^B has lost *wkʿsy,* "and my vexation," by haplography (*homoioteleuton*).

I have tarried So LXX: *ektetaka* = *hʾrkty* (Budde, Smith), used intransitively with a human subject only here (cf. Num 9:19,22) and preferable to MT *dbrty,* "I have spoken," as *lectio difficilior.* Note also Targ. *ʾwrkyt.* Hannah is explaining why she has lingered at the temple after the sacrificial meal. In defense of MT we might think of the seldom recognized Hebrew verb of motion *dbr,* "turn back, turn aside" (cf. M. Pope, *Song of Songs,* AB 7C [Garden City, N.Y.: Doubleday, 1977] 525-526). Thus we might retain MT and translate, "I have gone aside (to this place [*ʿad-hēnnâ*])."

18. *the woman . . . ate* MT: *wtlk h'šh ldrkh wt'kl*, "the woman went her way and ate." LXX: *kai eporeuthē hē gynē eis tēn hodon autēs kai eisēlthen eis to katalyma autēs kai ephagen meta tou andros autēs kai epien*, reflecting *wtlk h'šh ldrkh wtb' hlškth wt'kl 'm 'yšh wtšt*, "the woman went her way, and when she came to the (LXX^B *her*) chamber, she ate with her husband and drank." MT has lost *wtb' hlškth*, "and when she came to the chamber," by haplography after *ldrkh* (*homoioteleuton*), but the extra words at the end of LXX ("with her husband and drank") probably represent secondary expansion. Wellhausen strikes everything after *ldrkh*, but the point is that Hannah, somewhat encouraged by the words of Eli, is now willing to take nourishment (Budde). For a defense of MT, see Weingreen, "Rabbinic-Type Gloss."

and no longer wore her [disconsolate] expression Hebrew *ûpānêhā lō'-hāyû-lāh 'ôd*, lit. "and she no longer had her face." The expression has no real parallel, although Job 9:27 is sometimes cited: *'e'ezbâ pānay wĕ'ablîgâ*, "I shall abandon my face and be cheerful," that is, "I shall give up my sad expression and be cheerful." LXX here has *kai to prosōpon autēs ou synepesen eti*, from which some critics have reconstructed *wpnyh l' nplw 'wd*, "and her face was no longer fallen," a common enough expression—but too common: MT must be retained as *lectio difficilior*. No proposal, by the way, has yet accounted for the curious syntax with *pānêhā* in the first position. We expect some kind of disjunction.

20. *was pregnant* Placed before "when a year had passed" in LXX, but *ltqpwt hymym*, lit. "at the coming round of the days," refers to the coming round of the year, the time for the sacrifice mentioned in v 21 (Driver), not to the term of Hannah's pregnancy. We follow the arrangement of MT here.

21. *the seasonal sacrifice* MT adds *w't ndrw*, "and his vow," and LXX^B reflects a longer reading of the same kind (". . . and his vows and all the tithes of this land"). We know of no vow by Elkanah, and many critics have excised the words as secondary. But if so, what did the author of the expansion mean? Nowhere else is *ndr*, "vow," the object of *zbḥ*, "sacrifice." We must assume that the reading of MT is a vestige of a longer reading, whether expansive or original, to which LXX^L (cf. OL) gives a clue: *kai apodounai pasas tas euchas autou kai pasas tas dekatas tēs gēs autou*, "and to redeem (*lšlm*) all his vows and all the tithes of his land." Perhaps we should restore *w't ndrw lšlm w't kl m'śrwt 'rṣw*, "and to redeem his vow and all the tithes of his land," as original, assuming everything from *ndrw* to *'rṣw* to have been lost in MT by haplography.

to Yahweh So MT. LXX has "in Shiloh." Either reading may be original or both secondary.

22. *[I shall stay] . . . I have weaned him* The elliptical statement (see the NOTE) is expressed variously in the witnesses. MT has *'d ygml hn'r whb'tyw*, "[I shall stay] until the child is weaned, and then I shall bring him. . . ." LXX^B (*heōs tou anabēnai to paidarion ean apogalaktisō auto*) probably reflects *'d 'lwt hn'r k'šr gmltyhw*, "[I shall stay] until the child comes up, when I have weaned him. . . ." 4QSam^a preserves only *'d 'šr*, followed by a lacuna into which the reading of either MT or LXX will fit (assuming the slight modification of the latter to *'d 'šr y'lh hn'r*, etc.). The phrase *k'šr gmltw* appears in MT

in v 24, where it is redundant and syntactically awkward. LXX and 4QSam[a] omit the phrase in v 24. All of this suggests that it may be original in v 22. Thus we may hold a slight preference for the text of LXX[B].

he will appear . . . as a Nazirite forever See the second *Textual Note* at v 11. 4QSam[a] may be reconstructed here to read [*wnr'h*] *'t pn*[*y*] *yhwh wyšb lpny* [*yhwh šm 'd 'wlm wnt*]*tyhw nzyr 'd 'wlm kwl ymy* [*ḥyyw*], "and he will appear before Yahweh and remain before Yahweh there forever, for I shall dedicate him as a Nazirite forever all the days of his life." MT and LXX reflect a shorter text: *wnr'h 't pny yhwh wyšb šm 'd 'wlm.* Undoubtedly *lpny yhwh* in 4QSam[a] is a secondary expansion; cf. in v 11, *lpnyk* (4QSam[a]), *lyhwh* (MT). The concluding phrase, *kwl ymy ḥyyw* is probably secondary also, again under the influence of v 11. On the other hand, *wnttyhw nzyr 'd 'wlm* is original, having been lost in MT and LXX through an ordinary haplography caused by *homoioteleuton* (*'d 'wlm wnttyhw nzyr 'd 'wlm*). Cf. Josephus *Ant.* 5.347.

23. *May Yahweh confirm what you have said!* Reading *'k yqm yhwh hywṣ' mpyk,* lit. "May Yahweh indeed establish that which goes forth from your mouth!" with LXX (*alla stēsai kyrios to exelthon ek tou stomatos sou*) and 4QSam[a], which preserves [*'k yqm yhw*]*h hywṣ' mpyk.* MT has *'k yqm yhwh 't dbrw,* "May Yahweh establish his word!" but as yet there has been no word from Yahweh.

24. *Then she went up with him* So LXX: *kai anebē met' autou* = *wt'l 'tw.* This is supported by 4QSam[a], though the scroll actually reads *wt'l 'wtw,* "Then she took him up." This was an interpretation in fuller orthography of the same reading as that in the *Vorlage* of LXX in a time when the *nota accusativi* with suffix could replace the verbal suffix, as frequently in late biblical prose (GK §117b). MT has *wt'lhw 'mh,* "Then she took him up with her": the suffixed *Hip'il* verb is secondary, and *'mh* arose as a variant of *'tw* in an age when final *-ô* was still represented by *-h.*

to Shiloh . . . at Shiloh MT has simply *k'šr gmltw,* "when she had weaned him"; but, as noted above, this is repetitious and awkward. LXX has nothing at all after "to Shiloh." 4QSam[a] has *k'šr* followed by a gap with space for several words. F. M. Cross (personal communication) proposes the following solution: "We know that *k'šr* [*gmltw*] is too short to fill the space [in the scroll] and too long to permit a suitable reading if we include it. We should expect *k'šr* to introduce a reference to the customary pilgrimage of Elkanah. As long ago observed by Wellhausen, the text of LXX presumes that Elkanah went up with Hannah and the lad, taking the sacrifices, and after making his customary devotions killed the sacrificial calf which was specified to fulfill the vow of Hannah. Contrary to Wellhausen, there is every reason now to suppose that LXX preserves the more original account. Tentatively one may restore: *šylh k'šr 'lh 'yšh lzbḥ lyhwh šylh.* LXX has suffered a haplography, the scribe's eye jumping from the first *šylh* to the second *šylh.*" The defective MT was influenced by the expression *k'šr gmltyhw* in v 22 before it was lost there (see above), creating the present (tautological) reading.

with a three-year-old bull Reading *bpr mšlš* with LXX (*en moschō trietizonti*) and Syr. MT *bprym šlšh* shows a simple corruption, the *m* grouped with the wrong word. 4QSam[a] is expansive: [*bpr bn*] *bqr mšlš* (cf. Lev 4:3; etc.).

an ephah of flour After *mšlš* appears *wlḥm*, "and bread," in LXX (*kai artois*) and 4QSam[a], probably secondarily. MT has *'êpâ 'aḥat qemaḥ*, "one ephah (of) flour," but *'ḥt* is to be deleted as an expansion, having arisen after the corruption of *bpr mšlš* to *bprym šlšh*, "three calves."

24-25. *After they had gone . . . to Eli* The text at this point is seriously troubled, having become conflate in all witnesses and then, at least in MT, suffered further corruption. LXX[B] reads *kai eisēlthen eis oikon kyriou en sēlōm kai to paidarion met' autōn kai prosēgagon enōpion kyriou, kai esphaxen ho patēr autou tēn thysian hēn epoiei ex hēmerōn eis hēmeras tō kyriō kai prosēgagen to paidarion kai esphaxen ton moschon kai prosēgagen hanna hē mētēr tou paidariou pros ēlei*, reflecting *wtb' byt yhwh šylh whn'r 'mm wyb'w lpny yhwh wyšḥṭ 'byhw 't hzbḥ k'šr y'śh mymym ymymh lyhwh wtb' 't hn'r wyšḥṭ 't hpr wtb' ḥnh 'm hn'r 'l 'ly*, "And she came to the house of Yahweh in Shiloh, and the child was with them. And they went before Yahweh, and his father slaughtered the sacrifice as he did regularly to Yahweh. And she took the child, and he slaughtered the calf. And Hannah, the mother of the child, went to Eli." MT has a shorter text: *wtb'hw byt yhwh šlw whn'r n'r wyšḥṭw 't hpr wyby'w 't hn'r 'l 'ly*. "And she brought him to the house of Yahweh in Shiloh, and the child was a child (?). And they slaughtered the calf and brought the child to Eli." The unintelligible expression *whn'r n'r* is the remnant of a long haplography due to *homoioteleuton*, suggesting that the Hebrew tradition behind MT at this point was substantially the same as that behind LXX. Enough is preserved in 4QSam[a] to assure that it, too, had the full text. Both the requirements of space and the clear traces of *hzbḥ k'šr* make this reading certain. Thus:

[. . . *wtb' byt*] *yhwh šylh whn'r*
['*mm wyb'w lpny yhwh wyšḥṭ 'byhw 't*] *hzb*[*ḥ k*]*'šr*
[*y'śh mymym ymymh lyhwh wtb' 't hn'r wy*]*šḥṭ*
['*t hpr wtb' ḥnh 'm hn'r 'l 'ly* . . .]

All witnesses, in short, point to a reading similar to that of the *Vorlage* of LXX; but this long, repetitious text is manifestly a conflation of two shorter variants. Tentatively, we may reconstruct these as follows: (A) *wyb'w* (so LXX[L]; LXX[B] *wtb'*; MT *wtb'hw*) *byt yhwh šylh whn'r 'mm wyšḥṭ 'byhw 't hzbḥ k'šr y'śh mymym ymymh lyhwh wtb' 't hn'r* <*'l 'ly*>; (B) *wyb'w lpny yhwh wyšḥṭw* (so MT, LXX[L]; LXX[B], 4QSam[a] *wyšḥṭ*) *'t hpr wtb' ḥnh 't hn'r* (cf. MT, Vulg.; LXX[B] *'m hn'r*) *'l 'ly*. Variant A is redundant in its reference to Shiloh and echoes vv 3 and 24 in content. Variant B is evidently the superior reading.

26. *As surely as you live* MT here adds another *'ădōnî*, "my lord." Omit with LXX.

28. *For as long as he lives* LXX *pasas tas hēmeras has zē autos*, reflecting *kl hymym 'šr ḥy hw'* (cf. Syr., Targ.). MT *kl hymym 'šr hyh* (*hw'*) is patently corrupt.

Then she left him there and worshiped Yahweh The witnesses are at odds here because of the confusion caused by the insertion of the Song of Hannah

MT has simply, "So he worshiped Yahweh there" (*wayyištaḥû šām lĕyahweh*), referring, presumably, to Eli. LXX^B has nothing at all at this point, but after the song reads in 2:11: *kai katelipen auton ekei enōpion kyriou,* reflecting *wt'zbhw šm lpny yhwh,* "And she left him there before Yahweh." LXX^L follows MT in v 28, but in 2:11 reflects *wy'zbwhw lpny yhwh šm wyšthww lyhwh.* 4QSam^a in v 28 preserves [. . . *wt'zb*]*hw šm wtšth*[*w lyhwh* . . .]. This reading deserves preference. The presence of *šām* in MT indicates that the tradition behind it had some reference to the leaving of the child. As hinted by its varying position in LXX^B and LXX^L, *lpny yhwh* is probably secondary.

NOTES

1 1. *Ramathaim.* The name *rāmātayim* means "the Double Height." LXX renders it *harmathaim,* and the city is associated with Arimathea of the New Testament and identified with the village of Rempthis by Eusebius of Caesarea (*Onomasticon* 32.21-23; 144.27-29) and Jerome, who locates it in the region of Timnah (modern Khirbet Tibneh, ca. 9 miles NW of Bethel). If the ancient authorities are correct, the site is modern Rentis, ca. 16 miles E of Tel Aviv on the western slope of the hills of Ephraim. But this has been long disputed. For other possible locations, see W. F. Albright, *AASOR* 4 (1922/23) 112-113.

a Zuphite. Apparently Zuph was the eponymous ancestor of natives of an area of unknown extent in the vicinity of Ramathaim. The district is mentioned again in 9:5, where it turns out to be Samuel's home.

Elkanah . . . the son of Zuph, an Ephraimite. This genealogy is also given with slight variations (see the *Textual Notes*) by the Chronicler (I Chron 6:11-12,19-20 [English 6:26-27,34-35]), who ascribes to Elkanah a Levitical descent. In particular, Elkanah and Samuel are assigned to the Kohathite family of Levites, among whose responsibilities was the care of the ark (Num 3:31). This adjustment of Samuel's lineage may reflect the sense of theocratic propriety of the post-Exilic community. In the present account, Elkanah is an Ephraimite with no specified priestly connection.

2. *the first . . . the second.* Hannah is explicitly called the first wife. We learn below that she is also the favorite of her husband. Perhaps we are to conclude that it was her failure to bear him children that prompted Elkanah to marry a second time.

3. *regularly.* Hebrew *miyyāmîm yāmîmâ,* lit. "from days to days." The expression seems to connote "annual(ly)." At least this is the case unambiguously in its occurrences in Exod 13:10 and Judg 11:40. Note also *šānâ bĕšānâ* in v 7 below. Elkanah goes annually to Shiloh to perform the seasonal sacrifice (*zebaḥ hayyāmîm;* see the NOTE at v 21), which M. Haran (*VT* 19 [1969] 11-22) has described as a cultic-familial observance taking place once a year. It was, he says, distinct from the seasonal *ḥaggîm,* the agricultural pilgrim festivals.

Yahweh Sabaoth. That is, *yahweh ṣĕbā'ôt,* the national deity of Israel. This is a longer form of the name Yahweh, the derivation and original significance of which are disputed. Cf. the discussion of William H. Brownlee, "The Ineffable Name of God," *BASOR* 226 (1977) 38-46. Quite possibly *yahweh ṣĕbā'ôt* meant "He who creates the (heavenly) armies," an ancient cultic epithet of the high god 'El in his aspects as warrior and creator; see the discussion of Cross, *CMHE,* 68-71. Whatever its original significance it is here the proper name of the god of Israel, who guides the crucial events of the formation of the new state. Yahweh was believed to be specially present with the ark, the central object of the Israelite cult, which, as we learn below, was remembered as having been located at Shiloh in this early period. It was to worship before the ark of Yahweh that Elkanah went up to Shiloh.

Shiloh. Modern Khirbet Seilun, ca. 20 miles NNE of Jerusalem among the hills of Ephraim. An ancient cultic center, it was remembered as the central sanctuary of the Israelite cult at the time of Samuel's birth. Archaeological evidence suggests that it was not a city of major importance long before or after the late premonarchical period (see Marie-Louise Buhl and S. Holm-Nielsen, *Shiloh: The Danish Excavations at Tell Sailun, Palestine, in 1926, 1929, 1932, and 1963: The Pre-Hellenistic Remains* [Copenhagen: The National Museum of Denmark, 1969]; and most scholars have assumed that the shrine itself was destroyed in the course of the Philistine wars described later in c 4 (cf. Jeremiah's references to the ruins of Shiloh in Jer 7:12,14; 26:6,9), though it now seems that there is no archaeological evidence to substantiate this (cf. Bright, *History,* 181 and n. 5).

Shiloh occupied a prominent position in prophetic tradition, not only as the childhood home of Samuel, but as the city of Ahijah, the prophet associated with Jeroboam (I Kings 11:29*ff;* 14:1*ff*). Jeremiah too was descended from the Shilonite house of Eli (assuming that, as a member of a priestly family from Anathoth, he could trace his ancestry to Abiathar [cf. Jer 1:1; I Kings 2:26-27]).

Hophni and Phinehas. Both names are Egyptian. The house of Eli (and thus the old Shilonite priesthood) claimed Levitical descent, tracing its lineage back to Moses. For some of the implications, see Cross, *CMHE,* c 8 *passim.* On Egyptian names in the tribe of Levi, see Noth, *Israelitischen Personennamen,* 63.

4-7. The temporal relationship of the events described in these verses is subtle and can be discerned only by careful attention to grammatical detail. Two types of verbal sequences are used here. One of these, which expresses habitual or continued action in the past, employs independent prefixed verbs and suffixed verbs joined to the conjunction—hence in v 3 above *wĕ'ālâ,* "he used to go up." The other type of sequence, the common Hebrew vehicle for simple past narration, uses independent suffixed verbs and, most characteristically, prefixed verbs joined to the conjunction. The beginning of v 4 exhibits such a sequence: *wayhî hayyôm wayyizbaḥ 'elqānâ,* "One day when Elkanah was sacrificing. . . ." Such a protasis introduces simple past narration and requires an apodosis of the same type. This is found only near the end of v 7, viz. *wattibkeh,* "she wept." All of the intervening material, which is couched in the syntax of habitual action in the past, is therefore to be understood as parenthesis: *wĕnātan . . . yittēn . . . wĕkî'ăsattâ . . . ya'ăśeh . . . tak'īsennâ,* "he would give . . . he would give . . . she used to provoke her . . . he would do . . . she would provoke her. . . ." In the present translation, we repeat the protasis after the long parenthesis to help the reader resume his train of thought (the original found no such repetition necessary). We may render *wattibkeh,* "she wept," as "she began to weep" to conform to English idiom ("she wept" would suggest continued action). With *wĕlō' tō'kal* the Hebrew returns to the habitual sequence, in this case to indicate that Hannah refused to eat—hence our translation, "would not eat," preserving the durative sense of the verb.

5. *a single portion equal to theirs.* If this reading is correct (see the *Textual Note*), the narrator's point is that Elkanah accords to Hannah a special distinction disproportionate to her barren status. The motive for this preferential treatment is provided in the following clause, *kî 'et-ḥannâ 'āhēb,* "for it was Hannah that he loved," not simply, "for he loved Hannah," which would be *kî 'āhēb 'et-ḥannâ.* This also explains Peninnah's spiteful and rather brutal treatment of her co-wife and provides some justification for Elkanah's remonstrance in v 8, "Am I not better to you than ten sons?"

6. *her rival.* That is, Peninnah. The correct meaning of Hebrew *ṣārâ,* "rival wife, co-wife," already recognized in the ancient versions, was first given a modern scholarly treatment by Paul de Lagarde, *Mittheilungen* I (Göttingen, 1884) 125-134. The same term (**ḍarrat-*) is reflected in cognate languages (Syriac *'artā,* Arabic *ḍarratu*ⁿ) with similar force. Hebrew *ṣārâ* became virtually a technical, legal designation for a man's second wife in the Talmudic period, when bigamy was permitted (though not encouraged) until its general prohibition in the tenth century CE.

7. *the house of Yahweh* The expression *bêt yahweh* may refer to a tent-shrine or to a permanent temple. At least one major branch of Israelite tradition, of which II Samuel 7 is the chief exemplar, favors the former, insofar as it assumes that the ark never resided in a permanent sanctuary before the construction of Solomon's temple (note esp. II Sam 7:6 and cf. Pss 78:60 and 132:7). The two references to *hêkal yahweh,* unambiguously "the temple of Yahweh," in 1:9 and 3:3 below seem to belie this conclusion, and thus to represent a rival tradition.

8. *Am I not better to you than ten sons?* What does this mean? Perhaps Elkanah is saying, "Do I not treat you even better than would be appropriate if you had ten sons." See the NOTE to v 5 above.

9. *the doorpost of the temple of Yahweh.* Hebrew *mĕzûzat hêkal yahweh.* Strictly speaking, the *hêkāl* was the nave or temple proper at the back of which was the inner sanctuary (*dĕbîr*). Eli's chair is beside the doorpost at the entrance to the nave affording him a view through the vestibule (*'ûlām*) of Hannah, who presumably is praying at the entrance to the temple.

11. In Northwest Semitic tradition vows were expressed in stereotyped formulae. See Loren R. Fisher in *Ras Shamra Parallels,* 1. 147-152 and esp. 151-152. Hannah's vow is couched in poetry. After the extrametrical invocation of the deity follows a quatrain of long lines (syllable count in restored Hebrew: 12:13:13:13) and a couplet of short lines (8:9). Compare the verses of the

annunciation to Samson's mother in Judg 13:3-5 (cf. 13:7,13-14), where the poetry is somewhat more difficult to recover:

> . . . You were barren and had not given birth, (8)
> But you have become pregnant and will bear a son . . . (7)
> Drink no wine or strong drink! (7)
> Eat no unclean food! (7)
> Now you are pregnant and will bear a son. (8)
> Let no razor touch his head! (9)
> The child is to be a Nazirite of God from the womb . . . (8)

We may posit the existence of a stock of such poetry in early Israel stemming from the rites of Nazirite dedication, of which two examples have survived within the tales of Samson and Samuel.

offspring. Paraphrasing Hebrew *zera' 'ănāšîm,* lit. "seed of men." The frequently given translation "male child" is indefensible even though Hannah presumably intends a boy and, indeed, gets one. The expression, which is unique to this passage in the Hebrew Bible, may be an instance of periphrasis for metrical reasons.

I shall set him before you. Though it is not made explicit until v 22 (see the *Textual Note*), Hannah is pledging her child to the life of a Nazirite. For the pertinent regulations, see Num 6:1-21. A Nazirite was an individual specially dedicated to God by vows of separation, abstention from products of the vine, and regulation of cutting the hair. According to Israelite tradition such an individual was endowed with certain charismatic gifts as a warrior. Samson (Judg 13:5,7) is the chief example. Here Samuel is said to have been consecrated even before birth, as was Samson. In spite of the loss of the specification of his Nazirite status in MT, postbiblical Jewish tradition remembered Samuel as a Nazirite, as reflected in the Hebrew fragments to Sir 46:13 (see M. Z. Segal, *spr bn-syr' hšlm* [Jerusalem, 1958] 321) and in the Talmudic tractate Nazir 9.5.

strong drink. Hebrew *šēkār* (a fixed pair with "wine" in the repertoire of the Canaanite bard, as attested in Ugaritic as well as Hebrew poetry) refers to any intoxicating beverage, i.e. wine or beer.

17. *the request you have made of him.* Hebrew *šēlātēk 'ăšer šā'alt mē'immô,* foreshadowing v 27. This is the first in a series of wordplays involving the root *š'l,* "ask, request." See the NOTES to vv 20 and 27,28.

18. *to the chamber.* Hebrew *liškātâ.* Evidently this was a room in the temple where sacrificial meals were eaten, as in 9:22. The term "lishka" or "chamber" elsewhere refers to any of several kinds of rooms with various functions associated with the temple in Jerusalem.

19. *Ramah.* Elkanah's home is called Ramathaim only in v 1, elsewhere Ramah. This might be regarded as a satisfactory shorter form of the name of the Ephraimite village, but it is clear in subsequent chapters that the narrator is thinking of Ramah of Benjamin (modern er-Rām, ca. 5 miles N of Jerusalem). Apparently there is confusion in the tradition itself. The older narrative recorded Samuel's home as Ramathaim of the land of Zuph in the Ephraimite hills. In the course of the transmission of the story, the name became associated

with the much more familiar Benjaminite Ramah. The result is a mixed picture. In the present episode there is no barrier to maintaining the assumption that Ephraimite Ramathaim is intended.

Elkanah knew Hannah. The most common of the biblical euphemisms for sexual intercourse.

Yahweh remembered her. In such a context, the expression implies more than simple calling to mind. Remembering in the religious terminology of Israel and other Northwest Semitic societies referred to the benevolent treatment of an individual or group by a god, often, as in this case, in response to a specific plea (see the discussion of W. Schottroff in *TWAT* 1.507-518, esp. 514). Yahweh in his role as governor of childbirth (cf. 2:5b) has ensured the success of Hannah's union with her husband.

20. *Samuel, "because," [she said,] "it was from Yahweh that I requested him."* As explained in the NOTE on vv 27,28 below, a dominant feature in the original form of this story was its repeated wordplay on the verb *š'l*, "ask, request," culminating in the assertion *hû' šā'ûl lĕyahweh*, "He is dedicated (Saul!) to Yahweh." This fact in company with other considerations leads to the conclusion that Samuel's birth narrative has absorbed elements from another account describing Saul's birth (see the COMMENT). The explanation of the name Samuel in the present verse might be regarded as simply another instance of play on *š'l* because of the occurrence of *šĕ'iltîw*, "I requested him." But closer inspection is required. The Hebrew is *šĕmû'ēl kî miyyahweh šĕ'iltîw*, lit. " 'Samuel' because, 'From Yahweh I requested him.' " The syntax is important: *miyyahweh* stands in the emphatic first position suggesting that it and not the verb is the intended referent of the etymology. The name Samuel is being explained as if it were *šemē'ēl*, "He-who-is-from-God." Thus, "She named him 'He-who-is-from-God' because it was from Yahweh that she had requested him." The correspondence of *-mē'ēl* to *-mû'ēl* is no worse (or better) than that of *mē'āb* to *mō'āb* in the explanation of the name Moab in Gen 19:37. The purpose of this verse, then, is not to reinforce the etymological play on *š'l* but, on the contrary, to eclipse it or at least to modify it to the requirements of the name Samuel. This has no bearing, however, on the question of the original meaning of the name *šĕmû'ēl* from the point of view of the modern philologian. It displays archaic features and may already have been an ancient name in the time when the present story is set. In its original form the name was probably **šimuhū-'il-*, that is, "His-name-is-'El." Contraction of *-uhū* to *-û* and other changes attending the growth of the language led to the present form. (Nevertheless the name remains somewhat at variance with the normal morphological development of the language: we expect *šĕmô'ēl.*) The meaning of the name is clear. The suffix ("his") refers not to the deity but to the individual so named—thus, "His-name (i.e. the name on which he calls in worship) -is-'El." Compare the personal name *rĕ'û'ēl*, "Reuel," originally **ri'uhū-'il-*, "His-friend-is-'El." In such a context the "name" of a deity refers to his cultically available presence; the "name of Yahweh," for example, is intimately associated with the ark.

21. *the seasonal sacrifice.* Hebrew *zebaḥ hayyāmîm*, lit. "the sacrifice of days," and thus, "the annual sacrifice" (also 2:19; cf. 20:6). See the NOTE on "regularly" at v 3 above.

22. [*I shall stay*] *until the child goes.* Hebrew *'ad 'ălôt hanna'ar* (reconstructed; see *Textual Note*). Such an elliptical expression with *'ad* is unusual but not unexampled elsewhere. Cf. Judg 16:2: *'ad 'ôr habbōqer wahăragnûhû,* "[We shall wait] until the morning light, and then we shall slay him."

a Nazirite. See the NOTE on "I shall set him before you" at v 11.

24. *a three-year-old bull.* The expression *par měšulläš* (see the *Textual Note*) is elliptical, omitting the unit of time in question (years). As E. A. Speiser pointed out some time ago, this usage, which occurs elsewhere in Biblical Hebrew (Gen 15:9[*tris*]; cf. Ezek 42:6; Eccles 4:12), is also found in Nuzi Akkadian. Here, as in Gen 15:9 and ancient Mesopotamian cultic practice, the specification of age identifies the animal as of legal maturity for sacrifice. See *BASOR* 72 (1938) 15-17.

an ephah of flour. The standard measure of dry capacity was the homer or ass-load. The ephah was equal to a tenth of a homer, roughly half a bushel.

27,28. Scattered about the birth narrative are several occurrences of the verb *šā'al/hiš'îl,* "ask/hand over, dedicate," and related nouns. Thus in v 27 we read "my request (*šě'ēlātî*) which I asked (*šā'altî*) of him" (cf. v 17 and the NOTE) and in v 28 "I have dedicated him (*hiš'iltīhû*) to Yahweh . . . he is dedicated (*šā'ûl*) to Yahweh." We recognize in these passages wordplay upon the name of the child, a common feature of Old Testament birth narratives. Nevertheless it is impossible to derive *šěmû'ēl* from a form of *šā'al,* even on the basis of a popular and fanciful etymology. The notion that the author is proposing to us the monstrous contraction *šěmû'ēl* < *šā'ûl mē'ēl,* "asked of God," goes back at least to David Kimchi, the great medieval philologian; and other equally unlikely explanations have been offered. But at best the expressions in question bring the name Samuel to mind in a general way by virtue of assonance (Driver). It has not gone unnoticed, however, that the wordplay involved here applies much more naturally to the name Saul (*šā'ûl*). This raises the suspicion that within the narrative about Samuel's birth are elements taken from one about Saul's. The suspicion becomes almost a certainty when the narrative closes with the formula *hû' šā'ûl lěyahweh,* "he is dedicated to Yahweh," or quite simply, "he is Saul (= one who is dedicated, handed over) to Yahweh." This is the climax to which the previous wordplays have been building. In composing the story of Samuel's birth the narrator expropriated the force of the various plays for his own purposes (see the NOTE at v 20), but their original intent can still be discerned.

COMMENT

Israel remembered the appearance of its first great prophet as an event of singular importance. Samuel's career was regarded as a watershed in the sacred history, separating the days of the judges from the days of the kings, and the portentous story of his birth in the form it has come down to us leaves no doubt that something significant has occurred. It is easy to see that beyond the entertaining little melodrama of Hannah and Elkanah, the narrator is preparing us for a new departure in Israel's experience.

Yet the setting of the story is not new but old. The scene is Shiloh, an early shrine of Yahwism and, according to tradition, the last great center of Israelite worship before the monarchy. Here the old Elide priesthood still officiates. The story itself is reminiscent of the account of Samson's birth and seems to find its place among the ancient-most legends of Israel. But the rudiments of new ways are also here. The child whose birth is recounted is to become the single figure under whose direction the old system will dissolve in favor of the age of prophets and kings. And he is ascribed a hero's birth in a tale of miracles.

This at least is the perspective of the prophetic circles from which our story derives.[1] No king receives first consideration in the history of the incipient monarchy; instead it is Samuel, the prophet and anointer of kings, who dominates the scene. His birth sets in motion a chain of events that will begin with the inauguration of kingship in Israel and the rejection of Shiloh and the house of Eli and end with the election of David and the beginning of the worship of Yahweh in Jerusalem. Samuel's conception itself is miraculous, the answer to a barren woman's prayer, recalling details of the stories of Samson and even Isaac, not to mention New Testament figures. As in the case of Isaac, whose birth represented the fulfillment in principle of Yahweh's promise of posterity to Abraham, the gift of a son to Hannah makes possible the working out of the divine plan at a crucial juncture in the history of the people. We learn at the end of c 3 that Samuel is to be the mouthpiece through which Yahweh's will is communicated to this generation of Israelites as they undertake the heavy responsibilities of change. In other words the child is to become the prototype of the ideal prophet, a vessel of divine purpose and a director of human affairs. The prophetic point of view according to which our story received its primary shape clearly held Samuel's birth to be an event of unique importance.

Behind the narrative in its present form, however, we discern a complex interweaving of literary patterns, of which that concerned primarily with Samuel is only the most conspicuous.[2] The tragedy of Eli, for example, a theme to be developed in subsequent chapters, begins here as the old priest stolidly executes his office preparing unwittingly for his own downfall. As our discussion in the sections that follow will show, Samuel had no part in this tragedy in its earliest formulation, but in the prophetic version he is a leading figure. Basic to the present story, moreover, is the

[1] See LITERARY HISTORY in the Introduction.

[2] Among the recent treatments of the literary history of I Samuel 1 are Noth, "Samuel und Silo"; Garbini, "Osservazioni linguistiche"; Dus, "Geburtslegende Samuels"; Willis, "Anti-Elide Narrative Tradition" and "Cultic Elements."

motif of Nazirite birth and dedication, and here the source critic is most exercised. We expect the child born under such circumstances to be a warrior like Samson, but only the Samuel of c 7 will fulfill this expectation and only in a general way. The many-sided prophet of Ramah can hardly be compared to simple, heroic Samson. As we have already noted (see the NOTE at vv 27,28), the repeated wordplay on *š'l,* which applies so easily to Saul and so awkwardly to Samuel, provides the clue to the mystery of the prehistory of this part of the narrative. Other evidence strengthens the case that a story of Nazirite origins belonging originally to Saul was borrowed and built into the account of Samuel's birth.[3]

The latter conclusion involves such a radical impeachment of the integrity of the account that the considerations upon which it is based must be listed in detail. (1) The anticipatory wordplay on *š'l* in vv 17 and 27, which finds its resolution in v 28 in the assertion *hû' šā'ûl lĕyahweh,* "He is dedicated (Saul!) to Yahweh," is most decisive, as already explained in the NOTES. (2) The formal similarity between the introductory verse of this story (1:1) and that of the tale of the lost asses of Kish, Saul's father (9:1), is striking. It is quite possible that the identification of Kish and his genealogy originally stood at the beginning of a Nazirite birth narrative. In the present story the credentials are those of Elkanah, which may be patterned upon them. (3) As already noted, the points of contact between this account and that of Samson's Nazirite birth in Judges 13 are conspicuous. It may be argued, moreover, that Saul is much more easily described as a hero like Samson than is Samuel. To be sure Samuel does "judge" Israel and fight heroically against the Philistines in the account of the Israelite victory in c 7; but the report there is of a highly generalized sort —probably itself a product of prophetic revision—without clear parallels to the Samson saga. By contrast the narratives relating Saul's military exploits share specific features with the stories about Samson. Conclusive is the account of Saul's victory over Nahash the Ammonite (10:27b-11:11), where Saul is filled with heroic inspiration and anger in a fashion that recalls Samson's behavior in detail (compare 11:6 to Judg 14:6,19; 15:14; and see the NOTES at 11:6).[4]

The story of the birth of Samuel, therefore, has been built from diverse materials. Fundamental is an account of Saul's birth and Nazirite dedication which has been transferred to Samuel. The wordplay that animated the older version has been retained, probably because of the slight similarity in the sound of the two names, with some effort to divert its original intent (see the NOTE at v 20), but the entire account has been overlaid with

[3] Though long recognized, the implications of this fact were first systematically investigated by Hylander, *Samuel-Saul-Komplex,* 11-39.

[4] For further comparison of these two wrathful, self-willed heroes, see Dus, "Geburtslegende Samuels," 174-175.

the personal details of Samuel's childhood—his father's name, his mother's name, the name of his native village. The narrator has set the central episodes in Shiloh, thereby permitting himself to incorporate the beginning of the story of the fall of the house of Eli into the whole. It is not likely that the infant Saul was associated with Eli.[5] All else that we know of Israel's first king renders this generally improbable, and, in addition, the chronology is wrong: Eli's great-great-grandson will be Saul's priest at the battle of Michmash (see 14:3 and the NOTE). So the Shilonite apprenticeship is not an original element from the tradition but, like the transferral of Saul's birth narrative, an innovation in the prophetic revision of the material which works to the aggrandizement of Samuel, who will become heir to the lost authority of the house of Eli (see the COMMENT on 3:1-4:1a; cf. p. 16). This will be the subject of the material that follows Hannah's song of thanksgiving.

[5] The unlikelihood that Saul was a temple boy at Shiloh has been the chief barrier to the acceptance of the theory that his birth narrative underlies the present account. Cf. Noth, "Samuel und Silo," 394-396. Dus ("Geburtslegende Samuels") is to be credited with recognizing the independence of the Shiloh and Eli elements from the original Nazirite birth narrative.

II. THE SONG OF HANNAH
(2:1-10)

2 1 [Hannah] said:

My heart exults in Yahweh! (7)
My horn is raised by my god! (8)
My mouth is stretched over my enemies! (7)
I rejoice in my vindication. (8)
2 For there is no holy one like Yahweh, (7)
And no mountain like our god! (8)
3 Do not speak haughtily (8)
Or let arrogance out of your mouth! (8)
For Yahweh is a mindful god, (6)
And a god who balances his actions: (8)
4 The bows of the mighty are broken, (7)
While the feeble are girded with armor; (8)
5 The sated have hired out for bread, (8)
While the hungry are fattened on food; (8)
The childless wife has borne seven, (8)
While the mother of many sons is bereaved. (8)
6 It is Yahweh who slays and quickens, (8)
Who sends down to Sheol and brings up. (7)
7 It is Yahweh who makes poor and makes rich, (7)
Who debases and also exalts; (6)
8 Who raises the poor from the dust, (6)
From the scrap heap lifts the needy, (7)
To give them a seat with noblemen (7)
And grant them a chair of honor. (8)
For the straits of the earth are Yahweh's, (8)
And upon them he founded the world. (7)
9 He guards the way of his faithful, (7)
But the wicked perish in darkness. (9)

He gives to the vower his vow (6)
And blesses the years of the just. (8)
For no one can prevail by his own power; (7)
10 It is Yahweh who shatters his antagonists. (7)
Who is h[oly like Yahweh?] (6)
. . .
. . .
. . .
[He guards] the feet [of his faithful] (7)
. . .
. . . kin[g] . . .
Eli thunders in heaven! (7)
Yahweh judges the ends of the earth! (7)
Now may he give power to his king (7)
And raise the horn of his anointed! (7)

TEXTUAL NOTES

2 1. *[Hannah] said* Reading the shorter text of LXX[B] (= *wt'mr*), "And she said," in preference to MT *wttpll ḥnh wt'mr, "And Hannah prayed* and said" (so LXX[L]).

by my God Reading b'lhy on the basis of LXX (*en theō mou*) and OL. MT and 4QSam[a] (*rmh qrny by*[*hw*]*h*) repeat *byhwh*, "in, by Yahweh," which is poetically inferior and textually suspicious.

My mouth is stretched over my enemies! LXX seems to reflect *rḥb 'l 'wybym py* for MT *rḥb py 'l 'wyby*. The word order of the latter is more consistent with the two preceding lines.

1-2. *I rejoice in my vindication. For* Reading *śmḥty byšw'ty ky* with LXX, against MT *ky śmḥty byšw'tk*. The initial *ky*, absent in LXX, is a prosaizing addition. The final -*k* of MT is the remnant of a following *ky* reflected in LXX (*hoti*) and 4QSam[a], which reads [*k*]*y' 'yn qdwš kyh*[*wh*].

2. This verse is conflate in all witnesses. All have *ky 'yn qdwš kyhwh* (MT omits *ky;* see above). We posit a variant *ky 'yn qdwš bltk*, "For there is no holy one apart from you," retained in MT without *qdwš* and in LXX without *ky*. MT *w'yn ṣwr k'lhynw* and LXX *w'yn ṣdyq k'lhynw* (*kai ouk estin dikaios hōs ho theos hēmōn*) are also ancient variants. The former (which is superior) is also preserved in 4QSam[a]; cf. also M. Dahood in Fisher, *Ras Shamra Parallels* 2. 27. The following chart shows the original bicolon, its variants, and the texts reflected in the versions:

ORIGINAL:	*ky 'yn qdwš kyhwh*
	w'yn ṣwr k'lhynw
VARIANTS:	*ky 'yn qdwš bltk*
and	*w'yn ṣdyq k'lhynw*
MT:	*'yn qdwš kyhwh*
	ky 'yn bltk
	w'yn ṣwr k'lhynw
LXX:	*ky 'yn qdwš kyhwh*
	w'yn ṣdyq k'lhynw
	'yn qdwš bltk
4QSam[a]:	[*k*]*y' 'yn qdwš kyh*[*wh*]
	[*w'yn ṣdyq k'lwhynw*
	w'yn blt]*k*
	w'yn ṣwr k'lwhynw

3. *Do not speak haughtily* Reading *'l tdbrw gbhh.* LXX *mē kauchasthe kai mē laleite hypsēla,* "Do not boast and do not speak haughtily," seems to preserve two renderings of this, and (similarly) MT *'l trbw tdbrw gbhh gbhh,* "Do not continue to speak (?) haughtily, haughtily," seems to be a conflation of it in correct and corrupt form.

Or let . . . out Reading *'l yṣ',* "let not (arrogance) go out," on the basis of LXX. MT omits *'l.*

a mindful god Reading *'l d'wt,* lit. "a god of knowledge," with MT (on the plural, see Driver). LXX has *theos gnōseōs,* reflecting *'l d't,* with which 4QSam[a] agrees. We read the *lectio difficilior.*

And a god who balances his actions MT has *wl'* (*qĕrê: lô*) *ntknw 'llwt,* "And by him (?) actions are balanced." But we read *w'l tkn 'llwtw* on the basis of LXX *kai theos hetoimazōn epitēdeumata autou.*

4. *The bows . . . are broken* MT *qšt . . . ḥtym.* Poetic symmetry requires the plural, and the treatment of the verb as singular in LXX (*ēsthenēsen*) and 4QSam[a] (*ḥth*) must reflect a "correction" of *ḥtym* based on ignorance of the (masculine) plural form *qāšōt,* a rare byform of *qĕšātôt.* Cf. M. Dahood, *Ugaritic-Hebrew Philology* (Rome: PBI, 1965) 15.

5. *are fattened on food* MT (cf. Syr., Vulg.) *ḥdlw 'd;* see the NOTE. LXX has *parēkan gēn,* and whereas the first word corresponds to *ḥdlw,* the second corresponds not to *'d* but, as Marvin L. Chaney in a paper presented to the Society of Biblical Literature, October 25, 1974, has shown, to *ḥdl* (=*ḥld*), "world." This may be a case of dittography, as Chaney suggests, or of the conflation of different attempts to render the same original.

8. *with noblemen* Reading MT *'m ndybym,* the shortest in a group of readings, including *'m ndyby 'mym* (LXX[B] *meta dynastōn laōn*) and *'m ndyby 'm,* reflected by LXX[L] and many MSS. Compare also Ps 47:10[English 9]: *ndyby 'mym,* and Ps 113:8: *'m ndybym 'm ndyby 'mw* (so also the text of one Latin MS to I Sam 2:8: *cum principibus cum principibus populi sui*).

8b-10a$_{\alpha}$. *For the straits . . . kin*[*g*] . . . 4QSam[a] shows that both MT and LXX have suffered losses of material here. The scroll reads (on the reconstructions see below):

[*ky lyhwh mṣwqy 'rṣ wyšt*]
'lyhm tb[*l*] *wdrk ḥ*[*sydw yšmr wrš'ym bḥšk ydmw*]
ntn nd[*r*] *ln*[*wd*]*r wybrk š*[*nwt ṣdyq ky l' bkḥ ygbr 'yš*]
yhwh yḥt mr[*y*]*bw my q*[*dwš kyhwh*]
[ ]*tm bšlmh*[ ]
[ ]*rgly ḥ*[*sydw yšmr*]
[ ]*ml*[ ]

Except where noted below, this text is represented by our translation. MT has a much shorter reading: *ky lyhwh mṣqy 'rṣ wyšt 'lyhm tbl rgly ḥsydw yšmr wrš'ym bḥšk ydmw ky l' bkḥ ygbr 'yš yhwh yḥtw mrybw,* "For the straits of the earth are Yahweh's, and upon them he founded the world. He guards the feet of his faithful (*kĕtîb* singular, *qĕrê* plural), but the wicked perish in darkness. For no one can prevail by his own power. As for Yahweh, his antagonists (so *qĕrê*) will be shattered." LXX is also short, but it preserves other material: *didous euchēn tō euchomenō kai eulogēsen etē dikaiou hoti ouk en ischui dynatos anēr kyrios asthenē poiēsei antidikon autou kyrios hagios* = *ntn ndr lnwdr wybrk šnwt ṣdyq ky l' bkḥ ygbr 'yš yhwh yḥt mrybw yhwh qdwš,* "He gives the vower his vow and blesses the years of the just. For no one can prevail by his own strength: it is Yahweh who shatters his antagonist. Yahweh is holy!" This is followed in LXX by the remarkable intrusion of a long passage equivalent to Jer 9:22-23.

The full original reading cannot be recovered from this evidence. Both MT and LXX seem to have suffered haplography and partial restoration. The initial error in MT was probably a haplography caused by the similar sequences *wdrk ḥsydw yšmr* (see below) and *rgly ḥsydw yšmr.* Some of the lost material was restored, but not all, and the corruption spread into the succeeding lines. In the *Vorlage* of LXX the corruption may have begun with a haplography caused by *homoioarkton,* a scribe's eye skipping from *ky lyhwh* to *ky l' bkḥ,* after which only a part of the intervening material was restored (Wellhausen). 4QSam[a] has much material found in neither MT nor LXX; nor is its longer reading derived from any apparent source (as in the case of the Jeremiah 9 material in LXX). So this seems to be a case where our usual preference for a shorter reading must be set aside. The scroll, fragmentary as it is, seems to be the only surviving witness to the primitive text.

9. *He guards the way of his faithful* Our reconstruction of 4QSam[a] (*wdrk ḥ*[*sydw yšmr;* see above) is based partially on Prov 2:8. MT has *rgly ḥsydw yšmr,* "He guards *the feet* of his faithful," which 4QSam[a] and the primitive text seem to have read much later on, as surmised above.

10. *It is Yahweh who shatters* Reading *yhwh yḥt* with 4QSam[a], LXX. MT *yhwh yḥtw* interprets *yhwh* as *casus pendens,* thus, "As for Yahweh, (his antagonists) will be shattered."

Who is h[*oly like Yahweh?*] Our reconstruction of 4QSam[a] (*my q*[*dwš kyhwh*]; see above) takes a clue from LXX *kyrios hagios* = *yhwh qdwš,* "Yahweh is holy!" Cf. also v 2a.

Eli Restoring *'ly* (see the NOTE). The archaic divine name has caused considerable confusion in the text. MT reads *'lw,* showing the common confusion of *w* and *y*, and interprets the word as *'alā(y)w*, "against him." LXX *anebē* reflects a "correction" to *'lh*, "has gone up," leading to further corruption by the addition of *yhwh* before *'lh* to provide a subject and the insertion of the conjunction before *yr'm*. Thus the *Vorlage* of LXX must have read *yhwh 'lh bšmym wyr'm*, "Yahweh has gone up into heaven and thundered." The preservation of *wyr'm* in 4QSam[a] suggests that its text corresponded to that of LXX. For *yhwh* in the parallel stich, LXX reflects *hw'*, "He."

to his king So MT. LXX has *tois basileusin hēmōn*, "to our kings," which is clearly inferior, though "to our king" is possible even in view of the parallel.

NOTES

2 1. *My horn is raised*. The Hebrew idiom "raise, exalt the horn" (*hērîm qeren*) with its related expressions has not been fully explained. The major lexica list it as a figure of speech "denoting increase of might, dignity," the horn itself being "a symbol of strength" (BDB). According to Driver, therefore, the present allusion is to "an animal carrying its head high, and proudly conscious of its strength." There can be no denying any of this, but the following observations should also be made. First, as the related expression "cause a horn to sprout" (*hiṣmîaḥ qeren*, cf. *giddēa' qeren*, "cut off the horn") suggests, the allusion is to the growth of the horn itself, not simply the bearing of the animal. The individual whose horn Yahweh has raised is *conspicuously* fortunate (as in Ps 112:9-10, where the sight causes vexation to the wicked), because a horn is a conspicuous eminence (thus *qeren* may refer secondarily to a mountain [Isa 5:1 and probably II Sam 22:3 = Ps 18:3(English 2)] or, quite possibly, a tower or tall building [Lam 2:3]). An ancient couplet preserved in Num 23:22 and 24:8 reads: "El brought them out of Egypt / As the horns (*tô'ăpōt*, lit. 'eminences') of a wild ox for himself." The meaning is that God brought the Israelites out of Egypt to establish his own reputation, a theme ubiquitous in the exodus tradition. The exalted horn, then, is first of all a *visible* sign of success. Second, in certain cases it is clear that the raised horn refers specifically to progeny. Most explicit is the statement appended to the list of the children of Heman in I Chron 25:5: "All these were the children of Heman, the royal seer, in accordance with God's promise to raise up (his) horn: God gave Heman fourteen sons and three daughters." Note also the divine oath in Ps 132:17, "There [i.e. in Zion] I shall cause a horn to sprout for David," promising the establishment of a Davidic dynasty. In Deut 33:16b-17 the burgeoning of Ephraim and Manasseh is described in terms of the growth of the two horns of Joseph under the image of a wild bull. A third observation concerns the referent of the expression. The allusion is to the prominent attire of the dominant male animal, most especially of the wild ox (*rĕ'ēm*, the *bos primigenius*) as in Ps 92:11(English 10) and elsewhere, whose horns distinguish him from his retinue. The wild ox himself was a symbol of strength and virility throughout the ancient Near East. In summary then, we may conclude that the expression "exalt the horn" implies a significant elevation in condition involving some kind of visible distinction; in certain instances it refers specifically to the establishment of the lasting distinction of posterity. It does not follow necessarily that in the present passage the birth of a son was intended by the original composer of the poem, but this is quite possible. At the least the statement is susceptible to such a construction and gives a certain propriety to the placing of the song on Hannah's lips.

My mouth is stretched over my enemies. Or to paraphrase, "I have triumphed over my enemies!" The curious expression *hirḥîb peh ʿal,* "stretch the mouth over," refers to opening the mouth wide for swallowing something (Ps 81:11[English 10]) and is here and elsewhere applied figuratively to the defeat of one's enemy by swallowing him (the verbal form here is simply *rāḥab,* "is wide, stretched"). That this and not "mock" or "gloat" is the meaning in Ps 35:21, for example, is assured by v 25, where swallowing is mentioned specifically. Compare also Isa 5:14 (substituting *nepeš,* "throat," for *peh*), where the reference is to Sheol's gaping maw swallowing up the living (cf. Prov 1:12), a depiction of hell common also at Ugarit and elsewhere (see T H. Gaster, *Thespis,* rev. ed. [New York: Harper and Row, 1966] 206-207).

2. *no holy one . . . no mountain.* English idiom would require "no *other* holy one . . . no *other* mountain" to be strictly correct. Each noun is a common designation for a divine being. By "mountain" we render Hebrew *ṣûr,* which may mean "rock" or, as in the case of Ugaritic *ǵr,* "mountain."

3. *Yahweh is a mindful god.* Hebrew *'ēl dēʿôt yahweh* (see the *Textual Note*). William H. Brownlee ("The Ineffable Name of God," *BASOR* 226 [1977] 40-44) raises the interesting possibility of translating *yahweh* verbally here—thus, "The God of knowledge *makes things happen*" (43).

a god who balances his actions. As Brownlee has shown ("Ineffable Name," 43-44), this stich introduces the catalogue of reversals of fortune that follow in vv 4 and 5. The verb (*tōkēn*) refers to weighing, or rather balancing, and the succeeding list of antitheses shows the divine balancing out of human experience.

5. *are fattened on food.* Hebrew *ḥādĕlû ʿad.* This meaning of *ḥādal* (or more probably *ḥādēl*), already recognized in eighteenth-century lexica, has been "rediscovered" by D. Winton Thomas ("Some Observations on the Root *ḥdl,*" VTSup 4 [Leiden, 1957] 8-16) and (independently) by P. J. Calderone ("*ḤDL*-II in Poetic Texts," *CBQ* 23 [1961] 451-460; 24 [1962] 412-419). Arabic *ḫadula/ḫadila,* "be, become fat," is cognate, as are the old Babylonian adjective *ḫuddulu,* "fat" (as a physical characteristic) and proper name *ḫuddultu/ḫundultu,* "Fatso." The term *ʿad,* "food" (hence "prey, booty"), which also follows *ḥdl* in Job 14:6 (Calderone, 454-455) and Judg 5:7 (Marvin L. Chaney, unpublished), is identified by its parallelism to *lḥm,* "bread," to which compare the Ugaritic word pair *lḥm//mǵd* in *CTCA* 14.2.80-84 = Krt 80-84 (Calderone, 452-454).

the mother of many sons. Hebrew *rabbat bānîm,* lit. "(she who is) abundant of sons," according to a fairly common usage whereby the adjective *rab/rabbâ* receives nearer definition from a following genitive. One of David's heroes, for example, is called *rab pĕʿālîm*, lit. "(one who is) abundant of deeds," that is, "a man of many accomplishments." For a complete list, see BDB, 913; for the grammar, see GK §128x. To the entire stich cf. Jer 15:8-9.

6. *Sheol.* The realm of the dead, both as a place of judgment and a final residence. With regard to the former, note that according to the present verse Yahweh both consigns to and brings back from Sheol. See further the NOTE on "the straits of the earth" at v 8.

and brings up. Hebrew *wayyáʿal*, a finite verb after a series of participles. See GK §111u.

8. *Who raises the poor . . . a chair of honor.* Compare Ps 113:7-8. The Israelite poet drew upon a store of stock phrases and expressions to build his composition.

And grant them. Hebrew *yanḥillēm*, an imperfect verb in sequence with the preceding infinitive *lĕhôšîb*. For the grammar, see GK §114r.

the straits of the earth. These (*mĕṣūqê ʾereṣ*) are the great rivers of the underworld. The tradition of the foundation of the world upon the waters is well known in the cosmogonic lore of Israel (Ps 24:2, etc.) and other ancient Near Eastern societies. The verbal root of *māṣûq* is *ṣûq*, "be narrow," rather than the (doubtful) secondary formation *ṣûq* from common *yāṣaq*, "pour out." The English nouns "narrows, straits" referring to bodies of water are semantically comparable. The "straits of the earth" in Israelite tradition were also the swift-running waters where men were judged, and this is the context in which the succeeding bicolon is to be understood (cf. P. Kyle McCarter, "The River Ordeal in Israelite Literature," *HTR* 66 [1973] 403-412).

9. *He guards . . . in darkness.* The allusion is to the fate of the just and the wicked in "the straits of the earth," where judgment takes place, and thus finally to their fate in the mundane world. Those who have maintained a right relationship with Yahweh ("his faithful") have nothing to fear: their feet will not slip in the treacherous waters (cf. Deut 32:34-36a and "River Ordeal," p. 411). But the wicked will be lost forever in the gloom of the underworld.

9-10. *For no one . . . his antagonists.* That is, no one prevails over his antagonists alone; it is Yahweh (the name is in the emphatic first position as in vv 6 and 7) who is responsible for every success.

10. *Eli.* Those early commentators who proposed the restoration of *ʿelyôn*, "the Most High," here were on the right track (cf. II Sam 22:14 = Ps 18:14 [English 13]). The old divine name *ʿēlî*, now known from Ugaritic and frequently identified in Biblical Hebrew, might be translated "the Exalted One." See M. Dahood, "The Divine Name *ʿELĪ* in the Psalms," *TS* 14 (1953) 452-457; *Psalms I: 1-50*, AB 16 (1966) 45. Eli as a divine name is not to be confused with Eli as the name of the priest of Shiloh, except insofar as the former may be the theophorous element in the longer form of the latter (Dahood compares the personal name *yḥwʿly*, "May Eli give life," in the Samaria ostraca, nos. 55,60).

his king . . . his anointed. The concluding benediction suggests the original context of the song, viz. an occasion of royal thanksgiving, quite possibly the birth of an heir to the throne. On the royal title "anointed (one)," see the NOTE at 9:16.

COMMENT

The so-called "Song of Hannah" is an exclamation of pious thanksgiving acknowledging a great personal benefaction. The singer's good fortune is attributed to Yahweh, who is esteemed as an incomparable god and ascribed authority over universal justice. As the verses unfold, their chief burden becomes an affirmation of the relationship between divine justice and the human condition. The song as a whole, therefore, belongs to a fairly large category of biblical psalms which elaborate the declaration of a specific instance of God's beneficence with a general celebration of his sovereignty and grace.[1]

Hannah's psalm, with its sustained spontaneity and unity of purpose, is quite properly called a song. We can display its poetic symmetry most readily by enumeration of the lengths of the various cola in syllabic notation.[2] This has been provided parenthetically in the translation. Note that the psalm is composed uniformly of short lines (seven or eight syllables with isolated instances of six), producing a fast-paced, lyrical impression. The translator can reproduce this effect quite satisfactorily in English if he avoids discursive and periphrastic renderings (thus, "He guards the feet of his faithful" is better than "He guards the feet of those who keep faith with him"). The parallelism, too, tends to be bold and straightforward without extensive use of chiasm. The three lines which open the song, for example, are remarkably uniform, exhibiting in Hebrew the pattern *verb + noun with first person singular suffix + prepositional phrase,* thus:

'ālaṣ + libbî + bĕyahweh
rāmâ + qarnî + bē'lōhay
rāḥab + pî + 'al-'ôyĕbay.

This creates a sense of urgency, which is relieved only partially in the (slightly) divergent fourth line. Much of the rest of the song also reads without chiasm, including the final bicolon:

[1] For a partial list of these, which Claus Westermann calls "descriptive psalms of praise," see his *The Praise of God in the Psalms,* tr. Keith R. Crim (Richmond: John Knox, 1961) 122.

[2] Any calculation of syllables in lines of biblical poetry must be based on the ancient form of the language. This involves the elimination of (1) linguistic features affecting syllable count which appear in the Masoretic text as developments of Post-biblical Hebrew, such as segholation (e.g. read *qašt* for MT *qešet* in v 4), the so-called "rule of *šĕwa*" (e.g. read *bĕyĕšû'ātî* for MT *bîšû'āt*[*î*] in v 1), "triphthongization" of diphthongs (e.g. read *ḥayl* for MT *ḥāyil* in v 4), etc., and (2) prosaizing additions to a poetic text, such as *'ăšer,* most instances of *kōl,* many of *kî,* etc. Very few of the latter have been introduced into the present text, though we might excise the *kî* introducing v 8b, thus reducing the syllable count to 7:7.

wĕyitten-ʿōz lĕmalkô
wĕyārēm qeren mĕšîḥô.

Where it does occur chiasm is inconspicuous. Compare the next to the last bicolon of our poem:

ʿēlî baššāmayim yarʿēm	(ABC)
yahweh yādîn ʾapsî-ʾāreṣ	(AC'B')

to the similar couplet in II Sam 22:14 = Ps 18:14(English 13), where the chiasm is much more pronounced:

yarʿēm baššāmayim yahweh	(ABC)
wĕʿelyôn yittēn qôlô	(C'A').[3]

Only in v 8a, a stock passage (see the NOTE), is chiasm sustained beyond a single bicolon:

mēqîm·mēʿāpār dal	(ABC)
mēʾašpōt yārîm ʾebyōn	(B'A'C')
lĕhôšîb ʿim-nĕdîbîm	(AB)
wĕkissēʾ kābôd yanḥillēm	(CA').

Monotony, therefore, is not avoided by variations in the length of lines or multiformity in parallel structure but by the lively career of the song itself. The quick, trenchant verses reinforce the mood expressed in the lyrics, so that the effect of the whole is one of triumphant jubilation.

This jubilation has been placed not inappropriately on Hannah's lips, but the lyrics presuppose the monarchy (see the second NOTE at v 10), and the song cannot have been contemporary with the events to which the composers of the present narrative relate it. Its insertion may have taken place quite late in the literary history of the Samuel corpus: we have already noted the textual disturbance it occasioned (see the second *Textual Note* at 1:28).[4] But this says nothing at all about the date of the composition of the song itself. It is not, as some have supposed, a "late" piece, for it exhibits thematic and prosodic traits characteristic of early Israelite poetry.[5] Of special importance are its similarities to portions of Psalm

[3] "Yahweh thunders in the heavens, / And the Most High utters his cry!"

[4] See also G. Bressan, "Il cantico di Anna."

[5] Willis, "Song of Hannah," associates our poem with the earliest corpus of Israelite poetry, including Exodus 15, Judges 5, II Samuel 22 = Psalm 18, Habakkuk 3, and Psalm 68; but this judgment seems extreme, based as it is on several debatable textual decisions (the choice of *byhwh* [2] in v 1, the retention of the conflate text of v 2, the acceptance of the dittograph *gbhh* in v 3, etc.). W. F. Albright (*Yahweh and the Gods of Canaan* [Garden City, N.Y.: Doubleday, 1968] 20-22) defends a similarly early date ("the time of Samuel, though rather . . . the end of his life than . . . its beginning"), based largely on parallels to Deuteronomy 32, which he dates to the eleventh century B.C. Although the archaic features pointed to by Albright and Willis show the Song of Hannah to be early, an eleventh-century date is too high.

113, which seems more archaic throughout, and Deuteronomy 32, which may be contemporary with our poem or slightly later.[6] Nor can we overlook the references to the king. Provisionally we may date the Song of Hannah to the monarchical period, perhaps as early as the ninth or late tenth century.[7]

As we have already seen, the song is not wholly unsuited to its secondary context. The central theme is joy over an elevation in condition, quite possibly the birth of a child understood as a divine gift of posterity (see the NOTE at v 1). The three illustrations of reversal of fortune in vv 4-5 culminate poignantly in the case of the formerly barren woman who bears seven sons. So the little hymn is fitting enough on Hannah's lips. On a subtler but no less important level, moreover, these verses with their meditation upon the exaltation of the meek find the heart of the Samuel stories with singular directness. We are about to hear of the elevation of Samuel, of Saul, of David—indeed even of Israel herself—from humble circumstances to power and distinction. The Song of Hannah sounds a clear keynote for what follows.

Albright's contention that in the poem "kingship belongs to Yahweh" and not an earthly king is based on a very dubious treatment of the final lines, which devastates the parallelism, viz.:

It is Yahweh who judges the ends of the earth,
Giving power to His reign (*molkô*)
As He lifts the horns of His anointed one.

Like Willis, he retains the second *byhwh* in MT 1 (to which we have objected on textual grounds) as an instance of archaic repetitive parallelism. As for the criterion of Deuteronomy 32, see the following footnote.

[6] On Deuteronomy 32, see G. Ernest Wright, "The Lawsuit of God: A Form-Critical Study of Deuteronomy 32," in *Israel's Prophetic Heritage: Essays in Honor of James Muilenburg*, eds. B. W. Anderson and W. Harrelson (New York: Harper and Brothers, 1962) 26-67, esp. 57-58. Wright notes in particular the themes found in common in the Song of Hannah and the last speech of Yahweh in Deuteronomy 32, esp. v 39. His argument for a ninth-century date for the latter is forceful; for additional literature bearing on the date of Deuteronomy 32 see Eissfeldt, *Introduction*, 227, n. 14. On Psalm 113 see provisionally Willis, "Song of Hannah," 152–154.

[7] David Noel Freedman has developed a typology of the use of divine names in archaic Yahwistic poetry, according to which the Song of Hannah can be dated ca. 1000 B.C., later than Psalm 113 but earlier than Deuteronomy 32. See "Divine Names and Titles in Early Hebrew Poetry," in *Magnalia Dei: The Mighty Acts of God. Essays on the Bible and Archaeology in Memory of G. Ernest Wright* (Garden City, N.Y.: Doubleday, 1976) 55-107.

III. SAMUEL CONTRASTED WITH THE SONS OF ELI (2:11-26)

2 11 After [Hannah] had returned to Ramah, the child ministered
to Yahweh in the presence of Eli, the priest.
12 Eli's sons were worthless fellows, who did not acknowledge
Yahweh 13 or the priest's due portion from the people. Whenever
someone was sacrificing, the priest's servant was supposed to come
while the meat was boiling. In his hand would be a three-pronged
fork, 14 which he would thrust into the pot or kettle. Whatever the fork
brought up the priest was to keep for himself. But this is the way
they dealt with all the Israelites who came to sacrifice to Yahweh at
Shiloh. 15 Before they had even burned the fat, the priest's servant
would come to the man who was sacrificing and say, "Hand over
some meat to be roasted for the priest, for he will not accept boiled
meat from you!" 16 If the man should say, "Let [the fat] be burned
as usual; then take as much as you want!" he would reply, "No! Hand
it over now! Otherwise I shall take it by force." 17 The servants' sin
was very serious, because they were treating the offering of Yahweh
with contempt.
18 Meanwhile Samuel continued to serve in the presence of Yahweh
as a servant boy girt with a linen ephod. 19 From time to time his
mother would make him a little robe and bring it to him when she
came up with her husband to offer the seasonal sacrifice. 20 Then Eli
would bless Elkanah and his wife in these words: "May Yahweh repay you with offspring from this woman in place of the gift she has
dedicated to Yahweh!" Then when [Elkanah] returned home, 21 Yahweh favored Hannah so that she bore three sons and two daughters,
while the boy Samuel grew up in the presence of Yahweh.
22 When Eli had grown very old, he kept hearing what his sons
were doing to the Israelites; 23 so he said to them, "Why do you do
such things as these that I have been hearing from the people of Yahweh? 24 No, my sons! Do not do this! For they are not good reports
that I have heard the people of Yahweh spreading. 25 If one man
sins against another, gods may mediate for him; but if it is against

Yahweh that a man sins, who can intercede for him?" But they would not listen to their father (for Yahweh wanted to kill them).

26 All the while the boy Samuel continued to rise in the estimation of Yahweh and of men.

TEXTUAL NOTES

2 11. *After* [*Hannah*] *had returned to Ramah* Reading *wtlk hrmth* on the basis of LXX *kai apēlthen eis harmathaim.* The action continues from 1:28 where Hannah is the principal actor. MT *wylk 'lqnh hrmth,* "After Elkanah had returned to Ramah," arose after this connection was obscured by the intrusion of the song. MT also adds *'al-bêtô,* "to his home," as a gloss on *hārāmātâ* (if *'al* = *'el,* as often in the MT of Samuel; otherwise "along with his family"—cf. 1:21). On the additions to the beginning of the verse in LXX[BL], see the *Textual Note* at 1:28.

12-13. *Yahweh or the priest's due portion from the people* So construed by LXX. MT could be interpreted the same way but for the omission of *'et-* before *mišpaṭ,* "due portion" (this sense of *mišpāṭ* being assured by Deut 18:3 [so Wellhausen and most commentators]; see the NOTE). It is quite likely that this omission is the result of the intrusion of *yhwh* into a text which originally read *l' yd'w 't mšpṭ hkhn,* etc. The divine name is conspicuously superfluous at several points in this section. LXX *tou hiereōs para tou laou* = *hkhn m't h'm,* "of the priest from the people," is to be preferred to MT *hkhnym 't h'm,* "of the priest*s* *with* the people," in which the *m* has been associated with the wrong word (cf. Deut 18:3).

13,14. Appended to v 16 in 4QSam[a] is a long addition, which is apparently a doublet of the description of the priest's due portion in the present passage. It may have arisen from a dittography. It reads as follows (restorations proposed by F. M. Cross and, after *'m,* P. W. Skehan): *kbšlt* [*h*]*bśr yqḥ 't mzlg šlwš hšnym* [*bydw whkh*] *bsyr 'w bṗrwṙ* [*kw*]*l 'šr y'lh hmzlg yqḥ 'm* [*r' hw' w'm*] *ṭwb lbd mḥ*[*zh htnwph wšw*]*q hymyn,* "While the meat was boiling, he would take a three-pronged fork in his hand and thrust it into the pot or kettle. Whatever the fork brought up, whether bad or good, he would keep, along with the breast for the wave-offering and the right thigh." Corresponding to *kbšl* of v 13 (MT) is the unusual form *kbšlt,* possibly an irregular feminine stative infinitive (GK §45). On the shorter list of pots, see the *Textual Note* at v 14. In addition to certain minor changes from vv 13,14 of MT, this reading shows two interesting expansions. The expression "whether bad or good" applied to the portion retrieved by the fork betrays an interpretation of the passage akin to ours: the priest is to take whatever Providence provides him. In this light the addition is shown to be quite out of place in v 16+, where the topic is priestly abuse of privilege. The second expansion—"along with the breast for the wave-offering and the right thigh"—accommodates the passage to the regulation of priestly portions in the Tetrateuch. Cf. esp. Lev 7:31,32; Num 18:18; and the interpolation in the prescriptions for ordination of priests, Exod 29:26-28; cf. Lev 9:21.

14. *into the pot or kettle* MT here lists four kinds of vessels, LXX three, and 4QSam^{a} (in the addition to v 16; the scroll is not extant in v 14) only two. In view of the strong tendency of lists to conflate, the shortest deserves preference on *a priori* grounds at least. Cf. II Chron 35:13 (contrast LXX), which may have influenced this passage. The chief witnesses to the present list reflect:

MT (v 14)	*bkywr 'w*	*bdwd 'w*	*bqlḥt 'w*	*bprwr*
LXX (v 14)	*bsyr*		*'w bqlḥt 'w*	*bprwr*
4QSam^{a} (v 16 +)	*bsyr*			*'w bprwr.*

for himself Reading *lô* in preference to MT *bô,* "with it (the fork?)." Compare LXX *heautō.*

to sacrifice to Yahweh LXX^{B} *thysai kyriō,* reflecting *lzbḥ lyhwh.* MT has simply *šām,* "there," which seems unlikely before "in Shiloh," but there is no real basis for choosing between these readings.

15. *boiled meat* Reading *mĕbuššāl* with LXX^{B} (some Greek MSS reflect *bśr mbšl*). MT is expansive: *bāśār mĕbuššāl kî 'im-ḥāy,* "meat that is boiled (cooked), but only raw." At the end of the sentence, LXX^{B} also has an expansion: *ek tou lebētos,* "from the pot."

16. *If the man should say* MT reads *wy'mr 'lyw h'yš,* "And the man said to him," which is inconsistent with the habitual tenses elsewhere. We omit *'lyw* with LXX and restore *w'mr h'yš,* "And the man would say," or in this construction, "If the man should say. . . ." Both LXX and 4QSam^{a} are expansive, showing the influence of v 15. The former reads: *kai elegen ho anēr ho thyōn,* reflecting *wy'mr h'yš hzbḥ,* "And the man who was sacrificing said"; the latter: *w'nh h'yš w'mr 'l n'r hkwhn,* "And the man would answer and say to the priest's servant. . . ."

Let [the fat] be burned 4QSam^{a} *yqṭr hkwhn,* "let the priest burn," shows an explicating expansion. LXX *thymiathētō* reflects *yqṭr,* "let one burn." MT (cf. Syr.) has *qṭr yqṭrwn,* "let them burn," presumably under the influence of *yqṭrwn* in v 15. The original was probably *qṭr yqṭr,* "let one burn," the infinitive absolute having fallen out of 4QSam^{a} and LXX.

as usual MT *kayyôm,* reflected also in 4QSam^{a}, Syr., and probably LXX and Vulg. LXX conflates two interpretations of *kayyôm: prōton hōs kathēkei,* "first as is fitting"; and Vulg. three (!): *primum iuxta morem hodie,* "first according to custom today." The second interpretation in each case is most nearly correct. See the NOTE.

as much as MT, Syr. *k'šr.* 4QSam^{a} (cf. LXX) has *mkwl 'šr,* "all of it which." There is no basis for choosing between these variants.

No! So LXX, 4QSam^{a}, and MT *qĕrê.* MT *kĕtîb: lw,* "to him."

I shall take it Reading *wlqḥty.* MT *lqḥty* is the wrong tense: we expect *'qḥ* or *wlqḥty.* Many scholars have preferred to emend to the latter on the basis of LXX *lēmpsomai,* to which 4QSam^{a} now lends further support, reading *wlq[ḥty]* (but omitting the previous *w'm l'*). Driver defends MT, citing Num 32:23: *w'm l' t'śwn kn hnh ḥṭ'tm lyhwh.* But the cases are not the same, *ḥṭ'tm* having the force of English future perfect: "If you do not do so, *you will have sinned* against Yahweh."

by force MT *bḥzqh;* 4QSam^a *bḥzq.*

For 4QSam^a's long addition to v 16, see the *Textual Notes* at vv 13,14 and v 14 above.

17. *The servants' sin was very serious* All witnesses add *'t pny yhwh* or (possibly) *lpny yhwh,* but in different places. MT, 4QSam^a, LXX^L: "The servants' sin was very serious *before Yahweh.*" LXX^B: "The servants' sin *before Yahweh* was very serious." Most likely *'t pny yhwh* arose in anticipation of *'t pny yhwh* in v 18.

they were treating . . . with contempt Reading the shorter text of LXX and 4QSam^a (*n'ṣw*) in preference to MT *n'ṣw h'nšym, "the men* were treating with contempt" (so Syr., Vulg., Targ.).

20. *May Yahweh repay you* Reading 4QSam^a *yšlm y[hwh] lk* (so LXX^B: *apotisai soi kyrios*). MT has *yśm yhwh lk,* "May Yahweh establish for you." Cf. S. Talmon, "The Textual Study of the Bible—A New Outlook," in *Qumran and the History of the Biblical Text,* eds. F. M. Cross and S. Talmon (Cambridge, Mass.: Harvard, 1975) 347.

she has dedicated The reading of MT (*š'l*) is impossible. LXX, Syr., Vulg. reflect *hš'lt,* "you have dedicated." Many scholars have adopted the proposal of Budde to restore *hš'lh* on the basis of 1:28, and this now seems even more attractive in view of 4QSam^a *hš'yl[h].*

when [Elkanah] returned home LXX and 4QSam^a reflect *wylk h'yš lmqwmw,* "and the man went to his place." Syr., Targ. reflect *whlkw lmqwmm,* "and they would go to their place." MT *whlkw lmqwmw,* "and they would go to his place" is evidently a mixture of these two variants, viz. *wylk lmqwmw* (*h'yš* being expansive) and *whlkw lmqwmm.* If we choose the former we must ask who the subject is. It cannot be Eli, for the verb does not agree with *wbrk,* "would bless," in tense. It must, therefore, be Elkanah, hence the explicating addition of *h'yš* in 4QSam^a and the *Vorlage* of LXX. The change in tense signals a shift from habitual to conventional past narrative (see the NOTE at 1:4-7) and introduces a sequence which will include *wypqd . . . wtld,* "he favored . . . she bore. . . ."

21. *favored* Reading *wypqd* on the basis of 4QSam^a and LXX *kai epeskepsato* (cf. Syr.). MT has *ky pqd* (so Vulg., Targ.), an error for *wypqd.*

she bore Read *wtld.* All versions show simple expansions, which may be eliminated by comparison. MT, Vulg., Targ. have *wthr wtld,* "she conceived and bore." LXX^B and 4QSam^a have *wtld 'wd,* "she bore yet again" (an addition inserted to give precision). LXX^L conflates the readings represented in MT and 4QSam^a: *wthr 'wd wtld* (*kai synelaben eti kai eteken*).

in the presence of Yahweh Reading *lpny yhwh* with LXX and 4QSam^a. The reading of MT (*'m yhwh,* "with Yahweh") has been influenced by *'m yhwh* in v 26, where it is certainly original.

22. *very old* 4QSam^a adds a note giving Eli's exact age. See the *Textual*

Note to 4:14-16 for the notice (itself not original) from which this addition is derived.

he kept hearing 4QSam^{a} has *wyšm'*, simply "he heard." But the frequentative *wšm'* of MT is to be preferred as *lectio difficilior*—thus, "he kept hearing" or "he heard from time to time" (Driver).

what Reading *'t 'šr* with 4QSam^{a}, LXX^{BL} against MT *'t kl 'šr*, "everything that."

to the Israelites Reading *lbny yśr 'l* with LXX and 4QSam^{a} against MT *lkl yśr'l*, "to all Israel" (so Syr., Vulg., Targ.), which shows the influence of v 14.

The text of MT shows an interpolation at this point: *w't 'šr yškbwn 't-hnšym hṣb'wt pth̤ 'hl mw'd*, "and that they were lying with the women who served at the entrance to the Tent of Meeting." The reading is missing from LXX^{B} (but cf. LXX^{L} and Josephus *Ant.* 5.339) and 4QSam^{a}. It is couched in the technical terminology of the priestly legislation of the Tetrateuch (cf. Exod 38:8) and effectually links the present situation with the incident in Num 25:6-15 (see Cross, *CMHE*, 201-203). The interpolation may have arisen from an annotation by a post-Exilic scholar, who recognized in both stories etiologies of the ascendancy of the priestly descendants of Aaron (Zadok) over those of Moses (Abiathar). See further the COMMENT on 2:27-36.

23. *so he said . . . have been hearing* MT has *wy'mr lhm lmh t'śwn kdbrym h'lh 'šr 'nky šm' 't dbrykm r'ym*, "So he said to them, 'Why do you do such things as these that I have been hearing, that is, your evil deeds?' " The awkward structure is the result of a conflation of variant readings, viz. *kdbrym h'lh*, "such things as these," and *'t dbrykm r'ym*, "your evil deeds" (cf. S. Talmon, "Double Readings in the Massoretic Text," in *Textus*, vol. 1 [Jerusalem: Magnes, 1960] 180). We follow LXX^{B} in reading *wy'mr lhm lmh t'śwn kdbrym h'lh* (so LXX^{L}; LXX^{B} evidently reflects *kdbr hzh*, "such a thing as this") *'šr 'nky šm'*. Corresponding to *'t dbrykm r'ym* in MT, LXX^{L} has *mdbrym bkm*, "being said of you" (cf. Ps 87:3), and this reading is also suggested by the traces of 4QSam^{a}; though it is possible that this was original, having fallen out of LXX^{B} by haplography before *mpy* (*homoioarkton*), it is perhaps best to preserve the shorter reading of LXX^{B}.

from the people of Yahweh We read *mpy 'm yhwh*, lit. "from the mouth of the people of Yahweh," with LXX^{B} (which, however, has "from the mouth of *all* the people of Yahweh"; omit *kl* with LXX^{L}). MT has a variant: *m't kl h'm 'lh* (for *'lhym*?), "from all the people of God(?)."

24. *No . . . I have heard* 4QSam^{a} and LXX share a common, conflate reading. The scroll has [*'l bny ky lw' ṭwbh hš*]*mw'h 'šr 'nky šwm*[*' 'l t'śwn kn ky lw*]*' ṭwb*[*wt hšmw'wt*] *'šr* '[*n*]*y šwm'*, "No, my sons! For it is not a good report that I have heard! Do not do this! For they are not good reports that I have heard. . . ." MT has a shorter reading, but it does not reflect an earlier stage in the development of the text; instead it is a consequence of haplography in a text identical to that of 4QSam^{a} and LXX, a scribe's eye having jumped from the first *šm'* to the second—thus, *'l bny ky lw' ṭwbh hšm'h 'šr 'nky šm'*, "No, my sons! For it is not a good report that I have heard. . . ." We must choose between the conflate variants in the older text of 4QSam^{a} and LXX, viz.

(1) *ṭwbh hšm'h 'šr 'nky sm'* and (2) *ṭwbwt hšm'wt 'šr 'ny šm'*. In the present arrangement of 4QSam[a] and LXX it is variant (1) that is out of place, interrupting the original sequence *'l bny 'l t'śwn kn,* "No, my sons! Do not do this!" and our translation reflects a preference for variant (2).

the people of Yahweh spreading So MT: *m'brym 'm yhwh.* LXX seems to have read *m'brym,* "spreading," as *m'bdym,* "causing to serve(?)," and for *yhwh,* "Yahweh," LXX[B] reflects *'lhym,* "God." The syntax of this phrase is awkward and the use of the verb without precise parallels, but neither a superior text to that of MT nor a better interpretation of the received reading has been proposed. (Some critics restore *'tm,* "you," at the beginning or assume it to have been understood—thus, "namely, that you are causing the people of Yahweh to transgress"; cf. GK §116s.)

25. *If one man sins* MT: *'m yḥṭ' 'yš.* LXX, 4QSam[a]: *ḥṭw' yḥṭ'.*

gods may mediate for him Reading *wpllw* (i.e. *ûpīlĕlû*) *lw 'lhym.* In MT *lw* has fallen out by a simple haplography. In LXX (so probably 4QSam[a]) *'lhym* evidently was read *'l yhwh* (a likely corruption because of the virtual identity of *w* and *y* in MSS of the Hasmonaean and Herodian periods), producing *wpllw lw 'l yhwh,* "they may on his behalf appeal to Yahweh." On *'ĕlōhîm* with a plural verb, see the NOTE.

26. *continued to rise* Reading *hōlēk wāṭôb,* lit. "grew better and better," on the basis of LXX. For the idiom with the participle, cf. I Sam 17:41; II Sam 3:1; etc. MT inserts *wĕgādēl* (cf. v 21), an expansion that does not essentially change the sense of the shorter original.

NOTES

2 11. *ministered.* Hebrew *mĕšārēt,* which in such a context as this is specifically sacerdotal. Samuel is being presented as a priest.

12. *did not acknowledge.* Though we may suspect that "Yahweh" was not an original object of this verb (see the *Textual Note*), the sense is completely appropriate. To "acknowledge" or "know" Yahweh implies in such a context the maintenance by priests of a proper relationship with the god they serve, including especially the correct execution of cultic regulations. See W. Schottroff, *TWAT* 1.695; H. W. Wolff, "'Wissen um Gott' bei Hosea als Urform der Theologie," *EvT* 12 (1952-53) 533-554. The failure to acknowledge the "priest's due portion from the people" suggests, as the following verses explain, habitual abuse of the stipulated privilege.

13. *the priest's due portion from the people.* The livelihood of the priesthood was provided for in part by the reservation of specified portions of the sacrificial fare for priestly use. The passage that follows describes the way these portions were supposed to be determined at Shiloh. Whatever a random thrust of the fork brought out of a suppliant's pot became his contribution to the officiating priest, the supposition being that a fair portion was providentially de-

termined (an expansion in 4QSam[a] provides that the priest is to take it "whether it be bad or good"; see the *Textual Note*). In cultic regulations elsewhere the priestly portions are stipulated expressly. Deut 18:3 reserves for the priest the shoulder, jowls and stomach of each sacrificial animal. According to the priestly legislation of the Tetrateuch (Lev 7:28-36; etc.) he was to have the right thigh and the breast (for the expansion in 4QSam[a] to v 16+, see the *Textual Notes*). Nowhere in Pentateuchal legislation is there mention of such a procedure as the one here reported at Shiloh, and this may be an authentic recollection of pre-Deuteronomic practice. The expression "the priest's due portion from the people," however, echoes Deut 18:3, confirming the translation of *mišpāṭ* as "due portion" and not simply "custom."

was supposed to come. We so render *ûbā'*, "would come," to make clear that the practice described in vv 13-14 is a proper procedure in contrast to that in vv 15-16. But this is by no means self-evident in the text. Many commentators have regarded both passages as descriptions of corrupt practices. Accordingly, *gam bĕṭerem,* etc., at the beginning of v 15 would not be read "even before" but "moreover, before. . . ." Decisive, however, is the statement in v 15 to the effect that boiled meat will *not* be taken. This is not an amplification of the situation in vv 13-14 but a contradiction of it. Thus the more satisfactory interpretation is that vv 15-16 refer to the perversion of a practice described in its proper execution in vv 13-14.

a three-pronged fork. For a drawing of an excavated specimen of one of these three-tined "flesh-hooks" (*KJV*), see G. E. Wright, *Biblical Archaeology* (Philadelphia: Westminster, 1957) 143, fig. 95.

14. *the pot or kettle.* Distinct types of cooking vessels are intended (Hebrew *sîr* and *pārûr;* MT adds *kiyyôr, dûd,* and *qallaḥat*). The differences among the various types are not completely clear. See J. L. Kelso, "The Ceramic Vocabulary of the OT," *BASOR* Supplementary Studies 5-6 (1948), nos. 44, 39, 76, and 68. These designations may refer to ceramic or metal vessels, but the latter were preferred for cultic use.

15. *burned the fat.* The blood and fat of a sacrificial animal were reserved by regulation for the deity (Lev 17:6; Num 18:17; etc.). The blood was to be splashed on the altar and the fat burned or rather made to release smoke as incense. The practice described here violates the prohibition of the fat to the priests (Lev 3:16-17; 7:31; etc.).

16. *as usual.* Hebrew *kayyôm.* On this meaning of *kayyôm* and *kayyāmîm* (which confounded the ancient translators; see the *Textual Note*), see F. M. Cross, "Epigraphic Notes on Hebrew Documents of the Eighth–Sixth Centuries B.C.: II. The Murabba'at Papyrus and the Letter Found near Yabneh-yam," *BASOR* 165 (1962) 45, n. 44 (to line 5 of the Yabneh-yam letter).

18. *a linen ephod.* The regulations of the Jerusalem priesthood provided for an ornate garment called an ephod to be worn by the high priest; cf. the NOTE at 14:3. The ephod referred to here, however, is a simple garment of white linen, perhaps an apron or loincloth. Elsewhere white linen (Hebrew *bad*) is mentioned only as a fabric of priestly (or angelic!) vestments. David wears a linen ephod in his dance before the ark (II Sam 6:14). See most recently N. L. Tidwell, "The Linen Ephod," *VT* 24 (1974) 505-507.

19. *From time to time . . . the seasonal sacrifice.* Hebrew *miyyāmîm yāmîmâ . . . 'et-zebaḥ hayyāmîm.* As in 1:3,21 to translate these expressions "Year after year . . . the annual sacrifice" would be overprecise, even though an annual pilgrimage may in fact be involved here. See the NOTES at 1:3 and 21 and the remarks of Cross cited in the NOTE at 2:16 above.

a little robe. The *mĕʿîl* was an outer garment associated in priestly tradition with the ephod in the regalia of the high priest (Exod 28:4,31; etc.).

20. *the gift she has dedicated to Yahweh.* Hebrew *haššĕ'ēlâ 'ăšer hiš'îlâ lĕyahweh* (see the *Textual Note*). This statement echoes the play on *šā'al* in c 1 (see the NOTES at 1:20 and 27,28 as well as the COMMENT to 1:1-28).

25. *If one man sins . . . who can intercede for him?* Such an interrogative formulation was a common didactic device in the ancient world and is most appropriate to a father's admonition of his sons. Here "gods" renders Hebrew *'ĕlōhîm,* construed with a plural verb as in Exod 22:8(English 9), where the adjudicatory function of clan or household gods is called upon. See A. E. Draffkorn, "ILANI/ELOHIM," *JBL* 76 (1957) 216-224, esp, 218-219; de Ward, "Superstition and Judgment." Contrast Houtman, "Zu I Samuel 2:25."

Yahweh wanted to kill them. That is, Yahweh, as controller of destinies, would not permit Eli's sons to heed their father's good advice because it was his (Yahweh's) intention that they sin and die. The theology of this passage, though distasteful to modern sensibilities, is by no means unusual in the Old Testament. This is the same god who, in the Exodus story, "hardens Pharaoh's heart" (Exod 4:21; 7:3; 9:12; etc.), rendering him unable to release the Israelites, and then punishes him grimly for not doing so. Here, as in the Exodus story, the writer's point is clear: the events of history are directed by Yahweh with specific purposes in view. For further discussion of the problem, see Tsevat, "Death of the Sons of Eli."

COMMENT

The depravity of Hophni and Phinehas is now revealed. In their hands the cult of Yahweh at Shiloh has become corrupt. They are portrayed as greedy, impious priests as well as disobedient sons of a father who, though completely aware of the situation, is unable to influence them for the better. Again there is no suggestion that Eli himself is wicked. As in c 1 he is depicted as well intentioned, if clumsy and ineffectual, while direct responsibility for the corruption at Shiloh is attached to his sons.

The crimes of the Shilonite priesthood are explicitly recounted. Whereas the cultic procedures of the day provided sufficiently for the sustenance of the priests (vv 13-14a), at Shiloh the priests demanded more than their rightful share (vv 14b-16). The custom of thrusting a fork randomly into the boiling sacrificial vessel is not mentioned elsewhere in the Old Testament. It would seem to leave something to chance; and it must have been supposed that the priestly portion was providentially selected by this method. In any case the allowance is a modest one in contrast with the provisions made for the priesthood in Pentateuchal legislation (see the NOTE at v 13). It is not enough to satisfy the demands of the sons of Eli, who bully their clientele into compliance.

The evil in the house of Eli is set in greater relief by the contrasting example of the young Samuel, who also resides at Shiloh as he grows in favor with God and men. By a deliberate selection of terminology Samuel is implicitly characterized as a priest, ministering to Yahweh and clad in sacerdotal garments (see the NOTES at vv 11,18, and 19). The impact of such a characterization in such a context is unavoidable: the good and the wicked, the chosen and the rejected are set before us in an almost simplistic juxtaposition. We are prepared for the fall of the house of Eli and, with equal certainty, for a corresponding rise in the fortunes of Samuel.

This effect has been achieved by the most elementary of editorial techniques. Auspicious statements about Samuel provide a framework within which the description of the corruption of Eli's sons has been arranged. No attempt is made to integrate the two: this awaits the climax of the prophetic story of Samuel's childhood in c 3. In the present passage three notices concerning Samuel (vv 11,18-21, and 26) have been inserted at the beginning, middle, and end of the primary account (vv 12-17+22-25). The latter introduces the theme of Yahweh's displeasure with Shiloh. As explained in the Introduction (see pp. 25-26) it seems to have been an original part of the old story of the ark that continues in 4:1b-7:1 below, providing an explanation of Yahweh's departure from Israel and from Shiloh in particular. In the present arrangement of the material, however, it functions primarily as background for the story of Samuel's rise, preparing us for the theophany in c 3 and the confirmation of Samuel's prophetic office. "Before the sun of Eli set," says Genesis Rabbah 58:2, "the sun of Samuel rose." From the prophetic perspective, as from the Deuteronomistic (see the NOTE at 4:18), Eli was more than chief priest. He was ruler of Israel; but Samuel, not his own sons, will succeed him (cf. the COMMENT on 8:1-22).

IV. THE ORACLE AGAINST THE HOUSE OF ELI (2:27-36)

2 27 A man of God came to Eli and said, "Yahweh has spoken
thus: 'I revealed myself to your father's house when they were in
Egypt, slaves to the house of Pharaoh. 28 From all the tribes of Israel
I chose them to serve me as priests, to go up to my altar, to burn
incense, and to wear the ephod; and I gave to your father's house
all the oblations of the Israelites. 29 Then why do you look upon my
sacrifice and my offering with a selfish eye? Why do you honor your
sons more than me, letting them eat from the first part of all the
offerings of Israel before me?' 30 Therefore Yahweh, the god of Israel,
has spoken thus: 'I did say that your house and your father's house
would walk before me forever . . . but now (oracle of Yahweh) far
be it from me! For it is they who honor me that I shall honor, and
they who despise me will be accursed 31 The days are coming when
I shall cut off your descendants and the descendants of your father's
house, 32 so that there will not be an old man in your father's house
ever again. 33 One man shall I spare you at my altar to wear out his
eyes and use up his strength, but all the rest of your house will fall
by the swords of men. 34 And this, which will happen to your two
sons, Hophni and Phinehas, will be a sign to you: both of them will
die on a single day. 35 Then I shall raise up for myself a faithful priest
who will do as I intend and desire. I shall build for him a secure
house, and he will walk before my anointed forever. 36 Whoever remains in your house will come groveling to him for a bit of money,
saying, "Please assign me to one of the priestly offices, that I may
have a crust of bread to eat."'"

TEXTUAL NOTES

2 27. *and said* So LXX, 4QSam[a]. MT, Syr., Vulg., Targ. have *wy'mr 'lyw,* "and said *to him.*"

I revealed myself Reading *nglh nglyty* on the basis of LXX. MT *hnglh nglyty,* "Did I reveal myself . . . ?" is inappropriate and shows dittography of the preceding *h.*

slaves Reading *'bdym* with 4QSam[a] and LXX (*doulōn*); omitted in MT through haplography caused by *homoioteleuton* (*mṣrym 'bdym lbyt pr'h*).

28. *them* So MT; LXX repeats "your father's house."

to serve . . . as priests In view of the series of infinitives which follows, LXX *hierateuein* (*lĕkāhēn*) is to be preferred to MT *lĕkōhēn* (4QSam[a] *lkwhn*).

to wear the ephod So LXX[B], 4QSam[a]. MT, LXX[L] add *lpny,* "before me."

all the oblations of the Israelites LXX adds *eis brōsin,* reflecting *l'kl,* "as food." It is difficult to decide whether this is an explicating expansion or an original reading, which has fallen out of the text of MT by haplography (*yśr'l l'kl lmh*).

29. *Then why do you look . . . with a selfish eye?* LXX: *kai hina ti epeblepsas . . . anaidei ophthalmō.* MT: *lāmmâ tib'ăṭû . . . 'ăšer ṣiwwîtî mā'ôn,* "why do you *kick at*(?) . . . which I have commanded *as a refuge*(?)?" Cf. in v 32 (MT) *whbṭt ṣr m'wn.* The text of MT in vv 29-33 reflects a corrupt and highly conflate tradition. The clues to the recovery of the original text lie in the shorter reading of LXX[B], as first argued forcefully by Wellhausen. We follow here the reconstruction of F. M. Cross, who writes (personal communication): "First of all, *whbṭt ṣr m'wn* in 32a and *tb'ṭw . . . 'šr ṣwyty m'wn* in 29a are corrupt variants. We should argue that underlying the text of LXX[B] is a Hebrew reading: *tbyṭ . . . ṣrt 'yn.* 4QSam[a] has *tbyṭ . . .* [ ]. In 29a (MT), *ṣwyty* is a simple corruption of *ṣrt* (ignoring *matres lectionis*): *waw* and *reš* regularly are confused in the scripts of the third century B.C. In 32a (MT) *ṣr m'wn* is again a simple corruption of *ṣrt 'yn: mem* and *taw* are easily confused in the fourth century; *waw* and *yod* were virtually interchangeable in the late Hasmonean and early Herodian eras. For *ṣrt 'yn,* compare Gen 42:21 (*ṣrt npšw*) and the Rabbinic idiom *'yn ṣrh* and variants (called to my attention by Benzion Kaganoff), and, of course, LXX *anaidei ophthalmō.*" Thus we read *wlmh tbyṭ . . . ṣrt 'yn.* Contrast Seebass, "Text," 76-77.

letting them eat Conjectural. All readings in the witnesses are unsatisfactory. MT *lhbry'km,* "to fatten yourselves," is awkward grammatically; the question is asked of Eli in the singular. Moreover there is no hint of Eli's fattening himself along with his sons. We cannot, however, reconstruct an original without *k.* LXX *eneulogeisthai* reflects *lhbrk* "to be blessed" (cf. 4QSam[a] *lhbryk*), which is meaningless in the context. This may be a case of an early, deliberate corruption of such a reading as *lhbr(w)tm*, "to cause them to eat, to let them eat," to avoid the anthropomorphic implications of *lhbrwtm . . . lpny*, "to let them eat . . . ahead of me." The reading *lhbrkm* was retained with minor changes in the tradition behind LXX. After losing *lpny* MT restored some of the original sense and then reinterpreted *k* as part of the suffix (leading quite possibly to the further corruption of the first verb in v 29 to a plural).

from the first part MT *mr'šyt*. 4QSam[a] has the variant *mr'š*, but LXX *aparchēs* apparently agrees with MT.

of all the offerings of Israel 4QSam[a] has *kwl mnḥwt* [ ] (cf. Syr.), which is probably original. MT *kl mnḥt yśr'l* is pointed as singular (*minḥat*) but probably reflects the plural (*minḥōt*) in the older orthography. Cf. *rē'šît maś'ōtêkem* in Ezek 20:40.

before me Reading *lpny* or *l'yny* on the basis of LXX *emprosthen mou* (cf. OL), against MT *l'my*, "to my people."

30. *Yahweh . . . has spoken thus* LXX *tade eipen kyrios* = *kh 'mr yhwh;* MT *n'm yhwh*, "oracle of Yahweh." Either the reading of LXX is a reminiscence of *kh 'mr yhwh* in v 27 or the reading of MT is an anticipation of *n'm yhwh* in v 30b. The latter explanation seems more likely.

I did say Reading *'mwr 'mrty* with MT, Syr., Vulg., Targ. LXX, 4QSam[a] have *'mrty*, which has probably suffered haplography.

31. *your descendants and the descendants of your father's house* Reading *'t zr'k w't zr' byt 'byk* (MT *kĕtîb*) and vocalizing on the basis of LXX *'et-zar'ăkā*, etc. MT *qĕrê* vocalizes *'et-zĕrō'ăkā*, etc., "your arm and the arm of your father's house." The following verses require the sense of LXX here (but cf. Driver).

31b-32. MT reads in 31b,32: *mihyôt zāqēn bĕbêtékā wĕhibbaṭtā ṣar mā'ôn bĕkōl 'ăšer-yêṭîb 'et-yiśrā'ēl wĕlō'-yihyeh zāqēn bĕbêtĕkā kol-hayyāmîm*, "so that there will not be an old man in your father's house. And you will look (upon) the *affliction of the refuge* (?) upon anything which *makes Israel glad* (?); and there will not be an old man in your house ever again." LXX[B] and 4QSam[a] omit the whole of vv 31b and 32a. As indicated (see the first *Textual Note* at v 29), we follow the reconstruction of F. M. Cross, who writes: "At first look it appears that the text of 4QSam[a], LXX[B] has suffered haplography, *zqn bbytk* in v 31b to *zqn bbytk* [4QSam[a], LXX[B] *bbyty*] in 32b. There are serious problems with this explanation of the history of the text as shown most forcefully by Wellhausen. The text of 32a is certainly corrupt in MT. [As noted already, *whbṭt ṣr m'wn* in 32a and *tb'ṭw . . . 'šr ṣwyty m'wn* in 29a are corrupt variants; for the details see the same *Textual Note* at v 29.] Again, v 32a as it stands cannot be right. As Wellhausen has shown, 32a presumes that Eli sees the catastrophe which is to come upon his house; properly (with LXX[B], 4 Sam[a]) Eli witnessed only the death of his two sons, the *sign* of the later catastrophe to overtake his house. That is, the catastrophe of the prophecy is the slaughter of the Elides at Nob (I Samuel 22), and untimately the expulsion of Abiathar, the last of the Elides, from the high priesthood by Solomon (I Kings 2:27, where it is explicitly stated by the Deuteronomist that the prophecy of I Samuel 2 is fulfilled). In light of these data, Wellhausen is probably correct in taking the *Vorlage* of LXX (and 4QSam[a]) as the primitive text. . . . The two readings of MT (*mhywt zqn bbytk* and. *wl' yhyh zqn bbytk*) are in fact conflated variants (Wellhausen), not the trigger of an extensive haplography. *Lectio brevior praeferenda est.*" Of the two variants MT *wl' yhyh zqn bbytk*, "and there will not be an old man in your house," is probably to be preferred to LXX^B *kai ouk estai sou presbytēs en oikō mou* = *wl' yhyh lk zqn bbyty*, "and you will not have an old man in my house (i.e. the temple in Jerusalem)." For a different interpretation see Seebass, "Text," 76-82.

33. *his eyes . . . his strength* MT has "your eyes . . . your strength" (*'ynyk . . . npšk*), as a result of the spread of the corruption described above to v 33, where the older readings *'ynyw* (LXX^B, 4QSam^a) and *npšw* (LXX^B) referring to Abiathar have been shifted to apply to Eli under the influence of v 32 (Cross).

use up Reading *lhdyb* (or *lhd'yb*) for MT *l'dyb* with most commentators (cf. Lev 26:16).

will fall by the swords of men So LXX (*pesountai en rhomphaia andrōn*) and 4QSam^a *ypwlw bḥrb 'nšym*. MT, reading *ymwtw 'nšym*, "will die *as men* (?)," is obviously defective (cf. *ymwtw* in v 34 where it is original).

36. *a bit of money* MT, LXX^AL, and probably 4QSam^a add *wkkr lḥm*, "and a loaf of bread." The reading is absent in LXX^B, which is evidently superior (note the mention of bread at the end of the verse).

NOTES

2 27. *A man of God.* Hebrew *'îš-'ĕlōhîm*, a generalized designation used often of an oracle-giver or prophet. Another acceptable translation might be "holy man." Though more can be said about the role of the man of God in Israelite society (see the NOTE at 9:6), it is not really pertinent here, where the holy man's visit is simply a literary device of the Josianic historian. See the COMMENT.

Yahweh has spoken thus. Hebrew *kōh 'āmar yahweh*, the so-called prophetic "messenger formula." In the ancient world it was the responsibility of a messenger to repeat the words which had been given to him verbatim, so that messages characteristically were recited in the first person and prefaced by the naming of the sender in the formula, "So and so has spoken thus" (cf. Gen 45:9; etc.). The holy man or prophet, conceived of as the messenger of God, discharged his responsibility in the same way. In the present instance, therefore, the man of God is to be thought of as the bearer of a message from Yahweh to Eli.

your father's house. Eli traced his lineage to Moses (cf. the NOTE on "Hophni and Phinehas" at 1:3), and the reference here is to the house of Moses. See Wellhausen, *Prolegomena,* 142; Cross, *CMHE,* 196-197; and the COMMENT below.

in Egypt, slaves to the house of Pharaoh. The expression is reminiscent of the language of the Book of Deuteronomy. Cf. Deut 6:21; also 5:15; 15:15; 16:12; 24:18,22; etc.

28. *to wear the ephod*. The official garment of the high priest (see the NOTE at 2:18).

oblations. That is, the oblations were to provide their sustenance (cf. the addition of *l'kl*, "as food," in LXX, which, whether original or not, correctly interprets the statement; see the *Textual Note*). Compare Deut 18:1 and Josh 13:14 (MT). The cultic term *'iššeh*, "oblation," is incompletely understood, but its association with *'ēš*, "fire" (thus "fire offering" or the like) can no longer be maintained in view of Ugaritic *'iṯt*, "(votive) offering." See especially J. Hoftijzer, "Das sogenannte Feueropfer," in *Hebraische Wortforschung* [W. Baumgartner Volume] (Leiden: E. J. Brill, 1967) 114-134.

29. The condemnation of Eli is based upon the charges made against his sons in 2:11-26. The accusation may be paraphrased as follows: Yahweh made generous provision for the family of Eli (v 28b), but now Eli has acted greedily toward the sacrificial fare brought by the Israelites, permitting his sons to claim an unlawful share of it even before it was offered up to Yahweh. The charge that the priests have taken "the first part (*rē'šît*) of all the offerings of Israel" evidently refers to the practice described in vv 15-16 above. Ideally the first part of all offerings belonged to Yahweh (Ezek 20:40; cf. I Sam 15:21), except as otherwise stipulated in priestly law.

a selfish eye. Hebrew *ṣārat 'ayin*, lit. "narrowness of eye." See the *Textual Note*. The clues to the meaning of this unique biblical expression are postbiblical *ṣar 'ayin*, "selfish, envious," and *'ayin ṣārâ*, "ill will, selfishness, envy" (opp. *'ayin ṭôbâ*, "good will, liberality"). See Jastrow, 1071 and 1299.

30. *Therefore*. In the stereotyped formal structure of an oracle of doom this term (*lākēn*) occupies a pivotal position, marking the end of the accusation or diatribe and introducing the threat itself. Characteristically it is followed immediately by the messenger formula, "Yahweh has spoken thus" (see the NOTE at v 27). Cf. Micah 2:3; Amos 5:16; 7:17; etc.

I did say. Hebrew *'āmôr 'āmartî*. The force of the infinitive absolute is concessive, as in 14:43 (cf. *niglōh niglêtî* in v 27 above).

would walk before me. Hebrew *yithallěkû lěpānay*. Driver's remarks notwithstanding, the expression "walk about before someone" does not mean simply to behave in a manner pleasing to him. It implies the performance of a function on someone's behalf. The point here is that the descendants of Eli's ancestors were to perform the priestly offices Yahweh required. In v 35, to "walk before my anointed" means to function as a royal priest. Cf. also the two occurrences of the expression in 12:2 and the NOTE there.

far be it from me. The aversive exclamation *ḥālîlâ*, lit. *ad profanum*, refers to the foregoing statement. We might paraphrase the entire assertion: "Although I did say that your family would serve me as priests forever, I will now permit nothing of the kind!"

For it is they . . . will be accursed! Note the balanced phrases of the proverb. The author is quoting or paraphrasing a traditional maxim.

33. To the expression "one man shall I spare you" (*'îš lō' 'akrît lěkā*, lit. "one man shall I not cut off to you") compare the promise to David and Solomon in

I Kings 9:5, another thematic passage in the Josianic history of the kingdom. The present reference is to Abiathar, one of David's two high priests, who according to the older genealogies was descended from the house of Eli (Cross, *CMHE,* 196; Wellhausen, *Prolegomena,* 126). Solomon's banishment of Abiathar, who had opposed his succession to the throne, is interpreted in I Kings 2:27 as fulfillment of the present oracle. The expression "wear out his eyes and use up his strength" may point to the dotage of the old priest after his disgrace and exile to Anathoth (I Kings 2:26). The slaughter of the rest of the family is described in 22:11-23.

34. Eli will not witness the fulfillment of the oracle in the slaughter of the priests of Nob (22:11-23) and the final expulsion of Abiathar (I Kings 2:26-27), but he will see a sign to confirm the coming disaster, viz. the simultaneous deaths of Phinehas and Hophni. Compare the sign given in I Kings 13:13, part of another Deuteronomistic "man of God" passage (see the COMMENT).

35. As explained in the COMMENT, "the faithful priest" is Zadok, Abiathar's rival and successor. Our translation only incompletely reflects the Hebrew, in which "faithful" and "secure" are represented by a single word (*ne'ĕmān,* "firm, sure"). The repetition is deliberate: just as the priest will be firm in his allegiance to Yahweh, so Yahweh will make his tenure in office firm. This play on words recalls strikingly that on *bêt dāwîd* and *bêt yahweh,* "the house (dynasty) of David" and "the house (temple) of Yahweh," which animates II Samuel 7. For the latter, see Cross, *CMHE,* 246-247. Note especially that David's house is also to be "secure" (*ne'ĕmān*), according to II Sam 7:16.

as I intend and desire. Hebrew *ka'ăšer bilbābî ûbĕnapšî,* lit. "according to that which is in my heart (the seat of the intellect and will) and in my soul (the seat of desire and the appetites)." Cf. the Deuteronomic cliché "with all the heart and with all the soul" (Deut 4:29; 6:5; 10:12; etc.), which means "wholeheartedly, unequivocally."

he will walk before my anointed. That is, he will serve the king (as priest). See the NOTES at 2:30 (on the expression "walk before . . .") and 9:16 (on the royal title "anointed [one]").

36. That is, the non-Zadokite priests, excluded from the altar, will have to perform menial tasks in order to subsist. Such a situation developed as a consequence of the Josianic reform (II Kings 23:9) and was formalized by at least the time of Ezekiel (Ezek 44:10-16).

COMMENT

The consequences of the mischief at Shiloh are dire, and their disclosure is not long in coming. The house of Eli will fall; its descendants will be slain; the survivors will earn their bread as hierodules. Eli himself will live to see his grief certified, when his two sons die on the same day. All of this is announced to the old priest by an anonymous holy man in a long oracle of unrelieved gloom. There is, to be sure, a positive side to the message, but it offers no comfort to Eli. Yahweh will choose a new and faithful priest to do his bidding and will make his house secure forever. And who, we ask, is this happy individual? Our reading of 2:11-26 with its contrasting portrayal of Samuel and the Elides has inclined us to suppose that it is Samuel himself. Indeed we are bound to say that on the basis of our reading of the childhood narrative of Samuel up to this point and of the sequel to this passage in 3:1-4:1a, Samuel emerges incontestably as the successor to the prerogatives of the house of Eli. But the author of the present passage, which interrupts the story of Samuel, had something else in mind, and a closer look at the oracle is therefore in order.

This passage is replete with the devices and clichés of the Josianic historian. Many of these have been pointed out above in the NOTES. Of special importance are the similarities to the oracle in I Kings 13:1-3, where the destruction of Jeroboam's altar at Bethel is foretold:

> 1 A man of God came from Judah to Bethel with the word of Yahweh, while Jeroboam was standing beside the altar burning incense. 2 Crying out against the altar with the word of Yahweh, he said: "O altar, altar! Yahweh has spoken thus: 'A son will be born to the house of David, Josiah by name, who will slaughter upon you the priests of the high places who burn incense upon you, and human bones will be burned upon you!' " 3 He gave a sign that day, saying: "This is the sign that Yahweh has decreed: 'The altar will be torn down and the fat that is upon it spilled out!' "

In each case an anonymous man of God enters the stage and pronounces an oracle of doom. The phrases of I Kings 13 are the most boldly explicit in the Josianic history in their stipulation of the measures of the seventh-century reform; the reader is even relieved of the task of supplying Josiah's name. Seen in this light, however, the events foretold in the oracle against the house of Eli are not much more difficult to identify. The slaughter of the descendants of Eli must refer to Saul's massacre of the priests of Nob, the Elide refuge after Shiloh.[1] The "one man" of v 33, therefore, is certainly Abiathar, who according to 22:20 escaped the carnage at Nob and became David's high priest (jointly with Zadok; see below), as recorded in II Sam 20:25, only to be banished by Solomon to Anathoth for his support of the succession of Adonijah (I Kings 1:7; 2:26-27). The notice in I Kings 2:27 removes all doubt: "So Solomon deposed Abiathar from being priest to Yahweh, fulfilling the word of Yahweh that he had spoken against the house of Eli in Shiloh."

So the "faithful priest" of v 35 is not Samuel but Zadok, David's second

[1] See the NOTE at 21:2. The association of Nob with Shiloh, taken for granted by most scholars, rests on the fairly safe assumption that the Ahitub of 14:3, who was Eli's grandson, is identical with the Ahitub of 22:9,20, who was Abiathar's grandfather.

high priest (II Sam 15:24-37), who supported Solomon's cause (I Kings 1:22-39 *passim*) and became the unrivaled leader of the Jerusalem priesthood after the banishment of Abiathar (I Kings 2:35). The "secure house" is that of the Zadokites, whose authority was made absolute as a result of the Josianic reform; and, as explained in the NOTE, the beggared priests of v 36 are the non-Zadokites from outside of Jerusalem, who were reduced in status to minor cultic functionaries in the course of the reform. For the Josianic historian, then, the house of Eli, that is, the Shilonite priesthood, was representative of all claims to priestly authority outside of Jerusalem, and its rejection was the natural corollary of the election of the Zadokites.[2] In his own age the priests of the outlying areas, their shrines destroyed, were proceeding under orders to Jerusalem, where they found a modest subsistence, though interdicted from the service of the altar itself (II Kings 23:9).[3] The *vaticinia post eventum* in I Kings 13 and the present passage point, each in its own way, to this situation.

The Books of Samuel and Kings display a relentless march of history toward not only David, the chosen king, but also Jerusalem, the chosen city, and along with the latter, Zadok of Jerusalem, the chosen priest.[4] Inevitably this progression of events also involves the corresponding rejection of Saul and of Shiloh with its priesthood. The Josianic historian shaped his materials to demonstrate this movement of history unambiguously, and the present passage is characteristic of his craft. He fashioned it as a response to the account in his sources of the wickedness of the sons of Eli (2:11-26), itself based on an ancient narrative describing the departure of the ark from Shiloh.[5] But, as we have seen, the story of the fall of Eli's house functioned in the pre-Deuteronomistic prophetic history as part of the story of Samuel, to which we now return.

[2] Wellhausen (*Prolegomena,* 142-143) argued that priestly tradition traced Eli's ancestry to Moses and that Moses was intended as the recipient of the authorization referred to in vv 27-28. Zadok, a parvenu without Levitical genealogy but later incorporated into the line of Aaron, superseded Abiathar and the claims of the sons of Eli, who had traced their descent to Moses. Cross (*CMHE,* c 8) has extended the argument by strengthening the case for Zadok's claim to descent from Aaron and collecting considerable evidence for an ancient rivalry between Mushite and Aaronid priestly houses.

[3] The distinction thus implied between Jerusalemite and non-Jerusalemite priests is not fully developed in Deuteronomistic law but was an immediate and inevitable result of the Josianic reform. By the time of Ezekiel it had been formalized. See de Vaux, *Ancient Israel* 2. 361-366.

[4] The language used in the oracle to refer to the house of Zadok is reminiscent of that used elsewhere to refer to the house of David. See the NOTES at vv 33 and esp. 35.

[5] See the COMMENT on 2:11-26 and pp. 25-26 in the Introduction.

V. THE CALL OF SAMUEL
(3:1-4:1a)

3 1 In those days, when the boy Samuel was ministering to Yahweh in Eli's presence, the word of Yahweh was rare. There was no widespread vision.

2 At that time—(Now Eli, whose eyes had become so weak that he could no longer see, was lying down in his usual place; 3 the lamp of God had not yet been extinguished; and Samuel was lying in the temple where the ark of God was kept.) At that time 4 Yahweh called, "Samuel! Samuel!"

"Here I am!" he responded 5 and ran to Eli saying, "Here I am! For you called me."

But [Eli] replied, "I did not call. Return to bed!" So he went and lay down.

6 Again Yahweh called, "Samuel! Samuel!"

[Samuel] went to Eli and said, "Here I am! For you called me."

But [Eli] replied, "I did not call. Return to bed!" 7 (Samuel did not yet know God: the word of Yahweh had not yet been revealed to him.)

8 When Yahweh called, "Samuel!" for the third time, [Samuel] arose, went to Eli, and said, "Here I am! For you called me."

Then Eli realized that Yahweh was calling the boy. 9 "Go lie down," he said, "and if someone calls you, say, 'Speak! For your servant is listening.'" So Samuel went and lay down in his usual place.

10 When Yahweh came as on the previous occasions and stood calling, Samuel said, "Speak! For your servant is listening."

11 Then Yahweh said to Samuel, "I am about to do a thing in Israel
such that both ears of anyone who hears it will ring! 12 On that day I
shall carry out against Eli all that I have spoken concerning his house
from beginning to end. 13 I give him notice that I am passing judgment upon his house forever, because he knew that his sons were blaspheming God and did not restrain them. 14 Therefore have I sworn
concerning the house of Eli: 'The guilt of the house of Eli shall never be atoned for by sacrifice or by offering!'"

15 Samuel lay in bed until morning and then, getting up early,
opened the doors of the temple of Yahweh. He was afraid to report
the vision to Eli.
16 Then Eli said to Samuel, "Samuel, my son!" and he replied,
"Here I am!"
17 "What was the message that he spoke to you?" asked Eli. "Do
not conceal it from me! May God do thus and so to you if you conceal from me anything of the entire message he spoke to you!" 18 So
Samuel told him every word, concealing nothing from him, and [Eli]
said, "He is Yahweh. Let him do what seems best to him!"
19 As Samuel grew up Yahweh was with him, letting none of his
words fall to the ground, 20 and all Israel from Dan to Beersheba
knew that Samuel was confirmed as a prophet of Yahweh. 21 Yahweh
continued to appear at Shiloh when he revealed himself to Samuel,
4 1a and Samuel's words went out to all Israel.

TEXTUAL NOTES

3 1. *widespread* MT *niprāṣ;* LXX *diastellousa,* reflecting *prṣ* (interpreted as *pōrēṣ,* but to be read, perhaps, *pārūṣ*). The initial *n* of MT may be dittographic, but the expression is obscure. See the NOTE.

3. *the temple* So LXX^{B}. MT, LXX^{L} add "of Yahweh." Space considerations indicate that 4QSam^{a} followed LXX^{B} in omitting *yhwh* and then went its own way in also omitting *'šr šm 'rwn 'lwhym,* "where the ark of God was." One is tempted to regard this shorter reading as superior.

4. *Yahweh called, "Samuel! Samuel!"* So LXX^{B}, 4QSam^{a} and most commentators (cf. v 6[LXX], v 10[MT]). LXX^{L} has "Yahweh stood and called," anticipating v 10. MT has "Yahweh called *to* Samuel" (*'el-šĕmû'ēl*).

6. *"Samuel! Samuel!"* So LXX^{BL}. MT reads *šmw'l wyqm šmw'l,* " 'Samuel!' And Samuel arose. . . ."

"I did not call" MT adds *bĕnî,* "my son," absent in LXX (which adds here and in v 4 *se* = *lĕkā,* "to you").

7. *did not yet know God* Reading *ṭerem yēda'* for MT *ṭerem yāda'*. Though *yāda'* in the perfect admits of imperfect translation, *ṭerem* normally takes the imperfect as in the second half of the verse. We read "God" with LXX against MT "Yahweh," but there is no decisive reason for choosing between them.

9. *he said* Reading the shorter text of LXX^{B}. MT, LXX^{L} have, *"Eli* said *to Samuel."*

" 'Speak!' " So LXX^{B}. MT, LXX^{L} add, " 'Yahweh!' "

10. *and stood calling* Cf. LXX^B^. MT, LXX^L^ in reminiscence of previous vv add, "Samuel! Samuel!"

12. *against Eli* Reading *'al 'ēlî* with LXX (*epi ēlei*) and Syr., Targ., Vulg., against MT *'el-'ēlî*. These prepositions are so frequently interchanged in the MT of Samuel as hardly to require comment.

13. *because he knew* Reading *'šr yd'* or *b'šr yd'*. MT *b'wn 'šr yd'*, "for the iniquity that he knew," is most awkward. LXX has *en adikiais huiōn autou*, reflecting *b'wn bnyw*, "for the iniquity of his sons." Following Wellhausen, we assume that behind these witnesses lie two distinct readings, viz. (1) (*b*)*'šr yd'* and (2) *b'wn bnyw*, of which MT is a conflation. Reading (1) seems preferable in view of *wl' khh bm*, "and did not restrain them."

that his sons were blaspheming God Reading *ky mqllym 'lhym bnyw* on the basis of LXX. MT *ky mqllym lhm bnyw*, "that his sons were blaspheming *for themselves*," shows a deliberate scribal distortion for pious reasons, the passage being among those few recognized in Rabbinic sources as well as the Masoretic lists as belonging to the so-called "emendations of the scribes" (*tiqqûnê sôpĕrîm*).

14. *Therefore* So MT: *wlkn*. LXX: *kai oud' houtōs* = *wl' kn*, "But not so!" A Qumran fragment (4Q160) published by John M. Allegro in DJD 5.9-11, quotes the text somewhat differently, reading [. . . *k*]*y'* . . . , "Because (I have sworn). . . ."

15. *lay in bed . . . early* Reading *wyškb . . . 'd hbqr wyškm bbqr*, lit. "lay in bed until morning and got up early in the morning," with LXX. MT has lost *wyškm bbqr* by haplography after *hbqr* (*homoioteleuton*). The reading of 4Q160 is rather different throughout: [. . . *w*]*šmw'l škb lpny 'ly wyqwm* . . . , "[And] as for Samuel, he lay in bed before Eli and then arose. . . ."

to report the vision to Eli MT: *mhgyd 't hmr'h 'l 'ly*. 4Q160: *lhgyd 't hmś' l'ly*.

16. *Eli said to Samuel, "Samuel, my son!"* So LXX^B^, which reflects a Hebrew text reading *wy'mr 'ly 'l šmw'l šmw'l bny* (LXX^L^ omits the second *šmw'l*). MT *wyqr' 'ly 't* (many MSS: *'l*) *šmw'l wy'mr šmw'l bny*, "Eli summoned Samuel and said, 'Samuel, my son!' " is expansive. Cf. 4Q160: *wy'n 'ly ẇ*[*y'mr*], "Then Eli answered and [said . . .]."

17. *"What was the message that he spoke to you?"* So MT: *mh hdbr 'šr dbr 'lyk*. 4Q160: [*hw*]*dy'ny 't mr'h h'lwhym*, "Make known to me the vision of God!"

May God do thus and so to you So LXX. MT adds *wĕkōh yôsîp*, "and may he do thus and so again," according to the common idiom.

the entire message he spoke to you So MT. LXX adds *en tois ōsin sou*, "in your ears," which, though it might have fallen out of MT by haplography (*'lyk b'znyk*), is probably an old variant of *'lyk* preserved in LXX in a conflate tradition (*soi en tois ōsin sou* = *'lyk b'znyk*).

18. *concealing nothing from him* To *wl' kḥd mmnw* (MT, LXX^B^) the *Vorlage* of LXX^L^ adds *dbr* (*rhēma*), but in view of *'l n' tkḥd mmny* in v 17 it is clear that this is not necessary.

and [*Eli*] *said* We read *wy'mr* with MT, Vulg., Targ., against LXX, Syr., which have supplied *'ēlî* for clarification.

21. MT adds *bšlw bdbr yhwh,* "in Shiloh by the word of Yahweh," which may be regarded as expansion. For the text of LXX see the following *Textual Note.*

4 1a. Reading *wyhy dbr šmw'l lkl yśr'l,* lit. "and the word of Samuel was to all Israel" (so MT). LXX at this point (v 21+) has a much longer text. The first part of it can be explained as a displaced variant of v 20, viz. *kai episteuthē samouēl prophētēs genesthai tō kyriō eis panta israēl ap' akrōn tēs gēs kai heōs akrōn,* reflecting *wy'mn šmw'l lhywt nby'* (cf. LXX[L]) *lyhwh lkl yśr'l mqṣh h'rṣ w'd qṣh,* "So Samuel was confirmed to be a prophet of Yahweh for all Israel from one end of the land to the other end." LXX then goes on to read *kai ēlei presbytēs sphodra kai hoi huioi autou poreuomenoi eporeuonto kai ponēra hē hodos autōn enōpion kyriou,* reflecting *w'ly zqn m'd wbnyw hlkw whr' drkm lpny yhwh,* "And Eli grew very old, and his sons continued to act more and more wickedly in the presence of Yahweh." This might be regarded as further expansion, but we are inclined to assume that it was original, having fallen out of MT as part of the long haplography that affected 4:1 (see the *Textual Note* to 4:1b).

NOTES

3 1. *the word of Yahweh was rare.* The expression *dĕbar-yahweh,* "the word of Yahweh," functions in Israelite literature as a technical designation for an oracle or revealed message, communicated to man by Yahweh. The force of the assertion that the word of Yahweh was "rare" (*yāqār,* "precious, highly valued"), therefore, may be that direct divine communications were infrequent at the time of the events described. See also the following NOTE.

widespread vision. Hebrew (MT) *ḥazôn niprāṣ.* Whereas in Biblical Hebrew the *Nip'al* of *pāraṣ* is unique to this passage, the postbiblical evidence offers the meanings "broken through, spread abroad, unrestrained" (Jastrow, 1237). We assume with most commentators that the point of the present passage is that visions were restricted in number and infrequent at the time with which the story is concerned, or, in other words, that the incident that follows was something out of the ordinary. Thus we are not to suppose that Samuel (or even Eli) is unusually obtuse in his initial failure to realize what was transpiring. It seems quite likely, on the other hand, that the signification of the terminology of v 1 has, at least in part, been lost. The expression *ḥazôn niprāṣ* or *ḥāzôn pōrēṣ/pārūṣ* (see the *Textual Note*) may be a technical designation of some kind, perhaps referring to a cultic practice whereby visions were regularly obtained.

2-4. The expression *wayhî bayyôm hahû',* "At that time," introduces a syntactical sequence of ordinary past narration, which finds its continuation only in *wayyiqrā' yahweh,* "Yahweh called," at the beginning of v 4. All of the intervening material is parenthetical in accordance with a common device of Hebrew narrative. "That same day" is repeated in the translation for the convenience of the reader. Cf. 1:4-7 and the NOTE there.

2. *he could no longer see.* This allusion to Eli's failing eyesight seems extraneous, unless it is to indicate that the old priest will be unable to witness the coming apparition; but Eli is "in his usual place" in the vestibule while Samuel is in the nave with the doors closed (v 15; cf. the NOTES on 1:7 and 1:9). See the *Textual Note* to 4:14-16.

3. *the lamp of God had not yet been extinguished.* That is, it was not yet dawn. Lamps were burned in the sanctuary from evening until morning according to priestly regulations (Exod 27:20-21). Samuel's revelation apparently took place just before dawn.

in the temple where the ark of God was kept. The most sacred object of the Israelite cult is mentioned here for the first time in the story of Samuel. The ark is discussed in the COMMENT on 4:1b-11. It was kept in an inner sanctuary (*dĕbîr*) at the back of the nave or temple proper (*hêkāl*), where Samuel slept (see the NOTE at 1:9). Why Samuel's bed was here we are not told, but presumably he needed to be nearby in order to discharge some cultic responsibility.

4-5. Yahweh addresses Samuel from the ark, but unaccustomed as he is to divine communications (v 7), the boy mistakes the voice for that of Eli.

7. *Samuel did not yet know God.* That is, the special relationship with Yahweh that Samuel was to enjoy (vv 19-20) was not yet established. Contrast the statement concerning the sons of Eli in 2:12, and see the NOTE on that verse.

10. *Yahweh came . . . and stood.* Apparently the revelation to Samuel involved a vision as well as an audition.

11-14. The oracle has been largely revised in light of the insertion of the episode in 2:27-36. In their present form these verses contain Deuteronomistic language and explicit references to the previous oracle. See the following NOTES. Cf. especially Veijola, *Dynastie*, 35-37.

11. *both ears . . . will ring.* Cf. II Kings 21:12, where the same expression is used in another Deuteronomistic passage (Dtr_2 [see p. 15]; cf. Cross, *CMHE*, 285-286). The third and only other occurrence of the expression is in Jer 19:3, again an expansion (post-Jeremianic) in the same spirit (cf. John Bright, *Jeremiah*, AB 21, NOTE on 19:2-11 and COMMENT).

12. *I shall carry out . . . all that I have spoken.* The language is carefully chosen in the awareness that an oracle of doom has already been spoken against the house of Eli. As with *yāqēm* in 1:23 (see the *Textual Note*), *'āqîm*, "I shall carry out," means to give effect, carry out, or confirm what has been said previously. Cf. also 15:11,13. The expression "all that I have spoken" is an unambiguous reference to the oracle in 2:27-36.

13. *restrain them.* Hebrew *kihâ bām*. BDB, KB give "rebuke" as the meaning of *kihâ*. But this cannot be right; Eli did rebuke his sons (2:22-25). D. N. Freedman conjectures a relationship to *kāhâ*, "be weak" (cf. v 2)—thus, *kihâ*, "weaken, extinguish; repress, restrain."

14. Ordinarily the sins of the priests might be expiated by the presentation of specified offerings. Compare the ritual for the expiation of priestly sins in Lev

4:3-12, where the required victim is a bull. In this case Yahweh declares that he can never be propitiated.

15. *the doors of the temple.* These are the doors of the nave or temple proper (*hêkāl*), where Samuel slept (cf. the second NOTE at v 3). Samuel knows that when he opens them he will meet Eli in the vestibule—hence his apprehension.

17. *May God do thus and so to you.* An oath formula common in Biblical Hebrew (for a complete list, see Driver). The gravity of such an imprecation was assured by the invocation of God to enforce it, though the specification of the form such divine intervention was to take has been reduced to the formula "do thus (and so)," probably accompanied by some symbolic action.

19. *letting none of his words fall to the ground.* The Hebrew expression denotes "letting nothing he said be ineffective" or "letting nothing he said prove false."

20. *from Dan to Beersheba.* The phrase was a conventional way of describing the full extent of Israel. Dan (modern Tell el-Qâḍî), as the old Canaanite city of Laish was called after the Danite migration described in Judges 18, lay in the shadow of Mount Hermon at the traditional N extreme of Israelite territory. Beersheba on the other hand was located in the Judaean hills at the traditional S limit of the land. The modern site is Tell es-Sebaʻ, ca. 23 miles SW of Hebron.

a prophet of Yahweh. Samuel is now recognized by his contemporaries as having been engaged by Yahweh to do his bidding. The term that designates his office is *nābî'* (rendered *prophētēs* by the Greek translators, hence our term "prophet"), a noun probably of an archaic passive formation denoting "one summoned (for a specific assignment or office)." Cf. the Akkadian verb *nabû*, "call by name, call to duty," used especially of the calling of men by gods. Hebrew *nābî'* may thus connote "one called to duty by a god." This explanation, which remains the most satisfactory, was most vigorously argued by W. F. Albright; see *From the Stone Age to Christianity*, 2d ed. (Baltimore: Johns Hopkins, 1946) 231-232. The restriction of the duties of the *nābî'* to those of an oracle-giver as seen elsewhere in Israelite literature is out of spirit with the present material. As we have already begun to see, the prophetic history presents the office as all-embracing. Samuel the prophet is also priest, warrior, judge and governor.

COMMENT

That which was implied from the beginning is now made explicit. Samuel accedes to the office for which he has been prepared from the womb. This is the occasion anticipated in the wondrous story of his birth and hinted at in a succession of brief but auspicious notices about his early career at Shiloh. Heretofore he had served God in the temple, but "the word of Yahweh had not yet been revealed to him" (v 7). Now the moment has come and the channel is opened.

Nor is it accidental that the first message Samuel receives is a confirmation of the doom already forecast for the house of Eli. The term of his indentures is over and it is time for the apprentice to replace the master. Ancient Eli is almost a tragicomic figure. As when he mistook Hannah's quiet supplications for drunkenness, the old priest again presides over a holy misunderstanding; and again, when the reality of the situation finally impresses itself upon him, he responds with stolid piety. "He is Yahweh," concedes Eli. "Let him do what seems best to him!" (v 18). There is no wickedness in this pitiable old man, but neither is there the strength to combat wickedness, and Yahweh has found himself a strong man to lead Israel aright.

The literary critic will perceive that this is a turning point in the prophetic history. The author of the birth narrative, where the reuse of existing materials can be discerned, is also the author of this section, where it cannot. Apart from the Deuteronomistic revision of vv 11-14 (see the NOTES) I Samuel 3 is an original composition of our prophetic writer from beginning to end. In v 1a ("the boy Samuel was ministering to Yahweh in Eli's presence") he sets the stage and establishes a kinship between what follows and his own editorial insertions in the account of the wickedness of the sons of Eli (2:11,18-21, and 26; see the COMMENT on 2:11-26). He then presents the condemnation of the house of Eli as the crowning event to which the previous events have been building. By no means, however, is the episode entirely or even primarily retrospective. Samuel has entered upon his majority as a prophet and realized the destiny prepared for him before birth; his life's work now lies ahead, and this passage, the conclusion of the childhood narrative, points ahead to his exploits in c 7 and beyond. His role as the instrument by which a sorrowful message is communicated to Eli is his first assignment and marks a beginning. He has now been addressed directly by Yahweh, and the significance of this fact extends beyond the immediate circumstances; for the closing verses of the account make it clear that Samuel is henceforward to be the medium through which Yahweh will address his people. That is, Samuel is now a "prophet of Yahweh" (see the NOTE at v 20) and so recognized by his contemporaries. The present passage, therefore, can be grouped with Isaiah 6; Jer 1:4-10; Ezek 1:1-3:16 and the other so-called prophetic call narratives, with the important formal distinctions that the call of Samuel is told in the third person and contains no direct charge to prophesy. After the initial revelation, which here as in Isaiah 6 occurs in the temple, the prophetic relationship is established, and the prophet is henceforth obliged to function as a heavenly emissary. Samuel's further activities are to be viewed in this light.[1]

[1] See also Newman, "Prophetic Call."

In v 21 we are told that Shiloh continued to be the place where Yahweh revealed himself to Israel. Yet when Samuel, who is about to be given a well-deserved rest by the narrator, returns to center stage in c 7, he is no longer in Shiloh. And we never hear of Shiloh again. How and when did the change take place? We shall never be told directly, but the clues lie in the next section.

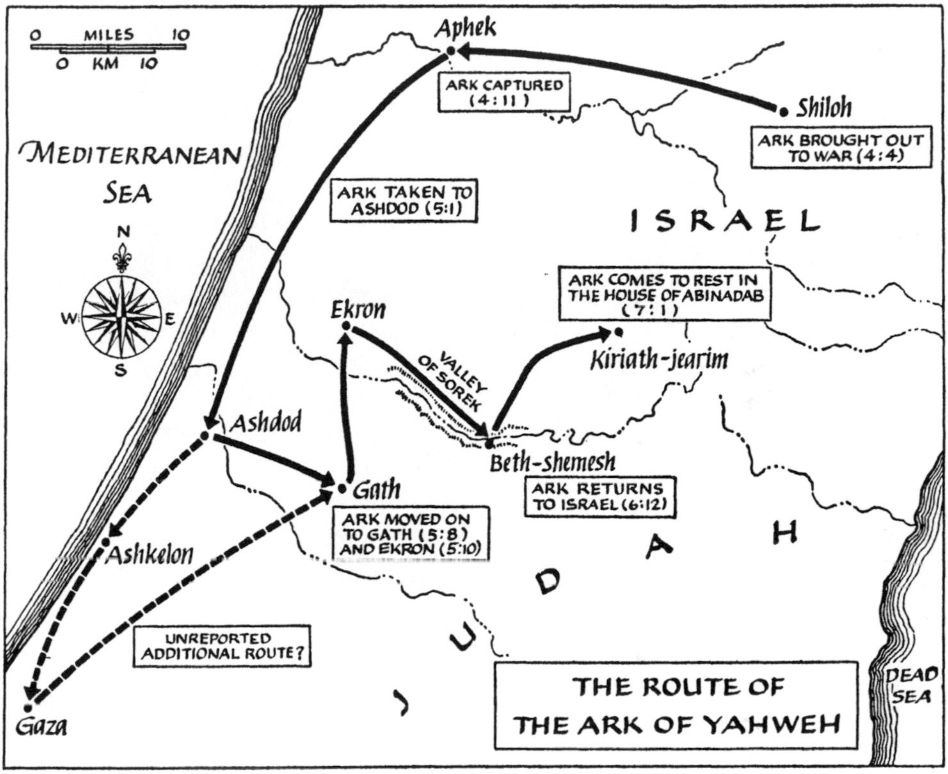

VI. THE BATTLE OF EBENEZER
(4:1b-11)

4 1b Eli grew very old, and his sons continued to act more and more
wickedly in the presence of Yahweh.
In those days the Philistines gathered to make war against Israel.
Israel marched out to meet them in battle and made camp at
Ebenezer. The Philistines were encamped at Aphek. 2 [They] drew up
their forces to engage Israel, and the battle lines were deployed.
Israel was routed by the advance of the Philistines, about four thousands being slain from the ranks in the field.
3 When the army returned to camp the elders of Israel asked, "Why
has Yahweh routed us today before the Philistines? Let us fetch the
ark of Yahweh from Shiloh! Let it go among us and rescue us from
the clutches of our enemy!" 4 So the army sent word to Shiloh to carry
over from there the ark of Yahweh Seated-upon-the-Cherubim. And
Eli's two sons, Hophni and Phinehas, were with the ark.
5 As the ark of Yahweh arrived in camp all Israel uttered a great
shout and the land resounded. 6 When the Philistines heard the shouting they thought, "What is this great shouting in the camp of the Hebrews?" Realizing that the ark of Yahweh had come to camp, 7 they
were afraid, thinking, "Gods have come to the camp! Alas for us! For
nothing like this has happened before. 8 Alas for us! Who will rescue
us from the clutches of these mighty gods? These are the gods who
struck Egypt with every kind of scourge and pestilence. 9 Fortify
yourselves and be men, you Philistines, or you must serve the Hebrews as they have served you! Be men and fight!" 10 And they did
fight; and Israel was routed and fled, every man to his own tent. The
slaughter was very great: there fell from Israel thirty thousands of the
infantry. 11 Also the ark of God was captured, and the two sons of Eli
perished.

TEXTUAL NOTES

4 1b. *Eli . . . against Israel* Reading *w'ly zqn m'd wbnyw hlkw hlwk whr' drkm lpny yhwh wyhy bymym hhm wyqbṣw plštym lmlḥmh 'l yśr'l,* all of which has been lost in MT through a long haplography, the scribe's eye having jumped from *yśr'l* at the end of *wyhy dbr šmw'l lkl yśr'l* in 4:1a to *yśr'l* at the end of the present reading. LXX preserves the longer text: *kai ēlei presbytēs sphodra kai hoi huioi autou poreuomenoi eporeuonto kai ponēra hē hodos autōn enōpion kyriou kai egenēthē en tais hēmerais ekeinais kai synathroizontai allophyloi eis polemon epi israēl* (3:21 +). Cf. the *Textual Note* to 4:1a.

to meet them Reading *lqr'tm* on the basis of LXX *eis apantēsin autois.* MT *lqr't plštym,* "to meet the Philistines," was expanded after the loss of the first part of the verse (see above).

Ebenezer Reading *'eben hā'ēzer* for MT *hā'eben hā'ēzer;* cf. 5:1; 7:12.

2. *and the battle lines were deployed* Reading *wattuṭṭaš hammilḥāmâ,* lit. "and the battle was deployed," which suits Hebrew idiom, in which a battle draws near (*qārĕbâ milḥāmâ*) and one sets a battle in order (*'ārak milḥāmâ*). We interpret the verb as *Qal* passive, repointing MT *wattiṭṭōš* accordingly. This verb is attested in the *Nip'al* with the meaning "be dispersed (of troops), be deployed" (Judg 15:9; II Sam 5:18,22; cf. the use of the *Qal* passive participle in I Sam 30:16). LXX has *kai eklinen,* taken by most scholars to reflect *wattēṭ,* "inclined," but such a usage is without parallel.

being slain Vocalizing *wykw* as *wayyukkû,* "and . . . were slain," with LXX, Vulg., Syr.; against MT *wayyakkû,* "and they slew."

3. *Let us fetch* MT, LXX^L^, Syr. add "to ourselves" (*'lynw*), probably a displacement of *'lhynw,* "our god," from its position after *yhwh* (see below).

the ark of Yahweh Read *'t 'rwn yhwh.* All witnesses are expansive. MT: *'t 'rwn bryt yhwh,* "the ark of the covenant of Yahweh." LXX^B^: *tēn kibōton tou theou hēmōn = 't rwn 'lhynw,* "the ark of our god" (*yhwh* having been lost after the addition of *'lhynw*). LXX^L^: *tēn kibōton tēs diathēkēs kyriou tou theou hēmōn* "the ark of the covenant of Yahweh, our god" (conflating the readings of MT and LXX^B^). Cf. also the LXX^(B)^ readings in vv 4 and 5 and the reading of MT and LXX in v 7.

4. *the ark of Yahweh* With LXX^B^, against MT, LXX^L^ "the ark of the covenant of Yahweh Sabaoth."

Eli's two sons So LXX, Vulg. MT adds *šām, "There* Eli's two sons . . ." which is reminiscent of 1:3 (Wellhausen). Stoebe defends its originality.

the ark So LXX^B^. MT, LXX^L^ again add *bryt h'lhym.*

5. *the ark of Yahweh* So LXX^B^. MT, LXX^L^: *'rwn bryt yhwh,* "the ark of the covenant of Yahweh."

6. *the shouting . . . this great shouting* Reading *'t trw'h . . . htrw'h hgdwlh hz't* on the basis of LXX^B^ (*tēs kraugēs . . . hē kraugē hē megalē*

hautē). MT inserts *qwl:* "*the sound* of the shouting . . . *the sound* of this great shouting." Cf. v 14.

7. *thinking* MT: *ky 'mrw,* "for they thought (said)"; LXX *kai eipon* = *wy'mrw,* "and they thought (said)."

Gods have come to the camp! Reading *b'w 'lhym 'l hmḥnh* with MT (which, however, has *b';* but cf. LXX and the plurals in v 8). LXX reflects *'lh h'lhym* (LXX[L] *h'lhyhm*) *b'w 'lyhm 'l hmḥnh,* "These are the gods (their gods)! They have come to them to the camp." The shorter reading is better: *'lh h'lhym* is an anticipation of *'lh* (*hm*) *h'lhym* in v 8b, and *'lyhm* is a corruption of *'lhym.*

Alas for us! Preceded in MT by a repetition of *wy'mrw,* "and they said"; omit with LXX. LXX adds "Rescue us, O Yahweh, today!" (*exelou hēmas kyrie sēmeron* = *hṣylnw yhwh hywm*), which is impossible in the mouths of the Philistines. Perhaps this was intended as the shout of the Israelites upon the arrival of the ark, arising as an expansion of v 5.

8. *mighty* LXX *stereōn* = *'byrym,* "mighty, powerful," is less likely to be original than MT *'dyrym,* "mighty, majestic," a divine epithet at Ugarit and in Israel (Pss 76:5; 93:4; cf. Ps 8:2,10[English 1,9]).

and pestilence MT has *bmdbr,* "in the wilderness," which is contrary to biblical tradition. But cf. LXX *kai en tē erēmō,* reflecting *wbmdbr,* understood as "and in the wilderness," but which may be read *ûbĕmō-deber,* "and with pestilence." The long form of the preposition is rare (archaic and poetic).

9. So MT, LXX[L], OL and (as the fragments show) 4QSam[a]. LXX[B] has suffered a long haplography, the scribe's eye jumping from the first *l'nšym* to the second *l'nšym* (or from *eis andras* to *eis andras* if the corruption was inner-Greek, occurring in an ancestor of the family LXX[B], rather than derived from the Hebrew *Vorlage* of LXX[B]). Thus LXX[B] has *krataiousthe kai ginesthe eis andras kai polemēsate autous* = *htḥzqw whyw l'nšym wnlḥmtwm,* "Take courage and be men and fight them!"

10. *And they did fight* Reading *wylḥmw;* cf. LXX[(B)], which adds the suffix as in v 9 (*kai epolemēsan autous,* "And they did fight *them*"). MT, LXX[L], Syr., Vulg., Targ. add *plštym* ("And *the Philistines* did fight"); omit with LXX[B], 4QSam[a].

11. *the two sons of Eli* Limitations in space show that 4QSam[a] uniquely omits *ḥpny wpnḥs,* "Hophni and Phinehas," which is here appended in all other witnesses. Compare the text of LXX in 4:17, where LXX[BL] omit *hophnei kai phinees* against MT in wording closely parallel to the present passage. The shorter reading in each context is probably original.

NOTES

4 1b. *the Philistines.* At the end of the Late Bronze Age coastal Syria-Palestine began to experience an inundation of Aegean invaders known as the Peoples of the Sea to the Egyptians, who were also troubled by them. One of these groups was designated Perasata or Persata in Egyptian records. These were the biblical Philistines, who entered relatively briefly into the history of Palestine, but long enough to give the land their name. In the years before the rise of monarchy in Israel they firmly controlled the coastal plain north of Gaza and must have posed a serious threat to the Israelites who occupied the inland mountains. Thereafter the relationship between Israel and the inhabitants of the Philistine plain was more often than not a hostile one. Philistia was regarded as a traditional enemy throughout the biblical period.

Ebenezer. The location is unknown. One might assume that it ought to be in the vicinity of Aphek, and indeed an outpost of Aphek, modern 'Izbet Ṣarṭah, is now often cited as a leading candidate. See further the NOTE at 7:12.

Aphek. The city was situated on an important access route from the coastal plain into the Ephraimite highlands, inevitably a locality contested by Israel and Philistia. The site, just E of Tel Aviv, is currently under excavation by the Institute of Archaeology of Tel Aviv University, under the direction of Moshe Kochavi.

2. *about four thousands.* The Hebrew reads, "about four thousands of men," or (perhaps) some twenty to fifty-six men. See the second NOTE at v 10 below.

3. *the elders of Israel.* The elders were senior tribesmen, seventy in number according to tradition (Num 11:16-17; cf. Exod 18:13-27; Deut 1:9-13), entrusted with important decisions.

"Why has Yahweh routed us . . . ?" Yahweh himself is seen as the agent of the disaster. The question is to some extent rhetorical, insofar as the speakers assume that the answer (viz. because the ark was absent) is self-evident.

go among us. In the ideology of Israelite warfare the presence of the ark in battle was tantamount to the participation of the deity on Israel's behalf. The ark traveled in the van of the army, from which position the divine warrior was believed to assault his enemies and lead the troops home in triumph (cf. Num 10:35-36).

4. *Yahweh Seated-upon-the-Cherubim.* Cf. II Sam 6:2. Hebrew *yahweh yōšēb hakkĕrūbîm,* a longer form of the divine name (see the NOTE at 1:3). That the full form, *yahweh ṣĕbā'ôt yōšēb hakkĕrūbîm,* meaning "He who is seated upon the cherubim creates the (heavenly) armies," was an original cultic epithet of the god of Israel at Shiloh was argued first by Otto Eissfeldt (see "Jahwe Zebaoth," in *Miscellanea Academica Berolinensia* [Berlin: Akademie-Verlag, 1950] 128-150, esp. 139-146). Cherubim were mythological beings with both human and animal features. They were an important element in the

royal iconography of Canaan, often depicted in association with the thrones of kings. This is the picture suggested by the present epithet, according to which Yahweh is conceived of as a seated monarch flanked by a pair of the sphinx-like creatures. That the ark itself was thought of as a cherub throne or in association with a cherub throne, as well as a battle palladium, is beyond doubt, though its precise significance was understood in various ways in various periods. See further the COMMENT. On the cherub-throne iconography of Shiloh and later Jerusalem, see Cross, *CMHE,* cc 2-3 *passim* and esp. 69; on the cherubim in general see especially the article of de Vaux cited in fn. 4 to the COMMENT below.

5. The arrival of the ark is greeted by the Israelite *tĕrû'â* or battle cry, a prolonged, menacing roar. Cf. G. von Rad, *Der heilige Krieg im alten Israel* [Göttingen: Vandenhoeck und Ruprecht, 1951] 11. In response to the cry, "the land resounded" (*wattēhōm hā'āreṣ*). The divine consternation or panic (*mĕhûmâ*) spread by stampede until it reached the camp of the Philistines. This *mĕhûmâ* was thought to be the weapon that in divinely directed warfare was finally decisive (Deut 7:23). Cf. 5:9 and esp. 14:15,20 and 22.

6. *the Hebrews.* Whereas the narrator himself uses the name "Israel," he portrays the Philistines speaking of "the Hebrews" (*'ibrîm;* so also 4:9; 13:3,19; 14:11; 29:3). The latter was evidently a generalized designation and not entirely synonymous with "Israelites" (14:21). Characteristically it was used of Israelites by foreigners, but the origin and precise significance of the term are disputed. See the NOTE at 14:21, where a fuller discussion is provided.

7. *Gods.* Aware of the claim that Yahweh rides upon the ark the Philistines are dismayed. The plural ("gods") is probably intended to indicate that the Philistines—themselves worshipers of several gods—assume the same of the Israelites. But very little is known about Philistine religion. It is clear that they eventually assimilated the culture of Palestine thoroughly, including the worship of Canaanite gods. The biblical writers associate the Philistines especially with the Semitic deity Dagon (see the NOTE at 5:2).

Alas for us! Hebrew *'ôy lānû,* the conventional cry of woe uttered in the face of sudden peril. See G. Wanke, "*'wy* und *hwy,*" *ZAW* 78 (1966) 215-218; W. Janzen, *Mourning Cry and Woe Oracle,* BZAW 125 (Berlin: Walter de Gruyter, 1972) 24-25.

8. The Philistines know the reputation of the god of Israel. The events that follow will parallel those of the exodus story closely, and this early allusion to Egypt prepares the reader to take notice of the connections.

9. *Fortify yourselves and be men.* The elegant phrases of the *KJV* come to mind: "Be strong, and quit yourselves like men." Evidently the charge to be men was a traditional exhortation to battle. In a fourteenth-century letter to the king of Egypt (*EA* 289:26-30) an enemy of Jerusalem is quoted urging his confederates on to insurrection as follows: "Be men (*lū amēlātunu* [!]) . . . and let us break with Jerusalem!" (translation based on suggestions by W. von Soden and W. L. Moran). The fuller expression ("Fortify yourself and be a man!") occurs in David's charge to Solomon (I Kings 2:2; cf. II Sam 13:28; etc.) with reference to the punishment of Joab and Shimei (vv 5*ff* should be read as following immediately upon v 2, notwithstanding the intrusive state-

ments in vv 3-4). Cf. also I Cor 16:13. See also Weinfeld, *Deuteronomy*, 11 and n. 5.

or you must serve the Hebrews as they have served you! In the Philistine wars as they are presented to us in these stories territory was not so much at issue as ascendancy. The conquered became slaves of the conquerors. Note the stakes in the Philistine's challenge in 17:9.

10. *every man to his own tent.* The military unification of Israel is dissolved. In the stories about this period the Israelites, when assembling to make war, vow not to return "every man to his own tent" until victory is assured (cf. Judg 20:8). To be sent "every man to his own tent" is to be dismissed from active duty (I Sam 13:2; etc.). To flee "every man to his own tent" is not simply to retreat but to abandon military service altogether. Thus the cry, "Every man to his own tent, O Israel!" (II Sam 20:1; I Kings 12:16), is an exhortation to members of the northern tribes to forswear their allegiance to the southern king.

thirty thousands of the infantry. Hebrew *šĕlōšîm 'elep raglî,* lit. "thirty thousands on foot." A figure of 30,000 is out of the question, and there is wide agreement that the designation "thousand" (*'elep*) denotes some kind of military unit of unspecified size. This assumption has been used to special advantage by G. E. Mendenhall in interpreting "The Census Lists of Numbers 1 and 26," *JBL* 77 (1958) 52-66: "There (Num 1) the units [thousands] vary in size from 5 men per unit . . . to over 14 men per unit" (63). Applying these figures to the present passage we may estimate the Israelite losses in the battle of Ebenezer at between 150 and 420 infantrymen in addition to the casualties suffered in the first engagement (v 2). These figures, though more plausible, still represent a grievous loss. Note that the total force Saul is able to muster in 11:8 is only 330 thousands or (again applying the data of Numbers 1) 1,650 to 4,620 men.

COMMENT

The scene now shifts from Shiloh to a battleground in the hills some twenty miles away. Here the Philistines, Israel's western neighbor and perennial foe, have amassed an army on the edge of the Ephraimite heartland, and the Israelites have gathered for the defense. Our attention is fixed on the two battlecamps and, for the moment at least, the situation at Shiloh is forgotten. In 4:1-7:1 the family of Eli enters into the story only briefly (in 4:4b,12-22) and Samuel not at all. Indeed as these events continue to unfold we shall seldom see any human participant rise above anonymity, for now the chief protagonist is no man but the ark of Yahweh itself.

What was the ark of Yahweh? The term traditionally rendered "ark" is *'ărôn,* meaning "box" or "chest,"[1] and our sources suggest that the ark was in fact a wooden chest in which were said to be deposited the tablets that Moses received on Sinai (Deut 10:5; etc.; cf. I Kings 8:9). Because it contained these "two tablets of the covenant"[2] the ark was often referred to as *'ărôn hā'ēdūt* (Exod 25:22; etc.) or *'ărôn habbĕrît* (Josh 3:6; etc.), that is, "the ark of the covenant." The former term is characteristic of the Tetrateuch, the latter of those writings especially influenced by the Deuteronomic legislation.[3]

More important for the interpretation of the present narrative, however, is the fact that the ark was venerated as the visible sign of the presence of Yahweh. It was Yahweh's footstool or podium (I Chron 28:2; cf. Pss 99:5; 132:7; Lam 2:1), above which was the divine throne itself, flanked in the manner characteristic of Canaanite royal thrones by a pair of winged sphinxes or cherubim.[4] Here, we are told, Yahweh appeared in a cloud (Lev 16:2) and addressed Israel (Exod 25:22; Num 7:89). Thus the Israelites fitted out the ark with crafted cherubim and provided the entire structure with rings and poles so that it might be carried about after the fashion of a royal litter (Exod 25:12-13; 37:3-5).

The conceptions of the ark as a covenant repository on the one hand and as a cherub throne on the other, however originally related,[5] have been thoroughly combined in the priestly legislation of the Tetrateuch, where no conflict between them exists. The adjacent Tetrateuchal narratives present the portable ark as the guiding center of the Israelite camp (Num 10:33-36), and this is also the case in the stories of the conquest, where the ark carried on its poles precedes the people across the Jordan

[1] The *'ărôn* of Gen 50:26 is a sarcophagus, and this is the most common meaning of Phoenician *'rn.* In II Kings 12:10,11 (English 12:9,10) and II Chron 24:8,10,11 the *'ărôn* is a chest used for the collection of funds for temple repairs.

[2] Referred to in the Tetrateuch as *šĕnê lūḥōt hā'ēdūt* (Exod 31:18; 32:15) and in Deuteronomy as *šĕnê . . . lūḥōt habbĕrît* (Deut 9:11,15).

[3] But the terminology alone is not a safe indicator of Priestly or Deuteronomic influence because of the tendency to expansion in the later transmission of the text.

[4] See the NOTE at v 4. This does not imply the existence of a throne as a separate cult object. The ark with its appurtenances could be thought of as Yahweh's throne as well as his footstool (Jer 3:16–17; cf. Ezek 43:7). On the cherubim, see especially R. de Vaux, "Les chérubins et l'arche d'alliance," *MUSJ* 37 (1960–61) 93-124.

[5] De Vaux has argued vigorously that there is no contradiction between these conceptions. Ancient Near Eastern parallels amply illustrate the practice of depositing treaty texts at the feet of divine images and of preserving sacred documents in sanctuaries under the protection of the gods. See "Les chérubins," esp. 118-122. But such citations cannot resolve the tension between the two concepts. To show that the ark conceived of as a receptacle might have been deposited at Yahweh's feet in no way explains its significance as a footstool. The religious formulations involved are very different. The footstool represents a sacral place where the deity is present and approachable, while the receptacle is important for what it contains and preserves. De Vaux has demonstrated a basis for the coalescence of the two concepts in Israelite religion, but it remains likely that each was discrete in origin.

(Joshua 3-4) and plays a decisive role in the siege of Jericho (Joshua 6). The primary importance of the ark as conceived in these accounts is military, and its presence in battle is regarded as essential. Without it victory is impossible (Num 14:44). In other words the ark as the visible sign of Yahweh's presence functioned in the ideology of Israelite warfare as a battle palladium for the armies of Israel. It was the source of security in conflict. Where the ark was there was Yahweh fighting on Israel's behalf.

This brings us back to the incident under discussion. Finding themselves overmatched in an initial engagement with the Philistines, the Israelites send to Shiloh for the ark. The plan, then, is to involve Yahweh in the hostilities directly; and the Philistines themselves perceive that, "Gods have come to the camp!" The details reflect Israel's sacred rites of war. The ark arrives, the troops set up their ritual roar (*tĕrû'â*), and a holy panic (*mĕhûmâ*) spreads itself abroad (see the NOTE at v 5). But this time the ark does not bring victory. The Philistines harden themselves to the task. The battle is lost, Israel routed, and the ark itself captured.

In the Introduction (see "The Ark Narrative," pp. 23-26) we accepted the arguments of P. D. Miller, Jr., and J. J. M. Roberts that the present account was composed only a short time after the events it describes. These events must have generated in their Israelite participants a peculiar sense of disorder. Here was solemn conviction flouted. The presence of the ark had not produced the expected result. The central question that would have been provoked is easy to formulate: How can the Philistines have defied the power of Yahweh and prevailed? As we shall see, the theological purpose of the ark narrative as a whole (2:12-17,22-25 + 4:1b-7:1) is to deal with this problem; it will affirm emphatically that Yahweh was in control of the events from the beginning. This requires that the initial question be posed in a different way: Given that Yahweh is in control, why has he permitted this defeat (cf. v 3) and the capture of his ark? The answer to this question, as Miller and Roberts have shown, is to be found in the account of the corruption of the Shilonite priesthood in 2:11-26, or rather in the parts of that account that belonged originally to the ark narrative (2:12-17,22-25). The ark was captured because Yahweh had chosen to abandon Israel on account of the wickedness of the Elides. The details in vv 4b and 11b are thus essential, not incidental remarks of the narrator, and the report to Eli that follows makes the point clear.

VII. THE DEATH OF ELI
(4:12-22)

4 12 A Benjaminite raced from the front and came to Shiloh that
same day with his clothes torn and dirt upon his head. 13 When he arrived—(Now Eli was in a chair atop the gate watching the road, for
he was anxious about the ark of God; but the man went inside the city
to make his report.) When he arrived the city began to cry out, 14 and
when Eli heard the noise of the outcry he asked, "What is this tumultuous noise?"

The man came quickly and reported to Eli. 15 [ ] 16 "I fled from
the front today," he said to him. And when [Eli] asked, "What was
the situation, my son?" 17 the messenger answered, "Israel fled before
the onslaught of the Philistines. Not only was there a great rout of the
army, but also your two sons are dead and the ark of God is captured." 18 As soon as he mentioned the ark of God, [Eli] fell backward from his chair over the gate-tower. His neck was broken and he
died, for he was old and overweight. He had judged Israel for twenty
years.

19 His daughter-in-law, the wife of Phinehas, was pregnant and
ready to give birth. When she heard the news of the capture of the ark
of God and the death of her father-in-law and husband, her labor
began, and she crouched down and gave birth. 20 When her time [to
give birth] came, she was about to die, and the women attending her
said, "Do not be afraid, for you have borne a son!" But she did not
respond or pay attention.

21 She called the child "Ichabod" in reference to the ark of God and
to her father-in-law and husband; 22 for she said, "Glory was exiled
from Israel when the ark of God was captured."

TEXTUAL NOTES

4 13. *Now Eli was in a chair* Reading *whnh 'ly 'l ks'* on the basis of LXX. MT inserts *yōšēb,* "sitting"; but it is difficult to see how this was lost if original and easy to see how it might have arisen in the shorter text (derived from 1:9?).

atop the gate watching the road Reading *'l* (or *'l*) *yd hš'r mṣph* (*'t*) *hdrk* on the basis of LXX *para tēn pylēn skopeuōn tēn hodon.* MT *yad* (the *kětîb* is *yk; yad* = *lěyad,* cf. Syr.) *derek měṣappeh,* "beside (the) road watching," is patently corrupt, although on the basis of the consonants alone of the last word one might read "beside the Mizpah road" (Wellhausen). But the reading of LXX is superior. For the interpretation of *'l yd,* see the NOTE.

the city So LXX. MT inserts *kol:* "the *entire* city."

14-16. *he asked . . . said to him* The text of LXX in these verses shows a conflation of two variant readings. It reads: *kai eipen tis hē phōnē tēs boēs* (so LXX^{AL}; LXX^{B}: *boē tēs phōnēs*) *tautēs kai ho anthrōpos speusas eisēlthen kai apēngeilen tō ēlei kai ēlei huios enenēkonta kai oktō* (so LXX^{L}; LXX^{B} omits *kai oktō*) *etōn kai hoi ophthalmoi autou epanestēsan kai ouk eblepen kai eipen ēlei tois andrasin tois periestēkosin autō tis hē phōnē tou ēchous toutou kai ho anēr speusas proselthen ēlei kai eipen autō,* reflecting a Hebrew text that read *wy'mr mh qwl hṣ'qh hz't wh'yš mhr wyb' wygd l'ly w'ly bn tš'ym wšmnh šnh w'ynyw qmw wl' yr'h wy'mr 'ly l'nšym hnṣbym 'lyw mh qwl hhmwn hzh wh'yš mhr wyb' 'l 'ly wy'mr lw,* ". . . he asked, 'What is this outcry?' The man came quickly and reported to Eli. (Now Eli was ninety-eight years old and his eyes were fixed—he no longer saw.) So Eli asked the men who were standing beside him, 'What is this tumultuous noise?' The man came quickly to Eli and said to him. . . ." The text of MT is shorter: *wy'mr mh qwl hhmwn hzh wh'yš mhr wyb' wygd l'ly w'ly bn tš'ym wšmnh šnh w'ynyw qmh wl' ykwl lr'wt wy'mr h'yš 'l 'ly,* ". . . he asked, 'What is this tumultuous noise?' The man came quickly and reported to Eli. (Now Eli was ninety-eight years old and his eyes were fixed—he could no longer see.) And the man said to Eli. . . ." We might assume that the parenthesis about Eli's age and blindness was original and that (A) *wy'mr mh qwl . . . wygd l'ly* and (B) *wy'mr 'ly l'nšym . . . wyb' l'ly* were variants conflated in LXX with MT preserving only the first in an older form of the text. But there are certain objections to this. The parenthesis about Eli's blindness is not necessary to variant A, which precedes it, but essential to variant B, in which Eli finds it necessary to appeal to the men standing around him. Moreover, the mention of his blindness is suspiciously reminiscent of the notice in 3:2 and seems to contradict the statement in v 13 of the present passage that he was watching the road. So we must assume that the parenthesis was a part of the second, much longer variant—thus: (variant A) *wy'mr mh qwl . . . wygd l'ly;* (variant B) *w'ly bn tš'ym . . . wyb' 'l 'ly wy'mr lw.* Of these, A is surely original. MT is to be explained as follows. Originally it shared the long, conflate reading of LXX (in A, MT *hhmwn hzh* is probably original, LXX *hṣ'qh hz't* being reminiscent of the preceding *hṣ'qh* in v 14) but suffered a long haplography, a scribe's eye skipping from the second *wy'mr* to the third (*wy'mr 'ly l'nšym . . . wyb' 'l 'ly wy'mr*). At the end, MT *wy'mr h'yš 'l 'ly* is a remnant of variant B showing simple expansion from *wy'mr lw* (LXX).

14. *this tumultuous noise* MT *qôl hehāmôn hazzeh,* lit. "this noise of tumult." So LXX in variant B (see above). Here LXX$^{(L)}$ reflects *qwl hṣ'qh* (*tēs boēs*) *hzh,* "this noise of shouting." MT is to be preferred. See the preceding *Textual Note.*

16. *"I fled from the front today"* Here MT and LXX reflect a single tradition, and the common ancestral text was conflate. MT has *'nky hb' mn hm'rkh w'ny mn hm'rkh nsty hywm,* "I am he who came from the front, and I fled from the front today." LXX reflects a similar reading: *'nky hb' mn hmḥnh w'ny nsty mn hm'rkh hywm.* LXX is to be preferred in its reading of *hmḥnh,* "the camp," for MT *hm'rkh* (1), "the front." But clearly the common ancestor of MT and LXX was a conflation of two variants. This conflation may be related to that identified above in the *Textual Note* to vv 14-16. There is scant basis for choosing between the variants. The second stands closer to the statement in v 12 (but this might also be used to argue against its originality), and the first seems to presuppose that Eli knew already that a messenger had arrived, which is hardly likely (see the NOTE at v 13). We should give the second variant a tentative preference and read *'ny nsty mn hm'rkh hywm.*

he said to him So LXX^{B}. MT: *"the man* said to *Eli."*

17. *your two sons* So LXX. MT adds *ḥpny wpynḥs,* an explicating expansion (cf. the *Textual Note* to v 11).

18. *As soon as he mentioned* Reading *khzkyrw* with MT. LXX *hōs emnēsthē* reflects *kzkrw,* "When he [viz. Eli] remembered," but MT is superior.

over the gate-tower MT *bĕ'ad yad haššaʻar.* LXX$^{(B)}$ *echomenos* probably also reflects *b'd yd* as a guess based on the Septuagint's usual treatment of prepositions compounded with *yd.* For the interpretation, see the NOTE at v 13.

twenty years With LXX against MT "forty" (cf. Josephus *Ant.* 5.359). See the NOTE.

19. *to give birth* Reading *lldt* for MT *llt* on the assumption of a simple scribal omission. A contracted form of the infinitive written phonetically (**-latt* < **-ladt*) is conceivable but unexampled elsewhere in Biblical Hebrew (for a possible Ugaritic parallel, see M. Dahood, *Ugaritic-Hebrew Philology* [Rome: PBI, 1965] 9).

of the capture . . . and the death Reading *'el hillāqaḥ . . . ûmût,* two infinitives construct serving as objects of the preposition *'el,* "concerning, about, of." MT vocalizes the second as a finite verb, *ûmēt.*

20. *When her time* [*to give birth*] *came, she was about to die* Reading *ûkĕ'ittāh mētâ* on the basis of LXX *kai en tō kairō autēs apothnēskei* (Klostermann) against MT *ûkĕ'ēt mûtāh,* "When her time of death came."

21. *Ichabod* Hebrew *'î kābôd.* LXX *ouai barchabōth* (so LXX^{B} with variants *barchabōd,* etc., in other MSS; LXX^{L} has *bariōchabēl*) represents *'wy*

kbwd, preserving two attempts to render the second element (1) by a form of *barys,* "heavy" (cf. v 18 above) and (2) by simple transliteration.

MT at this point inserts *l'mr glh kbwd myśr'l,* "saying, 'Glory is exiled from Israel!'" As the text of LXX shows, this is to be deleted as an alternative reading to v 22.

in reference to the ark of God Reading *'l 'rwn h'lhym* on the basis of the shorter text of LXX. MT has *'l hlqḥ 'rwn h'lhym,* "in reference to *the capture of* the ark of God," the insertion of the infinitive being reminiscent of v 19.

22. MT: *wt'mr glh kbwd myśr'l ky nlqḥ 'rwn h'lhym.* LXX = *wt'mr glh kbwd yśr'l bhlqḥ* (cf. MT in v 21) *'rwn h'lhym,* "for she said, 'The glory of Israel was exiled when the ark of God was captured.'" The difference between these variants is slight and the phraseology of each is paralleled (to MT cf. Hosea 10:5; to LXX cf. Micah 1:15; etc.). Our choice of MT is arbitrary.

NOTES

4 12-17. The structural parallel between the present episode and the report to David of Saul's death in II Sam 1:2*ff* is quite striking. The details may be outlined as follows. The two messengers, having fled from the battlefield with torn clothes and dirt-sprinkled heads (I Sam 4:12; II Sam 1:2), make their sorrowful reports in similar fashion:

I Sam 4:16-17	*II Sam 1:3-4*
	David said to him, "From where have you come?"
"I fled (*nastî*) from the front today," he said to him.	"I escaped (*nimlāṭtî*) from the camp of Israel," he said to him.
And when [Eli] asked, "What was the situation, my son?" the messenger answered, "Israel fled before the onslaught of the Philistines.	And when David asked him, "What was the situation? Tell me!" he said, "The army fled from the battle.
Not only was there a great rout of the army, but also your two sons are dead and the ark of God is captured."	Not only did a great many fall from the army, but also Saul and his son Jonathan are dead."

This is an example of the common use of a literary motif by different writers, who drew upon a common source or a shared repertoire of conventional narrative situations, a familiar feature of biblical prose.

12. *A Benjaminite.* The tribal territory of Benjamin was a small wedge of land between Jerusalem and Bethel. Saul himself was a Benjaminite—Rabbinic sources identified him with the anonymous refugee in the present story—and the little tribe plays a big role in the stories of this period. But why is this messenger identified as a Benjaminite? It is uncharacteristic of biblical narrative to

provide such details gratuitously (cf. the significance of the Amalekite messenger in II Samuel 1), but in this case the point escapes us.

that same day. The position of the expression after *wayyābō' šilōh*, "and came to Shiloh," calls attention to the fact that the courier's journey was completed in a single day. The distance from Ebenezer to Shiloh was nearly twenty miles, so that the run was a short marathon (Budde).

his clothes torn and dirt upon his head. The messenger's lack of grooming might be accounted for easily enough by his recent exertion, but we should also bear in mind that tearing the clothes and sprinkling the head with dirt were traditional signs of grief (cf. II Sam 1:2; etc).

13. See the NOTES at 1:4-7 and 3:2-4. The narrative sequence introduced by *wayyābō'*, "When he arrived . . . ," and resumed by *wattiz'aq kol-hā'îr*, ". . . the city began to cry out," is interrupted by a long parenthesis explaining in advance why Eli was not in the center of the city to witness the arrival and hear the first report. Eli was watching anxiously for the return of the ark. We are not told whether he noted with misgiving the arrival of a solitary traveler in mourning dress; but in any case, it is not necessary to appeal to the old priest's failing eyesight (cf. the NOTE at 3:2 and the *Textual Note* to 4:14-16). The issue is not what he saw but what he heard. After the parenthesis the narrative continues. "When he arrived" is repeated in the translation as an aid to the English reader.

atop the gate. Hebrew *'el-yad haššaʿar* or *ʿal yad haššaʿar* (see the *Textual Note*), lit. "on the 'hand' of the gate," i.e. on the side of the gate; but the expression does not mean "beside the gate" in the usual sense. The "hands" of a city gate are the two parallel walls which form the sides of the gateway (*derek haššaʿar*) analogous to the "hands" (= "banks") of a river (Exod 2:5; Num 13:29; Judg 11:26; Jer 46:6; Dan 10:4). Here a leader would take his position to judge the citizenry: (1) in II Sam 15:2 Absalom decides lawsuits "upon the 'hand' of the gateway" (*ʿal-yad derek haššaʿar*); (2) in II Sam 18:4 David stands "on the 'hand' of the gate" (*'el-yad haššaʿar*) to review the troops. In an instructive passage in Prov 8:2-3 Wisdom calls to men from "atop the towers along the road (*bĕrō'š-mĕrōmîm ʿălê-dārek*, cf. Prov 9:14) . . . / On the 'hand' of the gates at the city's entrance (*lĕyad-šĕʿārîm lĕpî-qāret*)." This explains the much discussed expression *bĕʿad yad haššaʿar* in v 18 below: Eli falls "over the 'hand' of the gate," i.e. over the wall to the street below.

17. *Not only . . . but also*. Hebrew (*wĕ*)*gam . . . wĕgam*. The expression implies a close relationship between the clauses so joined. So for example in 26:25 we read: *gam ʿāśōh taʿăśeh wĕgam yākōl tûkal*, lit. "Not only will you do but also you will prevail," i.e. "In whatever you undertake you will surely succeed!" Thus the force of the present statement is, "There was a great rout of the army and in its course your two sons were killed and the ark captured." The syntax has the further effect of emphasizing the last parts of the sentence (see the COMMENT).

18. *He had judged Israel for twenty years*. This notice is intended to incorporate Eli's career into the chronological framework of the preceding material (i.e. in terms of canonical divisions, the Book of Judges). How Eli the priest can also have been attributed judgeship by the tradition has puzzled scholars. Hertzberg would tentatively restore his name to the list of the "minor judges" of

Judges 10 and 12 ("Die kleinen Richter," *TLZ* 79 [1954] cols. 285-290). But the present notice is a Deuteronomistic expansion (see p. 16 in the Introduction), and every major figure between Joshua and Saul was a "judge" from the Deuteronomistic point of view. See Noth, *ÜS* 55 and the NOTE on "twenty years" at 7:2.

19-22. The relationship of the account of the birth of Ichabod to the section as a whole is difficult to determine. It is not really an organic part of the report of Eli's death and seems to have no necessary function in the larger story. It does serve to assure us that the line of Eli is not already blotted out after the death of the old man and his sons, but we learn later (in 14:3, where Saul's chaplain, Ahijah son of Ahitub, is identified as Ichabod's brother) that Phinehas had another son anyway. It is probably best to regard these verses as representative of a separate unit of tradition included in the ark narrative not because it was necessary to the author's purpose but because it was familiar.

19. *pregnant and ready to give birth.* Hebrew *hārâ lāledet* (see the *Textual Note*), a unique expression. Budde explains it as meaning "pregnant to the point of giving birth," but it may simply be an elliptical representation of *hārâ wattĕhî lāledet,* "(she was) pregnant and was ready to give birth."

her labor began, and she crouched down and gave birth. Hebrew *wattikraʿ wattēled kî nehepkû ʿālêhā ṣirêhā,* lit. "she crouched down and gave birth, for her pains had turned upon her," as in Dan 10:16 (metaphorically). An Israelite woman assumed a sitting or squatting position ("she crouched down") during parturition. In this instance the onset of labor is premature, induced by the shock to the mother (cf. Josephus *Ant.* 5.360).

20. Compare the account of the birth of Benjamin and death of Rachel in Gen 35:17,18: "When her labor was at its hardest, the midwife said to her, 'Do not be afraid, for this time, too, you have a son!' With her last breath—for she was dying—she named him Ben-oni, but his father called him Benjamin."

But she did not respond or pay attention. Hebrew *wĕlōʾ ʿānĕtâ wĕlōʾ-šātâ libbāh.* Two very different interpretations are possible. The one followed here and shared by all previous commentators assumes that the woman is despondent. She offers no reply to the words of comfort and in fact (according to the common meaning of *šît lēb,* "set the heart [upon], pay heed [to]") ignores them (though there is no reason, by the way, to conclude with Smith that she was unconscious). The alternative begins by recognizing that *šît lēb* may carry a stronger connotation, viz. of preoccupation with grief or misfortune (II Sam 13:20). Another sense of *ʿānâ* is also available. Thus read, "And she was not downcast and paid no heed (to her affliction)." This interpretation assumes that the words of comfort have had some effect or, more probably, that the woman is bearing her misfortune stoically. Faced with the loss of the ark she can have no thought for herself. There is no compelling reason to choose between these alternatives.

21. *Ichabod.* The tradition that the name (*ʾî-kābôd*) means "Inglorious"—a tradition as ancient as Josephus (who explains the name as *adoxia* in *Ant.* 5.360) and as contemporary as Washington Irving—may still be found in modern commentaries. But despite Ethiopic and Phoenician negatives the most instructive comparison is with Ugaritic *ʾiy,* "where is?" or "alas!" Cf. Biblical Hebrew *ʾî,* "alas!" in Eccles 4:10; 10:16. Note also the LXX association of the

term with *'ôy,* "woe!" Thus the name means, "Where is (the) Glory?" or "Alas (for the) Glory!" It belongs to a distinctive group of names referring to lamentation for an absent deity. Similar is the biblical name "Jezebel" (MT *'î-zebel,* perhaps erroneously for *'î-zĕbūl*), meaning, "Where is (the) Prince? / Alas (for the) Prince!" where "Prince" is the Phoenician version of a familiar epithet of the old storm god Ba'l-Haddu, the mourning for whose (ritual) absence is well known in both cult and epic (cf. *CTCA* 5.6.11-25 = 67:VI:11-25 and *passim,* and esp. 6.4.25-29 = 49:IV:25-29, which concludes *'iy 'al'iyn b'l 'iy zbl b'l 'arṣ,* "Where is 'Al'iyan Ba'l? Where is the Prince, Lord of the Earth?"). Compare the Ugaritic proper names *'iy-ba'lu,* "Where is Ba'l?" *'iy ṯôru,* "Where is Bull ('El)?" etc. Another biblical name that belongs to this group is the common priestly name *'î-tāmār,* "Ithamar" (Exod 6:23; etc.), the (cultic?) significance of which is hinted at by the story in Judg 11:30-40. The popular etymology of "Ichabod" given in the present passage, therefore, stands close to the original meaning of such a name, which should have had something to do with mourning for the departed "Glory" of Yahweh. The latter is to be understood as a technical designation for "the refulgent and radiant aureole which surrounds the deity in his manifestations or theophanies" (Cross, *CMHE,* 153, n. 30). That is, it was a ponderable sign of Yahweh's presence, especially associated with the tent of meeting (cf. G. von Rad, "The Tent and the Ark," in *The Problem of the Hexateuch and Other Essays* [New York: McGraw-Hill, 1966] 103-124, esp. 105) but also with the ark (on the antiquity of the association of the tent and the ark, see R. de Vaux, "Ark of the Covenant and Tent of Reunion," in *The Bible and the Ancient Near East* [Garden City, N.Y.: Doubleday, 1971] 136-151).

22. *exiled.* Hebrew *gālâ,* "is exiled, has gone into exile," not simply "has departed."

COMMENT

Old Eli's death is tragic. In life, as we have seen (cf. the COMMENTS on 1:1-28; 2:11-26; and 3:1-4:1a), he was not depraved or even inattentive to his duties as chief priest. In death he is concerned for Yahweh's ark to the end. It is not the news of the defeat of the Israelites that finishes him or even the tidings of the death of Hophni and Phinehas. The messenger's woeful report builds to a climax at the end of v 17, ". . . and the ark of God is captured." This is too much for the old priest. He tumbles backward over the wall and falls lifeless in the gate. The death of the grandfather is balanced by the birth of a grandson, but the cheerless event brings no hope to the cursed family. The child's mother, Phinehas' wife, can think only of the lost ark, and with her last breath she calls her luckless child Ichabod, "Alas for the Glory!" So as the tragedy of Eli ends, our attention is focused squarely on the ark, the story of which has only begun.

VIII. THE HARROWING OF THE PHILISTINES (5:1-12)

5 1 After the Philistines had captured the ark of God, they brought
it from Ebenezer to Ashdod. 2 Then [they] took it, brought it to the
house of Dagon, and set it up beside Dagon.

The Contest between the Gods

3 When the Ashdodites arose, there was Dagon fallen on his face
before the ark of Yahweh; so they raised up Dagon and put him back
in his place. 4 But when they arose the next morning, there was
Dagon fallen on his face before the ark of Yahweh. Dagon's head
and both his hands were broken off upon the threshold; only his trunk
was left intact. 5 (For this reason not even today do the priests of
Dagon or any who enter the house of Dagon tread upon the threshold
of Dagon in Ashdod.)

The Plague on the Philistines

6 And the hand of Yahweh was heavy upon the Ashdodites. He
ravaged them and afflicted them with tumors—both Ashdod and its
environs. He brought up mice upon them, and they swarmed in their
ships. Then mice went up into their land, and there was a mortal
panic in the city.

7 When the men of Ashdod saw that this was so, they thought, "The
ark of God must stay with us no longer, for his hand is hard upon us
and upon Dagon, our god." 8 So they summoned the Philistine lords
to them and said, "What shall we do about the ark of the god of Israel?"

"Let the ark of God be moved on [to us]," said the Gittites. So the
ark of God was moved on. 9 But after it was moved on to Gath, Yahweh's hand was upon that city—a tremendous panic! He afflicted the
men of the city, both young and old, and tumors broke out upon
them.

10 Then they sent the ark of God to Ekron. But when the ark of
God arrived in Ekron, the Ekronites complained, "Why have you

brought the ark of the god of Israel around to me to kill me and my
kin?" 11 So they summoned all the Philistine lords and said, "Send the
ark of the god of Israel away! Let it go back to its place and not kill
me and my kin!" For there was a very grievous panic throughout the
city when the ark of God came there: 12 those men who did not die
were afflicted with tumors, and the cry of the city rose up to the skies.

TEXTUAL NOTES

The text of c 5 is replete with problems. Both MT and LXX are seriously disturbed throughout. The chief source of difficulty seems to have been the tendency of the accounts of the plague in the various Philistine cities to conflate. The two elements of the plague, mice and tumors, along with the divine panic (*měhûmâ*) that ensues, appear and reappear, and it has become impossible to determine which was original where. The critical decisions made here, therefore, are occasionally arbitrary, and the text established must be regarded as an approximation.

5 2. *it* (1) So LXX^{L}, the *lectio brevior*. LXX^{B}: "the ark of Yahweh." MT: "the ark of God."

3. *When the Ashdodites arose* The witnesses are expansive. LXX^{B} adds *kai eisēlthon eis oikon dagōn kai eidon,* reflecting *wyb'w byt dgwn wyr'w,* "and went to the house of Dagon and looked. . . ." MT, LXX^{L} add *mmḥrt,* "on the morrow."

on his face Here and in v 4 read *'l pnyw* or *l'pyw* with LXX$^{(B)}$ *epi prosōpon autou* in preference to MT *lpnyw* (Wellhausen, Driver). MT, LXX^{L} add *'rṣh,* "on the ground."

the ark of Yahweh So MT. LXX has "the ark of God."

they raised up Reading *wyqmw* with LXX (*ēgeiran*), against MT *wyqḥw,* "they took."

3+. At the end of v 3, LXX^{B} adds a long passage equivalent to the reading of MT in v 6. It is out of place at this point. See the *Textual Note* to v 6.

4. *But when they arose the next morning* LXX^{B} *kai egeneto hote ōrthrisan to prōi* probably reflects *wyhy ky hškymw bbqr,* which is preferred by most commentators to the too abrupt MT *wyškmw bbqr.* MT, LXX^{L} again add *mmḥrt,* "on the morrow."

on his face See the *Textual Note* at v 3.

on the ark of Yahweh So MT, LXX^{L}. LXX^{B} has "the ark of the covenant of Yahweh."

Dagon's head . . . upon the threshold So MT. LXX has a long, repetitious text, perhaps reflecting a conflation of variant readings. It is not impossible that a longer reading was original, mentioning severed feet as well as hands (cf. LXX^{L}), but LXX is replete here with secondary problems, some of them insoluble, and it seems prudent to prefer the shorter text of MT.

only his trunk was left intact Read *rq gww nš'r 'lyw*, lit. "only his back was left upon him." MT *rq dgwn nš'r 'lyw*, "only Dagon was left upon him/it," is meaningless. LXX *plēn hē rhachis dagōn hypeleiphthē*, "only Dagon's spine was left," suggests that a word has fallen out of MT before *dgwn*. Most critics, therefore, would restore *gw dgwn* (or perhaps *gwyt dgwn;* cf. Dan 10:6, where this term is used specifically of the body as distinct from the extremities), "Dagon's trunk," or simply *gww*, "his trunk" (cf. Targ. *gwpyh 'št'r 'lwhy*). Wellhausen's ingenious suggestion to read *rq dgw*, "only his fish" (interpreting LXX *rhachis* as a reflection of *raq* and assuming a dittography of the *n* of *nš'r*) has not found wide acceptance, partly because of the failure of this solution to account for LXX *plēn* and partly because of doubt about the ichthyomorphic nature of the god Dagon (see the NOTE at v 2).

5. At the end of the verse, LXX(B) appends *hoti hyperbainontes hyperbainousin*, reflecting *ky dlwg ydlgw*, "but they leap over it." See the NOTE.

6. The textual problems that center on this verse are extensive and probably insoluble. The chief difficulty is presented by the introduction of mice in the text of LXX. There is no corresponding reference to mice in MT, where they are not mentioned until 6:4. The first impulse of the textual critic, therefore, is to exclude the reading of LXX as expansive. The problem, however, is that the statements concerning the mice attested in c 6 in all witnesses (viz. the statements in vv 5,11, and 18) seem to presuppose earlier mention of the mice. These, along with the reference in 6:4 (which appears in MT alone), are concerned with golden mice used as offerings; and the rationale for this use must be, as in the case of the tumors, the presence of the mice as an element in the plague. (To be sure, Wellhausen denied this, reasoning that mice may be understood as symbols of plague because of the universally known association of rats with pestilence. Accordingly, the mention of mice in LXX in 5:6 [and 6:1] might be rejected as secondary. Ingenious as this solution is, it is not really compelling and has not found wide acceptance.) We have the alternatives of acknowledging an early reference to the mice or excluding them altogether from the account. The latter solution, though it might be plausible to assume that references to the mice were introduced secondarily under the influence of their general association with plague, is untenable. The mice are attested by all witnesses in at least three places and cannot be excluded on textual grounds. So we are left with the necessity of assuming that LXX is correct in introducing the mice early. Support for this assumption comes from Josephus, who also introduces the mice at a position corresponding to 5:6 (*Ant.* 6.3), in accordance with the unanimous witness of LXX.

The principal witnesses read as follows:

1) MT: *wtkbd yd yhwh 'l h'šdwdym wyšmm wyk 'tm b'plym 't 'šdwd w't gbwlyh*, "And the hand of Yahweh was heavy upon the Ashdodites. He ravaged them and afflicted them with tumors—both Ashdod and its environs."

2) LXX^B: *kai ebarynthē cheir kyriou epi azōton kai epēgagen autois kai exezesen autois eis tas naus kai meson tēs chōras autēs anephyēsan myes kai egeneto synchysis thanatou megalē en tē polei* = *wtkbd yd yhwh 'l 'šdwd wy'l 'lyhm wyšrṣ lhm b'nywt wbtk 'rṣh 'lw 'kbrym wthy mhwmt mwt hgdwlh b'yr*, "And the hand of Yahweh was heavy upon Ashdod. He brought up against them (?) and it (?) swarmed among them in the ships, and in the midst of

their (?) land mice went up, and there was a mortal panic in the city." Note further that in 5:3 +, LXX^B appends the equivalent of MT in the present verse.

3) LXX^L: *kai ebarynthē hē cheir kyriou epi azōton kai ebasanisen tous azōtious kai epataxen autous eis tas hedras autōn tēn azōton kai to orion autēs kai epēgagen ep' autous myas kai exebrasan eis tas naus autōn kai eis meson tēs chōras autōn anephyēsan myes kai egeneto synchysis thanatou megalē en tē polei* = *wtkbd yd yhwh ʿl ʾšdwd wyšm ʾt hʾšdwdym wyk ʾtm bʿply(h)m ʾt ʾšdwd wʾt gbwlyh wyʿl ʿlyhm ʿkbrym wyšrṣw bʾnywtm wbtk ʾrṣm ʿlw ʿkbrym wthy mhwmt mwt hgdwlh bʿyr,* "And the hand of Yahweh was heavy upon Ashdod. He ravaged the Ashdodites and afflicted them with tumors—both Ashdod and its environs. He brought up mice upon them, and they swarmed in their ships. Then mice went up into the land, and there was a mortal panic in the city."

The evidence of LXX^B in 5:3+, a reading lost from 5:6 and subsequently restored in the wrong place, shows that it, too, originally shared the longer reading of LXX^L, which is generally superior (LXX^B having also lost the first *ʿkbrym,* "mice," by haplography after *ʿlyhm,* "upon them"). MT is defective, perhaps in consequence of haplography, a scribe's eye skipping from *gbwlh* to *hgdwlh* with subsequent loss of *bʿyr.* LXX^L is thus the best witness to the primitive text, and our translation follows it (except in reading *wyšmm,* "He ravaged them," with MT for LXX^L *wyšm ʾt hʾšdwdym,* "He ravaged the Ashdodites").

7. *the ark of God* So LXX; MT has "the ark of the god of Israel." In this chapter the longer expression is probably original only in its first occurrence in v 8, its third occurrence in v 10, and its first occurrence in v 11—all direct quotations of Philistine speech. MT lengthens the shorter expression here and twice in v 8, and LXX lengthens it once in v 11.

they thought Reading *wyʾmrw* for MT *wʾmrw* (cf. LXX).

8. *the ark of God* (*bis*) See the *Textual Note* to v 7. MT, LXX^L, 4QSam^a reflect *ʾrwn ʾlhy yśrʾl,* "the ark of the god of Israel." We follow LXX^B.

[*to us*] So LXX; omitted in MT, which is probably original.

So the ark of God was moved on Reading *wysb ʾrwn hʾlhym* on the basis of LXX (which adds "to gath"). MT has *wysbw ʾt ʾrwn ʾlhy yśrʾl,* "So they moved on the ark of the god of Israel."

9. *But after it was moved on to Gath* Reading ʾ[*ḥry*] *sbw gth* with 4QSam^a (cf. LXX^L). MT and LXX^B show corruption of *gth* to *ʾth* (*ʾtw*), resulting in the revision of MT to *hsbw ʾtw,* "(after) they moved it."

both young and old So MT. LXX^L adds "with tumors"; LXX^B adds "and afflicted them with tumors."

and tumors broke out upon them MT and LXX reflect variant readings, of which MT *wyśtrw lhm ʿplym* is evidently superior. LXX^B reflects *wyʿśw lhm hgtym ʿply(h)m,* "and the Gittites made tumors for themselves," which anticipates 6:5; *hgtym* is shown to be secondary by its differing location in LXX^B (after *lhm*) and LXX^L (before *lhm*). Thus the difference between LXX and MT is simply the variation between *wyʿśw* and *wyśtrw,* the obvious *lectio difficilior.* LXX^L shows further expansion: "and the Gittites made *golden* tumors for themselves, *and mice swarmed among them.*"

10. *Ekron . . . the Ekronites* So MT, 4QSam[a], Syr., Vulg., Targ. LXX has *eis askalōna,* etc. Ekron and Ashkelon are also confused in LXX in 7:14.

Why have you brought . . . around Reading *lmh hsbwtm* with LXX and 4QSam[a]. MT reads simply *hsbw,* "they have brought around" (cf. *hsbw* in v 9 of MT). F. M. Cross suggests that *lmh* may have fallen out of MT after *l'mr* (*homoioarkton*) and before *hsbw*(*tm*), which begins with *h.*

to me to kill me and my kin So MT, 4QSam[a]. LXX has instead "to us to kill us and our kin," which may represent an interpretation of the same Hebrew original. In any case the singular pronouns, which have good parallels elsewhere (Driver), are to be preferred as the more difficult reading.

11. *very grievous . . . when the ark of God came there* So LXX = *kbdh m'd ky b' 'rwn h'lhym* (cf. MT; LXX[B]: *'lhy yśr'l*) *šmh* (cf. 4QSam[a]: [. . . *š*]*ṁh*). MT *kbdh m'd yd h'lhym šm,* "The hand of God was very heavy there," is the result of haplography caused by the graphic similarity of the sequence *kbdh m'd* and *ky b' 'rwn* (*yd* having arisen from *-wn*).

panic MT *mhwmt mwt,* "mortal panic," (so Syr., Targ., Vulg.; cf. v 6) and 4QSam[a] *mhwmt yhwh,* "panic of Yahweh," (cf. Zech 14:13) are both expansions of *mhwmh* as reflected in LXX[(B)].

12. *those men who did not die* MT, 4QSam[a]: *wh'nšym 'šr l' mtw.* LXX has *kai hoi zōntes kai ouk apothanontes,* "Those who lived and did not die. . . ."

up to the skies Reading *'d hšmym* with LXX[L] *heōs tou ouranou* and 4QSam[a] [']*d h*[*šmy*]*m.* Cf. Syr. *'dm' lšmy'.* MT (cf. LXX[B]) has lost *'d* after the preceding *h'yr,* "the city."

NOTES

5 1. *Ashdod.* An ancient Canaanite center, the coastal city of Ashdod became one of the principal Philistine strongholds (see the NOTE at v 8). The site lay only a few miles inland, roughly in the center of Philistine territory.

2. *the house of Dagon.* That is, the temple of the god Dagon in Ashdod, which along with Gaza (see Judg 16:23 and the NOTE to vv 4-5 below) was long a center of his worship. The temple referred to here (or a later successor) was burned in 147 B.C. by Jonathan, the brother of Judas Maccabaeus (I Macc 10:83-84; 11:4).

Dagon. According to common practice our narrator refers to the cultic representation of Dagon simply as "Dagon." The name is that of a very ancient deity, probably of West Semitic origin, whose cult is attested in the West from Early Bronze Age Ebla in northern Syria to Roman Gaza at the southern extreme of the Philistine Plain. Unhappily, Dagon is one of those deities who seldom appear in myth, and as a consequence little is known of his character. Medieval Jewish commentators (Rashi, Kimchi) connected his name with a common Northwest Semitic word for "fish" (**dagg-/digg-,* hence **dagān* > *dāgōn,* "the one of the fish, the fish god"); but this has seldom been maintained in recent scholarship. Instead the name is now identified with a Semitic root (*dgn*) having to do with clouds and rain. This is credible enough for a fertility deity; and since among the few things we do know about Dagon is the fact that he was regarded as the father of the great storm god Baʿl Haddu, the identification is attractive. Evidently the common Northwest Semitic term for grain (Hebrew *dāgān*) is derived from his name (compare Latin *Cerealis, Cerealia,* from Ceres, the name of the Roman goddess of grain). Note also that the biblical form of the name reflects Phoenician *dāgōn* and not Hebrew *dāgān.* See further J. J. M. Roberts, *The Earliest Semitic Pantheon* (Baltimore: Johns Hopkins, 1972) 18-19 and nn. 95-105. There is as yet no way of knowing how soon after their arrival in Palestine the Philistines adopted the worship of Dagon, but it is clear that the biblical writers here and elsewhere regard Dagon as the national god of Philistia (cf. I Chron 10:10).

4-5. An etiological legend explaining why the threshold of the temple of Dagon was not trod upon is incorporated into the story at this point. To v 5 LXX adds, "instead they leap over it," and leaping over the threshold was a practice known, if not universally approved, in Israel as well (Zech 1:9). The Philistine custom seems to have survived, at least in Gaza, into the first centuries A.D. (cf. Delcor, "Jahweh et Dagon," 149). As the passageway into a sacred region the door and especially the threshold of a temple may be accorded a special character, and the history of religions records many instances of rites and customs associated with thresholds. (A modern bridegroom may still lift his new wife over the threshold.) In the present passage the sacred character of the threshold of the house of Dagon is traced fancifully to holy contamination resulting from contact with the broken extremities of the cultic image.

4. *threshold.* Hebrew *miptān,* rendered three (!) different ways by LXX. The term remains poorly understood, having been interpreted variously by modern scholars as "threshold" (BDB) and "podium (of an idol)" (KB). Though the latter meaning fits v 5 well enough, the former is absolutely necessary to v 4; so that unless we are prepared to see v 5 as reinterpreting the passage by interpolation and to suppose different meanings for the same term (which is certainly not impossible; cf. Stoebe), we must retain the translation "threshold." See H. Donner, "Die Schwellenhüpfer: Beobachtungen zu Zephanja 1,8f.," *JSS* 15 (1970) 42-55.

6. *the hand of Yahweh was heavy upon the Ashdodites.* That is, the holy power of Israel's god was loosed against them. The specific form this power took (viz. plague) is identified in the phrases that follow. For the background of this expression, see J. J. M. Roberts, "The Hand of Yahweh," *VT* 21 (1971) 244-251.

both Ashdod and its environs. Hebrew *'et-'ašdôd wĕ'et-gĕbûlêhā,* which is appended in rather clumsy apposition to *'ōtām,* "them." These words may have been added secondarily to specify *'tm* in light of the following phrase, *b'plym,* understood as "on (their) mounds, on (their) acropoles" (see the following NOTE). Although every major city was surrounded by smaller, dependent population centers, those of Ashdod seem to have had special importance. They are, at any rate, often mentioned: Josh 15:46 (cf. 47); I Macc 10:84; 11:4; cf. II Chron 26:6.

tumors . . . mice. The collocation of tumors and mice in this account has led most commentators since Martin Luther to identify the disease that ravaged the Philistines as bubonic plague. Cf. Driver, "Plague"; Brentjes, "'Beulen'-Epidemie"; Wilkinson, "Philistine Epidemic." The tumors are the chief pathognomic symptom, viz. the inflamed nodes or "buboes," which give the malady its name. The mice of course are the host of the plague bacillus and thus the agent of the spread of the disease. In antiquity plague was endemic to coastal areas, where infected rats might arrive by ship, and, indeed, a connection between rats and pestilence was recognized in early times. But the narrator of the present account is not suggesting any *causal* relationship between the mice and the misery of the Philistines, for he credits the afflictions of Israel's enemies solely to Yahweh.

The history of the text shows clearly the perplexity of early interpreters faced with the mention of tumors here. The word *'ōpel,* usually "hill, mound," seems also to have meant "swelling, tumor" (compare English "tumulus" and "tumor," both ultimately from Latin *tumēre,* "to swell"); hence *b'plym* of the ancient consonantal text was probably intended to be read *bo'ŏpālîm,* "(he afflicted them) with tumors." Evidently, however, *'ŏpālîm* (**'opláyim?*) could be understood to mean "buttocks" at the time the first Greek translation of the text was made. Hence the rendering of LXX is *eis tas hedras,* "(he smote them) in the seats, on the buttocks," and Josephus delicately concludes that the plague was one of dysentery (*Ant.* 6.3). Compare also the treatment of this episode in Ps 78:66 (*wayyak-ṣārāyw 'āḥôr*), which one recent commentator translates. "He smote his adversaries on the rear" (Dahood, *Psalms II,* 238 and NOTE). The MT, recognizing the problem, has repointed the text to be read *baṭṭĕḥōrîm,* introducing, whether for epexegetical (Hertzberg) or euphemistic (Driver) reasons, a term unambiguously connected with dysentery (BDB).

8. *the Philistine lords.* According to biblical tradition Philistia comprised five, semi-independent cities (Ashdod, Ekron, Gath, Ashkelon, and Gaza), each of which was ruled by a "lord." (The Hebrew word is **sarn*—Biblical [*séren*], plural *sĕrānîm*—but modern scholars believe the term to be traditionally and anciently Philistine and therefore non-Semitic in origin. Greek *tyrannos,* "[absolute] ruler, tyrant," though often compared, is itself of obscure etymology and is probably non-Hellenic in origin. Hieroglyphic Hittite *tarwanas,* a title of Neo-Hittite rulers, has been cited in the attempt to identify a common [Anatolian] ancestor of the Semitic and Greek terms.) Evidently the lords of the Philistines acted in concert in times of crisis, as in the present instance.

The Gittites . . . Gath. Another member of the pentapolis, Gath of the Philistines was the best known of the several Syria-Palestinian cities whose names included the common element *gat,* "winepress." Gath was a inland city, long disputed with Judah, but the site has never been satisfactorily identified. The leading candidate seems now to be Tell eṣ-Ṣâfî, ca. 12 miles E of Ashdod. See A. F. Rainey, "A Problem in Source Analysis for Historical Geography," *Eretz Israel* 12 (1975) *63-*76.

9. *a tremendous panic.* In Hebrew the main clause reads most awkwardly. One is tempted to delete either "the hand of Yahweh" (thus, ". . . there was a tremendous panic in the city . . .") or "a tremendous panic" (thus, ". . . Yah-

weh's hand was on the city . . ."); but there is no textual warrant for either change, and we must interpret the clause by appeal to anacoluthon. On the panic itself (*mĕhûmâ*) and its place in the Israelite ideology of warfare, see the NOTE at 4:5.

10. *Ekron.* Ekron, a third member of the pentapolis, lay ca. 19 miles inland at the N frontier of Philistine territory. The modern site is Khirbet el-Muqannaʿ.

11. *its place.* The term *māqôm,* although it is the common Hebrew noun "place," may connote a holy place or shrine or, as in v 3 above, the pedestal upon which a cultic image resided in its sanctuary. In the present instance, therefore, the Ekronites are urging that the ark of Yahweh be returned to a shrine of its own in Israel. Nor are they referring to any specific shrine (such as Shiloh): wherever Yahweh is content for the ark to remain will be its "place."

12. *the cry of the city rose up to the skies.* Compare Exod 2:23, where the closest parallel to this expression is found (Driver), and Exod 3:7,9; etc. The author's point is not simply that the lamentation was very loud. The cry has finally reached the skies ("heavens"); that is, the plight of the Philistines has come to the attention of the gods. When in the Exodus passages cited above the cry of the Israelites reaches God, he determines to intervene on their behalf. In the present story, of course, we expect no active intervention on the part of the gods, but the pattern is the same. The situation on earth has become intolerable, and the Philistines must discover through their "priests and diviners" (6:2) the divine solution to their problem.

COMMENT

The triumphant Philistines conduct the ark to Ashdod, where they set it up in the temple of their god. Evidently they intend Yahweh's footstool to reside in Dagon's house as an emblem of the ascendancy the latter has established, as they suppose, at Ebenezer. But when the "gods" are left to themselves at night, the unforeseen occurs. The Ashdodites, opening the temple for the day, discover the image of Dagon lying prostrate before the ark in a position of adoration. An attempt to preserve Dagon's dignity by restoring him to his sanctum proves futile, for the next morning brings the same result with the alarming complication that now the fallen statue is mutilated and defiled. Moreover the ark of Yahweh has become a costly trophy for the Philistines themselves, who are being wasted by a deadly plague launched from the hand of the Israelite god. In consternation the men of Ashdod transfer their baneful prize to Gath; but as the ark proceeds to the other Philistine cities in turn, pestilence and turmoil follow.

The purpose of the initial episode (vv 2-5) is to illustrate Yahweh's superiority to Dagon, a circumstance the preceding events have left in some doubt. It was the chief boast of Israel that her god was greater than the gods of other nations, and here he is pitted against the god of her ancient rival. This is a contest of national deities: Yahweh the god of Israel against Dagon the god of Philistia and, insofar as the Philistines were the quintessential enemy, of every hostile nation. The showdown itself—for this is in fact a test of strength—takes place off stage, and we may not ask what wonders occur in the darkened temple. But the result is clear: the god of Israel has triumphed. His rival is humbled.

The location of this divine contest in Ashdod, the city of Dagon, is not an insignificant detail. Yahweh—or rather the thing men may approach and expect to find him—has been brought here as a trophy of war. As noted in the Introduction (p. 24), it was the custom of the peoples of the ancient Near East to carry off the "gods" of a conquered enemy and deposit them in places of worship at home. Ample written records and plastic representations have survived depicting statues of deities transported by victorious armies.[1] Clearly a captured god was the final proof of the subjugation of a victim. Even more than human prisoners, it demonstrated the utter helplessness of the defeated army, for as the account of the ark's arrival in the Israelite camp in 4:5*ff* illustrates admirably, the god was the cohesive center of a fighting force and indeed of a people at large. Furthermore a captured god ensconced in the temple of a rival, insofar as earthly events were believed to mirror decisions made in heaven, might be regarded as palpable evidence of the subordination of one divine being to another, thus imputing authority to the claims of one people upon another.

All of this is in the background of the installation of the ark in the temple of Dagon. The holy object is to stand there as proof of the subservience of Israel. Yahweh, it seems, has been vanquished, for his ark is lodged in an alien house, discredited and neglected. But the events that transpire belie this impression. Though his ark has been captured, Yahweh has not been vanquished. His power remains. Indeed his complete mastery of the Philistines and their god leaves no doubt that the rout of Israel at Ebenezer and the deportation of the ark to Ashdod could not have been accomplished against his will. In other words, extraordinary as it may seem, it is Yahweh himself who has been guiding these events for purposes of his own. This theological claim was implicit already in the elders' cry, "Why has Yahweh routed us today before the Philistines?" (4:3). The disaster at Ebenezer did not mean that Yahweh had failed; in-

[1] See Delcor, "Jahweh et Dagon," 138-140, for a listing of biblical and extrabiblical examples. Miller and Roberts, *Hand of the Lord,* have shown that the ark narrative as a whole is best understood as an example of a literary genre in which the capture of a people's "god" or cultic image (in the present case of the ark, the closest Israelite equivalent) is interpreted theologically from the perspective of the vanquished army. See "The Ark Narrative" in the Introduction, pp. 23-26.

deed Yahweh was using the disaster for his own purposes. The force of this assertion, which lies at the heart of the entire story of the ark, would not have been lost on its ancient audience. The tale of Yahweh's vengeful rampage in captivity offered reassurance to the community. It contradicted the assumption that Yahweh might be humbled or spent. By withholding his hand from the Philistines at Ebenezer, Yahweh had created an opportunity not only to remove his ark from Shiloh and its wicked priests (cf. the COMMENT on 2:11–26 and pp. 25-26 in the Introduction) but also to demonstrate his power in the land of his enemies. The analogy with the exodus traditions that our narrator draws below (c 6) brings this purpose clearly into focus:

> "I might already have stretched out my hand and afflicted you and your people with a plague that would have wiped you from the earth, but instead I spared you for this reason, that I might exhibit my power through you[2] to make my name known in all the earth!" (Exod 9:15-16)

So at least a part of Yahweh's purpose is the creation of an occasion to display his awful power.

Yahweh's power expresses itself in the dreadful form of a plague. This is most characteristic. Compare the "census plague" of II Samuel 24, where Yahweh dispatches a sword-wielding lieutenant to strike down the people.[3] In the old poetic descriptions of the theophany of Yahweh as a divine warrior, plague also has a part:

> Before him went Plague!
> Pestilence marched at his heels! (Hab 3:5)

The role of plague in the exodus material need hardly be mentioned, and further examples could be cited. The point is that alongside the holy panic with which he dazzled the enemy (see the NOTE at 4:5), Yahweh's particular weapon is plague. When he exercises his terrible capacity for destruction, plague is most often the agent. Nor is this difficult to understand. Warfare in which casualties from wounds inflicted by the enemy exceed those from disease is a modern, indeed a twentieth-century phenomenon; and in the ancient world the divine origin of battlefield epidemics—or indeed of any disease—was never doubted. Plague was the weapon of the gods, and relief could be had only by appeasement of the gods. As the present story of plague continues, therefore, we shall find the Philistines much chastened and earnestly engaged in making atonement to the god of Israel.

[2] So LXX. MT has "show you my strength." See the commentaries.

[3] See I Chron 21:16, the equivalent of the text of which is read by 4QSam[a] in II Sam 24:16-17.

IX. THE RETURN OF THE ARK
(6:1-7:1)

6 1 When the ark had been in Philistine territory for seven months,
2 the Philistines consulted their priests and diviners, asking, "What
shall we do about the ark of Yahweh? Tell us how we may send it
back to its place!"
3 "If you are going to send back the ark of the god of Israel," they
said, "do not send it back empty-handed. Instead you must pay him
compensation. Then you will be healed. When you have been ransomed, why should his hand not turn away from you?"
4 "What is the compensation we should pay to him?" asked the
Philistines.
"Five golden tumors," they replied, "the number of Philistine lords
—for the same plague was upon you and your lords. 5 Make images
of your tumors and images of the mice that are wasting the land, and
give them to the god of Israel as tribute. Then perhaps he will lift his
hand from you and your god and your land. 6 Why harden your
hearts as the Egyptians and Pharaoh did? Is it not true that when
[Yahweh] had had his way with them, they let [the Israelites] go
free? 7 Now then, make ready a new cart and two milch cows that
have not been yoked; harness the cows to the cart; and drive home the
calves that are following them. 8 Then take the ark and place it in the
cart. As for the golden objects that you are paying him as compensation—these you shall place in the pouch beside it. Then let it go free.
9 But watch! If it goes up toward Beth-shemesh on the road to its own
border, then it was he who brought this great calamity upon us; but if
not, then we shall know that it was not his hand that struck us—it
was an accident that befell us."
10 The men did so. They took two milch cows and harnessed them
to the cart, having stabled their calves at home, 11 and put the ark
in the cart. 12 The cows went straight ahead on the way to Beth-
shemesh, going along one highway and lowing as they went. They
did not turn aside to the right or the left. The lords of the Philistines followed them as far as the border of Beth-shemesh.

The Ark's Arrival in Israel

13 The people of Beth-shemesh were gathering the wheat harvest
in the valley. When they looked up and saw the ark, they ran rejoicing to meet it. 14 The cart, having reached the field of Joshua, a Beth-
shemeshite, stopped there beside a great stone. So [the Beth-
shemeshites] split up the wood of the cart and offered the cows as a
holocaust to Yahweh. 15 The Levites took down the ark of Yahweh
and with it the pouch in which the golden objects had been put and
set them up on the great stone, while the men of Beth-shemesh offered
holocausts and made sacrifices to Yahweh that same day. 16 The five
lords of the Philistines watched and then returned to Ekron the same
day.

17 (These are the five golden tumors which the Philistines paid as
reparation to Yahweh: one for Ashdod, one for Gaza, one for
Ashkelon, one for Gath, and one for Ekron. 18 The golden mice corresponded in number to all the Philistine cities belonging to the five
lords, from fortified cities to peasant villages. Even now the great
stone upon which the ark of Yahweh was placed is in the field of
Joshua the Beth-Shemeshite.)

19 But no members of the priesthood had joined in the celebration
with the men of Beth-shemesh when they saw the ark of Yahweh, and
so he struck down seventy of the people. The people mourned because of the great calamity with which Yahweh had stricken them,
20 and the men of Beth-shemesh wondered, "Who can stand before
this holy thing? To whom will it go from us?" 21 They sent messengers
to the inhabitants of Kiriath-jearim to say: "The Philistines have returned the ark of Yahweh. Come down and get it!" **7** 1 So the men
of Kiriath-jearim came to get the ark of Yahweh and took it to the
house of Abinadab on the Hill. His son Eleazar they consecrated to
care for the ark of Yahweh.

TEXTUAL NOTES

6 1. *the ark* So LXX[B], the shortest reading. MT has "the ark of Yahweh" and LXX[L] "the ark of God."

1+. At the end of the verse LXX adds *kai exezesen* (LXX[L] *exebrasen*) *hē gē autōn myas*, reflecting *wtšrṣ 'rṣm 'kbrym*, ". . . and their land swarmed with mice." We retain the shorter text of MT, corroborated by 4QSam[a].

2. *priests and diviners* So MT. LXX adds, "and their magicians" (*kai tous epaoidous autōn,* i.e. *wlhrṭmyhm*), and 4QSam[a] apparently adds a fourth, viz. *wlm'wn[ny]m,* "and soothsayers" (the first three being lost through damage to the scroll but required by space). Such lists tend to expand, and the short MT should probably be retained despite the possibility of haplography (caused by *homoioarkton* or *homoioteleuton*) in the longer texts.

3. *If you are going to send back* Reading *'m mšlḥym 'tm* on the basis of LXX. MT has lost *'tm* through haplography before the following *'t.*

the ark of the god of Israel So MT. LXX[L], 4QSam[a] have "the ark of the covenant of Yahweh the god of Israel" (cf. LXX[B]).

When you have been ransomed Reading *wnkpr lkm* on the basis of LXX *kai exilasthēsetai hymin,* confirmed by 4QSam[a]: *nkpr l[km].* MT is corrupt here, reading *wnwd' lkm,* "And it will be known to you . . .". That this reading is difficult to construe with the following expression has long been recognized (Smith), but it has usually been retained because of the general prejudice in favor of MT. The rare grammatical form of the original (see the NOTE) may have contributed to the process of corruption in the tradition behind MT. For a defense of MT, see D. Winton Thomas, "Note."

4. *Five golden tumors* MT here adds *wḥmšh 'kbry zhb,* "and five golden mice," omitted in LXX[(B)] and 4QSam[a]. One could argue for expansion in MT or haplography in the other witnesses. The former seems preferable if only because "five golden mice" contradicts v 18, which indicates that there were golden mice to correspond to "all the Philistine cities . . . from fortified cities to peasant villages."

upon you and your lords So LXX. MT has *lklm wlsrnykm,* "upon all of them and your lords," which is unacceptable. LXX adds *kai tō laō,* "and the people," which may be omitted with MT, corroborated by 4QSam[a] (the end of the verse is not extant, but the space is insufficient for the longer reading of LXX). Doubtless this LXX plus is a vestige (*w'm*) of the reading *w'śytm,* which follows in MT but has been lost in LXX.

5. *Make images of your tumors* Reading *w'śytm ṣlmy 'plykm* with MT and probably 4QSam[a]: *[w'śytm ṣlmy 'p]l[yk]m.* LXX[(B)] has *kai tō laō* (see the previous *Textual Note*) *kai mys chrysous.* That is, *w'm w'kbry zhb,* ". . . and the people; and golden mice. . . ."

and images of the mice So 4QSam[a]: *wṣlmy 'kbrym.* MT, LXX have, "and images of *your* mice," under the influence of the suffix of *'plykm.*

the god of Israel So MT. LXX[B] reads "Yahweh" (*kyriō*), but except in v 2 the Philistines do not refer to the god of Israel by name. LXX[L] conflates the readings of MT and LXX[B]—thus, "Yahweh, the god of Israel."

7. *a new cart* So LXX[B]. Under the influence of the specification "two milch cows" MT here adds *'ḥt,* "one (new cart)," to which LXX[L], OL show correction.

two milch cows that have not been yoked So MT: *šty prwt 'lwt 'šr l' 'lh 'lyhm 'l.* LXX on the other hand has *dyo boas prōtotokousas aneu tōn teknōn,* "two firstborn cows without (their) young." The expression *aneu tōn teknōn* has been explained as an interpretation of *'šr l' 'lh 'lyhm 'l* in light of the verb *'wl,* "give suck" (Budde), but this reading is hardly difficult enough to have exercised a translator to such a degree. In any case *prōtotokousas* (here and in v

10) reflects an alternative to *'lwt*, probably *bkwrwt;* and it is probably best to regard LXX as entirely at variance here. Both MT and LXX might be regarded as expanded at this point (cf. the short reading in v 10), the one in light of such passages as Num 19:2, the other of the references to the calves below. But of the two, MT is probably to be preferred.

8. *the ark* So LXX^B. MT, LXX^L, OL: "the ark of Yahweh."

you shall place So MT. LXX reads "and you shall not place," construing "the objects of gold" as a second object of "place" above and regarding *mṣdw* (?), translated *ek merous autēs,* "(some) of its (the gold hoard's) parts," as the object here.

in the pouch Reading *b'rgz* with MT. LXX$^{(B)}$ shows two attempts to render the obscure term: (1) *en themati,* "in order"; and (2) *berechthan,* a (corrupt) transliteration with variants in other MSS. (See also LXX to vv 11 and 15.) Targ. *brgzt'* is evidently intended to associate the term with *rgz,* "quake, tremble"—thus, *b'rgz,* "with trembling." For *'argaz,* "pouch," see the NOTE.

let it go free That is, "send it away and it will go" (*wĕšillaḥtem 'ōtô wĕhālāk*); so MT. LXX: ". . . send it away and let it go free and it will go free." See the NOTE.

10. *The men* So MT. LXX reflects "The Philistines."

11. *the ark* So LXX^B. MT, Syr., OL: "the ark of Yahweh." LXX^L: "the ark of God."

All witnesses here append lists of the other items to be sent back with the ark (the box, the golden tumors, the golden mice), but the lists are at variance in arrangement and completeness. MT has *w't h'rgz w't 'kbry hzhb w't ṣlmy ṭḥryhm* (note that the *qĕrê* has intruded into the text in the last phrase—a sure sign of lateness). LXX^B reflects *w't h'rgz w't 'kbry hzhb* and LXX^L *w't 'kbry hzhb w't 'ply hzhb śmw b'rgz mṣdw* (*mṣrw?*). It is not likely that anything after *'t 'rwn,* "the ark," is original, expansion having arisen in one or more versions and subsequently influenced others.

13. *the ark* So MT. LXX: "the ark of Yahweh."

they ran rejoicing to meet it Reading *wyśmḥw lqr'tw* on the basis of LXX, *kai ēuphranthēsan eis apantēsin autēs.* Cf. Judg 19:3 (Wellhausen). MT, though defended by Stoebe, is clearly inferior: *wyśmḥw lr'wt,* "they ran rejoicing *to see.*"

14. *Joshua* MT *yĕhôšūa'* (cf. LXX^L). LXX^B has *hōsēe,* "Hosea."

stopped MT *wt'md.* LXX *kai estēsan* reflects *wy'mydw,* "they stood up, erected," the stone being understood as object and (apparently) the Beth-shemeshites as subject. MT is evidently to be preferred.

beside Reading *'m* with LXX$^{(L)}$. LXX^B, since it construes the stone as the object of the verb, reads, "beside *it* (*par' autē*)," but LXX^L preserves *para* alone. MT has a less elegant variant: *wšm,* "and there (was a great stone)."

15. *and made sacrifices* Reading *wyzbḥw zbḥym* with MT, LXX^L. LXX^B has lost *yzbḥw* by haplography.

18. *Even now the great stone* Reading *wĕ'ôd hā'eben haggĕdôlâ* on the basis of LXX, which joins MT in misreading *w'd* as *wĕ'ad,* "and to," after the previous *wĕ'ad* but not in altering *'bn,* "stone," to *'bl,* "meadow." Elsewhere in

the verse MT adds "until this day" (cf. LXX^{L}), which though unobjectionable is also unnecessary in view of *wĕʿōd* correctly understood, so that the shorter text of LXX^{B} should probably be retained.

19. The beginning of the verse is defective in MT: *wyk bʾnšy byt-šmš ky,* etc., "And he made a smiting among the men of Beth-shemesh when. . . ." Most commentators prefer LXX$^{(B)}$: *kai ouk ēsmenisan hoi huioi iexoniou en tois andrasin baithsamys hoti,* which, as shown by Klostermann (21), is to be retroverted into Hebrew as *wlʾ ḥdw* (not *śmḥw,* which LXX elsewhere [v 13] renders with *euphrainō,* not *asmenizō* as here) *bny yknyhw bʾnšy byt šmš ky,* "But the sons of Jeconiah did not join in the celebration with the men of Beth-shemesh when . . ." (to the translation of *ḥdw . . . b-* as "join with [in celebration]," cf. Job 3:6). The curious thing is that Yahweh smites the people of Beth-shemesh (i.e. the people in general, as the subsequent verses show, and not only the sons of Jeconiah) because of the absence of this group. Why was their absence important? Josephus, whose text seems to have lacked any mention of Levites as in v 15 of MT, LXX (see the NOTE at v 15), appears to have had a reading that provides a hint: he explains the smiting on the grounds that the Beth-shemeshites were not priests (*Ant.* 6.16). This suggests the possibility that *bny yknyhw* is a corruption of *bny hkhnym,* "the sons of the priests," that is, "members of the priesthood." Thus, recalling the secondary character of the notice about the Levites in v 15, we read *wlʾ ḥdw bny hkhnym bʾnšy byt šmš ky,* "But the sons of the priests did not join in the celebration with the men on Beth-shemesh when . . . ," that is, "But no members of the priesthood had joined in the celebration with the men of Beth-shemesh when. . . ." In other words the Beth-shemeshites were smitten because they had no priests among them, and Yahweh would not permit his ark to be approached with unclean hands. Note also in this regard that the problem at Beth-shemesh is expressed in sacerdotal terms ("Who can stand before this holy thing?"; see the NOTE at v 20) and that the solution to the problem is the transfer of the ark into the care of a properly consecrated priest (7:1).

when they saw the ark of Yahweh So LXX. MT has *ky rʾw bʾrwn yhwh,* "when they *looked into* the ark of Yahweh" (cf. Wellhausen, Driver). The latter may reflect an attempt to account for the smiting by appeal to cultic taboos (cf. Num 4:15,20; so Hertzberg) after the corruption of the beginning of the verse in MT.

of the people So MT. LXX has "of them" (i.e. of the sons of Jeconiah; see above).

All major witnesses here append the extraordinary gloss "fifty thousand men"! Josephus seems to have known nothing of such an assertion, and most critics prefer to relegate it to the margin.

20. *stand before* Reading *lʿmd* with MT and LXX^{L} (*parastēnai*). LXX^{B} *dielthein* reflects a corruption to *lʿbr,* "cross over, pass by."

this holy thing Reading *hqdš hzh* with LXX$^{(B)}$. 4QSam^{a} expands this to [*y*]*hwh hqdwš hzh,* "Yahweh, this holy one," and MT to *yhwh hʾlhym hqdš hzh,* "Yahweh, God, this holy one." Cf. the following *Textual Note.*

To whom will it go So MT. In this case it is LXX that expands, reading,

"To whom will the ark of Yahweh go. . . ." All these expansions are intended to identify the "holy one" or "holy thing" further.

7 1. *the ark of Yahweh* (*bis*) So MT. LXX has "the ark of the covenant of Yahweh" both times.

NOTES

6 1. *in Philistine territory*. Hebrew *biśdê pĕlištîm,* not "in the field of the Philistines," as though referring to some specific locality. The noun *śādeh* commonly means "field" or "open country," often as distinguished from the land occupied by a city. With respect to a city *śādeh* refers to the adjacent lands under control of the city. With respect to a nation or people it denotes the territory of the nation, urban and rural. Cf. Gen 32:4(English 32:3); etc. Smith cites the instructive instance of I Sam 27:7, according to which David, while residing in the city of Ziklag, is said to have lived *biśdê pĕlištîm*.

2. *diviners*. The diviners, as well as the magicians and soothsayers added here in the versions (see the *Textual Note*), were individuals skilled in eliciting communications from the divine realm. The specific practices involved are difficult to identify. The diviners (*qōsĕmîm;* cf. Arabic *qasama,* I. "cut, divide," X. "receive a portion [by lot]") may have dealt in the casting of lots or drawing of arrows (belomancy). The biblical writers, however, show no interest in such specifics, preferring to use the various terms—diviners, magicians, soothsayers —rather loosely as designations of the functionaries to whom other peoples resort and who are regarded in Israel as false and ineffectual (cf. Deut 18:10-14). In the present instance, however, the priests and diviners do succeed in ascertaining the proper method of returning the ark to Israel. The last fact has troubled those commentators who wish to find throughout the Bible a consistent and unrelieved denial of the efficacy of foreign religious practices. Hylander, for example, concluded that the divination must have been carried out by a captured Israelite priest! See *Samuel-Saul-Komplex,* 76-77.

how. Or perhaps "with what." Both meanings are possible for Hebrew *bammeh,* but the evidence of Micah 6:6 adduced by Driver (citing Keil) favors the latter. See also Campbell, *Ark Narrative,* 108-112, for a full discussion of the problem of interpretation posed by the double question.

its place. See the NOTE at 5:7.

3. Compare Exod 3:21, where, amid Yahweh's instructions to Moses concerning preparations for the escape from Egypt, it is said: "And when you go, you will not go empty-handed." There the Israelites were to receive gifts from the Egyptians, viz. "objects of silver, objects of gold (*kĕlê zāhāb,* the expression used below as a common designation of the golden tumors and mice), and clothing" (v 22). See also Exod 11:2; 12:35-36; Ps 105:37; and Ezra 1:6 (where the influence of the exodus tradition is also at work).

you must pay him compensation. Hebrew *hāšēb tāšîbû lô 'āšām*. The verb carries implications of requital (Gen 50:15; etc.) and the payment of tribute (II Kings 3:4; etc.). According to most lexica *'āšām* ranges in meaning from simply "guilt" in a few passages (Gen 26:10; etc.; cf. Arabic *'aṯima,* "sin, be guilty") to "propitiatory sacrifice, compensatory payment" or even "surrogate victim" in priestly regulations. All of the latter meanings are often grouped under the general term "guilt offering." See D. Kellermann in *TDOT* 1. 429-437. However, a survey of biblical references to the *'āšām* sacrifice will show that it is basically a substitutionary offering intended to draw off impurity. The impurity might have arisen in a variety of ways—from sin (whether deliberate or not), from disease, etc. See the list in Leviticus 5 and also note the instructions for purifying a leper by means of an *'āšām* in Leviticus 14. In other words an *'āšām* is an offering substituted for an unclean and therefore endangered individual. It is not necessarily concerned with sin at all. In the present passage the *'āšām* is compensation paid as protection against further suffering. See the following NOTE.

When you have been ransomed. Hebrew *wěnikkappēr lākem,* lit. "when it has been ransomed for you" (see the *Textual Note*). The form is anomalous but attested also in Deut 21:8, which in light of the Qumran evidence for the present reading can no longer be dismissed as a textual error (GK §55k). While the form is rare, the term itself, *kippēr,* is the common one for ritual purification. Though traditionally translated "atone," it seems rather to refer primarily to decontamination or purgation from (ritual) impurity. Human beings are the beneficiaries of such purgation, insofar as they escape the hazard of the impurities that are removed; but they are not the objects purged, and the expiation of sins is not necessarily involved. See J. Milgrom, "Atonement in the OT," *IDBSup* ad loc. In certain cases *kippēr* is to be thought of as virtually denominative from *kōper,* "ransom" (Milgrom), suggesting the removal of evil by payment of ransom or transferral to some substitutionary object. Instructive is the stipulation in Exod 30:12 that each Israelite enrolled in the census must pay half a shekel as *kōper napšô,* "a ransom for his life," as protection from plague (*negep*); thus they are said "to ransom (their) lives," *lěkappēr 'al-napšōtêkem* (vv 15,16). The present case is also an instance of decontamination by the payment of a ransom.

4-5. The Philistines discover the peculiar nature of the gift they must return with the ark. It is clear that the golden objects function in two ways. On the one hand they provide a compensatory sacrifice, carrying away the contamination from Philistia and with it the suffering. See the preceding NOTES. Thus they must correspond to the ransomed victims—the five lords and all their cities. On the other hand the objects also represent a payment of "tribute" (*kābôd,* not "glory"). Thus they are made of gold and have intrinsic worth.

5. *images of your tumors.* The possibility must be considered that part of the rationale for this peculiar gift is the wordplay on *'ōpel,* "tumor," and *'ōpel,* "acropolis." The latter referred to the fortified hill of a city, and the five Philistine cities that can unquestionably be said to have had *'ōpělîm* are those listed in v 17 below as corresponding to the golden *'ōpělîm.*

images of the mice. Muriform plague amulets have been recovered in the excavation of Near Eastern sites. See Brentjes, " 'Beulen'-Epidemie." The golden mice in the present account are not amulets, but the comparison is nonetheless instructive.

perhaps. The priests and diviners seem less confident than in v 3. But Biblical Hebrew *'ûlay* is somewhat stronger than English "perhaps." It implies an expectation of the desired (or feared) result (Gen 16:2; Num 22:11; etc.) and so stands somewhere between "perhaps" and "surely."

6. The argument of this verse may be rehearsed as follows: Why should the Philistines be obstinate and refuse to release the ark? The Egyptians were obstinate when the Hebrews were captive there and refused to release them; yet as soon as Yahweh had had his way with the Egyptians, they let the Israelites go. So what will the Philistines gain from obstinacy but further suffering? The implication is that such obstinacy serves no purpose except Yahweh's in his wish to display his power amidst the enemy. Unmistakable is the allusion to Exod 10:1-2 in the so-called "J" or Yahwistic materials of the exodus account: "Yahweh said to Moses, 'Go to Pharaoh! For I have hardened his heart and the hearts of his servants in order to set these signs of mine in their midst, so that you might recount to your sons and grandsons how I had my way with Egypt and how I set my signs in their midst and that you might know that I am Yahweh.'"

harden your hearts. Hebrew *tĕkabbĕdû 'et-lĕbabkem,* lit. "make your heart heavy." Compare the expressions *kābēd lēb,* "(the) heart is/was heavy," *hikbîd lēb,* "cause (the) heart to be heavy" (see Exod 10:1, quoted above), and *lēb kābēd,* "a heavy heart," all of which are to be found used in reference to the Egyptians and Pharaoh in the J material in the Exodus account, where E and P material use variations of *ḥizzaq lēb,* "strengthen, harden (the) heart," to express the same idea.

when [*Yahweh*] *had had his way with them.* Hebrew *ka'ăšer hit'allēl bāhem.* As noted the expression is reminiscent of Exod 10:2. The verb means to treat arbitrarily with a connotation of ruthlessness or cruelty. Cf. 31:4, where the wounded Saul chooses death "lest these uncircumcised come and have their way with me."

7. As in the case of the offering of gold (see the NOTE at vv 4-5), the method of return must be understood in two ways. On the one hand the cows are chosen as sacrificial animals intended to carry off the contamination from the Philistines. Thus it is stipulated that the cart must be new, i.e. not previously used and therefore ritually clean, and similarly that the cows must never have been yoked. In Numbers 19 a red cow "that has not been yoked" (v 2) is slaughtered and burned; its ashes are mixed with water to be used for all kinds of ritual cleansing. The cow is specifically called a *ḥaṭṭā't* (v 9), i.e. a purgative offering (see J. Milgrom, "The Function of the *ḥaṭṭā't* Sacrifice," *Tarbiz* 40 (1970) 1-8 [Hebrew]). Similarly in Deut 21:3 a cow "which has not been led under a yoke" is the offering prescribed to cleanse the community from the guilt of an unidentified murderer. On the other hand the animals are also carefully selected in an experiment designed to discover whether or not Yahweh was in fact involved in the plague (v 9). The cattle are completely untrained; they are milch cows forcibly separated from their calves; they are to be given no guidance on the road. If under such adverse circumstances the cattle

head straight for Beth-shemesh, neither wandering aimlessly nor turning homeward in search of their calves, then there can be no remaining doubt that Yahweh is guiding the events.

that have not been yoked. Hebrew *'ăšer lō' 'ālâ 'ălêhem 'ōl.* The suffix on the preposition is *-êhem,* not *-êhen* as we might expect after the feminine plural antecedent, *pārôt,* "cows." The same is true of the other possessive suffixes referring to the two cows in this verse (*bĕnêhem,* "their calves," and *mē'aḥărêhem,* "from after them"—here translated "the calves that are following them") and in vv 10 (*bĕnêhem,* "their calves") and 12 (*'aḥărêhem,* "[after] them"). Similarly the accusative suffix of *wayya'asrûm,* "and harnessed them," in v 10 is *-m,* not *-n,* the usual feminine plural verbal suffix. Despite GK §135o, it is difficult to avoid the conclusion that these suffixed pronouns preserve archaic dual forms, used here in reference to the yoke of cows, especially in light of Ugaritic grammar, which has a third person dual possessive suffix of common gender, viz. *-hm* (cf. Gordon, *UT* §6:10). Compare also Arabic *-humā.* See further the discussion of E. F. Campbell (*Ruth,* AB 7, 65) of the similar phenomenon in Ruth 1:8*ff,* with a list of other passages where the occurrence of dual pronominal suffixes is suspected.

8. *in the pouch.* Hebrew *bā'argaz.* The obscure term *'argaz,* which occurs only in I Samuel 6, is often rendered "box, chest" (BDB). It has this meaning in Postbiblical Hebrew, but this probably represents no independent evidence beyond one traditional interpretation of the present passage. More instructive are Syriac *rĕgāztā,* "wallet, bag," and Arabic *rigāzat,* "pouch, bag." The latter referred to a receptacle in which heavy stones were placed to give ballast to a small tent (which could also be called a *rigāzat*) borne on a camel. Some time ago Julian Morgenstern ("The Ark, the Ephod, and the Tent," *HUCA* 17 [1942-43] 251-255), comparing the ark to the portable tent-shrines of certain pre-Islamic Arabian tribes, argued for association of the *rigāzat* with Biblical Hebrew *'argaz.* Accordingly the *'argaz* would be a constant part of the paraphernalia of the ark in its earliest form, thus explaining the use of the definite article ("in *the* pouch"). Translations such as "saddlebag" (KB), therefore, are now often seen. While this explanation leaves a number of unanswered questions, others, including attempts to identify *'argaz* as a Philistine (Anatolian) term (E. Sapir, "Hebrew *'argaz,* a Philistine Word," *JAOS* 56 [1936] 272-281), have been less successful.

9. *toward Beth-shemesh on the road to its own border.* The most direct route from the Philistine Plain to Israelite territory was the Valley of Sorek (modern Wâdī eṣ-Ṣarâr), perhaps best known as the home of Delilah in the Samson stories (Judg 16:4). At the SW end of this valley lay Beth-shemesh ("House of the Sun," a name suggesting an early role as a shrine of the sun god[dess]), a city that plays no major role in the Bible but must have been constantly disputed by Philistia and Israel because of its location (cf. II Chron 28:18). The site is Tell er-Rumeilah near modern 'Ain Shems, some 20 miles W of Jerusalem in the Wâdī eṣ-Ṣarâr. See J. A. Emerton, "Beth-shemesh," *AOTS,* 197-206.

12. *went straight ahead.* Hebrew (MT) *wayyiššarnâ derek.* The verb is anomalous and the problem is threefold. First, we might expect *wayyīšarnâ;* but

examples of assimilation of *y* in such forms are available (GK §71). The second problem is more serious. We expect not *Qal,* which ought to mean simply "be straight," but *Piʿel,* which with *derek* can mean "go straight ahead" (literally, "straighten one's way"). The expected *Piʿel* may have influenced the Masoretic vocalization of the extant form. The third and most serious problem is the gender of the verb. We expect the feminine *wattiššarnâ,* since the cows (*happārôt*) are the subject, and Hertzberg is evidently correct in seeing a conflation of *wayyiššĕrû* and *wattĕyaššarnâ* here, at least in the Masoretic treatment of the form. There is no good evidence for a *y*-prefix third feminine plural verb in Hebrew (GK §47k), for both other examples that have been identified (Gen 30:38; Dan 8:22) occur in very troubled texts. In view of the dual suffixes in vv 8,10, and 12 (see the NOTE on "that have not been yoked" in v 7) it seems reasonable to conjecture that *wyšrnh* preserves an archaic dual verb form of common gender (cf. Gordon, *UT* §9.15).

They did not turn aside to the right or the left. The expression *sār . . . yāmîn ûśĕmōʾl* occurs only here outside of Deuteronomic and Deuteronomistic passages (cf. Prov 4:27), where it is used figuratively (but cf. Deut 2:27) of straying from the path of obedience to Yahweh.

13. *the wheat harvest.* The time of the wheat harvest was May/June. On the agricultural calendar in antiquity see G. E. Wright, *Biblical Archaeology,* 2d ed. (Philadelphia: Westminster, 1962) 183-187; note especially his comments on the silos excavated at Beth-shemesh. Apparently the modern schedule is different: see the observations of E. F. Campbell in *Ruth,* AB 7, 108.

14. *Joshua.* This individual is not mentioned elsewhere, but evidently the field bore his name in the time of the narrator (see v 18b).

holocaust. That is, a whole burnt offering, so called because the entire victim was consumed. The English word is derived from a Greek term used to translate Hebrew *ʿōlâ.* For the priestly regulations, see Lev 1:1-17; 22:17-25. Note that the cattle in our passage are somewhat irregular holocausts insofar as they are not males (Lev 1:3; 22:19).

15. Most commentators regard this verse, or part of it, as intrusive, inserted late in the literary history of the passage by a fastidious scribe, who insisted that the ark must have been handled by Levites, members of the official priestly tribe of Israel. Josephus' text seems to have had the verse, but without any reference to Levites; cf. *Ant.* 6.15. Beth-shemesh was among the so-called Levitical cities recorded in Josh 21:1-42 = I Chron 6:39-66(English 6:54-81); that is, it was assigned according to at least one tradition to the Levites as a special residence. Knowledge of this fact may have influenced the author of this interpolation. In any case Smith, Hertzberg, and others may be right in supposing that the statement is intended to "correct" the original version's implication that the "great stone" of v 14 was used as an altar. Instead, we are told, it was used simply as a resting place for the ark and the golden objects. But in fact it was precisely because of the *absence* of priests that Yahweh struck Beth-shemesh, a detail that must have become obscured in the texts of MT and LXX early enough to have contributed to the intrusion of Levites here (see the *Textual Note* at v 19).

17-18. These verses constitute an appendix to the narrative unit that concludes with the return of the Philistine lords to Ekron. Verse 18b may be considered in isolation from the rest. It is added to lend verisimilitude to the story. What it asserts is not so much etiological—i.e. designed to explain the presence of the stone as a well-known feature of the terrain—as evidential, and as such it must be regarded as an original part of the narrative. Verses 17-18a on the other hand serve only to specify and explain the numbers of golden tumors and mice. This unit probably represents an addition to the account providing the results of a later audience's analysis of the curious components of the *'āšām*. On the cities of the Philistine pentapolis, see the NOTE at 5:8.

20. *Who can stand before this holy thing?* Hebrew *mî yûkal la'ămōd lipnê haqqādôš hazzeh* (see the *Textual Note*). The expression *'āmad lipnê*, "stand before," connotes "attend upon" and is often used specifically of priests attending upon Yahweh and/or the paraphernalia of his sanctuary (cf. Deut 10:8; Ezek 44:15; II Chron 29:11; in the first of which the ark is mentioned explicitly). Most instructive is Judg 20:27-28: "And the Israelites inquired of Yahweh, for the ark was there [viz. at Bethel] in those days, and Phinehas, son of Eleazar, son of Aaron, was standing before it (*'ōmēd lipnāyw*) in those days. . . ." In other words the expression may be used specifically of priestly attendance upon the ark, and this is the issue here. Recognizing the cause of the calamity (". . . no members of the priesthood had joined in . . ." v 19) the Beth-shemeshites seek a suitable attendant, who is eventually found at Kiriath-jearim (7:1).

21. *Kiriath-jearim.* The name *qiryat yĕ'ārîm* means "City of the Forests." Earlier the same city seems to have been called *qiryat ba'al*, "City of Baal" (a name eschewed by the Israelites because of the unacceptable religious connotations), as in the list of Judahite cities (Josh 15:60) and the Benjaminite boundary lists (Josh 18:14; cf. LXX, v 15). In the description of Judah's N border it is called simply *ba'ălâ*, "Baalah" (Josh 15:9,10). The site is Tell el-Azhar, near modern Qaryet el-'Enab, ca. 8 miles NW of Jerusalem. In ancient times the city commanded a strategic hill at the juncture of the traditional tribal boundaries of Judah, Dan, and Benjamin. It was some 15 miles ENE of Beth-shemesh.

7 1. *the house of Abinadab on the Hill.* Abinadab, father of the priests Eleazar, Ahio (II Sam 6:3,4; I Chron 13:7), and Uzzah (II Sam 6:3,6,7,8; I Chron 13:7,9,10,11), lived "on the Hill." This may refer to a particular quarter of Kiriath-jearim. Y. Aharoni ("The Province-List of Judah," *VT* 9 [1959] 228-229) has suggested that the Hill was the older Benjaminite town as distinguished from a later, adjoining Judahite settlement. Compare "the Hill of Kiriath-jearim" in the list of Benjaminite cities in Josh 18:28 (emending MT *gb't qryt 'rym* to *gb't qryt* <*y'rym*> *'rym* on the assumption of a simple haplography) to the identification of Kiriath-jearim in the preceding Benjaminite boundary description as "a city of the Judahites" (Josh 18:14). As for the officiating priest there is no claim made for an official priestly connection for Abinadab and Eleazar, but the names are common in the Levitical pedigrees. Eleazar was also the name of a son of Aaron, the chief figure through whom the Levitical descent was traced. The name Abinadab also has Aaronid ties (Budde). Suggestive but obscure is the cryptic note in Josh 24:33 according to which Eleazar, the son of Aaron, was buried *"on the hill* of Phinehas, his son, which had been given to him in the hill country of Ephraim."

COMMENT

The return of the ark to Israelite territory concludes the story of its Philistine captivity. The release of the holy object is elaborated in an intricate ritual calculated to rid the land of the hostile influence, whatever its source might be, and the wonderful manner in which the untrained cattle proceed directly to Beth-shemesh demonstrates to the lords of the Philistines what their priests had already suspected, namely, that their recent misfortune was the work of the alien god whose ark they had captured.

The account is filled with similarities to biblical purgative rites. The prescription of a compensatory offering (*'āšām*), the notion of the ransom of the afflicted, and even the specific detail of the provision of unyoked cattle are all referable to known Israelite ritual (see the NOTES). It is not impossible, moreover, that the report reflects the details of certain Philistine practices. Part of an old Hittite ritual against plague reads as follows:

> If people are dying in the country and if some enemy god has caused that . . .
>
> They drive up one ram. They twine together blue wool, red wool, yellow wool, black wool and white wool, make it into a crown and crown the ram with it. They drive the ram on to the road leading to the enemy and while doing so they speak as follows: "Whatever god of the enemy land has caused this plague—see! We have now driven up this crowned ram to pacify thee, O god! Just as the herd is strong, but keeps peace with the ram, do thou, the god who has caused this plague, keep peace with the Hatti land!" They drive that one crowned ram toward the enemy.[1]

The resemblance to our account is superficial but striking, and in view of the common eastern Mediterranean background of the Hittites and the Philistines some kind of connection may be assumed.[2]

In the Hittite text the animal is an offering intended to placate the foreign god. In the biblical story the animals are first of all conveyors of the cart, but as their fate in Beth-shemesh shows, they have a sacrificial purpose as well. We have already noted this kind of multiplicity of purpose and ritual significance in the descriptions of the *'āšām* offering and the method of return (see NOTE at vv 4-5 and the first NOTE at 7), and the impression given by the whole is somewhat bewildering. Are the golden

[1] *ANET*[3], 347. The translation is that of Albrecht Goetze.
[2] See Mendenhall, *Tenth Generation*, 107.

objects tribute signifying submission to the sovereignty of Yahweh or are they compensatory gifts intended to rid the land of contamination? Are the cattle purgative offerings or part of a carefully designed experiment to test the role of Yahweh in the preceding events? Doubtless there is a mixture of elements here, and while one might be moved by this fact to attempt a painstaking analysis of literary accretions,[8] it seems sufficient to recall the fact that ritual practices are characteristically complex and multifaceted with respect to their interpretations and purposes, and it would probably be a mistake to attempt to resolve all the apparent duplications and contradictions here.

The end of the ark narrative comes with the return of the holy object to Israel and the ordination of a priest to care for it in Kiriath-jearim. It seems at first as if the Israelites will receive no better treatment from the ark of Yahweh than did the Philistines. In the Beth-shemesh episode seventy people (a gloss reads fifty thousand!) are slain immediately. If Miller and Roberts are correct in assuming that an actual plague coincided with the ark's sojourn in Philistia (*Hand of the Lord,* 74), we might assume further that the plague spread to the Beth-shemesh area, which was adjacent to Philistine territory. The purpose of this final episode, then, was to give a reason for this, since the larger explanation of the plague, viz. Yahweh's vindication from his enemies, would not apply here. It was a lack of priests in Beth-shemesh, the narrator says, that caused the problem. Yahweh would not be approached with unclean hands. But this final difficulty is resolved when Eleazar, a proper custodian for the ark at last, steps on stage.

[8] Rost (*Thronnachfolge Davids,* 129) isolated vv 5-9 as secondary. But compare Campbell, *Ark Narrative,* 166-168.

X. SAMUEL THE JUDGE
(7:2-17)

7 2 From the day the ark began to reside in Kiriath-jearim a long
time passed—twenty years—and all the house of Israel turned after
Yahweh. 3 Samuel said to all the house of Israel, "If it is with all your
heart that you are returning to Yahweh, you must remove the foreign
gods from among you, as well as the Asherim. You must fix your
heart on Yahweh and serve him alone. Then he will rescue you from
the grasp of the Philistines." 4 So the Israelites removed the Baals and
Astartes and served Yahweh alone.

5 "Let all Israel assemble at Mizpah," said Samuel, "and I shall
pray to Yahweh on your behalf." 6 So they assembled at Mizpaḥ and
drew water and poured it out before Yahweh. They fasted that day
and said, "We have sinned against Yahweh." Thus Samuel judged the
Israelites at Mizpah.

7 The Philistines heard that the Israelites had assembled at Mizpah,
and the lords of the Philistines went up against Israel. When the
Israelites heard, they were afraid of the Philistines. 8 So [they] said to
Samuel, "Do not refuse to cry out for us to Yahweh, your god, that he
may rescue us from the grasp of the Philistines!" 9 Samuel took a
sucking lamb and offered it whole as a holocaust to Yahweh; then
[he] cried out to Yahweh on Israel's behalf, and Yahweh answered him— 10 (Now while Samuel was offering the holocaust, the
Philistines had drawn near to attack Israel.) And Yahweh thundered
in a loud voice against the Philistines that day and so confounded
them that they were routed before the Israelites. 11 The men of Israel
sallied forth from Mizpah in pursuit of the Philistines, harrying them
as far as a point below Beth-car. 12 Samuel took a stone and set it up
between Mizpah and Jeshanah. He named it Ebenezer, explaining,
"To this point Yahweh helped us."

13 Yahweh humbled the Philistines, so that they did not cross the
border of Israel again. Yahweh's hand was upon the Philistines all the
days of Samuel: 14 the cities the Philistines had taken from Israel
were restored to Israel from Ekron to Gath, and Israel also recovered

the environs of these cities from Philistine control. There was peace, too, between Israel and the Amorites.

15 Samuel judged Israel all the days of his life. 16 He would go in a
circuit year by year to Bethel, Gilgal, and Mizpah, judging Israel in
all these places, 17 but he always returned to Ramah, for his home was
there. There too he judged Israel, and there he built an altar to Yahweh.

TEXTUAL NOTES

7 2. *turned after Yahweh* Reading *wypnw . . . 'ḥry yhwh* on the basis of LXX[B] *kai epeblepsen . . . opisō kyriou* and LXX[L] *kai epestrepsen . . . opisō kyriou* (Wellhausen, Budde, Smith). MT has *wynhw . . . 'ḥry yhwh.* The expression *nāhâ 'aḥărê . . .* does not mean "mourn for, lament after" (*RSV*), which elsewhere is *nāhâ 'al* (Ezek 32:18), and in any case such a statement would be pointless in the present context, since Yahweh has already returned. If MT were retained (as *lectio difficilior*), it would have to be interpreted as a pregnant construction with approximately the force of *wayyinnāhû wayyippĕnû 'aḥărê . . .*, "they lamented and turned after . . . ," or *wayyinnāhû wayyēlĕkû 'aḥărê . . .*, "they lamented and went after (Yahweh)." See the list of similar pregnant constructions with *'aḥărê* in GK §119gg. Cf. also Driver.

3. *as well as the Asherim* So LXX: *kai ta alsē* = *w't h'šrym.* MT has *wh'štrwt,* "and the Astartes," in anticipation of v 4.

6. *and poured it out* LXX adds "on the ground." Omit with MT.

and said MT adds "there." Omit with LXX.

7. *the Israelites* (1) So MT. LXX has "*all* the Israelites."

8. *Yahweh, your god* So LXX. MT has "our god." Cf. 12:19.

At the end of v 8 some witnesses, under the influence of 12:23, add: "And Samuel said, 'Far be it from me to revolt against Yahweh my god by not crying out on your behalf in prayer!' "

9. *and offered it* Reading *wayya'ălēhû* with LXX and MT (*qĕrê*), against MT (*kĕtîb*) *wy'lh.*

whole MT *kālîl,* "whole," which after *'ôlâ,* "holocaust," is redundant, suggests a gloss. But it is difficult to see in LXX *syn panti tō laō,* "with all the people," a genuine and meaningful variant. Wellhausen and Driver regard the latter as an interpretive rendering of a text identical to MT.

answered him So MT (*wy'nhw*). LXX, though almost certainly reading an identical text, shrinks from the literal interpretation and renders *epēkousen autou,* "hearkened to him." But as v 10b shows, the literal sense is intended here. See the NOTES.

12. *Jeshanah* Reading *hyšnh* on the basis of LXX *tēs palaias* and Syr. *yšn.* MT has *hšn.* See also the NOTE.

13. *Yahweh humbled the Philistines* Reading *wykn' yhwh ('t) plštym* on the basis of LXX. MT has *wykn'w hplštym,* "The Philistines were humbled. . . ." Note that elsewhere in this part of MT *plštym* appears without the definite article. Thus *-w* of *wykn'w* and *h-* of *hplštym* should probably be regarded as a remnant of the reading *yhwh* as preserved in LXX.

14. *were restored* So LXX (*kai apedothēsan*). MT has *wattāšōbnâ,* "(they) returned," which must be corrected to *wattûšabnâ.* Note that LXX inserts a second verb, reading, "The cities that the Philistines had taken from the Israelites (*sic*) were restored, *and they gave them back* (*kai apedōkan autas*) to Israel, etc."

from Ekron to Gath So MT, LXX^L. LXX^B has "from Ashkelon (as in c 5; see the *Textual Note* to 5:10) to *azob* (?)."

and Israel also recovered the environs of these cities So MT: *w't gbwln hṣyl yśr'l.* LXX is somewhat different: *kai to horion israēl apheilanto,* reflecting *w't gbwl yśr'l hṣylw,* "and they (the Israelites) recovered the territory of Israel. . . ."

16. *judging Israel in all these places* There are two problems to be noted here. MT has *wšpṭ 't yśr'l 't kl hmqwmwt h'lh,* which is literally "and (he would) judge Israel, all these places." Is *'t kl hmqwmwt h'lh* a gloss? Is *'t yśr'l* an anticipation of v 17? The solution adopted here is that of LXX, which reads *en* for the second *'t,* but it is not certain that LXX was reading a different text. The second problem arises from the fact that LXX reads *hēgiasmenois,* "holy places," corresponding to MT *mqwmwt,* "places." While it is possible that LXX was reading *mqdšym,* it seems more likely that the connotation of *mqwmwt* is reflected in the Greek translation. See the NOTE.

17. *he judged* Unaccountably, MT vocalizes *šāpāṭ.* See GK §29i,N.

NOTES

7 2. *twenty years.* The notice *wyhyw 'śrym šnh,* which interrupts the flow of the narrative, is probably a late insertion in the account. It is Deuteronomistic (Hertzberg) or at least in the spirit of the Deuteronomistic chronological system (cf. the NOTE at 4:18).

2b-4. Samuel's addresses to the people in vv 3 and 5 give the impression of duplication, and there is warrant for supposing that vv 3-4 represent an intrusion in the account. The expression *šwb 'l yhwh bkl lbb,* "return to Yahweh with all the heart," is a signal Deuteronomistic cliché, occurring elsewhere in well-established Deuteronomic and Deuteronomistic contexts: Deut 30:10; I Kings 8:48; II Kings 23:25. ("Returning" is itself a dominant leitmotiv of Deuteronomistic theology, as shown by H. W. Wolff in "Das Kerygma des deuteronomistischen Geschichtswerkes," *ZAW* 73 [1961] 171-186, esp. 178, reprinted in his *Gesammelte Studien zum alten Testament*, 2d ed. [Munich: Chr. Kaiser, 1973] 308-324; for *bkl lbb*, "with all the heart," alone, which is ubiquitous in Deuteronomy, cf. Josh 22:5; 23:14; I Sam 12:20,24; I Kings 8:23; 14:8; II Kings 10:31.) Other key expressions seem to be taken over from the editorial framework of the Book of Judges and from Judg 10:6-16 in particular. These include:

1) *hsyr 't 'lhy hnkr*, "remove the foreign gods," as in Judg 10:16. The expression also occurs in the Deuteronomistically edited account of the assembly at Shechem in Joshua 24 (v 23, cf. 14 LXX), as well as Gen 35:2 (cf. 4) and II Chron 33:15. For the expression *'lhy knkr*, "foreign gods," alone (the usual Deuteronomistic expression is *'lhym 'ḥrym*), cf. Jer 5:19 (in an Exilic or early post-Exilic prose interpolation) and Deut 31:16 (in an introduction to the Song of Moses). See also the NOTE on "the Asherim" below.

2) *'bd [yhwh] lbdw*, "serve [Yahweh] alone." Cf. Judg 10:16 (n.b. LXX[B]).

3) *hb'lym wh'štrwt*, "the Baals and the Astartes," as in Judg 10:6. Cf. Judg 2:13; 3:7; and I Sam 12:10.

It seems clear that vv 2b-4 should be isolated as Deuteronomistic interpolation based at least in part upon Judg 10:6-16. The latter, itself showing visible marks of Deuteronomistic editing, stands as a thematic introduction to Jephthah's judgeship and the second half of the Book of Judges as a whole (see Boling, *Judges*, AB 6A, 193; cf. Richter, *Bearbeitungen des "Retterbuches,"* 13*ff*). The purpose of the present interpolation, therefore, is to incorporate the story of Samuel into the Deuteronomistic theology of history as it is presented in the Book of Judges, where the premonarchical experience of Israel is related according to a rigid, fourfold pattern of apostasy, punishment, repentance, and deliverance. See further the COMMENT.

3. *the Asherim.* Cult objects of an unknown sort. Their prohibition is another commonplace in Deuteronomic (Deut 7:5; 12:3) and Deuteronomistic (I Kings 14:15,23; II Kings 17:10; 23:14; cf. Jer 17:2) contexts.

4. *the Baals and Astartes.* "Baal" (*ba'al*, "Lord") was the chief epithet of the great Canaanite storm god Haddu/Hadad, and "Astarte" (**'aštart*, Greek *astartē;* Masoretic *'aštōret* instead of **'ašteret* is probably a deliberate misvocalization to suggest *bōšet*, "shame") was the name of the greatest of the Canaanite goddesses. The plurals refer to the several local cults of Baal and Astarte, or rather of gods and goddesses in general, since Baal and Astarte can be regarded as typical names for (illicit) male and female deities in general.

6. *Mizpah.* The city appears as a place of assembly for "all Israel" in Judges 20-21 as well as the prophetic history of the rise of the monarchy in I Samuel (here and in 10:17-27). Note also the statement in I Macc 3:46 to the effect that it was an old place of prayer for Israel. It must have been an early center of worship of some kind. In the monarchical period it seems to have been a strategically important northern fortress of Judah, fortified early in the ninth century by Asa as a result of his disputes with Baasha of Israel (I Kings 15:16-22). It achieved a new distinction in the Exile, when it served as the Babylonian provincial capital and headquarters of Gedaliah after the destruction of nearby Jerusalem (II Kings 25:23). Its importance in the prophetic his-

tory of the rise of kingship suggests that it, along with nearby Ramah, was a major center of prophetic activity from at least the time of the fall of the northern kingdom (and probably earlier) down to the last days of Jeremiah (Jer 40:6). The location of ancient Mizpah is disputed. Older scholars often pointed to Nebi Samwil, an imposing height ca. 5 miles NW of Jerusalem, which takes its name from its traditional role as the burial place of Samuel; but the archaeological data seem to favor Tell en-Naṣbeh atop an isolated peak ca. 5 miles N of Jerusalem, which affords a clear view of the surrounding countryside including an important ancient road leading north and south. For this identification see J. Muilenburg in C. C. McCown et al., *Tell en Naṣbeh*. 2 vols. (Berkeley and New Haven, 1947) 1. 13-49; also Muilenburg, "Mizpah of Benjamin," *ST* 8 (1954) 25-42, and D. Diringer, "Mizpah," in *AOTS*, 329-342.

drew water . . . poured it out before Yahweh . . . fasted. The rites here described are otherwise unknown, at least from biblical sources. One might compare, however, the libations of water which during the Feast of Booths supplemented the customary wine offerings in the temple service, according to postbiblical sources. Water drawn from the pool of Siloam was poured out into a basin west of the great altar (Tosefta Sukkah 3.3); and on the seventh day of the festival, Hosh'anna Rabbah, there occurred "the rejoicing at the place of drawing" (*śimḥat bêt haššô'ēbâ*), according to Talmudic (Sukkah 50a) and Mishnaic (Sukkah 5.1-4) testimony. Lucian (or Pseudo-Lucian) claims to have witnessed a similar practice at Hierapolis, where twice a year water was drawn from "the sea" and poured out in the temple (*De dea Syria* 12-13, 48). The cleft into which the water was poured was believed to be that into which the Great Flood had subsided, and the Jewish custom, too, may have originally had something to do with the Flood tradition. There is also good evidence for a connection between the water libations and the hope for sufficient rainfall. See G. F. Moore, *Judaism*, 3 vols. (Cambridge, Mass.: Harvard, 1966) 2.44-46; Pedersen, *Israel*, 4.342-343, 424.

The relationship of all of this to the present incident is by no means clear. That the water rite is somehow penitential may be concluded from its association here with fasting and confession. One thinks of the calendrical proximity of the Day of Atonement (*yôm kippūr*), the only fast day on the old liturgical calendar, to the Feast of Booths (the former was the tenth day of Tishri, the seventh month, while the latter began on the fourteenth day). What we have, then, is almost certainly a ritual of community purification. Its form may reflect pre-Exilic practice at Mizpah, and some connection with the observance of the Feast of Booths and the Day of Atonement (or its antecedents) may be taken for granted. The details of the ceremony suggest a need for purification. Fasting and confession were intended to purge the community of guilt. Probably the water libation—which may have had its origin in a ceremony designed to ensure the autumn rainfall, a dearth of which was considered a sign of divine disfavor (cf. Zech 14:16-19)—was supposed also to wash away guilt. The need for such rites in the circumstances depicted here is indicated by the battle of Ebenezer and its consequences, insofar as such a disaster might be interpreted as a sure sign of communal uncleanness.

Thus Samuel judged the Israelites at Mizpah. Cf. the NOTE at 4:18. This statement has been appended by a Deuteronomistic hand to incorporate the career of Samuel into the succession of "judges" who ruled Israel between Joshua and Saul. See Noth, *ÜS*, 55, n. 3; so also Stoebe; cf. Hertzberg. The question of Deuteronomistic editing in this section is more fully addressed in the COMMENT.

7a. Note the general parallel to the story of another Mizpah assembly in Judges 20, where the enemy of Israel is not Philistia but Benjamin: "The Benjaminites heard that the Israelites had gone up to Mizpah . . . and the Benjaminites were gathered from their cities to Gibeah, to march out to battle with the Israelites" (20:3a,14). The close similarity in pattern displayed by the two accounts is obscured only by the discursive treatment of that in Judges 20.

7b-8. The general parallel to 12:18b*ff*, despite the heavy Deuteronomistic editing there, is striking. See also the *Textual Note* to v 8.

8. *"Do not refuse to cry out for us. . . ."* The expression is idiomatic and doubly pregnant; it is difficult to capture in English. The Hebrew is *'al-taḥărēš mimmennû mizzĕ'ōq,* lit. "Do not keep silent from us, from crying out. . . ." This combines one pregnant construction, viz. *'al-taḥărēš mimmennû,* "Do not keep silent from us, do not withdraw from us in silence" (GK §119ff; cf. Ps 28:1), with another, viz. *'al-taḥărēš mizzĕ'ōq,* "Do not keep silent from crying out, do not keep silent so as not to cry out" (GK §119y).

9. *whole as a holocaust.* Hebrew *'ōlâ kālîl,* lit. "a holocaust, a whole burnt offering." The two terms are more or less synonymous in Israelite usage, and the expression seems redundant, suggesting a gloss (but see the *Textual Note*). In Ps 51:21(English 51:19), where both terms may be intrusive, the two stand together again. On the holocaust see the NOTE at 6:14.

9-10. The syntax of these verses must be carefully noted. Verse 10a is original but parenthetical, supplying the audience with incidental information necessary to the story. The verbal syntax interrupts the flow of the narrative: *wayhî šĕmû'ēl ma'ăleh . . . ûpĕlištîm niggĕšû . . . ,* "while Samuel *was offering* . . . the Philistines *had drawn near*. . . ." The verbs that stand in the mainstream of the narrative, however, have the ordinary form for past narration: *wayyiz'aq šĕmû'ēl . . . wayya'ănēhû yahweh . . . wayyar'ēm yahweh,* "Then Samuel cried out . . . and Yahweh answered him . . . and Yahweh thundered. . . ."

Failure to recognize that v 10a is parenthetical discursion, a common enough feature of the narrative art of Biblical Hebrew (see the NOTES at 1:4-7; 3:2-4; 4:13; etc.), obscures the connection between Yahweh's "answering" and his "thundering." The latter specifies the way in which Yahweh answered Samuel Though interrupted by the parenthesis the two verbs function in virtual hendiadys: "Yahweh answered in thunder/thundered an answer."

10. *Yahweh thundered in a loud voice.* Elsewhere in the Bible Yahweh's intervention in human affairs is often described in the language of the storm. Thus Yahweh often "thunders" in the older hymns, as in I Sam 2:10; II Sam 22:14 = Ps 18:14(English 18:13); and Psalm 29, as well as in Exilic and post-Exilic literature (cf., for example, Isa 29:6; Job 37:4-5; 40:9). For a discussion of the storm theophany in Canaan and Israel see Cross, *CMHE,* 147-194.

and so confounded them. Hebrew *wayhummēm.* The verb means to throw into confusion and panic and is used especially with Yahweh as subject and an enemy as object within a holy war context (Exod 14:24; 23:27; Josh 10:10; Judg 4:15). Cf. especially II Sam 22:15 = Ps 18:15(English 18:14) and Ps 144:6, where the term is used to describe the effect upon the enemy of Yahweh's lightning ("arrows") in a storm theophany context. On the related noun *mĕhûmâ,* see the NOTE at 4:5.

11. *as far as a point below Beth-car.* Hebrew *'ad-mittaḥat lĕbêt kār.* The city of Beth-car is not mentioned elsewhere, and its location is unknown. Verse 12 seems to imply that Samuel erected his monument at the point to which Israel had harried the Philistines, and that point should be the place below Beth-car mentioned here. The first location between Mizpah and Jeshanah that comes to mind is the great sanctuary of Bethel, situated on a high ridge a few miles N of Mizpah (see the NOTE at v 16), but it is difficult to see in *bêt kār* a corruption, deliberate or otherwise, of *bêt-'ēl.* Many commentators, denying any connection between the location of the monument and the point to which the enemy was harried (see the NOTE at v 12), have sought Beth-car to the W of Mizpah in the direction of the Philistine homeland. Both 'Ain Kârim, ca. 3 miles W of Jerusalem, and Beth Horon the lower (Beit 'Ur et-Taḥtā), ca. 12 miles NW of Jerusalem, have been proposed. The ancient versions were equally at a loss (Targ., "Beth-sharon"; Syr., "Beth-jashan").

12. The plain meaning of the verse is that Samuel erected a stone at the spot to which the rout of the Philistines extended, viz. somewhere between Mizpah and Jeshanah, specified in v 11 as "a point below Beth-car." The statement *'ad-hēnnâ 'ăzārānû yahweh* thus means, "To this point (thus far) Yahweh helped us." The expression *'ad-hēnnâ* can refer to time ("up till now, hitherto") as well as space, but the latter alone makes sense of the context. It is difficult to see the need for Wellhausen's emendation of *'ad-hēnnâ* to *'ēd hî' kî,* "This is a witness that. . . ."

Jeshanah. See the *Textual Note.* If the reading is correct, this is a city mentioned twice in the Old Testament, here and in II Chron 13:19, where it is an Israelite border city disputed with Judah. It has been identified with Isanas, the site of a victory of Herod the Great (Josephus *Ant.* 14.458) and modern Burj el-Isâneh, ca. 17 miles N of Jerusalem.

Ebenezer. That is, *'eben hā'ēzer,* "Stone of Help." Behind this popular explanation of the place name we discern a cultic designation, viz. "Stone of the Helper" or even "Stone of the Warrior." (On the question of the two Hebrew roots, *'zr* I [**'ḏr*] and *'zr* II [**ǵzr*], see P. D. Miller, "Ugaritic *ǵzr* and Hebrew *'zr* II," *UF* 2 [1970] 159-176.) The noun *'ēzer* is a suitable designation for a deity, often applied to Yahweh (Pss 33:20; 70:6(English 70:5); 115:9,10,11; etc.). The relationship of this Ebenezer, located N of Mizpah, to the site of the great battle in c 4 (see the NOTE at 4:1) is problematic, especially since that Ebenezer is supposed to have existed already before the foundation of this one. But it is clear that a certain symmetry is intended between the two battles of Ebenezer, and perhaps the two sites are to be identified (see the COMMENT). The Bible provides plenty of examples of the anachronistic mention of a place name in advance of the narrative describing the foundation of the place so named. (Bethel, for example, is named by Jacob in Gen 28:19, though already mentioned in connection with Abraham as early as Gen 12:8.)

On the whole v 12 may be described as etiological. That is, insofar as it relates the incident described in the preceding verses to a location that was well known in the time of the writer, it provides an explanation of the name of the place. Ebenezer, then, was connected in popular memory with the Israelite defeat described in c 4. It was a familiar spot in the time of our prophetic narrator, who attributed its foundation to Samuel.

13-14. Samuel's military career is summarized and concluded in a formulaic pattern known from the Book of Judges. The pertinent passages are Judg 3:30; 4:23-24; 8:28; and 11:33b (cf. 9:56-57, which probably comes from the same hand). All of these describe the subjugation of an enemy expressed by the verb "humble" (Judg 4:23; I Sam 7:13) or "be humbled" (Judg 3:30; 8:28; 11:33b; cf. the *Textual Note*). Most commentators since Noth have regarded this as evidence of further Deuteronomistic editing, intended to incorporate the career of Samuel into the Deuteronomistic scheme. Birch (*Rise of the Israelite Monarchy,* 20) has pointed out that the expression "Yahweh's hand was upon . . ." and the use of the designation "Amorites" for the non-Israelite inhabitants of the land (see below) are also characteristic of Deuteronomistic usage. On the other hand it would be a mistake to regard these verses with their exaggerated assertions about the pacification of the land as cut out of whole cloth by a Deuteronomistic hand. It is characteristic of Deuteronomistic summations to incorporate synopses of source materials. The far-reaching claims of these verses reflect the spirit of the prophetic writer who fashioned the story of Samuel. Yahweh's complete subjugation of foreign and domestic enemies alike is a part of the careful negative preparation for the people's demand for a king. See further the COMMENT.

14. *from Ekron to Gath.* On these cities see the NOTES at 5:8 and 5:10. Both were disputed border cities. The writer's point is that all such cities were controlled by Israel during Samuel's lifetime, and that the Philistines were confined to a minimal home base.

the Amorites. Biblical narrative influenced by Deuteronomy or by the so-called Elohistic portions of the Tetrateuch uses this term as an ethnic designation for the entire pre-Israelite population of Palestine and Transjordan. The exceedingly complicated background of the designation has no importance here. The writer's point is simply that during Samuel's career the Israelites were at peace with those who remained of the indigenous population as well as with the Philistines, who, like the Israelites, were regarded as latecomers. In other words, Israel was safe from internal as well as external threat.

15-17. These remarks provide an editorial transition from the close of the account of Samuel's career, as signaled by the formulaic summation in vv 13-14, to the events of c 8. Such a transition is required because in 8:1 we find the great prophet an old man, and it is clear that a long time has passed. It seems likely that the prophetic author of the foregoing told other tales about Samuel, but the Deuteronomistic editor whose hand can be recognized in the formulaic v 15 (cf. Judg 3:10; 10:2,3; 12:7,8,10,11,13,14; 15:20; 16:31; see also the NOTES at 4:18; 7:6) has not preserved them. Instead we are presented with a summary. In the stories that follow and probably also in stories that have not been preserved, Samuel appears at a variety of places, including Mizpah (in the present chapter as well as in the account of Saul's election in 10:17-27a), Gilgal (where the kingship is "renewed" in 11:14-15 and Saul's disobedience is recorded in cc 13 and 15), and Bethel (nowhere in the extant tradition though many episodes occur in its vicinity), as well as Ramah, Samuel's home. Viewed critically this variety of appearances is to be explained as a result of the (prophetic) editorial pattern of the larger narrative, which tends to subject everything to the supervision of Samuel. A Deuteronomistic hand has harmonized the several accounts by explaining that Samuel exercised his sacral and political authority on an annual circuit.

16. *He would go in a circuit.* The syntax of the Hebrew (*wĕhālak . . . wĕsābab*) expresses repeated action in the past (GK §112f), hence, "he used to go around, would go in a circuit."

Bethel. A shrine of first importance throughout the history of Israel, Bethel was traditionally Benjaminite (Josh 18:22) but in fact Ephraimite throughout most of its (Israelite) history, serving as one of the two principal sanctuaries of the northern kingdom (I Kings 12:29). The site is the modern village of Beitîn, ca. 10 miles N of Jerusalem. According to the notice in Judg 20:27 the ark had been in Bethel before its removal to Shiloh, but the city plays no direct role in the stories of Samuel and Saul, though it is mentioned from time to time and the action often takes place in its vicinity.

Gilgal. See the NOTE at 11:14.

17. *an altar to Yahweh.* The purpose of this reference to an altar is not clear. Perhaps it has etiological significance for a familiar holy place at Ramah (Hertzberg, Stoebe). Note that our Deuteronomistic editor is not squeamish about this particular altar insofar as the events described take place before the arrival of the ark in Jerusalem and the ark is not involved. Cf. the NOTE at 6:15.

COMMENT

The account of Samuel's victory over the Philistines, though a rough mixture of various elements, occupies a pivotal position in the great study of political leadership and divine sanction that now stands as the first half of the First Book of Samuel. It gazes backward with satisfaction to Samuel's boyhood, giving new significance to his prophetic commission, and at the same time looks suspiciously ahead to the rise of kingship, insofar as it presents Israel's premonarchical institutions as absolutely sufficient. Here the first part of the larger story finds its conclusion: we have seen how leaders were made and unmade in the theocracy that was Israel before the kingdom, and now we see how leadership functioned, as a situation that has threatened Israelite society with complete dissolution is miraculously set right through the intervention of Yahweh's prophet.

The curtain opens on a scene of confusion and danger. Though penitent, the people are scattered and helpless. The Philistines seem none the worse for their recent embarrassment and pose as serious a threat as ever. Now Samuel, of whom we have heard nothing for some time, returns to center stage. He gathers the people and invokes Yahweh on their behalf. When the Philistines advance on the assembled Israelites, they are quickly repulsed, put to flight, and finally subjected to the will of Israel. Indeed the entire land is pacified under the administration of Samuel. So when the curtain closes harmony prevails and all is secure.

The climactic scene is that of the battle itself. And significantly it is not an army of Israel or even Samuel himself who stampedes the invading Philistines; instead it is Yahweh, Samuel's god, roaring from the skies and broadcasting his wonderful, crippling panic, who routs the enemy. Samuel is an intercessor, not a general—or rather he is a general who makes war by prayer.[1] The prophet invokes the god and the god thunders in reply. The field is won by divine warfare, and the Israelites have nothing to do but take up the pursuit of the Philistines as they rush precipitously into the hills. So the primary tenet of the Israelite ideology of warfare underlies this account: victory belongs to Yahweh, and the proper human posture in battle is one of confidence and patience.[2]

As in c 4 the geographical focus of the battle is a place called Ebenezer. This is no coincidence. It is clearly the author's intent to show that the damage done in the earlier conflict has been perfectly repaired by the Israelite victory described here. The symmetry between the two battle stories is therefore of particular importance. The Israelites were attacked at Ebenezer in the first battle and routed; in the second battle they harry the Philistines as far as Ebenezer. So the former state of affairs is exactly restored. (On the problems of the identification of the two Ebenezers, see the NOTES at vv 11-12.)

All of these considerations point to the prophetic hand that gave the stories of Samuel their basic shape, for they tend to enhance the reputation

[1] The intercessory role of the prophet and his special function in holy warfare were two important aspects of the prophetic view of leadership. On the former see, for example, von Rad, *Old Testament Theology* 2.51-52. On the latter see R. Bach, *Die Aufforderungen zur Flucht und zum Kampf im alttestamentlichen Prophetenspruch*, WMANT No. 9 (Neukirchen, 1962); P. D. Miller, "The Divine Council and the Prophetic Call to War," *VT* 18 (1968) 100-107.

[2] See especially G. von Rad, *Der heilige Krieg im alten Israel* (Göttingen: Vandenhoeck und Ruprecht, 1958) *42ff, 56ff*. Richter has pointed out (*Traditionsgeschichtliche Untersuchungen*, 181*ff*) that our account finds its closest parallel among holy war passages in the story of Joshua's victory over a coalition of five Amorite states in Joshua 10. The narrative elements shared by the two accounts include an enemy assault (in each case by a coalition of five states!), a petition by the people to Joshua/Samuel, the participation of Yahweh in the actual battle, the language of the storm theophany (hail in Joshua 10, thunder in I Samuel 7), the rout and headlong flight of the enemy.

of Samuel, the prophet, and they demonstrate the sufficiency and theological propriety of non-royal leadership. But in contrast to other sections where we have found this writer's touch to be most conspicuous, there seems to be little doubt that the present section has been expanded by a later hand. In particular there is a general similarity between vv 3 and 5, which scholars have long recognized as a clue to the composite character of c 7.[3] As pointed out in detail in the NOTES, characteristically Deuteronomistic themes and expressions are found in certain verses, and we are justified in speaking of substantial Deuteronomistic supplementation here. The latter takes the form of additions of new passages of Deuteronomistic material (vv 2aβ,2b-4,6b) and of summaries of original material available to the Deuteronomistic editor but not preserved in full (vv 13-14,15-16). The purpose of this augmentation, as already explained (the NOTE at vv 2b-4), was to incorporate the age of Samuel into the Deuteronomistic theology of history, but the revision of the original material was not so thoroughgoing as to diminish its force. The prophetic narrative of the second battle of Ebenezer (vv 5-6a,7-12, and the original material underlying vv 13-16) remains dominant.

Whether the latter was fashioned by a prophetic writer out of whole cloth we cannot say. It does seem likely that the account of Samuel's success in the Philistine wars drew its inspiration from certain statements about David's early career. Note the general parallels in (1) the battle reports in I Sam 7:7-11 and II Sam 5:17-25, as well as the statements about (2) the recovery of captured lands in I Sam 7:14a and II Sam 8:1, (3) the administration of justice in I Sam 7:15 and II Sam 8:15, and perhaps (4) the pacification of the land in I Sam 7:14b and II Sam 8 *passim.* The position of the ark narrative in its present context effectually gives to Samuel the distinction of having presided over the restoration of order in Israel, a distinction originally David's, and the notices about David's achievements just cited may have provided our prophetic writer with a model for his description of Samuel's accomplishments. In any case it seems impossible to decide whether or not long-standing traditions about the prophet himself lie behind any part of the present account.[4]

In the episode that follows the Israelites will approach Samuel with a demand. We have been carefully prepared for that moment, and the present chapter is the climax of the preparation. All is well in Israel. Yahweh

[3] See especially Birch, *Rise of the Israelite Monarchy,* 11-21.

[4] A number of scholars (most significantly Noth, *ÜS,* 55) have admitted the possibility that vv 16-17 preserve some ancient traditions of a career of Samuel as a judge, perhaps in the narrow, judicial sense. But this overlooks the summary character of this notice, already described above. A. Weiser has championed the larger defense of authentic traditions in cc 7 and 8; see "Samuels 'Philister-Sieg,'" "Samuel und die Vorgeschichte des israelitischen Königtums," and the corresponding sections in *Samuel.*

rules by his prophet. The land is secure. We have seen a major crisis met and surmounted under Samuel's leadership. Our narrator would have us believe that at this point in history the people of Israel could perpetrate no greater breach of trust, no more arbitrary exercise of self-will, no more senseless deed of vanity than to demand for themselves a human king.

THE ADVENT OF KINGSHIP

XI. THE DEMAND FOR A KING
(8:1-22)

8 1 When Samuel grew old he appointed his sons as judges in Israel.
2 (The name of his firstborn son was Joel and the name of his second
was Abijah. They were judges in Beersheba.) 3 But his sons did not
go his way: they turned aside after private gain, accepting bribes and
subverting justice. 4 So the men of Israel gathered and came to Samuel at Ramah. 5 "You yourself have grown old," they said to him,
"and your sons have not gone your way. So now, appoint us a king to
judge us in the manner of all the other nations!"

6 Samuel was distressed that they said, "Give us a king to judge us,"
and he prayed to Yahweh. 7 But Yahweh said to Samuel, "Listen to
the people, whatever they may say to you! For it is not you they have
rejected; rather it is I they have rejected from ruling over them. 8 As
they have always done to me from the day I brought them up from
Egypt until this very day—for they abandoned me and served other
gods—thus they are doing to you, too. 9 So now, listen to them! Yet
you must solemnly warn them: tell them of the justice of the king who
will rule over them!"

The King's Justice

10 Samuel reported all the words of Yahweh to the people who were
requesting a king of him. 11 "This will be the justice of the king who
will rule over you," he said. "Your sons he will take and assign to his
chariot and his cavalry, and they will run before his chariot. 12 He will
appoint for himself captains of thousands and captains of hundreds
from them. They will do his plowing, harvesting, and grape-gathering
and make his weapons and the equipment of his chariotry. 13 Your
daughters he will take as perfumers and cooks and bakers. 14 Your
best fields and vineyards and olive groves he will take and give to his
servants. 15 Your seed crops and vine crops he will tithe to make gifts
to his officers and servants. 16 Your best slaves, maidservants, and cattle, and your asses he will take and use for his own work; 17 and your

flocks he will tithe, too. You yourselves will become his slaves.
18 Then you will cry out because of the king you have chosen for
yourselves, but Yahweh will not answer you then."
19 But the people refused to listen to Samuel. "No!" they said.
"There shall be a king over us! 20 Then we, too, shall be like all the
other nations: our king will judge us and march out before us and
fight our battles."
21 When Samuel had heard all the words of the people, he repeated
them in the ears of Yahweh, 22 and Yahweh said to Samuel, "Listen
to them and make them a king!"
Then Samuel said to the men of Israel, "Go, each man to his own
city!"

TEXTUAL NOTES

8 2. So MT. LXX has, "These were the names of his sons: the firstborn was Joel, and the name of the second was Abijah, etc." Josephus' report that the sons judged in Bethel as well as Beersheba (*Ant.* 6.32) is without support in the extant versions (see the NOTE at v 2).

3. *his way* Hebrew *bĕdarkô*, "(in) his way" (so LXX, MT *kĕtîb*). MT *qĕrê* has *bidrākāyw*, "in his ways," under the influence of *bidrākêkā* in MT in v 5.

4. *the men of Israel* So LXX here and in v 22. MT has "*all the elders* of Israel" here, but agrees with LXX in 22. See also the *Textual Note* to 11:3.

5. *your way* So LXX. MT: "your ways" (see the *Textual Note* to v 3 above).

So now Reading *wĕʿattâ* with LXX (*kai nyn*). MT has *ʿattâ* alone, which is not in accord with the best Hebrew style.

7. *whatever they may say to you* Reading *kʾšr yʾmrw lk*, lit. "according as they may say to you," with LXX^{B} (*katha an lalēsōsin soi*). Cf. Gen 44:1; etc. MT has *lkl ʾšr yʾmrw ʾlyk*, "to everything that they may say to you" (cf. LXX^{L}), to which compare 12:1.

8. *to me* Inserting *lî* with LXX into the text of MT after *ʿāśû*, where it has fallen out through a simple omission. Though there is no evident cause for such an omission, *lî* seems necessary before *gam lāk*, "to you, too," at the end of the verse (so Wellhausen and most commentators, following an original suggestion of Thenius; contrast Stoebe).

11. *and they will run* Hebrew *wĕrāṣû* in sequence after *yiqqāḥ wĕśām* . . . , "he will take . . . and assign (them). . . ." So MT. LXX *kai protrechontas* evidently reflects *wrṣym* (cf. Wellhausen).

12. *captains of thousands and captains of hundreds* The complete list

found elsewhere in such passages as Exod 18:21 is here reflected in Syr. MT has only "thousands" and "fifties"; LXX "thousands" and "hundreds" (so Josephus *Ant.* 6.40). While Syr. is clearly expansive, there is no compelling reason to choose between the two shorter readings.

to do his plowing, harvesting, and grape-gathering MT has only the first two, LXX^{B} only the second two. Wellhausen argues that MT and LXX are reading a common original on the grounds that *therizein,* "to harvest, reap," may translate *ḥrš,* "plow" (based on the imperfect parallel of 13:20,21) but does not mention LXX^{L}, which adds to the beginning of LXX^{B} *kai arotrian tēn arotriasin autou,* which must reflect *lḥrš ḥryšw,* "to do his plowing." Thus the witnesses reflect:

MT	*lḥrš ḥryšw wlqṣr qṣyrw*
LXX^{B}	*lqṣr qṣyrw wlbṣr bṣyrw*
LXX^{L}	*lḥrš ḥryšw wlqṣr qṣyrw wlbṣr bṣyrw*

We should probably conclude that MT and LXX^{B} are haplographic, each in its own way. LXX^{L}, then, preserves the primitive reading. 4QSam^{a}, by the way, shows traces of the first of the three phrases ([*lḥr*]*š ḥ*[*ryšw*]) and space considerations suggest that it shared the reading of MT.

13. *perfumers* Syr. reflects instead *rqwmwt,* "embroiderers," on which see Wellhausen.

16. *Your . . . maidservants* MT and 4QSam^{a} have synonyms: *špḥwtykm* and *'mhwtykm,* respectively.

cattle Reading *bqrkm* or *bqrykm* on the basis of LXX *boukolia* in preference to MT *bḥwrykm,* which, though defended by Stoebe ("Anmerkungen") is plainly inferior. "Your young men," as it would have to be understood, would be out of place here in the list.

and your asses The adjective *haṭṭôbîm,* "best," follows the several nouns it modifies as in v 15, but *w't ḥmwrykm,* "and your asses," stands after the adjective. This might be a late addition to the text, and one is tempted to excise it with Dhorme; but no textual warrant exists. Cf. also the *Textual Note* to v 17 below.

and use for his own work MT *w'śh lml'ktw,* a rather curious construction. 4QSam^{a} has *w'św lml'ktw,* "and they will work at his business" (?) or perhaps "and they will be used (cf. Ps 139:15) for his work." LXX reflects *w'śr lml'ktw,* "and tithe (them) for his work," but this is inappropriate in view of the restriction already implied in *haṭṭôbîm,* "best," and MT is to be preferred to 4QSam^{a} as *lectio difficilior.* See the NOTE.

17. *and your flocks he will tithe, too* Reading *wṣ'nkm y'śr* on the basis of LXX, Syr., Vulg., and 4QSam^{a}; MT omits *w,* "and." As with *w't ḥmwrykm* in v 16 (see above), this statement stands in awkward isolation.

18. *Then . . . then* Hebrew *bayyôm hahû' . . . bayyôm hahû',* lit. "on that day . . . on that day" (MT). The second time LXX reflects instead *bymym hhm,* "in those days" (cf. 4QSam^{a}: [ ] *hhm*).

18 +. At the end of the verse LXX adds *hoti hymeis exelexasthe heautois basilea,* reflecting *ky 'tm bḥrtm lkm mlk,* "because you will have chosen a king for yourselves." Omit with MT and 4QSam^{a}.

19. *No!* Reading *lō'* with MT (some Hebrew MSS have *lō*, "to him"). LXX *lô lō'* (*autō ouchi*) combines two interpretations in a single text (cf. 12:12 MT). On the rare daghesh in MT, see Driver and GK §20g.

NOTES

8 2. *Joel . . . Abija.* The names of Samuel's sons find their place in the Levitical genealogy attributed to him by the Chronicler (see the NOTE at 1:1). The two sons are also identified in I Chron 6:13(English 6:28), though the Hebrew text has lost the name of Joel (cf. the versions). In a list of Kohathite Levites (I Chron 6:18[English 6:33]), Joel, son of Samuel, appears as father of Heman, chief singer to David and Solomon; and the name Joel occurs elsewhere in the ancestry of Elkanah and in Kohathite genealogies in general. As we have already noted, the latter were the Levitical family specially charged with the care of the ark (Num 3:29-31; cf. 4:4-15).

Beersheba. The location of the headquarters of the two sons comes as a surprise. For the most part the Samuel stories take place in a tightly circumscribed region, roughly the traditional territory of the tribe of Benjamin and immediately adjacent areas. By contrast, the mention of Beersheba takes us far away. Indeed the city lay at the traditional S extreme of Israelite territory, so that it was coupled with the N outpost of Dan in the expression "from Dan to Beersheba" to designate the full extent of the land (see the NOTE at 3:20). Some scholars have viewed this as warrant for postulating an authentic southern connection in the Samuel tradition (cf. especially Weiser, *Samuel*, p. 30); others have regarded it as totally artificial, calculated to give an "all Israel" dimension to the narrative. Josephus, on the other hand, knows a tradition according to which one son was situated in Bethel and the other in Beersheba (*Ant.* 6.32).

3. *they turned aside after private gain.* Hebrew *wayyiṭṭû 'aḥărê habbāṣa'*. The noun *beṣa'* refers to ill-gotten gain, and as the parallel in Exod 23:2 shows (Driver), the verbal expression suggests inappropriate influence. Evidently the simple meaning is that the sons used their offices to enrich themselves.

4. *Ramah.* Samuel's home, as in 7:17. Cf. the NOTE at 1:19.

5. *appoint us a king . . . other nations.* Cf. Deut 17:14, where Moses instructs the people as follows: "When you come into the land which Yahweh, your god, is giving you, and occupy it and settle in it and say, *'I shall appoint myself a king in the manner of all the other nations* around me,' then appoint yourself a king whom Yahweh, your god, chooses. . . ." The present writer, whose work we have described as "proto-Deuteronomic" (see "The Prophetic History" in the Introduction, esp. pp. 21-23), was acquainted with the tradition of the inauguration of kingship as it also appears in the Deuteronomic corpus. See the COMMENT.

6. *Samuel was distressed.* Literally, "The thing was bad in the eyes of Sam-

uel." But why is Samuel displeased? Is it because he takes the request as a personal betrayal, as v 7 seems to imply, or because he objects to its religious impropriety? From the prophetic point of view the former is the equivalent of the latter, insofar as the prophet is the chosen vehicle through which the theocracy operates; so if Samuel's indignation is self-directed, it is nonetheless righteous and proper. See further the NOTES and COMMENT on 12:1-25.

7. This verse gives explicit statement to the narrator's belief that the demand for a king is tantamount to a rejection of Yahweh's rule. Kingship is presented as divinely ordained (cf. vv 9,22), but by an exasperated deity. Clearly Yahweh's permission does not include his approval. Thus the narrator reconciles (somewhat awkwardly, one must admit) his conviction about the theological inadmissibility of the office of king with the unavoidable fact of history that Israel did, after all, become a monarchy.

from ruling over them. Or, "from being king over them" (*mimmĕlōk ʿălêhem*), a translation that renders the import of Yahweh's declaration even more clearly. The verb is a simple denominative from *melek,* "king."

8. It is widely agreed that this verse represents a Deuteronomistic interpolation in the narrative, designed to incorporate the present incident into the larger pattern of repeated apostasy according to which Deuteronomistic theology understood Israel's historical experience (cf. the NOTE at 7:2b-4). Characteristic Deuteronomistic expressions appearing here include:

1) *mywm hʿlty ʾtm mmṣrym wʿd hywm hzh,* "from the day I brought them up from Egypt until this very day." Cf. II Kings 21:15. The expression *ʿad hayyôm hazzeh* is ubiquitous in Deuteronomic and Deuteronomistic literature.

2) *ʿzb ʾt yhwh,* "abandon Yahweh." So Josh 24:16,20; Judg 2:12,13; 10:6,10,13; I Sam 12:10. See Richter, *Bearbeitungen des "Retterbuches,"* 58*ff.*

3) *ʿbd ʾlhym ʾḥrym,* "serve other gods, as in Josh 23:16; 24:2,16; Judg 10:13; I Kings 9:6; cf. II Kings 21:21. The phrase is common in the Book of Deuteronomy itself. Note that the last two expressions frequently occur together in Deuteronomistic and Deuteronomistically edited contexts.

9. *Yet you must solemnly warn them.* Hebrew *ʾak kî-hāʿēd tāʿîd bāhem.* This is formal legal language. In the future the people will not be able to claim they were not aware of what was in store for them. The force of the unique *ʾak kî,* "yet only, except that," is restrictive. For the expression *hāʿēd tāʿîd bāhem,* cf. Gen 43:3(*bis*); I Kings 2:42, etc.

the justice of the king. The Hebrew word here translated "justice" (*mišpāṭ*) may also mean "judgment, ordinance" and "way, custom, manner." In this case it refers to the justice of the king who is to come, i.e. the way he will exercise his authority as judge (thus not "the law of the king," though the issue has been much discussed; cf. Langlamet, "L'institution de la royauté," 186, n. 46), and there is a nuance of meaning that relies upon wordplay involving *mišpāṭ* and the related terms. The people have asked for "a king to judge us" (*melek lĕšopṭēnû,* v 5), and they are to be warned about "the justice of the king" (*mišpaṭ hammelek*).

10. *who were requesting.* Hebrew *haššōʾălîm.* The king the people have requested (*šāʾal*) turns out to be *šāʾûl,* "the requested one," that is, Saul. Recall

the different kind of play on this name that occurs residually in Samuel's birth narrative (see esp. the NOTE at 1:27,28).

11. *his chariot . . . run before his chariot.* The royal chariot was customarily escorted by a team of runners—a practice first mentioned in connection with Saul (21:8; 22:17)—who also guarded the door of the palace when the king was in residence (I Kings 14:27 = II Chron 12:10). See further, de Vaux, *Ancient Israel* 1.123-124, 221.

12. *He will appoint for himself.* The grammar is difficult. Following S. R. Driver (*A Treatise on the Use of the Tenses in Hebrew,* 3d ed. [Oxford: Clarendon, 1892] §206, 278-279) we interpret the force of the infinitive construct *wĕlāśûm* as essentially that of a finite verb with "your sons" the implied subject; it derives its tense value from its position in continuation of *yiqqaḥ,* "he will take," and carries an implication of purpose. In effect then, the form is a periphrastic infinitive, comparable, for example, to verbs in the periphrastic conjugations of Greek or Latin, and with the following *lô* it may be rendered, "And they will be for appointing for himself" or, less awkwardly, "He will appoint for himself . . . from them." (We assume with Smith that *wĕlāśûm* is elliptical for *wĕhāyû lāśûm.*) The simplifying explanation offered in GK §114p is less satisfactory.

captains of thousands . . . hundreds. That is, military officers of varying rank. The division of the tribes of Israel into military units of thousands, hundreds, fifties, and tens was, according to tradition, Mosaic in origin (Exod 18:21; Deut 1:15). In general these units represented the organization not of the professional standing army of the state but rather the forces conscripted from the people. The officers here referred to, however, should probably be thought of as permanently recruited servants of the king.

14. *his servants.* The title "servant of the king" (*'ebed hammelek*) referred not to a menial functionary but to a ranking member of the court. This is clear not only from the biblical evidence (e.g. II Kings 22:12 = II Chron 34:20; II Kings 25:8) but also from surviving Israelite (and other Northwest Semitic) seals inscribed with this title after proper names. So the "servants" in question here are royal courtiers, who as feudatories of the king, receive grants of land confiscated from the people, a practice known also at Ugarit (cf. Mendelsohn, "Samuel's Denunciation of Kingship," 19-20; A. F. Rainey in Fisher, *Ras Shamra Parallels* 2.97-98).

15. *tithe.* The Hebrew verb (*'āśar*) is denominative from *'eśer,* "ten," and means "take the tenth part of." Cf. English "to tithe" from Old English *teothian,* which is denominative from *teothe,* "a tenth part." As distinct from the tithe that supported the religious institutions (Deut 14:22-29; 26:12-15)—itself ultimately based on the model of a feudal society with Yahweh as king—the tithe referred to here was apparently a tax levied upon agricultural products for the support of the royal estates. Cf. Mendelsohn, "Samuel's Denunciation of Kingship," 20-21; A. F. Rainey in Fisher, *Ras Shamra Parallels* 2.95-97.

officers. Hebrew *sārîs* is a loanword from Akkadian (Assyrian) *ša rēši,* "one at the head, officer." The Assyrian title, because it was often applied to officials who were emasculated as a requirement for their positions (harem keepers, but also military commanders, etc.), acquired the meaning "eunuch." The term most frequently has this sense in the several languages that borrowed it, Hebrew among them; but the broader meaning "officer" seems to be indicated in certain biblical passages including the one under consideration here where "officers" are grouped with "servants" (see above).

16. *and use for his own work.* Hebrew *wĕʿāśâ limlaʾktô* (see the *Textual Note*). There is no precise parallel to this expression, but cf. Exod 28:24; Lev 7:24; and Ezek 15:5.

18. The language of this verse is generally reminiscent of that of the editorial framework of the material concerning the period of the judges, according to which the Israelites repeatedly suffer oppression, cry out to Yahweh, and receive deliverance. The characteristic verb for the people's appeal (*zāʿaq*), found in Judg 3:9,15; 6:6,7; 10:10 (cf. I Sam 12:8), also occurs here. Accordingly some scholars have regarded this verse as Deuteronomistic interpolation. But this is not a necessary conclusion. The characteristic terminology (including *zāʿaq*, as explained in the NOTE at 12:6-15) is ultimately derived from a pre-Deuteronomistic scheme (see the second NOTE at 11:3 for bibliography). Moreover the pattern of oppression by a foreign enemy, appeal by the people, and deliverance by Yahweh acting through a deliverer—so rigidly stereotyped elsewhere—is absent here. Israel's misery is to come from her king. There is no enemy to be defeated. There is no question of the raising up of a deliverer. Indeed the identification of this verse as secondary rests entirely upon the occurrence of *zāʿaq*, "cry out," a common verb with no necessary association with any particular Hebrew style or historical theology.

Yahweh will not answer you. That is, Yahweh will not respond to your self-inflicted misery. Contrast 7:9, where Yahweh does respond when Samuel, the prophet, cries out on the people's behalf.

22. Exeunt omnes. The prophetic narrator dismisses the people. They will be reconvened at Mizpah (10:17), where the kingmaking prescribed in the last verse will take place; but it is necessary now to clear the stage and introduce the actor who will play the major part in the scenes that follow. This bit of dramaturgy enables our narrator to include here the old story about Saul and the lost asses of Kish.

COMMENT

After the account of the pacification of the land in 7:5-14 the biblical narrative suddenly becomes silent. Years pass—how many we are not told. The details of Samuel's subsequent career have been reduced to the synopsis in 7:15-17, and when the story resumes he is already an old man sharing administrative responsibilities with two feckless sons. The events that now transpire have special importance in Israel's record of her own history, for the clamor for a king described here was—at least according to the present shape of the tradition—the decisive event that determined the future of the nation. Henceforward Israel's experience would be dominated by the deeds of her kings, for better or for worse.

The delegation that calls upon Samuel at Ramah confronts him with what amounts to a popular demand. The people wish to be ruled by a king. Samuel is old and cannot be expected to serve much longer. His sons are unworthy of succeeding him. Specifically, they are corrupt (v 3). The parallel with the sons of Eli is striking, especially when we recall that according to our prophetic narrator Samuel was Eli's designated successor (see COMMENT on 2:11-26). The meaning of this is plain to see: no one, not even Samuel, can expect to hand down his authority as leader of Israel to his sons. As in the case of Hophni and Phinehas—to which we might add that of Abimelech in Judges 9 (with Hertzberg), though there are important differences—the succession is shown to be undesirable because of the character of the sons. This is the danger of hereditary succession, and our narrator, as if the case of the well-intentioned but incompetent Eli had not sufficed, makes it completely clear with the case of the paragon Samuel.

So a new leader is needed. But this is not all the people have in mind. Why a king? Why will another judge not do? The change the people have in mind is not simply one of leaders but rather of institutions of leadership. The approaching end of Samuel's career and the unworthiness of his sons provide the occasion for the demand, but they do not create it. Clearly the people think of kingship as a military advantage (v 20; cf. the NOTE on "the justice of the king" at v 9), and it might be argued that a king is requested out of military necessity. Israel's pre-monarchical institutions have become inadequate to cope with new political realities, especially the Philistine threat. The story of the demand for a king, thus interpreted, portrays the people of Israel taking action as a result of their own assessment of the exigencies of their situation. But such an interpretation, though it corresponds to our modern evaluation of the conditions surrounding the birth of the Israelite monarchy, cannot be derived from the text. As we have seen, the pre-monarchical institutions are presented in this material as completely adequate, indeed as ideal (see the COMMENT on 7:2-17), and the people's insistence upon change must be seen as a strange denial of this plain fact.

So the inquiry into the people's motivation must proceed along other lines. A clue is provided by the proclamation in v 20 (cf. v 5), "Then we, too, shall be like all the other nations." The people demand a change because they are not content with what in the narrator's opinion was their proper sphere of life. They are motivated by a perverse and self-destructive urge to rise above themselves. As Adam and Eve in the Yahwistic primeval history desired to become "like gods" (Gen 3:5), so their descendants desire to become "like the nations." The people are naive, almost childlike. They want a king who will march before them in splendid array (v 20). Even when sternly warned they seem unable to comprehend the danger in the thing they seek. Everywhere the lineaments of the Eden story are apparent. We have here a reflection of a traditional pattern, found more than once in the Hebrew Bible, which presents men striving to exceed divinely appointed boundaries and holds the tragic consequences up to view. The people demand a king of Samuel because they want to be like the other nations; but this is precisely what they are not supposed to be. As our narrator sees it, they are a special community, divinely provided for and uniquely privileged. Now they seek a new status that in their impetuosity they regard as more glorious; but in the seeking they repudiate their only true glory.

Chapters 7 and 8, therefore, stand in a reciprocal relationship. Together they present the case, positively and then negatively expressed, for the theocratic ideal of the kingship of Yahweh as it was cherished in prophetic circles. As we saw, the positive argument in c 7 appealed to the picture of a peaceful and secure Israel, ruled by Yahweh through his prophet. The negative argument, developed in the present episode, points to the folly of abandoning such perfect conditions in pursuit of a vain desire. It then goes on to express in plain detail the new conditions under which the people must expect to live. Living under a human king, it is said, will be a difficult and ignominious experience for the people. It will contrast with the life they seek in a fashion that is darkly ironic. Kingship will be a curse for them. Their king will enslave them. Again the analogy of the Eden story is important: life after the rebellion will be hard, not splendid.

The elaborate and specific description of "the king's justice" in vv 11-19 reflects a long and bitter experience with kingship. In the Introduction we considered the possibility that the prophetic history of the origin of the monarchy, in which the present chapter is a key passage, was composed in the north at about the time of the fall of Samaria in circles that may also have played a part in the origin of the Deuteronomic movement.[1] It is important in this regard to note the relationship between I Sam 8:1-22 and Deut 17:14-17. The latter shows an acquaintance with the tradition of the origin of the monarchy in Israel by popular demand as also presented in our passage. It reads:

> When you come into the land that Yahweh, your god, is giving you, and take possession of it, and settle in it, and say, "I shall set a king over me like all the nations around me!" you must set over you a king from among

[1] Many scholars have tried to find substantial Deuteronomistic reworking in c 8, and some agree with Noth that the whole is "Deuteronomistically formulated through and through" (*ÜS*, 57). Compare most recently Clements, "Deuteronomistic Interpretation." Our own findings with respect to Deuteronomistic supplementation here are minimal—the criterion of characteristic language requires that only v 8 must certainly be isolated (see the NOTES at vv 5,8, and 18).

> your kinsmen: you cannot place over you a foreigner who is not your kinsman. But [your king] must not multiply horses for himself, and he must not take the people back to Egypt in order to multiply horses, for Yahweh has said to you, "You will never return that way again!" Also [your king] must not multiply wives for himself, lest his heart turn aside, and he must not greatly multiply gold for himself.

Both passages view monarchy as an institution that tends to become corrupt and must be introduced with much circumspection. Both list offenses of which Israel's kings were guilty. It has not gone unnoticed that the list of excesses in the Deuteronomy passage recalls in detail the description of the reign of Solomon, especially in I Kings 10 and 11. Although one cannot cull from the biblical record examples of each of the royal offenses in the catalogue in the present passage,[2] many kings are portrayed as involved in the kind of greedy abuse of power that is implied here, and the list of offenders includes not only names like Rehoboam and Ahab, but those of David and Solomon as well. The prophetic circles out of which our narrative (and perhaps the Deuteronomic law code) arose, disciplined by their negative theological valuation of monarchical government, were inclined to remember these unfavorable details in the history of the two kingdoms with special clarity. Thus they have placed in the mouth of Samuel, their great spokesman, a sardonic commentary on kingship couched in phrases that combine the genres of curse, oracle, and paternal instruction.

In spite of it all, however, there is to be a king. He is not to be welcomed, but he is to be indulged. And in a sense kingship receives a divine sanction here, even if only in a backhanded way, for Yahweh himself consents to the appointment. There still remains, however, the selection of an individual to fill the office. Who will be the king? If we expect an immediate search among the noblemen of Israel for an eligible candidate, we shall be disappointed, for now our attention turns to an obscure village a few miles away, where a Benjaminite youth is about to set out in search of lost asses belonging to his father.

[2] Many can be illustrated by appeal to the records of Israel's predecessors in Canaan, as shown especially by Mendelsohn, "Samuel's Denunciation of Kingship" (see also A. F. Rainey's critique of Mendelsohn's observations in Fisher, *Ras Shamra Parallels*, cited in the NOTES above). This is no reason, however, to suppose that the present passage necessarily reflects an early Israelite warning against kingship. The Israelite monarchy was of the Canaanite type, and such corruption might be found in any age. Still it should be noted that Mendelsohn and others have dated the substantial content of Samuel's warning as early as a time contemporary with the events described.

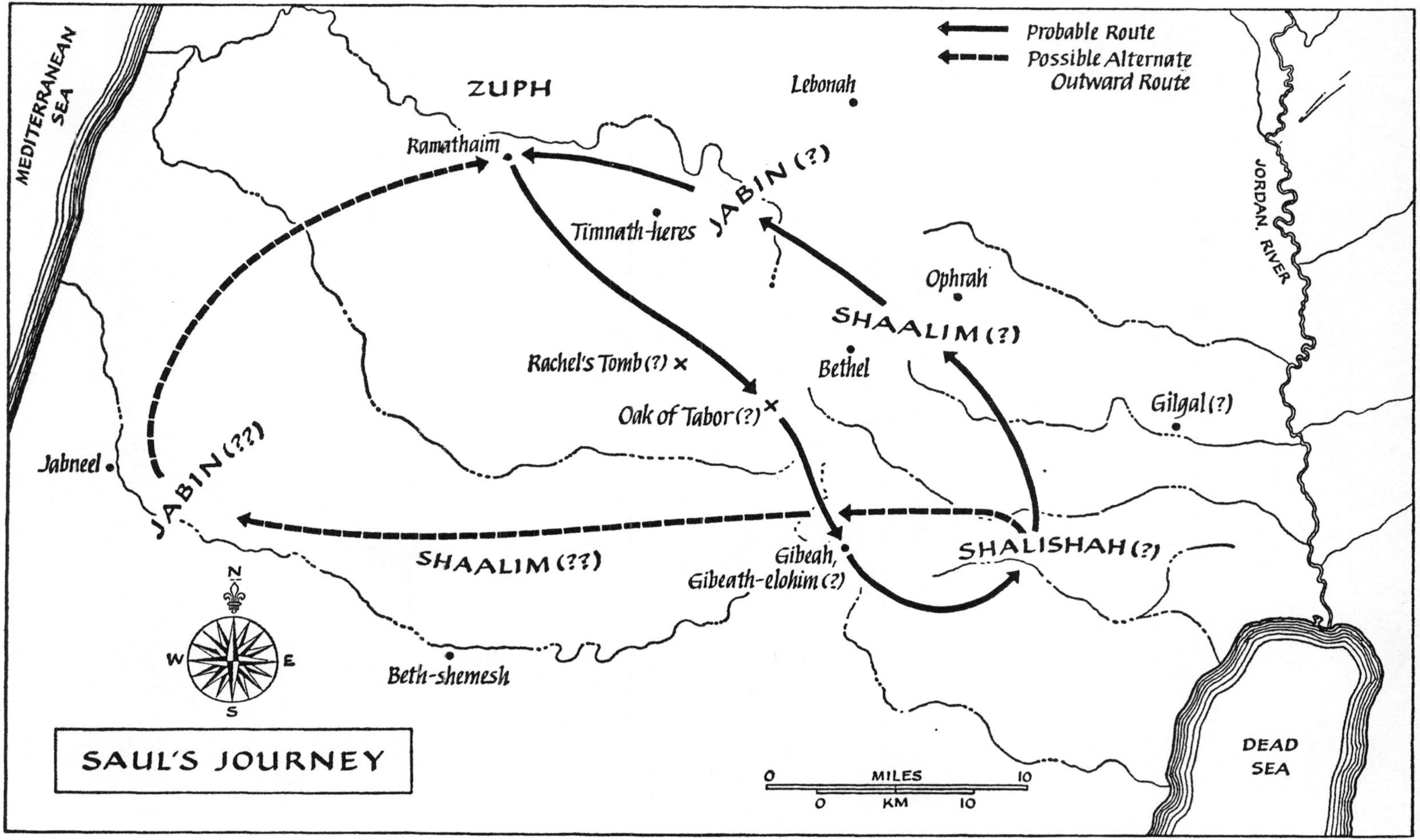
SAUL'S JOURNEY
Probable Route
Possible Alternate Outward Route
MEDITERRANEAN SEA
ZUPH
Ramathaim
Lebonah
JABIN (?)
Timnath-heres
JORDAN. RIVER
Ophrah
SHAALIM (?)
Bethel
Rachel's Tomb (?)
Oak of Tabor (?)
Gilgal (?)
Jabneel
JABIN (??)
SHAALIM (??)
Gibeah, Gibeath-elohim (?)
SHALISHAH (?)
Beth-shemesh
N
W
E
S
MILES
KM
0
10
0
10
DEAD SEA

XII. THE ANOINTING OF SAUL
(9:1-8, 10, 9, 11-27; 10:1-16)

9 1 There was a man from Gibeah of Benjamin, whose name was
Kish, the son of Abiel, the son of Zeror, the son of Becorath, the son
of Apiah—a Benjaminite and a powerful man. 2 He had a son, whose
name was Saul, a handsome young man. None of the Israelites was
more handsome than he! From his shoulder upward he was taller than
all of the rest of the people.

The Lost Asses of Kish

3 Now some asses that belonged to Kish, Saul's father, were lost,
and Kish said to Saul, his son: "Take one of the servants with you,
and go search for the asses!" So taking one of his father's servants
with him Saul went to search for the asses of Kish, his father. 4 They
crossed through the hill country of Ephraim—they crossed through
the land of Shalishah and did not find them; they crossed through the
land of Shaalim, and there was nothing there; they crossed through
the land of Jabin and did not find them.
5 When they came to Zuph, Saul said to the servant who was with
him, "Come, let us return, lest my father stop thinking about the asses
and worry about us instead!"
6 But [the servant] said to him, "There is a man of God in this city,
and the man is honored—everything he says is sure to come to pass!
Now let us go! Perhaps he will advise us about the journey we have
undertaken."
7 "If we do go," said Saul to his servant, "what shall we take to the
man? For the bread in our bags is used up, and there is none to take
to the man of God as a gift. What do we have?"
8 Again the servant replied to Saul, "I find I have a quarter of a
shekel of silver. Give it to the man of God, and he will advise us
about our journey!"
10 "What you say is good!" said Saul to his servant. "Come, let us
go!" So they went to the city where the man of God was.

9 (Formerly in Israel when a man went to inquire of God, he said,
"Come, let us go to the seer!" For someone who today would be
called "the prophet" was formerly called "the seer.")

11 As they were going up the ascent to the city, they met some girls
coming out to draw water and asked them, "Is the seer here?"

12 "He is," they told him in reply. "Right ahead of you! Now, just
today, he has come to the city, for the people have a sacrifice today
on the high place. 13 When you come into the city, you will find him
about to go up to the high place to eat, for the people will not eat
until he comes, since it is he who blesses the sacrifice and afterwards
the guests eat. So go up right away, for just now you will find him!"

14 So they went on up to the city, and when they came into the
midst of the gate, there was Samuel coming out toward them on his
way up to the high place.

15 Now one day before Saul's arrival Yahweh had disclosed to Samuel the following: 16 "At this time tomorrow I shall send you a man
from Benjamin. You will anoint him prince over my people Israel,
and he will free my people from the grip of the Philistines. For I have
seen the affliction of my people, and their cry has come to me."
17 Then when Samuel saw Saul, Yahweh told him, "Here is the man
of whom I spoke to you! This one shall muster my people!"

18 Saul approached Samuel in the midst of the gate. "Tell me," he
said, "where is the home of the seer?"

19 "I am the seer," said Samuel in reply to Saul. "Go up before me
to the high place and eat with me today! I shall send you on your way
in the morning and tell you about everything that is on your mind.
20 As for the asses lost to you these three days, do not be concerned
about them, for they have been found. And to whom do the riches of
Israel belong if not to you and to your father's house?"

21 "Am I not a Benjaminite," replied Saul, "from the smallest of the
tribes of Israel and from the humblest clan of all the tribe of Benjamin? Then why have you spoken to me this way?"

22 Samuel took Saul and his servant and brought them into the
chamber. He gave them a place at the head of the guests, of whom
there were about thirty. 23 Then Samuel said to the butcher, "Fetch
the portion I gave you—the one I told you to set aside"; 24 and when
the butcher had separated the thigh and served it to Saul, he said,
"That which remains is set before you. Eat! For it was kept for you
until the appointed time [. . .]"

So Saul ate with Samuel that day; 25 and when they had gone down
from the high place to the city, they made a bed for Saul on the roof,
26 and he slept.

The Anointing of Saul

At the break of dawn Samuel called to Saul on the roof, "Get up,
and I shall send you on your way!" So Saul got up, and he and Samuel went outside.

27 As they were going down through the outskirts of the city, Samuel said to Saul, "Speak to the servant! Let him pass on ahead of us!
But as for you, stay here for the moment, and I shall inform you of
the word of God." **10** 1 Then taking a vial of oil Samuel poured it
over [Saul's] head, kissed him, and said, "Has not Yahweh anointed
you prince over his people Israel? It is you who will muster the people
of Yahweh! It is you who will free them from the grip of their enemies all around!

"And this will be the sign for you that Yahweh has anointed you
prince over his estate: 2 when you depart from me today, you will
meet two men near Rachel's Tomb in the territory of Benjamin
[. . .], and they will say to you, 'The asses you went to seek have
been found. Your father has given up the matter of the asses and is
worried instead about you, saying, "What shall I do about my son?"'

3 "When you pass on from there, you will come to the Oak of
Tabor, where three men will meet you as they go up to God at Bethel.
One will be carrying three kids; one will be carrying three bags of
bread; and one will be carrying a jug of wine. 4 They will greet you
and offer you two wave offerings of bread, which you will take from
them.

5 "After this you will come to Gibeath-elohim, where there is a
Philistine prefect. When you reach the city, you will encounter a band
of prophets coming down from the high place. In front of them will
be harps, tambourines, clarinets, and lyres; and they themselves will
be prophesying. 6 Then the spirit of Yahweh will rush upon you, and
you will prophesy along with them and be turned into another man.
7 When these signs have befallen you, do whatever your hand finds to
do, for God will be with you!

8 "Go down ahead of me to Gilgal, for I shall come down to you to
offer holocausts and to make communion offerings. Seven days you

must wait until I come to you; then I shall tell you what you are to do."

9 When [Saul] turned to depart from Samuel, God gave him another heart, and all these signs came to pass that same day.

Saul among the Prophets

10 When he came from there to Gibeah, there opposite him was the
band of prophets! The spirit of God rushed upon him, and he
prophesied in their midst. 11 When all those who had known him
previously saw him prophesying with the prophets, the people said to
each other, "What has happened to the son of Kish? Is Saul, too,
among the prophets?" 12 Then one of them responded, "And who is
their father?" Therefore it became a proverb: "Is Saul, too, among
the prophets?"

Saul's Homecoming

13 When Saul had finished prophesying and gone home, 14 his uncle
asked him and his servant, "Where did you go?"

"To seek the asses," he said. "When we saw that they were nowhere to be found, we went to Samuel."

15 Saul's uncle said, "Tell me what Samuel said to you!"

16 "Why, he told us that the asses had been found!" said Saul to his uncle. But of the matter of the kingdom he told him nothing.

TEXTUAL NOTES

9 1. ***from Gibeah of Benjamin*** One might read *mbny ymyny*, "of the Benjaminites," on the basis of LXX *ex huiōn beniamein* (cf. 22:7; Judg 19:16). MT *mibbin-yāmîn*, "from Benjamin" (?), is anomalous (we expect *mibbin-yāmîn*) and probably defective. But either reading is superfluous in view of the identification of Kish as "a Benjaminite" below, and Wellhausen is probably correct in suspecting (without textual warrant) an original *mgb't bn ymyn*, "from Gibeah of Benjamin," on the analogy of 1:1 and Judg 13:2.

Zeror MT *ṣĕrôr;* LXX^{B} *ared;* LXX^{L} *sara.* Read MT. The name evidently means "Flint"; cf. Noth, *Israelitischen Personennamen,* 225.

Becorath So MT (*bĕkôrat*). The versions give some support for reading *bākîr,* a masculine equivalent of the well-attested feminine proper name *bĕkîrâ.* Either name (*bĕkôrat* or *bākîr*) would mean "Firstborn."

Apiah MT *'ăpîaḥ* (cf. LXX^B^ *aphek*). The name may mean "Sooty, Dusky": cf. *pîaḥ*, "soot." For a different interpretation, see Noth, *Israelitischen Personennamen*, 227.

a Benjaminite Reading *'îš yĕmînî* on the basis of LXX^L. MT, LXX^B reflect *ben-'îš yĕmînî*, "the son of a Benjaminite," preserving an old doublet, *bn/'yš ymyny*. In view of the previous identification of Kish as a Benjaminite in all versions, his further identification as "a Benjaminite" seemed superfluous; thus MT, LXX^B have attached the (conflate) designation to Apiah as "a son of a Benjaminite" whose patronymic was unknown. But Wellhausen's likely conjecture concerning the previous reading (see above) eliminates the problem. LXX^L evidently preserves an original, shorter reading here. Cf. S. Talmon, "Double Readings in the Massoretic Text," in *Textus* I (Jerusalem: Magnes, 1960) 165.

3. *go search* The three imperatives so rendered (lit. "Arise! Go! Search!") are singular in MT, plural in LXX. This must be related to the confusion over the number of the verbs in v 4. See below.

So taking . . . of Kish, his father We read the text of a long plus in LXX^L: *kai anestē saoul kai parelaben hen tōn paidariōn tou patros autou met' autou kai eporeuthē zētein tous onous keis tou patros autou,* reflecting *wyqm š'wl wyqḥ 't 'ḥd mn'ry 'byw 'tw wylk lbqš 't 'tnwt qyš 'byw,* lit. "And Saul arose and took one of his father's servants with him and went to seek the asses of Kish, his father.' This is omitted in both MT and LXX^B, but it is shared by Syr. Normally such a long, repetitive passage would be rejected out of hand as scribal expansion. But the transition to v 4 in MT and LXX^B is much too abrupt. In view of the tendency of the MT of Samuel to haplography, therefore, we prefer to retain the longer reading here. Such repetition is not uncharacteristic of the best Hebrew style. Compare, for example, the instructions in 6:7*ff* and their execution in 6:10*ff*.

4. In this verse MT shows a perplexing mixture of singular and plural verbs. We read plurals uniformly with LXX, Vulg. (so Wellhausen, Driver, and most critics). The grave difficulties surrounding the toponymy of Saul's itinerary are discussed in the NOTES.

5. *When they came . . . Saul said* Hebrew *hēmmâ bā'û . . . wĕšā'ûl 'āmar.* The syntax of MT (*perfect + perfect*) is rather unusual, as explained in the NOTE. LXX^B reflects a text that has reverted to the more common sequence *participle + perfect,* as in vv 11,27, etc. Thus *hēmmâ bā'îm . . . wĕšā'ûl ā* "As they came . . . Saul said . . . ."

Zuph MT *ṣûp;* LXX^B *seip* (= *ṣyp*). Cf. the second *Textual Note* to 1:1. MT, LXX^L have "*the land of* Zuph" under the influence of the preceding place names. Omit with LXX^B.

6. *But* [*the servant*] *said to him* Reading *wy'mr lw* with MT. LXX adds "the servant" for clarity, just as we must insert it in English to avoid ambiguity.

Now let us go! Reading *'th nlkh*. MT: *'th nlkh šm*, "Now let us go *there!*" LXX: *w'th nlkh*, "*So* now let us go!" Neither of these little expansions is necessary.

7. *his servant* So MT, OL. LXX adds, "who was with him," as in v 5.

8. *Give . . . !* Reading *wĕnātattâ* on the basis of LXX *kai doseis* in prefer-

ence to MT *wĕnātattî*, "So let me give. . . ." On the imperative force of the construction, see Driver.

9. The statement that follows here as v 9 in all witnesses evidently arose as a marginal gloss. It is preserved here between vv 10 and 11, where it causes least disruption to the narrative. The word it explains (*rōʾeh*, "seer") occurs in v 11. See further the NOTE.

For someone who today would be called . . . "the seer" So MT. LXX is somewhat different: "For the prophet the people formerly called 'the seer.'"

12. *Right ahead of you!* Reading *hnh lpnykm* on the basis of LXX *idou kata prosōpon hymōn*. MT has *hnh lpnyk mhr*, "Right ahead of you (sing.)! Hurry!" (cf. Josephus *Ant.* 6.48). Wellhausen argues plausibly that the singular is out of place here in view of the plurals in vv 11 and 13 and the previous *ʾôtām*, "them," in v 12; that the *m* of *mhr* belongs to the preceding word, as in the *Vorlage* of LXX; and (following a suggestion by P. A. de Lagarde) that *hr* is a remnant of *hrʾh*, "the seer," added by a scribe to make the subject explicit.

Now, just today Reading *ʿth khywm* on the basis of LXX *nyn dia tēn hēmeran* (Wellhausen, Driver). MT has *ʿth ky hywm*, ". . . now. For today. . . ." The expression *khywm* means "just today, just now," as in v 13 below and Neh 5:11.

13. *and afterwards* So LXX, Syr., Vulg.; MT omits "and."

for just now you will find him! So LXX. MT has *ky ʾtw khywm tmṣʾwn ʾtw*, "for him—just now you will find him!" Though parallels exist for the longer text of MT, we must omit the first *ʾtw* with LXX (despite the indignant objections of Wellhausen and Driver).

14. *into the midst of the gate* All major witnesses read "into the midst of the city" (but cf. Sahidic, "into the gate of the city"), but most commentators prefer to change *hʿyr* to *hšʿr* in light of v 18 (MT). The extant reading probably reflects the influence of *hʿyr* in the opening clause. Note that LXX has suffered the corruption again in v 18 (see below).

15. *Saul's arrival* So MT: *bôʾ-šāʾûl*, "the coming of Saul." LXX: "the coming of Saul *to him*."

16. *from Benjamin* So LXX. MT: "from *the land of* Benjamin."

the affliction of my people Reading *ʾt ʿny ʿmy* or *ʾt lḥṣ ʿmy* (cf. Exod 3:9) on the basis of LXX, Targ. MT omits *ʿny/lḥṣ*, "affliction."

18. *in the midst of the gate* So MT. The confusion in v 14 (see the *Textual Note* above) has extended to this verse in the tradition behind LXX, which reads, "in the midst of the city" (so 4QSam[a]: [*btwk h*]*yr*).

19. *"I am the seer"* So MT (*ʾnky hrʾh*). LXX has *egō eimi autos*, reflecting *ʾnky hwʾ*, "I am he," corroborated by 4QSam[a] [*ʾnky hw*]*ʾ ʿl*[*h*], "I am he. Go up. . . ." There is no basis for choosing between these variants.

eat Reading *wʾkl* or *wʾklt* (sing.) on basis of LXX *kai phage*, in preference to the inappropriate plural (*wʾkltm*) of MT.

20. *these three days* That is, "today, the three days": *hayyôm šĕlōšet hayyāmîm* (MT). The definite article in *hayyāmîm* may be retained on the grounds that the particular three days that have just passed are referred to (so Smith, Driver; but cf. Wellhausen, Budde, GK §134m).

the riches Reading *ḥămūdôt,* "the riches, treasures," on the basis of LXX *ta hōraia.* MT has *kol-ḥemdat,* "every treasure."

your father's house So LXX. MT: *"all of* your father's house."

21. *a Benjaminite* So MT. LXX: "a man, a Benjaminite."

from the smallest of the tribes of Israel Reading *mqṭn šbṭy yśr'l* (cf. LXX). MT has *miqqĕṭānê,* "from the smallest ones (pl.)," possibly by attraction to *šibṭê,* "tribes."

and from the humblest clan of all the tribe of Benjamin Reading *wmhšpḥh hṣ'rh mkl šbṭ bnymn* on the basis of LXX[B] *kai tēs phylēs tēs elachistēs ex holou skēptrou beniamein.* MT has *wmšpḥty hṣ'rh mkl mšpḥwt šbṭy bnymn,* "and my clan is the most humble of all the clans of the tribes (*sic*) of Benjamin." At least the plural *šbṭy,* "tribes," in MT must be corrected to the singular. With regard to the other variation, there is no basis for choice.

22. *thirty* So MT. LXX: "seventy" (so Josephus *Ant.* 6.52). Numbers tend to become exaggerated, and in the absence of other data the smaller is to be preferred.

24. *the thigh* Hebrew *'et-haššôq,* reflected by LXX *tēn kōlean.* To this MT adds the troublesome reading *wh'lyh.* Evidently the Masoretes understood this as a prepositional phrase given substantive force by the article, used here as a kind of relative. Thus *'et-haššôq wĕhe'ālêhā,* "the thigh and that which was upon it." LXX[L] and other Greek MSS seem to share the addition of MT: *kai to ep' autēs,* "and that which was upon it." But such a construction is otherwise unknown in Biblical Hebrew (see Driver). The old suggestion of Abraham Geiger to read *wĕhā'alyâ,* "and the fatty tail," has been the most popular explanation of the problem (so Wellhausen, Budde, Driver, Smith), assuming that *wh'lyh* was inserted by a scribe who knew the regulation that the fatty tail was supposed to be reserved along with the thigh (Exod 29:22; Lev 3:9; 7:3; 8:25; 9:19). 4QSam[a] offers new evidence; reading *[h]'lyṅh* (= *h'lywnh,* "the upper [thigh?]"), to which perhaps compare Josephus *Ant.* 6.52, *merida basilikēn,* "a royal portion." But until a certain reading is proposed, it is safest to follow the short text of LXX[B], which reflects *'t hšwq* alone.

That which remains is set before you. Eat! So MT. LXX, Targ., Vulg.: "Behold that which remains! Set it before you and eat!"

it was kept for you MT *šmwr lk.* LXX[B] *tetheitai soi* seems rather to reflect *śym lk,* now confirmed by 4QSam[a]: *[ś]ym lk.* This reading is reminiscent of *śym lk* immediately above and is evidently inferior to that of MT.

At the end of v 24a there occurs a series of words, the interpretation of which remains quite elusive. MT has *l'mr h'm qr'ty,* "saying, 'The people have I summoned' "(?). LXX[B] reads *para tous allous* (LXX[L]: *para tou laou*) *apoknize,* "beside the others (LXX[L]: 'from the people'). Nip (it) off!" Precisely what Hebrew reading this reflects is impossible to guess (see the commentaries). Unfortunately 4QSam[a] preserves only two letters: *l'*[ ]. The conjectures of modern scholars are legion and diverse, but uniformly unsuccessful. Of these the most popular is probably Budde's: read *l'kl 'm hqr'ym,* "to eat with the guests." This gives good sense but is not supported by the textual data. Stoebe supposes two divergent variants: "(for at the appointed time) I have summoned the people" and "for at the appointed time it was kept for you"; these readings, he suggests, were artificially joined by *l'mr*. But in the absence of a full explanation of the evidence of LXX the problem must be considered unsolved.

25,26. *they made a bed . . . and he slept* Reading *wyrbdw lš'wl 'l hgg wyškb* on the basis of LXX *kai diestrōsan tō saoul epi tō dōmati kai ekoimēthē*. MT *wydbr 'm š'wl 'l hgg wyškmw*, "and he spoke with Saul upon the roof. And they arose early . . ." is plainly inferior. See also Josephus *Ant.* 6.52.

26. *on the roof* Reading *'l hgg* with LXX, *epi tō dōmati*. The preposition has fallen out of the text of MT (*kĕtîb: hgg*), but the Masoretes have partly solved the problem by pointing the noun to be read as if with the so-called "*he*-locale" (*qĕrê: haggāgā*).

he and Samuel So LXX. MT adds *šnyhm*, "the two of them."

27. *Let him pass on ahead of us!* Reading *wy'br lpnynw* (cf. LXX, Syr.). MT adds a second *wy'br*, "And he passed on."

10 1. *Has not Yahweh . . . over his estate* So LXX: *ouchi kechriken se kyrios eis archonta epi ton laon autou epi israēl kai su arxeis en laō kyriou kai su sōseis auton ek cheiros echthrōn autou kyklothen kai touto soi to sēmeion hoti echrisen se kyrios epi klēronomian autou eis archonta*, reflecting *hlw' mšḥk yhwh lngyd 'l 'mw 'l yśr'l w'th t'ṣr b'm yhwh w'th twšy'nw myd 'ybyw msbyb wzh lk h'wt ky mšḥk yhwh 'l nḥltw lngyd*. MT has lost everything between *hlw'* and *ky* owing to haplography triggered by the repeated sequence *mšḥk yhwh* (*lngyd*).

2. *in the territory of Benjamin* The obscure sequence *bṣlṣḥ* follows in MT, where it is evidently taken to be a place name ("Zelzah"?); but nearer definition of the location is out of place here, following the foregoing phrases (which a place name should precede). LXX^B has *hallomenous megala*, "leaping greatly" (?). The first term may reflect some form of the verb *ṣlḥ*, "rush upon, spring upon" (or perhaps *ṣl'*, "limp"; see below). The second, since *megala* is not used adverbially in LXX, is probably a transcription in origin. Other Greek MSS (cf. OL) have in addition *en sēlō en bakalath*, which is certainly transcription. Combining these data we might conjecture an original *bṣl'm bmqlwt*, lit. "in their limping on staffs"; thus, "(You will meet three men) . . . as they hobble on their staffs." (The *maqqēl* was a traveler's staff [Gen 32:11(English 32:10); Exod 12:11] or a shepherd's stick [cf. 17:40], but it might also be a wand of divination [Hosea 4:12], and there may be some question of divination here—the three travelers do have knowledge somehow of the lost asses. On the place of "limping" in mantic rites, see R. de Vaux, "The Prophets of Baal on Mount Carmel," in *The Bible and the Ancient Near East*, tr. D. McHugh [Garden City, N.Y.: Doubleday, 1971] 240-241.) But if this is assumed, MT is all the more difficult to explain. Preceding *hallomenous megala*, LXX^L adds *mesēmbrias* (Vulg. *meridie*), perhaps reflecting *bṣhrym*, "at noon" (?): and there are still other readings. The problem remains unsolved.

3. *When you pass on* MT *wĕḥālaptā*, which is not used elsewhere of human travel. See the NOTE.

Tabor So MT (*tābôr*), LXX^B (*thabōr*); cf. Targ. LXX^L has *tēs eklektēs* = *bḥwr*, "Bahur."

three bags of bread Reading *šlšt klwby lḥm* on the basis of LXX *tria ag-*

geia artōn. MT has *šlšt kkrwt lḥm*, "three *loaves* of bread." 4QSam[a] has *šlš[t k]l[wby] kkrwt [lḥm]*, "three bags of loaves of bread." Evidently *klwby* and *kkrwt* are ancient variants conflated in the text of 4QSam[a].

4. *two wave offerings of bread* MT *šty lḥm*, "two of bread," obviously shows the loss of a word, and it is supplied by LXX (*dyo aparchas artōn*) and 4QSam[a] ([*šty t*]*ṅwpwt lḥm*).

5. *prefect* So LXX (treated two ways), Syr. MT has "prefects."

8. *Gilgal* So MT. LXX (wrongly), "Gilead."

to make communion offerings MT (cf. LXX[L]) *lzbḥ zbḥy šlmym*. LXX[B] omits *lzbḥ* by haplography.

9. At the beginning of the verse MT *whyh* is to be corrected to *wyhy* (GK §112uu).

10. *from there* So LXX, as required by the sense. MT: "there."

12. *one of them* Reading *'îš mēhem* on the basis of LXX, *tis* (*ex*) *autōn*, in preference to MT, *'îš miššām*, "one from there." But cf. Stoebe. We cannot be certain. See the NOTE.

their father So MT, 4QSam[a]. LXX, Syr., OL: "his father." See the NOTE.

13. *home* MT *hbmh*, "to the high place," makes no sense, and LXX *eis ton bounon* = *hgb'th*, "to Gibeah," is incompatible with v 10. The conjectural emendation of *hbmh* to *hbyth* followed here is that of Wellhausen, who might have cited Josephus *Ant*. 6.58, in support.

14. *his uncle* So LXX. MT, 4QSam[a]: "Saul's uncle."

15. *Saul's uncle* So MT. LXX: "the uncle . . . to Saul."

16. At the end of the verse MT and other witnesses (including 4QSam[a]) add; "(that) which Samuel had said." Omit with LXX[B].

NOTES

9 1. This introductory notice is reminiscent of that in 1:1 in form. For the implications see the COMMENT on 1:1-28, where the possibility is considered that a Nazirite birth narrative belonging to Saul was rewritten and applied to Samuel. Note that the present story begins with Kish, not Saul, as its focus—a fact that has given scholars some pause (e.g. Birch, "Anointing of Saul," 57). Originally the narrative may have gone on to describe the miraculous birth of Saul, an episode in which his father (and mother) starred, as in 1:1-28. Cf. Judges 13.

Gibeah of Benjamin. The ancient city, also called Gibeah of Saul (11:4; 15:34 [MT]), occupied a prominent height (thus its name *gib'â*, "hill") of considerable strategic importance on the NS ridge of hills between Ramah and Jerusalem. The modern site is Tell el-Fûl, ca. 3½ miles N of Jerusalem. See Paul Lapp, "Tell el-Fûl," *BA* 28 (1965) 2-10.

Kish . . . son of Apiah. Saul's genealogy is not elsewhere mentioned except in I Chron 8:33 and 9:39, where the father of Kish is identified as Ner. But there is no textual warrant to assume the loss of a name in the present list, and the Chronicler may have "corrected" his sources to conform to his interpretation of the confusing explanation of the relationship between Saul and Abiner given in c 14. For the details, see the NOTE at 14:50,51. The names given here seem to be correct: Ner was Kish's brother, not his father.

a Benjaminite. See the NOTE at v 21.

a powerful man. The title *gibbôr ḥayil* often carries a military connotation (Josh 1:14; 8:3; 10:7; etc.), but this does not exhaust its meaning, as is sometimes assumed. Basically the expression describes social standing and implies economic power. It may be used in reference to a nobleman or wealthy citizen, such as Jeroboam (I Kings 11:28) or Boaz (Ruth 2:1). The *gibbôrê ḥayil* are the taxable gentry (II Kings 15:20), who in the feudal hierarchy of the monarchy are associated closely with the court (II Kings 24:14; I Chron 28:1), where the feudatory obligation of military service is especially important. Thus while the expression may have referred originally to military prowess (though to be sure *ḥayil* may mean "wealth" as well as "[physical] strength"), it became applicable to any high-ranking citizen (cf. I Chron 9:13)—hence our translation, "a powerful man," which is neutral with regard to wealth or strength, but also literal. We are not to conclude, in short, that Saul's father was a soldier but rather that he was a substantial citizen.

2. *a handsome young man.* Hebrew *bāḥûr wāṭôb,* suggesting that Saul at the time was a young man about to enter upon adult life (*bāḥûr*) and that he was attractive in his physical appearance (*ṭôb*). Both details are important. Saul has attained his majority and is ready to assume adult responsibilities, though to be sure he has no knowledge of the extraordinary responsibilities being prepared for him. Also he is conspicuously handsome. The attribution of good looks is a traditional part of the biblical presentation of an Israelite hero or heroine, e.g. Joseph (Gen 39:6), David (I Sam 16:12), Esther (Esth 2:7), the infant Moses (Exod 2:2), and so on. The quality is to be interpreted as a physical symptom of special divine favor.

some asses that belonged to Kish. Hebrew *hā'ătōnôt lĕqîš,* not to be translated "*the* asses of Kish," which would leave the unusual periphrastic construction used to express the genitive unrepresented. Such a circumlocution is normally employed to *avoid* determination of the first noun (e.g. *bēn lĕyîšay* in 16:18, meaning "a son of Jesse," since *ben yîšay* would mean "the son of Jesse"). In the present case *'ătōnôt qîš* would be the natural way to express "the asses of Kish." By contrast the sense of the construction used here is "certain ones of/some of the asses of Kish," the force of the definite article being the identification of those particular asses with which the incident about to be narrated will be concerned. The same construction is used in 14:16, where *haṣṣōpîm lĕšā'ûl* does not mean "the watchmen of Saul" but rather "certain ones of the watchmen of Saul" or "some of Saul's watchmen." This function of the article in Biblical Hebrew narrative, while not common, is well attested (as in II Sam 15:13, "a certain messenger"; 17:17, "a certain maidservant"; etc.). So in the present instance it is necessary neither to delete the article as dittographic (Budde, Dhorme, Driver, etc.) without textual support from the versions nor to conclude (with Hertzberg, Stoebe) that *all* of the asses of Kish were lost, threatening Saul's family with economic ruin. The apparent reason for the journey was less important than that, as the dramatic irony of the tale requires.

one of the servants. Hebrew *'et-'aḥad mēhannĕ'ārîm.* Though not in fact determined by any genitive, *'aḥad* is governed so closely by the prepositional phrase that follows it that it is marked by the *'ēt* particle and given construct state form. See Driver for parallels supporting both anomalies.

4. The journey Saul and his servant undertake leads them across the full extent of the Ephraimite hills. The first three phases of the search, each with its negative result, are described in the phrases that follow. "The hill country of Ephraim" is a general description of the itinerary; "Shalishah," "Shaalim," and "Jabin" specify the territories visited. Identification of the geographic features designated is very difficult, and most commentators have preferred to abandon the task as hopeless. The solution adopted here at least has the advantage of identifying the toponyms with fixed points along a direct route to Samuel's home.

Shalishah. MT *šālīšâ,* Syr. *šlyšh,* LXX^{B} *selcha,* OL *seliha.* The region may also be mentioned in II Kings 4:42, where it is said that a delegate from Baal-shalishah (read *mibba'ălê šālīšâ,* "from the lords/leading citizens of Shalishah"?) supplied Elisha with provisions at Gilgal. This suggests that the land of Shalishah lay in NE Benjamin or SE Ephraim (the old identification of Baal-shalishah with the village of Kefr Thilth, near Shechem, has nothing to recommend it but linguistic coincidence), and thus that Saul began his search, as we might expect, "in his own backyard."

Shaalim. MT *šĕ'ālîm,* LXX^{L} *segaleim;* LXX^{B} *easakem.* The region is nowhere else mentioned but can probably be identified with "the land of Shual (*šû'āl*)," mentioned later as being in the direction of Ophrah from Michmash (see the NOTE at 13:17). If this is correct, the land in question must have been the region N of Bethel in the central hills. A plausible alternative identification links Shaalim with Shaalbim (*ša'albîm;* Judg 1:35; etc.), modern Selbît, N of Beth-shemesh. Accordingly, Saul's journey would be proceeding almost due westward. But if, as we surmise, Shaalim is to be located N of Bethel, Saul is traveling northwestward, directly toward Ramathaim.

Jabin. As generally agreed MT *'ereṣ yĕmînî,* "the land of Benjamin" (!), cannot be correct. Saul, who has been traveling for some time, is about to reach the land of Zuph. To assume that he has somehow doubled back to Benjamin leaves any reconstruction of the itinerary in shambles. An original, less familiar toponym has been distorted in MT in favor of the ubiquitous designation of Saul's tribal homeland. (One factor contributing to the confusion may have been the [spurious] identification of Ramathaim with Ramah of Benjamin that characterizes the prophetic revision of the material.) Other versions preserve more likely but still ambiguous readings (LXX^{L} *iabein,* LXX^{B} *iakeim,* OL *lamin*), and the original can be restored only conjecturally. If the northwestward route proposed above is correct, we must look to the region between Ophrah and Ramathaim. Dominating this area is the site of Timnath-heres (modern Khirbet Tibneh, near which Jerome locates Ramathaim; see the NOTE at 1:1), and a corruption of *tmnh* to *ymny* (so MT) is certainly plausible. A second possibility is Lebonah (modern Lubban, a few miles NW of Shiloh), by which the location of Shiloh is fixed in Judg 21:19; here again a corruption of *lbnh* to *ybnh* (cf. LXX[L]) or *lmnh* (cf. OL) is quite possible. If on the other hand the westward route through Shaalbim is the correct one, this region is almost certainly to be identified with Jabneh (*yabneh*, II Chron 26:6), that is, Jabneel, the major city in the Philistine Plain N of Ekron, known to Greek speakers as Jamnia (*iamnia*), due W of Shaalbim and ca. 3 or 4 miles from the coast (modern Yebnā).

5. *When they came . . . Saul said. . . .* Hebrew *hēmmâ bā'û . . . wĕšā'ûl 'āmar . . .* See the *Textual Note*. The sequence of perfect verbs suggests immediacy, as in v 17 (see Gk §164b with the examples cited in (b)(3) and footnote 1). Saul has become more and more discouraged as the journey has progressed, and upon arrival in the land of Zuph he suddenly resolves to turn back.

Zuph. The district in which Ramathaim, Samuel's home, was located. (See the NOTE at 1:1, where Elkanah, Samuel's father, is called a Zuphite and is said to be descended from a certain Zuph, who is evidently the eponymous ancestor of the region.) Providentially (v 16) Saul's wanderings have brought him to Samuel.

lest my father stop thinking about the asses. Hebrew *pen-yeḥdal 'ābî min-hā'ătōnôt*, lit. "lest my father desist from the asses." For *ḥādal min* followed by a substantive, meaning "have no more to do with, cease concern for," cf. Isa 2:22.

6. *a man of God*. In general a man of God was a professional holy man. He was thought of as possessing special skills and powers enabling him to invoke the aid of supernatural forces. His role in society is best illustrated by reference to the stories about Elijah and Elisha, who might be categorized as paradigmatic men of God. The miracles ascribed to them include healings of the sick or even dead (I Kings 17:17-24; II Kings 4:18-37), provision of much food from little (I Kings 17:7-16; II Kings 4:42-44), and so on. To be sure Elijah and Elisha also prophesy, for the ability to know unseen things, whether past, present, or future, is also within the province of the man of God. But the designation "man of God" (*'îš hā'ĕlōhîm*) itself carries none of the special force of "prophet" (*nābî'*) in the particularized sense of the latter, as used by the prophetic narrator of the Samuel stories. We should expect to find a man of God in neighboring societies as well as Israel or Judah, duly recognized in the community for his special powers regardless of which god or gods have granted him authority. This is not to say, however, that a man of God might not also be identified as a prophet. Indeed this identification is regularly made in the biblical literature, as it is in Samuel's case. But when an individual such as Saul's servant mentions a man of God, we are to think of no more than a recognized holy man, itinerant as in the case of Elijah and Elisha or locally resident as Samuel seems to be in the present narrative, to whom one might appeal for assistance with problems ranging from illness to barrenness to famine. In this case Saul and his servant plan to appeal to the visionary powers of the local man of God in the hope that he may provide some information about their journey. As characteristically happens in such tales when intercourse with the supernatural

is involved, the information received is quite different from the information expected.

he will advise. Hebrew *yaggîd,* the first in a series of occurrences in the story of the verb *higgîd,* "inform, make known," which is etymologically related to *nāgîd,* the title bestowed upon Saul in 10:1 below. The frequent use of *higgîd* (9:6,8,18,19; 10:15,16[*bis*]) is one of the techniques employed to heighten the fundamental irony of a young man's unknowing quest for a kingdom: Saul in his innocence asks the man of God to inform (*higgîd*) him about the lost asses, but what he is informed is that he is to be prince (*nāgîd*) over Israel. See also Buber, "Erzählung," 126, 142.

7. *"If we do go."* Here, as in II Sam 18:22, a protasis introduced by *wĕhinnê* has approximately the force of an emphatic conditional clause.

what shall we take . . . ? Saul is concerned about his inability to provide a local dignitary with an appropriate token of greeting (*tĕšûrâ,* see below) before requesting assistance. But the matter of the gift is not mentioned again after this conversation, and the inclusion of an extraneous incident violates the usual economy of Biblical Hebrew narrative. These facts, combined with the interest in the terms "seer" and "prophet" expressed in v 9, raise the question whether originally an attempt was made here to correlate somehow the expression *nābî',* "(What) shall we bring?" with the term *nābî',* "prophet," and thus to explain by the kind of fanciful etymology of which biblical prose is so fond the change of terminology recorded in v 9.

is used up. Hebrew *'āzal,* a verb that is rare in prose. E. Lipiński (*Studies in Aramaic Inscriptions and Onomastics* I [Louvain: Leuven University, 1975] 43-44) cites an instructive parallel from the Sefire treaties of the ninth century B.C., viz. *Sef* I.B.39 (*KAI* 222).

gift. The term *tĕšûrâ* occurs only here in Biblical Hebrew, and the text has been suspected. The versions show confusion but do not suggest an alternative reading. Many commentators would associate the term with *š'r,* "be left over, remain," and translate. "And there is nothing left over to take, etc." But the meaning "gift (of greeting)" is supported by the context and by Rabbinic tradition (see Jastrow, 1703) and is not without philological basis. The best attested meaning of the Hebrew verb *šwr* is "see, look upon." Thus we might understand *tĕšûrâ* as "gift of greeting" on the analogy of Akkadian *tāmartu,* "gift of greeting," a common derivative of *amāru,* "see." (In Akkadian *tāmartu* fundamentally refers to "an occasion of seeing one another," from which it takes the meaning "a gift given upon seeing someone, especially the king," and hence "tribute.") See now S. M. Paul in *Biblica* 59 (1978) 542-544.

8. *I find I have.* Literally, "There is found in my hand. . . ." The expression *nimṣā' bĕyādî* is used in preference to a more common phrase like *yēš lî,* "I have," to suggest that the money seems to have turned up adventitiously, solving the problem of the lack of a suitable gift. The implication is clear: though the travelers themselves are quite unaware of it, their journey is being divinely directed. See further the COMMENT.

a quarter of a shekel. The shekel (*šeqel*) was the basic unit of weight. A shekel of silver probably weighed something less than one-half ounce, and though from time to time it must have varied considerably in purchasing power, we may presume that the gift of a quarter of this amount would have been regarded as neither penurious nor especially munificent.

9. This antiquarian notice (less disruptive here than in its received position between vv 8 and 10) was not part of the original narrative (see the *Textual Note*). But we may not conclude that it derives from a time when *rō'eh*, "seer," was an obsolete term requiring editorial explanation. After all, Samuel is called *hārō'eh* regularly by the Chronicler (I Chron 9:22; 26:28; 29:29). Instead the notice is redactional, intended to harmonize the present tale, in which Samuel is called "seer" and "man of God," with the preceding material, in which he is called "prophet." It is clear, however, that the author of the notice considers *nābî*, "prophet," to be the primary, contemporary designation and that he regards *rō'eh* as somewhat old-fashioned. In this sense, then, the purpose of the notice is to explain an outmoded term that might be confusing to his audience (cf. Ruth 4:7). For *nābî*, "prophet," see the second NOTE at 3:20. *Rō'eh* means quite literally "seer," insofar as it is in origin a participial form of the common Hebrew verb "to see." As in the case of "man of God" (see the NOTE at v 6 above) it lacks the specialized sense of *nābî'* and is instead a generalized term for a soothsayer or diviner.

11. *the ascent to the city*. An "ascent" (*ma'ăleh*) was any ascending pathway. It might have been a slope, a ramp or even a stairway, leading (in this case) to the city gate. For defensive purposes Palestinian cities and villages were most often built on hills, and Ramathaim evidently was no exception.

some girls coming out to draw water. Out of necessity cities were located near springs supplying fresh water, and it was the traditional duty of girls and young women to fetch water daily.

12. *the high place*. A "high place," so called because the Hebrew term (*bāmâ*) implies a hill or other raised ground, was a local area where worship in all its forms took place. The site, which might be open to the air or elaborated with buildings, was often outside the walls of the city, as in the present case (cf. v 14). See further de Vaux, *Ancient Israel* 2.284-288. Deuteronomic theology condemned high places because of its own emphasis on a single, central place of worship. Thus the expression often carries a negative connotation, suggesting non-Yahwistic, syncretistic, or at least illicit cultic practice. The Josianic historian, therefore, praises his patron for destroying the high places (II Kings 23:8-9,19-20) and evaluates other kings accordingly. The present passage with its unflinching association of Samuel and a high place is pre-Deuteronomic in origin and has escaped editorial censorship.

13. *the people will not eat until he comes*. In certain kinds of sacrifice the portions not reserved for the deity were given to the people "to eat before Yahweh" (Deut 12:18). In this case the feast will be delayed until the arrival of Samuel, who is to bless or consecrate the sacrifice, a function otherwise unknown in the Old Testament.

14. *the gate*. See the *Textual Note*. The gate of a walled city was an elaborate structure, providing not only a line of defense at the most vulnerable part of the fortifications but also an arena for a variety of civic activities. It was a meeting place, a market place, and by ancient tradition the place of the dispensation of justice.

Samuel. Abruptly the anonymity of the seer vanishes, and he turns out to be Samuel himself. See the COMMENT.

15-17. With the exception of this parenthesis the entire tale of the lost asses of Kish is told as seen through the eyes of Saul. Here, however, we are supplied with background information that neither Saul nor any mortal man (but Samuel) could have known.

15. *Yahweh had disclosed to Samuel.* Literally, "Yahweh had uncovered Samuel's ear." The idiom implies disclosure of something previously unknown to or even kept secret from the hearer (as in 20:2,12[MT],13; 22:8[*bis*],17) and may be used, as in the present instance, of a revelation to a man by a god (cf. II Sam 7:27).

16. *anoint.* Anointment refers to rubbing or smearing with a sweet-smelling substance. The practice involved a symbolic transfer of sanctity from the deity to an object or person and thus was essentially a sacramental act. The unguent employed was animal fat or, as in the present case, vegetable oil (see the NOTE at 10:1), so that in origin the sacramental principle must have been similar to that of the practice of ritual ingestion of food; that is, the divine virtue, believed to be especially present in living things, was directly transferred to the sanctified individual. There are biblical references to the anointment of altars and other cultic objects. Cultic personnel might also be anointed, and in fact unction came to be regarded as distinctive of and necessary to priestly office (Exod 40:12-15). But in Israel anointing was first of all a royal rite. The Books of Samuel and Kings report the anointing of Saul, David (I Samuel 16), Solomon (I Kings 1:39), and so on. The king was "the anointed one" or "messiah" (Hebrew *māšîaḥ*) of Yahweh. The ceremony was believed to impart something of the sanctity of the national god to the king. Thus after he is anointed Saul is told that "the spirit of Yahweh will rush upon [him]" (10:6; cf. 10:10); and the connection between unction and inspiration is drawn even more closely in David's case (see 16:13).

prince. Hebrew *nāgîd.* The term has an archaic passive form (C. Brockelmann, *Grundriss der vergleichenden Grammatik der semitischen Sprachen* [Berlin: vol. 1, 1908; vol. 2, 1913; reprinted Hildesheim: George Ohms, 1961], §138c) shared by a sizable group of Hebrew nouns of office including, among others, *nābî'*, "one who is nominated; prophet" (see the NOTE at 3:20). Cf. also *māšîaḥ,* "one who is anointed; messiah" (see the preceding NOTE). Most instructive is the common noun *nāśî'*, "chieftain," with the original meaning "one who is raised up, elevated (to office)." Similarly *nāgîd* can be interpreted as "one who is made known, singled out, designated (for office)," that is, "designee." It seems to have referred to (1) someone designated for a particular office who has assumed its duties (i.e. the incumbent in an office) as well as (2) someone who though designated for an office has not yet begun to serve. In the first sense it occurs as the title of officials both priestly (Jer 20:1; Neh 11:11; I Chron 9:11,20; II Chron 31:12,13; 35:8) and military (I Chron 12:28[English 12:27]; 13:1; 27:4), as well as a variety of others (I Chron 26:24; II Chron 28:7). In every case the *nāgîd* is an individual singled out from among others as leader. Accordingly the king seems once to be called *nĕgîd 'am,* "the one designated (from among) the people," in II Kings 20:5. But this is not certain. The expression in II Kings 20:5 is missing from LXX and does not appear in the synoptic passage in Isaiah 38. Nowhere else is a reigning king unambiguously called *nāgîd* (Isa 55:4 is likely but uncertain). Overwhelmingly *nāgîd* is a title attributed to a king *before* he begins to reign (I Sam 9:16; 10:1; 25:30). When applied to a reigning king the reference is to his designation as *nāgîd* before becoming king (II Sam 5:2; 6:21; 7:8[= I Chron 17:7]; I Kings 14:7; and probably 16:2). Thus the term regularly refers to the king-designate. Indeed a king might single out one of his sons as *nāgîd* or "crown prince" to the exclusion of the others (I Kings 1:35; II Chron 11:22). T. N. D. Mettinger (*King and Messiah,* 151-184) has argued plausibly that the responsibility of the reigning king to designate (*lĕhaggîd,* I Kings 1:20) the heir to his throne was the point of origin of the term *nāgîd,* "crown prince," as a royal title (I Kings 1:35). It follows from all of this that Saul will be anointed as king-designate or (crown) prince. He has been singled out from among the people to become king and lead Israel in war. For the significance of anointment as *nāgîd* in the prophetic ideology of kingship, see the COMMENT.

For I have seen . . . has come to me. Compare the strikingly similar language of Exod 3:9: "The cry of the Israelites has come to me, and also I have seen the oppression (*laḥaṣ*) with which the Egyptians are oppressing them."

17. For the syntax, which implies immediacy ("The moment Samuel saw Saul, Yahweh told him . . ."), see the NOTE at v 5 above.

muster. The verb *ʿṣr* commonly means "restrain, hinder" or even "retain, shut in" in Biblical Hebrew. Here, used with the preposition *bĕ-,* it has usually been rendered "rule," since "restrain" is inappropriate and "rule" is conceivable, if "restrain" is understood "in the sense of *coercere imperio*" (Driver). But it is less likely to mean "restrain" in the sense of "coerce" than "retain" in the sense of "gather, assemble, muster," especially in light of the common noun *ʿăṣārâ/ʿăṣeret,* "assembly." The point is that Saul is to be the one who will muster the weak and scattered forces of Israel in a strong army of defense.

18. *"Tell me."* Hebrew *haggîdâ-nāʾ lî.* See the NOTE on "he will advise" at v 6 above. The irony in this question is keen. The audience knows now that Samuel has instructions to designate (*lĕhaggîd,* as in I Kings 1:35) Saul as designee (*nāgîd*). Innocently Saul says *haggîdâ-nāʾ lî,* by which he means only "tell me, inform me" though it might mean "designate me."

20. *these three days.* See the *Textual Note.*

to whom do the riches of Israel belong. Samuel's meaning is as obscure to Saul as it is clear to the audience. Saul is to be king of Israel and therefore owner, in a sense, of all her wealth. Why then should he concern himself about a few stray asses?

21. Saul protests his own unworthiness (cf. 15:17), the customary response of individuals called into divine service in the Bible (Exodus 3-4; etc.). In particular, Saul appeals to the humbleness of his origins. To this should be compared Gideon's expostulation: "But my lord, how shall I free Israel? My thousand is the weakest in Manasseh, and I myself am the humblest in my family!" (Judg 6:15). The exaltation of the humble to positions of power is a common folklore motif (cf. the COMMENT on 2:1-10), which serves to underline the supernatural aspect of certain biblical stories. It is significant that

Saul comes from the humblest clan of the smallest tribe, because it emphasizes the miraculous nature of his rise to the throne.

a Benjaminite. According to the boundary description in Josh 18:11-20 the tribal territory of Benjamin was a little wedge of land centered on the ridge of hills that runs from Jerusalem N to Bethel. Despite its important historical role as a buffer zone between the northern and southern kingdoms, Benjamin was best known in tradition as the smallest of the tribes. In particular the lore about the twelve sons of Jacob remembered Benjamin as the youngest. Thus Saul is astonished at the importance Samuel seems to attribute to him, a member of the humblest tribe.

tribes . . . clan. The traditional social structure of ancient Israel was hierarchical, comprising families, clans, and tribes. The family (*bêt 'āb,* lit. "father's house") was the immediate family of the head of a household, including the wives and children of his married sons. A group of families living in the same vicinity constituted a clan (*mišpāḥâ*) with an independent organization whereby certain political and religious functions were shared. A tribe (*šēbeṭ*) was a group of several clans. For further details, see de Vaux, *Ancient Israel* 1. 4-10. For particulars about Saul's clan, see the NOTE at 10:21.

22. *the chamber.* That is, the "lishka," a room associated with the high place where sacrificial meals were eaten (see the NOTE at 1:18).

24. *had separated the thigh.* Hebrew *wayyārem . . . 'et-haššôq.* This is the so-called "thigh of consecration" (*šôq hattĕrûmâ:* Exod 29:27; Lev 7:34; 10:14,15; Num 6:20), that part of a sacrificial animal (viz. the right rear leg or thigh) reserved for the priests and their families. In Priestly usage the verb *hērîm* means "set apart, separate, reserve" (not "raise up"), as shown by J. Milgrom ("The *šwq htrwmh,*" *Tarbiz* 42 [1973/74] 1-11), and here it describes the separation of the priestly share from the portion of meat. Saul is being treated as if he were a priest! See the COMMENT.

That which remains. That is, the thigh remains, since presumably the rest of the meat has been distributed to the other guests.

25. *on the roof.* The roof was breezy and cool, the appropriate sleeping place for an honored guest.

26. *At the break of dawn.* Literally, "when the dawn arose," contrary to English idiom.

27. *the word of God.* In simplest terms "the word of God" refers to the expressed intention of the deity conveyed to man by some medium, in this case a seer (cf. the NOTE at 3:1). Samuel is keeping his promise of the previous day to send Saul on his way with the information he had come to acquire; but unless the young Benjaminite is very obtuse indeed, his extraordinary treatment on the previous evening will have led him to expect to learn more from Samuel than the whereabouts of the strayed livestock.

10 1. *a vial of oil.* On anointing in general see the NOTE at 9:16, above. In 16:1,13 a horn is used (see the NOTE at 16:1). The vessel in question here is probably a small clay flask or juglet. The ointment itself may be spiced olive oil. A recipe for anointing oil given in Exod 30:22-25 includes oil of myrrh, cinnamon, sweet cane, and cassia in a base of olive oil.

his estate. Hebrew *naḥălātô.* The noun refers to landed property, inalienably held by an individual, whether acquired by inheritance, military victory, feudal grant, or other means. See provisionally P. K. McCarter and R. B. Coote, "The Spatula Inscription from Byblos," *BASOR* 212 (December 1973) 20-21, where we rely on unpublished work of H. O. Forshey. Yahweh's estate, mythically conceived, is the land won in the conquest, hence Israel.

2-6. It is unclear whether one of the events predicted in these verses or the combination of them all is the confirmatory sign to which Samuel refers in the preceding verse. (In the notices about the fulfillment of the predictions in vv 7 and 9, "signs" is plural, but there the meaning is not "confirmatory tokens" but "wondrous events." See the NOTES at vv 7 and 9 below.)

2. *Rachel's Tomb.* According to Gen 35:16-20 and 48:7 Rachel died giving birth to Benjamin while en route from Bethel to Ephrathah. This must be the Benjaminite Ephrathah in the vicinity of Kiriath-jearim (see NOTE to 6:21), as recognized long ago by Franz Delitzsch. See the evidence cited in Cross, *CMHE,* 94-95, n. 16; also Tsevat, "Interpretation of I Samuel 10:2,"; E. Vogt, "Benjamin geboren 'eine Meile' von Ephrata," *Biblica* 56 (1975) 30-36. The glosses in Genesis linking the location to Bethlehem are based on an erroneous identification with Ephrathah of Judah, the home of David's clan (see the NOTE at 17:12) and the site of a present-day "Rachel's Tomb" erected by the Crusaders. The northern locality is intended here (cf. Jer 31:15).

3. *When you pass on.* Hebrew *wĕḥālaptā.* When intransitive the verb usually refers to the passing of something inanimate, something fleeting or transitory. Its use here is most curious, but the textual evidence seems to support the reading.

the Oak of Tabor. Evidently this tree was located near Bethel, but it is not mentioned elsewhere and the exact site is unknown. The text is not altogether certain (see the *Textual Note*). Hebrew *'ēlôn* refers to a great tree, usually marking some kind of a shrine. The translation "oak" is not intended to be precise; "terebinth" is also possible. Based on an old suggestion by H. G. A. Ewald a number of commentators have attempted to associate this tree with the oak mentioned in the notice in Gen 35:8, under which Rebekah's nurse Deborah was buried, and the Palm of Deborah mentioned in Judg 4:5 (Dhorme, Hertzberg), but there is no sound basis for such an identification.

as they go up to God at Bethel. The three men will be on their way to worship at Bethel with kids, bread, and wine to be offered in sacrifice. For the expression *'ālâ 'el hā'ĕlōhîm/yahweh,* "go up to God/Yahweh," meaning "present oneself before God/Yahweh (for purposes of worship, entreaty, etc.)," see Exod 19:3,24; 24:1,12; 32:30; Deut 10:1; etc. On Bethel, see the NOTE at 7:16.

4. *two wave offerings of bread.* "Wave offering," the traditional (originally Rabbinic) translation of *tĕnûpâ,* is somewhat misleading. The ritual involved lifting, not waving, the sacrificial fare "before Yahweh" in ceremonial dedication before reserving it for the priests. See J. Milgrom, "The Alleged Wave Offering in Israel and the Ancient Near East," *IEJ* 22 (1972) 33-38. As in the incident of the consecratory thigh (v 24), therefore, Saul is again being given the priestly share of a sacrifice (cf. Num 18:11; etc.). See the COMMENT.

5. *Gibeath-elohim.* That is, "the Hill of God" (*gib'at hā'ĕlōhîm*), which is

probably the longer name of Gibeah of Benjamin, Saul's home, since people "who had known him previously" (v 11) are there. The identification is also favored by the parenthetical expression, "where there is a Philistine prefect" (see below), which points ahead to 13:3, where the city seems to be understood as Gibeah of Benjamin (see 13:2). But many commentators have rejected this identification: for a list of other proposals see Stoebe.

where there is a Philistine prefect. This notice is immaterial at this point and probably secondary, having been added along with the instructions in v 8 as preparation for c 13. See the NOTES at 10:8 and 13:3.

a band of prophets. The hand that shaped the stories of Samuel and Saul viewed the prophet as a sober mediator between God and man, whose leadership responsibilities were unlimited except by the divine will itself and whose complete integration into the social structure could therefore be taken for granted. But here we encounter another aspect of the phenomenon of prophecy. These prophets, like Samuel, are recipients of divine inspiration, but in them it expresses itself in the form of ecstatic practices of an orgiastic type, which set them apart from other individuals. Examples of such supernormal group behavior abound in the annals of the religions of the world—the case of the various orders of dervishes in Islam is only the most obvious—and on the basis of these parallels one can fill out the scant biblical evidence to give a fairly complete description of an Israelite prophetic troop of the type Saul encounters. Expressions of possession by the spirit of God must have included singing and dancing to the accompaniment of such musical instruments as those listed here in v 5, and the rites may have involved self-flagellation or mutilation as well (cf. I Kings 18:28). In addition we should think of more sedate displays of ecstasy, such as trances and ecstatic fits (cf. 19:22-24), among these several activities, which taken together are collectively called "prophesying" (*mitnabbĕ'îm*). By all accounts such behavior is highly contagious, as Saul himself discovers.

harps, tambourines, clarinets, and lyres. All of these were commonly used in celebrations and processions. The harp (*nēbel*) and lyre (*kinnôr*) were the most popular stringed instruments, while the tambourine (*tōp*), a small double-membraned drum that was carried and beaten with the hand, was the most widely used percussion instrument. The clarinet (*ḥālîl*), though often wrongly translated "flute," was in fact a primitive woodwind, especially associated with occasions of extreme emotionalism. See further E. Werner, *IDB*, s.v. "Musical Instruments."

6. *the spirit of Yahweh will rush upon you.* Hebrew *wĕṣālĕḥâ ʿālêkā rûaḥ yahweh*, a stereotyped expression for divine inspiration in the stories of the martial exploits of Samson and Saul (Judg 14:6,19; 15:14; I Sam 11:6), where the hero is empowered by virtue of Yahweh's spirit to perform wondrous feats of arms. The "spirit of Yahweh" (*rûaḥ yahweh*, more properly the "breath of Yahweh") refers in such a situation to the vital force of the deity, that is, to the invigorating power of God as experienced by a human being. In the passages just noted, therefore, the hero experiences the spirit as an explosive surge of strength. The present case, though it shares the formulaic terminology, is somewhat different, insofar as the onrush of spirit finds expression not in the heroic

animation of the warrior but in prophetic ecstasy instead (so 10:10; cf. also 16:14 and the NOTE there). See further the NOTE at 16:13. On *ṣlḥ,* "rush (upon)," see H. Tawil in *JBL* 95 (1976) 405-413.

you will . . . be turned into another man. Hebrew *wĕnehpaktā lĕʾîš ʾaḥēr.* The reception of inspiration was believed to involve a loss of self, or rather, the emergence of a new self.

7. The meaning of this instruction is: surrender yourself to any impulse in the assurance that it is of divine origin. For a different use of the idiom "whatever your hand finds" see 25:8.

these signs. "Signs" in this case means "wondrous things," as in the hendiadytic combination *ʾôtôt ûmôpĕtîm,* "signs and wonders" = "wondrous signs" (Deut 4:34; etc.), and has nothing to do with Samuel's prediction of a confirmatory sign in v 1 above. See the NOTES at 10:2-6 above and 10:9 below.

8. This verse is editorial and secondary. Its purpose is to prepare the reader for the account of the rejection of Saul in 13:7b-15. See also the second NOTE at 10:5 above.

Gilgal. See the NOTES at 11:14; 13:4.

holocausts. See the NOTE at 6:14.

communion offerings. Hebrew *zibḥê šĕlāmîm,* i.e. offerings of a common meal with the deity. These were the common blood sacrifices, differing from the holocausts in that the victims were not offered whole but in part, the remainder being eaten by the priests or supplicants themselves.

9. *God gave him another heart.* Hebrew *wayyahăpok lô ʾĕlōhîm lēb ʾaḥēr,* lit. "God turned another heart to him." Compare the turning of Saul into another man in v 6 above; the two expressions are about equivalent in import. The present statement is rather curious at this point, and its position in the text has been questioned. Hertzberg, for example, moves it to the end of v 10.

all these signs came to pass that same day. This is probably a summary that has replaced the recitation of the first two predicted events. "Signs," as in v 7 (see the NOTE there), here refers to "wondrous things," not the sign promised to Saul in 10:1 as a token of confirmation.

11-12. These verses provide an etiology of a current expression, viz. "Is Saul, too, among the prophets?" A second, different explanation of the origin of this saying is given in 19:19-24. Note that although both passages speculate about the origin of the saying, neither gives any direct information about its meaning. That is, neither passage explains the way the expression was used or with what purpose. Yet we may assume that it *was* in common use in the time of the writer; indeed in v 12 it is called a *māšāl,* "proverb." This need occasion no surprise: a familiar saying requires no explanation to those who know and use it, as the original audience of this material evidently did. The modern reader, however, can only guess at the meaning of the proverb. In doing so we must give close attention to the structure of the question itself. It is the name Saul that is marked by the intensive particle *gam.* Thus the force of the expression must be, "Is Saul, too, among the prophets?" that is, "Is even Saul (in addition to others) among the prophets?" In common use this saying may have been applied to situations involving participation in a particular group or activity by an individual who for one reason or another would not have been expected to participate. It may have thus implied that such a group had absorbed everyone, even the least likely person. Such a saying might easily have arisen from popular familiarity with Saul's reputation as an antagonist of the prophets. When someone would find an unlikely individual involved in some group, therefore, he would say, "Is Saul, too, among the prophets?" Other recent conjectures include those of Eppstein, "Was Saul among the Prophets?" and Sturdy, "Original Meaning."

12. *one of them.* Does this refer to one of the bystanders or one of the prophets themselves?

"And who is their father?" This cryptic question has no obvious meaning. The commentaries are filled with speculation, based sometimes on the reading "his father" (see the *Textual Note*) and sometimes on the present reading; but no suggestion yet proposed is entirely satisfying. It may be helpful to recall that the leader of a group of prophets was called "Father" by his followers (II Kings 2:12; 6:21; 13:14). Perhaps, then, "And who is their father?" implies "And who (but Saul himself) is their leader?" That is, it is a reply to the question, "Is Saul, too, among the prophets?" signifying "Yes, indeed! In fact he is their leader!"

13-16. Saul's concealment of his special status from his family may be compared to the similar behavior of Samson (Judg 14:4,6; cf. 14:16). What reason Saul had for his secrecy is not immediately apparent. (Jewish tradition records that the reason was humility: see, for example, the Midrash Tanḥuma, *Wayyiqrā'* §4.)

14. *his uncle.* Hebrew *dôdô.* It is surprising to find Saul's uncle here instead of Kish, his father. If there was something in the story to prepare us for this, it has been lost. But the primary point remains: Saul keeps the secret of the kingdom even from his own kinsman. Is this Ner (14:50)? D. R. Ap-Thomas ("Saul's 'Uncle,'") has proposed a very different interpretation of these events. With reference to the notice in 10:5 about the Philistine prefect at Gibeah he argues that *dôd* here means "(Philistine) governor" and that Saul is concealing his appointment from the Philistines as a matter of military discretion.

COMMENT

Saul makes his first appearance in the Bible as an agreeable young man, motivated only by a sense of family duty, unassuming, deferential, and, as far as we can see, without high ambition. He is a private citizen from a mountain town in Benjamin, and the rather quaint tale of his search for the lost asses of Kish provides relief from the public affairs of Israel that so dominated the preceding material. To be sure the audience has not forgotten that a king is about to be crowned and can see in the humble beginnings of the story the promise of a lofty finish, but the disclosure of Saul's election is made under such commonplace circumstances as to create a false atmosphere of inconsequentiality. The dutiful son of a man of property searches in vain for some strayed asses and as a last resort stops in a remote city to inquire of the local seer. Such is the basic plan of the story. Yet behind this unremarkable sequence of events a higher purpose is working itself out. Saul's journey has brought him unawares into public life. In Yahweh's name the seer anoints him prince over Israel, king-designate of all the tribes.

It is this tension between the ordinary and the extraordinary, the mundane and the supermundane, that animates the little tale and raises it above the level of an entertaining but ordinary vignette. Saul, the hero and the only figure with whom the account is really concerned, is innocently blind to the reality behind the appearance. The process of discovery that he undergoes, his growth from simplicity to awareness, is shared by the audience, and thus the story finds its interest. We are not told that he was astonished to find himself expected by the seer, but we may assume it. There is no doubt that the unexplained remark about all the riches of Israel sets the young man thinking about himself, for in his confusion he protests his own insignificance; but to his query, "Then why have you spoken to me this way?" there is no reply. Instead he finds himself at a sacrificial banquet as the honored guest, served a special portion that has been reserved for him! The process of disclosure is completed the next morning when Saul is anointed prince over Israel. Now he hears the word of God (9:27) and knows.

As we share in Saul's self-discovery, the story provides us with other clues to the momentous reality that underlies the seemingly trivial circumstances. At first glance the category of accident seems to play a major part —the asses are lost by misfortune; the travelers fortuitously stop within sight of the city of an honored seer; and so on. But we come quickly to suspect that it is not chance that is guiding events. Behind all of these apparently accidental occurrences the hand of Providence may be discerned. An excellent example of the subtlety with which this is conveyed to the audience is the incident of the quarter shekel (9:7-8,10). The lack of a suitable gift threatens at the last moment to prevent Saul from consulting the seer, but a bit of silver turns up in the servant's possession as if by accident (see the NOTE at 9:8). It is no accident. And there is no reason to report such an incident except as a clue to the providential direction of the entire adventure.

As we have already implied, the story's creative tension between appearance and reality is reflected in the character of the king-designate himself. Saul, although he bears physical signs of divine favor (NOTE to 9:2; cf. the NOTE at 10:23) that might be recognized by a discerning observer, is only a youth, and his condition in life is hardly auspicious. He is of Benjamin, the smallest of the tribes of Israel, and of Matri (10:21), the humblest of the clans of Benjamin. Yet here again appearances prove deceptive: Saul will be king. The fact that these are not ordinary circumstances is thus more strongly underlined. A man from little Benjamin will be king of all Israel! Yahweh, who exalts the meek (see the COMMENT on 2:1-10), must have done this!

Saul is now Yahweh's anointed and as such is entitled to the sacral privileges of the recipient of that distinction. Twice he is given sacrificial portions of food usually reserved for priests (see the NOTES at 9:24 and 10:4), and this points tellingly to his new status, for Israelite kingship had an important sacerdotal aspect (cf. Ps 110:4; etc.) that seems to have been refuted only in postmonarchical times.

But the basic stratum of the present story, which is free from the kind of searching examination of the royal office that we encountered in earlier material, seems to derive from the traditional lore of the monarchical period. Moreover, the narrative features outlined above reflect, according to the opinion of many modern scholars, the peculiar genius of the Israelite storyteller. That is, the story of the handsome young man who, seeking lost asses, finds a kingdom, is an old folk tale. This assessment must be correct at one level. The theme is certainly worthy of a folk tale, and other features typical of the genre are here, including the fantastic nature of many events and especially the anonymity of people and places that characterizes the beginning of the story.[1] But further reading exposes an irregularity in the fabric of the account that bears on this assessment.[2] The "man of God" or "seer" of vv 6-13 turns out to be Samuel himself in vv 14*ff*. While at the beginning of the story he goes unnamed and Saul and the servant do not recognize him, at the end Saul refers to him as though known to everyone (10:14). The anonymous seer is a suitable folklore character, but the famous prophet is not. If this is a folk tale at base, it has been overlaid with other material. The nameless city has been identified with Ramathaim, the nameless seer with Samuel. Furthermore and most especially, the concept of anointment as *nāgîd* or "prince" over Israel has found its way into the account.[3] This can hardly be considered a folkloristic element, since as we shall see, it belongs to a series of passages that express an important part of the prophetic ideology of the royal office. The introduction of all these features into the story shows that it too received reworking in the process of its inclusion in the prophetic history of the rise of monarchy in Israel.

The focus of the story in its revised form is the anointing of Saul to the

[1] The classic formulation of this position is that of Gressmann, esp. 33-35. Gressmann stresses the characteristic folklore elements of timelessness and the anonymity of people and places as well as the fabulous theme and generally unrealistic atmosphere.

[2] For detailed lists of discrepancies in the narrative see Hertzberg, Stoebe; cf. also Birch, "Anointing of Saul," 56.

[3] See Boecker, *Beurteilung der Anfänge des Königtums*, 13-14; Birch, "Anointing of Saul," 61-66; Richter, *Vorprophetischen Berufungsberichte*, 13-29.

office of *nāgîd,* "prince, king-designate" (see the NOTE at 9:16), by the prophet Samuel. From the prophetic point of view the designation of an heir to the throne (*nāgîd*) was a divine prerogative, and the unchecked practice of blood succession, because it seemed to interfere with Yahweh's free choice of the ruler, was one of the things that made kingship hateful. Reference to appointment as *nāgîd* is made again and again in prophetic speeches about the making and unmaking of kings: I Sam 9:16; 10:1; 13:14; II Sam 5:2 (where a prophet does not speak, but an old oracle is quoted); I Kings 14:7; 16:2; cf. II Sam 7:8. As these passages show, Yahweh was believed to appoint whom he pleased as "prince," and conversely such an appointment was considered prerequisite to office. Because Saul was the first king, his kingship might be regarded as archetypal and thus from the prophetic viewpoint could not have been flawed by omission of the sacred ritual of designation by a prophet. So it was that an old story describing the revelation of his future kingship by a seer was developed into the present account. Saul has been designated "prince" and his election as king can proceed.

Formally Saul's anointment as *nāgîd* is couched in a stereotyped pattern of call to office visible also in the calls of Gideon (Judg 6:11-16) and Moses (Exodus 3-4) and, in less complete form, in the several prophetic vocation accounts of the Books of Kings.[4] This comes as no surprise, since we are already aware of our narrator's regard for prophetic vocation as an ideal. Nor, then, is it really surprising to find Saul's inspiration express itself in prophetic fashion. After leaving Samuel and arriving in Gibeath-elohim, Saul is possessed by the spirit of God and to the confusion of old acquaintances joins a band of ecstatics as they "prophesy." The point is not that Saul has become a prophet—he is never called by the title—but that he has experienced inspiration legitimately and is now open and receptive to the spirit of Yahweh. In anticipation of later events we might add that this kind of openness to the supernatural has its hazards. Saul's receptivity to visitations of spirit will bring him little happiness.

In biblical literature the reception of a divine call to office is usually depicted as a thoroughly private experience, and the case of Saul is no exception. The anointment described here is not public. Indeed a special point is made of the privacy of the act: the servant is sent on ahead (9:27), leaving Saul alone with Samuel. In fact it is accurate to speak of a *secret anointing,* for not only does Saul receive his consecration in private, but also he avoids public disclosure of "the matter of the kingdom," concealing his new status even from his family (10:16). However this secrecy

[4] Both Birch and Richter (see the preceding footnote) have developed this point in detail, and the form-critical discussion need not be repeated here. Note that Richter considers the vocation accounts of Saul as ancestral to those of the prophets, whereas we have found it to be a retrojection of a later pattern on an early figure.

motif is finally to be understood,[5] it functions in the larger story of Saul's rise as a device that permits a prior anointing of Saul without upstaging his dramatic revelation in the materials that follow. His open frenzy at Gibeath-elohim adumbrates his inspired heroism in the Ammonite wars (see 10:27b-11:15) but only in an incomplete way, and his public secrecy about the anointing assures that no one will suspect his election until the lots have fallen in the following episode.

[5] The fact of the matter is that it has never been fully explained. Saul's behavior is certainly related to that of Samson, who hides his inspired feats of strength from his parents (see the NOTE at 10:13-16), and the theme may stand somehow in the background of the much discussed secrecy motif of the Gospel of Mark.

XIII. THE ROYAL LOTTERY (10:17-27a)

10 17 Samuel summoned the people to Yahweh at Mizpah. 18 He
said to the Israelites, "Yahweh, the god of Israel, has spoken thus: 'I
brought Israel up from Egypt and rescued you from the clutches of
Egypt and of all the kings who oppressed you, 19 but you today have
rejected your god, the one who delivers you from all your ills and
hardships, and have said, "No! You shall set a king over us!" Now
then, take up your positions before Yahweh by your tribes and your
clans!' "

20 Then Samuel presented all the tribes of Israel, and the tribe of
Benjamin was taken. 21 So he presented the tribe of Benjamin by
clans, and the clan of Matri was taken. So he presented the clan of
Matri man by man, and Saul, the son of Kish, was taken. But when he
looked for him, he could not be found.

22 So once again [Samuel] inquired of Yahweh, "Has the man
come here?"

"There he is," said Yahweh, "hidden among the gear!" 23 So
[Samuel] ran and brought him out; and when he took his place
among the people, he was taller than all the rest of the people from
his shoulder upward!

24 Then Samuel said to all the people, "Do you see him whom
Yahweh has chosen—that there is no one else like him among all the
people?" And all the people shouted and said, "Long live the king!"

25 Then Samuel declared the Law of the Kingdom to the people. He
wrote it in a document and laid it up before Yahweh.

When Samuel sent the people away, each to his own home, 26 Saul,
too, went to his home in Gibeah, and with him went those stalwart
men whose hearts Yahweh had touched. 27a But there were worthless
men who said, "How can this fellow save us?" They spurned him and
brought him no gift.

TEXTUAL NOTES

10 17. *the people* So MT. LXX: "all the people."

18. *Israel* So MT. LXX: "the Israelites," under the influence of the previous reference.

from the clutches of Egypt So MT, as in Judg 6:9. LXX "from the clutches of Pharaoh, king of Egypt," is probably a simple expansion.

19. *your god* So MT. LXX, *ton theon = h'lhym,* "God."

No! So LXX, Vulg., Syr., Targ. (cf. 8:19 MT). MT has *lw,* "to him." Thus, ". . . you . . . have rejected your god . . . and have said *to him.* . . ."

and your clans Reading *wlmšpḥtykm* on the basis of LXX[B], *kai kata tas phylas hymōn,* as required by v 21. MT, LXX[L] have *wl'lpykm,* "and (by) your thousands."

21. *by clans* Reading *lmšpḥwt* with LXX. MT (*qĕrê*) has "by *its* clans" (cf. Josh 7:16). The *kĕtîb* of MT is *lmšpḥtw,* and the *w* may have arisen from dittography of the following conjunction.

In the middle of the verse MT has suffered a long haplography. We read *wtlkd mšpḥt mṭry wyqrb 't mšpḥt mṭry lgbrym* (cf. Josh 7:17) *wylkd š'wl bn qyš* on the basis of LXX[BA] (cf. LXX[L])—hence our rendering, ". . . and the clan of Matri was taken. So he presented the clan of Matri man by man, and Saul, the son of Kish, was taken." The eye of the scribe of MT jumped from the first *mṭry* to the second, leaving (after subsequent loss of the now meaningless *lgbrym,* "man by man") *wtlkd mšpḥt hmṭry wylkd š'wl bn qyš,* ". . . and the clan of Matri was taken. And Saul, the son of Kish, was taken."

21b-23. We follow LXX in reading certain verbs in this verse and the next two as singular in contradiction to MT's plurals (". . . when *they* looked for him . . . *they* inquired of Yahweh . . . *they* ran and brought him out . . ."). Samuel is the implied subject of each, and this is made explicit once in LXX (in v 22), probably secondarily. In English, too, it is necessary to include "Samuel" once or twice to avoid confusion. The plurals of MT represent another means of surmounting the problem.

22. *"Has the man come here?"* LXX *ei erchetai ho anēr entautha = hb' h'yš 'd hlm.* MT has *hb' 'wd hlm 'yš,* which Driver renders, "Is there still (i.e. besides ourselves) any one come hither?" But probably the original of MT was *hb' 'd hlm* (*'ad-hălōm,* as in II Sam 7:18) *h'yš,* "Has the man come here?" When *'ad* was misinterpreted as *'ôd,* leaving an unintelligible question ("Has the man come here again?"), the definite article was dropped from *'yš* to give the sense supposed by Driver.

24. *Do you see . . .* MT *harrĕ'îtem,* as also in 17:25 (cf. the *Textual Note* to 1:6). See GK §22s.

among all the people So MT (*bkl h'm*). LXX has instead *en pasin hymin,* reflecting *bklkm,* "among you all." Choice between these variants is arbitrary.

shouted MT *wyr'w,* for which LXX has *kai egnōsan,* i.e. *wyd'w,* "(and all the people) knew." This is another case of simple confusion of *r* and *d,* which were virtually indistinguishable throughout much of the history of their use. Cf. the *Textual Note* to v 27a below.

25. *the Law of the Kingdom* So MT (*mšpṭ hmlkh*), LXX^{L}, OL. LXX^{B} *to dikaiōma tou basileōs* = *mšpṭ hmlk,* "the Law of the King," is reminiscent of 8:9,11. MT is to be preferred as *lectio difficilior.*

in a document So LXX. MT, "in *the* document," reading the same consonantal text. Note also that MT could be translated, "in *a certain* document."

each to his own home LXX, 4QSam^{a} read, *"and they went* each to his own *place."*

26. *with him* So MT. Omitted by LXX, which instead has "with Saul" at the end of the verse.

stalwart men Reading *bny hḥyl* with 4QSam^{a} and LXX *huioi dynameōn.* MT, omitting *bny* after the somewhat similar sequence *'mw,* has *hḥyl* alone (thus, ". . . and with him went *the army* . . .").

Yahweh So 4QSam^{a} (*yh*[*w*]*h*), LXX. MT: "God."

27a. After "gift" MT adds *wyhy kmḥryš,* "And he was like someone who keeps silent." But this is to be corrected to *wyhy kmw ḥdš* and read with what follows. See the *Textual Note* to "About a month later" at 10:27b-11:1 below. The source of the corruption in MT is again the confusion of *r* and *d,* as in v 24 above.

NOTES

10 17. Samuel summons the people to Yahweh; that is, he calls a holy convocation. The purpose is to consult Yahweh to determine his choice for king. Thus the passage follows up on the instructions given Samuel in 8:22: "Listen to [the people] and make them a king!" The events in 9:1-10:16 have intervened off stage, but the present material continues the story of the popular demand for a king.

Mizpah. See the NOTE at 7:6. Again the location of the pan-Israelite assembly at Mizpah betrays the provenance of the passage. This episode derives from the same prophetic hand that shaped the story of Samuel and reported the people's willful demand for a king. See the COMMENT.

18. *Yahweh . . . has spoken thus.* The prophetic messenger formula (see the NOTE at 2:27). The phrase marks what follows as an oracle of Yahweh. More specifically, the succeeding remarks take the form of an oracle of judgment. That is, an accusation contrasting the good things Yahweh has done for the people (v 18) with their rebellious behavior (v 19a) is followed by an announcement of the response Yahweh is making ("Now then . . ." v 19b). These are the formal elements that appear in one arrangement or another in every judgment oracle (see C. Westermann, *Basic Forms of Prophetic Speech,*

tr. Hugh Clayton White [Philadelphia: Westminster, 1967] *passim*). Notably, however, in the formal position of the announcement of judgment itself, stand instructions for the choice of the king. For the implications, see the COMMENT.

18-19. *I . . . but you.* The pronouns stand in the emphatic position at the beginning of each clause, thus highlighting the contrast between what Yahweh has done and what Israel has done.

18. *I brought Israel up . . . the kings who oppressed you.* Israel's good treatment by Yahweh is recited in stereotyped phrases. (Note that the closest parallel by far to the language here is that of Judg 6:7-10, a very late insertion in the Gideon story [missing in 4QJudges[a], an unpublished fragment from Qumran Cave 4; see Boling, *Judges*, NOTE at 6:7-10].) Inclusion of such references to the Exodus and the premonarchical era in this context effectually emphasizes the sufficiency of non-royal rule in the spirit of cc 7 and 8. On the significance of the verb *lḥṣ*, "oppress," see the NOTE on "the one who delivers you" in v 19 below.

the kings. Hebrew *hammamlākôt* instead of the more common *hammĕlākîm*, as in Phoenician (*mmlkt*). Cf. Dahood, *Psalms II*, AB 17, 151, and the literature cited there. The recognition of this meaning seems to go back to Caspari. Note that *hammamlākôt* is construed (correctly) with a masculine participle (*hallōḥăṣîm*), a fact that confused earlier commentators, who read the noun as "kingdoms."

19. *you . . . have rejected your god.* The accusation is pointedly reminiscent of 8:7.

today. We need not conclude that the Mizpah assembly occurred on the same day as the demand for a king. Hebrew *hayyôm*, "today," may mean no more than "now, at this time," in a general reference to current events.

the one who delivers you. Hebrew *'ăšer-hû' môšîa' lākem;* see Driver for parallels. The rather unusual construction emphasizes that in the writer's view Yahweh and no other is properly the savior (*môšîa'*) of Israel. The syntax warrants such a paraphrase as: "Today you have rejected your god—he who alone is the one to deliver you. . . ." Thus it anticipates and casts a shadow over the search of the people of Jabesh-gilead for "one to deliver us" (*môšîa' 'ōtānû*) in 11:3, where the deliverer turns out to be Saul, the king. Similarly, the use of *lḥṣ*, "oppress," in v 18 above looks ahead to the oppression of Israel by another king, viz. Nahash (see 10:27b). The narrator's choice of words, then, is an important part of his preparation for the episode to follow. In the past, he says, when kings oppressed Israel, Yahweh was the deliverer. In their ingratitude the people have forgotten this, and in their demand for a king they have rejected Yahweh. We are thus prepared to give a wholly unfavorable interpretation to the story of a human deliverer's rescue of Israel from the oppression of a king.

"No! You shall set a king over us!" The reference is to the events of c 8 in general and to 8:19 in particular.

19b-21bα. Saul is chosen king by lot. Though the word "lot" (*gôrāl*) is not used here, the technical terminology of lot casting may be discerned. When the people have taken up their positions before Yahweh, i.e. before some place where he was believed to be cultically present, Samuel presents (*hiqrîb*) them (cf. Exod 29:4,8; 40:12,14; etc., all of which refer to the presentation of individuals at the entrance to the Tabernacle) by tribes, clans, and individuals, and lots are cast among them until the king is selected ("taken," *nilkad*). The outcome of the lottery was believed to be divinely determined. For further details see the NOTES at 14:40-42.

19. *tribes . . . clans.* For the social organization of ancient Israel see the NOTE at 9:21.

21. *the clan of Matri.* The name of Saul's clan (*maṭrî*) is mentioned nowhere else, a situation that has led to sporadic unsuccessful attempts to emend the text.

22. *So once again* [*Samuel*] *inquired of Yahweh.* Hebrew *wayyišʾal ʿôd bĕyahweh.* The lot casting was a kind of inquiry, but here Samuel requests (and receives) an oracle. Here again we find wordplay involving the name Saul (*šāʾûl*) and the verb "ask, inquire" (*šāʾal*). Samuel asks Yahweh for the man, who is *ipso facto* "one asked" (*šāʾûl*) of Yahweh. Cf. the NOTES at 1:27,28, and 8:10. We have seen the name *šāʾûl* "explained" four ways: (i) as "one requested" of God by Hannah; (ii) as "one dedicated" to Yahweh by Hannah; (iii) as "one demanded" of Samuel (and Yahweh) by the people; and now (iv) as "one inquired after" by Samuel. See further the COMMENT.

the gear. Hebrew *hakkēlîm,* which can refer to almost any kind of equipment or paraphernalia, so that exactly where Saul was hiding is something we cannot know with certainty. He may have been concealed in a stockpile of weapons or a store of cultic utensils or, as many translators have supposed, a collection of baggage.

23. *he was taller.* Cf. 9:2. Saul's kingly stature is unmistakable, and like his good looks (NOTE at 9:2) it was a mark of divine favor. Saul literally "stands out" among the people.

24. *him whom Yahweh has chosen.* Cf. 16:8,9,10; II Sam 6:21; I Kings 8:16; etc. In biblical tradition David is preeminently the chosen one of Yahweh, but at this point in the history of the kingdom the slogan is applicable to Saul. Cf. also Deut 17:14. See further the NOTE at 15:23b.

"Long live the king!" Or rather, "Let the king live!" (*yĕḥî hammelek*), a phrase used throughout the historical books of the Bible to express the popular acclamation of the king (I Kings 1:25,34,39; II Kings 11:12 = II Chron 23:11).

25. *the Law of the Kingdom.* It is difficult to disassociate this "Law of the Kingdom" (*mišpaṭ hammĕlūkâ*) from the "justice of the king" (*mišpaṭ hammelek*) of 8:11-18, as the textual tradition of LXX bears witness (see the *Textual Note*). Smith, for example, explains that, "The document [describing 'the justice of the king'] is laid up before Yahweh as a testimony, so that when [the people] complain of tyranny they can be pointed to the fact that they have brought it upon themselves." But it seems more likely in the present circumstances that the people are advised of the regulations under which the new kingdom will operate and thus that *mišpāṭ* here means "law, ordinance" or even "constitution" rather than "justice" as in c 8. We might also compare Deut 17:18, where it is said of the king that, "When he sits on his royal throne, he shall write for himself in a document a copy of this law, which is in the keeping of the Levitical priests"; but the law referred to there is "the Teaching" (*hattôrâ*), i.e. the Deuteronomic legal corpus itself. It is probable that the

Law of the Kingdom referred to in the present passage is a lost or unidentified document that prescribed the operation of the kingdom. What privileges it granted king and people and what limitations it imposed on each we cannot know. It is true, however, that the very existence of such a document implies a certain regulation of the monarchy according to principles deriving, in the view of the present story, from the prophet Samuel.

26,27a. *stalwart men . . . worthless men.* The contrast between *bĕnê haḥayil* and *bĕnê bĕliyya'al* is deliberately drawn. The former expression may mean soldiers or warriors ("the sons of strength, the sons of the army"), but it specifically connotes loyalty: the *bĕnê haḥayil* are those men who may be depended upon for loyal service (cf. esp. II Sam 2:7; I Kings 1:52: also I Sam 14:52; 18:17; II Sam 13:28; etc.). On the other hand the *bĕnê bĕliyya'al,* lit. "sons of worthlessness," are just what the designation suggests, scoundrels and riffraff (cf. 2:12 above); and a traitor or disloyal individual is often called *ben/'îš bĕliyya'al* (II Sam 20:1; etc.).

26. *whose hearts Yahweh had touched.* Hebrew *'ăšer nāga' yahweh bĕlibbām,* a unique expression.

27a. *this fellow.* Hebrew *zeh,* contemptuously. Cf. 21:16. GK §136b.

They spurned him. The Hebrew verb *bzh* means "show contempt for, despise" and often implies repudiation (Gen 25:34) or a refusal or rejection of loyalty (II Sam 6:16; 12:9,10).

gift. Hebrew *minḥâ* often refers to tribute paid to a king by people under his sway (Judg 3:15; etc.). We have no other evidence for a gift of homage following the election of a (new) king, but this is certainly the issue at stake here. To fail to bring a gift is to refuse fealty.

COMMENT

The secret choice of Yahweh is now publicly disclosed: the sacred lot designates Saul, the son of Kish, with all the tribes looking on. Israel receives her king amid the acclamation of the people, and the tension between the seen and the unseen that animated the preceding section evaporates. To be sure, the old state of affairs continues for a moment as Saul lies "hidden among the gear," his new identity known only to Yahweh and Samuel; but when the young giant is brought out to stand among his subjects, his royal qualities are there for all to see. Some may still question his ability to rule Israel, but none can deny that he is the chosen king.

The account is a continuation of the story in 8:1-22, which concluded with Samuel's dismissal of the people after he had been instructed by Yahweh to "Listen to them and make them a king!" (8:22). Now Samuel reconvenes the people to carry out the instruction. The present section also shares the spirit of cc 7 and 8. The place of convocation is Mizpah, as in 7:5*ff* (see the NOTES at 7:6 and 10:17), and Samuel, the prophet, presides over the assembly. Nor does the old man miss the opportunity to berate the people, as he reminds them once again of Yahweh's past kindnesses and their own ingratitude (vv 18-19a). All of these things mark the present episode as a part of the prophetic narrative of the story of Samuel and the rise of kingship, into which all the older materials, such as the tale of the lost asses of Kish in its original form, have been absorbed and to which all subsequent (esp. Deuteronomistic) materials have been appended.

Whether an older source can be discerned even here is a matter for debate.[1] Undoubtedly the tradition of Saul's imposing height was an old one, and his presentation to the people in v 24 seems to lack any pejorative overtone. Nor indeed is there anything necessarily "anti-monarchical" about the procedure of his election. The use of the sacred lot guarantees the freedom of Yahweh's choice, but this is no objection. Saul was also freely chosen by Yahweh in the old story of the lost asses of Kish, and since he is the first king the question of blood succession simply does not arise. So we cannot rule out the possibility that our prophetic narrator was working with traditional materials here.

If so, however, he has cast those materials in a most unfavorable light. This he accomplished by the use of more than one literary device. First of all, as remarked upon in the NOTES, the election is prefaced with an oracle delivered by Samuel, which is formally a prophetic judgment speech.[2] Precisely in the position where an acquaintance with such forms of speech leads us to expect an announcement of judgment we find the instructions for the election of the king (v 19b). It would be overstating the case only slightly to say that this arrangement implies that the gift of a king is a kind of punishment. Certainly it is here thought of as a kind of negative judgment or even curse (see the COMMENT on 8:1-22) which the people have brought upon themselves. We might paraphrase as follows: Yahweh has protected the people unfailingly since the Exodus (v 18). He alone is their deliverer (see the NOTE at v 19). Yet they have rejected him and demanded an earthly king (v 19a). Well then, they shall have their king (v 19b), and (it is implied) this will be punishment enough!

In this light the similarity between the narrative of Saul's selection by lot and the accounts found elsewhere in the Bible of the use of the lottery

[1] Eissfeldt (*Komposition,* 7) argues for a source division of the material, distinguishing between an account of Saul's election by lot (10:17-$21b_{\alpha}$) and an (earlier) account of proclamation by reason of Saul's stature ($21b\beta$-27). In this conclusion he is partly followed by Noth (*ÜS,* 54-60) and Birch (*Rise of the Israelite Monarchy,* 42-54).

[2] See especially the NOTE at v 18. Birch ("Choosing of Saul") is to be credited both with recognizing the formal structure of 10:17-19 and with demonstrating its non-Deuteronomistic character.

to determine a hidden offender becomes significant. The passages in question are Joshua 7 and I Sam 14:38-44—the only other detailed reports of the use of the sacred lots in the Bible. The formal similarities among the three passages are striking, but in the other examples the purpose of the lot casting is to discover an unknown guilty individual, in the one case Achan and in the other Jonathan. While it is certainly true that lot casting was used for other purposes than the exposure of a criminal (including, indeed, the designation of individuals for office), the combination of features that appears here—an oracle of judgment followed by the injunction to cast the lots—casts a shadow over Saul's election. Again it would be overstating the case to say that all of this means Saul is guilty of something—that will come later—but there is a clear if subtle implication that he is an offending party by virtue of the election itself.

As if he were somehow aware of these things, Saul hides; so that when his lot is taken, he cannot be found (v 21). But we are not told *why* he hides. Is his motive modesty (cf. 9:21) or timidity? As we have already remarked (NOTE to 10:13-16), Rabbinic Judaism did in fact regard him as a model of humility, at least partly on the authority of this passage. Probably, however, to seek Saul's motive is to miss the point. The purpose for which this little incident is told is wordplay, and its chief interest is Saul's name. Samuel inquires of (*šā'al*) Yahweh, "Has the man come here?" When the man is found, then, he is *šā'ûl,* "the one asked (of Yahweh)," that is, "Saul" (see the NOTE at 10:22). But in any case this turn of events does not present Saul as a bold and eager aspirant to the new office. Yet it does serve the purposes of the drama, insofar as it preserves until the climactic moment the anonymity of the king-designate in spite of his conspicuous height; for once they have set eyes on him the people, as we have said, cannot refrain from acknowledging his reign. "Long live the king!"

Finally, however, we should note with Wellhausen (and others before him) that "Saul is at this point only king *de jure;* he does not become king *de facto* until after he has proved himself."[3] The proving of Saul is the subject of the next section.

[3] *Prolegomena,* 250.

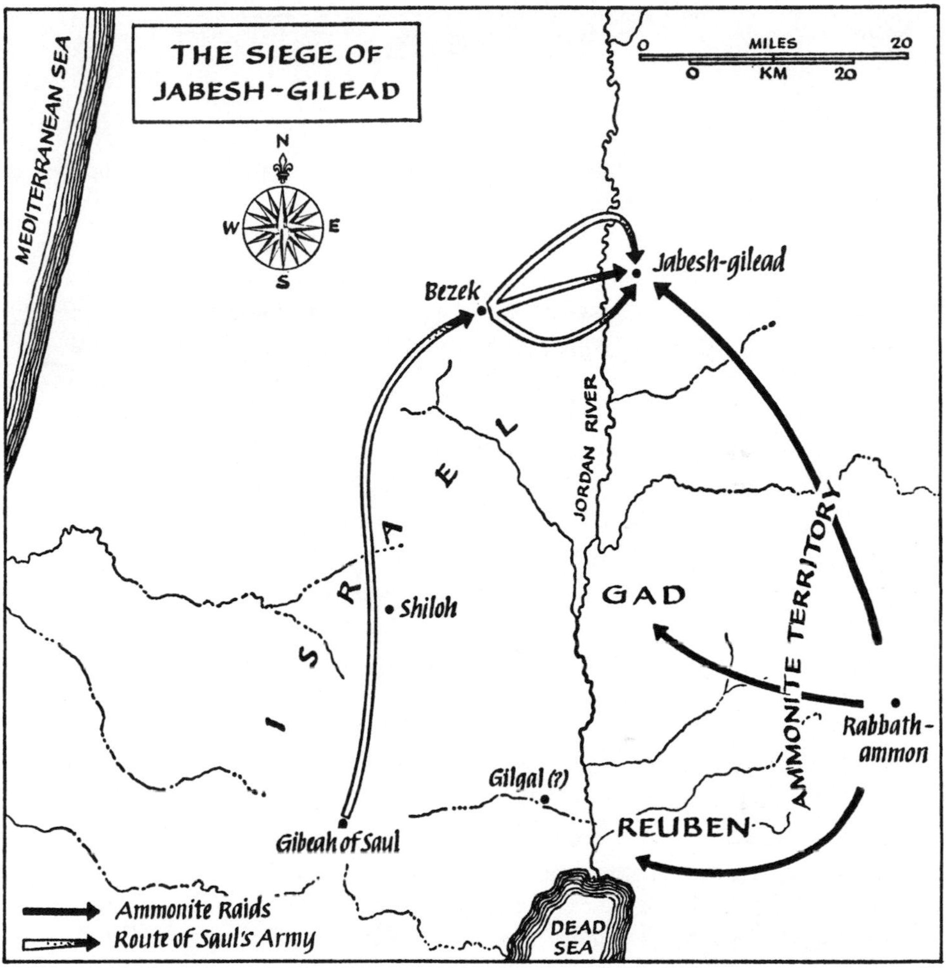
THE SIEGE OF JABESH-GILEAD
MEDITERRANEAN SEA
N
W
E
S
0 MILES 20
0 KM 20
Jabesh-gilead
Bezek
JORDAN RIVER
ISRAEL
Shiloh
GAD
AMMONITE TERRITORY
Rabbath-ammon
Gilgal (?)
REUBEN
Gibeah of Saul
DEAD SEA
Ammonite Raids
Route of Saul's Army

XIV. THE PROVING OF SAUL
(10:27b-11:15)

10 27b Now Nahash, the king of the Ammonites, had been oppressing the Gadites and the Reubenites grievously, gouging out the right
eye of each of them and allowing Israel no deliverer. No men of the
Israelites who were across the Jordan remained whose right eye
Nahash, king of the Ammonites, had not gouged out. But seven thousand men had escaped from the Ammonites and entered into Jabesh-
gilead.

About a month later **11** 1 Nahash the Ammonite went up and
encamped against Jabesh-gilead, and all the men of Jabesh said to
Nahash, "Make a treaty with us, and we shall serve you!"

2 "On this condition I shall make a treaty with you," Nahash the
Ammonite told them, "that the right eye of each of you be gouged
out! Then I shall make it a reproach upon all Israel!"

3 "Let us alone for seven days," said the elders of Jabesh to him,
"while we send messengers throughout the territory of Israel. Then if
there is no one to deliver us, we shall come out to you."

4 When the messengers came to Gibeah of Saul and reported the
news in the hearing of the people, all the people began to weep aloud.
5 Now just at that time Saul was coming in behind the oxen from the
field, and when he asked, "Why are the people weeping?" they
repeated the news of the men of Jabesh. 6 When Saul heard this news,
the spirit of God rushed upon him! He became enraged 7 and seizing
a yoke of oxen dismembered them and sent them throughout the territory of Israel by messengers, saying, "Whoever does not come out
after Saul (and after Samuel), thus let it be done to his oxen!" Then
the fear of Yahweh fell upon the people, and they gathered together
as one man. 8 [Saul] mustered them at Bezek: three hundred thousands of Israelites and thirty thousands of men of Judah.

9 [Saul] said to the messengers who had come, "Thus you shall say
to the men of Jabesh: 'Tomorrow deliverance will be yours when the
sun has grown hot!'" So the messengers went and informed the men
of Jabesh, and they rejoiced. [. . .]

10 Then the men of Jabesh said [to Nahash the Ammonite], "Tomorrow we shall come out to you, and you may do with us whatever seems good to you."

11 The next day Saul positioned the army in three groups. They entered the camp during the morning watch and battered the Ammonites until the day had grown hot; those who survived were so scattered that no two of them remained together.

12 Then the people said to Samuel, "Who was it who said, 'Saul shall not reign over us!'? Give us the men and we shall put them to death!"

13 But Samuel said, "No one shall be put to death this day, for
today Yahweh has brought about deliverance in Israel! 14 Come!"
[he] said to the people. "Let us go to Gilgal and there renew the
kingship!" 15 So all the people went to Gilgal and there made Saul
king in the presence of Yahweh in Gilgal. There, too, they made communion offerings before Yahweh, while Saul and all the men of Israel celebrated exuberantly.

TEXTUAL NOTES

10:27b-**11**:1. We read the text of a long passage that is unique to 4QSam[a] among the surviving witnesses, though it was present also in the Greek text used by Josephus (see *Ant.* 6.68-71). It cannot be regarded as secondary, for it introduces completely new material with no epexegetical or apologetic motive. The scroll reads as follows (the reconstruction is that of F. M. Cross): *[wn]ḥš mlk bny 'mwn hw' lḥṣ 't bny gd w't bny r'wbn bḥzqh wnqr lhm k̊[wl 'y]n ymyn wntn 'y[n mwšy]' l[y]śr'l wlw' nš'r 'yš bbny yśr'l 'šr b'[br hyrdn 'š]r l[w' n]q̊r̊ lw nḥ[š mlk] bny [']m̊wn kwl 'yn ymyn w[h]n šb't 'lpym 'yš [nṣlw myd] b̊n̊ẙ 'mwn wyb'w 'l ybš g̊l'd wyhy kmw ḥdš wy'l nḥš h'mwny wyḥn 'l ybyš [gl'd] wy'mrw kwl 'nšy ybyš 'l nḥš* VACAT *[h'mwny krt] l[nw bryt wn'bdk]*. The sentence reading *wyhy kmw ḥdš . . . 'l ybyš [gl'd]*, "About a month later . . . against Jabesh-gilead," is written supralinearly on the scroll in the hand of the original scribe, who inadvertently omitted it the first time (his eye having skipped from the first "Jabesh-gilead" to the second) and subsequently corrected his own mistake. MT and LXX have lost everything from "Now Nahash . . ." to ". . . and entered into Jabesh-gilead" (*wnḥš . . . wyb'w 'l ybš gl'd*), an extraordinary case of scribal oversight. The omission apparently was not haplographic—there seems to be nothing in the text to have triggered it. A scribe simply skipped an entire paragraph of his text.

10 27b. *About a month later* Reading *wyhy kmw ḥdš* with 4QSam[a], as

suggested also by LXX *kai egenēthē hōs meta mēna,* which however specifically reflects *wyhy kmḥdš* (cf. Gen 38:24), obscuring the unusual (archaic and poetic) form of the preposition. The latter reading has been corrupted in MT to *wyhy kmḥryš* (see the *Textual Note* to 10:27a).

11 1. *Nahash* (2) LXX again adds "the Ammonite." Omit with MT.

2. *I shall make a treaty with you* Reading the shortened expression *'krt lkm* with MT (cf. 22:8), the word *bryt,* "treaty," being omitted in a kind of ellipsis. But it is also possible that the longer text of LXX, which reflects *'krt lkm bryt,* is primitive, *bryt* having fallen out before the following *bnqwr.* Space requirements indicate that 4QSam[a] shared the longer reading of LXX.

3. *the elders of Jabesh* Reading *zqny ybyš* with MT. LXX *hoi andres iabeis* = *'nšy ybyš,* "the men of Jabesh," is reminiscent of v 1 (cf. vv 9,10).

to you MT has *'lyk,* "to you (sing.)," as required by the context. The elders are speaking "to him," and the imperative "Let us alone" (*herep lānû*) is singular. LXX has *pros hymas* = *'lykm,* "to you (pl.)."

5. *behind the oxen* MT *'aḥărê habbāqār.* LXX[B] *meta to prōi* interprets the same consonantal reading as *'aḥărê habbōqer,* "after the morning." LXX[L] (cf. OL) *prōi katopisthen tōn boōn,* "early, behind the oxen," represents a conflation of the readings of MT and LXX[B].

6. *the spirit of God* So MT, as in 10:10. LXX has "the spirit of Yahweh," as in 10:6; 16:3.

enraged LXX adds *ep' autous* = *'lyhm,* "on account of them," i.e. on account of the news. Omit with MT.

7. *by messengers* So LXX[B]. MT, LXX[L] have "by *the* messengers," identifying them with the men sent from Jabesh. But the Jabeshite messengers are sent on a different errand in v 9.

upon the people Reading the shorter text of MT. LXX has "upon the people of *Israel,*" and space requirements indicate that 4QSam[a] shared this longer reading.

they gathered together LXX *kai eboēsan,* "and they shouted," reflects a consonantal Hebrew text *wyṣ'qw,* which however should read as *Nip'al,* not *Qal.* Hence *wayyiṣṣā'ăqû,* "and they gathered." MT has *wyṣ'w,* "and they came out," which is reminiscent of the preceding summons.

8. *at Bezek* So MT (*bbzq*). LXX[B] has *abiezek en bama,* reflecting *hbzq bbmh,* "at Bezek on the high place." (LXX[L]: *en rama* = *brmh,* "at Ramah"; Josephus: *en bala,* "at Balah"[?].) We thus recognize two early variants, *bbzq* and *bbmh,* of which the former is to be preferred as *lectio difficilior.*

three hundred thousands . . . thirty thousands These are the figures given in MT. LXX has 600,000 Israelites and 70,000 Judahites, the latter being confirmed by 4QSam[a] (the figure for the former is not extant on the scroll). Josephus has 700,000 and 70,000. Since such numbers tend to become exaggerated rather than understated, we prefer the smaller figures of MT.

9. *[Saul] said* That is, *wy'mr,* "and he said," as reflected by LXX *kai eipen.* MT has *wy'mrw,* "and they said." Cf. the *Textual Note* to 10:21b-23.

to the men of Jabesh So LXX, which has *tois andrasin iabeis,* reflecting *l'nšy ybyš* or perhaps *l'yš ybyš* (cf. MT). MT adds *gl'd,* ". . . -gilead."

Tomorrow deliverance will be yours The principal witnesses differ only slightly here (MT: *mḥr thyh lkm tšw'h;* LXX^{B} = *mḥr lkm htšw'h;* LXX^{L}, OL = *mḥr lkm thyh htšw'h*), and all yield approximately the same sense, viz. "Tomorrow deliverance will be yours. . . ." The text of LXX^{B}, therefore, is shortest and best (*thyh* being shown to be secondary by its varying position). 4QSam^{a} preserves a small fragment of a divergent text: [. . .]*myhwh htš[w'h* . . .], ". . . from Yahweh the deliverance . . ." (cf. Ps 37:39). Space requirements suggest that the fuller text of the scroll read: *mḥr lkm myhwh htšw'h,* "Tomorrow deliverance will be yours from Yahweh." This may reflect corruption of a text originally identical to that of LXX^{L}, OL, in anticipation of v 13 below.

went So MT. LXX adds "to the city."

and they rejoiced. [. . .] Something seems to have been lost here, and although only a small fragment is preserved, 4QSam^{a} had a longer text at this point. The surviving portion reads: [. . .]*lkm ptḥw hš['r* . . .], ". . . to you. Open the gate. . . ." This seems to be the remnant of a speech by Nahash, who has returned at the end of the agreed upon time (see the following *Textual Note*).

10. [*to Nahash the Ammonite*] The name is necessary for clarity in English, and it has also been added to the text of LXX; but the shorter text of MT, which omits it, is probably original. Nahash was probably speaking in the lost material at the end of v 9 (see above) and needed no further identification here.

whatever seems good to you LXX *to agathon enōpion hymōn* = *'t hṭwb lpnykm;* MT *kkl hṭwb b'ynykm.* These are more or less equivalent idiomatic expressions, and there is no basis for choice between the variants.

11. *the Ammonites* So LXX, OL, Syr. and some MSS of MT and Targ. MT has "Ammon."

12. *Saul shall not reign* Reading *š'wl l' ymlk* on the basis of LXX *saoul ou basileusei* (cf. Syr., Targ.). MT has *š'wl ymlk,* "Saul shall reign," which is contradictory to the context. Driver argues for MT as follows: "The sense of the words is indicated by the tone in which they are uttered—either affirmatively, in a tone of irony, or, more probably, interrogatively."

13. *Samuel* So LXX. MT has "Saul" (so LXX^{BmgA}, OL; cf. Josephus).

14. *Come!* So MT (*wy'mr šmw'l 'l h'm lkw wnlkw,* lit. "And Samuel said to the people, 'Come! Let us go . . .'"). LXX reflects *wy'mr šmw'l 'l h'm l'mr nlkw,* "And Samuel said to the people, *saying,* 'Let us go. . . .'"

15. *and there made Saul king* Reading *wymlkw šm 't š'wl* with MT. LXX has *kai echrisen samouēl ekei ton saoul eis basilea,* reflecting *wymšḥ šmw'l šm 't š'wl lmlk,* "and there Samuel anointed Saul king" (cf. Josephus). Though the reading of LXX does not really contradict 10:1*ff* (so Stoebe), where Saul is anointed "prince" (*nāgîd*) but not "king" (*melek*), the unelaborated version of MT seems better. Both are suited to the spirit of the account.

communion offerings MT *zbḥym šlmym,* lit. "communion offering sacrifices." LXX reflects *zbḥym wšlmym,* "sacrifices *and* communion offerings." Either reading is acceptable.

Saul (2) With MT we read *šm š'wl,* "there Saul," which in the tradition behind LXX has been corrupted to *šmw'l,* "Samuel." Note that *šm,* "there," immediately succeeds each of the three verbs describing what the people did after going to Gilgal: *wymlkw šm . . . wyzbḥw šm . . . wśmḥ šm,* ". . . and they made (Saul) king there . . . and they sacrificed there . . . and (Saul and all the men of Israel) rejoiced there. . . ."

NOTES

10 27b. *Nahash, the king of the Ammonites.* The Ammonites were a Semitic people who spoke a Canaanite language similar to Hebrew and maintained an autonomous state on the Transjordanian Plateau during a time period roughly equivalent to that of the independent existence of the Israelite state(s), ca. twelfth to sixth centuries B.C. The territory of ancient Ammon was approximately centered on its capital city, Rabbath-ammon, modern Amman. Of Nahash, king of the Ammonites during Saul's reign and the beginning of David's, we know only what we are told here. In II Sam 10:1,2 = I Chron 19:1,2 he is mentioned (in connection with the exploits of his son Hanun) as a benefactor of David, but without further explanation. It is true, however, that Ammon and Israel shared a mixed history, sometimes as allies, often as enemies. Each nation seems to have regarded the E bank of the Jordan as its own.

oppressing. Hebrew *lōḥēṣ*. See the NOTE at 10:18.

the Gadites and the Reubenites. That is, the Transjordanian tribes of Israel and immediate neighbors of the Ammonites.

and allowing Israel no deliverer. Hebrew *wĕnōtēn 'ên môšîa' lêyiśrā'ēl,* as reconstructed by F. M. Cross, who compares, in addition to v 3 below, II Kings 13:5. Apparently the point is that by his mutilation of every able-bodied Israelite Nahash hoped to prevent Israel from finding a leader able to deliver them (cf. Josephus, who elaborates with further interpretation of his own).

Jabesh-gilead. Generally speaking Gilead was that part of Israel that lay E of Jordan or, more narrowly conceived, the tribal territories of Gad and Reuben. Jabesh, one of the principal cities of Gilead, is now usually identified with Tell Abū Kharaz, ca. 20 miles S of the Sea of Galilee on the E bank of the Jordan. (Contrast Noth, *History,* 167, n. 3.) The city is closely associated in biblical tradition with Gibeah, Saul's home. According to Judges 21 the inhabitants of Jabesh were all but exterminated by their fellow Israelites for having failed to join in a punitive expedition against Gibeah; in the present episode Saul of Gibeah rescues Jabesh from defeat and humiliation; and later we shall see the men of Jabesh willing to endure hardship in order to give Saul and Jonathan an honorable burial (31:8-13).

About a month later. Viz. than Saul's return to Gibeah (10:26-27); cf. Josephus *Ant.* 6.68. The material in v 27b, as the Hebrew syntax shows (cf. 1:9b; etc.), is parenthetical, providing the reader with needed information about events that have transpired off stage. The expression "About a month later" resumes the narrative thread from 10:27a.

11 1. *Make a treaty with us.* The Jabesh-gileadites propose a treaty whereby

Jabesh would be bound to the Ammonite king as a vassal city ("we shall serve you") and Nahash as suzerain would give assurances of good treatment and protection. See further G. Mendenhall, *IDB*, s.v. "Covenant." (C.1.a.).

2. *a reproach*. A visible token of shame and humiliation. Compare 17:26.

3. *the elders of Jabesh*. The elders of a city were its senior male citizens, usually entrusted with important decisions. Cf. the NOTE at 4:3.

if there is no one to deliver us. Hebrew *'im 'ên môšîa' 'ōtānû*. The use of the term *mōšîa'*, "deliverer" (Judg 3:9,15; cf. II Kings 13:5) and the related noun *tĕšû'â*, "rescue," in vv 9 and 13 below, along with the general pattern of the deliverer called to war in Yahweh's name, links the present account to the "deliverer" stories of the Book of Judges. Cf. the COMMENT. See Richter, *Bearbeitungen des "Retterbuches"* and *Traditionsgeschichtliche Untersuchungen*, 319*ff*, for a discussion of the pre-Deuteronomic "savior book" of Judges 3-9. Recall that we have already been prepared unfavorably for the application of the term "savior/deliverer" to Saul: see the NOTE at 10:19.

4. *Gibeah of Saul*. See the NOTE at 9:1. The distance was some forty-two miles as the crow flies.

6. *the spirit of God rushed upon him!* See the NOTE at 10:6. In the account of Saul's anointing the onrush of divine spirit expressed itself in the form of prophetic ecstasy, but here Saul, like Samson (Judg 14:6,19; 15:14), is inspired to undertake heroic feats of arms. See Beyerlin, "Königscharisma bei Saul," who makes this distinction and then goes on to distinguish both types of charisma from the royal charisma later possessed by Saul and his successors.

He became enraged. Hebrew *wayyiḥar 'appô mĕ'ōd*, lit. "and his anger (nose) burned greatly," as in Judg 14:19, where rage is a sympton of Samson's inspiration as well.

7. The fundamental assumption of this bizarre method of summoning help was that all Israelites were obliged by mutual pledge to come to the aid of any Israelite in time of military need. (The grim parallel in Judg 19:29 would prevent us from concluding that as king Saul has special privileges to summon the people, even if we assumed that he was considered already to be king by the author of the present account. See the COMMENT.) Thus the symbolic dismembering of the oxen may be regarded as a kind of conditional curse: may the oxen of anyone who does not respond to the summons as agreed suffer the same fate! Ancient parallels, moreover, suggest that the threat might have been more direct, wishing that the people themselves, not their oxen, would be slain, for the practice of dismembering an animal to muster the troops seems to have had its origin in covenant-making ceremonies, which often involved dismemberment of animals accompanied by an oath ("May I suffer the fate of these animals if I am not true to the terms of this agreement!"). See Wallis, "Paralelle," and R. Polzin, "HWQY' and Covenant Institutions in Israel," *HTR* 62 (1969) 227-240.

(*and after Samuel*). These words are redactional and secondary, added by the writer who incorporated the old story in 10:27b-11:11, in which Samuel had no place, into the larger prophetic history of the rise of kingship. See the COMMENT.

the fear of Yahweh. The expression (*paḥad yahweh*) most often refers to a kind of paralyzing dread that disables the enemies of Israel (II Chron 17:10; etc.) in a way similar to that of the *mĕhûmâ*, "(divine) panic," unleashed on the Philistines in the story of the captivity of the ark (see the NOTE at 4:5). But here, as in II Chron 14:13(English 14:14), the "fear" is upon the Israelites themselves, spurring them to battle and victory.

8. *Bezek*. This city is not mentioned elsewhere, but it can be identified with modern Khirbet Ibziq, ca. 12 miles NE of Shechem on the W slope of the Jordan Valley opposite Jabesh-gilead. Josephus says that it was a march of ten schoenes (ca. forty to fifty miles) from Bezek to Jabesh (*Ant.* 6.79), but he seems to have confused the city with the Bezek of Judg 1:4-5, near Jerusalem. In fact the distance from Bezek to Jabesh was little more than ten miles.

thousands. That is, contingents. See the NOTE at 4:10.

9. According to Josephus (*Ant.* 6.76) Saul's message of reassurance was sent to Jabesh *before* he summoned the tribes, and his promise was "to come to their aid on the third day and to conquer the enemy before the sun rose, so that the ascending sun might see them victorious and released from their fears."

11. Saul divides his forces into three groups and surrounds the Ammonite camp. The strategy is similar to but less elaborate than that used by Gideon in his raid on the Midianite camp (Judges 7). Compare also the account of Abimelech's attack on Schechem in Judges 9. For *rā(')šîm*, "(military) groups, companies," see also 13:17(*bis*),18(*bis*) below, as well as Judg 7:16,20; 9:34,37,43,44(*bis*); and Job 1:17.

At this point Josephus (*Ant.* 6.80) goes on to say that Saul, "not satisfied with merely having rescued Jabesh, made an expedition against the territory of the Ammonites, subdued it all, and having taken much booty, returned home a famous man." Though this campaign is not mentioned in extant texts of the Bible, it may have been described in the fuller text known to Josephus, which often preserved original readings like the one at the beginning of this section (see the *Textual Note* to 10:27b - 11:1).

12. The reference is evidently to the factious behavior of the "worthless men" of 10:27a. Saul, by his heroism, has erased all doubts about his ability "to deliver," a key term in 10:27a and 10:27b - 11:11 (see the NOTE at v 3 above). The brief notices in 10:26-27a and 11:12-15 thus form a bracket around 10:27b - 11:11, serving to point up the significance of Saul's victory over the Ammonites. Before, though his kingship was formally declared, its desirability lacked demonstration; but now there can be no basis for doubting his ability to lead the armies of Israel.

13. *Yahweh has brought about deliverance*. Hebrew *ʿāśâ yahweh tĕšûʿâ*. The reference is to the deliverance of Jabesh, with a direct allusion to v 9, ". . . deliverance will be yours . . ." (*lākem tĕšûʿâ*). On the significance of the term *tĕšûʿâ* in pre-Deuteronomistic tradition, see the second NOTE on v 3 above.

14. *Gilgal*. The modern site remains unlocated. Past proposals have included two villages near Tell es-Sultan (Jericho), viz. Khirbet Mefjir and Khirbet en-Nitleh. The ancient city was an important Benjaminite shrine and place of sacrifice near Jericho. Here Saul's kingship is "renewed," and here also it will be repudiated (13:7b-15a).

"Let us . . . renew the kingship!" Hebrew *ûnĕḥaddēš . . . hammĕlûkâ*. Since Saul has already been proclaimed king at Mizpah, his office need not be granted again. Thus the kingship is simply "renewed" at Gilgal. Most commentators regard this as an editorial attempt to accommodate an older story of Saul's proclamation as king to the later one in 10:17-27a. See the COMMENT.

15. *communion offerings*. See the NOTE at 10:8.

COMMENT

Those who questioned the prowess of the young king found hidden in the gear at Mizpah could hardly have been accused of unreasonable skepticism. As far as they were concerned Saul's abilities had not been proven. To be sure he was the manifest choice of Yahweh, and it was their refusal to accept that fact as a basis for loyalty that earned them their designation as "worthless men" by the narrator. But these were people who needed to be shown. "How," they asked, "can this fellow save us?"(10:27a).

In 10:27b-11:11 the new king's ability to save is demonstrated. An appeal goes out from a besieged city to all Israel, and it is Saul of Gibeah who comes to the rescue. In a fit of inspiration he summons the tribes, and his leadership, which seems to emerge spontaneously, is never questioned. He guides an army of 30 contingents in a surprise attack on the camp of the enemy, and the strategy is devastatingly successful. The enemy is routed, and when the fighting is over, the advantage of Saul's leadership seems so obvious that those who had doubted him before find themselves in danger for their lives.

The story of Saul's victory in 10:27b-11:11 is thus a single narrative unit embraced by notices about the response to his kingship in 10:26-27a and 11:12-15. Clearly the purpose of this arrangement is to show that Saul, who was already king *de jure*, has now become king *de facto* (see the COMMENT on 10:17-27a) and earned the loyalty of all Israel. Yahweh's new plan for the leadership of his people is now in effect.

It is widely recognized[1] that Saul's deliverance of Jabesh-gilead belongs to a type of story, best known from the Book of Judges, in which an enemy threat is averted by an Israelite hero whom Yahweh has raised up from among his countrymen. These were the tales of the so-called "major

[1] The classic description of the continuities between the stories of the "major judges" and those of the kingship of Saul is A. Alt, "The Formation of the Israelite State in Palestine," in his *Essays in Old Testament History and Religion*, tr. R. A. Wilson (Garden City, N.Y.: Doubleday, 1968) 223-309. See also Cross, *CMHE*, 219*ff* and bibliography.

judges" (Judg 3:7-16:31), each of whom rescued some part of Israel from a foreign threat. The present story is another such account, with two notable exceptions. First, though the threat itself is localized in Gilead, all of Israel is involved in the proceedings. Second, Saul unlike the others becomes king. Thus the temporary and geographically limited leadership exercised in time of crisis by each of the deliverers of the Book of Judges is transformed in Saul's case into a permanent, pan-Israelite office, which will persist after the elimination of the Ammonite threat.

It follows that our account represents a development in the category of the story of the deliverer, which shows the temporary, "charismatic" type of leadership evolving into kingship. In positing such an origin for the new office, moreover, it presents kingship itself in a distinctive light. The king, it implies, is the successor to the heroes of the age of the judges. His office is legitimized by divine selection, and his powers are derived from divine inspiration. These concepts contrast sharply with the elements of dynastic succession and permanent authority in Davidic kingship and hark back, as most scholars assume, to an old northern ideal of monarchy.[2] This ideal, according to which each new king came to office through the free selection of Yahweh and might as quickly lose his position in consequence of divine disapproval, found its prototype in the reign of Saul. It seems to have prevailed in the time of the early monarchs of the northern kingdom[3] and, after the interruption of the Omri dynasty, to have returned full force with Jehu's revolution.[4] As we should expect, it enjoyed the sympathy and support of the prophetic party, who naturally favored the limitations it imposed upon the king.[5] It is not surprising, therefore, to find an account of Saul's charismatic "judging" of Israel among the sources of a prophetic history of the rise of kingship.

We should note quickly, however, that this old story does not share the extreme outlook of the larger narrative into which it has been incorporated. Saul, inspired by Yahweh in a way that moves him to fight but not to prophesy (see the NOTE at 11:6), defeats the enemy and is acknowledged as king by the people. This implies a concept of limited monarchy but not suspicion of human kingship in any form. The latter view, which dominates the stories of Samuel and to some extent those of Saul in their present form, was characteristically prophetic, as we have already seen.

[2] See Alt, "The Monarchy in the Kingdoms of Israel and Judah," *Essays*, 310-335, esp. 315-321; Cross, *CMHE*, 222, n. 1.

[3] See I Kings 11-16. Tradition remembered both Jeroboam and Baasha as kings who acquired rule through acts of divine intervention, and each had a son who failed to survive the attempt to succeed his father.

[4] II Kings 9-10. Of course Jehu set up a dynasty of his own (II Kings 12-13), though he may not have so intended.

[5] Again according to the record of the Books of Kings. On the relationship between northern prophecy and the ideal of limited kingship, see Cross, *CMHE*, 223-229.

The story of Saul's rescue of Jabesh-gilead in its original form presupposed no public clamor for a king and, despite the editorial manipulation of v 14 (see the NOTE), no prior installation of Saul. Instead the old story probably belonged to a cycle of tales about Saul, which combined legendary and semi-historical materials into a singly, loosely organized narrative. This collection must have contained at least Saul's Nazirite birth story (see the NOTE at 1:27,28), the original of the tale of his search for the lost asses of Kish, and the present account of his victory over Nahash, as well, perhaps, as some of the later materials concerning Saul's reign.[6] No doubt there were other stories which have not survived; we have only those materials that our prophetic narrator found suitable and useful. In any case the original Saul cycle must have been much like our present Samson cycle (Judges 13-16) in its combination of traditional elements and marvelous tales (see also the COMMENT on 1:1-28).

Saul, however, is not so shrouded in legend as Samson, and we must reckon with the influence of historical memory on the record of his public deeds, of which this is the first reported. The base of operation from which Saul fought the Philistines and thus consolidated his kingdom seems very likely to have included parts of Gilead as well as Benjamin, especially in view of the strong traditional associations between Jabesh and Gibeah (see the NOTE at 10:27b). Hence the story of his victory over Nahash may preserve considerable historical information amid its mixture of legendary and typical features.[7] Saul may indeed have become Israel's first recorded king in the wake of a decisive victory at Jabesh in Gilead.

In any case Saul is formally established as king at this point in the biblical record. The leadership of Samuel, to which we have become so accustomed, must now pass away as Saul assumes the duties of his new office. Or so it might seem! But the materials that follow show that Samuel still has a part to play.

[6] See "The Saul Cycle" in the Introduction (LITERARY HISTORY). The original interrelationship among these materials before their collection into a single cycle is more difficult to surmise. For reasons given in the COMMENT on 1:1-28 we should suppose an original connection between Saul's Nazirite birth story and the account of his deliverance of Jabesh. The story of the lost asses of Kish, on the other hand, seems likely to have arisen independently.

[7] The historical value of c 11 has been taken for granted by most scholars. For bibliography see Langlamet, "L'institution de la royauté," 167, nn. 27-28.

XV. SAMUEL'S FAREWELL
(12:1-25)

12 1 Samuel said to all Israel, "I have listened to you—to everything you said to me—and have made you a king. 2 And now the king
walks before you, and as for me, I am old and gray and my sons are
among you. Yet it was I who walked before you from my youth until
this very day 3 Here I am! Accuse me before Yahweh and before his
anointed! Whose bull have I taken? Whose ass have I taken? Whom
have I wronged? Whom have I abused? From whom have I taken a
bribe or a pair of shoes? Accuse me, and I shall repay you!"
4 But they said, "You have not wronged or abused us! You have
not taken anything from anyone!"
5 So he said to them, "Yahweh is witness against you today—and
his anointed is witness—that you have found nothing in my hand!"

Israel's History of Apostasy

6 "Yahweh is witness," he said, "who appointed Moses and Aaron
and who brought your fathers up from Egypt. 7 Now then, present
yourselves, and I shall enter into judgment with you before Yahweh
and recount for you all of Yahweh's kindnesses, which he did for you
and your fathers. 8 When Jacob went to Egypt, the Egyptians
oppressed them, and your fathers cried out to Yahweh. So Yahweh
sent Moses and Aaron, and brought your fathers out of Egypt, and
settled them in this place. 9 But they forgot Yahweh, their god. So he
sold them to Sisera, the commanding officer of Hazor, and to the Philistines and to the king of Moab, and they fought against them.
10 Then they cried out to Yahweh and said, 'We have sinned! For we
have abandoned Yahweh and served the Baals and Astartes! Now
then, rescue us from our enemies, and we shall serve you!' 11 So [Yah-
weh] sent Jerubaal and Bedan and Jephthah and Samson and rescued
you from your enemies on every side, and you lived securely. 12 But
when you saw that Nahash, the king of the Ammonites, had come
against you, you said, 'No! A king shall rule over us!'
13 "And now here is the king you have chosen! Yahweh has ap-

pointed a king over you! 14 If you fear Yahweh's commands, if both
you and the king who rules over you follow after Yahweh, your god,
then he will rescue you. 15 But if you do not obey Yahweh and rebel
against Yahweh's commands, then the hand of Yahweh will be upon
you and your king to destroy you."

The Power of the Prophet

16 "Now then, present yourselves and see this great thing that Yahweh is about to do before your eyes! 17 Is it not wheat harvest today?
I shall call upon Yahweh, and he will send thunder and rain. Then
you will understand and see that the evil you have done in requesting
a king for yourselves is great in Yahweh's eyes." 18 So Samuel called
upon Yahweh, and Yahweh sent thunder and rain that day; and all
the people became greatly afraid of Yahweh and Samuel.

19 All the people said to Samuel, "Intercede on behalf of your servants with Yahweh, your god, that we might not die! For in requesting a king for ourselves we have added another evil to all our sins."

20 "Do not be afraid!" said Samuel to the people. "You yourselves
have done all this evil. Yet do not turn away from Yahweh: rather
serve Yahweh with all your heart! 21 Do not turn away after nothingness, which cannot help and cannot save—for such things are nothingness! 22 For Yahweh will not abandon his people on account of his
great name, since Yahweh chose to make you into a people for himself.

23 "And as for me, far be it from me to sin against Yahweh by ceas-
ing to intercede on your behalf! I shall instruct you in the good and
fair way. 24 Yet you must fear Yahweh and serve him truly with all
your heart, for you have seen the great things he has done for you;
25 and if you act wickedly, both you and your king will be swept
away!"

TEXTUAL NOTES

12 2. *I am old and gray* Reading *zqnty wśbty* with MT. LXX[B] reflects a text which read *zqnty wyšbty,* "I am old and will sit down," and LXX[L] conflates the two readings. But MT is evidently correct.

3. *or a pair of shoes? Accuse me* Reading *wn'l(ym) 'nw by* on the basis of LXX *kai hypodēma apokrithēte kat' emou.* Cf. Sir 46:19. MT, confused by

the arcane reference to shoes (see the NOTE), has revised the text to read *w"lym ʿyny bw*, "and covered my eyes with it." See E. A. Speiser, "Of Shoes and Shekels."

4. *they said* So MT. LXX adds "to Samuel."

wronged or abused So MT. LXX has three verbs, and the correspondence between the verbs in MT and LXX here (and in v 3) is uncertain. In any case we should read the shorter text.

5. *So he said to them* So MT. LXX: "So Samuel said to the people."

today MT *hywm hzh*, rendered twice by LXX (*sēmeron en tautē tē hēmera*).

5,6. At the end of v 5 and the beginning of v 6 MT reads *wy'mr ʿd wy'mr šmw'l 'l hʿm*, to which we may restore a second *ʿd* after *hʿm* with LXX. Thus, "And he said, 'Witness.' And Samuel said to the people, 'Witness. . . .'" This is a conflation of shorter and longer variants, viz. *wy'mr ʿd* and *wy'mr šmw'l 'l hʿm ʿd*. LXX^{B} reinterprets the former as *wy'mrw ʿd*, "And *they* said, 'Witness,'" and similarly LXX^{L} attempts to understand the text by reading *wy'mr hʿm ʿd*, "And *the people* said, 'Witness.'" But in fact the text is conflate in all versions and the shorter reading of the two involved in the conflation, viz. *wy'mr ʿd*, is to be preferred (note the same kind of expansion at the beginning of each of the last two verses in LXX) and belongs at the beginning of v 6.

6. *from Egypt* So LXX. MT: "from the land of Egypt."

7. *and recount for you* Reading *w'gydh lkm* on the basis of LXX *kai apangelō hymin*. These words are omitted from MT, and although the cause of their omission is not evident, they must be included as grammatically necessary (Driver).

8. *Jacob* So MT. LXX adds "and his sons," perhaps in anticipation of the plural pronoun in the following expression ("the Egyptians oppressed *them*," though as noted below this reading, too, is preserved only in LXX, the *Vorlage* of which may have read "him"); but in any case the name is to be understood as collective for the nation. See the NOTE.

to Egypt, the Egyptians oppressed them Reading *mṣrym wyʿnm mṣrym*, lit. "to Egypt, Egypt oppressed them," on the basis of LXX *eis aigypton kai etapeinōsen autous aigyptos*. MT reads *mṣrym* alone; the rest has fallen out by simple haplography, the scribe's eye jumping from the first *mṣrym* to the second. Space considerations indicate that $4QSam^{a}$ shared the longer reading of LXX.

brought out . . . settled The verbs are singular with Yahweh as subject (so LXX). MT has plurals, understanding Moses and Aaron as subjects. But Moses and Aaron did not settle the people in Canaan.

9. This enumeration of enemies is quite sketchy in comparison to the stories of Judges 3-16. Josephus (*Ant.* 6.90) is somewhat more complete, listing the Assyrians (Judg 3:7-11), the Ammonites (Judges 11, unless Josephus is thinking of Judg 3:13), the Moabites (Judg 3:12-30), and the Philistines (Judges 3:31; 13-16); but the textual significance of all of this is difficult to assess.

Sisera, the commanding officer of Hazor So MT. LXX^{L} (cf. LXX^{BA}) has "Sisera, the commanding officer of Jabin, the king of Hazor" (cf. Judg 4:2-3, etc.), which looks like simple expansion.

10. *and said* Reading *wy'mrw,* "and they said," with LXX and MT *qĕrê.* MT *kĕtîb* has *wy'mr,* "and *he* said."

11. The names of the great heroes of the Book of Judges given here do not conform to the canonical arrangement, nor do they correspond to the list of enemies given in v 9. These problems and others have led to confusion in the text. Two of the names, Jerubaal and Jephthah, are not in doubt. The two others, Bedan and Samson, are less certain. Interestingly enough, Josephus has only "Jephthah and Gideon" (*Ant.* 6.90; see below).

So [Yahweh] sent Reading *wyšlḥ* on the basis of LXX *kai apesteilen.* MT adds "Yahweh" for clarity.

Jerubaal So MT, LXX[L], and 4QSam[a] ([*y*]*rb*:*l*). LXX[B] has *ieroboam.* "Jeroboam," here and in II Sam 11:21 (where there is no doubt that the hero of Judges 6-9 is meant).

Bedan and Jephthah LXX (cf. Syr.) has "Barak and Jephthah," MT "Bedan and Jephthah." Clearly "Bedan" (*bĕdān*) is to be preferred as *lectio difficilior,* "corrected" in the tradition behind LXX to *bārāq,* the familiar hero of Judges 4-5. But how are we to explain "Bedan"? Rabbinic tradition (Babylonian Rosh ha-Shanah 25a) speculated that the name means "from Dan" and identified Bedan as the great Danite hero Samson (so Kimchi, who says it means "son of Dan," as if **ben-dān* > *bĕdān*). An attractive modern suggestion has been made by Zakovitch ("*bdn* = *ypth* [1 Sam 12:11]"), who identifies the Gileadite Bedan of I Chron 7:17 with the Gileadite Jephthah of Judges 11, whom he assumes to have had two names in a fuller tradition, exactly like Gideon-Jerubaal. He takes the original reading here to have been *bdn,* later glossed (correctly) as *ypth.* A still later scribe, ignorant of the identification, arranged the text to read two different names (*w't bdn w't ypth*) as it now stands. Though Zakovitch does not cite it, the evidence of Josephus (*Ant.* 6.90), who lists only "Jephthah and Gideon," as if he knew that "Bedan" would be superfluous (on the omission of the fourth name see below), lends some support to his argument.

Samson So LXX[L], Syr. But MT, LXX[BA] have "Samuel," which many critics prefer on the grounds that the reading "Samson" was substituted to preserve Samuel's modesty (Smith, etc.), and it is true that "Samuel" is not by any means inappropriate in view of 7:2-17. Josephus (*Ant.* 6.90) omits the name altogether, leading to the suspicion that it may have arisen as a secondary expansion in a shorter list.

12. *you said, 'No!'* So LXX, Syr. (thus *wt'mrw l'*). MT: *wt'mrw ly l',* "you said *to me,* 'No!'" Cf. 8:19, LXX.

At the end of the verse MT adds *wyhwh 'lhykm mlkkm,* ". . . but Yahweh, your god, was your king!" This is an expansion in the spirit of the text, but an expansion nonetheless.

13. *you have chosen!* So LXX[B]. MT (cf. LXX[L]) has *'šr bḥrtm 'šr š'ltm,* "whom you have chosen, whom you requested." Evidently the last two words were added to correct the contradiction of 10:24, where it is said that the king was chosen by Yahweh.

14. *your god* MT *'lhykm* (cf. 4QSam[a]: [*'l*]*whyk*[*m*], of which LXX *poreuomenoi* = *hwlkym* ("going"?) is probably a corruption (Wellhausen).

then he will rescue you Assuming that LXX[L] is correct in its unique reading (*kai*) *exeleitai hymas* = *whṣylkm.* 4QSam[a], though not extant here, has a space requiring four to six letters (*whṣlkm?*). In any case something is needed after the last conditional clause. To be sure, Driver accepts MT, describing the whole as "protasis, ending with an aposiopesis," and is followed in this by Stoebe and others; but this is to accuse Samuel (or at least a Deuteronomistic writer) of some rather bewildering speechmaking. Although the suppression of the entire apodosis is attested elsewhere (see GK §§159dd,167a), it seems so apt to confuse in this situation as to be most unlikely. We must conclude that in MT *whṣlkm* fell out after *'lhykm.*

15. *and your king to destroy you* MT has *b'bwtykm,* "and upon your fathers," which is impossible (thus Targ., Syr. interpret it as *"as it was* upon your fathers"; cf. Stoebe). It is a corrupt remnant (reminiscent of v 7; cf. vv 6,8) of *wbmlkkm l'bydkm,* "and upon your king to destroy you," as reflected by LXX[L] *kai epi ton basilea hymōn exolothreusai hymas* (cf. LXX[B], the *Vorlage* of which had lost *l'bydkm* by haplography after *wbmlkkm*). Contrast Weiss, "Main du Seigneur," who proposes the reading *wbbtykm,* "and upon your houses."

21. *turn away* After these words MT inexplicably adds *kî.* Omit with LXX.

23. *I shall instruct you* Preceded in LXX by *kai douleusō tō kyriō,* which reflects *w'bdty 't yhwh,* "and I shall serve Yahweh." Omit with MT.

in the . . . way Reading *badderek* (Budde, Smith). The same consonants are vocalized in MT as *bĕderek,* thus "in the way of the good and the fair." LXX reflects *'t hdrk,* thus "(I shall teach you) the good and fair way," but the expression usually takes the preposition (Pss 25:8; 32:8; Prov 4:11).

24. *truly with all your heart* MT *b'mt bkl lbbkm.* LXX reflects instead *b'mt wbkl lbbkm,* "truly *and* with all your heart."

for you have seen Reading *ky r'ytm* on the basis of LXX *hoti eidete.* MT has *ky r'w,* "for see!" which is unsuitable.

NOTES

12 1. Samuel's opening statement harks back directly to 8:22, where he was instructed by Yahweh to "Listen to [the people] and make them a king." The chain of events would follow smoothly enough from the account of Saul's election at Mizpah (10:17-27a) were it not for the fact that the narrator has interrupted himself by the incorporation of the story of Saul's victory over the Ammonites (10:27b-11:15). We are obliged, therefore, to think of the present episode as occurring at Gilgal (11:15), not Mizpah.

2. *the king walks before you . . . I . . . walked before you.* The juxtaposition is deliberate and important: the king has replaced the prophet. The expression "walk before" (*hithallēk lipnê*) means to perform a function on someone's behalf, as explained in the NOTE at 2:30. Samuel is reminding the people that al-

though the king serves them now, it was he, Samuel, who served them in years past. The verses that follow draw out the contrast further.

3. Samuel protests against his deposition by the people on the grounds that his leadership has been just. His objection to their lack of confidence is couched in language identical to that used by Moses on a similar occasion (Num 16:15). Von Rad, "Early History," has popularized the view that this verse belongs to an ancient formal category of cultic self-justification, also represented in the Old Testament by such passages as Deut 26:13-14; Job 31; etc. The form, he says, belonged originally to any of those "various occasions when the individual worshipper was expected to bear witness to the divine law by making some kind of profession" and "did so in a series of negative statements, in which he professed himself innocent of any transgression of certain particular commandments." But even if this is so, it must not lead us to overlook the special function of Samuel's "negative confession" in the present context. It represents a kind of companion piece to the description of "the way of the king" in 8:11-18, to which it returns our attention. The key word there as here is *lāqaḥ*, "take." Samuel has taken nothing from the people, not an ox, an ass, or any kind of bribe; the king will take their sons, daughters, crops, slaves, and livestock. Samuel's purpose is to show the people once and for all how foolish they have been. Though they were blind before (8:19-20), now that it is too late they will finally realize that Samuel, the prophet, has been a just leader and that his channel to Yahweh is direct (see vv 16*ff* below). See further the COMMENT.

3,5. *and before his anointed . . . and his anointed is witness.* These notices have been taken by some commentators as evidence of a favorable attitude toward the monarchy in 12:1-5, despite the contrary tone of the rest of the chapter. The king, they say, is here presented as a guarantor of the law, before whom Samuel must justify his life (Stoebe). But c 12, especially its pre-Deuteronomistic stratum (see below), is uniformly critical of the monarchy. There is no sense, moreover, in which these two notices are organic to the compositional unit of vv 1-5. Elsewhere the new king is called "king" (v 2) not "anointed of Yahweh," and it is not the king but the people who absolve Samuel (v 4). Indeed both references to the anointed of Yahweh have the look of secondary insertions, especially that in v 5, which breaks up the syntax of the sentence quite awkwardly: "So he said to them, 'Yahweh is witness against you today—and his anointed is witness—that you, etc.' " Even if original the notices merely acknowledge the new authority of the king; they do not further condone it.

3. *a pair of shoes.* The rather curious reference is explained by an antiquarian notice in Ruth 4:7, according to which, "It (was the custom) formerly in Israel with reference to redemption and exchange that to confirm any such matter a man would slip off his shoe and give it to his companion. This, then, was the method of attestation in Israel." E. A. Speiser ("Of Shoes and Shekels," 155) has gone on to show that the practice served "to validate arrangements by circumventing legal obstacles." As Speiser points out, this clarifies Samuel's assertion: "In his capacity as judge he had never accepted bribes or gratuities from any litigant; what is more, he had had nothing to do

with cases where the law could be circumvented through some technicality." Cf. also Amos 2:6; 8:6.

6-15. This long retrospect on Israel's history of apostasy is one of a series of reflective speeches by major figures, including Joshua (Joshua 23-24), Samuel and Solomon (I Kings 8:12-61), inserted at important junctures in the history by a Deuteronomistic writer as vehicles for his editorial point of view (cf. Noth, *ÜS*, 5). The original continuation of v 5 is found in vv 16*ff* (n.b. the duplication in vv 7 and 16), where Samuel goes on to reinforce his self-defense with a demonstration of his ability to communicate with Yahweh; and although those latter verses show marks of Deuteronomistic annotation (see below), vv 6-15 represent a self-contained and completely Deuteronomistic composition, which may therefore be isolated for discussion. Characteristically Deuteronomistic expressions occurring here include:

1) *zʿq ʾl yhwh,* "cry out to Yahweh," which is derived ultimately from the pre-Deuteronomistic sin-outcry-deliverance scheme of the stories of the so-called "major judges" (see the NOTE at 11:3 for bibliography). Cf. Judg 3:9,15; 6:6,7; 10:10. See also the NOTE at 8:18.

2) *škḥ ʾt yhwh,* "forget Yahweh," as in Judg 3:7. Cf. Weinfeld, *Deuteronomy*, 367, n. 6.

3) *mkr byd PN,* "sell (the Israelites) to (an enemy)," which also comes ultimately from the pre-Deuteronomistic framework of the stories of the great deliverers. See Judg 2:14; 3:8; 4:2; 10:7; cf. Deut 32:30.

4) *ʿzb ʾt yhwh,* "abandon Yahweh," as in Judg 2:12,13; 10:6,10,13; I Sam 8:8. Cf. the NOTE to 8:8.

5) *ʿbd ʾt hbʿlym (wʾt hʿštrwt),* "serve the Baals (and Astartes)." So Judg 2:11,13; 3:7; 10:6,10. Cf. I Sam 7:4.

6) *yrʾ ʾt yhwh,* "fear Yahweh," as in Josh 4:24; I Kings 8:40,43. The expression is ubiquitous in the Book of Deuteronomy itself.

7) *ʿbd ʾt yhwh,* "serve Yahweh." So Josh 22:5 and 24:14. Cf. the stronger expression in 7:4 and Judg 10:16 (LXX^{B}). Again the phrase is common in the Book of Deuteronomy (and indeed in pre-Deuteronomic literature, though its use to describe loyalty to Yahweh in contrast to apostasy is primarily Deuteronomic and Deuteronomistic, as pointed out by Weinfeld, *Deuteronomy*, 332).

8) *šmʿ bqwl yhwh,* "hear Yahweh's voice, obey Yahweh," as in Josh 24:24; etc. The expression alone is not distinctively Deuteronomistic.

6. *"Yahweh is witness."* In v 5 the meaning of this expression was clear: Yahweh is a divine witness to the people's acknowledgment of Samuel's innocence. Here it is less clear. Evidently Yahweh is being invoked as witness to the past behavior of the people. In view of the covenantal patterning of vv 6-15 (see the COMMENT) it seems appropriate to compare this to the invocation of divine witnesses that customarily introduced a treaty. See D. J. McCarthy, *Treaty and Covenant* (Rome: PBI, 1963) 141. But it is also true that the expression serves to cement the intrusive passage into the narrative and thus can be explained satisfactorily enough as a redactional device introduced to smooth the transition to the new material.

who appointed Moses and Aaron. Hebrew *ʾăšer ʿāśâ ʾet-mōšeh wĕʾet-ʾahărōn.*

The expression is unusual in that *'āśâ* alone does not elsewhere mean "appoint." We expect it to be followed by a term denoting office or function (cf. Driver). Our translation assumes that the reference is to the traditions recorded in Exodus 2-4.

9-11. The focus of Samuel's reflection is the period of the judges, which from the Deuteronomistic point of view closed with the appointment of the first king. This age is presented in the Book of Judges as a series of acts of apostasy, each of which was punished by subjugation to an enemy, until the repentant people were again freed by a deliverer raised up by Yahweh. This cyclical pattern of apostasy-subjugation-petition-deliverance is also reflected here, though only a brief selection of the foes and deliverers known from the canonical record is given.

9. *Sisera.* See Judges 4-5.

the Philistines. The most prominent enemy; see the NOTE at 4:1b. Cf. Judges 3:31; 13-16.

the king of Moab. Presumably the reference is to Eglon, the Moabite king who subdued Israel and enslaved her people for eighteen years according to Judg 3:12-30.

10. *the Baals and Astartes.* That is, local cults of foreign gods and goddesses. See the NOTE at 7:4.

11. *Jerubaal.* According to the existing (composite) account, another name for Gideon. The reference is to Judges 6-8.

Samson. See Judges 13-16.

12. This verse gives the impression that the people's demand for a king (8:1-22) was a response to the new threat posed by Nahash the Ammonite (11:1-15), as if the materials available to the Deuteronomistic author of this retrospective summary differed from those of the extant text either in arrangement or extent. Accordingly some commentators have assumed that Nahash was mentioned before c 8 in an earlier version of the story; but although we have now recovered further information about Nahash and his raids in Transjordan (see the *Textual Note* to 10:27b-11:1), this information, too, belongs with c 11 and not earlier. We must conclude, therefore, either that the Deuteronomistic author of this verse knew an independent tradition with a different view of the relationship between the events related in cc 8 and 11 (Stoebe) or, as seems more likely, that he made a free interpretation of the existing materials (Noth, *ÜS*, 60). In either case the new slant given by the assertion that the people made their demand in response to the Ammonite threat is quite important, inasmuch as it forces a different interpretation of the inauguration of kingship. Yahweh's gift of a king cannot be understood here, as it is in the larger narrative, as a unique act of divine condescension in response to a wicked and willful human act, but rather it must here be interpreted, as Stoebe points out, as another gracious provision for Israel's deliverance from deserved danger in the series of such provisions that extends through the record of the age of the judges.

15. *the hand of Yahweh will be upon you.* The Israelites, if they are disobedient, will suffer holy punishment inflicted by the awesome power of their god.

For the background of this expression, see J. J. M. Roberts, "The Hand of Yahweh," *VT* 2 (1971) 244-251. Cf. the NOTE at 5:6.

16-25. Though there is further Deuteronomistic annotation in these verses (19b,20b-22,24-25), they preserve in basic outline the original continuation of vv 1-5. Samuel, having contrasted his own righteousness as leader of the people to the selfish cruelty they have been told to expect from the king, goes on to demonstrate anew his ability to communicate with Yahweh and Yahweh's willingness to respond.

17-18. The allusion to the wheat harvest marks the season as early summer (see the NOTE at 6:13), when rain rarely fell. R. B. Y. Scott ("Palestine, climate of," *IDB*, 3.622-623) writes: "The long, rainless summer begins [in Palestine] in May or June and lasts until September. . . . Rain is rare in June except in the extreme N, and is almost unheard of in July and August (cf. II Sam. 21:10). . . ." Thus the thunderstorm here sent by Yahweh at Samuel's behest cannot be misinterpreted by the people as a natural occurrence: it is so extraordinary as to be unambiguously supernatural in origin. The point of the incident is not so much that Yahweh thunders at the people to express his displeasure (though that is an important element) as that he exhibits his willingness to respond to Samuel, his prophet, as earlier in 7:9-10. The point of the narrator is clear: a prophet is the proper and divinely sanctioned channel between man and God, and in this respect the request for a king is a great evil. Thus it is that when the storm begins, the people become afraid "of Yahweh *and Samuel.*"

19. Finally chastened, the people call upon the intercessory power of the prophet, as they used to do in moments of trouble before they made their fatal demand (cf. 7:8). The second half of this verse with its reference to all the previous sins of the people is probably a Deuteronomistic interpolation.

20-25. The structure of Samuel's argument with its contrasting emphatic pronouns (*'attem . . . gam 'ānōkî,* "You yourselves . . . And as for me . . .") is the key to a correct understanding of the reply. "You brought this evil upon yourselves," says Samuel in effect. "*I* have done nothing to harm you. Moreover, I shall continue to act on your behalf, as I always have. So do not be afraid!"

In the text as it now stands each half of the reply (20a and 23) is elaborated by further sentences in characteristically Deuteronomistic language (20b-22 and 24-25). Stereotyped Deuteronomistic expressions occurring here include:

1) *swr m'ḥry yhwh,* "turn away from Yahweh," used by the Josianic historian in reference to a king (II Kings 18:6). On the general use of *swr,* "turn away," for apostasy in Deuteronomic and Deuteronomistic contexts, see Weinfeld, *Deuteronomy,* 339.

2) *'bd 't yhwh bkl lbb,* "serve Yahweh with all the heart," as in Josh 22:5; cf. Deut 10:12; 11:13. For "serve Yahweh" alone, see above, NOTE at 6-15, no. 7. For the common cliché "with all the heart" alone, see the NOTE to 7:2b-4.

3) *l'śwt lw l'm,* "to make into a people for himself," as used (with other verbs) in II Sam 7:24 (cf. 23), as well as Deut 28:9; 29:12(English 29:13).

4) *yr' 't yhwh*, "fear Yahweh." See the NOTE at vv 6-15.

5) *b'mt*, "truly." Frequently attached to the expression "serve Yahweh," as in this case (cf. Josh 24:14) or to some other Deuteronomistic cliché, such as "walk before Yahweh" (said of the king; cf. I Kings 2:4; 3:6).

21. This verse moves beyond the usual Deuteronomistic polemic against the worship of "other gods" and raises the question of idolatry. Its use of *tōhû*, "nothingness," in reference to idols is reminiscent of Isa 41:29 (cf. 44:9). Thus we may have here a late (post-Deuteronomistic) addition to the text.

22. Since Israel is known as Yahweh's special people, it would reflect badly on his own reputation if he were to cast them off. Cf. Ezek 20:9, where Yahweh explains that despite the sins of the people he did not abandon them "for the sake of my name, so that it would not be defiled in the eyes of the nations . . . before whom I had made known that I would bring [Israel] out of the land of Egypt."

23. Samuel pledges to continue his services to Israel as an intercessor and teacher, roles from which prophets are not excluded by the inauguration of kingship. Excluding the Deuteronomistic interpolation in vv 24-25, this concludes Samuel's farewell, which thus ends with a reference to the future role of the prophet under the monarchy. See further the COMMENT.

COMMENT

With Israel's new leader in office Samuel must settle his account with the people. It is their king who "walks before" them now, and Samuel's term of service, at least in the old form, is over. The sequence of events initiated by the audience at Ramah has reached its conclusion. In obedience to Yahweh's command (8:22) and the people's own mandate, Samuel has given Israel her first legitimate king. Only in the present episode, however, do the people come to appreciate the price of the king, for it is here that they recognize for the first time the importance of what they have given away. In their zeal to be "like all the other nations," they have forgotten the privileges of their national uniqueness and scouted the advantages of prophetic rule. Now, reminded of the fairness of Samuel's administration and made to acknowledge it (vv 3-5), and called upon to witness a new demonstration of the prophet's intimacy with Yahweh (vv 16*ff*), they realize at last how foolish they have been. But it is too late. They have their king, and there can be no return to the old way. They must attach their hope to the only remaining provision for their welfare: Samuel even now will continue to pray for them and instruct them "in the good and fair way."

As this summary suggests, Samuel's farewell address in its pre-Deuteronomistic form represents another important chapter in the prophetic narrative of the establishment of kingship in Israel. It is retrospective to a great extent, reviewing ideas projected earlier in order to give them final clarity; but its crucial contribution is a new one, for as we shall see, v 23, in which Samuel pledges further service in the future, purports to be nothing less than the formal initiation of the prophet's new role in the era of the kingdom.

All of this is organized according to a threefold scheme in which (1) the prophet is contrasted to the king, (2) the power of the prophet is demonstrated, and (3) the shape of the continuing office of the prophet is foretold:

1) *The prophet contrasted to the king.* As pointed out in the NOTE at v 3 above, Samuel's self-justification in vv 1-5 harks back to his description of "the way of the king" in 8:11-18. The key term in both speeches is the verb *lāqaḥ*, "take."[1] Samuel has taken nothing from the people. By contrast the king must be expected to take everything they have and enslave them. The implication is clear. Prophetic rule, as exemplified by the career of the paradigmatic prophet, is just rule. This follows, we are to assume, from the peculiar circumstances of the prophet's call and his continuing relationship with Yahweh. These circumstances do not pertain to the office of king, and Israel's king will behave as kings do everywhere, viz. selfishly and cruelly.

2) *The prophet's power demonstrated.* Verses 16*ff* recall our attention to the fact that it is Yahweh's pleasure to respond to the entreaty of his prophet. Samuel calls and Yahweh answers, exactly as in the prophetically confected account of Samuel's victory over the Philistines (7:9-10). The thunderstorm, therefore, is not only an expression of divine wrath; it is a demonstration of the special powers of the prophet—powers of which the people were so aware before (cf. 7:8) but seem to have forgotten since. This view of the prophetic office is the same as that which animates the story of the drought in the days of another prophet, Elijah, who at one point says, "As Yahweh, the god of Israel, whom I serve, lives, there shall be no dew or rain these years except at my word!" (I Kings 17:1). The prophet is Yahweh's chosen servant, and any attempt to supplant his authority is an evil that "is great in Yahweh's eyes." Realizing this, the people become "greatly afraid of Yahweh and Samuel," as we are told, and they beg Samuel to intercede for them with Yahweh, whom they refer to in this case as Samuel's god (v 19)—a usage found also in 7:8, where the intercessory role of the prophet and his special relationship to Yahweh are also central. Again the implication of the incident is clear. The prophetic office is unique in its privileges of communication with Yahweh. By their

[1] This has also been recognized by Boecker, *Beurteilung der Anfänge des Königtums,* 70. Cf. Weiser, *Samuel,* 40.

demand for a king the people have forfeited the special opportunity this situation offered them, and since prophetic rule was Yahweh's own choice, they have incurred divine condemnation.

3) *The future of the prophetic office foretold.* The surprise in Samuel's farewell message is neither the protestation of his own righteousness nor the appeal to the displeasure of his god. These things we might have expected. The real surprise is his promise to continue to serve. Justice does not require this, since a solemn warning was given (see the NOTE at 8:9), and though they plead for it, the people have no right to expect Samuel to "Intercede . . . with Yahweh . . . that we might not die!" Samuel's pledge in v 23, therefore, is undeserved by its beneficiaries, the Israelites. It amounts to a special provision for the succor and preservation of the people, which comes on the very brink of disaster, and it is a God-given provision, inasmuch as it arises from the terms of Samuel's prophetic relationship with Yahweh. To abandon the people even at this point would be to sin against Yahweh (v 23a). Instead Samuel will continue to serve. And he will do so in two ways: (1) by interceding with Yahweh on their behalf; and (2) by instructing them "in the good and fair way." Here then is inaugurated a new role for the prophet in Israel. In the past he discharged, in the view of the present narrative, a wide variety of duties both religious and secular; but now with a king in Israel the duties of the prophet are to be more circumscribed. He has become the figure familiar to us from the prophetic books themselves, who is assigned to play two roles corresponding to the two parts of Samuel's pledge, as the people's intercessor with Yahweh on the one hand and as the moral conscience of the kingdom on the other. These are the irreducible aspects of the prophetic office, which in the idealized cases of the great prophets like Moses and Samuel are combined with a number of others, and which, under less than ideal conditions when the leadership prerogatives that the prophets claim are denied them by the people, remain alone.

As detailed in the NOTES this key chapter in the prophetic narrative of the rise of kingship has been expanded by a Deuteronomistic hand into a reflective summary of the period of the judges and an exhortation to good behavior in the coming age of the kings. The primary expansion is found in vv 6-15, as betrayed by the conspicuous duplication of vv 7 and 16;[2] other additions include 19b(?),20b-22,24-25. Thus Samuel's farewell belongs to the series of Deuteronomistically formulated passages that according to Martin Noth provide the organizational framework for the Deuteronomistic history as a whole.[3] These appear in the story at major junctures, where each presents a retrospect on preceding events and a preview of the future, thus dividing the larger history into epochs In this

[2] Verse 6 is redactional. See the NOTE.

[3] *ÜS*, 5. Noth evidently regarded c 12 as wholly Deuteronomistic (cf. 59-60).

scheme I Samuel 12 marks the watershed between the end of the period of the judges and the beginning of the age of kingship.

More specifically, Samuel's farewell in its present form belongs to a subset of the passages indentified by Noth, which also includes the dedicatory speech and prayer of Solomon in I Kings 8:12-61 and the farewell discourses of Joshua in their Deuteronomistically revised form (Joshua 23-24). These three speeches serve to reiterate the Deuteronomic exhortations of Moses in each new era down to the day of the completion of the temple, so that the words of these four key figures (Moses, Joshua, Samuel, Solomon) provide an ongoing theological line of reference for the Deuteronomistic history of the pre-temple period. See further LITERARY HISTORY in the Introduction.

The farewell speeches of Joshua and Samuel in particular may be set apart for comparison. They renew the Deuteronomic covenant at the two critical passages in the history after the entrance into the land and before the erection of the temple: (1) at the time of the completion of the conquest and the beginning of Israel's life in the land, and (2) at the end of the age of the judges and the beginning of life under the kings. In other words, the two passages describe the repetition and restoration at these crucial moments of Israel's solemn promise of obedience to Yahweh with all its accompanying sanctions and contractual obligations. The covenantal form of Joshua 24 is well known, and the lineaments of covenantal patterning may also be discovered in the present passage.[4] The two speeches share a number of formal features characteristic of covenant renewal:

1) *Introduction* (I Sam 12:7; Josh 24:1). The people take up their positions in formal array to hear the words of the covenant mediator.

2) *Antecedent History* (I Sam 12:8-12; Josh 24:2-13). The history of the relationship between Yahweh and Israel is reviewed with special emphasis upon the good things Yahweh has done for the people in the recent past. This historical prologue is crucial in that it demonstrates Israel's indebtedness to Yahweh and thus the propriety of her obedience to the terms of the covenant.

3) *Transition to the Present: "And now . . ."* (I Sam 12:13; Josh

[4] James Muilenburg, "The Form and Structure of the Covenantal Formulations," *VT* 9 (1959) 347-365, esp. 361-365; McCarthy, *Treaty and Covenant,* 141-144; Birch, *Rise of the Israelite Monarchy,* 68-70; Klaus Baltzer, *The Covenant Formulary,* tr. D. E. Green (Philadelphia: Fortress, 1971) 66-68. On the other hand, F. Brent Knutson (in Fisher, *Ras Shamra Parallels* 2. 171-173) denies the presence of treaty formulations here, arguing that the structure of c 12 as a whole does not suggest treaty influence and that while some features of the chapter are similar to certain treaty elements, there is nothing similar in many verses. But the verses Knutson identifies as lacking covenantal features (1-7,16-19,21-24) correspond generally to those we have identified as pre-Deuteronomistic (1-5,16-19a,20a,23). The treaty influence is in the Deuteronomistic overlay.

24:14). The expression *wĕʿattâ* functions as a kind of ligature, connecting the recital of Yahweh's past kindnesses to the present situation upon which they impinge. Thus the covenant is related to the present moment and the people may be enjoined to renew their loyalty.

4) *Requirements* (I Sam 12:20b-21; Josh 24:14). In the present passage the things required of the people by the covenant relationship are implied in the blessings and curses (see below) and also listed separately in vv 20b-21. In Joshua 24 the requirements are in effect epitomized in the double injunction to serve Yahweh and cast away other gods.[5]

5) *Blessings and Curses* (I Sam 12:14-15,24-25; Josh 24:20). The future prosperity of the people is attached to obedience to the requirements of the covenant. Failure to obey and serve Yahweh will bring disaster. Thus the alternatives of right and wrong behavior as detailed in the Deuteronomic corpus itself are presented anew in each generation with the consequences of disobedience fully in view. In the present passage the king is included in the terms of these sanctions for the first time.

As we have already noted in regard to other Deuteronomistic interpolations in our story (see 7:3-4; 8:8; and the corresponding NOTES), the purpose of such expansion is to incorporate the account of the rise of kingship into the Deuteronomistic theology of the period of the judges with its fourfold scheme of apostasy, punishment, repentance, and deliverance. The special concern with questions of leadership and theocracy that dominates the primary narrative is thus subordinated to issues of obedience and service, and most especially of fidelity in contrast to apostasy (v 10). Israel is portrayed as the adherents of Deuteronomistic theology saw it, i.e. as a fickle, backsliding nation upon whom the good choice must be repeatedly urged.

From any perspective, however, the age of Samuel is now over. To be sure, the life's work of the old prophet is not yet completed, for there is a greater king than Saul still to be anointed; but the new era has dawned. Samuel's few remaining tasks are important, but he will no longer be the center of interest in the narrative.

[5] In covenant renewal passages a detailed list of stipulations, such as that which characterizes the original covenant itself (in this case Deuteronomy 12-26), is unnecessary and may be replaced by a generalized call to obedience.

XVI. A NOTICE ABOUT SAUL'S KINGSHIP (13:1)

13 1 Saul was . . . years old when he began to reign, and he reigned . . . years over Israel.

TEXTUAL NOTE

13 1. This notice is missing in LXX^B and defective in all witnesses in which it survives. LXX^B probably reflects scribal suppression of an obviously corrupt text, a practice attested elsewhere. (F. M. Cross [personal communication] compares II Sam 4:1,2, where the name Mephibosheth, which was originally in the text [cf. LXX], has been suppressed in MT because it is an obvious error for Ishbosheth.) The scribes preferred to suppress or leave blank rather than correct. MT has *bn šnh š'wl bmlkw wšty šnym mlk ʿl yśr'l,* "Saul was a year old (!) when he began to reign, and he reigned two years over Israel." The first part of this statement exercised the ingenuity of the ancient commentators and translators considerably. Targ. has *kbr šn' dlyt byh ḥwbyn š'wl kd mlk,* "Like a one-year-old who has no sins was Saul when he became king." Some MSS of LXX^L (oe_2; bc_2 = MT) record Saul's age as thirty, but this is probably an estimate or at best a figure derived from other sources (cf. II Sam 5:4). The information concerning the length of Saul's reign inspires little more confidence. The reading of MT in this clause is also represented by most of the versions (LXX^L, etc.), but the time is too short—surely Saul reigned for more than two years! Josephus, who has nothing to say at this point (*Ant.* 6.95), elsewhere gives the rounded figures of twenty (10.143) and forty (6.378; cf. Acts 13:21). Wellhausen is probably correct in supposing *šty,* "two," to be a corrupt duplication of the following *šnym,* "years." It seems likely, then, that originally the numbers were lacking in both clauses: "Saul was ______ years old when he began to reign, and he reigned ______ years over Israel." See further the NOTE.

NOTE

13 1. This notice was inserted by the Deuteronomist in the spirit of his chronological framework for the stories about subsequent kings (cf. II Sam 2:10; 5:4; I Kings 14:21; 22:42; etc.), but the figures were not available to him or (if he had them) were subsequently lost.

XVII. A BROKEN APPOINTMENT
(13:2-15)

13 [2]Saul picked himself three thousands from Israel: two thousands were under [his] command at Michmash in the hill country of Bethel, while one thousand was under Jonathan's command in Geba of Benjamin; the rest of the army [Saul] dismissed, each to his own tent.

[3]Jonathan slew the Philistine prefect who was in Gibeah, and the
Philistines were told, "The Hebrews have revolted!" Saul blew the
horn throughout the land, [4]and all Israel was told, "Saul has slain the
Philistine prefect! Indeed, Israel has become obnoxious to the Philistines!" So the army rallied behind Saul at Gilgal.

[5]The Philistines, meanwhile, had gathered to fight with Israel.
They brought up three thousands of chariotry, six thousands of cavalry, and an army like the sand on the seashore in number against Israel, and came up and encamped at Michmash, east of Beth-aven.
[6]When the men of Israel saw that they were hard pressed, the people
hid themselves in caves, thickets, fissures, dugouts, and pits, [7]and
crossed the fords of the Jordan to the territory of Gad and Gilead.

But Saul was still in Gilgal with all the army trembling behind him.
[8]He waited seven days until the time Samuel had stipulated, but Samuel did not come to Gilgal, and the army began to drift away from
him. [9]So [he] said, "Bring the holocaust and the communion offer-
ings to me!" And he offered up the holocaust. [10]But as soon as he
had finished offering [it] up, Samuel arrived! So Saul went out toward him to greet him.

[11]"What have you done?" said Samuel.

Saul replied, "When I saw that the army had begun to drift away from me and that you did not come in the appointed number of
days and that the Philistines were gathering at Michmash, [12]I said
to myself, 'Now the Philistines will come down against me at Gilgal—but I have not entreated Yahweh's favor!' So I took it upon myself to offer up the holocaust."

[13]"You acted foolishly," said Samuel to Saul. "If you had been

careful of the appointment that Yahweh, your god, gave you, then [he] would have established your kingship over Israel forever!
14 But now your kingship will not endure! Yahweh will seek out a man of his own choosing. He will appoint him as prince over his people, for you were not careful of what Yahweh appointed you."
15 Then Samuel set out from Gilgal and went his way, while the remnant of the army went up after Saul to meet the fighting force, going from Gilgal toward Gibeah of Benjamin. Saul mustered the people who were with him—some six hundred men.

TEXTUAL NOTES

13 2. *three thousands* So MT. When it is understood that a "thousand" is a military unit (see the NOTE at 4:10), there is no need to add "of men," as do LXX, Syr.

from Israel So MT. LXX^B: "from *the men of* Israel"; LXX^L: "from *the sons of* Israel."

at Michmash in the hill country of Bethel So LXX^B; other MSS, including MT and LXX^L, have "at Michmash *and* in the hill country of Bethel," as though one thousand was located in each place. It is more likely that the second prepositional phrase is intended to identify the site of Michmash. See the NOTE.

Geba Where we find Jonathan in 13:16. The similarity of the names of the Benjaminite cities *gib'â*, "Gibeah," and *geba'*, "Geba," has caused endless confusion in the text of cc 13 and 14. Elsewhere further difficulties arise from a third name, *gib'ōn*, "Gibeon." Despite numerous attempts it seems unlikely that a comprehensive solution to these problems can be found. Each occurrence of one of these names must be evaluated on its own merits, and (unhappily) textual evidence must always be eyed with suspicion. Here MT has *gib'â* (so Syr., Targ., Vulg.); LXX *gabaa* (so LXX^L; LXX^B *gabee*) is ambiguous but seems to reflect *gb'*, "Geba."

3. *Gibeah* MT has *gb'*, "Geba" (see the *Textual Note* at 13:2). LXX *en tō bounō*, "on the hill," points to Gibeah. Cf. 10:5.

and the Philistines were told, "The Hebrews have revolted!" Reading *wyšm'w plštym l'mr pš'w h'brym*, lit. ". . . and the Philistines heard, saying, 'The Hebrews have revolted!'" All principal witnesses have *wš'wl tq' bšwpr bkl h'rṣ*, "and Saul blew the horn throughout the land," before *l'mr*, but it is out of place at this point. It is characteristic of foreigners, not Israelites, to use the term "Hebrews" (see the NOTE). Moreover, as Driver points out, the intrusive clause fits naturally before v 4.

The Hebrews So MT: *h'brym*. LXX *hoi douloi* reflects *h'bdym*, "the slaves," an example of the frequent confusion of *r* and *d*.

have revolted Reading *pš'w* on the basis of LXX *ēthetēkasin.* MT *yšm'w,* "Let (the Hebrews) hear!" shows the influence of the intrusive clause about Saul's horn blowing.

Saul blew the horn throughout the land See above.

4. *rallied* MT *wayyiṣṣā'ăqû.* LXX[B(L)] (cf. OL) have *kai anebēsan,* "(and they) came up," an inner-Greek corruption of *kai aneboēsan* (attested in some MSS), "(and they) shouted," reflecting *wyṣ'qw,* a consonantal reading identical to that of MT. Cf. the third *Textual Note* at 11:7.

5. *Israel. They brought up . . . against Israel* Reading *yśr'l wy'lw 'l yśr'l* on the basis of LXX *israēl kai anabainousin epi israēl.* MT, which reads *yśr'l,* has lost the rest by haplography.

three So LXX[L], Syr. MT, LXX[B] have "thirty."

Beth-aven So MT. LXX: "Beth-horon." Syr.: "Bethel" (correctly). See the second NOTE at v 2.

6. *saw* In MT the verb has a plural form (*r'w*) after the collective singular subject (*'yš yśr'l,* "the men of Israel"); in LXX the verb is singular (*eiden* = *r'h*). Either is possible, but the reading of LXX is better in view of the subsequent collective singular *lw,* "to them," in both MT and LXX.

that they were hard pressed MT reads *ky ṣr lw ngś h'm,* "that they were hard pressed, that the people were oppressed," and Dhorme (followed by Hertzberg, Stoebe, and others) argues that this represents a conflation of ancient variants. The variants were *ky ṣr lw,* retained here, and (as the obscure reading of LXX[BA], *mē prosagein auton,* "not to bring him near" [?], may suggest) *ky ngś,* "that he was oppressed/hard pressed" (cf. Wellhausen).

thickets Most critics emend MT *ḥwḥym* to *ḥwrym,* "holes," following a suggestion of Ewald (cf. 14:11). But surely the *lectio difficilior* is original. It means "brambles, thickets," unless it has an otherwise unattested meaning that is more appropriate here. LXX renders it *mandrais,* "enclosed spaces," using a Greek term (*mandra*) which, like Hebrew *ḥwḥ,* can refer to the setting of a ring. Perhaps we should translate it as "enclosures."

7. *and crossed the fords of the Jordan* Reading *wy'brw m'brwt hyrdn* for MT *w'brym 'brw 't hyrdn,* "and Hebrews crossed the Jordan" (cf. LXX). See Wellhausen, Budde, etc. Stoebe defends MT.

8. *He waited* MT (*kĕtîb*) *wyyḥl,* a *Pi'el* without elision of *y.* MT (*qĕrê*) *wayyôḥel* is reminiscent of *tôḥēl,* "you must wait," in Samuel's instructions in 10:8 above.

until the time Samuel had stipulated Reading *lmw'd 'šr 'mr šmw'l,* lit. "until the appointed time that Samuel had said," on the basis of LXX, Targ. In MT *'mr* has fallen out after *'šr.*

9. *"Bring . . . to me!"* So MT. LXX: "Bring, that I may make. . . ."

11. *you did not come* So MT. LXX adds "as you arranged" (*hōs dietaxō*).

13. *If* Revocalizing *MT lō',* "not" ("You did not follow, etc.") as the hypothetical particle *lū'* (*lû'*) with Wellhausen and others, following an old suggestion of Ferdinand Hitzig.

the appointment that Yahweh, your god, gave you We read *'t mṣwt yhwh 'lhyk 'šr ṣwk,* lit. "the instruction of Yahweh, your god, that he instructed you," with MT, but the reading reflected by LXX (*'t mṣwty 'šr ṣwk yhwh,* "my instruction which Yahweh instructed you") is not demonstrably inferior. On the translation "appointment," see the NOTE.

15. MT has suffered a long haplography in the first part of the verse, a scribe's eye having skipped from the first "from Gilgal" to the second; thus, *wyqm šmw'l wy'l mn hglgl gb't bnymn,* "Then Samuel set out and went up from Gilgal toward Gibeah of Benjamin." On the basis of LXX (*kai anestē samouēl kai apēlthen ek galgalōn eis hodon autou kai to katalimma tou laou anebē opisō saoul eis apantēsin* [*opisō;* cf. Driver] *tou laou tou polemistou autōn paragenomenōn ek galgalōn eis gabaa beniamein*) we restore *wyqm šmw'l wylk mn hglgl ldrkw wytr h'm 'lh 'ḥry š'wl lqr't 'm hmlḥmh wyb'w* (cf. Driver) *mn hglgl gb't bnymyn.* The variation between *wy'l,* "and (he) went up," and *wylk,* "and (he) went," is probably secondary, *wylk* having been changed in the tradition behind MT to *wy'l* after the loss of *ldrkw,* "(on) his way."

NOTES

13 2. *thousands.* Military contingents. See the NOTE at 4:10.

Michmash in the hill country of Bethel. The modern site is the mountain village of Mukhmas, ca. 7 miles NE of Jerusalem and 3 or 4 miles S of Beitîn, ancient Bethel (see the NOTE at 7:16). For the topography, see the NOTE at 13:16.

Geba. The site of the ancient Benjaminite stronghold is the modern village of Jeba', ca. 6 miles NNE of Jerusalem. For the topography of Geba in relationship to Michmash, see the NOTE at 13:16.

3. *the Philistine prefect who was in Gibeah.* Cf. 10:5. If our geography is correct (see the fourth *Textual Note* to 13:2), Saul's home town is depicted as the location of an outpost charged with securing Philistine control of occupied Benjaminite territory. Jonathan's assassination of the prefect or governor is an act of rebellion and initiates the long war between Philistia and Israel that continues throughout Saul's lifetime.

The Hebrews. As usual the Israelites are called "Hebrews" in the speech of foreigners (cf. the NOTE at 4:6); but see the NOTE at 13:21.

4. *at Gilgal.* The mention of Gilgal (see the NOTE at 11:14) brings to mind Samuel's instructions in 10:8 and the ceremony described in 11:14-15. We are to assume that Saul has remained there: the notice in 13:2, like that in 13:1, is summary; it describes the general deployment of Saul's forces, and does not mean that he was at Michmash at the time of Jonathan's assassination of the prefect.

5. *at Michmash, east of Beth-aven.* See the NOTE at 13:2. The name *bêt 'āwen,* which means "House of Wickedness," is used by Hosea (4:15; 5:8; 10:5) as a pejorative substitute for Bethel ("House of God"), and Bethel is

probably also intended here and in 14:23 below. The name appears also in Josh 18:12 and 7:2, and the latter passage, because it reads in MT *'m byt 'wn mqdm lbyt 'l,* "near Beth-aven to the east of Bethel," has been cited as evidence for an independent Beth-aven; but the text of MT in Josh 7:2 is the result of a conflation of two readings and should be corrected to read *'m byt 'l,* "near Bethel" (so LXX^B).

6. Archaeological evidence shows that the caves of Palestine often provided refuge for people in danger. On the walls of a cave near Lachish, for example, are incised what seem to be the prayers of a refugee from the Babylonian onslaught of 588-586 B.C. The inscriptions on the W and S walls read *nqh yh 'l ḥnn nqh yh yhwh,* "Spare (me), O merciful God! Spare (me), O Yahweh!" and *hwš'* [*y*]*hwh,* "Save (me), O Yahweh!" See J. Naveh, "Old Hebrew Inscriptions in a Burial Cave," *IEJ* 13 (1963) 74-96; and for this interpretation, F. M. Cross, "The Cave Inscriptions from Khirbet Beit Lei," in *Near Eastern Archaeology in the Twentieth Century* [Nelson Glueck Volume], ed. J. A. Sanders (Garden City, N.Y.: Doubleday, 1970) 299-306, esp. 302.

7. *Gad and Gilead.* Like Gilead (cf. the NOTE at 11:1) Gad was used as a general designation for Israelite lands E of the Jordan, but properly it was the territory of the tribe of Gad, which together with that of Reuben made up Gilead. For the boundaries, see Josh 13:24-28 (cf. Num 32).

7b-15a. The older record of Saul's hostilities with the Philistines is interrupted at this point by the insertion of an account of Saul's indictment by Samuel told from a prophetic perspective. The reference in v 8a is to Samuel's instructions in 10:8, where Saul was told to wait at Gilgal until Samuel arrived. There Saul was a young man still living in his father's house; here he is king of Israel and has a grown son of his own. Yet according to the timetable of the prophetic author of 10:8 and 13:7b-15a, only seven days have passed since Saul's completion of the journey Samuel started him on in 10:2*ff*! In the older, unamended version of the story the events of cc 13-14 were supposed to have taken place long after Saul's return from the search for his father's asses.

9. *the holocaust and the communion offerings.* Cf. the NOTES at 6:14 and 10:8. According to 10:8 Samuel had intended to make these offerings himself.

13,14. The incident reaches its climax in Samuel's abrupt indictment of Saul, which takes the form of an oracle of judgment (cf. Birch, *Rise of the Israelite Monarchy,* 80-83). The prophet's words derive their force from play on the verb *ṣiwwâ* and the related noun *miṣwâ.* The semantic range of the former includes both "command" and "appoint," so that it can be used at once of Yahweh's commanding Saul to wait for Samuel at Gilgal and of Yahweh's appointing a new king in Saul's place. A connection is deliberately drawn between Saul's appointment as king and his appointment with Samuel. The charge in v 13 that Saul should have "been careful of the appointment that Yahweh, your god, gave you" (*šāmartā 'et-miṣwat yahweh 'ĕlōhêkā 'ašer ṣiwwāk*) delicately balances the two ideas: Saul did not keep the appointment (with Samuel), and so also he did not carefully execute his appointment (as king). Now Yahweh will find Saul's successor and appoint him (*wayṣawwēhû*) king-designate, since Saul did not keep/carefully execute his appointment.

13. *your kingship over Israel forever! / your kingship will not endure.* It is not Saul's reign that is at stake. It is his dynasty. See the COMMENT.

14. *a man of his own choosing.* Hebrew *'îš kilbābô,* lit. "a man according to his own heart." This has nothing to do with any great fondness of Yahweh's for David or any special quality of David, to whom it patently refers. Rather it emphasizes the free divine selection of the heir to the throne (*nāgîd,* "prince"), as the alternative to the endurance of Saul's "kingship [dynasty!] over Israel forever" (see the preceding NOTE and the COMMENT). As its use in 14:7 shows, the expression *klbb,* "according to (one's) heart," has to do with an individual's will or purpose. Compare Ps 20:5(English 20:4):

> *yitten lĕkā kilbābekā*
> *wĕkol 'ăṣātĕkā yĕmallē'*
> May he give to you according to
> your heart,
> And your every purpose may he
> fulfill!

The present passage, therefore, asserts the freedom of the divine will in choosing a new king in the spirit of the prophetic theology of leadership already described in the COMMENT on 9:1-10:16. So also Jer 3:15: *wĕnātattî lākem rō'îm kĕlibbî,* "And I (Yahweh) shall give you shepherds (= kings) of my own choosing. . . ."

COMMENT

The cries of popular acclamation for Saul have hardly subsided before his kingship is censured by Yahweh's prophet. As political events in the hills around Bethel rush toward a major conflict with the Philistines, Saul bides his time impatiently at Gilgal looking for the arrival of Samuel. There was to have been a wait of seven days (10:8; cf. the NOTE at 12:7b-15a), but when the time finally expires Saul is far from relieved and confident. His army is deserting, and in his anxiety not to do battle without first having "entreated Yahweh's favor" he takes it upon himself to make the offerings Samuel was to have made. So when the old prophet arrives, he finds the victims already upon the altar. "You acted foolishly," says Samuel, and he abruptly declares that Saul's kingship is condemned.

As pointed out in the NOTES, the narration of the incident is animated by a rather subtle play on words in Samuel's final speech that unobtrusively but effectively directs our attention toward one central theme, viz. the relationship between kingship and obedience to Yahweh. On the surface this is the story of a broken *appointment:* for failing to keep the terms of the meeting precisely as stipulated Saul is judged blameworthy. He has disobeyed Yahweh, or rather Yahweh's prophet. Thus he has violated the terms of his *appointment* as king. Kingship requires obedience. The *appointment* of the prince or king-designate (*nāgîd*), therefore, will go not to Saul's son but to "a man of [Yahweh's] own choosing." Saul's kingship will not endure; his son will not succeed him. There is going to be a new king.

Here again we recognize the prophetic theology of political leadership that structures the stories of Samuel and Saul in their present form. The prophet is Yahweh's official spokesman and thus is not to be gainsaid or disobeyed. Kingship is suspect. It will be tolerated but, as we now see, only as subject to the controlling authority of the prophet. Most dubious is the dynastic aspect of kingship, since it interferes with the free divine election of the king as exercised through the prophets. Yahweh must have "a man of his own choosing" as king (see the NOTE at v 14); and only if a man is obedient to Yahweh can he hope for his son to be chosen to succeed him as king.

Here again, too, we can see that the prophetic perspective has been forwarded by a reworking of older material—in this case, it seems, by a simple insertion. The larger literary unit is that which describes the battle of Michmash Pass and the cursing of Jonathan; into this the report of the Gilgal incident has been introduced. Verses 3-7a,15b (on which see the COMMENT to 13:16-14:23a) represent the beginning of the account of the battle of Michmash Pass, as directly continued in vv 16*ff*. The insertion, then, includes vv 7b-15a (and possibly also 4b). The new arrangement is somewhat awkward for the geography of the story: the audience is shunted unceremoniously from the vicinity of Gibeah (v 3) to Gilgal (v 7b, cf. 4b) and then back to Gibeah (v 15). But the prophetic writer makes his point amid the confusion.

The older story that began with Jonathan's rebellion-provoking assassination of the Philistine prefect at Gibeah (vv 3-4 above) will continue in the pitched battle that is about to ensue.

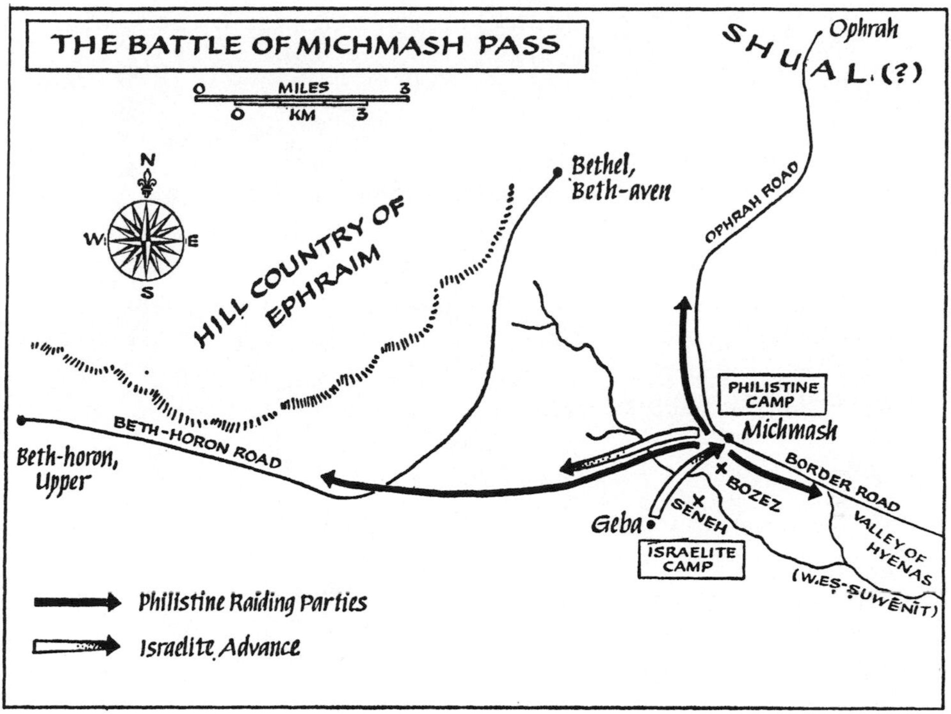
THE BATTLE OF MICHMASH PASS
0 MILES 3
0 KM 3
N
W
E
S
HILL COUNTRY OF EPHRAIM
Bethel, Beth-aven
Ophrah
SHUAL (?)
OPHRAH ROAD
PHILISTINE CAMP
Michmash
BORDER ROAD
BOZEZ
SENEH
Geba
ISRAELITE CAMP
VALLEY OF HYENAS
(W. EṢ-ṢUWENIT)
Beth-horon, Upper
BETH-HORON ROAD
Philistine Raiding Parties
Israelite Advance

XVIII. THE BATTLE OF MICHMASH PASS (13:16-14:23a)

13 16 Saul, his son Jonathan, and the troops who were with them
were staying in Geba of Benjamin, and the Philistines had encamped
at Michmash. 17 From time to time a certain raiding party came out
of the Philistine camp in three squadrons: one squadron would take
the Ophrah road toward the land of Shual, 18 another would take the
Beth-horon road, and still another would take the border road
overlooking the Valley of Hyenas.

Israel Disarmed

19 There was no smith to be found in all the land of Israel, for the
Philistines had said to themselves, "The Hebrews might make swords
or spears!" 20 So all Israel would go down to the Philistines to repair
any of their plowshares, mattocks, axes, or sickles. 21 The price was a
paim for plowshares and mattocks and a third of a shekel for picks
and axes or setting an ox-goad. 22 So at the time of the battle of
Michmash neither sword nor spear was available to any of the soldiers who were with Saul and Jonathan—only Saul and his son
Jonathan had them.

The First Engagement

23 A Philistine outpost had advanced into Michmash Pass.
14 1 That same day Saul's son Jonathan said to the servant who
carried his weapons, "Come, let us cross over to the Philistine outpost
on the other side!" But he did not inform his father— 2 Saul was on
the outskirts of Geba sitting under a pomegranate tree, which was on
the threshing floor, and with him were about six hundred men, 3 as
well as Ahijah, son of Ahitub, brother of Ichabod, son of Phinehas,
son of Eli, the priest of Yahweh at Shiloh, who was wearing the
ephod—so the army did not know that Jonathan had gone.

4 Now within the pass through which Jonathan planned to cross to
the Philistine outpost there were rocky crags, one on each side: the

name of the one was Bozez and of the other Seneh; 5 the one crag was to the north opposite Michmash and the other to the south opposite Geba.

6 Jonathan said to the servant who carried his weapons, "Come, let us cross over to the outpost of those uncircumcised! It may be that Yahweh will give us victory, for nothing can prevent Yahweh from gaining victory, whether by many or by few!"

7 "Do whatever you have in mind," said his weapon-bearer. "I shall be with you! We are of the same mind!"

8 So Jonathan said, "We shall cross over to the men and show ourselves to them. 9 If they say to us, 'Stand still until we come to you!'
we shall stay where we are and not go up to them; 10 but if they say,
'Come up to us!' we shall go up, for Yahweh will have given them into our power. That will be the sign for us."

11 When the two of them showed themselves to the Philistine outpost, the Philistines said to themselves, "Hebrews, coming out of the
holes where they hid themselves!" 12 The men of the outpost called to
Jonathan and his weapon-bearer. "Come up here to us," they said, "so that we may show you something!"

Then Jonathan told his weapon-bearer, "Come up after me, for
Yahweh has delivered them into the power of Israel!" 13 Jonathan
climbed up on his hands and feet, his weapon-bearer behind him; and when [the Philistines] turned toward [him], he struck them down, his weapon-bearer dispatching them behind him (with darts and crude flint weapons).

14 In this first engagement Jonathan and his weapon-bearer struck
down about twenty men. 15 There was a convulsion in the camp and
in the field: all the soldiers of the garrison and in the raiding party, too, shuddered; then the earth shook, and it became an awesome convulsion!

The Rout of the Philistines

16 Some of Saul's watchmen in Geba of Benjamin saw that the
camp was surging back and forth; 17 so Saul said to the troops who
were with him, "Call the roll to see who has gone from us!" And when they called the roll, Jonathan and his weapon-bearer were not
there. 18 Then Saul said to Ahijah, "Bring the ephod!" (for he was
wearing the ephod at that time before Israel). 19 But as Saul was talking to the priest, the confusion in the Philistine camp was growing

greater and greater; so [he] said to the priest, "Withdraw your hand!"

20 Saul and all the soldiers who were with him assembled and marched to the battle, where the swords [of the Philistines] were turned against each other in a very great panic. 21 As for the Hebrews who had sided previously with the Philistines and gone up into the camp, they too turned to be with Israel under Saul and Jonathan;
22 and when all the Israelites who had been hiding in the hill country of Ephraim heard that the Philistines had fled, they too pursued them in the fighting.

23a So Yahweh gained victory that day for Israel.

TEXTUAL NOTES

13 16. *in Geba of Benjamin* So MT, LXX, and the topography is decisive: see the NOTE. After "Benjamin" LXX (cf. Syr., OL) adds *kai eklaion*, "and they wept"; omit with MT.

17. *From time to time . . . came out* In view of the succeeding imperfects MT *wyṣ'* should be vocalized *wĕyāṣā'* and read as a converted perfect expressing repeated action in the past. MT reads *wayyēṣē'*, simply "came out." See also the NOTE to vv 17,18.

18. *the border road* So MT: *drk gbwl*. LXX(B): "the Geba road" (= *drk gb'*).

the Valley of Hyenas MT adds *hammidbārâ*, "toward the wilderness," i.e. the wilderness of Jordan, for clarity. Omit with LXX[BL].

19. *had said to themselves* That is, *'āmĕrû* (so LXX, MT *qĕrê*). MT *kĕtîb* (*'mr*) is defective.

20. *would go down* Repointing MT *wayyērĕdû*, "went down," as *wĕyārĕdû*. The verb was originally intended to indicate repeated action in the past, as in the case of *wĕhāyĕtâ* in the next verse.

to the Philistines Restoring *'l hplštym* in MT, which has lost *'l* after *yśr'l*. LXX *eis gēn allophyloi* = *'rṣh plštym*, "to *the land of* the Philistines" (cf. Targ.), might be original, but the loss of *'rṣ*(*h*) is difficult to explain.

sickles MT repeats the previous word for "plowshare" (*mḥrštw*) in a slightly different form. We read *ḥrmšw* on the basis of LXX *drepanon*, "scythe, sickle." In v 21, however, the same Greek word seems to correspond to MT *drbn*, "ox-goad," and Wellhausen proposes to restore *drbnw* here; the similarity of sound between the Hebrew and Greek words might have influenced the rendering (as in v 21). But the corruption of *ḥrmšw* to *mḥrštw* is easier to understand.

21. *The price* Hebrew *pĕṣîrâ*. See the NOTE.

and a third of a shekel for picks Reading *wšlšt hšql lqlšwn* (for the noun *qilšôn,* "pick," see Gordis, "Note"), a sequence that is ripe for haplography. Thus MT (*wlšlš qlšwn,* "and for three picks" [?], where initial *l-* has arisen in a long succession of words with initial *l-*) and LXX (*kai treis sikloi eis ton odonta* = *wšlšt šql*[*ym*] *lšn,* "and three shekels for the tooth") preserve corrupt remnants.

22. *So at the time of the battle of Michmash* MT reads *whyh bywm mlḥmt,* "So it would happen on the day of battle (that) . . ."; that is, "So whenever there was a battle. . . ." Thus MT understands this to be continuation of the description of the situation that used to prevail: no specific battle is meant. But *mlḥmt* is a construct form and a governing noun must have been lost. LXX, then, is probably correct in adding *machemas,* "Michmash," here. The original was *wyhy* (changed in MT to *whyh* after the loss of *mkmš*) *bywm mlḥmt mkmš,* lit. "So it happened on the day (LXX, 'days') of the battle of Michmash (that). . . ."

23. LXX adds "and he did not inform his father," a misplaced duplicate of the last part of 14:1.

14 2. *Geba* Though MT, LXX, and Targ. all point to "Gibeah," topographical considerations seem to require "Geba," especially in view of v 16 below where Saul's watchmen see the battle raging at Michmash Pass. Gibeah —even on its outskirts—is too far away. For a different explanation see Stoebe, "Topographie."

on the threshing floor Reading *bĕmô gōren.* The long form of the preposition has confused later scribes, as in 4:8 and 10:27b (= 11:1); thus MT reads *bĕmigrôn,* "in Migron" (under the influence of Isa 10:28?). See further the NOTE.

and with him were So LXX. MT "and *the troops who were* with him were. . . ."

3. *Eli* So MT (correctly). LXX: "Levi."

Yahweh So MT, LXX^{L}. LXX^{B}: "God."

4. *rocky crags, one on each side* MT *šn hslʿ mhʿbr mzh wšn hslʿ mhʿbr mzh,* lit. "a certain tooth of rock on this side and a certain tooth of rock on that side." LXX^{B} seems to render the statement twice: (1) *akrōtērion petras enthen kai akrōtērion petras enthen* = *šn* (?) *hslʿ mhʿbr wšn* (?) *hslʿ mhʿbr;* and (2) fragmentarily, *kai odous petras ek toutou* = *wšn hslʿ mzh.* As LXX^{B} suggests, *mhʿbr* (*enthen*) and *mzh* (*ek toutou*) are not both necessary; they may represent a conflation in MT of variant readings.

5. *crag* So MT (*šēn,* lit. "tooth"). LXX^{B} has *hodos,* "road, path," but as Driver points out this must be an inner-Greek corruption of *odous,* "tooth."

to the north That is, *mṣpwn.* MT precedes this with *mṣwq,* "as a pillar (?)," a corrupt anticipation of *mṣpwn* (Driver); delete with LXX, OL.

6. *will give us victory* Emending MT (cf. LXX) *yʿśh . . . lnw,* "will do for us," to *ywšyʿ . . . lnw* (without textual support). The corruption arose from a simple metathesis of *š/ś* and *ʿ* in the old orthography (*yšʿ* > *yʿś*). Many critics have defended MT here (Smith, Stoebe), but the correction seems likely in view of *lhwšyʿ,* "to gain victory," in the following clause (cf. v 23 below).

7. *Do whatever you have in mind* Reading *ʿśh ʾšr* (so LXX^{L}; LXX^{B}

reflects *kl 'šr) lbbk nṭh lw*, lit. "Do that which your heart inclines to," with LXX against MT *'śh kl 'šr blbbk nṭh lk*, "Do all that is in your heart! Turn!(?)"

We are of the same mind! Reading *klbby klbbk*, lit. "My heart is like your heart!" (cf. LXX). MT has lost *klbby* by haplography.

9. *Stand still* So MT. LXX adds "there."

10. *if they say* So MT. LXX adds "to us."

to us So LXX (*pros hēmas* = *'lynw*). MT has "against us" (*'lynw*); but cf. v 12.

That Reading *zh* with LXX. MT *wzh*, "And that," shows dittography of the preceding *w*.

11. *showed themselves* So MT. LXX: "went."

12. *the outpost* MT has *hammaṣṣābâ*, a form unique to this passage. The previously used form (*hammaṣṣāb*) is reflected by LXX^{B} *messaph*.

13. *and when [the Philistines] turned toward [him]* Reading *wypnw lpny ywntn* on the basis of LXX *kai epeblepsen kata prosōpon iōnathan*, against MT *wyplw lpny ywntn*, "and they fell before Jonathan," which is too abrupt.

he struck them down Inserting *wykm* with LXX. Omitted in MT.

(*with darts and crude flint weapons*) This notice now stands at the end of v 14 in all versions, but it probably arose as a marginal gloss at the end of v 13, intended to identify the weapons of Jonathan's weapon-bearer in view of 13:19-22 above (Wellhausen). We read *bḥṣym wb'bny ṣrr* (or *wbṣrry*) *hśdh* on the basis of LXX^{BA} *en bolisi kai en kochlaxin tou pediou*. LXX^{L}, OL add *kai en petrobolois*, "and with slingstones," but as noted by Wellhausen this is a gloss explaining *kochlaxin*, "pebbles." MT has *kbḥṣy m'nh ṣmd śdh*, traditionally rendered, "as it were within half a furrow, an acre of field," or the like; but MT is plainly corrupt. The initial *k* is not reflected in LXX, but the next five letters are identical in MT and the *Vorlage* of LXX. The sequence *b'bny* has been corrupted in MT to *nh* as a result of haplography of *'b* after *b* and subsequent confusion of *b* for *'*. The distortion of *ṣrr* to *ṣmd* is not difficult to understand, especially in view of the close similarity of the forms of the letters *r* and *d*. (Some consideration must also be given to the reading *bḥṣbym* = *baḥăṣûbîm*, "with hewn [stones]," at the beginning, especially in view of the evidence of Syr., which reflects *kḥṣbym*, and the initial *k* of MT.) For a different solution to this old crux, see Driver, "Old Problems Re-examined."

15. *in the camp and in the field* Reading *bmḥnh wbśdh* with LXX in preference to *bmḥnh bśdh*, "in the camp in the field," of MT.

all the soldiers of the garrison . . . shuddered The text is most awkward and may be over full (Stoebe). MT reads: *wbkl h'm hmṣb whmšḥyt ḥrdw gm hmh*, "and among all the soldiers. The garrison and the raiding party shuddered —they, too!" We read *wkl 'm hmṣb*, etc. (cf. Targ., Syr., Vulg.). LXX^{B} has a still longer text: *kai pas ho laos hoi en messaph kai hoi diaphtheirontes exestēsan kai autoi ouk ēthelon poiein* (LXX^{L} *ponein*), as if the original read, ". . . and all the soldiers, both those in the garrison and those in the raiding party, shuddered, and they were not willing *to act* (?; LXX^{L} 'to toil'?)." See further Wellhausen, Smith, Stoebe.

and it became an awesome convulsion So MT: *wthy lḥrdt 'lhym*, lit. "and it became a convulsion of God" (see the NOTE). LXX reflects *wthy ḥrdt yhwh*, "and there was a convulsion of Yahweh." Cf. Wellhausen.

16. *the camp* So LXX^{B} (LXX^{L} adds "of the Philistines"). MT *hhmwn*, "the confusion," seems to anticipate v 19.

was surging back and forth Reading *nmwg hlm whlm* on the basis of LXX *tetaragmenē enthen kai enthen*. MT *nmwg wylk whlm*, "was surging and went (?) and . . . (?)" is untranslatable (cf. Driver). The corruption of *hlm* to *wylk* may have begun with anticipation of *wylk hlwk wrb*, "was growing greater and greater" in v 19.

17. *Jonathan and his weapon-bearer were not there* So MT (*'yn ywntn* . . .). LXX reflects *l' nmṣ' ywntn* . . . , "Jonathan and his weapon-bearer were not found."

18. Strangely enough MT has the ark in place of the ephod in this verse: *hgyšh 'rwn h'lhym ky hyh 'rwn h'lhym bywm hhw' wbny yśr'l*, ". . . 'Bring the ark of God'—for the ark of God was present [?] at that time—'and the Israelites!'" With most critics we read the text reflected by LXX^{BL}: *hgyšh h'pwd ky hw' nś' h'pwd bywm hhw' lpny yśr'l*. Contrast Davies, "Ark or Ephod."

19. *as Saul was talking* Repointing MT *'ad dibber šā'ûl* as an infinitive construction, *'ad dabbēr šā'ûl*, with Stoebe following Smith, who compares Judg 3:26 and Exod 33:22.

20. *assembled* So MT: *wayyizzā'ēq*. It is true, as Smith points out, that elsewhere "this is used of the people who are summoned to war, not of the leader who summons them." But there is no supporting parallel for reading *wayyiz'aq* (cf. LXX^{A} *kai aneboēsen*), "shouted." LXX^{BL} have *kai anebē*, suggesting *wy'l*, "went up," but this may be an inner-Greek corruption of *kai aneboēsen*.

21. *the Hebrews* So MT: *h'brym*. LXX: *hoi douloi* = *h'bdym*, "the slaves." Cf. the *Textual Note* to 13:3.

and gone up So LXX. MT adds *'mm*, "with them."

they too turned Reading *sbbw gm hmh* on the basis of LXX *anestrophēsan kai autoi*. MT has misdivided the words and reads *sbyb wgm hmh*, ". . . round about. And they, too. . . ."

NOTES

13 16. As explained in the NOTES to 13:2, Geba and Michmash were Benjaminite cities only a mile or two apart in the rugged hill country S of Bethel. They were separated by a deep ravine, a part of what is now called the Wadi eṣ-Ṣuwēnīṭ, a narrow but strategically important pass from the Jordan Valley into the Ephraimite hills. This is the setting for the battle of Michmash Pass: the Philistines command the hilltop site that overlooks the ravine from the N, while the Israelites are encamped to the S. See further Stoebe, "Topographie," esp. 271-272, 275*ff*.

17,18. From time to time (see the *Textual Note* to v 17) the Philistines, in order to maintain their control of Israelite territory and probably in response to the act of rebellion described in 13:3, would make a raid on the surrounding countryside, sending squadrons N, W, and E as follows:

17. *the Ophrah road toward the land of Shual.* Ophrah (*'oprâ*) is listed as a Benjaminite city in Josh 18:23; it is probably identical to Ephron (*'eprôn*) in II Chron 13:19 and (according to the evidence of Jerome) to Ephraim (*'eprayim*) in II Sam 13:23 (cf. John 11:54), modern eṭ-Ṭaiyibeh, ca. 5 miles N of Mukhmas (ancient Michmash) and 4 miles NE of Beitîn (ancient Bethel). For the land of Shual, see the third NOTE at 9:4.

18. *the Beth-horon road.* Raids to the W followed the road toward Beth-horon, or rather the two Beth-horons, Upper (modern Beit 'Ur el-Foqa) and Lower (modern Beit 'Ur et-Taḥta); the former was some 10 miles due W of Michmash. This squadron evidently followed the main highway that ran from Bethel past the two Beth-horons and on down into the Philistine Plain, the route of the Philistine retreat described in 14:23b.

the border road overlooking the Valley of Hyenas. The Valley of Hyenas or Zeboim (*ṣĕbō'îm*) is probably the modern Wadi Abū Ḍabā', SE of Mukhmas (Michmash), which like the Wadi Ṣuwēnīṭ flows into the Wadi Qilt and so into the Jordan. Perhaps the border road was so called because it led to the border of the tribal territory of Benjamin (near Debir or the Adummim pass?).

19-22. The Philistine army of occupation denied Israel the wherewithal to arm itself. This parenthetical notice serves not only to portray the restrictions imposed by Philistine rule but also to emphasize the importance of divine help in the Israelite victory described below. See the COMMENT.

20. *plowshares.* Perhaps we should simply render "plows" or "plowtips." A plow of this period was a simple metal blade attached to a wooden handle. The moldboard plow, on which the blade could be distinguished as a share, came later.

21. *The price.* Hebrew *happĕṣîrâ.* The word is otherwise unknown, and the present translation is a guess from context. Cf. Bewer, "Notes," 45-46. Others render it "Sharpening" or "The (price for) sharpening" (KB). Cf. Driver, "Hebrew *pĕṣîrâ.*"

a paim. The term *payim* occurs only here in the Hebrew Bible but is known from a series of inscribed stone weights found in various excavations in Palestine. The average weight of the stones marked *pym* (= *paym;* thus MT *pîm* is wrong) is 7.616 grams (= 0.268 oz.) or about two-thirds of a shekel (see the NOTE at 9:8). Cf. O. R. Sellers, *IDB,* s.v. "Weights and Measures," B. 4.b,d,f,g. In other words the Philistine smiths charged two-thirds of a shekel (presumably of silver) for a new plow or mattock and half that amount for repairing an ax or a goad.

23. Up until now the narrator has been setting the stage. Now the action begins, signaled in Hebrew by the story's first verb in the converted imperfect, the standard vehicle for past narration. An outpost has advanced from the Philistine camp onto the slope of the ravine that separates Michmash from Geba and the Israelites.

14 2. The picture of the ruler sitting on the threshing floor at the gate of the city is age-old. A Late Bronze Age poem from Ugarit describes the Canaanite hero Daniel as follows:

'apnk dn'l mt rp'i
'aphn ǵzr mt hrnmy
ytš'u yṯb b'ap ṯǵr
tḥt 'adrm dbgrn
ydn dn 'almnt
yṯpṭ ṯpṭ ytm

Then Daniel, man of Rapi'u,
Ghazir, man of Hrnmy,
Sits erect before the gate
Under the mighty tree which is
    on the threshing floor.
He judges the cause of the widow,
Decides the case of the orphan.

CTCA 17(= 2 Aqht).5.4-8; 19(= 1 Aqht).1.19-25

Compare also I Kings 22:10, where the kings of Israel and Judah are described before a battle "sitting on their respective thrones, dressed in their robes, on the threshing floor at the entrance of the gate of Samaria." Just as Saul consults Yahweh here (vv 18-19) by means of the ephod, so also the two kings inquire of their prophets. For the Canaanite Daniel, too, the threshing floor is a place of theophany (*CTCA* 17.5.4*ff*) and (apparently) divination (19.1.19*ff*).

about six hundred men. Cf. 13:15.

3. *Ahijah, son of Ahitub.* Saul's chaplain is the great-grandson of Eli, priest of Shiloh (for Eli and Phinehas, see cc 1-4 *passim;* for Ichabod, see 4:19-22). He is the son of Ahitub and therefore the brother of Ahimelech, priest of Nob and father of Abiathar (22:9,11,12,20).

the ephod. The ornate ephod and breastpiece described in Exodus 28 and 39 made up the distinguishing costume of the chief priest in the Jerusalem cult. Ahijah's ephod in the present passage represents similar authority. In these tales it functions primarily as a means of consulting Yahweh (see below, NOTE to vv 18,19; cf. 23:6) and must have contained a pocket or compartment for the Urim and Thummim (cf. 28:30) used by Saul in 14:41,42 (see the NOTE).

4,5. Jonathan has in mind a pass or ford through which the intervening wadi can be crossed, but within the pass on his side is a large outcropping of rock called Seneh and within the pass on the other side is a second rock, Bozez. These names suggest the difficulty of crossing: (1) *senneh* (so MT) means "the Thorny One" (cf. *sĕneh,* "thornbush"; Empire Aramaic *sanyā',* "thornbush"); (2) *bôṣēṣ* means "the Gleaming One" (cf. Arabic *baṣṣa,* "glitter, shine, gleam") or "the Miry One" (cf. *bōṣ,* "mire"; *biṣṣâ,* "swamp").

6b. Compare the words of Judas Maccabaeus, brother of another Jonathan who figured prominently in the history of Michmash (I Macc 9:73), which read almost like a midrash on the present verse: "And Judas said: 'It is easy for many to be overpowered by a few; nor is it different before Heaven to save by many or by few! For not on the size of the army does victory in battle depend: rather it is from Heaven that strength comes!" (I Macc 3:18-19).

11. Cf. 13:6.

13. *dispatching them.* Hebrew *mĕmôtēt.* As in 17:51 the *Polel* of *mwt,* "die," refers to dispatching or "finishing off" someone already wounded and near death. So also Judg 9:54; II Sam 1:9,10,16.

15. *the raiding party.* See 13:17-18 above.

an awesome convulsion. Hebrew *ḥerdat 'ĕlōhîm,* lit. "a shuddering of God." For this intensifying use of *'ĕlōhîm,* see D. Winton Thomas, "A Consideration of Some Unusual Ways of Expressing the Superlative in Hebrew," *VT* 3 (1953) 209-224. The point here is that the convulsion has reached superhuman proportions; there is divine participation in Jonathan's exploit. See further the COMMENT.

16. *Some of Saul's watchmen.* Hebrew *haṣṣōpîm lĕšā'ûl.* See the first NOTE at 9:3.

18,19. In his confusion Saul summons his chaplain and commands him to seek divine guidance by means of the ephod (see the NOTE at 14:3 above) or rather the Urim and Thummim contained in it (see the NOTE at 14:40-42). It is not clear exactly what Saul hopes to discover with the oracular equipment, except that he intends in general to ask Yahweh's will. But he does not carry the intention through: in the heat of the moment he interrupts the consultation and marches precipitately into battle (v 20). This is another example of the fatal impetuosity that every part of the tradition attributes to Saul (13:9; 14:24; etc.).

20. *a very great panic.* Hebrew *mĕhûmâ gĕdōlâ mĕ'ōd.* See the NOTE at 4:5. Like "the awesome convulsion" of v 15 this panic is ultimately of divine origin. In their consternation the helpless Philistines actually fight against each other, so that the Israelites, though lacking suitable weapons (13:19*ff*) and greatly outnumbered (cf. 13:5) easily win an advantage.

21. *the Hebrews.* As already noted (NOTE at 4:6) the term *'ibrî,* "Hebrew," appears most often in the Bible as the designation of an Israelite in the speech of foreigners (or in speeches by Israelites to foreigners: Exod 3:18; Jonah 1:9; etc.); the only clear exceptions in narrative materials to this generalization occur in Gen 14:13 (see below), in the story of Moses, where the ethnic distinction between Egyptians and Hebrews is crucial (Exod 1:15; 2:11,13), and in the present passage. The term is also used in legal (Exod 21:2; Deut 15:12) or quasi-legal (Jer 34:9,14) material, where matters of kinship require emphasis. It seems clear, then, that "Hebrews" is an *ethnic* term distinct from *religio-political* designations such as "Israel," "sons of Israel," etc. But the question of the background and original meaning of the term is a difficult one. Scholars have long entertained the possibility of a connection between *'ibrî* and *'apiru,* a title applied to certain peoples of disputed cultural background and affiliation who are referred to in second-millennium B.C. texts from Mesopotamia, Egypt, and Syria-Palestine, most often as enemies of established societies. There is still no agreement whether the *'apirū* were in fact nomadic tribesmen who inhabited the fringes of urban civilization making occasional attempts to seize land (so most recently M. C. Astour, *IDBSup,* s.v. "Habiru") or disenfranchised people of mixed origin, who banded together out of mutual interest (see Mendenhall, *The Tenth Generation,* c V). It has become increasingly difficult, however, to defend any direct connection between *'apiru* and *'ibrî.* All scholars agree that the former was never an ethnic designation (though this could have been a pe-

culiar, secondary development in Israel; cf. Mendenhall). Moreover the philological correspondence cannot be forced to work: (1) the development *'apir-* > *'ipr* has no indisputable parallel, and (2) the variation of *p* and *b* is unlikely, especially in view of the Ugaritic evidence that *'apiru* was the Northwest Semitic original (on both points see Astour). Study of the *'apiru* phenomenon may still be quite instructive to students of the early history of Israel (so Astour as well as Mendenhall), but it is doubtful that it will shed any light on the meaning of the ethnic designation "Hebrew." So it seems best to maintain the old opinion that *'ibrî* is simply a gentilic of *'ēber,* "region beyond," i.e. "the region beyond the Euphrates (*'ēber hannāhār*), Mesopotamia," used in Israelite tradition to distinguish the family of Abraham (thus the reference in Gen 14:13 to "Abram the Hebrew") from the indigenous population of Canaan and from foreigners (cf. already GK §2b); n.b. Josh 24:2,3. It follows that the Hebrews referred to here are people of recognized kinship to the followers of Saul who allied themselves politically with the Philistines in the past. They are not "Canaanites" or "Amorites" in the technical biblical sense of either term (cf. the NOTE at 7:14); they are not Philistines; they are different from Israelites only insofar as they have been aligned politically with the Philistines. It is easiest to assume that originally they were loyal Israelites who defected to the enemy in times of distress and who now return as the fortunes of war change again. See further the COMMENT.

22. Cf. 13:6; 14:11.

pursued. Hebrew *wayyadbĕqû* instead of the expected form *wayyadbîqû* (Judg 18:22). See GK §53n.

COMMENT

The details of the great Israelite victory at Michmash Pass together with Saul's thwarted follow-up campaign (see 14:36*ff*) provide the context for an important anecdote about the king and the king's son. As we shall see, this is finally a story about Saul and Jonathan, and an interest in them is the reason it has come down to us at all. But the report of the battle itself is not without its own interest. The old story (for there is no evidence of late reworking here) provides plausible information about political circumstances at a crucial juncture in the rise of the Israelite state.

The general situation in Palestine is clear. It is a time of Philistine occupation, or at least of a strong Philistine military presence, in the central hill country. The "Hebrews" who live there (see the NOTE at v 21) are subject to certain constraints; in particular they are deprived of the wherewithal to arm themselves (13:19-22). In their allegiance to Israel, the political entity of which Saul is leader, they are fickle (cf. v 21), though Israel has a natural claim on their loyalty. Saul's armies, deployed in the hills around Bethel to the north of Gibeah (13:2), represent an organized resistance force.

In the immediate background is Jonathan's assassination of the Philistine prefect at Gibeah, an act of open rebellion in consequence of which Israel became the object of the vindictive fury of their enemies, who with Israelites fleeing before them move into Michmash threatening the center of Saul's base of power (13:3-7a). So at the beginning of the present section we find Philistines and Israelites encamped face-to-face across Michmash Pass. Saul and his men are dug in at Geba, while the invaders seem content for the time being to remain at Michmash, periodically sending out razzias into the surrounding countryside.

The Israelite successes in the great battle that finally ensues force the army of occupation to withdraw, leaving Saul's leadership in the central hill country unchallenged for the moment at least. Again he commands the loyalty of those "Hebrews" who had fled or defected to the enemy (14:21-22). All "the hill country of Ephraim" (v 22) rallies behind him in the south. The Philistines will return to threaten Judah in the south (17:1; 23:1) and Jezreel in the north (cc 29-31 *passim*), but there is nothing in our sources to suggest that the territory around Gibeah, the heartland of Saul's kingdom, is not secure hereafter.

As is usual with biblical accounts of Israelite victories the story of the battle of Michmash Pass leaves no doubt about the ultimate reason for the favorable outcome. It has nothing to do with armed might. Whereas the Israelites are inadequately armed (13:19-22), their enemies have chariotry, cavalry, and "an army like the sand on the seashore in number" (13:5). The hope of the underdogs is in their god: "It may be that Yahweh will give us victory, for nothing can prevent Yahweh from gaining victory, whether by many or by few!" (14:6). The narrator takes pains to make us aware that Yahweh is guiding Jonathan's initial incursion (14:9-10, cf. 12b), and once the battle rages, he shows the decisive factor to be neither the heroism of Jonathan and his weapon-bearer nor even the timely arrival of Saul and his army (14:20a); rather it is the heaven-sent "awesome convulsion," spreading under the Philistine positions and touching off a "very great panic" (see the NOTES at 14:15 and 20), that wins the field. Then with the issue decided and Israel in hot pursuit of the retreating Philistines the narrator steps forward to make his point explicit. "So," he concludes (14:23a), "Yahweh gained victory that day for Israel."

It is also characteristic of the Israelite theology of warfare, nonetheless, that a mortal man may play a central role. The human agent of Yahweh's victory in this case is Jonathan. It was he who provoked the crisis in the first place (13:3), and it is he who starts the fight and ignites the Israelite troops. But the exploits of Jonathan belong to a longer story that finds its conclusion in the strange events of 14:23b-46, apart from which their significance cannot be fully understood. So we must postpone further commentary at this point and return to the Israelite battle camp.

XIX. THE CURSING OF JONATHAN
(14:23b-46)

14 23b As the fighting passed by Beth-aven, the entire army was
with Saul—some ten thousands of men. But then the fighting scattered into every city in the hill country of Ephraim.
24 Saul made a great blunder that day. He adjured the army as follows: "Cursed be the man who eats food before evening has come and
I have avenged myself upon my enemies!" So none of the soldiers
tasted food.
25 Now there was honeycomb on the ground, 26 and when the army
came upon [it], its bees had left; but there was no one who would
raise his hand to his mouth, for the soldiers feared the oath. 27 Jonathan, however, had not heard his father put the army under oath, so
he reached down with the staff that was in his hand, dipping it into
the comb of honey. When he raised his hand to his mouth, his eyes
brightened.
28 One of the soldiers spoke up and said, "Your father has put the
army under oath, saying, 'Cursed be the man who eats food today!' "
29 "My father," said Jonathan, "has brought trouble to the land!
Look, my eyes are brightened because I ate a bit of this honey.
30 How much better then that the soldiers had eaten from their
enemy's spoil which they found today, for now the slaughter among
the Philistines would have been greater!"
31 When they had defeated the Philistines that day at Michmash,
the soldiers were completely exhausted, 32 and [they] pounced on the
spoil. They took sheep, cattle, and calves and slaughtered them on the
ground; then [they] ate [the meat] with the blood. 33 When it was reported to Saul that the soldiers were sinning against Yahweh by eating [meat] with the blood, he said, "You have acted faithlessly! Roll
a large stone here to me!" 34 Then [he] said, "Spread out among the
army and say, 'Let each man bring his ox or his sheep to me and
slaughter it here! But do not sin against Yahweh by eating [meat]
with the blood!" So each of the soldiers brought whatever he had at

hand and slaughtered it there. 35 (Thus Saul built an altar to Yahweh.
It was the first altar to Yahweh he built.)

36 Then Saul said, "Let us go down after the Philistines tonight! We
shall plunder them until the light of morning and leave them not a
man!"

"Do whatever seems best to you!" was the reply.

But the priest said, "Let us approach God!" 37 So Saul inquired of
God: "Shall I go down after the Philistines? Will you deliver them
into Israel's power?" But he received no answer that day.

38 "All officers of the army!" said Saul. "Come here! Look into this
and learn on whose account this sin has come about today! 39 For as
Yahweh lives, who brings victory to Israel, even if it is on account of
Jonathan, my son, he shall surely die!" None of the soldiers made a
reply to him, 40 so he said to all Israel, "You will be on one side, and I
and my son Jonathan will be on the other side."

"Do what seems best to you!" said the soldiers to Saul.

41 "O Yahweh, god of Israel!" said Saul. "Why have you not answered your servant today? If this guilt is on my account or on account of Jonathan, my son, then, O Yahweh god of Israel, give Urim!
But if it is on account of your people Israel, give Thummim!" Saul
and Jonathan were taken, and the soldiers went free. 42 Then Saul
said, "Cast between me and Jonathan, my son! Let him whom Yahweh takes die!" And though the soldiers said, "Let it not be so!" to
[him], Saul prevailed upon [them], and they cast lots between him
and Jonathan, his son. And Jonathan was taken.

43 "Tell me," said Saul to Jonathan, "what have you done?"

Jonathan told him. "With the tip of the staff that was in my hand,"
he said, "I tasted a bit of honey. Now here I am, about to die!"

44 Saul said, "May God do thus and so to me and thus and so
again! But you shall surely die this day!"

45 But the soldiers said to Saul, "Shall he who has gained this great
victory in Israel die today? As Yahweh lives, not a hair of his head
shall fall to the ground, for God was with him in what he did this
day!" So the army rescued Jonathan, and he did not die.

46 Then Saul went up from his pursuit of the Philistines, and the
Philistines returned to their place.

TEXTUAL NOTES

14 23b. *Beth-aven* So MT. LXX^{L}, OL: "Beth-horon." The rest of the verse has been lost in MT, which preserves only a remnant of the beginning of v 24 (see below). LXX^{B} has the original text intact: *kai pas ho laos* (LXX^{L} *israēl*) *ēn meta saoul hōs deka chiliades andrōn kai ēn ho polemos diesparmenos eis holēn polin en tō orei tō ephraim* [24]*kai saoul ēgnoēsen agnoian megalēn en tē hēmera ekeinē*, from which we may reconstruct (following Wellhausen) *wkl h'm* (*yśr'l*) *hyh 'm š'wl k'śrt 'lpym 'yš wthy hmlḥmh npwṣt bkl h'yr bhr 'prym* [24]*wš'wl šgh šggh gdwlh bywm hhw'*, lit. ". . . and the entire army (Israel) was with Saul—some ten thousands of men. But then the fighting scattered into every city in the hill country of Ephraim. Saul made a great blunder that day. . . ." Note that Wellhausen also regards *eis holēn polin* (=*bkl h'yr*, "into every city") as a translational doublet of *en tō orei* (= *bhr*, "in the hill country"). On the text of this passage as a whole, contrast Seebass, "Text von I Sam. XIV 23b-25a," 74-75.

24. *Saul made a great blunder that day* Reading *wš'wl šgh* (or *šgg*) *šggh gdwlh bywm hhw'* on the basis of LXX *kai saoul ēgnoēsen agnoiam megalēn en tē hēmera ekeinē* (Wellhausen; see the preceding *Textual Note*). MT is corrupt: *w'yš yśr'l ngś bywm hhw'*, "The men of Israel were hard pressed on that day" (cf. 13:6).

he adjured MT: "*Saul* adjured." Omit the proper name with LXX.

25. The beginning of v 25 is highly corrupt in all witnesses. MT reads: *wkl h'rṣ b'w by'r wyhy dbš 'l pny hśdh*, ". . . and all the land went into the forest, and there was honey on the ground. . . ." LXX^{B} reads: *kai pasa hē gē ērista kai iaar* (cf. LXX^{A}; LXX^{BL} *iaal*) *drymos ēn melissōnos kata prosōpon tou agrou*, reflecting *wkl h'rṣ ṭ'm lḥm* (?) *wy'r* (rendered two ways in LXX) *hyh dbš 'l pny hśdh*, ". . . and all the land tasted food and a honeycomb was (honey) on the ground. . . ." Based upon suggestions made by Wellhausen, we may reconstruct the history of the corruption as follows. The original probably read *wy'r hyh 'l pny hśdh*, "And honeycomb was on the ground . . ." or as we have rendered it here, "Now there was honeycomb on the ground. . . ." The noun *dbš*, "honey," was introduced as a marginal gloss to the rare term *y'r*, "honeycomb" (see the NOTE) and then found its way into the text in its present position. Meanwhile *wkl h'rṣ ṭ'm lḥm*, ". . . and all the land tasted food," had arisen as a (corrupt) variant of the preceding *wl' ṭ'm kl h'm lḥm*, ". . . and none of the soldiers tasted food." In MT *hyh dbš*, became *wyhy dbš*, "And there was honey . . ." leaving *wy'r* to be associated with the foregoing. Thus there arose by further corruption the reading *wkl h'rṣ b'w by'r*, ". . . and all the land went into the forest." In the tradition behind LXX an earlier but already corrupt stage in this development was preserved. The Greek translators rendered *wy'r* in two ways, by simple transcription (*kai yaar/yaal*) and by (*kai*) *drymos*, "(and) a forest."

26. *its bees had left* Reading *hlk dbrw,* that is *hālak dĕbōrô,* with most critics. MT *hēlek dĕbāš,* "(there was) a flow (?) of honey" is most awkward, and the emendation of the second word to *dbrw* seems to be supported by LXX *lalōn.*

but there was no one who would raise his hand to his mouth We read *w'yn mšyb ydw 'l pyw,* "but there was no one who would return his hand to his mouth. . . ." MT has *mśyg.* for *msyg,* "who would bring back," or perhaps *mgyš,* "who would bring near," but most critics prefer to read *mšyb* with LXX (*epistrephōn*), Targ. (*mtyb*), and OL (*qui convertebant*).

27. *it* Reading *'tw* (= *'ōtô*) or revocalizing MT *'wth* as *'ôtô.* MT reads *'ôtāh* by attraction to the feminine noun *yādô,* "his hand."

brightened So Targ., Syr., Vulg. and MT *qĕrê* (*wattā'ōrĕnâ*). MT *kĕtîb* is *wattir'enâ,* "saw." LXX^B *kai aneblepsan* may also reflect *wt'rnh* (Stoebe).

28. At the end of the verse MT adds *wy'p h'm,* "and the soldiers were exhausted" (LXX *kai exelythē ho laos*). The statement is disruptive at this point. It must have arisen as a marginal note, anticipatory of v 31 and explanatory of Jonathan's remarks in vv 29-30, which eventually found its way into the text. See further Wellhausen.

29. *said Jonathan* So MT, confirmed by 4QSam^a, OL. LXX *kai egnō iōnathan kai eipen* = *wyd' ywntn wy'mr,* "And Jonathan knew and he said. . . ." Wellhausen asks if this longer reading may have been original, its corruption in MT having contributed to the intrusion of *wy'p h'm* at the end of v 28.

Look LXX *ide* = *r'h,* "Look!" (sing.). MT has the plural *r'w.* Cf. the *Textual Note* to "saw" at 13.6 (cf. Wellhausen).

30. *How much better then that* Reading *'ap kî,* lit. "yea, that . . ." in the sense of "how much more that . . ." (cf. 21:6) with LXX^B. MT (cf. LXX^L) adds *lû'* (thus, "how much better then *if* . . ."), but this seems unnecessary, and the shorter reading may be retained.

for now MT again adds *l',* understood this time as *lō',* "not"—thus, "for now the slaughter . . . has not been great." Omit with LXX$^{(B)}$.

the slaughter . . . would have been greater Reading *rbh hmkh* with 4QSam^a and LXX *meizōn hē plēgē.* MT has *rbth mkh,* "slaughter was (not) great."

31. *at Michmash* So LXX. MT has *mmkmš 'ylnh,* "from Michmash to Aijalon," which is retained in most modern translations. The reference to Aijalon, a city that lay a few miles SW of Beth-horon, has been introduced for precision under the influence of v 23b. But the author of vv 31-35 intended only to identify the battle of Michmash in a general way. The short text of LXX is to be preferred.

32. *pounced on* MT *wy'ś* is incomprehensible. Read *wy'ṭ* with LXX (so LXX^L [*kai hōrmēsen;* cf. 15:19]; LXX^B *kai eklithē* reflects *wyṭ,* "inclined [after]"), Syr., as confirmed by 15:19. In 4QSam^a, though the verb is not extant, the succeeding preposition is *'l* (MT *l-*), which would be impossible with *wy'ś.*

the spoil So LXX, MT *qĕrê* (*haššālāl*). MT *kĕtîb: šll.*

They took So MT. LXX: "*the people* (*soldiers*) took."

33. *he said* So MT. LXX: "*Saul* said."

here Reading *hlm,* "here, hither," with LXX (*entautha*) in preference to MT *hywm,* "today, now."

34. *Spread out* MT: *pūṣû,* "Spread out! Scatter!" from the verb *pwṣ.* 4QSam[a] has *npṣw,* that is, *nipṣû,* "Spread out! Scatter!" as if from *npṣ* (cf. 13:11).

to me So MT (*'ly*). Or perhaps read *hlm* with LXX (*entautha*). Smith, following a suggestion of Klostermann, emends MT to read *'l yhwh,* "to Yahweh."

and slaughter it here LXX^{AL}, Syr. add "and eat." Omit with LXX^{B}.

whatever he had at hand Reading *'yš 'šr bydw,* lit. "each one, that which was in his hand" (cf. LXX). MT has *'yš šwrw bydw,* "each with his bull in his hand." MT at this point adds *hlylh,* "at night," which is not found in LXX^{B} but is represented at the end of the verse in LXX^{L}. The word is clearly intrusive. Perhaps it was added marginally in a text ancestral to MT as a correction of *lylh* in v 36 (see below) and found its way into the text at this point.

35. *built* LXX^{B}, Syr. add "there." Omit with MT, LXX^{L}.

37. *But he received no answer* That is, "But he did not answer him" (*wl' 'nhw*); so MT, LXX^{B}. LXX^{L}: "But *Yahweh* did not answer him."

38. *All officers of the army* Reading *kl pnwt h'm* with MT. LXX^{B} reflects *kl pnwt yśr'l,* "all the officers of *Israel,*" an insignificant variation, whereas in LXX^{L} the rare term *pnwt* has become *mšpḥwt*—thus *kl mšpḥwt h'm,* "all the *clans* of the people."

on whose account Reading *bmy* on the basis of Vulg. (cf. LXX) in preference to MT *bmh,* "on what account, wherein, how." Admittedly the evidence is ambiguous, but the reading seems required by v 39 (". . . even if it is *on account of Jonathan* . . .") and has been preferred by a majority of critics since Wellhausen. One cannot deny the force of Stoebe's objection that either reading makes the point with sufficient clarity.

39. *it is* We read *yešnāh,* following Wellhausen and others. MT has *yešnô* (cf. 23:23), but this conflicts with the feminine antecedent (*ḥṭ't,* "sin," not the masculine *h'wn,* "guilt," as in our reconstruction of v 41), and the evidence of LXX (*apokrithē* = *y'nh*) favors our reconstruction. The reading of MT evidently anticipates *yšnw* in v 41 (restored). See below.

40. *all Israel* So MT, LXX^{B}. LXX$^{AL(\text{and two MSS of B})}$, OL have "all *the men of* Israel."

on one side . . . on the other side So MT: *l'br 'ḥd . . . l'br 'ḥd.* LXX, confused by the similarity of *r* and *d,* reads *eis douleian . . . eis douleian,* as if *l'bdh . . . l'bdh,* "for service . . . for service," or the like.

41. *O Yahweh* So LXX. MT: "to (*'el* < **l-,* vocative *lamed?*) Yahweh."

Why . . . Thummim We follow LXX: *ti hoti ouk apekrithēs tō doulō sou sēmeron ē en emoi ē en iōnathan tō huiō mou hē adikia kyrie ho theos israēl dos dēlous kai ean tade eipēs* (so LXX^{A}, Syr.; LXX^{B} has *eipē dos dē* in anticipation of *dos dē* below) *en* (so LXX^{L}, Syr.; omitted by LXX^{B}) *tō laō sou israēl dos dē hosiotēta* = *lmh l' 'nyt 't 'bdk hywm 'm yš by 'w bywntn bny h'wn hzh yhwh 'lhy yśr'l hbh 'wrym w'm yšnw* (?; cf. OL *aut si ita est*) *b'mk yśr'l hbh tmym.* The only obscure point in the reconstruction of the Hebrew is the correspondence of *eipē(s)* to *yšnw,* on which see Wellhausen. MT has suffered a long haplography caused by *homoioteleuton,* the scribe's eye skipping from the *yśr'l* that preceded *lmh* to the *yśr'l* that preceded *hbh tmym,* and only *hbh tmym* (vocalized *hābâ tāmîm,* "give truth, wholeness") remains. See further, Toeg, "Textual Note"; and contrast Noort, "Weitere Kurzbemerkung."

42. Again MT has lost a large part of the verse, reading *wy'mr š'wl hpylw byny wbyn ywntn bny wylkd ywntn,* "Then Saul said, 'Cast between me and Jonathan, my son!' And Jonathan was taken." After *byny wbyn ywntn bny* we may reconstruct the text following LXX^(B): *hon an kataklērōsētai kyrios apothanetō kai eipen ho laos pros saoul ouk estin kata* (so LXX^L; LXX^B omits *kata*) *to rhēma touto kai katekratēsen saoul tou laou kai ballousin ana meson autou kai ana meson iōnathan tou huiou autou kai kataklēroutai iōnathan* = *'t 'šr ylkd yhwh ymwt wy'mr h'm 'l š'wl l' yhyh kdbr hzh wyḥzq š'wl b'm wypylw bynw wbyn ywntn bnw wylkd ywntn.* The eye of the scribe of MT jumped from the sequence *byny wbyn ywntn bny* to *bynw wbyn ywntn bnw* (*y* and *w* being almost indistinguishable in MSS of many periods) and lost everything that intervened.

44. *to me* Missing in MT but supplied by LXX, Syr., Vulg. Driver, comparing I Kings 19:2, asks if "to me" might be understood but originally unexpressed and supplied secondarily in the traditions that display it.

this day Reading *hywm* with LXX (*sēmeron*). MT has *ywntn,* "Jonathan."

45. *Shall he . . . die today* Reading *hhywm ymwt 'šr,* etc., with LXX. MT: *hywntn ymwt 'šr,* etc., "Shall Jonathan die, he who has gained this great victory in Israel?" Cf. the preceding *Textual Note.*

As Yahweh lives Hebrew *ḥy yhwh,* which in MT (cf. LXX^AL) is preceded by *ḥlylh,* "far be it." This is superfluous and may have arisen as corrupt dittography of *ḥy yhwh.* Omit with LXX^B.

for God was with him in what he did this day Reading (with MT) *ky 'm 'lhym 'śh hywm hzh,* lit. "for with God he acted this day!" LXX misunderstands the sequence *'m 'lhym* (properly *'im 'ĕlōhîm,* "with God") and renders, "for the people of God (*'am 'ĕlōhîm*) made this day!" (LXX^L *hoti eleon,* "for mercy . . ." is an inner-Greek corruption of *hoti ho laos,* "for the people . . ." [so LXX^BA]).

the army rescued Jonathan So MT: *wypdw h'm 't ywntn.* LXX *kai proseuxato ho laos peri iōnathan* reflects *wytpll h'm b'd ywntn,* "the army interceded on behalf of Jonathan" (cf. 12:19,23), a variant with equal claim to originality. Josephus' text seems to have conflated the variants (*Ant.* 6.128).

NOTES

14 23b. At first the army fought together, and communications were good. But when the battle became dispersed, problems developed. See v 27.

Beth-aven. See the NOTE at 13:5.

24. *a great blunder.* Hebrew *šĕgāgâ,* "blunder," refers to a mistake made out of ignorance or carelessness, an inadvertence. See Jacob Milgrom, "The Cultic *šggh* and Its Influence in Psalms and Job," *JQR* 58 (1967) 115-125. When one

commits a *šĕgāgâ,* says Milgrom (118), "he is conscious of his act . . . but not of its consequences." Saul's mistake, then, is not to be thought of as a deliberate act of wrongdoing but as a blunder; he fails to foresee the unfavorable effect it will have on the army and the consequences of the battle (cf. Jonathan's remarks in vv 29-30).

He adjured. Hebrew *wayyō'el* in place of the expected form **wayyō(')l.* See GK §76d.

Cursed be the man who eats food. Saul imposes a fast upon the army in an attempt, apparently, to influence Yahweh by a grandiose gesture of self-denial.

25. *honeycomb.* Hebrew *ya'ar* (vv 25,26) or *ya'ărâ* (v 27) is in fact quite obscure. It occurs only here and in the Song of Songs (5:1), where it is also associated with honey, with this meaning (elsewhere *ya'ar* means "forest"). No cognate is known in any language, and the meaning is guessed from v 27.

27. *his eyes brightened.* That is, he was refreshed. Cf. v 29 and Ps 13:4 (English 13:3); Ezra 9:8; etc.

31-35. These verses read like an interpolation: the momentum of the story is interrupted, and Jonathan is not involved at all. Probably the details of this little incident belonged originally to a separate tradition (about Saul's "first altar to Yahweh"?); see, e.g., Jobling, "Saul's Fall," 373. In the present shape of the narrative the unit is fairly well integrated into the whole. The cultic sin the people commit is another negative consequence of Saul's rash oath. The famished troops (encouraged by Jonathan's remarks in v 30?) seize the captured livestock as soon as the battle is won and the oath's prohibition no longer in force; but in their haste they ignore the requirements of the cult of Yahweh.

32. *then* [*they*] *ate* [*the meat*] *with the blood.* Hebrew *wayyō(')kal hā'ām 'al haddām.* The expression *'ākal 'al* means simply "eat with," the prepositional phrase referring to something eaten along with the main food (so, e.g., Exod 12:8, "They will eat the meat that night. . . . With bitter herbs they will eat it [*'al mĕrōrîm yō(')kĕlūhû*]"); so it is wrong to diminish the crime by rendering *"over/upon* the blood" (Hertzberg, Stoebe). In fact the people here violate the fundamental rule against eating blood, which was supposed to be reserved for Yahweh. Though arising from the notion that blood as the vital fluid, the essence of life itself (cf. Gen 9:4; Lev 17:11; Deut 12:23), was properly a food for gods alone, the prohibition survived in both Deuteronomic (Deut 12:23-27) and Priestly (Lev 19:26 in precisely the present form; cf. Ezek 33:25) regulations.

34. The stone permits the blood to drain from the meat. This could not be done when the animals were slaughtered "on the ground" (v 32).

36. *"Let us approach God!"* That is, let us inquire of God about the prospects for the expedition you propose (cf. 30:8). Probably the ephod is to be used again as in 14:18*ff*.

38. *officers.* Hebrew *pinnôt,* lit. "corners," in the sense of cornerstones of the community, as in Judg 20:2 and Isa 19:13 (cf. Zech 10:4; Ps 118:22).

this sin. Saul assumes, probably correctly, that the divination has failed because of some hidden sin by which Yahweh is offended; his first impulse is to expose the guilty party. Cf. v 41.

40-42. This is Saul's second recorded experience with a lottery; in the first he was chosen king (cf. the NOTE at 10:19b-21bα). Nowhere in the Old Testament are we given more detail about the actual procedures of lot casting than in the present passage. The lots can give one of two answers, viz. Urim or Thummin (see below), so that when it is a matter of choice among several individuals, they must be divided into two groups for each cast (vv 40,42). After each division the lots are "cast" (*hippîl,* v 42), one side is "taken" (*nilkad,* vv 41-42) and the other "goes free" (*yāṣā',* v 41), until the individual in question is discovered. This terminology is more or less fixed in the lot-casting passages of the Bible. See J. Lindblom, "Lot-casting in the Old Testament," *VT* 12 (1962) 164-178.

41. *Urim . . . Thummim!* These terms refer to the counters of the lottery, the two possible results of each cast—thus, *'ûrîm,* "accursed, condemned," and *tūmmîm,* "pronounced whole, acquitted." They were kept in the "breastpiece of judgment" (*ḥōsen hammišpāṭ*) of the priest's ephod (cf. Exod 28:30; Lev 8:8) and are evidently the things "cast" in the present passage, so that they must have been objects of some kind, probably marked with the first and last letters of the alphabet (*'* for *'ûrîm* and *t* for *tūmmîm*); but their form and appearance are unknown (pebbles, dice, sticks and arrows have all been proposed).

44. *May God do thus and so to me and thus and so again! But. . . .* See the NOTE at 3:17. Of this use of *kî* with oath formulae (cf. GK §149d) Driver lists the following as further examples: II Sam 3:9 (*kî . . . kî*), 35 (*kî 'im*); I Kings 2:23; 19:2; to which we should probably add I Sam 20:13.

COMMENT

The conclusion to the story of the battle of Michmash Pass focuses attention squarely on Saul and Jonathan. For the most part the public events have been recounted now, and the narrator, whose interest is finally in the affairs of the king, turns to the intimate. He gives us a vignette of high literary quality.[1] Saul, in the rash, headstrong manner that characterizes everything he does (see below), has bound the people by oath to a fast for the duration of the battle, evidently hoping that such a gesture will be pleasing to Yahweh and ensure his support for Israel's cause. The people, though spent with the exertion of battle, honor their oath and eat nothing until the battle is won, but Jonathan, who has not been informed of the fast, helps himself to some honeycomb that the army has happened upon. As the curse goes into effect, the oracle falls silent (v 37), alerting Saul that something is wrong. Without hesitation he begins to search doggedly

[1] See Blenkinsopp, "Jonathan's Sacrilege," who is reminded of the style of the Yahwistic stratum of the Tetrateuch and points to an intriguing structural parallel between our honeycomb episode and the story of the Fall in Genesis 2-3 (both passages involve a prohibition of eating, condemnation of the eater, etc.).

and somewhat self-righteously for the source of the problem, and when the sacred lot identifies Jonathan as the perpetrator, only the intervention of the army can save the young hero from his father's hand.

The portrayal of Saul in this material (13:2-7a,16-14:46) is very much like that in the old story of David's rise to power, which underlies most of cc 16*ff* (see LITERARY HISTORY in the Introduction). He is not depraved. He is capable of some success as the leader of Yahweh's people. But he is a man abandoned by his god. Indeed he seems ill-fated, for most of what he attempts goes awry. As we have seen (cf. the NOTE at 14:18,19), his character is flawed by a lack of good judgment and a kind of reckless impetuosity which thwart his own purposes—even the noble ones—again and again. The adjuration of the people is ill advised but not ill intended (cf. the NOTE on "a great blunder" at v 24). As suggested above and in the NOTE at v 24, the fast is imposed as a means of gaining divine favor for the Israelite cause. But we have the opinion of Jonathan as stated in vv 29-30 and the testimony of the consequences themselves to show that Saul's judgment has failed him here.

It was because of this portrayal of Saul, we may assume, that the prophetic author of 13:7b-15a and 15:1-34 selected the account of the battle of Michmash Pass and the cursing of Jonathan out of what must have been a fairly large amount of material concerning Saul's Philistine wars.[2] It shows what he believed to have been true about Saul, viz. that he was rash and presumptuous in his relationship to Yahweh and that he tried to manipulate the divine will through ritual formality (14:24; cf. 13:12; 15:15). To be sure, the prophetic writer's judgment of this behavior was much harsher than that of the narrator of the older story, but the picture is the same.

So the old story in cc 13-14 has survived because it illustrates the failings of Saul. Just as surely, however, it demonstrates the heroism of his son. Although as we have seen, there is no room for doubt that it is finally Yahweh who has "gained victory" (*hôšîa'*) for Israel in the battle of Michmash Pass (cf. 14:6,23,39 and the COMMENT on 13:16-14:23a), it is also clear that Jonathan is the human savior, and the report of his deed exhibits at least some of the characteristics of the stereotyped stories of the so-called "major judges" (see the COMMENT on 10:27b-11:15).[3] In the words of the soldiers (14:45), it is Jonathan who "has gained this great

[2] A number of scholars have recognized that the inclusion of this older material served the redactional purpose of the author of the rejection accounts. See Stoebe; Jobling, "Saul's Fall," 371-372.

[3] Compare Schicklberger, "Jonatans Heldentat," who attempts to identify an originally independent hero legend about Jonathan underlying 14:1-23a. Similarly Jobling, "Saul's Fall," esp. 372-375, argues that the larger pericope 'grew up around a story about Jonathan's exploit that existed at an earlier stage without reference to Saul.

victory (*'āśâ hayšû'â haggĕdôlâ hazzō't*)." With a son like Jonathan, then, Saul might seem to be about to establish a dynasty that will promise Israel continued security. But in the midst of this decisive battle, at the military pinnacle of his reign, he inadvertently lays a solemn curse upon the crown prince. Jonathan seems doomed and the hopes inspired by his heroism seem forfeit. It is true that the people rescue the condemned man, but this fact alone cannot restore the mood of optimism and success that prevailed earlier in the day. As Hertzberg stresses, the old story of the battle of Michmash Pass and the cursing of Jonathan leaves us in a condition of gloomy uncertainty about Saul. We do not yet know what is to become of him, but we look ahead to the events to come with little hope for him left.

XX. FURTHER NOTICES ABOUT SAUL'S KINGSHIP (14:47-52)

14 [47] Saul seized territory outside of Israel: he fought against its enemies on every side—against Moab, the Ammonites, Edom, the king of Zobah, and the Philistines—and wherever he turned he was victorious [48] and acquired power. Also he defeated Amalek, rescuing Israel from the clutches of its plunderers.

[49] The sons of Saul were Jonathan, Ishvi, and Malchishua. The names of his two daughters were as follows: the name of the firstborn was Merob, and the name of the younger was Michal; [50] and the name of Saul's wife was Ahinoam, the daughter of Ahimaaz. The name of the commander of his army was Abiner, the son of Ner, Saul's uncle. [51] (Kish, the father of Saul, and Ner, the father of Abiner, were sons of Abiel.)

[52] The fighting against the Philistines was severe all the days of Saul, and whenever [he] saw a powerful man or a stalwart man he recruited him for himself.

TEXTUAL NOTES

14 47. *Saul seized territory* We read *wš'wl lkd ml'kh.* MT has *wš'wl lkd hmlwkh,* "And Saul seized the kingship . . ."; and LXX^{B} (cf. LXX^{L}) has a double reading, viz. *kai saoul elachen ton basileuein kataklēroutai ergon,* interpreting the text as *wš'wl lkd hmlwkh* (= MT) on the one hand and as *wš'wl lkd ml'kh* on the other. The latter is more likely to be original for the following reasons: (1) it is *lectio difficilior,* "kingship" (*mlwkh*) being everywhere the issue in the preceding Saul stories and no doubt in the front of the scribe's mind; (2) *lākad* is not elsewhere used of assuming kingship or any office, but it is a common term for acquiring property; (3) Saul does not seize the kingship at this point, rather he has been king now for some time by all accounts. For *ml'kh,* "territory," see the NOTE.

Edom So MT. LXX: "*the sons of* Edom/Edomites." LXX^{L} (cf. LXX^{B})

here adds *kai eis ton baithroōbei* = *wbbyt rḥb*, "(and against) Beth-rehob"; cf. Judg 18:28; etc. This name is appropriate to the context and might be original (Budde), but there is no apparent motive for its loss in MT, and it may have arisen under the influence of the association of Beth-rehob with Zobah in II Sam 10:6. 4QSam^a is not extant at this point, and space considerations permit but do not require the longer reading.

the king of Zobah So LXX, 4QSam^a. MT: "the *kings* of Zobah."

he was victorious Reading *ywšʿ* on the basis of LXX^B *esōzeto*. MT reads *wršyʿ*, "he acted wickedly"; this corruption seems tendentious (see the commentaries), but the letters *w* and *r* were especially liable to confusion in scripts of the third and early second centuries B.C. Cf. LXX^L *epeblepsen*, "he gazed," as if reading *yšʿh* (from *šʿh*, "look at, gaze at").

48. *power* Hebrew *ḥayil* (see the NOTE). LXX has *dynamin aunanein*, and some (Schulz) have supposed the second term to reflect *'wnym*, "strength," a variant of *ḥyl*. It is more likely, however, that *aunanein* arose as a corrupt duplicate of *dynamin* in the Greek MS tradition (n.b. the similarity of the majuscules *delta* and *alpha*).

its plunderers MT *šshw*, vocalized *šōsēhû*, has long been supposed to conceal a plural defectively spelled (for *šsyhw*; cf. BDB, GK §91k, Driver). 4QSam^a now confirms this, reading [*š*]*syw*.

49. *Ishvi* That is, *yišwî* (so MT); cf. Noth, *Die israelitischen Personennamen*, 227-228, n. 17. The evidence of LXX (LXX^L has *iessiou;* cf. LXX^B) favors *yšyw*, and many commentators have reconstructed the name as *'îšyô*, "Man of Yahweh," an official, theologically corrected variation of *'îšbaʿal* (*'ešbaʿal*), "Man of Baal," identified as a son of Saul in I Chron 8:33 and 9:39 and elsewhere euphemistically called *'îš-bōšet*, "Man of Shame" (II Sam 2:8; etc.). But we cannot be sure that *yšwy*/*yšyw* is Ishbosheth. There is no textual evidence for the spelling *'yš-* here, and the present enumeration of Saul's sons, which omits Abinadab (cf. 31:2), cannot in any case be made to correspond to the information given elsewhere. The evidence of 4QSam^a is tantalizingly ambiguous. The scroll has: *yhwntn wẙš*[*w*]*mlkyšʿ*, "Jonathan and . . . and Malchishua." The space is too generous for *-yw* or *-wy*, but a name such as *yšyhw* (cf. I Chron 12:7[English 12:6]) is possible, as is *yšbʿl* (cf. II Sam 23:8 [LXX^L, OL]) or even *yšbšt* (cf. II Sam 23:8 [LXX^BA]). Note also that after "Malchishua" LXX^L and certain other MSS add, "and Eshbaal" (cf. I Chron 8:33; 9:39). The original reading remains elusive.

Merob So 4QSam^a (*mrwb*) and LXX (*merob*), against MT *mērab*. The same contrast exists between MT and LXX^(AL) in 18:17,19.

Michal So MT (*mykl*) and 4QSam^a (*mkl*), against LXX *melchol* (= *mlkl*). Cf. the *Textual Note* at 18:20.

Abiner Here written *'bynr* (= *'ăbînēr*) in MT, elsewhere (defectively) *'bnr* and thus misvocalized *'abnēr*, "Abner."

51. *sons* MT has simply "son," as do 4QSam^a and LXX (though LXX is further complicated by the intrusion of *huios iamein* = *bn ymyn* after "Abiner"; restore *bny ymyny*, "(were) Benjaminites [?]); but "sons" is most likely (see the NOTE) and confirmed by Josephus (*Ant.* 6.130).

NOTES

14 47-48. This summary of the campaigns of Saul suggests that he succeeded not only in consolidating Israel's own holdings (see the COMMENT on 13:16-14:23a) but in gaining further holdings in adjacent territories to the N, E, and S.

47. The noun *mĕlā(')kâ,* though it frequently means "property" (as in 15:9; so also Exod 22:7,10[English 22:8,11]), does not elsewhere refer to *landed* property or territory unambiguously; but note its use in II Chron 17:13 in a summary description of the reign of Jehoshaphat of Judah: ". . . and he had extensive property [*mĕlā(')kâ rabbâ*] in the cities of Judah. . . ."

outside of Israel. That is, *'al yiśrā'ēl,* lit. "above (and beyond) Israel" or "in addition to Israel" (cf. Ezek 25:10; etc.), or even "adjoining Israel" (cf. Ezek 48:24-28; etc.).

Moab. The ancient kingdom of Moab occupied a narrow strip of plateau land some 60 miles long overlooking the E and NE shore of the Dead Sea. It was bordered by Edom on the S and, though the N reaches of Moab were claimed in theory by the Israelite tribe of Reuben, Ammon on the N. The language and material culture of the Moabites were similar to those of Israel, and the people of Moab figure prominently in the biblical record.

the Ammonites. See the NOTE at 11:1.

Edom. Edom is regarded in biblical tradition as a brother nation to Israel (cf. Genesis 25), and in fact the relationship between the two peoples was a kind of sibling rivalry, often of a bitter and even violent kind, that lasted into the Roman Period in Palestine. The homeland of the Edomites lay S and SE of the Dead Sea, bordering on Moab to the N.

Zobah. Zobah (ṣôbâ) was an important Aramaean city-state centered on the W slope of the Anti-Lebanon mountains N of Israel. Hadadezer, a later king of Zobah, who figures prominently among David's enemies (II Sam 8:3-12 = I Chron 18:3-8; II Sam 10:6-8), is called "son of Rehob" (*rĕḥōb*) in II Sam 8:3,12. Are we to assume that Rehob is the king of Zobah referred to in the present passage?

48. *and acquired power.* Hebrew *wayya'aś ḥayil.* As Deut 8:17-18 and Ezek 28:4 clearly show, the expression *'āśâ ḥayil* means not simply "do valiantly" (cf. Driver: "lit. *made might,* i.e. displayed prowess, performed deeds of valor") but "make/acquire power (= wealth)" (cf. also E. F. Campbell, *Ruth,* AB 7, the NOTE on 4:11). Often it is specifically a question of land possession, as probably in Pss 60:14 = 108:14(English 60:12 = 108:13); 118:15,16 and certainly in Num 24:18: "Edom shall be dispossessed . . . while Israel acquires power (*'ōseh ḥāyil*)!" The point here is that Saul, in consequence of his campaigns against neighboring states, extended his domain beyond the borders of Israel in several directions.

Amalek. The Amalekites are the archetypal plunderers in biblical tradition, and it may be that the present reference is to raiding bandits in general. But specifically Amalek (*'ămālēq*) was the name of a nomadic tribe that inhabited the desert S of Judah (see further the NOTE at 15:7); they play a major role in the story of Saul's rejection in 15:1-34.

49. Of the sons of Saul only Jonathan plays an important role in the stories we have. The names and even the number of the others are uncertain (see the *Textual Note*), though they are listed five times in the Bible:

I Sam 14:49	Jonathan, Ishvi, and Malchishua
I Sam 31:2 = I Chron 10:2	Jonathan, Abinadab, and Malchishua
I Chron 8:33; 9:39	Jonathan, Malchishua, Abinadab, and Eshbaal

Merob. See 18:17-19 (§ XXIV-B).

Michal. David's first wife. See 18:20*ff*.

50. *Ahinoam, the daughter of Ahimaaz*. Neither Saul's wife nor his father-in-law is elsewhere mentioned. David also married a woman named Ahinoam (25:43; etc.), but presumably there was no relationship to Saul's wife.

Abiner. Abiner held the important position of commander of the army during his cousin's reign and is mentioned from time to time in the stories about Saul (17:55[*tris*],57; 20:25; 26:5,7,14[*tris*],15), but he attained even greater power during the brief reign of Ishbaal (II Sam 2:8*ff*) until slain by David's commander of the army, Joab (II Sam 3:27).

50,51. The relationship of Abiner to Saul is confused in the tradition. The appositive "Saul's uncle" at the end of v 50 is ambiguous: does it refer to Ner or Abiner? That is, is Abiner Saul's cousin or uncle? If Abiner were Saul's uncle, Ner would be his grandfather, and this contradicts 9:1, where Saul's grandfather is identified as Abiel. So the evidence of the Samuel passages is that Abiner was Saul's cousin and thus that Ner was his uncle, and this seems to gain support from I Chron 9:36, where Ner (in 8:30 *nēr* has fallen out before *nādāb*) and Kish (presumably Saul's father) are listed as brothers (though their father is called *yĕ'î'ēl*, "Jeiel," not Abiel). Josephus (*Ant*. 6.130) supports this interpretation of the relationship. The parenthesis in v 51 was evidently added to make this clear, and though it has come down to us in a form that makes little clear (see the *Textual Note*), it accomplishes its purpose when restored. However, the problem of I Chron 8:33 = 9:39 remains: there it is said that Ner was Kish's father. This contradicts 9:1 but agrees with the interpretation of 14:50 that identifies Abiner as Saul's uncle. Until a better solution is proposed, we must assume that this was an error on the Chronicler's part, arising perhaps from misinterpretation of the information given in the present passage.

52. This verse stands somewhat in isolation here. It looks ahead to the continuation in 16:14*ff* of the older materials, from which it is separated by the prophetic stories of Saul's rejection and David's anointing in 15:1-16:13. Cf. Mettinger, *King and Messiah*, 34.

a powerful man. Hebrew *'îš gibbôr;* that is, a brave warrior, but cf. the NOTE at 9:1. At one level this notice anticipates 16:18, where David is so described.

a stalwart man. Hebrew *ben ḥayil;* see the NOTE at 10:26,27.

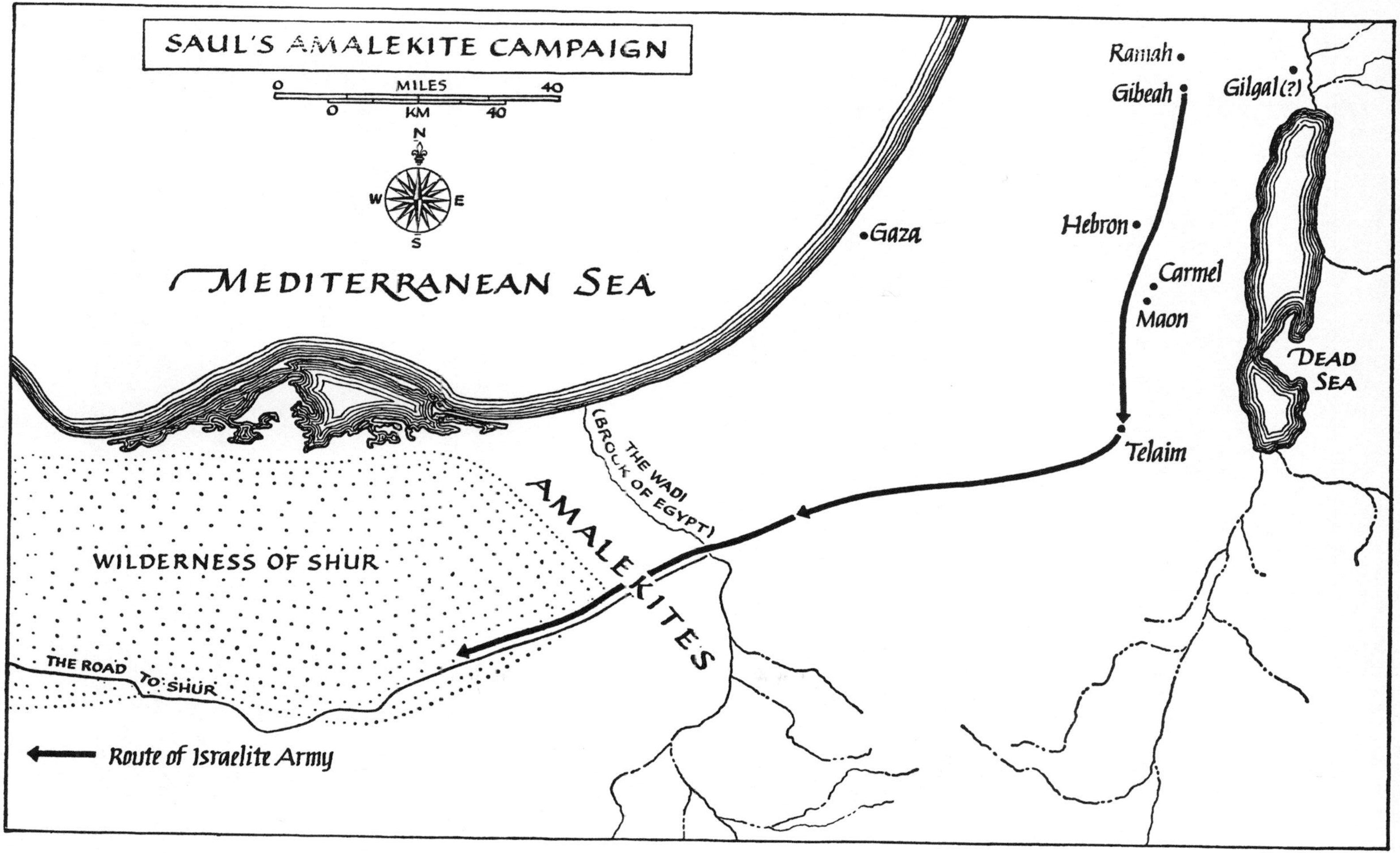
SAUL'S AMALEKITE CAMPAIGN
0
MILES
40
0
KM
40
N
W
E
S
MEDITERRANEAN SEA
Gaza
Ramah
Gibeah
Gilgal (?)
Hebron
Carmel
Maon
DEAD SEA
Telaim
THE WADI (BROOK OF EGYPT)
AMALEKITES
WILDERNESS OF SHUR
THE ROAD TO SHUR
Route of Israelite Army

XXI. THE REJECTION OF SAUL
(15:1-34)

15 1 Samuel said to Saul, "It was I whom Yahweh sent to anoint you
king over Israel. Now then, listen to what I have to say! 2 Yahweh
Sabaoth has spoken thus: 'I have taken account of what Amalek did
to Israel when [Amalek] confronted them on the road as they were
coming up from Egypt. 3 Now, go! Strike down Amalek, and put
them and everything that belongs to them under the ban, and have no
pity on them! Slay both man and woman, both weaned and nursing
child, both ox and sheep, both camel and ass!' " 4 So Saul summoned
the army and mustered it at Telaim—two hundred thousands of foot
soldiers and ten thousands of the men of Judah.

5 Then Saul went to the city of Amalek and lay in wait in the Wadi.
6 To the Kenites [he] said, "Go! Get away from Amalek, lest I sweep
you away with them, for you dealt kindly with the Israelites when
they were coming up from Egypt." So the Kenites went away from
Amalek.

7 Saul harried Amalek from the Wadi toward Shur on the border of
Egypt. 8 He captured Agag, king of Amalek, alive, though he put all
the people under the ban with the edge of the sword. 9 Saul and the
army spared not only Agag but also the best of the flock and the herd
—the fat ones and the young—and every good thing, and they were
unwilling to put them under the ban; but all the property that was
despised and rejected they did put under the ban.

10 So the word of Yahweh came to Samuel: 11 "I repent of having
made Saul king, because he has turned away from following me and
does not carry out my commands!"

Samuel was enraged and cried to Yahweh throughout the night.
12 Then [he] rose early to meet Saul in the morning; but [he] was
told that Saul had gone to Carmel (he was erecting a monument to
himself) and then turned and gone on down toward Gilgal.

When Samuel came to Saul he had just offered up as holocausts to
Yahweh the first parts of the booty he had taken from Amalek; 13 and

when Samuel drew near to [him], Saul said to him, "May you be blessed by Yahweh! I have carried out Yahweh's command."

14 "Then what," said Samuel, "is that bleating in my ears and the lowing that I hear?"

15 "I brought [the animals] from Amalek," said Saul, "for the soldiers spared the best of the flock and the herd in order to make a sacrifice to Yahweh, your god. The rest I put under the ban—"

16 "Stop!" said Samuel to Saul. "Let me tell you what Yahweh said to me last night."

"Say on!" he told him.

17 So Samuel said, "Is it not true that though you were small in
your own eyes you became head of the tribes of Israel? Yahweh
anointed you king over Israel, 18 sent you on a mission, and said to
you, 'Go put those sinners, the Amalekites, under the ban, and fight
with them until you have exterminated them!' 19 Then why did you
not listen to Yahweh? Why did you pounce on the spoil and do what
was wrong in Yahweh's eyes?"

20 "Because I listened to the soldiers!" said Saul. "When I went on
the mission on which Yahweh sent me, I brought back Agag, the king
of Amalek, but I put Amalek under the ban. 21 And the soldiers took
sheep and cattle from the spoil—the first parts of what had been
banned—to sacrifice to Yahweh, your god, at Gilgal."

22 But Samuel said,

"Is Yahweh as pleased with holocausts and sacrifices
as with obeying the voice of Yahweh?
Obedience is better than sacrifice,
attentiveness than the fat of rams!
23 For rebellion is the sin of divination,
and presumption the wickedness of idolatry!
Because you have rejected Yahweh's command,
he has rejected you from being king!"

24 "I have sinned!" said Saul. "I have violated Yahweh's instructions and your command, for I feared the soldiers and listened to
them. 25 But now, take my sin away! Return with me, and I shall
prostrate myself before Yahweh!"

26 But Samuel said to Saul, "I will not return with you! Because you rejected Yahweh's command, Yahweh has rejected you from being

king over Israel!" 27 Then when Samuel turned to go, [Saul] caught
hold of the skirt of his robe, and it tore away. 28 Samuel said to him,
"Yahweh has torn the kingship of Israel away from you this day and
has given it to your neighbor, who is more worthy than you. 29 (Yes,
and Israel's Everlasting One does not deceive and does not repent,
for he is not a man that he should repent!)"

30 "I have sinned," said [Saul], "yet honor me before the elders of
my people and before Israel. Return with me, and I shall prostrate
myself before Yahweh, your god!" 31 So Samuel returned with Saul,
and he prostrated himself before Yahweh.

32 Then Samuel said, "Bring Agag, the king of Amalek, to me!" So
Agag came to him in fetters.

"Would death have been as bitter as this?" said Agag.

33 "Just as your sword has made women childless," said Samuel,
"so shall your mother be childless among women!" And Samuel
hewed Agag to pieces in the presence of Yahweh in Gilgal.

34 Then Samuel set out for Ramah, and Saul went up to his home in
Gibeah.

TEXTUAL NOTES

15 1. *over Israel* So LXX^{B}. MT, LXX^{A}: "over his people, over Israel." LXX^{L}: "over Israel, his people."

to what I have to say We read *ldbry,* lit. "to my words." MT has *lqwl dbry yhwh,* "to the sound of the words of Yahweh" (cf. LXX^{L}). LXX^{B} has *lqwl yhwh,* "to the voice of Yahweh." This evidence points to early variants, viz. *ldbry* and *lqwl yhwh.* The latter was preserved in the tradition behind LXX^{B}, and the two were combined in that behind MT. Syntactical considerations suggest that *ldbry,* "to my words," was original. The emphatic position of *'ōtî,* "me," at the beginning of Samuel's remarks (thus, "It was I whom, etc.") makes no sense otherwise. We might paraphrase as follows, "Since I am the one whom Yahweh sent, you must listen to me!"

2. *when [Amalek] confronted them on the road* MT has *'šr śm lw bdrk,* "when he placed . . . against him on the road," as if something has fallen out of the text. Attempts to recover an obscure military usage of *śym,* "place," by reference to the highly corrupt text of I Kings 20:12 (Driver, Stoebe) fail completely. We restore *'šr qrhw bdrk,* "when he confronted him," which is almost certainly read by LXX (*hōs apēntēsen autō en tē hodō*) and is further supported by Deut 25:18. MT remains unexplained.

3. *Now* So MT. LXX: "And now."

and put . . . and have no pity on them MT reads: *whḥrmtm 't kl 'šr lw wl' tḥml 'lyw,* "and put (pl.) everything that belongs to him under the ban, and have no pity (sing.) on him"; but *whḥrmtm 't kl* is to be corrected with LXX to *whḥrmtw w't kl,* "and put (sing.) him and everything." LXX$^{(B)}$ reads: *kai iereim kai panta ta autou kai ou peripoiēsē ex autou kai exolethreuseis auton kai anathematieis auton kai panta ta autou kai ou pheisē ap' autou,* reflecting *whḥrmtw (?) w't kl 'šr lw wl' tḥml 'lyw whḥrmtw (whḥrmtw) w't kl 'šr lw wl' tḥml 'lyw.* Thus LXX$^{(B)}$ conflates two translations of the same text. Note especially that *whḥrmtw,* "and put him under the ban," is rendered three ways: (1) *kai iereim,* as if a proper name (cf. v 8, LXX^{B}); (2) *kai exolethreuseis auton,* "and utterly destroy him"; and (3) *kai anathematieis auton,* "and put him under a curse."

4. *at Telaim* That is, *ṭělā'îm* (Driver, Budde, etc.); cf. the place name *ṭelem* in Josh 15:24 and see the NOTE below. MT vocalizes *baṭṭělā'îm,* "with the lambs" (cf. Targ., Syr., Vulg.). LXX: *en galgalois,* "in Gilgal."

two hundred . . . ten So MT. LXX$^{(B)}$: "four hundred . . . thirty." The smaller numbers are more likely to be original.

5. *the city* So MT. LXX has "the cities," as adopted by Budde. See Smith, Stoebe. Cf. the NOTE.

and lay in wait Reading *wy'rb* (i.e. *wayye'ěrōb*) on the basis of LXX *kai enēdreusen.* MT has *wayyāreb,* "and struggled," from which some critics have attempted to recover a defectively written *Hip'il* of *'rb* (*wayyāreb* < *wayya'ărēb*) meaning "he prepared an ambush"; but the *Hip'il* of *'rb* is otherwise unattested, and the sense of the *Qal* suits the context.

6. *Go! Get away . . .* Reading *lk wsr* on the basis of LXX *apelthe kai ekklinon.* MT has *lkw srw rdw,* "Go! Get away! Go down. . . ."

Amalek So LXX^{L}. MT, LXX^{B}: "the Amalekites."

lest I sweep you away The consonantal text is *pn 'spk,* which MT (*pen-'ōsīpěkā*) understands as a *Hip'il* from *ysp* (*pace* Driver) and which LXX (*mē prosthō se,* "lest I add you") understands in exactly the same way (*pace* Stoebe). Thus, "lest I add you (to him)"; cf. Prov 10:22. But the old suggestion of P. A. de Lagarde to read *pen-'espěkā* or the like is surely correct (cf. Targ.), especially in view of Gen 18:23, and has been adopted here.

the Israelites So LXX^{BL}. MT: "*all* the Israelites."

the Kenites (2) So LXX. MT has lost the definite article.

7. *from the Wadi* MT, LXX have "from Havilah" (*mḥwylh*), but as long recognized this reading has been influenced by the description of the Ishmaelite homeland in Gen 25:18, which has wording almost identical to the present passage. The location of Havilah is unknown but thought to be somewhere on the W edge of the Arabian Peninsula, far away from the scene of the present story. We need to restore a place name here that is both geographically appropriate and vulnerable to corruption to *ḥwylh.* Wellhausen's proposal to read *mṭl'ym,* "from Telaim" (cf. v 4 above), has received wide approval, but as Smith observes, Saul had advanced well beyond Telaim when the fighting began. The most suitable reconstruction is *mnḥl,* "from the Wadi." It was "at the Wadi" that Saul "lay in wait" while warning the Kenites, and in view of Gen 25:18 the corruption of *mnḥl* to *mḥwylh* is understandable.

toward Shur on the border of Egypt MT: *bw'k šwr 'šr 'l pny mṣrym.* LXX = *'d 'šwr 'l pny mṣrym.* The variants *bw'k* and *'d* may be original to the present passage and Gen 25:18 respectively. LXX *'šwr,* "Asshur"(?), must have arisen from confusion caused by the sequence *šwr 'šr,* "Shur, which . . ." (cf. MT). The same variation is visible in the (conflate) text of Gen 25:18: *'d šwr 'šr 'l pny mṣrym b'kh 'šwrh,* "as far as Shur on the border of Egypt, in the direction of Asshur." There *b'kh 'šwrh* arose as a marginal variant of *'d šwr* and then found its way into the text at its present position.

8. *though he put . . . under the ban* So MT: *hḥrym* (cf. LXX^{L}). LXX^{B} again treats this as a proper name (cf. the *Textual Note* at v 3 above) and adds a second verb: *iereim apekteinen,* "though he killed (all the people), namely, Iereim . . ." or "though Iereim killed (all the people). . . ."

the people So MT, LXX^{BA}. LXX^{L}: "his (i.e. Agag's) people."

9. *the army* So MT. LXX: "*all* the army."

Agag So MT, LXX^{L}. LXX^{B} adds "alive" (cf. v 8).

the fat ones Reading *haššĕmēnîm* (cf. Syr., Targ. *wšmyny'*) as in Ezek 34:16 (Wellhausen) or *hammišmannîm* (cf. Isa 10:16) as reflected by LXX *tōn edesmatōn,* "and the victuals" (= *hammašmannîm;* cf. Neh 8:10). MT has *hammišnîm,* "the double portions" (?).

and the young MT has *w'l hkrym,* but repetition of *'l* is out of place and it may be deleted on the basis of LXX *kai tōn ampelōnōn* = *whkrmym,* "and the vineyards."

all the property that was despised and rejected Reading *kl ml'kh nbzh wnm'st* on the basis of $LXX^{(B)}$ *pan ergon ētimōmenon kai exoudenōmenon* in correction of the unintelligible text of MT (*kl hml'kh nmbzh wnms 'th*).

11. *was enraged* MT *wyḥr,* which, as recognized by Smith, is confirmed by LXX *kai ēthymēsen,* "and (Samuel) was disheartened"; cf. the treatment by LXX of II Sam 6:8 = I Chron 13:11. Contrast Budde, Driver.

12. *rose early to meet* So MT (*wyškm . . . lqr't*). LXX reflects *wyškm wylk lqr't,* "rose early *and went* to meet," conforming to the usual idiom. See the NOTE.

Saul (1) So MT (correctly). LXX has "Israel," but the confusion in LXX between Samuel and Saul below has influenced the reading.

[*he*] (2) Reading "Samuel" with MT, LXX^{AL}. LXX^{B}: "Saul."

Saul (2) So MT, LXX^{AL}. LXX^{B}: "Samuel."

he was erecting MT *whnh mṣyb,* which has the force of a parenthetical expression. In LXX this has been reduced to ordinary narration: *wyṣb* (*kai anestaken*).

and then turned and gone on down So MT: *wysb wy'br wyrd,* lit. "and turned and passed on and gone down." $LXX^{(B)}$ has "and then turned (his) chariot (*to harma* = *hmrkbh*) and gone down."

12,13. *When Samuel came to Saul . . . and when Samuel drew near to* [*him*] So LXX: *kai ēlthen samouēl* (so LXX^{L}; omitted in LXX^{B}) *pros saoul kai idou autos anepheren holokautōsin tō kyriō ta prōta tōn skylōn hōn ēnenken ex amalek kai parageneto* (so LXX^{B}; LXX^{L} has *kai ēlthen*) *samouēl pros saoul* = *wyb' šmw'l 'l š'wl whnh hw' h'lh 'lwt lyhwh 't r'šyt hšll 'šr lqḥ m'mlq wyqrb šmw'l 'l š'wl.* MT has lost almost the entire passage in consequence of a long haplography caused by *homoioteleuton,* the scribe's eye having jumped from the first *šmw'l 'l š'wl* to the second. Thus only *wyb' šmw'l 'l š'wl* remains in MT, where it is understood as introductory to v 13.

13. *Yahweh's command* So MT (*'t dbr yhwh*). LXX *hosa elalēsen kyrios* reflects *'t 'šr dbr yhwh,* "that which Yahweh commanded," understanding *dbr* as a verb.

15. *I brought* [*the animals*] So LXX. MT: "*they* brought them."

from Amalek So LXX. MT: "from an Amalekite."

I put under the ban So LXX. MT: "*we* put under the ban."

16. *he told him* Reading *wy'mr lw* with LXX, MT (*qĕrê*). MT (*kĕtîb*): *wy'mrw lw,* "*they* told him."

17. *Is it not true . . . the tribes of Israel?* We read MT: *hlw' 'm qṭn 'th b'ynyk r'š šbṭy yśr'l 'th.* LXX seems to be defective here. The first part of the statement is close to MT: *ouxi mikros su ei enōpion seautou* (so LXX^L with MT, Syr., OL; LXX^B *autou*), "Are you not (too) small in your own (LXX^B "his") eyes. . . ." Further on, however, LXX shows the influence of 9:21. LXX^L (cf. LXX^B) continues *eis hēgoumenon ek skēptrou beniamein tēs elachistoteras phylēs tou israēl,* reflecting *lr'š mšbṭ bnymyn hṣ'rh mšpḥt yśr'l,* "to be head (?), being from the tribe of Benjamin, the humblest of the family/families of Israel." In short, LXX offers no alternative to retention of the difficult text of MT.

18. *to you, "Go . . ."* Reading *lk lk* with LXX. MT omits one *lk:* "(and said,) "Go. . . ."

sinners LXX adds *eis eme* = *lî,* "against me."

until you have exterminated them Reading *'d klwtk 'tm* on the basis of LXX *heōs syntelesēs autous* (cf. Syr., Targ.) or perhaps *'d klwtm,* "until they are exterminated" (so Wellhausen, Driver, Smith). MT has what seems to be a mixture of these readings, viz. *'d klwtm 'tm,* "until they have exterminated them."

19. *did you pounce* MT *wt'ṭ.* LXX^B: *all' hōrmēsas tou thesthai,* "(but) you rushed to get for yourself" (= *wt'ṭ lqḥt* [?]).

20. *to the soldiers* So LXX (cf. v 24). MT "to Yahweh" is reminiscent of the preceding verse.

21. *to sacrifice to Yahweh, your god* So MT: *lzbḥ lyhwh 'lhyk.* LXX reflects *lpny yhwh 'lhynw,* "in the presence of Yahweh, our god."

23. *presumption* MT *hapṣar,* on the form of which see Driver. LXX *epagousin,* "they urge on," seems to reflect *pṣrw* or perhaps *hp(y)ṣw* (Smith), which could have arisen from the reading of MT in the third century B.C. when *r* and *w* were especially easily confused.

the wickedness of idolatry Reading *'wn htrpym* with LXX^B *ponos therapeian* (*htrpym* having first been transcribed, then modified into a Greek noun). MT has *'wn whtrpym,* "wickedness *and* idolatry." LXX^L renders the first word twice, as *pono(u)s* (so LXX^B) and as *adikia* = *'wn,* "crime, iniquity" (cf. Symmachus). The latter (*'wn*) is a better parallel to *ḥṭ't,* "sin," but the textual evidence is too sparse to displace *'wn,* which is also intelligible.

he So MT. LXX and other MSS: "Yahweh," anticipating v 26.

from being king So MT: *mmlk,* probably to be vocalized *mimmĕlōk* (cf.

LXX, OL), not *mimmelek* (MT). LXX adds "over Israel," again in anticipation of v 26.

25. *Yahweh* So MT. LXX adds "your god" (cf. vv 21,30).

27. *turned* MT *wysb* (*wayyissōb*). LXX reflects *wysb* (*wayyassēb*) . . . *'t pnyw*, "turned his face," that is, "turned away" (cf. I Kings 21:4).

[Saul] caught hold of Reading *wyḥzq* with MT. Syr., 4QSam[a] (cf. Vulg.) agree with LXX in adding "Saul" for clarity.

and it tore away So MT: *wyqr'* (vocalized as *Nip'al: wayyiqqāra'*). LXX (cf. Syr.): *kai dierrēxen auto,* "and (he) tore it," as if reading *wyqr'hw* (*wayyiqrā'ēhû*) but perhaps reading *wyqr'* (= MT) interpreted as *wayyiqra'* with object understood.

28. *the kingship of Israel* MT has *mmlkwt yśr'l,* which Wellhausen corrected to *mmlkt yśr'l* (contrast Driver, Stoebe). The first word may be a conflation of *mlkwt* and *mmlkt.* 4QSam[a] has [ ]*mlkwt,* with no trace of a preceding *m-* on leather and scarcely room for it against the right margin. Read tentatively *mlkwt yśr'l.* LXX reflects *mmlktk myśr'l,* "your kingship from Israel," evidently under the influence of I Kings 11:11 (LXX).

from you MT *m'lyk* (cf. I Kings 11:11 [MT]). LXX *mydk* (I Kings 11:11 [LXX]; cf. I Kings 11:31).

29. *Yes, and Israel's Everlasting One* Reading *wĕgam nēṣaḥ yiśrā'ēl* with MT (see the NOTE). LXX suggests an interesting variation: *kai diairethēsetai israēl eis duo kai . . . = wnḥṣh yśr'l (lšnym) w- . . . ,* "and Israel will be divided in two. And (Yahweh) . . ." (cf. Ezek 37:22). This is an attractive alternative to the suspiciously obscure divine epithet of MT, but as all critics have observed, a reference to the division of the kingdom seems quite out of place here. Moreover the text suggested by LXX leaves the rest of the verse without an explicit subject (thus LXX[L] finds it necessary to add "the Holy One of Israel" further on).

deceive MT *yšqr* (cf. Num 23:19). LXX, 4QSam[a] have *yšyb,* "retract" (?). The confusion of *q* and *b* was possible in fourth-century scripts, of *r, w,* and *y* in third.

a man So MT. LXX: "like a man."

30. *said [Saul]* Reading *wy'mr* with MT; LXX has "said Saul."

before the elders of my people and before Israel So MT, LXX[AL]. LXX[B]: "before the elders of Israel and before my people."

31. *and he prostrated himself* So LXX[BL], 4QSam[a]. MT: "and *Saul* prostrated himself. . . ."

32. *in fetters* MT *m'dnt,* which occurs only here and in Job 38:31. LXX[BL], evidently thinking of the verb *m'd,* "slip, totter," render this as *tremōn,* "trembling," to which LXX[L] adds a second conjecture, viz. *ex anathōth,* "from Anathoth." The best treatment of this old crux is that which goes back at least to Kimchi. In Job 38:31 the word seems to stand in parallelism with a word meaning "bands"; it may thus be related by metathesis to the verb *'nd,* "bind" (Prov 6:21; Job 31:36). Thus read, "in bands, fetters." Cf. M. Pope, *Job,* AB 15, NOTE on 38:31a. On this problem and the next, see also Talmon, "1 Sam. xv 32b."

Would death have been as bitter as this? So LXX: *ei houtōs pikros ho thanatos* = *hkn mr hmwt*, lit. "Would the bitterness of death have been thus?" (see the NOTE). That is, Agag now sees that it would have been better if Saul had not spared him. MT *'kn sr mr hmwt*, "Surely the bitterness of death is past!" is quite inappropriate though preferred by most translators. In fact it arose from dittography of *mr*. See further Talmon, "1 Sam. xv 32b."

33. *said Samuel* So MT. LXX adds "to Agag."

hewed . . . to pieces MT *wyšsp;* LXX *kai esphaxen* (on both, see the NOTE). LXX^L (cf. OL) adds a second attempt to render this rare term, viz. *huiou (s)aser*, a corrupt and partially Hellenized transcription.

34. *Gibeah* So LXX. MT: "Gibeah of Saul."

NOTES

15 1. *It was I whom Yahweh sent.* Hebrew *'ōtî šālaḥ yahweh.* The pronoun stands in the emphatic position; the prophet is asserting his own prerogative. He was the divinely appointed kingmaker, he says, and therefore his instructions must be obeyed by the king—or rather, Yahweh's instructions as transmitted through the kingmaker must be obeyed by the king.

2. *Yahweh Sabaoth.* That is, *yahweh ṣĕbā'ôt,* a longer form of the divine name *yahweh.* See the NOTE at 1:3.

Yahweh Sabaoth has spoken thus. The so-called prophetic messenger formula. See the NOTE at 2:27.

Saul is sent on a campaign against the Amalekites (on whom see the NOTE at 14:48) in retaliation for their ancient attack on Israel at the oasis of Rephidim during the journey from Egypt to Canaan (Exod 17:8-13). At that time, after the attackers had finally been repulsed by the Israelite army under Joshua's leadership, Yahweh swore to "blot out the memory of Amalek from under the skies," and Moses predicted perpetual holy war against the Amalekites (Exod 17:14-16). The phrasing of Saul's instructions point in detail to the passage that stands isolated in Deut 25:17-19, where Moses reminds the people of their responsibility when settled in the Promised Land to carry out Yahweh's sentence upon Amalek: "Remember what Amalek did to you on the road when you were coming out of Egypt, how they confronted you on the road when you were faint and weary, cutting off at your rear all who were straggling behind you, and with no fear of God! So when Yahweh, your god, gives you rest from all your enemies on every side in the land that Yahweh, your god, is going to give you to take possession of as your estate, you must blot out the memory of Amalek from under the skies! Do not forget!"

3. *the ban.* The grimmest of the rules of Israelite holy war were those requiring the imposition of the *ḥērem* or "ban." The verb *heḥĕrîm,* "put under the ban," actually means "consecrate" (cf. common Semitic **ḫrm,* "be separate, sacred"), and to put under the ban was to devote to Yahweh, i.e. to consecrate as

Yahweh's share. In application this meant the extermination of every living thing that was captured, including men, women, children, and even livestock. According to Deut 20:10-18 the ban was in effect for Palestinian cities only, that is, for "those peoples' cities that Yahweh, your god, is giving you as an estate" (v 16); non-Palestinian enemies were normally exempt. The Amalekites, however, though not strictly residents of Palestine, were an exception to the exemption, or rather the target of a special directive, as noted above (cf. Deut 25:19).

4. *summoned.* Hebrew *wayšammaʿ*, the *Piʿel* of *šāmaʿ*, "hear"; only here and in 23:8 in the Hebrew Bible.

Telaim. If *ṭĕlāʾîm* is identical with *ṭelem* in Josh 15:24, it was a city in the Negeb of uncertain location but not far from the Negebite Ziph (*not* the Ziph of 23:14, etc.), modern Khirbet ez-Zeifeh, some 32 miles due S of Hebron; cf. also 27:8. Telaim belonged to Judah (n.b. the reference in this verse to the presence of ten contingents of Judahite soldiers).

5. *the city of Amalek.* The writer seems to be unfamiliar with the name of the city (Smith, Stoebe), unless in fact it was *ʿîr ʿămālēq*, "Amalek City." But it is surprising to find the desert-dwelling Amalekites associated with a city at all, and we must suspect the accuracy of the tradition if not the text.

in the Wadi. Hebrew *bannaḥal*, which might be read simply "in the wadi"; but a specific place seems to be indicated here and in v 7 (see the *Textual Note* to v 7), and *nahal*, "wadi," may be a short form of *naḥal miṣrayim*, "the Wadi/Brook of Egypt," as in Ezek 47:19; 48:28. The Brook of Egypt marked the traditional S boundary of the Promised Land (Num 34:5; etc.); it is the modern Wadi el-ʿArîsh, which drains into the Mediterranean some 50 miles S of Gaza.

6. Saul warns the Kenites in sufficient time for them to escape. They were a tribe of metalworkers or smiths (*qênîm*), who inhabited the desert S of Israel and Judah. The specific act of "kindness" (*ḥesed*, "kindness, loyalty, faithfulness [to a legal arrangement]"; cf. the NOTE at 20:8) here referred to is unknown, but according to biblical tradition the Kenites were intimately associated with Israel during the journey of the latter through the wilderness (see esp. R. de Vaux, "Sur l'origine kénite ou madianite du Yahvisme," *Eretz Israel* 9 [W. F. Albright Volume, 1969] 28-31). The implication of the present passage that they later settled among the Amalekites corresponds to a notice to that effect that appears in Judg 1:16 (reading *hʿmlqy*, "the Amalekites," with most critics for MT *hʿm*, "the people"; cf. Moore, *Judges*, 34).

7. *from the Wadi toward Shur on the border of Egypt.* See the *Textual Notes.* The Amalekites are driven from the Brook of Egypt on the border of Israelite territory along the N margin of the Sinai Peninsula in the direction of the Wilderness of Shur, which lay to the NE of Egypt. See the map on p. 257.

8. *Agag, king of Amalek.* Mentioned only here and Num 24:7 and 23 (correcting MT with LXX, v 24; see W. F. Albright, "The Oracles of Balaam," *JBL* 63 [1944] 222). Notably, however, Haman, who in the Book of Esther is the antagonist of Mordecai, a Benjaminite descended from Kish, is called *ʾăgāgî*, "(the) Agagite" (Esth 3:1, etc.).

12. *rose early to meet.* Hebrew *wayyaškēm . . . liqrā't,* a pregnant construction with the force of "rose early *and went* to meet" (cf. the *Textual Note*), to which compare 6:13 (Driver).

Carmel. A small town in Judah near Maon (see the NOTE at 25:2a; cf. Josh 15:55), which provides the setting for David's encounter with Abigail and Nabal (25:2-42). The modern site is Tell el-Kirmil, ca. 7 miles S of Hebron.

Gilgal. The scene of Saul's previous encounter with Samuel (13:7b-15a). Cf. the NOTE at 11:14.

holocausts. That is, whole burnt offerings; see the NOTE at 6:14.

15. Saul's self-defense is based on two excuses: (1) it was the army, not he, who spared the animals (cf. v 21 below); and (2) the animals were not brought back for selfish reasons but to be offered up to Yahweh, whom Saul identifies to Samuel as "*your* god" (cf. 7:8; 12:19). The first excuse is contradicted by what we were told in v 9, and the second turns out to be theologically unacceptable (see below).

for. Hebrew *'ăšer* (cf. 20:42; 26:23), which Driver describes as "*a link,* bringing the clause which it introduces into relation with what precedes: here the relation is a causal one, *in that, forasmuch as. . . .*"

17. *small in your own eyes.* The reference is evidently to 9:21, where the young Saul marvels that he, a humble Matrite of Benjamin, is being accorded royal treatment.

22-23. Cf. Isa 66:2b-4:

> This is the man on whom I set my gaze:
> One who is humble and contrite in spirit
> and trembles at my word.
> He who slaughters a bull slays a man!
> He who sacrifices a sheep breaks a dog's neck!
> He who lifts up an offering raises up (*mērîm*)
> a boar!
> He who makes a memorial of frankincense
> blesses Wickedness!
> As they have chosen their ways,
> As their souls delight in their abominations,
> So I shall choose their torment
> And bring their horror upon them!
> For when I called, no one answered,
> And when I spoke, they did not listen!
> Instead they did what I thought evil,
> And chose that in which I take no delight!

Samuel's rebuke of Saul is also couched in poetry, and both passages belong to the long tradition of prophetic attack on hollow cultic practice. The present verses, then, could easily find a place among the harangues of the so-called "writing" prophets (e.g. Hosea 6:6; Amos 5:21-24; etc.). What Yahweh requires is diligent obedience, without which the prescribed acts of the cult, ordinarily good and proper in themselves, become vain deeds of hypocrisy.

23a. Rebellion (*mĕrî*) and presumption (*peṣer*[?]), because they involve a kind of rejection of Yahweh, are equivalent to apostasy, as suggested by reference to forbidden forms of divination and the worship of idols (on both see below).

divination. That is, *forbidden* divination: *qesem* (cf. Deut 18:10; II Kings 17:17; etc.). Consultation by means of the Urim and Thummim was quite acceptable in Israel (see the NOTE to 14:40-42), but *qesem* was most often associated with foreign practices (Num 22:7) and false prophecy (Jer 14:14).

idolatry. Or rather, "teraphim" (*tĕrāpîm*), here used as a generalized term for idols, as in II Kings 23:24. For the older, more specific meaning, see the NOTE at 19:13.

23b. Cf. Hosea 4:6. The verb "reject" (*mā'as*) implies the formal repudiation of a relationship (so 8:7[*bis*]; 10:19; 15:26; 16:1,7; cf. Judg 9:38); it is the legal opposite of "choose" (*bāḥar;* cf. 16:7,8; also II Kings 23:27; Isa 41:9; etc.). Just as Yahweh *chose* Saul (10:24), so now he has *rejected* him.

24-31. The story in its present form seems to have two conclusions: (1) vv 24-29, in which Saul confesses his sin, asks Samuel to return to Gilgal with him to worship, and is sharply refused; and (2) vv 30-31, in which Saul confesses his sin, asks Samuel to return to Gilgal with him to worship, and is obliged.

24. *and your command.* A touch most characteristic of the prophetic perspective; see the COMMENT.

27-28. As Brauner, "To Grasp the Hem," has shown, Old Aramaic (*'ḥz bknp*) and Akkadian (*sissikta ṣabātu*) equivalents of Biblical Hebrew *heḥĕzîq bakkānāp,* "seize the hem, catch hold of the skirt," suggest that the expression refers to a gesture of "supplication, importuning, submission." When Samuel turns to go, Saul grasps the skirt of his robe (*mĕʿîl,* Samuel's characteristic garment; cf. 2:19; 28:14) as a final, deferential plea for mercy; but the fabric gives way, and the angry prophet turns the accident into a symbolic act: the tearing away of the hem represents the tearing of the kingdom away from Saul. Cf. I Kings 11:29*ff*. For a very different interpretation of the incident see Conrad, "Samuel und die Mari-'Propheten.' "

29. This statement seems intended to discourage further expostulation from Saul; that is, it implies: Yahweh has rejected you, and since Yahweh does not change his mind, there is no reason for further discussion. But the contradiction of v 11 ("I [Yahweh!] repent . . .") that this statement ("Israel's Everlasting One . . . does not repent . . .") contains is so blatant that we must question its originality. It may be a late addition to the text (derived from Num 23:19?), penned by a redactor to whom the suggestion of a divine change of mind was unacceptable.

Israel's Everlasting One. Hebrew *nēṣaḥ yiśrā'ēl,* only here in the Hebrew Bible; but cf. I Chron 29:11, where *nēṣaḥ* is an attribute of Yahweh. The epithet may have had currency very late in the biblical period (when the present verse was inserted).

32. *"Would death have been as bitter as this?"* That is, *hăkēn mar-hammāwet,* lit. "Would the bitterness of death have been thus?" To *mar-hammāwet* compare Old Aramaic *mr ḥy',* "the bitterness of life," which as E. Lipiński has

shown (*Studies in Aramaic Inscriptions and Onamastics I* [Louvain: Leuven University Press, 1975] 38), is used euphemistically in the Sefire treaties of the eighth century B.C. (*Sef* I,B,31) as the equivalent of "the bitterness of death."

33. *Samuel hewed Agag to pieces in the presence of Yahweh.* The verb (*wayšassēp*) is unique to this passage, and its meaning must be derived from the context and its treatment in the versions (BDB: "hew in pieces"; KB: "cut in pieces," comparing Postbiblical Hebrew *šṣp*, "dissever"). LXX renders it *kai esphaxen*, "and (Samuel) slaughtered," using a verb that suggests sacrificial butchering. This fact and the phrase "in the presence of Yahweh" suggest that Agag suffered a ritual death. Ritual dismemberment was a punishment for covenant violation (see the first NOTE at 11:7), and perhaps we can conclude that the crime of the Amalekites described in v 2 (cf. the NOTE) was considered all the more heinous because it involved violation of a covenant with Israel of which we have no knowledge. Compare, similarly, the reference to the "kindness" or covenant loyalty of the Kenites in v 6.

COMMENT

If Israel is to have a king, then the king must assume responsibility for prosecuting Israel's ancient grievances. It is in this spirit that Yahweh assigns to King Saul the task of punishing Amalek "for what he did to Israel" on the way up from Egypt (Exod 17:8-16; Deut 25:17-19; see the NOTE at v 2 above). The Amalekites are to be put under the ban, that is, exterminated to the last man, woman, child, and animal, and Saul is entrusted with the realization of Yahweh's ancient vow to that effect (Exod 17:14). But Saul, though quick enough to respond (vv 4*ff*), is not punctilious in executing the details of his instructions: Agag, the Amalekite king, is not slain but taken alive, and the choicest of the livestock are led back to Gilgal for sacrifice. Israel's first king, whose dynastic claims have already been forfeited by a similar kind of disobedience (see the COMMENT on 13:2-15), has failed another crucial test and now must accept the repudiation of his own reign. Yahweh, he learns, has rejected him as king.

Whatever the antiquity of the tradition of Saul's Amalekite campaign,[1]

[1] That some account of a victory over the Amalekites was part of the oldest traditions about Saul's reign is clear from the summarizing notice in 14:48. Weiser "I Samuel 15," regards the present story as an independent narrative unit, older than and originally independent of the collection of anti-monarchical materials in cc 8, 10, 12, and 13 to which it now belongs. For Weiser the tradition most distinctively reflects the predicament of Israel's first king in his struggle between the will of the people on the one hand and the prophetically transmitted will of Yahweh on the other.

it comes to us wholly as a part of the prophetic reworking of the Saul materials. Again Samuel, the prophet, plays a central role: his authority as Yahweh's official spokesman is given its usual special stress (cf. vv 1,24 and the corresponding NOTES), and indeed, as in 7:8 and 12:19, Yahweh is described as *his* (Samuel's) god (vv 15,21,30)! The prophetic duties he is called upon to discharge here include summoning Israel to holy war[2] and delivering the oracle of judgment to Saul.[3] As explained in the COMMENT on 13:2-15, the prophetic narrator is principally concerned in these stories with obedience to the (prophetically transmitted) word of Yahweh, and the relationship of obedience to tenure in the royal office. Now this is made most explicit: "Because you have rejected Yahweh's command," Saul is twice (vv 23 and 26) told, "he has rejected you from being king!" Related to all this as a kind of negative corollary is the characteristic prophetic mistrust of sacrifice (or any ritual practice) as a substitute for obedience to divine command (Jer 7:21-26; etc.) "Obedience is better than sacrifice," says Samuel (v 22).

This narrative unit, together with the account of David's anointing that follows, holds a pivotal position in the First Book of Samuel. Heretofore Samuel and Saul have occupied center stage; hereafter, except in the strange tale of the seance at En-dor (28:3-25) and in the account of Saul's death (31:1-13), David will be the constant focus of attention.

From one perspective, then, this section serves as a prophetically oriented conclusion to the story of Saul's rise to power which began in 9:1. As implied in the NOTE at v 23b, the notice of the *rejection* of Saul in vv 23,26 of the present chapter forms an inclusion with the reference in 10:24 to his *choosing* as described in 9:1*ff*. Ironically enough, it was Samuel's capitulation to the importunate "voice of the people" (8:9,22; 12:1) that led to Saul's election in the first place, and now it is because Saul has listened to "the voice of the people," i.e. to the soldiers, (vv 20,24) that he is dismissed—democracy is no more acceptable a replacement for prophetic theocracy than is monarchy! Thus the prophetic story of Saul's rise, which began with a stern warning against kingship in any form (see the COMMENT on 8:1-22), ends with an outright rejection of the first king. Saul's dynastic hopes have already been shattered (13:7b-15a), and now his own demise is in view.[4]

[2] On the prophetic function of proclaiming the wars of Yahweh, see Cross, *CMHE*, 226-227.

[3] Birch, *Rise of the Israelite Monarchy*, 97-103, argues that the form of the prophetic judgment speech has influenced the composition of the entire chapter.

[4] At least since Wellhausen (*Prolegomena*, 258-260) there has been a general tendency to view these two passages, 13:7b-15a and 15:1-34, as doublets reflecting a single tradition in two discrete sources. Indeed Wellhausen, who regarded c 15 as older, described it as the "original" of which the material in c 13 is "the copy" (259). Even those commentators like Hertzberg who recognize the important

From another perspective, however, this story looks ahead. It prepares the reader for the change that comes in 16:14, after which David will be the protagonist, Saul at most the antagonist. As Wellhausen put it, "Chap. xv is the prophetic introduction to this change."[5] Or rather, as we shall see, c 15 in combination with 16:1-13 is the prophetic introduction to the change; for the succeeding story of the anointing of David, also told from the prophetic perspective, provides the sequel to the present narrative made necessary by the allusion in v 28 to a neighbor of Saul's to whom the kingdom of Israel is being given.

---

differences between the two stories, have tended to maintain the view that they are two versions of the same incident, ascribing the developmental relationship between them to the craft of a redactor. "For the compiler of the whole work," writes Hertzberg, "the details of ch. 13, which has no express mention of the rejection, represent the lightning, while the storm breaks in ch. 15." But in fact the condemnation of Saul's dynasty and the rejection of his own right to rule were separate issues requiring, in the view of the prophetic writer who shaped these stories, individual treatment. 13:7b-15a and 15:1-34 come from the same hand and describe different moments in the progressive denunciation of Saul (so, correctly, Birch, *Rise of the Israelite Monarchy*, 105-108).

[5] *Prolegomena*, 261.

THE RISE OF DAVID

XXII. THE ANOINTING OF DAVID
(15:35-16:13)

15 35 Never again before he died did Samuel see Saul; yet [he]
grieved for Saul, because Yahweh had repented of making [him] king
over Israel. **16** 1 But Yahweh said to Samuel, "How long will you
grieve for Saul, when I have rejected him from being king over Israel?
Fill your horn with oil and go! I am sending you to Jesse of
Bethlehem, for I have found me a king among his sons."

2 "How can I go?" said Samuel. "When Saul hears, he will kill me!"

But Yahweh said, "Take a heifer with you and say, 'It is to sacrifice
to Yahweh that I have come.' 3 Then summon Jesse to the sacrifice,
and I shall let you know what you are to do. You will anoint the one I
point out to you."

4 Samuel did as Yahweh had said. When he came to Bethlehem, the
elders of the city came trembling out to meet him. "Is your visit
peaceful, O seer?" they said.

5 "It is peaceful!" he said. "It is to sacrifice to Yahweh that I have
come. Receive sanctification and celebrate with me today!" Then he
sanctified Jesse and his sons and summoned them to the sacrifice.

6 When they came he looked at Eliab and thought, "Surely his
anointed stands before Yahweh!" 7 But Yahweh said to Samuel, "Do
not look upon his appearance or his stature—I have rejected him!
For it is not as a man sees that God sees: a man looks into the face,
but God looks into the heart."

8 Then Jesse summoned Abinadab, who presented himself to Samuel; but [Samuel] said, "Yahweh has not chosen this one, either." 9 So
Jesse presented Shammah, and [Samuel] said, "Yahweh has not chosen this one, either."

10 When Jesse had presented his seven sons to [him], Samuel told
Jesse, "Yahweh has chosen none of these." 11 And [he] asked Jesse,
"Are these all the lads?"

"There is still the youngest," he said. "He is shepherding the flock."

So Samuel told Jesse, "Have him brought, for we shall not sit down
to eat until he comes."

12 [Jesse] had him brought: he was ruddy and attractive, handsome to the eye and of good appearance. "Up!" said Yahweh. "Anoint him, for he is the one!"

13 So Samuel took the horn of oil and anointed him in the midst of his brothers, and the spirit of Yahweh rushed upon David from that day forward.

Then Samuel went up on his way to Ramah.

TEXTUAL NOTES

16 1. *to Jesse of Bethlehem* MT *'l yšy byt hlḥmy,* lit. "to Jesse the Bethlehemite." LXX[L] = *'l yšy byt lḥm,* "to Jesse, to Bethlehem" (cf. v 4); LXX[B] = *'d (hēos eis) byt lḥm,* "as far as/to Bethlehem."

2. *Take* Reading *qḥ* with 4QSam[b], LXX, Syr. MT has *tqḥ,* "you will take."

3. *to the sacrifice* Reading *lzbḥ* with LXX against MT *bzbḥ,* which shows the influence of the corruption in v 5 of MT (see the *Textual Note* there). The preposition *l-* is correct with *qr',* "summon" (cf. *wyqr' lhm lzbḥ,* "and summoned them to the sacrifice," at the end of v 5 in all witnesses).

I MT is strengthened by the emphatic pronoun *'nky.* It was apparently missing in the *Vorlage* of LXX and may have fallen out by *homoioarkton* before *'wdy'k,* "I shall let you know. . . ." We tentatively read MT.

You will anoint So LXX[B]. MT, LXX[L] add "for me."

4. *as Yahweh had said* So MT: *'t 'šr dbr yhwh,* lit. "that which Yahweh had said." LXX reflects *'t kl 'šr dbr lw yhwh, "everything* which Yahweh had said *to him."*

"Is your visit peaceful, O seer?" they said MT has *wy'mr šlm bw'k,* "and he said, 'Your coming is peace(ful)'" (see Driver for a rather impressive defense of MT). We read *wy'mrw hšlm bw'k hr'h* with LXX and 4QSam[b] ([ ] *hr'h*).

5. *and celebrate with me today* Reading *wśmḥw 'ty hywm* on the basis of LXX[BA] *kai euphranthēte met' emou sēmeron,* in preference to MT *wb'tm 'ty bzbḥ,* "and come with me to (?) the sacrifice" (so Wellhausen, Budde, Smith, Dhorme; contrast Hertzberg, Stoebe).

7. *For it is not . . . into the heart* Reading *ky l' k'šr yr'h 'dm yr'h h'lhym ky 'dm yr'h lpnym wh'lhym yr'h llbb* on the basis of LXX[(B)] *hoti ouch hōs emblepsetai anthrōpos opsetai ho theos hoti anthrōpos opsetai eis prosōpon ho de theos opsetai eis kardian.* The text of MT is defective (*yr'h h'lhym* having fallen out by *homoioarkton*), reading *ky l' 'šr yr'h h'dm ky h'dm yr'h l'ynym wyhwh yr'h llbb,* "For it is not what (the) man sees, for (the) man looks into *the eyes,* but *Yahweh* looks into the heart." Space considerations suggest that 4QSam[b] shared the longer reading of LXX. See Cross, "Oldest Manuscripts," 170.

8. *Abinadab* So MT (*'ăbînādāb*); cf. I Chron 2:13. Here and in the Chronicles passage LXX has "Amminadab" (*ameinadab* = *'ammînādāb*), a name that appears in David's lineage elsewhere (Ruth 4:19-20; cf. Matt 1:4; Luke 3:33).

who presented himself Reading *wayya'ăbōr,* lit. "and he passed by," with LXX (*parēlthen*). MT *wayya'ăbīrēhû,* "and presented him, caused him to pass by," anticipates *wayya'ăbēr* in vv 9,10; but *wayya'ăbēr,* "and (Jesse) presented PN," in subsequent verses is equivalent to *wayyiqrā' 'el-PN wayya'ăbōr,* "and (Jesse) summoned PN, and he presented himself," here.

Yahweh So MT, LXX^AL, Syr. LXX^B: "God."

9. *Shammah* So MT (*šammâ*) as in 17:13, and LXX^(B) (*sama*). Elsewhere, however, the name is spelled *šm"* (I Chron 2:13; 20:7; II Sam 21:21 [*qĕrê*]), *šm'h* (II Sam 13:3,32), and *šm'y* (II Sam 21:21 [*kĕtîb*]).

11. *There is still the youngest* So LXX: *eti ho mikros* = *'wd hqṭn.* MT expands to read *'wd š'r hqṭn,* "The youngest still remains."

He is shepherding So LXX^B. MT, LXX^L: "*And* he is shepherding. . . ."

we shall not sit down to eat MT *l' nsb.* The verb *sbb* had this sense at least in later Hebrew (Sir 32:1), and LXX^B (*kataklithōmen*) seems to have understood *nsb* this way in the present case (so also Targ.; cf. Driver). On the problem in general, see especially Stoebe.

until he comes So LXX^B. MT, LXX^AL add "here."

12. *ruddy and attractive* Conjectural. MT (cf. LXX) has *'dmwny 'm,* "ruddy with (handsomeness to the eyes, etc.)," which is awkward (despite 17:42, where *w'dmny 'm yph mr'h* is surely an expansion inspired by the present verse). We may reconstruct with some confidence: *'dm wn'ym,* "ruddy (cf. Cant 5:10) and attractive."

of good appearance So MT: *ṭwb r'y,* lit. "good of appearance." LXX^(B) adds *kyriō* = *lyhwh,* "to Yahweh," in reminiscence of v 7b above.

Yahweh So MT. LXX adds "to Samuel."

Anoint him, for he is the one So MT, LXX^L: *mšḥhw ky zh hw'.* LXX^B reflects *wmšḥ 't dwyd ky zh* (*hw'*) *ṭwb,* "And anoint David, for this one is good!" Cf. the *Textual Note* on "of good appearance" above.

NOTES

15 35. The statement that Samuel never again during his lifetime saw Saul is compatible with 28:3-25, since there the interview takes place after the prophet's death, but it is in direct contradiction of 19:18-24, where Saul follows David to Samuel at Ramah. The latter passage, which also duplicates certain aspects of 10:10-12, must be regarded as a late insertion into the story of David's flight (see the COMMENT on 19:18-24).

16 1. *Fill your horn with oil.* That is, for anointing the new king (v 13). Cf. the NOTES at 9:16 and 10:1. In this case the oil flask is a horn, as in I Kings 1:39, where Zadok anoints Solomon.

Jesse. According to the genealogical list preserved in I Chron 2:3-12 (cf. Ruth 4:17-22) Jesse was a Judahite of the house of Perez (Ruth 4:12; cf. Genesis 38) and the grandson of Boaz and Ruth.

Bethlehem. The village lay ca. 6 miles S of Jerusalem in the richest part of Judah. Departing from Ramah (cf. 15:34) a traveler to Bethlehem could take the main NS road that followed the spine of the highlands of Benjamin and Judah and passed close to both towns.

6. *Eliab.* Jesse's eldest son (I Chron 2:13).

his anointed. See the second NOTE at 9:16.

8. *Abinadab.* Jesse's second son (I Chron 2:13).

9. *Shammah.* Jesse's third son, elsewhere called Shimea (see the *Textual Note*).

10. *his seven sons.* The complete list is given in I Chron 2:13-15: "Now Jesse became the father of his firstborn, Eliab, and Abinadab, his second, and Shimea, his third, Nethanel, the fourth, Raddai, the fifth, Ozem, the sixth, David, the seventh." But the present verse implies that there were seven sons *besides* David, and 17:12 below asserts this explicitly; moreover, in I Chron 27:18 (MT) a brother of David named Elihu is mentioned. Accordingly, we might insert Elihu into the list in I Chronicles 2, as has actually been done in the text of the Peshiṭta. But it is more likely that we should read "Eliab" in I Chr 27:18 and leave the text of I Chronicles 2 as it stands; the notice in 17:12 is probably dependent on the present passage at some point. The hand that wrote "seven sons" in this verse may have erred out of careless fidelity to the tradition that Jesse had seven sons, or alternatively the tradition itself may have been mixed. C. H. Gordon in a review of U. Cassuto, *The Goddess Anath,* in *JAOS* 72 (1952) 181, traces the problem to a lost epic account of David's anointing in which seven and eight appeared in climactic poetic parallelism, cf. *CTCA* 14.1(= Krt 8-9).14-21; 15(= 128).2.23-24. "Any impartial reader of the account of how Samuel eliminated the older brothers of David and dramatically chose the youngest to be king," writes Gordon, "will see that the treatment is epic, however prosaic the language." See further the COMMENT.

11. *to eat.* That is, to eat that part of the sacrifice not reserved for the deity. See the NOTE at 9:13.

12. *attractive . . . handsome . . . of good appearance.* Divine favor usually has physical symptoms; see the NOTE at 9:2.

13. *the spirit of Yahweh rushed upon David.* See the NOTES at 10:6 and 11:6. Here the onrush of divine spirit follows immediately upon the anointing and remains "from that day forward." Moreover, as we are about to discover, Yahweh's spirit has departed from Saul (v 14).

COMMENT

Having rejected one king Yahweh sends Samuel to Bethlehem to find another. The task proves more difficult even than the nervous prophet, who fears the reprisal of Saul, expects; for as the sons of Jesse pass before him, they are refused, each in turn. Finally, however, the youngest is brought in from the pastures and immediately confirmed by Yahweh as his chosen king. Samuel pours the oil over David's head, and Yahweh's spirit takes charge of him.

The story derives its interest from the folklore motif of the seventh son (or the eighth: see the NOTE at v 10) who rises above his brothers. David is *haqqāṭān,* "the youngest" (v 11), and his selection over Eliab and the others emphasizes the miraculous nature of the incident as a whole and points in particular to the freedom of the divine choice in the naming of a king. As in the case of the election of a man from the smallest clan of the smallest tribe to be the first king (cf. the NOTE at 9:21), the break here with the expected or conventional shows Yahweh's free involvement in the events. And David, when he arrives at last, displays all the physical symptoms of divine favor: he is "ruddy and attractive, handsome to the eye and of good appearance" (v 12; cf. also the NOTE).

In spite of the last fact, however, we are warned—or rather Samuel is warned—not to trust in appearances, since "it is not as a man sees that God sees" (v 7). Despite Eliab's appearance and stature, which evidently are imposing, he is not Yahweh's choice. Some scholars have discerned in this a veiled attack on the theme of Saul's beauty and great height, as it appears in 9:2 and especially 10:23. "Eliab is something of a 'new Saul,' so that in his rejection Saul is denounced in effigy."[1] Indeed as T. N. D. Mettinger has shown, this episode is reminiscent of the story of Saul's election by lottery (10:17-27a) in a number of ways.[2] If Samuel is not using the lots in the examination of Jesse's sons, he is using something similar which gives "yes" and "no" answers. Moreover David, like Saul, turns up missing at the climactic moment and must be brought in from offstage. Finally certain connections in vocabulary exist between the two passages, such as, for example, the use of *bāḥar,* "choose," in reference to Yahweh's election of a king (10:24; 16:8,9,10). It seems clear that the story of David's anointing is fashioned at least partly in light of 10:17-27 and that both 10:17-27a and 16:1-13 reflect prophetic reaction to the

[1] Mettinger, *King and Messiah,* 175.
[2] Ibid., 176-179.

older tradition of Saul's election that lies behind the story of the divine lottery in its present form (see the COMMENT on 10:17-27a). Popular acclaim of the handsome, towering son of a powerful Benjaminite nobleman is replaced by the free divine selection of a shepherd boy from Judah.

This, then, is yet another major chapter in the prophetic reworking of the older materials about the early history of the monarchy. Again the prophet Samuel is the central figure, and again the propriety of divine election of the king by prophetic anointing is demonstrated. The story of David's election forms a brace with that of Saul's rejection in the immediately preceding material, and together they provide a prophetically oriented transition to the history of David's rise to power (see also the COMMENT on 15:1-34).[8] We are being prepared to understand the decline in the fortunes of Saul and corresponding rise in those of David in light of the prophetic theology of kingship as developed in the preceding chapters. Hereafter the prophetic writer who shaped this material will be content to remain out of sight, letting the older narrative pass by without comment, except when he makes a brief appearance in c 28. What follows immediately belongs to the old story of David's rise to power.

[8] In contrast, some scholars regard 16:1-13 (or 15:1 - 16:13) not as a prophetic introduction to the history of David's rise but as an original and organic part of the older complex. See especially Weiser, "Legitimation des Königs David"; Grønbaek, *Aufstieg Davids*, 25-27, 37-76. The position taken here stands closer to that of Veijola, *Die ewige Dynastie*, 102, n. 156. II Sam 12:7, which might be urged in objection since it seems to allude to an anointing of David before his deliverance from Saul, is, as Mettinger (*King and Messiah*, 29-30) points out, secondary in its present context and late (and prophetic!); and contrast II Sam 5:3, which seems aware of no previous prophetic anointing of David at the time of his popular anointing at Hebron, to the synoptic passage in I Chron 11:3, which acknowledges the good offices of Samuel, suggesting that the story preserved in 16:1-13 had become a fixed part of the tradition by the time of the Chronicler (so Ward, "Story of David's Rise," 13-14).

XXIII. DAVID'S ARRIVAL AT COURT (16:14-23)

16 14 The spirit of Yahweh departed from Saul, and an evil spirit
from Yahweh began to haunt him. 15 Saul's servants said to him, "An
evil spirit of God is haunting you! 16 Let our lord speak: your servants stand ready before you! Let us seek out someone who knows
how to play the lyre, so that when the evil spirit comes upon you,
he may play and you will be well and it will let you alone."
17 So Saul said to his servants, "Find me a man who plays well, and
bring him to me!"
18 Then one of the attendants spoke up. "I have noticed," he said,
"that Jesse the Bethlehemite has a son who knows how to play, a
powerful man, a warrior, skilled in speech, and handsome—and Yahweh is with him."
19 So Saul sent messengers to Jesse to say, "Send me your son
David, the one who is with the flock!" 20 Jesse took an ass, ladened it
with an omer of bread, a skin of wine, and a kid, and sent it to Saul in
the care of his son David. 21 When David came to Saul and presented
himself to him, [Saul] loved him so much that he became his weapon-
bearer; 22 and Saul sent word to Jesse, "David shall remain in my
service, for he has found favor in my eyes!"
23 Thereafter, whenever the spirit of God would come upon Saul,
David would take up the lyre and play, and Saul would find relief and
be well, and the evil spirit would depart from him.

TEXTUAL NOTES

16 15. *of God* So MT. LXX, Syr., under the influence of v 14, have "of Yahweh." Cf. vv 16,23.

16. The beginning of the verse presents certain unusual features in Hebrew, and this seems to have led LXX into an erroneous emendation. MT (cf. LXX^L) reads *y'mr n' 'dnnw 'bdyk lpnyk ybqšw*, lit. "Let our lord speak: your

servants are before you! Let them (= us) seek out. . . ." LXX^B evidently reflects *y'mrw n' 'bdyk lpnyk wbqšw l'dnnw,* "Let your servants speak in your presence, and (let them) seek out for our lord. . . ." Tentatively we follow MT (so Stoebe), though many critics have found reason to prefer LXX (Wellhausen, Driver, Budde, Smith). Syr., which might be expected to adjudicate in a case like this, is no help here, having suffered a long haplography from *hnh n'* in v 15 to *y'mr n'* in the present verse.

the evil spirit So LXX^B. MT (cf. LXX^L) adds "of God" in reminiscence of v 15.

he may play MT *wngn bydw,* lit. "he will play with his hand." For *bydw,* "with his hand," LXX has *en tē kinyra autou,* "on his lyre," which may be an inner-Greek corruption of *en tē cheiri autou,* "with his hand," influenced by the reference to playing the lyre in the first part of the verse.

and it will let you alone Reading *whnyḥh lk* on the basis of LXX *kai anapausei.* This was lost in MT by haplography after *wṭwb lk,* "and you will be well."

18. *handsome* MT *'yš t'r,* lit. "a man of form." LXX *anēr agathos tō eidei* reflects the fuller version of the expression, viz. *'yš ṭwb t'r,* "a man good of form" (cf. I Kings 1:6).

19. *to say* MT: *wy'mr,* "and said." LXX = *l'mr,* "saying."

the flock So MT, LXX^L. LXX^B: "your flock."

20. *an ass . . . an omer of bread* LXX^L and OL preserve the original reading, viz. *ḥmwr wyśm 'lyw 'mr lḥm.* MT (*ḥmwr lḥm*) and LXX^B (= *'mr lḥm*) have suffered similar haplographies, a scribe's eye having jumped from *ḥmr* to *'mr.*

21. The original, as reflected in MT, admits of such ambiguity (MT: lit. "And David came to Saul, and he stood before him, and he loved him greatly, and he became his weapon-bearer.") that LXX^L finds it necessary to introduce explicit subjects ("Saul . . . David") into the last two clauses. The same is necessary in English.

23. *the spirit of God* So MT. LXX^B (cf. Syr.) has "an evil spirit," in anticipation of the second part of the verse, and LXX^L combines the two readings.

NOTES

16 14. In ancient tradition a person once touched by divine spirit can never again be free. When Saul loses place to David and Yahweh's spirit falls upon the young Bethlehemite (16:13), an evil spirit arrives in Gibeah as though rushing into the vacuum Saul's loss of favor has created. Another way of saying this is that the infusion of spirit is never neutral. It may endow with special powers, or it may breed misery; and indeed the spirit now torments Saul. We may speak of mental illness if we want—Saul manifests some symptoms of par-

anoia, others of manic-depressive illness—but surely Hertzberg is correct to stress the fact that "Saul's suffering is described theologically, not psychopathetically or psychologically." The evil spirit is "from Yahweh" and will play its part in the working out of the divine plan.

15. *Saul's servants.* A king's servants (*'ăbādîm*) are not menial functionaries but high ranking members of the court, as explained in the NOTE at 8:14.

16. *someone who knows how to play the lyre.* As the first modern biblical scholar observed (quite possibly thinking of Saul), "Music is good to the melancholy" (Spinoza, in the preface to Part IV of his *Ethics*), and reliance on the apotropaic function of music was common to every ancient society confronted by demons. So Saul's servants propose to enlist the services of a musician to turn away the evil spirit and soothe the melancholia of their lord. On the lyre (*kinnôr*), cf. the NOTE at 10:5.

18. *a powerful man.* That is, a member of a family of standing, a *gibbôr ḥayil;* see the NOTE at 9:1.

a warrior. Hebrew *'îš milḥāmâ,* lit. "a man of war." This suggests that he is a trained fighter, but contrast 17:33 and see the COMMENT to the story of David and the Philistine champion in the section that follows.

skilled in speech. The ideal Israelite hero was clever with words, as the stories of Jacob, Joseph, Esther, Daniel, and the rest (except Moses) show.

handsome. Another characteristic of the ideal young man. See the NOTES at 9:2 and 16:12.

Yahweh is with him. This part of the description explains all of the previous parts: the young man's success, strength, manners, and looks are the result of divine favor. The expression "Yahweh is with him/David" now becomes a kind of leitmotiv running through the stories of David and Saul. "David was successful in all his undertakings, for Yahweh was with him" (18:14). The attendant who speaks here hardly realizes the importance of what he says, though his words adumbrate David's rise to power. Nor indeed does Saul see the implications. He is eager now to have a servant bestowed with Yahweh's favor, and he will soon rely on that favor for his servant's safety in a time of grave danger (17:37), but when he comes to understand what it all means, he will fear his servant because Yahweh is with him (18:28-29a).

20. *an omer of bread.* Hebrew *'ōmer leḥem* (see the *Textual Note*). The omer, not to be confused with the much larger homer, was a dry measure equivalent (according to Exod 16:36) to 1/10 ephah (cf. the NOTE at 1:24), or a bit more than two dry quarts. Elsewhere only in 25:18 (see the *Textual Note*) and Exodus 16.

21. [*Saul*] *loved him.* Without doubt the meaning is that Saul was greatly pleased with David, that he felt great affection for him; but as pointed out by W. L. Moran ("The Ancient Near Eastern Background of the Love of God in Deuteronomy," *CBQ* 25 [1963] 78-79) the language of love can be found "used to describe the loyalty and friendship joining . . . king and subject" in extrabiblical ancient Near Eastern texts from a wide span of time, and in the Amarna materials in particular the king of Egypt "is expected to love his vassal" (cf. *EA* 121:61; 123:23; 158:6). So as J. A. Thompson has suggested ("Significance of the Verb *Love*"), the verb "love" (*'āhēb*) may also have a political nuance here, as it seems to in the stories of David and Jonathan that

follow. The king has given official recognition to the young man, has made a kind of lêgal commitment to him; that is, he has "loved" him and appointed him to be his weapon-bearer, an intimate servant of the king.

COMMENT

It is an exciting moment in the biblical drama when David first steps on stage. To be sure, the prophetic writer has already introduced him to us in the preceding story of Samuel's visit to Bethlehem (see the COMMENT on 15:35 - 16:13), and the composite tradition of the received Hebrew Bible offers a complete alternative account of his first meeting with Saul (see § XXIV-B); but in the primary narrative to which the rest was added he makes his first appearance here. So according to the oldest tradition available to us (see pp. 27-30 in the Introduction) David came to court as a musician and royal weapon-bearer.

As for Saul, he appears here as a man abandoned by God; that is, in the words of the text, the spirit of Yahweh has left him. We are not yet told why. Though the writer of 15:1 - 16:13 has prepared us quite thoroughly to understand Saul's abandonment from the prophetic point of view, we shall find no such overt message in this older material itself. Only the events themselves will show what Yahweh is doing. For the time being we know that Saul has lost his old charisma and also that he has fallen prey to an evil spirit, an indication of an incipient inability to rule (understood, by the way, as a consequence not of depravity, as implied by 13:7b-15a and 15:1-34, but of illness).

In pointed contrast to the developing impotence of Saul is the array of the newcomer's abilities and qualities. He is "a powerful man, a warrior, skilled in speech, and handsome" (v 18). Most especially, "Yahweh is with him." Again we are not told what exactly this means—subsequent events will work that out (cf. the last NOTE at v 18)—but this is an auspicious introduction for the young musician, who seems to possess a kind of magical ability to relieve the fits of the ailing king. Moreover, Saul instantly conceives for David a strong emotional and professional loyalty (see the NOTE at v 21) and makes him his weapon-bearer.

So in this brief passage three of the major themes of the stories that follow are introduced: (1) Saul is in decline; (2) Yahweh is with David; and (3) Saul is deeply attached to the younger man. At least two other themes are prepared for in a general way, viz. that of David's unshakable loyalty to Saul and Israel and that of David's military prowess. Both of these find full expression in our story. This, then, is the beginning of the history of David's rise to power, an old narrative setting forth these themes and others, which is preserved with only minor alterations in the materials that follow; see "The History of David's Rise" in the Introduction (LITERARY HISTORY, pp. 27-30).

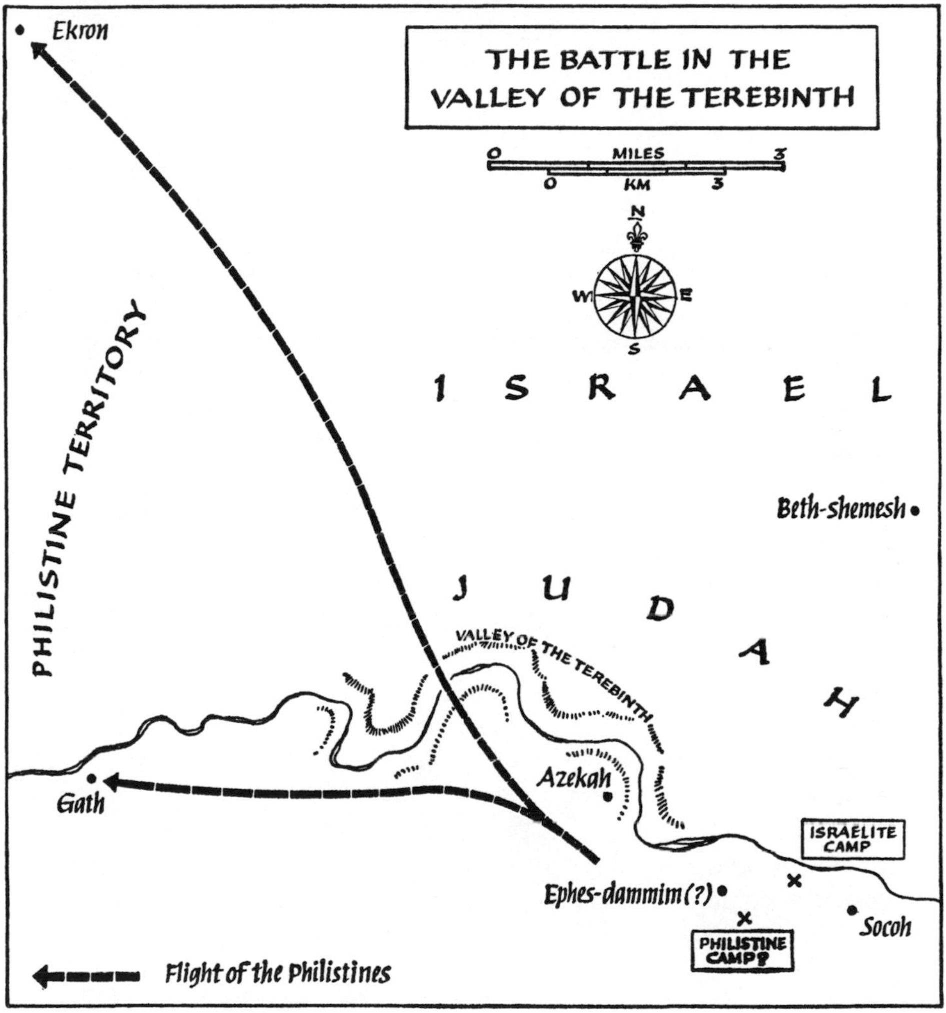

XXIV-A. DAVID AND THE PHILISTINE CHAMPION (17:1-11, 32-40, 42-48a, 49, 51-54)

17 [1]The Philistines had gathered their forces for battle, coming together at Socoh of Judah, and encamped between Socoh and Azekah
at Ephes-dammim. [2]So Saul and the men of Israel assembled, encamped in the Valley of the Terebinth, and deployed themselves to
meet the Philistines in battle.
[3]Now the Philistines were stationed upon a hill on one side, and
the Israelites were stationed upon a hill on the other side, and there
was a valley between them. [4]And there marched forth from the ranks
of the Philistines a certain infantryman from Gath whose name was
Goliath. (His height was four cubits and a span!) [5]A helmet was
upon his head, and he was dressed in a plated cuirass. (The weight of
the cuirass was five thousand bronze shekels!) [6]Bronze greaves were
upon his shins, and a bronze scimitar was slung between his shoulder
blades. [7]The shaft of his spear was like a weavers' heddle rod. (Its
blade weighed six hundred iron shekels!) And a shield-bearer preceded him.
[8]He stood calling to the ranks of Israel and said to them, "Why
should you march out in battle array? Am I not a Philistine? Are you
not servants of Saul? Select a man for yourselves, and let him come
down to me! [9]If he is successful in fighting with me and slays me,
we shall become your slaves. But if I am successful and slay him, then
you will become our slaves and serve us. [10]I defy the ranks of Israel
this day," continued the Philistine, "give me a man and let us fight together!"
[11]When Saul and all of Israel heard these words from the Philistine, they were dismayed and greatly frightened. [32]But David said to
Saul, "Let my lord's heart not sink within him! Your servant will go
and fight with that Philistine."
[33]"You cannot go and fight with that Philistine," said Saul to
David, "for you are only a lad, and he has been a warrior since his
youth!"

34 But David said to Saul, "When your servant was herding sheep
for his father and a lion or a bear would come and carry off a sheep
from the flock, 35 I would chase after him, strike him down, and
snatch [it] from his mouth. Then if he attacked me, I would grab him
by his throat, knock him down, and kill him. 36 Lion and bear alike,
your servant struck them down! So the uncircumcised Philistine will
be like one of them: shall I not go and strike him down and remove
the reproach from Israel today? For who is that uncircumcised fellow
that he should defy the ranks of the Living God? 37 Yahweh, who
protected me from the lion and the bear, will protect me from that
Philistine!"

"Go!" said Saul to David. "For Yahweh will be with you!" 38 Then
[he] dressed David in a uniform with a bronze helmet for his head
39 and girded [him] with his own sword over his uniform. But David,
after he had tried once or twice to walk, said to Saul, "I cannot walk
in these, for I have never practiced!" So they took [the armor] off
him. 40 Then taking his stick in his hand he selected five smooth
stones from the wadi and put them into his shepherd's bag—into the
pouch—and with his sling in his hand he approached the Philistine.

42 When the Philistine looked and saw David, he disdained him
because he was only a lad. 43 "Am I a dog," [he] said to [him], "that
you come after me with a stick?" And [he] cursed David by his god.
44 "Come to me," [he] said to David, "that I may give your flesh to
the birds of the sky and the beasts of the field!"

45 But David said to the Philistine, "You come against me with
sword and spear and scimitar, but I come against you with the name
of Yahweh Sabaoth, god of the ranks of Israel, which you have defied
this very day! 46 And Yahweh will hand you over to me, and I shall
strike you down and cut off your head! I shall give your corpse and
the corpses of the Philistine camp to the birds of the sky and the wild
animals of the land! Then all the earth will know that there is a
god in Israel, 47 and all those assembled here will know that it is
not by sword or spear that Yahweh gives victory! For the battle is
Yahweh's and he will hand you over to us!"

48a Then the Philistine rose up and came toward David. 49 David
reached into the bag, took out a stone and slung it, striking the Philistine in his forehead. When the stone sank into his forehead, he fell on
his face to the ground. 51 David ran up and stood beside him. He took
his sword and dispatched him, cutting off his head.

When the Philistines saw that their champion was dead, they fled.
52 The men of Israel and Judah rose up shouting and chased after
them as far as the approaches to Gath and the gates of Ekron, and
the Philistine wounded fell along the Shaaraim road all the way to
Gath and Ekron.

53 When the Israelites returned from their pursuit of the Philistines,
they looted their camp. 54 David took the Philistine's head and
brought it to Jerusalem, but his weapons he put in his own tent.

TEXTUAL NOTES

17 1. *Ephes-dammim* MT *ʾps dmym* (= *ps dmym,* I Chron 11:13). LXX^{B} *ephermem,* LXX^{L} [*s*]*apharm*[*e*]*in,* and OL *in ramoam in sepherme* point to *sprmym* or the like. There is little upon which to base an evaluation of this evidence. See further the NOTE.

2. *in the Valley of the Terebinth, and deployed themselves* So MT: *bʿmq hʾlh wyʿrkw* (cf. LXX^{L}). LXX^{B} reflects *bʿmq ʾlh ʿrkw,* "in the valley. *These* deployed themselves. . . ." Read MT.

3. *and . . . a valley* MT *whgyʾ* (cf. Josephus [*Ant.* 6.171]). Curiously, LXX$^{(B)}$ has *kyklō,* "in a circle," at this point. This most often represents *sbyb,* but here it is probably a defective representation of *kai ho autōn* (LXX^{A}) = MT.

4. *from the ranks* So LXX$^{(B)}$ (*ek tēs parataxeōs* = *mmʿrkt*). MT *mmḥnwt,* "from the *camps,*" is out of place. As v 3 shows, the two armies have already left camp.

a certain infantryman See the NOTE.

four cubits and a span So LXX^{BL}, Josephus (*Ant.* 6.171), and 4QSam^{a}, which preserves []ʾ*rbʿ*[ʾ]*mwt wzrt.* MT, LXX^{A} have "*six* cubits and a span." Stoebe suspects LXX of rationalizing, but a scribe would hardly have diminished David's feat willingly; an exaggeration is more likely. Better still is the mechanical explanation discovered by Michael D. Coogan, viz. *šš ʾmwt,* "six cubits," in anticipation of *šš mʾwt,* "six hundred," in v 7.

A helmet So LXX^{B}. MT, LXX^{L}: "A *bronze* helmet."

bronze shekels So MT. LXX: "bronze *and iron* shekels."

6. *greaves* MT vocalizes *mṣḥt* as singular (*miṣḥat*) and LXX^{B}, Syr. read it as plural (*miṣḥōt*). But we expect a dual (*miṣḥātê*), and LXX^{L} (= *mṣḥtw* < *mṣḥty?*) may preserve a vestige of one.

7. *shaft* Reading *ʿēṣ,* "wood, shaft," as in II Sam 21:19, for MT *ḥṣ,* "arrow." So Syr., LXX^{B} (*ho kontos,* "the shaft") and LXX^{L} (*to xylon,* "the wood").

Its blade So LXX^{B}. MT: "The blade *of his spear.*" LXX^{L}: "The blade *that was upon it.*"

8. *in battle array* So MT: *l'rk mlḥmh,* lit. "to deploy for battle." LXX^{B} (cf. LXX^{L}) adds *ex enantias hēmōn* = *lqr'tnw,* "opposite/against us" (cf. v 2).

a Philistine So LXX. MT: "*the* Philistine," in anticipation of the designation used in vv 10,11, etc.

servants of Saul So MT: *'bdym lš'wl.* LXX = *'brym wš'wl, "Hebrews and* Saul."

Select The consonantal text of MT (*brw*) is correct. Read *bōrû* (MT *qĕrê: bĕrû,* "eat"?), as reflected by LXX *eklexasthe.* For *brr,* "select," cf. I Chron 7:40.

12-31. Here in MT and other MSS appears a long addition which is missing from the text of LXX^{B}. See § XXIV-B.

32. *my lord's heart* So LXX (*kardia tou kyriou mou* = *lb 'dny*). MT *lb 'dm, "a man's* heart" (so Syr.).

34. *a lion or a bear* Reading *h'ry whdwb* (cf. LXX, Syr.). In v 36 of MT the *'t* particle marking *hdwb* as accusative was inadvertently lost at some point. It was restored marginally, but subsequently found its way into the text at the wrong point, viz. in the present verse. Hence MT: *h'ry w't hdwb.*

35. *his throat* MT has *bzqnw,* "his beard" (so Syr.), but as Stoebe observes, this may make sense with reference to a lion, but not to a bear. The translation of LXX (*tou pharyngos autou,* "his throat") reflects *bgrwnw* (Budde), from which the reading of MT arose by confusion of *g* for *z* and *rw* for *q* (the latter being possible especially in scripts of the late Hasmonean and early Herodian periods). No doubt the scribe of MT was thinking ahead to the struggle with the Philistine, in which case the reference to the beard would be entirely apropos.

36. *Lion and bear alike* Reading *gm 't h'ry wgm 't hdwb* (cf. LXX^{AL}, Syr., etc.). For the text of MT (*gm 't h'ry gm hdwb*), see the *Textual Note* to v 34 above.

So the uncircumcised Philistine . . . the Living God So LXX$^{(B)}$: *kai estai ho allophylos ho aperitmētos* (LXX^{L} + *houtos;* cf. MT) *hōs hen toutōn ouchi poreusomai kai pataxō auton kai aphelō sēmeron oneidos ex israēl dioti tis ho aperitmētos houtos hoti* (so LXX^{L}; LXX^{B} *hos*) *ōneidisen parataxin theou zōntos* = *whyh hplšty h'rl* (*hzh*) *k'ḥd mhm hlw' 'lk whktyw whsyrty hywm ḥrp myśr'l ky my h'rl hzh ky* (*'šr*) *ḥrp m'rkt 'lhym ḥyym.* Contrast MT: *whyh hplšty h'rl hzh k'ḥd mhm ky ḥrp m'rkt 'lhym ḥyym,* "So that uncircumcised Philistine will be like one of them, because he has defied the ranks of the Living God!" Josephus, too (*Ant.* 6.183), seems to have known this shorter version. It is difficult to decide whether the longer text of LXX reflects original material or secondary expansion. Critics who favor the latter explanation (Stoebe; cf. Smith) point to the almost identical wording of 17:26 as a probable source of the intrusive material. But v 26 is part of the material missing from LXX^{B}, which displays the longer reading here. Moreover MT as it stands seems rather abrupt. Tentatively, we assume that MT has suffered haplography from *h'rl hzh* (*k'ḥd m-*) to *h'rl hzh* (*ky ḥrp m-*), which has been partially repaired by the restoration of *k'ḥd mhm* (cf. Budde).

37. At the beginning of the verse MT, LXX^{AL} and other MSS add, "And

David said," which is retained by Wellhausen, Driver, Smith, Budde, and Stoebe, primarily on the grounds that although superfluous in Greek it is "in accordance with Hebrew idiom" (Driver). But this is entirely beside the point. The translator of LXX did not exclude things that were not in keeping with Greek style, and the absence of the words here where no textual motive for their loss can be discerned shows LXX^{B} to have had a shorter text. The words are an expansion in MT (to which LXX^{AL} have been corrected), added to re-identify the speaker of an unusually long speech.

from that Philistine So MT. LXX, Syr.: "from that *uncircumcised* Philistine."

38. *in a uniform* MT has *mdyw wntn,* "(in) *his* uniform *and will place* (?)" (cf. Syr., LXX^{L}). LXX^{B} *mdyn,* "in a uniform," is probably correct: MT *mdyw* anticipates v 39, and *wntn* is syntactically impossible. Cf. Budde.

for his head At the end of the verse MT, LXX^{AL}, Syr. add *wylbš 'tw šrywn,* "and dressed him in armor" (cf. 17:5). Omit with LXX^{B}.

39. *and girded [him] with his own sword* So LXX^{B}. MT: "David girded himself with his (= Saul's) sword. . . ."

after he had tried once or twice to walk Reading *wyl' llkt p'm wp'mym,* lit. "and he was unable to go once or twice," on the basis of LXX^{B} *kai ekopiasen peripatēsis hapax kai dis* (Budde). MT has *wy'l llkt ky l' nsh,* "and he was willing to walk but (?) had not practiced (wearing armor)." This shows not only corruption by metathesis in the verb (*wy'l* for *wyl'*) but also interference from the succeeding material (*ky l' nsyty* "for I have never practiced" (cf. LXX^{L}).

So they took [the armor] off him So LXX (= *wysrwm m'lyw,* lit. "And they took them off him"). MT has *wysrm dwd m'lyw,* "And *David* took them off."

40. *smooth stones from the wadi* MT *hlqy 'bnym mn hnḥl,* lit. "smooth ones of stones from the wadi." LXX$^{(B)}$ *lithous teleious,* "perfect stones" is an (inner-Greek) error for *lithous leious,* "smooth stones," or even *leious lithous* (so many MSS).

into his shepherd's bag—into the pouch Reading *bkly hr'ym 'šr lw bylqwṭ.* So all witnesses, except that MT has ". . . bag *and* into. . . ." It is quite likely that *bkly hr'ym 'šr lw* arose as a gloss to the unique *bylqwt* (Wellhausen, Budde, Smith).

the Philistine So MT. LXX: "the Philistine man."

41. MT and other MSS add a verse here, which is missing from LXX^{B}. See § XXIV-B.

42. *When the Philistine looked and saw David* Reading *wybṭ hplšty wyr'h 't dwd* with MT. LXX^{B} reflects *wyr'h glyt 't dwd,* "When Goliath saw David," having lost *wybṭ hplšty* by simple haplography, a scribe's eye having jumped from *hplšty* at the end of v 40 (which preceded v 42 immediately in the *Vorlage* of the OG) to *hplšty* in the present verse. After this loss it was necessary to specify the subject, hence the insertion of *glyt.*

a lad The verse originally ended with *n'r,* "lad," but it has been expanded on the basis of 16:12 (where MT has *'dmwny 'm yph 'ynym wṭwb r'y,* "ruddy with handsomeness to the eyes and good of appearance"; see the *Textual Note* to 16:12). Here MT (cf. LXX) adds *w'dmny 'm yph mr'h,* "and ruddy with handsomeness of appearance."

43. *Am I a dog* So MT. LXX^B: "Am I *like* a dog?" LXX^L: "I am not a dog, am I?"

with a stick So Syr., LXX^B (*en rhabdō* = *bmql*). MT: *bmqlwt,* "with sticks." Smith conjectures *bammaqelet,* but such a form is unattested. Here LXX^B continues with a longer text, viz. *kai lithous kai eipen daueid ouchi all' ē cheirō kynos,* "'. . . and stones?' And David said, 'No! But something worse than a dog!'" (as if, *wb'bnym wy'mr dwd l' ky 'm r' mklb*). One might make a case for the originality of the longer reading, which is also known to Josephus (*Ant.* 6.186), by assuming haplography triggered by confusion of *bmql* and *mklb;* but tentatively we read the shorter text of MT, LXX^{AL}, Syr.

44. *and the beasts of the field* So MT: *wlbhmt* (which should be pointed as plural; cf. LXX^B) *hśdh.* LXX^{AL} reflect *wlḥyt h'rṣ,* "to the wild animals of the land," in anticipation of v 46. LXX^B reflects a mixture: *wlbhmwt h'rṣ,* "to the beasts of the land."

45. *Yahweh Sabaoth, god of the ranks of Israel* So MT, LXX^{AL} (*yhwh ṣb'wt 'lhy m'rkwt yśr'l*). LXX^B reflects *yhwh 'lhy ṣb'wt m'rkwt yśr'l,* "Yahweh, god of the armies (= Sabaoth), the ranks of Israel" (cf. Syr.).

this very day So LXX. Construed by MT with the following verse.

46. *And Yahweh will hand you over to me* Reading *wsgrk yhwh bydy,* lit. "And Yahweh will enclose you in my hand," with LXX. MT *ysgrk,* etc. "Yahweh will enclose . . ." (LXX reflects *hywm,* "today," after "Yahweh"; delete with MT).

your corpse and the corpses Reading *pgrk wpgr* with LXX (for *pgr,* "corpses [collectively]," cf. Amos 8:3). MT has lost part of the reading by *homoioarkton;* thus *pgr,* "the corpses. . . ."

in Israel So LXX, Syr. MT: "(that there is a god) *to* Israel," that is, "that Israel has a god."

48a. We read *wyqm hplšty wylk lqr't dwyd* with LXX^B. MT (cf. LXX^{AL}) has *whyh* (*sic;* cf. GK §112uu) *ky qm hplšty wylk wyqrb lqr't dwd,* "When the Philistine rose up, he came and drew near to meet David. . . ."

48b. MT and certain other MSS have additional material here which is missing from LXX^B. See § XXIV-B.

49. *a stone* So MT. LXX: "*one* stone."

into his forehead So MT. LXX^B (cf. LXX^L, OL), by way of interpretation, precedes this with *dia tēs perikephalaias* = *b'd hkwb',* "through the helmet."

50. Here MT and other MSS add a verse missing from LXX^B. See § XXIV-B.

51. *beside him* So LXX^B (*ep' autou* = *'lyw*). MT, LXX^{AL}: *'l* (MT *'l*) *hplšty,* "beside *the Philistine.*"

He took his sword MT, LXX^{AL} add *wyšlp mt'rh,* "and drew it from its sheath," which M. Dahood (in Fisher, *Ras Shamra Parallels* 1.185) defends on the grounds of the parallelism of "sword" and "sheath" (cf. Jer 47:6; Ezek 5:1); and it is true that this kind of incidental expansion is not characteristic of MT.

cutting off his head So LXX^{B}, Syr. MT, LXX^{AL} add "with it (the sword)."

52. *after them* So LXX$^{(B)}$. MT (cf. LXX^{L}): "the Philistines."

Gath So LXX^{BL}. MT *gy'*, "Gai" or "a valley"? Cf. Wellhausen, Driver.

Ekron So MT. LXX: "Ashkelon"; cf. 5:10 and 7:14; see the *Textual Note* at 5:10.

along the Shaaraim road MT *bĕderek šaʿărayim* (cf. Josh 15:36). LXX *en tē hodō tōn pylōn* reflects *bdrk hšʿrym*, "on the road of the gates," on which see Wellhausen.

53. *they looted* So MT: *wyšsw* (cf. LXX^{L}). LXX^{B} *kai katepatoun*, "And they tramped down," probably reflects *wyšpw* (as if from *šwp*, "tread upon"). Confusion of *s* and *p* was possible especially in scripts of the second century B.C. Cf. the *Textual Note* to 23:1, where the same word has led LXX into a double rendering.

NOTES

17 1. *Socoh of Judah.* Of the two villages called Socoh that Judah claimed (Josh 15:35, cf. 48) this was the more prominent. Situated in the Shephelah some 14 miles W from Bethlehem toward Philistine territory, it was strategically important to the Israelites and Philistines alike, and between them it was long disputed (cf. in addition to the present passage, II Chron 11:7; 28:18). The modern site is Khirbet ʿAbbad near the village of Khirbet Shuweikeh, which preserves the ancient name.

Azekah. A few miles NW of Socoh lay the fortress of Azekah (Josh 15:35), modern Tell ez-Zakariyeh, which controlled the main road across the Valley of the Terebinth (see below), where the Israelites encamped.

Ephes-dammim. Probably identical to Pas-dammim, the site of the exploits of Eleazar, one of David's heroes (I Chron 11:13; cf. II Sam 23:9 [cf. Driver]). The modern site may be Damun, ca. 4 miles NE of ancient Socoh.

2. *the Valley of the Terebinth.* That is, the Valley of Elah (*'ēlâ*, "terebinth"), now called the Wadi es-Sant, immediately S of and parallel to the Wadi eṣ-Ṣarâr (Valley of Sorek; cf. the NOTE at 6:9) in the series of valleys that cross the Shephelah draining the highlands of Judah onto the Philistine Plain.

4a. *a certain infantryman.* Hebrew *'îš habbênayim*, lit. "the man-in-between, a certain man-in-between" (*bênayim* being a substantive formed from the preposition *bên*, "between"). The expression is unique to this passage in the Old Testament, and the ancient versions were confused by it (Targ. treats it as if *'îš mibbênêhem*, "a man from between them"); but the reading of MT is confirmed by its frequent appearance (in the plural) in the so-called War Scroll at Qumran, where it connotes "infantrymen" or perhaps simply "men involved in battle" (J. Carmignac, "Précisions apportées au vocabulaire de l'Hébreu Biblique par la guerre des fils de lumière contre les fils de ténèbres," *VT* 5

[1955] 356-357; cf. also LXX *anēr dynatos* in the present passage). Roland de Vaux ("Single Combat in the Old Testament," in *The Bible and the Ancient Near East* [Garden City, N.Y.: Doubleday, 1971] 122-135, esp. 124-125) has argued that the expression specifically means "champion," that is, "a man who steps out to fight between the two battle lines" and thus "one who enters into single combat between two armies" or alternatively "one who takes part in a fight between two" and thus "a champion in a single combat"; the Qumran usage, says de Vaux, reflects a weakening of the original force of the expression or even ignorance of its older meaning. There is no reason, however, to doubt the Qumran interpretation; "a man who steps out to fight between the two battle lines" would be an infantryman, but not necessarily a champion; and though the Philistine infantryman in the present story turns out to be a champion, it does not follow that *'îš (hab)bênayim* must mean "champion."

Gath. One of the cities of the Philistine pentapolis; see the NOTE at 5:8.

Goliath. The name *golyat* is not Semitic but "Philistine," perhaps Anatolian; cf. the terminative element *-yat* to Hittite *-wattaš*, Lydian *-uattes* (see W. F. Albright, *CAH* II, c 33, p. 30; cf. Frauke Gröndahl, *Die Personennamen der Texte aus Ugarit* [Rome: Pontifical Biblical Institute, 1967], 297). The name appears only here in the entire account; elsewhere David's adversary is simply called "the Philistine" (also 19:5; but contrast 21:10; 22:10, where "Goliath" may be secondary), and most scholars (contrast Stoebe) now assume that he was anonymous in the original version of the story. The name (along with the detail of the comparison of the shaft of his spear to a weavers' heddle rod; cf. the NOTE at v 7) was imported from II Sam 21:19 (cf. I Chron 20:5), where it is said that Elhanan, one of David's heroes, slew Goliath the Gittite. A. M. Honeyman's harmonizing suggestion that David *was* Elhanan (i.e. that "Elhanan" was his personal name, "David" being a throne name) has also received some support (see "The Evidence for Regnal Names among the Hebrews," *JBL* 67 [1948] 23-24), but this assumption creates more problems than it solves—how could Elhanan/David have come to be thought of as one of his own heroes? Nor is it necessary to assume that this entire story once had Elhanan, not David, as its hero (so, e.g., Grønbaek, *Aufstieg Davids*, 95 and n. 66); certain details of the Elhanan tradition have attached themselves artificially to an unrelated story of a duel of David's own.

4b. This notice about the Philistine's height is the first in a series of parentheses (4b, 5b, 7aβ) intended to call attention to the great size and power of David's opponent and thus to emphasize the miraculous aspect of the shepherd lad's victory.

four cubits and a span. A cubit was the distance from a man's elbow to the tip of his middle finger (ca. eighteen inches), a span from the tip of the thumb to the tip of the little finger of his splayed hand (ca. nine inches). According to tradition, then, the Philistine was some six feet nine inches tall—a true giant in an age when a man well under six feet might be considered tall—and the figure even became exaggerated in some circles to a fantastic nine feet nine inches (see the *Textual Note*).

5-7. The description of the giant's armor serves not only to emphasize further the inequality of the coming contest but to divulge to the alert reader the one vulnerable spot on the giant's body, viz. his forehead. His head, body, and legs are well shielded; only his face is exposed. A sword-wielding warrior cannot threaten him, but a slinger. . . . Incidentally, the giant's armor and weapons as described here are not distinctively "Philistine" or Aegean. Some of the terms were originally non-Semitic (*kôba'*, "helmet," *širyôn*, "cuirass"; see below), but it is not likely that these were "Philistine" in origin, and in any case they had come into full currency in Biblical Hebrew. Certain items, such as the plated armor and the scimitar, are distinctively Oriental; and only the javelin's throwing ring (see below) is without known Asiatic parallel. That David's opponent is no "Mycenaean hoplite" has been shown clearly by K. Galling ("Goliath und seine Rüstung," in VTSup 5 [1966] 150-169), who finds the armor to be a diverse collection of offensive and defensive weapons combined by the narrator from a variety of places and styles to emphasize the formidability of the Philistine champion.

5. *A helmet*. The common word in Biblical Hebrew for helmet, *kôba'*, was probably not Semitic in origin, as the alternate spelling *qôba'* (v 38) shows; cf. perhaps, Hittite *kupaḫis*, "hat, cap?" See E. Sapir, "Hebrew 'Helmet,' a Loanword, and Its Bearing on Indo-European Phonology," *JAOS* 57 (1937) 73-77. The present helmet is not the feathered headdress of the early Philistines but something more substantial; cf. Galling, "Goliath und seine Rüstung," 155, 163.

a plated cuirass. Hebrew *širyôn qaśqaśśîm*. As in the case of *kôba'/qôba'*, "helmet," *širyôn*, *širyān/siryōn*, "cuirass, (body-)armor," is a term of non-Semitic origin (Hurrian?; cf. E. A. Speiser, "On Some Articles of Armor and Their Names," *JAOS* 70 [1950] 47-49), which became common in Biblical Hebrew as a term for body-armor covering the entire torso (like English "cuirass") or, more strictly, for the breastplate alone (also like "cuirass") as in I Kings 22:34 = II Chron 18:33. The particular cuirass in question here is of *plate* or *scale* armor (*qaśqaśśîm;* cf. Deut 14:9,10; Lev 11:9,10,12, where the scales of fish and other marine life are so described), a well-known Egyptian and especially Asiatic (but not Mediterranean-Aegean) style; see Y. Yadin, *The Art of Warfare in Biblical Lands* (New York: McGraw-Hill, 1963) 1. 196-197; 2. 354; Galling, "Goliath und seine Rüstung," 161-162.

five thousand bronze shekels. Cf. the NOTES on shekels at 9:8 and 13:21. The Philistine's cuirass weighed some 125 pounds 15 ounces!

6. *greaves*. Hebrew *miṣḥātayim* (cf. the *Textual Note*). They were probably made of molded bronze encircling the entire calf, like later Greek greaves, and padded inside with leather.

scimitar. Hebrew *kîdôn*, a heavy, curved, flat-bladed, Oriental sword with a cutting edge on the outer (convex) side of the blade. See G. Molin, "What Is a *kidon?*" *JSS* 1 (1956) 334-337; Galling, "Goliath und seine Rüstung," 163-167. Cf. also the first NOTE at v 51 below.

7. *spear*. Hebrew *ḥănît*, the spear proper (cf. 13:19,22; 19:10; etc.) but in this case apparently a kind of javelin; see below.

like a weavers' heddle rod. A detail imported secondarily from II Sam 21:19 = I Chron 20:5. The comparison suggests that the shaft of the spear was equipped with a thong and ring for slinging, that is, it was a type of javelin known to have been used in Greece and Egypt, which resembled the wooden rod and rings used to lift the heddle in weaving. At least this is the explanation of the obscure comparison given by Yadin, "Goliath's Javelin and the *mᵊnôr 'origîm,*" *PEQ* 86 (1955) 58-69.

six hundred iron shekels. More than fifteen pounds! Note that the spearpoint is made of iron (more correctly, of steel), which was the practice from the beginning of the Iron Age, whereas the armor is bronze, which continued to be used when extreme hardness was not required down into Roman times.

9. But as pointed out by Nübel (*Davids Aufstieg,* 24-25), there is nothing in subsequent stories to suggest that the Philistines in fact become Israel's slaves after David slays their champion.

10. *I defy the ranks of Israel.* Compare esp. II Sam 21:21. The verb "defy" (*ḥērēp*) implies not only defiance and provocation but also open contempt (cf. the NOTE at 11:2). As de Vaux says ("Single Combat," 123), "This is only one step short of hurling insults, which happens as soon as the two adversaries confront each other."

33-37a. Saul objects (v 33) not so much on the grounds of David's youth and small stature as of his lack of training and experience (cf. vv 38-39 below). David is "only a lad"; that is, he is here at the front as a servant (as *na'ar,* "lad," must often be translated; cf. English "knave," which originally meant "boy, lad," like German *Knabe,* but came to mean "(boy)servant" [and also, unfortunately, "rogue," so that it cannot be employed to translate *na'ar*]) and not a combatant, whereas the Philistine is a professionally trained and battle-seasoned soldier, "a warrior since his youth." David's reply (vv 34-36) speaks precisely to this issue: his training as a shepherd has given him experience of this kind of situation. Moreover (v 37a) he trusts in Yahweh's special protection.

34-35. The verbs in David's speech are suffixed forms joined to the conjunction, indicating habitual or repeated action in the past (cf. the NOTE on 1:4-7); thus ". . . would come and carry off . . . would chase . . . strike down and snatch . . . would grab . . . knock down and kill. . . ." The single exception is *wyqm,* "(Then if) he attacked . . ."; read *wqm?* Driver further notes that the articles in *hā'ărî,* "*the* lion," and *haddôb,* "*the* bear," are generic —thus, "if some lion or bear would come, etc."

36. *the reproach.* Hebrew *ḥerpâ,* on which see the NOTES at 11:2 and 17:10.

the Living God. Hebrew *'ĕlōhîm ḥayyîm,* always used to stress the reality and effectiveness of the god of Israel (Deut 5:26 and esp. Jer 10:10) and most often, as in the present passage, to censure those who would dare to mock or otherwise revile Yahweh (II Kings 19:4,16 = Isa 37:4,17; Jer 23:36, cf. I Sam 17:26 in § XXIV-B).

38-39. Saul offers his champion the protection of a warrior's uniform and his (Saul's) own sword, but when David is equipped with it all, he finds he cannot walk! This incident gives a lighthearted touch to the narrative, while serving the serious purposes of reemphasizing David's lack of training ("I have never practiced!"; cf. the NOTE to vv 33-37a above) on the one hand and calling attention to his vulnerability (cf. v 45 below) on the other; and both of these things point to his complete dependence upon Yahweh.

40. *his stick.* Hebrew *maqlô,* presumably his shepherd's staff and not a weapon. In the battle the stick serves the purpose of distracting the Philistine from David's real weapon (v 43), but we need not assume David planned it that way. Stoebe, who is anxious that David have both hands free to load his sling, finds contamination in the tradition from II Sam 23:21.

the wadi. The Valley of the Terebinth; see the NOTE at v 2 above.

45-47. *with sword and spear and scimitar . . . with the name of Yahweh. . . .* David draws out the contrast between the weapons: those of the Philistine are the usual implements of warfare; David's own is the "name" of his god, that is, Yahweh's peculiar power as it is specially available to Israel. This is a struggle of the strong against the weak—but the weak fortified by the strength of Yahweh. So the fall of the Philistine, says David, will show the world that inferiority at arms is unimportant to Israel, which relies solely on its god for victory. At this point, then, the central theological assertion of the story is most explicit, and it is easy to understand why the tradition of David's victory over the Philistine had a special appeal to the little nation that struggled through most of its existence in conflict with vastly more powerful neighbors. See further the COMMENT.

45. *Yahweh Sabaoth, god of the ranks of Israel.* Cf. the NOTE at 1:3. The expression *'ĕlōhê ma'arkôt yiśrā'ēl,* "god of the ranks of Israel," reads like a kind of word-by-word paraphrase of *yahweh ṣĕbā'ôt,* understood as "Yahweh of the armies (of Israel)." But cf. W. Eichrodt, *Theology of the Old Testament,* tr. J. A. Baker (Philadelphia: Westminster, 1961) 1.192-193.

47. *all those assembled here.* Hebrew *kol haqqāhāl hazzeh,* lit. "all this assembly." Although *qāhāl* can refer specifically to a religious convocation (Neh 5:13; etc.), it quite commonly describes a gathering of men at arms (Num 22:4; Ezek 16:40; 38:15; etc.), and it is difficult to accept its occurrence as decisive evidence in favor of Hertzberg's argument for an original cultic setting for this story (cf. also Hertzberg, "Mizpa," *ZAW* 47 [1929] 161-196); but see the COMMENT.

51. *his sword.* Hebrew *ḥarbô;* but we were not told in vv 5-7 that the Philistine had a *ḥereb,* and we know that David had none of his own. Presumably then the reference is to the *kîdôn,* "scimitar," a specific term of which *ḥereb,* "sword," is the generic.

and dispatched him. Hebrew *waymōtĕtēhû,* on which see the NOTE at 14:13.

52. *the Shaaraim road.* The city of Shaaraim is also mentioned in the list of the cities of Judah in Josh 15:36 immediately after Socoh and Azekah. The exact site is unknown but it must have been to the W in the direction of the Philistine cities Gath and Ekron, on which see the NOTES at 5:8 and 5:10.

54. *Jerusalem.* A striking anachronism: Jerusalem was not in Israelite hands until the beginning of David's reign (cf. II Sam 5:6-9). Perhaps there was a tradition in Jerusalem that Goliath's head was preserved there as a kind of "relic" (cf. Hertzberg). See also the following NOTE.

his weapons he put in his own tent. But the sword, at least, shows up at Nob in the temple in 21:10. Accordingly some scholars prefer to read *b'hl yhwh,* "in the tent(-shrine) of Yahweh," here in place of *b'hlw*, "in his own tent" (cf. Galling, "Goliath und seine Rüstung," 151, n. 5). In view of the Nob connection and the impropriety of the reference to Jerusalem we may ask with several scholars (e.g. de Boer, "1 Samuel xvii") if Jerusalem has displaced Nob here. See further the COMMENT.

COMMENT

Of all David's exploits the one that is best known is the first. The story of the shepherd lad who by courage, cunning, and faith overcomes the gigantic champion of the enemy and brings victory to his people has all the elemental appeal of a fairy tale. The plot is uncomplicated and forceful, the characters almost archetypal. None of the subtleties of the account of the battle of Michmash Pass or the later stories of David and Saul are found here. The Philistine is perfectly terrifying in his sheer, malevolent power and perfectly hateful in his bold defiance of Israel. Saul is quite simply appalled: he and his army are disarmed by fear and completely helpless. David is able; or rather he is *uniquely* able, since the rest of Israel is powerless. There is nothing deficient, however slightly so, about David's courage; there is nothing tentative about his resolution. He acts without hesitation and fells the Philistine with cleverness and consummate skill. Only to Yahweh does he appeal for assistance, and here again his conduct is impeccable: his confidence in the power of his god is absolute.

The very simplicity that gives the story of David and the Philistine its lasting appeal—the idealizations and absolutes of which it is composed—also calls into question its originality as a part of the oldest narrative of the rise of David. The subtlety and realism of other episodes are missing here. In some respects, moreover, the episode fits most uncomfortably at this point. Certain details seem to be, in the words of Wellhausen, "in contradiction both with what goes before and with what follows it. According to xvi. 14-23, David, when he first came in contact with Saul, was no raw lad, ignorant of the arts of war, but 'a mighty valiant man, skilful in speech, and of a goodly presence'; and according to xviii. 6 the women sang at the victorious return of the army, 'Saul has slain his thousands of the Philistines, and David his tens of thousands,' so that the latter was the leader of Israel beside the king, and a proved and well-known man. Evidently something of a different nature must originally have stood between xvi. 23 and xviii. 6."[1] But surely, one might reply, the story of David and the Philistine has a clear and important function in the devel-

[1] *Prolegomena*, 263-264

opment of the larger narrative, for it demonstrates at the outset David's superiority to Saul as a war leader and "savior" of Israel. This is true enough; but the evidence cited by Wellhausen suggests that originally this point was made in a different way, a way equally clear but somewhat less melodramatic. David the warrior (16:18) entered the battle camp in the Valley of the Terebinth as Saul's weapon-bearer (16:21) and, to the amazement of everyone, acquitted himself so manfully in the ensuing battle as to surpass the king himself in heroism, so that although Saul slew thousands, David slew tens of thousands and won the hearts of the people (18:7). So as J. H. Grønbaek and others have argued,[2] we are entitled to think of one story overlying another here; that is, an older account of an Israelite victory led by Saul and especially David has been largely displaced by a sensational account of David's single combat with a Philistine champion.

Why then was the older narrative so revised? Surely it made the point of David's superiority to Saul well enough already. A part of the answer must be that the legend of David and the Philistine had simply become so well known that it found its way inevitably into the text. We know that according to one circle of tradition David came to the front not as a trained warrior but as a shepherd lad visiting his brothers in arms and that such a version of the story was interpolated into the present narrative at a very late date (see § XXIV-B). We also know that the prophetic story of David's anointing by Samuel stressed David's youth and his shepherd's duties (see 15:35-16:13). Clearly the picture of the young David that held sway in the popular imagination was that of a shepherd boy standing bravely among warriors. The oldest material we have already presents him as a young shepherd (cf. 16:19), and it seems to have been this element that became the focus of the popular stories that grew up around his memory. Of these the favorite must have been that of his victory over a Philistine champion in single combat, so that inevitably, as we have just said, it made its way into the larger narrative.

The story of the contest with the Philistine must have been nurtured for a long time in Jerusalem, the City of David.[3] It displays the kind of idealization of the founder of the southern dynasty that one would expect in the capital of Judah, and it shares the basic outlook of several other passages, also introduced secondarily into the old narrative about the rise of David,

[2] In particular, Grønbaek (*Aufstieg Davids*, 90-92) speaks of a "combination of the tradition of a battle with the Philistines in northwestern Judah, in which Saul decisively puts the enemy to flight, with the narrative of David and Goliath"; these elements, he says, have been closely woven together in such a way as to put Saul into David's shadow. It should be stressed, however, that in *both* traditions Saul is put in David's shadow. See below.

[3] This is suggested by, among other things, v 54. But there is also some evidence to suggest that the tradition belonged originally to Nob. See the NOTES at v 54.

which seem to be of Jerusalemite and probably Josianic origin (20:11-17,23,40-42; 23:14-18,19-24a; 24:2-23; 25:28-31; see pp. 16-17 in the Introduction). In its present form, moreover, it has a highly symbolic form. Here is David, the type of the Israelite king, doing battle with an enemy who is the very embodiment of threatening, destructive power. Some scholars even assume a cultic background for the account: here, they say, is the ritual battle of the king and the chaos monster, the forces of order and destruction.[4] But the reference to the assembly (*haqqāhāl*) in v 47, to which these scholars appeal, need not be taken cultically (see the NOTE), and the universalizing reference to "all the earth," which they cite as evidence of a ritual setting, is better understood in another way, as explained below. Nevertheless Grønbaek, Hertzberg, and the others are surely correct in one respect. Many of the symbolic elements that gave such ritual battle accounts their appeal all over the ancient Near East are also present here, as we have seen, and this fact must account at least in part for the popularity of the present story, whether or not it was ever associated directly with any cultic practice.

Another symbolic aspect of our story deserves mention insofar as it points directly to the central theological assertion of the account (see the NOTE at vv 45-57). Here is David, small, apparently defenseless, with none of the bearing or equipment of a trained soldier—the perfect personification of the tiny nation of Judah. And against him stands the gigantic enemy, heavily armed and evidently irresistible, as the enemies of Judah so often seemed. David has no real hope in force of arms, and despite his courage and wit he finally must rely on the one good hope that Judah, too, had in times of danger. "You come against me with sword and spear and scimitar," he cries to the Philistine, "but I come against you with the name of Yahweh Sabaoth, god of the ranks of Israel!" (v 45). He means to win the contest so that "all the earth will know that there is a god in Israel" (v 46). The theological implications are clear: it is Yahweh who gives victory, and he may give it to the weak (Israel) in order that his power might be known to all. This is a theme that runs throughout the Bible, finding its most vehement spokesman in Ezekiel[5] during the Exile when interest in the question of Yahweh's honor among the nations was most acute. It underlies the entire story of David and the Philistine in its present form and

[4] Grønbaek, *Aufstieg Davids,* 94-95, where Goliath is described as the "Verkörperung und Historifikation der Chaosmacht"; also "Kongens kultiske function i det forexilske Israel," *DTT* 20 (1957) 1-16, where the notion is entertained that all this was dramatically represented in the Jerusalem temple as part of a New Year's festival. Hertzberg's idea of a cultic background is rather different: see the article cited in the NOTE at v 47.

[5] On Ezekiel's formula, "Then you/they will know that I am Yahweh," and its theological significance, see W. Zimmerli, *Erkenntnis Gottes nach dem Buche Ezechiel* (Zurich, 1954) 65*ff*.

rises to the surface in the taunt speeches, where it is given full articulation in the mouth of David.

So the growth of the story of David and Goliath, as we have described it here and in the NOTES, involved several stages: (1) the foundation was an old story of an Israelite victory over the Philistines near Socoh, which Saul led but in which David played a prominent role, overshadowing the king; this story was incorporated into the larger story of David's rise to power by its compiler; (2) it was subsequently displaced in large part by the popular legend of young David's victory over a Philistine champion, which came into the text in a highly idealized and symbolic form; (3) certain details—the name of the Philistine, the distinctive metaphor about the shaft of his spear (v 7)—were "attracted" to the story from a similar legend about Elhanan, one of David's heroes (see the NOTES at vv 4 and 6); and (4) a complete, alternative account of David's arrival and victory over Goliath was interpolated somewhat heavy-handedly into some manuscripts of the completed story after the distinctive textual traditions had already begun to develop. This last stage, which we have not yet considered in detail, is the subject of the section that follows.

XXIV-B. DAVID AND THE PHILISTINE CHAMPION: A SECOND ACCOUNT (17:12-31, 41, 48b, 50, 55-58; 18:1-5, 10-11, 17-19, 29b-30)

17 12 Now David was the son of an Ephrathite named Jesse from
Bethlehem of Judah, who had eight sons. In the days of Saul the man
was old, advanced in years. 13 [His] three oldest sons had gone after
Saul to war. (Now the names of his sons who had gone to war were
Eliab, the firstborn, Abinadab, the second, and Shammah, the third.)
14 David was the youngest, *and though the three oldest had gone after*
Saul, 15 *David went back and forth from Saul's side to shepherd his*
father's flock in Bethlehem.

16 Once, *when the Philistine had drawn near morning and evening*
to take his stand for forty days, 17 Jesse said to David, "Take your
brothers this ephah of parched grain and these ten loaves of bread!
Run it over to the camp and give it to your brothers! 18 These ten cuts
of cheese you must take to the commander-of-a-thousand. As for your
brothers, check to see that they are well and receive their token.
19 Saul and they and all the men of Israel are in the Valley of the
Terebinth fighting with the Philistines."

20 So David rose early the next morning and, having left his flock
with a keeper, picked up [the food] and set out as Jesse had instructed him. When he reached the encampment, the army was just
marching out to the battle lines, giving the shout for war. 21 Israel and
the Philistines moved into position, battle line facing battle line!

22 David left the gear he had with him in the care of a keeper and
ran toward the battle line. When he arrived he inquired after the welfare of his brothers, 23 and while he was speaking with them, the infantryman was making his way up (Goliath, the Philistine, was his
name, from Gath) from the ranks of the Philistines. *So when he*
spoke the usual words, David heard him.

24 All the men of Israel, when they saw the man, fled from him and
were very frightened. 25 "Men of Israel!" someone had said, "Do you

see this man who comes up, that it is to defy Israel that he comes?
Well, the man who strikes him down the king will reward with great
wealth! He will give him his own daughter and will make his father's
house free in Israel!"

26 But David had been speaking to the men who were standing with
him. So he said, "What will be done for the man who strikes down
that Philistine and takes [this] reproach away from Israel? For who is
this uncircumcised Philistine that he should defy the ranks of the Living God?"

27 Then the soldiers told him what had been said. "Thus and so will
it be done for the man who strikes down [the Philistine]," they said.

28 When Eliab, his older brother, heard him speaking with the men,
[he] became angry with David. "Why have you come down?" he
said. "With whom did you leave those few sheep in the wilderness? *I*
know your impudence and your naughty scheme: it is to watch the
fighting that you have come down!"

29 "So what have I done now?" said David. "It was only talk, was it
not?" 30 And he turned away from him to someone else and spoke as
before, and they gave him an answer like the previous one. 31 *The
things David said were overheard and reported to Saul, who sent for
him. . . .*

41 Then as the Philistine, with the man who carried his shield in
front of him, drew closer and closer to David, 48b David ran quickly
to the battle line to meet [him]! 50 Taking hold of sling and stone he
struck down the Philistine and killed him—though there was no
sword in David's hand!

55 When Saul saw David going out to meet the Philistine, he had
said to Abiner, the commander of the army, "Whose son is that lad?"

"By your life, O king!" said Abiner, "I do not know!"

56 "Then inquire whose son the youth is," said the king.

57 So when David returned from striking down the Philistine,
Abiner took him and brought him before Saul with the Philistine's
head still in his hand.

58 "Whose son are you, lad?" Saul asked him.

"The son of your servant Jesse the Bethlehemite," said David.

18 1 By the time [David] finished speaking with Saul, Jonathan
found himself bound up with David. Jonathan loved him like himself!

2 Saul took [David] at that time and would not let him return to his
father's house, 3 and Jonathan and David made a covenant, because

[Jonathan] loved him like himself. 4 Jonathan took off the robe he had on and gave it to David along with his uniform, his sword, his bow, and his belt. 5 Then Saul put [David] in charge of the men of war, and he marched out and came in, succeeding in whatever Saul would send him to do. It was pleasing to all the army and also to the servants of Saul.

10 *The next day an evil spirit of God rushed upon Saul, and he prophesied in his house. Now David was playing music as at other times, and there was a spear in Saul's hand;* 11 *and Saul brandished the spear, thinking, "I shall pin David to the wall!" But David evaded him twice.*

17 Then Saul said to David, "Here is my older daughter, Merob: I shall give her to you as a wife if only you will become one of my stalwart men and fight the wars of Yahweh!" (*For Saul had said to himself, "My hand must not be upon him. Let the hand of the Philistines be upon him!"*)

18 "Who am I?" said David to Saul. "And who are my kinsmen in Israel that I should become the king's son-in-law?" 19 So when it was time to give Merob, Saul's daughter, to David, she was given to Adriel the Meholathite as a wife.

29b *So Saul became David's constant enemy;* 30 *but* when the Philistine commanders marched out, as often as they marched out David was successful—more than any other of Saul's servants—and his name was held in great esteem.

TEXTUAL NOTES

17 12. *Now David was the son of an Ephrathite* We read *wdwd bn 'yš 'prty*. LXX^{A} reflects *wy'mr dwd*, etc.: "And David, the son of an Ephrathite, said . . ."; omit *wy'mr* with MT. More troublesome is the fact that MT adds *hzh* after *'prty* (cf. LXX^{A}), as if to connect the inserted material with the foregoing: "Now David . . . *this very one* . . ." (cf. Vulg.); but the word is unacceptable on grammatical grounds (Driver) and is omitted here, though the omission is without clear support from the ancient witnesses (cf. Syr.)

old, advanced in years MT (cf. LXX^{A}) has *zqn b' b'nšym*, an impossible combination that invites two reconstructions: (1) *zqn b' bšnym*, as reflected in our translation (so LXX^{L}, Syr.); and (2) *zqn b'nšym*, "old among men." Though certain objections can be raised against either (cf. Wellhausen, Driver), the former seems preferable.

13. *had gone* Expressed twice in all the principal witnesses, first at the beginning of the verse (*wylkw*) and second in the sequence *hgdlym hlkw 'ḥry š'wl*. The second verb is suspicious not only because it is superfluous but also because *hlkw* appears again immediately below, and the entire sequence *hgdlym hlkw 'ḥry š'wl* recurs in v 14 below (Driver); we omit *hlkw*, though without clear textual support.

Now the names So MT, LXX^A^. LXX^L^: "Now *these were* the names . . ." (cf. Exod 1:1).

his sons So LXX^A^. MT, LXX^L^: "his *three* sons."

the firstborn So MT. LXX^AL^: "*his* firstborn."

the second So LXX^L^. MT, LXX^A^: "*his* second."

the third So MT, LXX^L^. LXX^A^: "*his* third."

16. *to take his stand* LXX^L^, OL, Syr. add "before Israel." Omit with MT, LXX^A^.

17. *to David* So LXX^A^. MT: "to David, *his son.*"

this ephah of parched grain So MT: *'ypt hqly' hzh*. LXX^A^ has lost "of parched grain" in consequence of an inner-Greek haplography (*oiphei tou alphitou toutou*).

these ten loaves of bread We read *w'śrh hlḥm hzh*. The *h-* of *hlḥm* has fallen out of MT after the preceding *-h*.

and give it Reading *wtnh* on the basis of LXX *kai dos* = *wtnh*, which has fallen out of MT after *hmḥnh*.

18. *and receive their token* MT *w't 'rbtm tqḥ*. Cf. LXX^L^ *kai to ersouba autōn lēmpsē*, "and receive their *ersouba*," the transcription reflecting bewilderment over the rare noun *'ărūbâ*, "token, pledge" (Prov 17:18). The same difficulty led other versions into error. OL *et cum quibus ordinati sunt*, "and with whom they are arrayed," suggests *w't 'rktm;* and LXX^A^ *kai hosa an chrēzōsin*, "and whatsoever they require," points yet another step away to *w't ṣrktm* (Cappellus *apud* Smith).

19. *Saul and they* MT (cf. LXX^L^) *wš'wl whmh*, etc. LXX^A^ (cf. Syr.) seems to reflect *wš'wl hw'* . . . , "Now as for Saul, he and all the men of Israel, etc.," in which case the verse would not be a part of Jesse's speech but a narrator's parenthesis.

20. *was just marching out* Reading *yṣ'* (*yōṣē'*) for MT *hyṣ'*. See Driver.

22. *a keeper* So LXX^A^. MT (cf LXX^L^) has *šwmr hklym*, "a *gear*-keeper."

23. *from the ranks* So MT *qĕrê*, LXX: *mm'rkwt*. MT *kĕtîb: mm'rwt*, "from the *caves* (!)"

30. *and they gave him* So LXX^L^. MT, LXX^A^: "and *the people* gave him."

50. *Taking hold of sling and stone* Reading *wyḥzq bql' wb'bn* on the basis of the shorter text of LXX^L^. MT, LXX^A^ have *wyḥzq dwd mn hplšty bql' wb'bn*, "So David proved stronger than the Philistine with sling and stone," an expansion designed to blend the statement into its secondary context as a kind of a summary. After "stone" LXX^L^ adds an expansion of its own, viz. "on that day," which may be omitted with MT, LXX^A^.

55. *Whose son is that lad?* Reading *bn my hn'r hzh* on the basis of LXX. MT: *bn my zh hn'r 'bnr*, "Whose son is the lad, Abiner?"

56. *the youth* So Mt. LXX: "*this* youth."

18 1. LXX^L is somewhat at variance and fuller throughout.

5a. So LXX^L. MT (cf. LXX^A) inverts the order and reads the first clause ambiguously: "And David marched out . . . ? . . . in whatever Saul would send him to do he succeeded, and Saul put him in charge of the men of war."

11. *brandished* MT *qĕrê* (cf. Syr.) has *wayyāṭel,* "hurled"; but read *way-yiṭṭōl,* "took up, brandished," on the basis of LXX *kai hēren* (cf. Targ.).

17. *Merob* See the *Textual Note* to 14:49.

18. *my kinsmen* The rare word *ḥayyî* was glossed by *mšpḥt 'by,* "my father's clan," and eventually misvocalized as *ḥayyay,* "my life," in MT (LXX^A understands it as *ḥayyê,* "the life of"), which now reads "my life, my father's clan" (cf. LXX^A). The *Vorlage* of LXX^L seems to have lost *ḥyy* altogether, but we cannot doubt its originality.

19. *to David* LXX^L adds "as a wife"; omit with MT, LXX^A.

she was given So MT, LXX^A: *why' ntnh,* expanded in LXX^L to read *why' yr'h 't dwd wntnh* (*kai autē ephobēthē ton daueid kai edothē*), "she *was afraid of David and* was given. . . ."

NOTES

17 12-15. The beginning of this account, which originally existed as an independent narrative (see the COMMENT), has been modified slightly to accommodate it to its new context. It is clear that it once began with an introduction of Jesse, not David, in a fashion similar to that of the stories in which we first met Samuel (1:1*ff*) and Saul (9:1*ff*), where the fathers, Elkanah and Kish, were first introduced before their more famous sons were mentioned; but now its opening sentences stand as parenthetical material within the main narrative and begin with a reference to David as someone already known to the audience. Note especially the redactional character of vv 14b-15: this is designed to harmonize the two stories, in one of which David is already in the service of Saul while in the other he is still at home with Jesse.

12. *an Ephrathite.* Hebrew (*'îš*) *'ĕprātî.* Though elsewhere in the Bible (e.g. 1:1 above) *'ĕprātî* is used as a gentilic of Ephraim (perhaps referring primarily to a tribal subdivision called Ephrathah in the vicinity of Kiriath-jearim; see the NOTE at 10:2), here it is the gentilic of the Judahite Ephrathah, evidently a tribal subdivision of the Calebites (cf. I Chron 2:19,24,50; 4:4) inhabiting the region around Bethlehem, with which it is closely associated (Ruth 4:11; Micah 5:1(English 5:2); I Chron 4:4). See E. F. Campbell, *Ruth,* AB 7, NOTE on 1:2.

eight sons. On the problem of the number of Jesse's sons, see the NOTE at 16:10. The present notice, since it belongs to materials that came into the text late, may have been adjusted to the redactor's understanding of 16:10 and cannot be considered independent evidence.

17. *this ephah of parched grain.* On the ephah, about half a bushel, see the NOTE at 1:24. For parched grain, see the NOTE at 25:18.

18. *cuts of cheese.* Hebrew *ḥărīṣê heḥālāb,* lit. "slices of milk."

19. Another reference to the primary narrative (17:1-2).

23. *the infantryman.* Hebrew *'îš habbênayim* (see the NOTE at 17:4). Clearly the redactor who inserted this material into the primary narrative wanted us to understand the definite article as rendered here ("*the* infantryman, *the aforementioned* infantryman"); but when this account stood alone, the Philistine champion was first introduced at this point, and the force of the article was meant to be "*a certain* infantryman," exactly as in 17:4. This is assured by the parenthetical notice about his name and hometown, which was appropriate enough as part of the independent account but is superfluous here.

So when he spoke the usual words. A redactional condensation. In the independent form of this account the Philistine's challenge must have been reported here in full.

25. *He will give him his own daughter.* See 18:17-19 below.

free. Hebrew *ḥopšî* is an adjective meaning "free," most often used in reference to persons emancipated from slavery (Exod 21:2; etc.) but applicable to other situations as well. In the present passage it seems to imply exemption from taxes and other obligations to the palace. A number of scholars have sought to connect the term to the Akkadian (especially Amarna, Nuzi, Alalakh) noun *ḫupšu* and the Ugaritic noun *ḫpṯ/ḫbṯ*. Both of the latter designate a particular social class in the lower part of the economic order, and this is contrary to Israelite usage, where there is no evidence of a distinct *ḥopšî* class (cf. de Vaux, *Ancient Israel* 1.88). Nevertheless a connection has often been argued: see especially I. Mendelsohn, "The Canaanite Term for 'Free Proletarian,'" *BASOR* 83 (1941) 36-39; J. Gray, "Feudalism in Ugarit and Early Israel," *ZAW* 54 (1952) 49-55, esp. 54-55; and cf. recently N. P. Lemche, "*ḥpšy* in 1 Sam. xvii 25," *VT* 24 (1974) 373-374, and O. Loretz, "Ugaritisch-Hebräisch *ḪB/PṮ, BT ḪPṮT-ḤPŠJ, BJT HḪPŠJ/WT,*" *UF* 8 (1976) 129-131. A more instructive semantic parallel to Hebrew *ḥopšî* has been drawn by A. F. Rainey (in Fisher, *Ras Shamra Parallels* 2.104), who compares the Akkadian adjective *zaki,* which in the Akkadian texts from Ras Shamra can be used to describe an emancipated slave (RS 16.250:21-22) or a soldier who, because of a brave deed at arms, has been granted freedom by the king from service to the palace (RS 16.269:14-16). The latter, as Rainey observes, affords a striking parallel to the offer made here by Saul.

26. The language is almost identical to that used in the main narrative, the influence of which may be felt at this point. See 17:36 and the NOTES there.

28. Eliab, Jesse's oldest son (16:6), scolds his little brother, accusing him of sneaking into camp with a boy's curiosity about war. This is the only hint we get that tradition told of a strain in David's relationship with his brothers similar to that in the story of Joseph.

31. This verse seems to be entirely redactional, penned by an editor who interpolated the alternative account of David's arrival at court into the primary narrative. It serves to smooth the transition from the inserted material in vv 12-30 back to the report of Saul's conversation with David in vv 32*ff*. But in fact no such conversation took place in the alternative account in its independent form: David is introduced to Saul for the first time *after* his battle with the Philistine (vv 57*ff* below).

41,48b,50. In this alternative account the duel between David and the Philistine is described in the barest essentials. Contrast the detailed version in the primary narrative: vv 40,42-48a,49,51a.

55. *Abiner*. See 14:50 and the NOTE there.

18 1. *Jonathan found himself bound up with*. Hebrew *nepeš yĕhônātān niqšĕrâ bĕnepeš dāwīd*, lit. "Jonathan's life was bound up with David's life." Cf. Gen 44:30-31, where Judah says to Joseph, "Now then, when I come to your servant my father, and the boy [i.e. Benjamin] is not with us, then, since [my father's] life is bound up with [the boy's] life, when he sees that the boy is not there, he will die. . . ." In this and the present case, then, the expression refers to inseparable devotion. Jonathan, in other words, is so taken with David that he becomes vitally devoted to him in affection and loyalty. The political overtones identified by J. A. Thompson and others in the use of the verb "love" in the stories about David and Jonathan (see below and the NOTES at 16:21 and 18:16) have emboldened Peter Ackroyd ("The Verb Love") to speculate on the use of *niqšar*, "be bound," here as involving a similar kind of double meaning in light of *qāšar*, "conspire," used by Saul in 22:8,13.

Jonathan loved him like himself. As explained in the NOTE at 20:17, where the same thing is said in the primary narrative, this statement hints of political loyalty just as it describes personal affection.

3-4. Jonathan and David enter into a *bĕrît*, "covenant," that is, a solemn pact. But if there is more meant here than a deep bond of friendship—and the political nuance of the statement that Jonathan "loved [David] like himself" suggests that there is (see above)—then what is the significance of the covenant? The details about the gift of Jonathan's clothes, which seems to be a kind of "sign" or formal gesture that seals the pact, may provide a clue. "The deep and beautiful symbolism of [the gift of the clothes] seems to have been overlooked so far," writes T. N. D. Mettinger (*King and Messiah*, 39). "It seems to me that the motif here has royal overtones. . . . Seen in light of the fact that the word *mĕʿîl* can denote a royal robe, Jonathan's robe is part of his princely apparel. When he hands it over to David he at the same time gives up and transfers his particular position as heir apparent. There is thus a legal symbolism in the act." (Actually Mettinger was anticipated in this line of thought by J. Morgenstern ["David and Jonathan," 322] and others). In other words, if Mettinger is correct, Jonathan is shown here to transfer his privilege of succession willingly to David out of his admiration and affection for him and the loyalty he spontaneously feels toward him.

5. The conspicuous position of military leadership from which David wins the loyalty of the people comes about in quite a different way in the primary narrative (see 18:12a and the COMMENT on 18:6-8a,9,12a,13-16).

It was pleasing to. . . . Lit. "It was good in the eyes of . . ."—another expression with political overtones (cf. II Sam 3:19; etc.). David's leadership has the approbation and political consent of both the general populace and the ranking members of Saul's court (his "servants"; cf. the NOTE at 8:14).

10-11. This duplicate of the incident in 19:9-10 seems out of place at this point. The offer of Merob to David that follows belongs to the aftermath of the battle with Goliath (see the NOTE at 17-19 below), and if we are correct in regarding 17b as redactional, no unpleasantness between David and Saul should have intervened. The introduction of this incident into the alternative account of David's arrival at court, then, would seem to belong to its redactional "correction" toward the primary narrative (see the COMMENT), in which the offer of Michal follows the beginning of David's estrangement from Saul.

17-19. In the primary account it is Michal, Saul's younger daughter, who is offered to David (cf. 14:49; 18:20*ff*), and there the offer is made to entrap David (cf. 18:21a,25b). In the present case, however, Merob is offered in consequence of Saul's promise quoted in v 25 above. So we must suspect v 17b of being redactional, part of the process of "correcting" the alternative account to the pattern of the primary account (see the COMMENT).

17. *one of my stalwart men.* That is, one of my loyal supporters. See the NOTE at 10:26,27.

and fight the wars of Yahweh. Cf. 25:28 and the NOTE there.

18-19. David seems to decline the offer, and Saul gives Merob to another man.

19. *Adriel the Meholathite.* The town of Abel-meholah was E of the Jordan (modern Tell el-Maqlûb, a few miles E of Tell Abū Kharaz, ancient Jabesh-gilead, on the Wadi Yâbıs), and we have already noted Saul's strong ties with Gilead (cf. the COMMENT on 10:27b-11:15). According to II Sam 21:8-9 Adriel, there called "the son of Barzillai," and Merob (so LXX^{L}, MT^{MSS}, cf. Syr.; MT, LXX^{B} have "Michal"; cf. Glück, "Merab or Michal") had five children, who were executed by the Gibeonites.

29b. This half-verse shows the influence of the primary narrative and of vv 28-29a in particular. It is redactional, smoothing the transition back to the alternative account, in which the alienation of Saul and David seems to have come later. See the COMMENT.

COMMENT

The material collected here, though it appears in the received Hebrew text (MT) and in those Greek MSS that regularly show correction toward MT (especially LXX^{AL}), is missing entirely from the Codex Vaticanus (LXX^{B}), the most direct witness to the Old Greek in I Samuel. It seems clear, then, that it was not in the Old Greek. It is easiest to conclude, moreover, that it was also absent from the Hebrew tradition behind LXX and indeed from the primitive text of Samuel itself, having been introduced into the tradition behind MT at some point after its divergence from the ancestral tradition of LXX in the fourth century B.C. (see TEXT AND VERSIONS in the Introduction).

Many critics, however, have followed Wellhausen in supposing that the evidence of LXX reflects a subsequent *shortening* of an original longer text intended to give the story balance and economy. That is, because the primitive text at this point was composite and self-contradictory, the shortening was undertaken for harmonistic purposes. Apart from the general lack of satisfactory parallels to such a phenomenon, this hypothesis founders on a number of specific obstacles (for what follows, see esp. Caird [p. 857], Stoebe). There is no thematic unity in the received text of 17:1-18:30 (or even in 17:1-18:5), and a number of duplications exist especially in the two accounts of David's introduction to Saul in 16:14-23 —presupposed in 17:1*ff*—and 17:57*ff*). Though it is true that similar observations might be made about many a biblical passage of unquestioned *textual* integrity, still it is quite difficult to understand why an editor who was removing contradictions so boldly would not remove them all, and the shorter text of 17:1-18:30 is far from harmonious with the materials that precede and follow it (see the COMMENT on § XXIV-A). Nor on the other hand is everything that is supposed to have been removed inharmonious with what remains: why, for example, would the report of Jonathan's covenant with David in 18:1-4 have been deleted? Most damaging to the "shortening" hypothesis, however, is the fact that the materials missing from LXX^B, when collected by themselves as they are here, can be seen to form a more or less complete narrative of their own. This strongly suggests that they represent the bulk of a full alternative account of David's arrival and early days at court that was interpolated *in toto* into the primary narrative at some time subsequent to the divergence of the ancestral textual traditions that lie behind MT and LXX. This alternative account, then, was absent in the primitive version of I Samuel and is, at least from the perspective of the textual critic, properly *excursus* material.

The events of David's early days at court as portrayed in this alternative account may be summarized as follows. (1) David was a shepherd boy from Bethlehem whose older brothers were soldiers in Saul's army fighting against the Philistines. (2) The lad came to the front to visit his brothers and was indignant to hear the insulting challenge of a Philistine champion before whom the Israelite soldiers cowered. At this point David and Saul were entirely unacquainted (in contradiction of the report of their previous meeting in the primary narrative [16:21*ff*]). (3) David, though not a trained soldier (16:18 notwithstanding), undertook the duel himself and managed to slay the Philistine with his sling. (4) Saul, who had seen David going out to fight without knowing who he was, had the boy hero brought to him. When David had been presented, he was given a position in the army as a reward (contrast 18:12a). (5) As David talked with Saul, his son Jonathan became devoted to him and afterwards made a solemn pact with him. (6) In keeping with his promise to do so (see 17:25), Saul offered his older daughter, Merob, to David as a wife, but David refused her on the grounds of the humbleness of his station in life. (7) In the end David became a successful war leader in Saul's services. At this point the alternative account becomes silent, but we might suppose that it went on, in material that was not inserted into our text and so has not survived, to tell its own version of many of the tales that follow.

The interpolation of the alternative account seems to have involved a minimum of redactional harmonization. No doubt some materials—we cannot be certain how much—were omitted as superfluous because they duplicated existing materials in the primary narrative. Other parts of the story, such as the report of the Philistine's challenge in v 23, were probably reduced to summary form for the same reason. A small number of harmonistic expansions were evidently found necessary as well (these are printed in our translation in italics and discussed in the NOTES), such as that in v 15 where David, who in the alternative account is home with Jesse at this point but in the primary narrative is with Saul, is said to be shuttling back and forth between Bethlehem and the Philistine front. There seems also to have been some attempt, and here we are on less certain ground, to revise the alternative account toward the pattern of the primary narrative (the material so affected is also italicized here and discussed in the NOTES). In particular, since the alienation of David and Saul did not take place so quickly in the alternative account—David's position of military command is given him not as an excuse for removing him from the palace, as in 18:12a, but as a reward for his heroism, and Saul's daughter is offered not to entrap David, as in 18:20*ff*, but, as we have said, in keeping with the pledge made in 17:25—some attempt has been made to introduce the motif of Saul's jealousy earlier (see the NOTES at 18:10-11 and 17-19). But in general the outline and details of the alternative account in its original, independent form remain visible.

Although this account did not find its way into the text of the primary narrative until at least the fourth century B.C. (see above), it does not follow that its date of composition was late. It may have circulated for some time independently before its appropriation by a redactor to fill its present position.[1] But there is little in it from which we might guess its antiquity. The view of David as a shepherd boy—itself very ancient (cf. Ps 78:70-71)—is closer to that of the popular legend about David's battle with the Philistine champion than to that of the older narrative which the legend now overlies (see the COMMENT on § XXIV-A), and it may have been attracted to its present position as one consequence of the superimposition of the one upon the other. That is, once the tale of David's victory over the Philistine was introduced into the older narrative about

[1] So Nübel (*Davids Aufstieg*, 22) is at least potentially correct in regarding the passages omitted from LXX as the more reliable version of the Goliath story.

David's rise to power by the Josianic historian (see the COMMENT on § XXIV-A), it began to attract more material from the same circle of tradition. Thus this alternative account of David's early days at court may have belonged to the idealized David traditions that had long circulated in Jerusalem[2] and, assuming that they continued to be cherished in royalist circles in the Exile, survived into the postexilic period.

[2] That is, those traditions now reflected in the secondary additions to the old narrative of David's rise (20:11-17,23,40-42; 23:14-18,19-24a; 24:2-23; 25:28-31), as well as the story of David and the Philistine champion that overlies the narrative in cc 17-18. Note again that the prophetic tradition also, though very different in theological outlook, shares the picture of David as a shepherd boy (cf. 16:1-13), suggesting that this view was also held in the northern kingdom.

XXV. SAUL'S JEALOUSY OF DAVID
(18:6-8a, 9, 12a, 13-16)

18 6 Dancing women came out from all the cities of Israel to meet David with tambourines and celebration and lutes.

> 7 Saul has slain his thousands,
> And David his ten thousands!

sang the women.

8a It was vexing to Saul, who thought, "They credit David with ten thousands, but me they credit only with thousands!" 9 Saul eyed David from that day on: 12a [he] began to fear [him] 13 and sent him away, appointing him a commander-of-a-thousand, so that he went out and came in before the army.

14 David was successful in all his undertakings, for Yahweh was with him; 15 and although Saul, seeing how successful he was, lived in fear of him, 16 all Israel and Judah loved [him], since it was he who went out and came in before them.

TEXTUAL NOTES

17:55 - 18:5. These verses represent additional materials interpolated into MT and certain other MSS but missing in LXX^{B}. See § XXIV-B.

18 6. In MT (so LXX^{AL}) the verse begins with a clause that was probably introduced editorially to smooth over the interpolation of 17:55 - 18:5. It reads *wyhy bbw'm bšwb dwd mhkwt 't hplšty*, "When they came, when David returned from slaying the Philistine. . . ." Note that the clause is conflate, combining two readings, viz. (1) *wyhy bbw'm*, "When they came . . ." and (2) *wyhy bswb dwd mhkwt 't hplšty*, "When David returned from smiting the Philistine. . . ." This same kind of conflation seems also to be represented in the rest of the verse as it appears in MT (cf. LXX^{AL}). It reads: *wtṣ'nh hnšym mkl 'ry yśr'l lšwr* (*qĕrê: lāšîr*, "to sing") *whmḥlwt lqr't š'wl hmlk btpym bśmḥh wbšlšym*, "Women came out from all the cities of Israel to sing, and dancing women (*hmḥlwt* = *hmḥllwt*) to meet Saul, the king, with tambourines, with

celebration, and with sistrums." Our translation follows the shorter text of LXX^B throughout: *kai exēlthon hai choreuousai eis synantēsin daueid ek pasōn poleōn israēl en tympanois kai en charmosynē kai en kymbalois* = *wtṣ'nh hmḥllwt lqr't dwd mkl 'ry yśr'l btpym wbśmḥh wbšlšym.* MT has combined a reading similar to this ([*wyhy bšwb dwd mhkwt 't hplšty*] *wtṣ'nh hmḥlwt mkl 'ry yśr'l btpym,* etc.) with another, slightly different reading ([*wyhy bbw'm*] *wtṣ'nh hnšym mkl 'ry yśr'l lqr't šw'l hmlk btpym,* etc.). The infinitive *lšyr* may have been introduced to accommodate the double subject, thus "women . . . to sing" and "dancing women to meet Saul."

7. *the women* So LXX^B. MT: *hnšym hmśḥqwt,* "the women, who were making merry." LXX^L reflects *hnšym hmḥllwt,* "the women, who were dancing."

8a. *It was vexing to Saul* Reading *wyr' hdbr b'yny š'wl,* lit. "The thing was evil in the eyes of Saul," on the basis of LXX^B *kai ponēron ephanē to rhēma en opthalmois saoul* (to which is added *peri tou logou toutou,* "on account of this speech"; cf. MT). MT (cf. LXX^L) has *wyḥr lš'wl m'd wyr' b'ynyw hdbr hzh,* "And Saul became very angry, and this thing was evil in his eyes."

8b. At the end of v 8 MT (cf. LXX^{AL}, Syr.) adds *w'wd lw 'k hmlwkh,* "And there remains for him only the kingship!" Omit with LXX^B.

10-11. MT and certain other MSS here add an episode which is not found in the text of LXX^B. See § XXIV-B.

12a. MT, LXX^{AL} here add as v 12b: *ky hyh yhwh 'mw wm'm š'wl sr,* "because Yahweh was with him but had departed from Saul."

13. *and sent him away* So LXX. MT: "and *Saul* sent him away."

16. *before them* So MT. LXX: "before *the people*" (cf. v 13).

NOTES

18 6. *tambourines.* Hebrew *tuppîm;* see the NOTE at 10:5.

lutes. Hebrew *šālīšîm,* perhaps so called because it had three (*šālōš*) strings. The term occurs only here in the Hebrew Bible, and the meaning is surmised from the similarity of the name to *šalaštu,* a Mesopotamian lute-like instrument. Some translators, following a different line of reasoning, render the term "triangles."

7. The women's song is a poetic couplet:

hikkâ šā'ûl ba'ălāpāw
wĕdāwīd bĕrībĕbōtāyw.

The use of *hikkâ* with *bĕ-* + noun serving as direct object is unique in the Hebrew Bible to this poem (= 21:12; 29:5; but other passages come close [cf. especially II Sam 23:10]; *hikkâ* with *bĕ-* + [plural] noun elsewhere means "wreak slaughter among . . ."), which may be an ancient victory chant. If so, we may ask whether any invidious comparison was originally intended. The word pair *'ălāpîm,* "thousands," and *rĕbābôt,* "ten thousands," is a standard way of expressing a very large number in parallel lines of poetry; cf. the assurance of protection from plague in Ps 91:7: "A thousand may fall at your side,/ Ten thousand at your right hand, / But to you it will not come near!"; that is, though a great many may perish in your sight, you yourself will be safe (cf. also Ps 144:13; Deut 32:30; etc.). The same pair occurs frequently in Ugaritic poetry with the same force; e.g. *CTCA* 4(=51).1.27-29, which describes the luxurious handiwork of Kothar-wa-Ḫassis, the craftsman god:

yṣq ksp l'alpm
ḫrṣ yṣqm lrbbt
He casts silver by the thousands,
Gold he casts by the ten thousands.

The meaning is not that there is more gold than silver here, but simply that Kothar is being very generous in his use of precious metals (cf. *CTCA* 24 [= 77].20-21; for a list of occurrences of this word pair in both Ugaritic and Biblical Hebrew, see Fisher, *Ras Shamra Parallels* 1.114). The original meaning of our little couplet, therefore, may have been, "Saul and David have slain a great many of the enemy!" a victory chant may actually be as old as the wars of Saul. See Stanley Gevirtz, *Patterns in the Early Poetry of Israel,* Studies in Ancient Oriental Civilization 32 (University of Chicago, 1963) 14-24. But in a review of Gevirtz's study D. N. Freedman has addressed the same point, arguing that "the biblical writer may still have been right in seeing in the episode and the offending couplet an occasion for Saul's outburst. The very fact that David was accorded equal treatment with the king in the song (which is the point of Gevirtz's argument) would be sufficient to arouse the suspicions of any monarch, and especially of one insecure in his position and jealous of his prerogatives. It is the other pair in the couplet (Saul//David) which provides the clue to the king's reaction. For this is the only example of standard number-parallelism, among all those cited by [Gevirtz], in which there is a significant distinction of subjects: Saul and David. Once the king's suspicions had been triggered by this coupling of names, he might well have seen in the otherwise innocuous number-parallelism of the song further evidence of a plot to displace him" (see *JBL* 83 [1964] 201-202).

9. *eyed.* Hebrew *'ôyēn* (MT *qĕrê*), the participle of a verb derived denominatively from *'ayin,* "eye." The verb occurs nowhere else in the Hebrew Bible, but it is well known in Postbiblical Hebrew (Jastrow, 1053-1054) in *Pi'el* (as generally with denominatives, and perhaps we should restore *'iyyēn* here, especially in view of the *kĕtîb/qĕrê* confusion) meaning "look carefully, etc." The implication is that Saul has begun to be *envious* of David, in consequence of the women's *invidious* comparison (cf. Latin *invidēre,* "to look askance at," which comes to mean, "to envy"; thus *invidia,* "envy," whence English *envy*). In Phoenician the verb *'yn* could even mean "look at (with the Evil Eye)," as in the second incantation text from Arslan Tash (A. Caquot and R. du Mesnil du Buisson, "La second tablette ou 'petite amulette' d'Arslan Tash," *Syria* 48 [1971] 391-406), lines 8-9: *brḥ 'yn bdr,* "Begone, O (Evil) Eyer, from (my) house!"; and *'ayin* in Postbiblical Hebrew often meant

specifically "the Evil Eye." (Cf. the secondary meaning of Latin *invidēre,* scil. "look at with an evil eye.") But there seems to be no suggestion of the Evil Eye here beyond the general malevolence of Saul's gaze with its caution, suspicion, and increasing jealousy.

13. *he went out and came in before the army.* The expression *yāṣā' lipnê,* "go out before . . ." is used of leading troops in battle, as in 8:20 (cf. II Sam 5:24; etc.), and "go out and come in" (*yāṣā' ûbā'*) often describes the activity of a soldier in battle, as in 29:6 (cf. Josh 14:11; etc.). The fuller expression found here, "go out and come in before . . ." occurs also in the account of the commissioning of Joshua in Num 27:17; it refers specifically to military leadership.

14. *for Yahweh was with him.* The explanation of David's success and his charismatic appeal to the people; cf. the NOTE at 16:18.

15. *how successful he was.* Hebrew *'ăšer hû' maśkîl mĕ'ōd,* lit. "that he was very successful," a rare object clause introduced by *'ăšer;* cf. GK §157c.

16. *all Israel and Judah loved* [*him*]. The love that the people have for David goes beyond an affectionate response to his personal charisma. As both W. L. Moran and J. A. Thompson (see the NOTE at 16:21) have argued, *'āhēb,* "love," seems to have a political connotation here. In the Amarna archive the love of subjects indicates loyalty to their lord and may be used to describe factional loyalty to rival leaders; cf. *EA* 138:71-73, where it is said, "Behold the city [viz. Byblos]! Half of it loves the sons of Abdi-ashirta [an instigator of rebellion] and half of it loves my lord [viz. the king of Egypt and legitimate sovereign]!" In the present case, to Saul's chagrin, it is *all* Israel and Judah who love David. That is, all Israel and Judah have given their loyalty to the young man who leads them in war, and it is partly out of his recognition of this state of affairs (cf. 18:28) that Saul has come to fear David. In other words ". . . if we see in this attachment, as the [extrabiblical] evidence encourages us to do, an essential requirement of the king-subject relationship, then the writer implies that the people at [this] point were already giving David *de facto* recognition and allegiance, which his actual leadership and success in a sense justified" (Moran, "Love of God," 81).

COMMENT

This brief section, which describes the onset of Saul's jealousy of David, provides our clearest statement of the principal themes in the early part of the old narrative about David's rise to power.

The first of these has to do with Saul: every action he takes relative to David—whether motivated by goodwill, as in 16:21-22, or fear and suspicion, as in the present passage, or downright malice, as later in 18:20-27—contributes to David's success. So it is that when he sends David away out of envy and fear (vv 12a,13), he does not thereby eliminate the threat he perceives in his popular lieutenant, but, on the contrary, enlarges it; for David's new post as a commander-of-a-thousand is one from which the loyalty ("love"; see the NOTE at v 16) of the people is easily won.

The second theme, which concerns David, is a corollary of the first. Everything the younger man does, whether out of a desire for personal gain (cf. 18:26 and the COMMENT on 18:20-21a,22-27) or not, brings him promotion and glory. Our narrator is quite explicit. "David was successful in all his undertakings," he says, going on to explain, "for Yahweh was with him." The latter assertion is, as we have already seen (see the NOTE at 16:20), the theological leitmotiv of the stories of David and Saul. David's success is divinely given and, as we shall see, cannot be thwarted by his own lack of selfishness or excessive ambition any more than by Saul's opposition. In other words, both men are caught up in something larger than themselves, in events in which they must participate but cannot finally control. The next episode illustrates this last point particularly well.

XXVI. DAVID'S MARRIAGE TO MICHAL (18:20-21a, 22-27)

18 20 Michal, Saul's daughter, had fallen in love with David, and
when Saul was told, he saw it as an opportunity. 21a "I shall give her
to him," [he] thought. "She will be an enticement to him, and he will
fall into the hands of the Philistines!"
22 So Saul instructed his servants, "Speak to David privately and
say, 'The king favors you, and all his servants love you! Now then,
you should offer yourself as a son-in-law to the king!'"
23 When Saul's servants spoke these things to David, David said,
"Does it seem to you a trifling thing to offer oneself as a son-in-law to
the king? Well, as for me, I am poor and humble!"
24 Saul's servants informed him of the things David had said.
25 "Say this to David," said Saul. "The king wants no bride-price except a hundred Philistine foreskins, so that he might have vengeance
upon the royal enemies." (For Saul intended him to fall into the
hands of the Philistines.)
26 Once [Saul's] servants had reported these words to David, David
saw it as an opportunity to offer himself as a son-in-law to the king.
27 [He] and his men went up and slew a hundred of the Philistines, and he brought back their foreskins to the king, offering himself
as a son-in-law to the king. So [Saul] gave him his daughter Michal
as a wife.

TEXTUAL NOTES

18 17-19. Here in MT and certain other MSS appears an account of Saul's offer of Merob, his older daughter, to David. See § XXIV-B.

20. *Michal* So MT (*mîkal*). LXX: *melchol* (= *mlkl?*); Syr. *mlky'l.* Cf. 14:49 and the *Textual Note* there.

and when Saul was told Reading *wygd* (= *wayyuggad*) *š'wl* with LXX in preference to MT *wygdw lš'wl*, "and (when) they told Saul . . ." (cf. vv 24, 26 below).

21a. *and he will fall into the hands of the Philistines* So MT: *wtyhy bw yd plštym*, lit. "and the hand of the Philistines will be upon him." But the clause is ambiguous. MT understands *wthy* as *ûtěhî*, "*and* (the hand of the Philistines) *will be*," and *bw*, "upon him," as referring to David; but *wthy* might be read *wattěhî*, "*and* (the hand of the Philistines) *was*," and *bw* might be taken to refer to Saul. Thus, "and the hand of the Philistines was upon (Saul)," that is, Saul was hard pressed at the time by the Philistines. This is in fact the interpretation made in LXX^{B}, which also makes "Saul" explicit.

21b. At this point MT adds *wy'mr š'wl 'l dwd bštym tthtn by hywm*, "So Saul said to David for the second time (?), 'You will become my son-in-law today!' " This is a redactional expansion, added to facilitate the interpolation of vv 17-19. See § XXIV-B. To *bištayim*, "for the second time," cf. Job 33:14, and for the interpretation of this phrase and of the notice as a whole by the ancient translators and commentators, see S. Talmon, "The Textual Study of the Bible—A New Outlook," in *Qumran and the History of the Biblical Text*, eds. F. M. Cross and S. Talmon (Cambridge, Mass.: Harvard, 1975) 363 and n. 175 (396).

22. *Now then* So MT: *w'th*, "and now." LXX = *w'th*, "and *you*."

23. *humble* So MT (*nqlh*, "lightly esteemed, unimportant, humble"). LXX seems to reflect *l' nkbd*, "not honored."

25. *except* Reading *ky 'm* with LXX (*all' ē*) and many Hebrew MSS. MT omits *'m*.

Saul intended him to fall into Reading *š'wl ḥšb 'tw lnpl b-* on the basis of LXX *saoul elogisato auton embalein*. MT is somewhat different: *š'wl ḥšb lhpyl 't dwd b-*, "Saul intended to cause David to fall by. . . ."

26 *[Saul's] servants* Reading *'bdyw*, "his servants," with MT. LXX shuns the ambiguity ("*Saul's* servants"), and this is also necessary in English.

27. The verse is preceded in MT (at the end of v 26) by *wl' ml'w hymym*, lit. "And the days were not yet filled," that is, "Before the time had passed . . ." (cf. LXX^{AL}). This does not appear in LXX^{B} and probably arose marginally (perhaps, as Wellhausen and others have supposed, to emphasize David's eagerness). The same marginal plus seems to have found its way into the text in fragmentary condition farther on in the verse as well, where LXX^{AL} (*kai eplērōsen autas*) reflect *wyml'm*, "and he paid them in full" (MT: *wyml'wm*, "and they paid them in full"), after "their foreskins"; but no true parallel for this use of *ml'*, "fill," exists, and again the shorter text of LXX^{B} (= *wyb' dwd 't 'rltyhm lmlk wythtn* [MT *lhthtn* as in v 26] *bmlk*, "and David brought back their foreskins to the king and offered himself as a son-in-law to the king") must be preferred.

a hundred So LXX^{BL}. MT, OL have "two hundred," as if David brought double the required amount. Is this a scribal exaggeration or is it original, LXX having been "corrected" to v 25? The issue is decided by II Sam 3:14, where the lower price is cited.

So [Saul] gave him So LXX^{B} = *wytn lw*, "So he gave him." MT, LXX^{AL}:

wytn lw š'wl, "So *Saul* gave him"; and the explicit subject is also necessary in English.

as a wife So MT (*l'šh*). LXX$^{(B)}$ = *lw l'šh, "to him* as a wife," that is, "as his wife."

NOTES

18 20. *Michal.* Saul's youngest daughter (see 14:49). Michal's love foreshadows that of her brother Jonathan: not even the king's family is immune to David's personal appeal! See also the COMMENT.

he saw it as an opportunity. That is, *wayyīšar haddābār bĕ'ênāyw,* lit. "the thing was right in his eyes," said here of Saul and in v 26 of David. This expression is a key to the interpretation of the incident. Each man sees the marriage prospect as an opportunity to further his own cause. For Saul it is a chance to place David in mortal danger without casting suspicion on himself. For David it is a chance to advance his position at court substantially and innocently. Each plan is good, and each involves certain risks; but the factor determining success is not the relative soundness of the plans or even their relative ethical merit, but the ever present ingredient of special favor in the story: "David was successful in all his undertakings, for Yahweh was with him" (18:14).

22. *all his servants love you.* As already noted (see the NOTE at 18:16) the use of *'āhēb,* "love," in such a context carries political implications; it goes beyond a statement of affection to suggest freely given loyalty and partisanship. The "servants" in question are the high-ranking members of Saul's court (see the NOTES at 8:14 and 16:15), and David is being tempted by them with the fact that he already has a natural base of power at court—a fact he must know to be true.

22b-25. Becoming a *ḥātān,* "son-in-law, bridegroom" (hence the denominative verb *hitḥattēn,* "offer one's self as a *ḥātān*"), involved payment of a "bride-price" (*mōhar;* also Gen 34:12; Exod 22:16[English 22:17]) to the bride's father. According to R. de Vaux (*Ancient Israel* 1.27), "A similar custom, with the same name (*mahr*), is found among the Palestinian Arabs of to-day. The *mahr* is a sum of money paid by the fiancé to the girl's parents. Its amount varies from village to village, and according to the family's income. . . ." Since the practice in ancient Israel seems to have been the same, it is no wonder that David accounts himself too "poor and humble" to enter into a royal marriage. But it seems also to have been the prerogative of the father to set the amount of the *mōhar* (cf. Gen 34:12), and so Saul cunningly places it at "a hundred Philistine foreskins," a bride-price within David's reach but likely, as Saul supposes, to cost the prospective bridegroom his life.

26. *David saw it as an opportunity.* See the NOTE at v 20 and the COMMENT.

COMMENT

David's rise to prominence at court has been so rapid that his betrothal to Saul's own daughter comes as no great surprise. In what seems to have been a very short time he has ascended from court musician (16:18-19) to royal weapon-bearer (16:21) to popular hero (18:6-8) to commander-of-a-thousand (18:13), and now he becomes son-in-law to the king. The palace intrigue that shrouds the betrothal gives the story its interest and illustrates well what we have said already about the divinely directed march of events in which both Saul and David are consciously but helplessly caught up.

Saul initiates the betrothal himself, hoping to use Michal as a lure to entrap David (vv 21a,25b). "He saw [Michal's love for David] as an opportunity," explains our narrator (v 20). Note that the same expression is used of David's motivation at the end of the episode when the unorthodox bride-price has been reported to him. "David saw it as an opportunity," we are told, "to offer himself as a son-in-law to the king." These two statements at the beginning and end of the episode form an inclusion that gives the section its literary unity and calls attention again to the dynamic of the relationship between the two men. Everything Saul does to thwart David's rise works ironically to David's advantage; every opportunity Saul attempts to seize for himself turns in the end into an opportunity for David.

It must also be pointed out that David's marriage to Michal, though at one level just another example of Saul's machinations turned to David's advantage, has a special significance of its own. Marriage to the king's daughter gives David a certain claim to membership in the royal house of Israel, which he will later, when already king of Judah, use to justify his succession to the northern throne as well (cf. II Sam 3:12*ff*). In other words there is great political significance to this little episode, and in reporting it our narrator is looking ahead to David's assumption of kingship over Israel and the question of legitimacy that will arise.[1] It has even been supposed that a formal rule of son-in-law succession is assumed to be in effect here.[2] But whatever the case, the entire issue remains unexpressed. It is true that the loyalty ("love"; see the NOTE at v 22) he

[1] Noth (*History*, 184, n. 1) and others have doubted the historicity of a marriage between David and Michal during Saul's lifetime (contrast Bright, *History*, 188, n. 23). Historical or not, the story suits perfectly the purposes of our narrator, who is concerned to demonstrate the legitimacy of David's rise to power and succession (see LITERARY HISTORY in the Introduction, pp. 27-30).

[2] See Morgenstern, "David and Jonathan."

commands among Saul's servants is mentioned to David as a favorable part of his candidacy, but from David's viewpoint the question seems to be entirely an economic one—he is too poor to pay a royal bride-price—and it would be reading too much into v 26 ("David saw it as an opportunity . . .") to assume that it implies that he already has the kingship in mind.

In the nearer future is David's flight from court, in which Michal is instrumental (19:8-17), and the present story prepares directly for that. Moreover, the important theme of the love of Saul's own family for David (cf. 16:21) is further developed here in the declaration of Michal's love in v 20. This theme reaches its maturity in the episode that follows.

XXVII. JONATHAN'S INTERCESSION ON BEHALF OF DAVID (18:28-29a; 19:1-7)

18 28 When Saul saw that Yahweh was with David and all Israel
loved him, 29a [he] came to fear David even more. **19** 1 [He] spoke to
his son Jonathan and to all his servants about killing David. But
Jonathan, Saul's son, was deeply fond of David, 2 and [he] told
David, "Saul is seeking to kill you! Take care in the morning! Keep
hidden in some secret place! 3 *As for me, I shall go out and stand beside my father in the field where you are.* As for me, I shall speak to
my father about you, and whatever I learn I shall tell you."

4 Jonathan spoke well of David to Saul, his father. "Let the king
not sin against his servant David," he told him, "for he has not sinned
against you. The things he has done are very good. 5 He took his life
in his own hands when he slew the Philistine and won a great victory
for all Israel. You rejoiced when you saw it, so why should you
commit a sin of innocent blood by killing David without cause?"

6 Saul heeded Jonathan, "As Yahweh lives," [he] swore, "[David]
shall not be killed!" 7 So Jonathan summoned David and reported all
these words to him. Then [he] brought David to Saul, and he served
him as before.

TEXTUAL NOTES

18 28. *When Saul saw* So LXX^{BL}. MT: "When Saul saw *and knew. . . .*" See further below.

all Israel loved him Reading *kl yśr'l 'hbw* with LXX^{B} (cf. 18:16). MT has *mykl bt š'wl 'hbthw,* "Saul's daughter Michal loved him" (LXX^{L} combines the two readings). After the insertion of vv 29b-30, which separated this material from that in 19:1*ff,* v 28 was interpreted strictly as a conclusion to the account of David's marriage to Michal (in fact it is a transitional remark connecting that episode with the story of Jonathan's intercession). Thus (MT), "When

Saul saw ('this,' viz. that David had won Michal), he realized not only that Yahweh was with David but that even Michal, his own (so LXX[L]) daughter, loved him, and he came to fear David even more."

29-30. Verse 29 begins *wywsp* (cf. LXX; MT *kĕtîb: wy'sp*) *š'wl lr' mpny dwd 'wd,* after which MT adds further material treated in § XXIV-B.

19 2. *Saul* So LXX[B]. MT, LXX[AL]: "Saul, *my father.*"

Take care Preceded in MT (cf. LXX[L]) by *w'th,* "And now." Omit with LXX[B].

in the morning So MT (*bbqr*). LXX *aurion prōi,* "tomorrow morning," may reflect *mḥr bbqr* but is more likely to be a conflation of two renderings of *bbqr* alone.

Keep hidden in some secret place That is, *wnḥb't wyšbt bstr* (cf. LXX), the order of which is illogically inverted in MT. The sequence *wnḥb't wyšbt,* lit. "And hide and remain . . ." is a good example of verbal hendiadys and thus should be rendered, "Remain hidden . . ." or "Keep hidden. . . ."

4. *his servant* So MT, LXX[L]. LXX[B]: "*your* servant."

very good So LXX[BL]. MT: "very good *for you.*"

5. *and won a great victory* MT, LXX[B] have *wy'ś yhwh tšw'h gdwlh,* "And *Yahweh* won a great victory," but this is beside the point here where it is David's exploits that are under discussion. Nor does the further expansion displayed by LXX[L], Syr. alter the situation (= *wy'ś yhwh bydw,* etc., "And Yahweh won *by his* [*David's*] *hand,* etc."). The introduction of the divine name was secondary. We read *wy'ś tšw'h gdwlh.*

for all Israel. You rejoiced when you saw it MT *lkl yśr'l r'yt wtśmḥ,* lit. "for all Israel. You saw and rejoiced. . . ." LXX[(B)] reflects *wkl yśr'l r'w wyśmḥw,* "And all Israel saw and rejoiced. . . ." There is little reason to prefer one of these readings to the other.

7. *and reported* So LXX[BL]. MT: "and *Jonathan* reported."

NOTES

18 28. David's success in the Michal affair forces Saul to admit to himself what the audience already knows, viz. that Yahweh is with David (see the NOTE at 16:18) and that all Israel is committed to him ("*loves* him"; see the NOTES at 16:21 and 18:16 and also the NOTE at 18:20).

29a. *to fear.* The infinitive appears in MT as *lērō',* a most irregular form; we expect *lĕyir'â* (Deut 4:10; etc.) or at least *lîrō'* (cf. Josh 22:25), and we must suspect *lērō'* to be an error for *līrō'* (= *lîrō'*); so GK §69n (cf. Driver).

19 2-3. Jonathan's instructions contain a seemingly irreconcilable contradiction. On the one hand he tells David to hide while he sounds out his father, after which he will report Saul's reaction to David; on the other he says he will speak with Saul "in the field where you are," as if the plan was for David to overhear, in which case Jonathan's subsequent report (v 7) would be unnecessary. We are forced to assume an incomplete mixing of two versions of the plan here (cf. especially Hertzberg). In the first, which fits more comfortably with the account in its present form, Jonathan plans to speak with Saul in an unnamed location while David hides in "some secret place," known to Jonathan but also unnamed; then Jonathan will summon David out of hiding and make his report. In the other, represented here only by the words, "As for me . . . where you are," Jonathan will speak to Saul while David hides nearby within hearing of their conversation; then David can decide whether to flee or return to court without further consultation with Jonathan. The latter plan shows marked similarities to that in 20:18-24 and may have been influenced by that account.

4. *Jonathan spoke well of David.* As intercessor Jonathan "spoke well" (*waydabbēr ṭōb,* lit. "spoke a good/beautiful [word]") concerning David to his father; that is, he said favorable things about him. Compare in the Amarna archive the entreaties to the royal scribe that conclude most of the letters of Abdi-ḫeba, a fourteenth-century king of Jerusalem, requesting that the scribe act as Abdi-ḫeba's advocate and "speak good/beautiful (*banāti*) words" to the king (*EA* 286:62-63; 287:67; 288:64-65; 289:49). See *ANET,* 487-489. For the rather different expression *dibbēr ṭôbâ,* "speak/promise a good thing," see the NOTE at 25:30.

The things he has done are very good. The general meaning of this statement is clear without explanation, but a more precise understanding can be gained by appeal to the repertoire of convenantal terminology so frequently drawn upon in the stories of Saul, David, and Jonathan—terms like "love" (NOTES to 16:21; 18:16; 20:17; etc.), "loyalty" (NOTES to 15:6; 20:8), and "goodness," all of which may carry legal and political nuances in addition to their common meanings. It is "good(ness)" (*ṭôb*/*ṭôbâ*) that occurs in the present passage: "The things he has done are very good (*ma'ăśāyw ṭôb mĕ'ōd*)." As recent studies of biblical and extrabiblical materials have shown, "good(ness)" describes the proper treatment of one another by partners in a formal political relationship; in particular, to "do good" (Hebrew *ṭôb*[*â*] *'āśâ*) is to treat one's lord, vassal, or ally (as the case may be) in the right way; to "seek good" is to act as a friend or loyal ally (cf. the NOTE at 24:10). See esp. W. L. Moran, "A Note on the Treaty Terminology of the Sefîre Stelas," *JNES* 22 (1963) 173-176; A. Malamat, "Organs of Statecraft in the Israelite Monarchy," *BAR*³, 195-199; D. R. Hillers, "A Note on Some Treaty Terminology in the Old Testament," *BASOR* 176 (1964) 46-47. While we are not dealing here with diplomatic treaties (the principal concern of the articles just cited), the same language applies *mutatis mutandis* to the formal relationship of king and subject. The things David has done have been good, says Jonathan; that is, he has acted consistently with the loyalty he owes his king. Cf. also 24:18-20 later, where this nuance is even more clear.

5. See the COMMENT on § XXIV-A, where it is suggested that the "great victory" was the major concern of that account before its overlay with the story of David's duel with the Philistine champion. If the present passage was part of the oldest narrative of David's rise to power, as we assume, then the words "when he slew the Philistine and" may reflect secondary adjustment to the present shape of c 17.

commit a sin of innocent blood. Jonathan implores his father not to incur the mortal contamination of bloodguilt by slaying a person who does not deserve to die. See especially Pedersen, *Israel,* 420-425. As the references to the shedding of innocent blood in the severe condemnation of King Manasseh of Judah show (II Kings 21:16; 24:4[*bis*]), the avoidance of bloodguilt was of supreme importance for the ruler who would not pollute his kingdom with his own sin. This is a lesson Saul will never really learn and one with which David himself will struggle (cf. 22:22, etc., and especially the COMMENT on 25:2-25).

6. Saul's volatile personality is not without its lucid (and penitent) moments, when he recognizes that David's behavior toward him has been consistently just; cf. esp. 26:21,25 below.

COMMENT

Saul's jealousy has become morbid suspicion, and he speaks with his courtiers about taking David's life. Fear of David has begun to obsess him now, and the obsession will grow as the story develops; but on this occasion an intercessory word from Jonathan is enough to soften his father's resolve. Saul's actions are always unpredictable where David is concerned —he is not yet and in fact never will be (cf. the NOTE at v 6) entirely hostile toward the younger man—and the incident ends in reconciliation. Nevertheless, this little episode, however harmonious its closing, effectively serves the function of introducing a new and alarming state of affairs: David's life is now in danger.[1]

This passage also introduces us to the theme of Jonathan's loyalty to David. That is, the narrative is designed to show not only that David is now in mortal danger but that he has found help from Jonathan, the king's son, and that it is willing, eager help. We have been told already that Michal, Saul's daughter, loved David (18:20), and we have known since the report of David's arrival (16:21) that Saul, too, his present jealousy notwithstanding, is devoted to him. But the theme of David's irresistibility, even to the family of the man he is to supplant as king, is given its clearest statement in the portrayal of his relationship to Jonathan, the heir apparent to the throne of Israel. We have already seen that the tradition made much of this relationship (18:1-4), but in the primary narrative the present passage is its first expression; it will be further developed in the episode recorded in 20:1 - 21:1.

[1] This is the function of this section in the larger narrative, and it is an important function. Thus, though it may show some influence from 20:1 - 21:1 (cf. Grønbaek, *Aufstieg Davids,* 111-113) and from c 17 (cf. the NOTE at v 5 above), it is not, as Wellhausen described it, "a pointless and artificial passage" (*Prolegomena,* 264), or a late insertion.

XXVIII. DAVID'S FLIGHT FROM COURT
(19:8-17)

19 8 Again there was war, and David marched out to fight with the
Philistines. He inflicted a great defeat upon them, and they fled before
him.

9 Then an evil spirit of God came upon Saul as he was sitting in his
house with his spear in his hand, while David played. 10 Saul tried to
strike David with the spear, but he broke away from Saul, who stuck
the spear in the wall. Then David fled and escaped.

11 That same night Saul sent officers to David's house to guard it, so
that he might have him killed in the morning; but David was informed by Michal, his wife. "If you do not save yourself tonight," she
said, "you will be killed tomorrow!" 12 and [she] let David down
through the window. When he had got away safely, 13 Michal took
the teraphim and, placing a tangle of goats' hair at its head, laid it on
the bed and covered it with a blanket; 14 then when Saul sent officers
to arrest David, she said that he was ill.

15 Next [Saul] sent the officers to see David, saying, "Bring him up
from the bed to me, so that he can be put to death!" 16 And when the
officers arrived, there was the teraphim upon the bed with the tangle
of goats' hair at its head!

17 "Why have you betrayed me like this?" said Saul to Michal.
"You have let my enemy go, and he has escaped!"

But Michal told Saul, "He said, 'Let me go! Why should I kill
you?' "

TEXTUAL NOTES

19 8. *there was war* So MT, LXX^{A}. LXX^{B} adds "against David." LXX^{L} adds "against the Philistines."

a great defeat So MT. LXX: "a *very* great defeat."

9. *of God* So LXX^{B} (cf. LXX^{L}). MT: "of Yahweh."

10. *to strike David with the spear* Reading *lhkwt 't hḥnyt bdwd,* lit. "to strike the spear into David," on the basis of LXX[(B)] *pataxai to doru eis daueid.* MT has *lhkwt bḥnyt bdwd wbqyr,* "to strike with the spear into David and into the wall," that is, "to pin David to the wall with the spear," to which cf. 18:11 (§ XXIV-B).

11. *That same night* So LXX[(B)]; *kai egenēthē en tē nykti ekeinē = wyhy blylh hhw'* (cf. Wellhausen). MT attaches these words (in defective form) to the end of v 10 (*blylh hw'*). Cf. also F. M. Cross, "Oldest Manuscripts," 171.

to guard it, so that he might have him killed Reading *lšmrw lhmytw* (so LXX). MT *lšmrw wlhmytw,* "to guard it *and* to have him killed," shows dittography of the first *w.*

14. *she said* So MT. LXX: "*they* said."

15. *Next [Saul] sent the officers to see David* MT: *wyšlḥ š'wl 't hml'kym lr'wt 't dwd* (cf. LXX[L], Vulg., Syr.). We may eliminate *š'wl,* "Saul," with LXX[B], but otherwise LXX[B] is defective here, omitting *'t hml'kym lr'wt* because of haplography caused by *homoioteleuton* (*'t . . .'t*). Space requirements show that 4QSam[b] shares the longer reading. See Cross, "Oldest Manuscripts," 171.

17. *He said* So LXX[B]. MT: "He said *to me.*"

Why should I kill you? That is, "(Let me go), or else I shall kill you!" LXX has *ei de mē thanatōsō se = w'm l' 'mytk,* "and if not I shall kill you!"[?]), but MT *lmh 'mytk* is surely original.

NOTES

19 8. This notice provides a transition from v 7, in which Saul and David are reconciled, to vv 9-10, in which Saul tries to take David's life. David's military successes described here provide an occasion for the renewal of Saul's jealous madness.

9-10. This incident is duplicated in 18:10-11, which stands among the additions to the story of David's early days at court (see § XXIV-B).

9. *an evil spirit of God.* Cf. 16:14-15 and see the NOTE at 16:14.

10. *but he broke away.* Hebrew *wayyipṭar,* which occurs intransitively only here in Biblical Hebrew (elsewhere "set free"; cf. II Chron 23:8), but the meaning is clarified by reference to extrabiblical resources. Akkadian *paṭāru* is normally transitive ("loosen, set free, ransom") but in peripheral Old and Middle Babylonian and notably in the Amarna letters from Jerusalem may mean "depart" (*EA* 287:46; 289:39) or "defect" (*EA* 286:8,35; 289:44; 290:12,17-23). Moreover, not only "set free" but also "depart" are attested meanings for *pāṭar* in Postbiblical Hebrew.

11-17. This story is a direct continuation of 18:27—in the original tradition David's house was guarded on his wedding night—but the connection was broken in the course of the compilation of the larger narrative of David's rise to power in order to permit the inclusion of other materials.

12. [*she*] *let David down through the window.* In Josh 2:15, where Rahab

helps Joshua's spies make a similar escape, it is explained that the house was built into the city wall, so that someone leaving the house through the window would escape detection by anyone within the city walls. Perhaps, since David does not encounter Saul's guards outside, we are to assume that the same is true here (Hertzberg). Cf. also II Cor 11:32-33.

13. *the teraphim.* In Genesis 31 the narrator refers to Laban's household idols as his "teraphim" (vv 19,34-35), whereas Laban himself calls them his "gods" (v 30). The term *ṭĕrāpîm,* which may be singular or plural, refers to an idol or idols, most often (it seems) of the household type (*penates*). They seem to have had a role in divination (Ezek 21:26[English 21:21]; Zech 10:2; cf. the NOTE at 15:23a) and can perhaps be identified with the "gods" which adjudicate in clan or household law in Exod 21:6; 22:7-8 (cf. 2:25 above and the NOTE there); but in other passages (15:23; cf. II Kings 23:24) the use of teraphim is condemned. It is obvious that the teraphim kept in the home of David and Michal was of human size and shape.

a tangle of goats' hair. Hebrew *kĕbîr hā'izzîm,* the interpretation of which is uncertain. *Kābîr* occurs only here in the Hebrew Bible, and its meaning must be guessed from apparently related words, like *kĕbārâ,* "sieve," *makbēr,* "blanket" (?; only II Kings 8:15), and *mikbār,* "grating"—hence **kbr,* "interwine," and *kābîr,* "something intertwined, netted." Accordingly some scholars have thought of *kābîr* as a kind of mosquito- or fly-net. But cf. Cant 4:1, where the young woman's hair is compared to a flock of goats. The *kābîr* of the present passage probably serves as a wig, and it may be a woven piece of material or simply an interwined tangle of goats' hair. The function of the definite article is that described in GK §125r (". . . placing *a certain* tangle . . .").

15. *from the bed.* Hebrew *bammiṭṭâ* means "*in* the bed," but English idiom requires "from" to represent faithfully Saul's command. This use of the preposition *bĕ-* with verbs of motion is now generally recognized as a feature Biblical Hebrew shared with Phoenician and Ugaritic.

17. *Why should I kill you?* That is, "Or else I shall kill you!" a use of the interrogative in keeping with good Hebrew idiom (see GK §150e and especially Driver). David threatened Michal, she says. But she is lying.

COMMENT

As we might have guessed on the basis of 18:20 and the account of Jonathan's intercession on behalf of David in § XXVII, Saul's daughter shows greater loyalty to her husband than to her father. In a fast-paced and entertaining story—the ruse of the idol and bedclothes is a nice touch—Michal contrives David's escape from their home and Saul's watchmen, and the first chapter—the "Gibeah phase"—in the story of David's rise draws to a close. Hereafter the action takes place in the deserts and villages of Israel and Judah, for David will never again return to Saul's court.

XXIX. SAUL AMONG THE PROPHETS
(19:18-24)

19 18 As for David, after he had gotten safely away, he went to
Samuel at Ramah and told him about everything Saul had done to
him. Then he and Samuel went to stay in the camps.

19 When Saul was told that David was in the camps at Ramah,
20 [he] sent emissaries to arrest David. But when they saw the assembly of prophets prophesying with Samuel presiding over them, the
spirit of God came upon Saul's emissaries, and they began to prophesy. 21 When Saul was told, he sent other emissaries, but they, too,
prophesied; and though [he] sent emissaries for a third time, they,
too, prophesied.

22 So [Saul] went to Ramah himself. When he arrived at the cistern
of the threshing floor that was upon the bare height, he made
inquiries. "Where are Samuel and David?" he asked, and someone
said that they were in the camps at Ramah. 23 As he walked toward
the camps at Ramah, the spirit of God came upon him, too, and he
went along, prophesying as he went, until he came to the camps at
Ramah. 24 Then he stripped off his clothes, prophesied in front of [the
prophets], and lay naked all that day and night.

It is for this reason that they say, "Is Saul, too, among the prophets?"

TEXTUAL NOTES

19 18. *in the camps* Apparently treated by MT as a place name (*qĕrê: bĕnāyôt; kĕtîb: bnwyt*) here and elsewhere in the story. For the translation, see the NOTE. LXX adds "at Ramah," anticipating v 19.

20. *But when they saw the assembly of prophets* Reading *wyr'w 't qhlt hnby'ym* on the basis of LXX$^{(B)}$ *kai eidan tēn ekklēsian tōn prophētōn* in preference to MT *wyr' 't lqht hnby'ym,* "But when *he* saw the (?) of proph-

ets. . . ." The corruption of *qhlt* to *lqht* in MT may have been promoted by the preceding infinitive *lqḥt,* "to arrest."

prophets prophesying So MT: *hnby'ym nb'ym* (cf. LXX^AL^). The second word was lost in the *Vorlage* of LXX^B^ by haplography.

and they began to prophesy That is, *wayyitnabbĕ'û,* to which MT in anticipation of v 21 adds *gam-hēmmâ,* "they, too."

21. *When Saul was told* LXX *kai apēngelē* reflects *wygd* (understood as *wayyaggēd,* "When [one] told [Saul] . . ."), which might be read *wayyuggad* as in v 19 (MT). Here MT has *wygdw,* "When *they* told (Saul). . . ."

22. At the beginning of the verse LXX has *kai ethymōthē orgē saoul,* reflecting *wyḥr 'p š'wl,* "And Saul became angry. . . ." There is no trace of such a reading in MT, and in the absence of a clear motivation for the loss of the clause from the longer text, we must consider this a case of simple expansion (Wellhausen).

at the cistern . . . upon the bare height Reading *'d bwr hgrn 'šr bšpy* on the basis of LXX *heōs tou phreatos tou halō tou en tō sephei.* MT has *'d bwr hgdwl 'šr bśkw,* "at the big cistern (?; GK §126x) that was *in Secu* (?)."

23. *he walked* MT adds *šm,* "there"; LXX^B^ adds *ekeithen* = *mšm,* "from there." Omit both with LXX^L^.

and he went along, prophesying as he went MT *wylk hlwk wytnb',* lit. "and he went, going and prophesying"; see the NOTE. LXX *kai eporeueto prophēteuōn* seems to reflect a simplification, viz. *wylk mtnb',* lit. "and he went, prophesying. . . ."

24. MT inserts *gm hw',* "he, too," into each of the first two clauses ("Then he, too, stripped off his clothes, and he, too, prophesied . . ."). Omit with LXX^(B)^.

in front of [*the prophets*] Reading *lpnyhm,* lit. "in front of them," with LXX^B^. MT: "in front of *Samuel.*"

NOTES

19 18. *Ramah.* Samuel's home (see the NOTE at 1:19) lay only two or three miles to the N.

the camps. The precise form of the noun is uncertain (see the *Textual Note*), but iṭ is probably related to *nāweh* (plural construct, *nĕ'ôt*), "pasturage, abode (of shepherds)." The meaning has been elucidated by comparison to Akkadian *nāwum,* "pasturage, steppe," which at Mari refers to the encampments of West Semitic nomadic or seminomadic tribes (see especially A. Malamat, "Mari and the Bible: Some Patterns of Tribal Organization and Institutions," *JAOS* 82 [1962] 146). In the Bible, then, a *nāweh* is a shepherd's camp pitched outside a city (Jer 33:12; etc.), and the use of the same or similar noun in this story (19:18,19,22,23[*bis*]; 20:1) suggests that "the prophetic fraternities of Israel [also] dwelt in such settlements" (Malamat).

20,21. The prophets are pictured in an assembly (*qĕhillat hannĕbî'îm;* cf. Deut 33:4; Neh 5:7) over which Samuel is presiding (*'omēd niṣṣāb,* lit. "standing holding a position," that is, "standing in the position of authority" or "standing in charge"; for *niṣṣāb 'al,* "be in charge of," cf. Ruth 2:5,6). The activity of the company is prophecy, that is, group ecstasy (see the third NOTE at 10:5) animated by the spirit of God (the NOTE at 10:6), which spreads contagiously to each newly arriving troop of Saul's emissaries in its turn.

22. *the cistern of the threshing floor that was upon the bare height.* We are to visualize the distraught king standing on a windswept hill in front of the city of Ramah. "Cistern" (*bôr*) refers to a pit dug in the ground and sealed with plaster for water storage. Since this one is located at the "threshing floor" (*gōren*) and thus probably near the gate of the city, we may assume it is a communal water source for Ramah; cf. the mention of young women coming out of the gate of Ramah to draw water in 9:11. "Bare height" (*šĕpî*) normally refers to a hot (Jer 4:11), dry (Isa 41:18) hill where nothing grows (Isa 49:9; cf. also Jer 14:6); like the threshing floor it sometimes appears as a place of mourning (Jer 3:21; 7:29) and religious ritual (cf. Jer 3:2; etc.).

23. *and he went along, prophesying as he went.* Hebrew *wayyēlek hālôk wayyitnabbē',* a rare construction. We expect a second infinitive absolute (*wĕhitnabbē'*) to be coordinated with the first (as in 6:12: *hālĕkû hālōk wĕgā'ô,* "[the cows] went along . . . lowing as they went") rather than an imperfect consecutive; but other examples of the present arrangement exist (II Sam 16:13; cf. 13:19). See Driver; GK §113st.

24. *stripped off his clothes . . . and lay naked.* Yet another form of ecstatic behavior. Driver supposes that *'ārōm* does not mean "naked" but something more modest, "i.e. as Is. 20,2. Mic 1,8 without the upper garment, and wearing only the long linen tunic, which was worn next the skin."

It is for this reason. . . . Cf. 10:12. For the second time we are given an explanation of the origin of the old saying, "Is Saul, too, among the prophets?" (see the NOTE at 10:11-12); but this time Saul appears in a less favorable light. As already pointed out (see the NOTE at 16:14) Saul's experience with divine inspiration has taken a downward turn. The spirit of Yahweh now haunts him rather than helps him. And in contrast to the encounter described in 10:10-12, here he meets the prophetic troop as an unwelcome intruder, indeed as an enemy. He is now more a victim of prophetic inspiration than a beneficiary of it; he participates in the prophesying as a sufferer, an invalid, and the ecstasy is for him a disease.

COMMENT

Once he is safely out of Gibeah, David makes his way to the prophetic encampments near Ramah where he confers with Samuel. This is the first in a series of interviews between David and various individuals who assist his escape, viz. Samuel, Jonathan, and Ahimelech of Nob, to each of whom he goes in turn.[1] All of them are important people—Ahimelech and Jonathan may be said to represent "church and state" to some extent—so that their support of the fugitive hero is especially significant. A new theme, for which we were prepared by Michal's part in the preceding incident, is introduced here: David is protected from Saul by the leading citizens of Saul's kingdom.

It is doubtful, however, that this episode is an original part of the old narrative about David's rise to power. Some scholars have thought it so,[2] but most have followed Wellhausen[3] in considering it a secondary insertion. It presupposes David's acquaintance with Samuel and therefore the story told in 15:35-16:13, which, as we have seen (the COMMENTS on 15:1-34 and 15:35-16:13), belongs to a secondary, prophetically oriented introduction to the history of David's rise. Accordingly, we might conclude that the present passage is yet another piece from the prophetic hand that shaped the earlier stories of Samuel and Saul. But two difficulties cast doubt on this conclusion. First, it was the prophetic author of 15:35 who told us that Samuel would never see Saul again before he died, a statement most difficult to reconcile with the assumption that the present story, in which Saul lies naked before the old prophet's eyes, derives from the same writer. Second, this section offers an alternative explanation of the origin of the saying, "Is Saul, too, among the prophets?" to that given in 10:10-12, which may itself have been part of the prophetic elaboration of the old folktale about Saul's search for the lost asses of Kish (see the COMMENT on § XII) and was in any case a part of the finished narrative as it left the hand of the prophetic writer; it seems unlikely that the same writer would introduce a variant explanation. We are obliged by these facts to regard 19:18-24 as a late addition to the narrative in the spirit of the prophetic revision of other materials but of independent origin, which was introduced in order to report another bit of tradition about David, Saul, and Samuel, which may have grown up as an explanation of —or a midrashic reinterpretation of (cf. Budde)—the saying "Is Saul, too, among the prophets?" in circles where the alternative explanation was not known or not accepted. We have some reason to believe that Saul was remembered with increasing hostility as the years went by—recall, for example, MT's suspicious corruption of the assertion that "wherever he turned he was victorious" in 14:47 to "wherever he turned he acted

[1] Grønbaek (*Aufstieg Davids,* 114, cf. 264) makes a neat observation about the craft of the compiler in the material that contains these interviews (19:18-22:23): each of the visits is introduced by *wayyābō',* "and (David) went" (to Samuel in 19:18, to Jonathan in 20:1, to Ahimelech in 21:1; cf. 21:11b), and a certain serial unity is thereby imparted to the section as a whole.

[2] Nübel (*Davids Aufstieg,* 32-33) argues on stylistic grounds that it is an original continuation of the flight story.

[3] See *Prolegomena,* 267-268.

wickedly"—and this late piece certainly puts him in an unfavorable light. Indeed as Grønbaek points out,[4] this account, in which the onrush of divine spirit is an expression of Saul's loss of favor and a means of protecting the man who will displace him, can be read as a kind of parody of 10:10-12, in which Saul's inspiration is a manifestation of his anointing as *nāgîd*. So this is a late addition to the narrative from a writer who, though not identical to the prophetic writer whose work we see elsewhere in our story, nevertheless shared his prophetic perspective and wanted to add Samuel to the list of David's abettors, and who even surpassed the earlier writer in his contempt for Saul. In the next episode, after a transitional notice from the hand of the author of this insertion (see the NOTE at 20:1a), we return to the older narrative.

[4] *Aufstieg Davids,* 116-117, 264. So also Stoebe; Mettinger, *King and Messiah,* 77.

XXX. DAVID AND JONATHAN
(20:1-21:1)

20 1 David fled from the camps at Ramah and came before Jonathan. "What have I done?" he said. "What is my crime? How have I
sinned against your father, that he should seek my life?"
2 "Heaven forbid!" [Jonathan] said to him. "You shall not die! My
father does nothing great or small without revealing it to me, so why
should [he] conceal such a thing from me? This cannot be!"
3 But in reply David said, "Your father knew that I have your
favor; so he thought, 'Jonathan must not know about this, lest he take
counsel [with David].' But indeed, as Yahweh lives and as you yourself live, he has sworn a pact between me and Death!"
4 Then Jonathan said to David, "What do you desire? I shall do it
for you!"
5 "Tomorrow is the New Moon," David said to [him], "and I am
supposed to take my place at dinner. Let me go and hide in the field
until evening. 6 If your father misses me, say to him, 'David asked my
permission to run to Bethlehem, his city, for the whole clan has a seasonal sacrifice there.' 7 If he says, 'Very well,' then your servant is
safe, but if he becomes angry, you will know that he intends evil.
8 Now deal loyally with your servant, for you have brought your servant into a covenant of Yahweh with you. If there were any guilt in
me, you could kill me yourself! So why should you turn me over to
your father?"
9 "Heaven forbid!" said Jonathan. "If I learn that my father intends
that evil should come upon you . . . [?] . . . I shall inform you!"
10 Then David asked [him], "Who will tell me if your father answers you harshly?"

Jonathan's Plea for His Family

11 "Come!" Jonathan told David. "Let us go out into the field!"
And when they had gone out into the field together, 12 [he] said to
David, "Yahweh, god of Israel, is witness that I shall sound out my

father at about this time tomorrow as to whether he is well disposed
toward David or not. Then I shall send word to you in the field.
13 May God do thus to Jonathan and thus again, but if my father
wishes to bring evil against you, I will reveal it to you and send you
away, so that you may go safely! And may Yahweh be with you as he
was with my father! 14 If I remain alive, deal loyally with me; but if I
die, 15 never cut off your loyalty from my house. And when Yahweh
cuts off each of the enemies of David from upon the face of the earth,
if 16 the name of Jonathan is cut off from the house of David, then
may Yahweh call David to account!" 17 So again Jonathan swore to
David out of his love for him, for he loved him as he loved himself.

Jonathan's Plan

18 "Tomorrow is the New Moon," said Jonathan, "and you will be
missed when your place is vacant. 19 But on the third day you will be
long gone; then come to the place where you hid on the day of the
deed and wait beside that mound. 20 As for me, on the third day I
shall shoot an arrow from the side [of the mound] aiming toward a
target. 21 When I send the servant to go and find the arrow, if I say to
[him], 'The arrow is on the near side of you! Fetch it!' come, for
you will be safe! As Yahweh lives, there will be nothing wrong! 22 But
if I say to the lad, 'The arrow is on the far side of you!' go, for Yahweh will have sent you away! 23 And as for the matter of which you
and I have spoken, Yahweh will be a witness between you and me
forever!" 24 So David hid in the field.

The Feast of the New Moon

At the time of the New Moon the king sat down at the table to eat.
25 He sat at his seat as usual, against the wall. Jonathan sat opposite
him, and Abiner was at Saul's side. David's place was vacant; 26 yet
Saul said nothing that day, for he thought, "By some mischance he is
not clean."

27 But on the day after the New Moon—the second day—when
David's place was [still] empty, Saul said to Jonathan, his son, "Why
has the son of Jesse not come to the table either yesterday or today?"

28 "David asked my permission [to go] to Bethlehem," replied
Jonathan to Saul. 29 "He said, 'Let me go, for we are having a clan

sacrifice in the city, and as for me, my brothers have commanded my
presence. Now if I have your favor, let me be free to go and see my
brothers!' It is for this reason that he has not come to the king's
table."

30 Then Saul's anger was kindled against Jonathan. "You son of a
rebellious servant girl!" he said to him. "Do I not know that to your
own disgrace and to the disgrace of your mother's nakedness you are
in league with the son of Jesse? 31 For as long as the son of Jesse is
alive upon the earth, you will not establish your kingship! Now then,
have him brought to me, for he is a dead man!"

32 "Why should he be killed?" replied Jonathan to Saul. "What has
he done?" 33 But when Saul raised his spear against him to strike
him, [he] realized that his father was so intent upon evil that he
would kill David, 34 and [he] sprang up from the table in a burning
rage and would eat no food on the second day of the New Moon, because his father had humiliated him so.

The Appointment

35 In the morning Jonathan went out into the field with a small lad
for the appointment with David. 36 He said to the lad, "Run find the
arrow that I am going to shoot!" And as the lad ran, he shot the
arrow, causing it to fly toward the city. 37 When the lad came to
the spot where Jonathan had shot the arrow, Jonathan called after
the youth to say, "The arrow is on the far side of you, is it not?"
38 And again he called after the lad, "Hurry! Be quick! Do not stand
still!" So Jonathan's lad picked up the arrow and brought it to his
master. 39 (Now the lad knew nothing; only Jonathan and David
knew what was meant.)

40 Then Jonathan gave his weapons to his lad and told him to return to the city. 41 When [he] had gone, David arose from beside the
mound, fell on his face, and did obeisance three times. Then they
kissed each other and wept over each other [. . . ? . . .], 42 and
Jonathan said, "Go in peace! For we two have sworn in Yahweh's
name: 'Yahweh will be between me and you and between my seed
and your seed forever!' "

21 1 Then David departed, and Jonathan returned to the city.

TEXTUAL NOTES

20 1. *and came before Jonathan . . . he said* Following the word order of LXX^{BL}, lit. "and came before Jonathan and said." MT: "and came and said before Jonathan."

2. [*Jonathan*] *said* We read *wy'mr,* "he said," with MT against Syr., LXX, "*Jonathan* said"; but it is necessary to supply the name in translation for clarity.

My father does Reading *l' y'śh 'by* with MT *qĕrê* and LXX. MT *kĕtîb* has *lw 'śh 'by*, etc., "If my father had done. . . ."

nothing great or small So MT: *dbr gdwl 'w dbr qṭn.* LXX^{B} reflects *dbr qṭn* (retained by Smith as *lectio brevior*), the result of a simple haplography, a scribe's eye having skipped from the first *dbr* to the second.

3. *But in reply David said* Reading *wyšb* (*wayyāšeb*) *dwd wy'mr,* lit. "But David made return and said" (Wellhausen; cf. LXX *kai apekrithē daueid . . . kai eipen*). MT *wyšb' 'wd dwd,* "and David swore again," anticipates the latter part of the verse. As stressed by Wellhausen, David has not yet sworn once; *'wd* probably arose from a dittography of *dwd,* which through further corruption gave rise to the new verb. (LXX inserts "to Jonathan," and Syr. "to him," both of which may be deleted with MT.)

lest he take counsel [*with David*] MT has *pn y'ṣb,* "lest he (Jonathan) be grieved"; but David would not credit Saul with being concerned with his son's feelings at this point. LXX^{B} preserves the original reading in *mē ou boulētai,* reflecting *pn yw'ṣ,* "lest he take counsel." The readings of LXX^{L}, OL, Syr., all of which state approximately that "(Jonathan must not know about this), lest *he tell David,*" support the reading of LXX^{B}.

he has sworn a pact Difficult. MT reads *ky kpś',* and those critics who insist upon making sense of the MT have succeeded here by positing a noun *peśa',* "step," and reading, "(it is) only about a step (between me and death)!" (cf. Driver, et al.). But LXX reflects a more intelligible reading. LXX^{B} has *hoti kathōs eipon empeplēstai,* "because, as I have said, he is sated," apparently reflecting *ky k'šr 'mrty nśb';* but the last word can be read instead as *nšb'*—hence "as I have said, he has sworn (an oath). . . ." LXX^{L} is better still; it omits *k'šr 'mrty,* which may have arisen by expansion. Thus read *ky nšb'* with LXX^{L}.

between me and Death So MT, LXX^{BL}. LXX^{A}, OL, Syr.: "between me and *your father.*"

4. *What do you desire?* Reading *mh t'wh npšk,* lit. "What does your soul desire?" on the basis of LXX *ti epithymei hē psychē sou,* in preference to MT *mh t'mr npšk,* "What does your soul *say?*"

5. *and I am supposed to take my place* So MT, LXX^{L}: *w'nky yšb 'šb.* LXX^{B} reflects *w'nky l' 'šb,* "and I shall *not* take my place. . . ." Contrast Wellhausen, Driver.

at dinner That is, *l'kwl,* "to eat." MT (cf. OL) has *'m hmlk l'kwl,* "to eat *with the king.*" Omit "with the king" with LXX[BL].

until evening So LXX[BL]. MT: "until *the third* evening," anticipating v 35.

7. *but if he becomes angry* So MT: *w'm ḥrh yḥrh lw.* LXX *kai ean sklērōs apokrithē soi* = *w'm qšh y'nk,* "but if he answers you harshly," anticipates v 10 below.

8. *with your servant* Reading *'m 'bdk* with LXX, Syr., Targ. MT has *'l 'bdk, "upon* your servant."

in me So MT. LXX: "in *your servant.*"

9. Before the concluding clause (*'gyd lk,* "I shall inform you") something has been lost. MT has *wĕlō' 'ōtāh,* thus, "and I shall *not* [read *lū'*, "surely"?] inform you of *it.*" LXX has *kai ean mē ē eis tas poleis sou egō apangelō soi* (= *wl' 'l 'ryk 'nky 'gyd lk,* "and if he is/he is not [*l'* being rendered two ways in LXX] . . . to your cities, I myself shall inform you"?). None of the efforts to make sense of all this has proved convincing; see the commentaries.

10. *if* Reading *'m* with LXX in preference to MT *'w mh,* "or what."

11. *Let us go out* So MT, LXX[L]. LXX[B]: *kai mene,* "And tarry. . . ."

12. *Yahweh, god of Israel, is witness* MT has only *yhwh 'lhy yśr'l,* "Yahweh, god of Israel," but as Smith points out, this is preceded in Syr. by *nshd,* "is witness," evidently reflecting *'d,* which may have fallen out of MT after *dwd,* "David," and LXX *oiden* = *yd',* "knows," though it now *follows* the divine name, could represent a corruption of the same original. This case is strengthened by the evidence of Josephus (*Ant.* 6.230), whose long paraphrase suggests that his text reflected both *'d* and *yd'* in conflation. Thus we read *'d yhwh 'lhy yśr'l.* By contrast Stoebe, who finds MT intelligible as it stands ("By Yahweh, the god of Israel . . ."), argues for preferring it as *lectio brevior.*

tomorrow MT (cf. LXX) adds *hšlšyt,* "the third (day)," in anticipation of the actual events in vv 24b*ff*. Cf. the *Textual Note* to "until evening" at v 5.

or not. Then So MT: *wl' 'z* (though in the present arrangement of the accents *wl'* is grouped with the following words rather than the preceding). LXX[B] *kai ou mē* is obscure (= *wl' 'l?*), and LXX[L] seems to omit everything between "David" and "I shall send."

in the field So LXX. MT has instead *wglyty 't 'znk,* "and I shall reveal it to you," in anticipation of the following verse.

13. *God* So LXX. MT, OL: "Yahweh."

if my father wishes to bring evil against you We restore *yyṭb 'l 'by lhby' 't hr'h 'lyk,* lit. "(if) it seems good to my father to bring evil upon you." All witnesses are defective. MT has *yyṭb 'l 'by 't hr'h 'lyk,* "(if) it seems good to my father . . . evil upon you," and we must assume that *lhby'* was lost because of its similarity to *'l 'by.* LXX has *anoisō ta kaka epi se* = *'by'(?) 't hr'h 'lyk,* "(that) I should bring evil upon you," and the cause of its corruption is not apparent.

14-15. *If . . . but if . . . if* MT has *wĕlō' . . . wĕlō' . . . wĕlō',* which might be retained and repointed *wĕlū' . . . wĕlū' . . . wĕlū'* (deleting *'im* following the first *wĕlū'*), as preferred by most critics (so LXX, Syr., Vulg.) Another *l',* which appears in MT in the second clause of v 14 (". . . and you do *not* deal loyally with me . . ."), may be omitted with LXX[B].

14. *deal loyally* Reading *wʿśh . . . ḥsd,* lit. "do loyalty," with LXX^B^. MT, LXX^AL^ have *ḥsd yhwh,* "the loyalty *of Yahweh."*

but if I die So LXX (= *wl'* [see above] *mwt 'mwt*). MT (*wl' 'mwt*) understands the clause as apodosis to the preceding (". . . and then I shall not die").

16. *the name of Jonathan is cut off from* Reading *ykrt* (i.e. *yikkārēt;* cf. LXX^AL^ *exarthēnai, exarthēsetai,* of which LXX^B^ *heurethēnai,* "to be found," is probably an inner-Greek corruption) *šm yhwntn mʿm byt dwd* with LXX. MT *wykrt yhwntn ʿm byt dwd,* "and Jonathan cut (a covenant) with the house of David," is clearly inferior.

then may Yahweh call David to account That is, *wbqš yhwh myd dwd,* lit. "then may Yahweh seek (it) from the hand of David." In fact the witnesses reflect ". . . from the hand *of the enemies* of David" (so MT; LXX^B^ has lost *ek cheiros,* "from the hand," through an inner-Greek haplography caused by the similarity of the sequence to the following *echthrōn,* "of the enemies"), but *'yby,* "enemies," is probably an addition "inserted to avoid an imprecation on David" (Smith; cf. Dhorme).

17. *So again Jonathan swore to David* So LXX^L(cf. B)^. MT: "So again Jonathan *caused David to swear. . . ."* Cf. the first *Textual Note* at v 3 above. As Wellhausen has explained, the reference here is to Jonathan's oath in vv 12-13.

out of his love for him So MT (cf. LXX^AL^): *b'hbtw 'tw,* which has fallen out of LXX^B^ before the following clause (MT: *ky 'hbt npšw 'hbw*), which also appears somewhat differently in LXX.

18. *said Jonathan* MT, LXX^AL^ add "to him." Omit with LXX^B^.

19. *But on the third day you will be long gone* Reading *wšlšt trd m'd* with the consonantal text of MT. MT interprets this as *wĕšillaštā tērēd mĕ'ōd,* lit. "And you will do for the third time, you will go down exceedingly," that is, "And you will go down (?) for a third time exceedingly." LXX (cf. Syr., Targ.) corroborates MT's interpretation of *wšlšt* as a verb, but reflects *tpqd,* "you will be missed," in place of the difficult *trd m'd,* which must be original (*tpqd* having arisen under the influence of v 18). We interpret *wšlšt* as *wišlīšit* (cf. *haššĕlīšit* in MT, vv 5, 12), "and a third," that is, "on the third day (of the festival)." The expression *trd m'd* must be understood in light of Judg 19:11, where *hayyôm rad* (read *rād*) *mĕ'ōd* must mean, "the day has wandered exceedingly," that is, "the day was long gone," as the context shows. The verb *rwd* means "wander, go astray, be absent" (cf. Jer 2:31, "Why do my people say, 'We shall stay away [*radnû*]! We shall not come again to you!' "). Thus here we read *tarūd mĕ'ōd,* "you will be long gone." The point is that on the third day of the festival David will be regarded as long gone and not looked for, in contrast to the situation that will prevail on the first day as described in the previous verse. Thus it will be safe for him to return in secret.

the place So MT, LXX^L^. LXX^B^: "your place."

beside that mound So LXX^B(cf. A)^: *para to ergab ekeino* = *'ṣl h'rgb hl'z,* for which MT has *'ṣl h'bn h'lz,* "beside the (*'lz?*) stone" (cf. LXX^L^, Syr.).

20. *As for me, on the third day I shall shoot an arrow from the side* [*of the mound*] MT has *w'ny šlšt hḥṣym ṣdh 'wrh,* "And as for me, I shall shoot

three arrows to (?) the side. . . ." But there is no reason for Jonathan to mention *three* arrows at this point, and in fact there is no mention of such a number in vv 35*ff*. LXX treats the word as a verb: *trisseusō*, as if *'šlš*—thus, "I shall shoot a third time"(?). Wellhausen's proposal to render the *Vorlage* of LXX (*'šlš . . . 'wrh*) as "I shall shoot on the third day," has received wide acceptance because it fits the story. But it is difficult to see how the verb *šlš* could mean "do something on the third day." We must understand *šlšt* as *šĕlīšīt*, "on the third day" (see the first *Textual Note* to v 19). MT *hḥṣym ṣdh* shows a misdivision of words caused by the use of the noun *ḥṣy*, "arrow," which is much less common than *ḥṣ*, "arrow." We read *hḥṣy mṣdh* (*miṣṣaddô*), lit. "a certain arrow from its (viz. the mound's) side"; the *-h* of *mṣdh* might be an archaic *mater* for *-ô*, or it may have arisen by attraction to the feminine antecedent *h'bn*, which has replaced *h'rgb* in MT (thus *-h* = *-āh*). LXX omits *ṣdh* altogether, having lost it, perhaps, before *'wrh*.

aiming Reading *lšlḥ*, lit. "to send (it)." Cf. LXX. MT adds *ly*, "for myself."

21. *the arrow* (*bis*) So LXX[BAL], OL (= *hḥṣy*). MT "the arrows" is in conformity with the (spurious) "three arrows" of v 20 in MT; see above.

there will be nothing wrong So MT: *w'yn dbr*, lit. "and there will be nothing." LXX[L]: "and there is no *evil* (*poneros*) thing"; LXX[B] (curiously): "and there is no thing *of Yahweh* (word of Yahweh?)."

22. *The arrow* See the *Textual Note* to v 21.

23. *a witness . . . forever* Reading *'d 'd 'wlm* on the basis of LXX *martys . . . heōs aiōnos* and Targ. *shyd 'd 'lm'*. MT *'d 'wlm*, "forever," has lost one *'d* by haplography. See Finkelstein, "Ignored Haplography."

24. *at the table* So LXX, 4QSam[b]: *'l hšlḥn*. MT has *'l* (*qĕrê: 'el*) *hlḥm*, "to the meal" (cf. v 27).

25. *his seat . . . against the wall* Reading *'l mwšbw . . . 'l hqyr* with LXX[L]. LXX[B], MT: *'l mwšbw . . . 'l* (MT *'l*) *mwšb hqyr*, "his seat . . . at his wall seat."

Jonathan sat opposite Reading *wyqdm yhwntn*, lit. "and Jonathan was in front," on the basis of LXX *kai proephthasen ton iōnathan* (as if, "and he [Saul] arrived before Jonathan"). MT has *wyqm yhwntn*, "and Jonathan arose."

26. *By some mischance he is not clean* Reading *mqrh hw' blty ṭhwr*, which in MT (cf. the versions) is conflated with a second, less distinctive reading (viz. *mqrh hw' l' ṭhwr*) identical in meaning to the first. Thus MT: *mqrh hw' blty ṭhwr hw' ky l' ṭhwr*. See S. Talmon, "Double Readings in the Massoretic Text," in *Textus* 1 (Jerusalem: Magnes, 1960) 173-174.

27. *to the table* So LXX, 4QSam[b]. MT: *'l hlḥm*, "to the meal." Cf. the *Textual Note* to v 24 above.

28. [*to go*] The infinitive is lacking in MT and Syr. The other versions supply it in various forms and at various points in the sentence, suggesting that the situation in MT is primitive. Perhaps, then, Stoebe and others are correct in regarding it as stylistically expendable.

to Bethlehem LXX adds "his city." Omit with MT.

29. *and as for me . . . my presence* Reading *w'ny ṣww ly 'ḥy* with 4QSam[b]

(cf. LXX). MT has *whw' ṣwh ly 'ḥy,* "and he, my brother, has commanded my presence"; but *'ḥy* is surely plural. F. M. Cross suggests (personal communication) that the reading *whw',* "and he," arose by metathesis of *w'ny,* "and as for me," and corruption of *ny* to *h* (a confusion most likely to have occurred in scripts of the fourth and third centuries B.C.)—thus, *w'ny* > *wh'* > *whw'*.

30. *Saul's anger was kindled* So MT. LXX, 4QSam^b add "greatly" (*sphodra, m'd*).

You son of a rebellious servant girl! Reading *ben na'arat hammardût,* lit. "Son of a young woman of rebellion!" with LXX, which, however, misinterprets *hmrdwt* as a plural participle and therefore *n'rt* as plural also—thus, "Son of rebelling young women!"; similarly 4QSam^b has [*bn*] *n'rwt mrdt,* "Son of rebelling young women!" or "Son of young women of rebellion!" MT: *bn n'wt hmrdwt,* "Son of a perverse woman (as if *n'wt* = *Nip'al* participle, feminine singular of *'wh*) of rebelliousness!"; see further Driver.

you are in league Reading *ḥbr 'th* with LXX (*metochos . . . su*), against MT *bḥr 'th,* "you choose. . . ."

31. *you will not establish your kingship* LXX *ouch hetoimasthēsetai hē basileia sou* reflects *l' tkn mlkwtk* with the verb interpreted as *tikkôn*—thus, "Your kingship will not be secure." But Jonathan as yet has no kingship, and we should vocalize the verb as *tākîn,* "you will establish." Thus 4QSam^b is correct in adding the *'t* particle: *l' tkn 't mmlkt.* This reading was altered in MT to *l' tkwn 'th wmlkwtk,* "you and your kingship will not be secure," an interpretation similar to that of LXX.

him . . . to me So MT: *'tw 'ly.* LXX *ton neanian* = *h'lm,* "the youth" (". . . have *the youth* brought . . .").

32. *to Saul* So LXX^BL. MT, LXX^A, Syr. add, "his father and said to him . . ."; 4QSam^b adds, "his father and said. . . ."

33. *raised* MT has *wyṭl,* vocalized *wayyāṭel,* "but (Saul) *hurled.*" Read instead *wayyiṭṭōl,* "but (Saul) took up, raised," with LXX (*kai epēren*). Cf. 18:11 (§ XXIV-B).

against him So MT. LXX: "against Jonathan."

to strike him So MT: *lhktw.* LXX *tou thanatōsai auton* reflects *lhmytw,* "to kill him," in anticipation of the same infinitive later in the verse.

that his father . . . would kill David The expression is the same as in vv 7, 9: *klth hr'h m'm* [*š'wl*], lit. "evil was determined by Saul," that is, "Saul was intent upon evil." Here we read with LXX: *ky klth hr'h hhy' m'm 'byw lhmyt 't dwd,* lit. "that the aforesaid evil was determined by his father even to the point of killing David." MT for *klth hr'h hhy'* has only a remnant, *klh hy',* which will yield no translation. Wellhausen's (unnecessarily) simpler solution (read *klth hy',* thus "that his father was determined to kill David") has enjoyed the support of most subsequent critics but lacks the corroboration of any ancient witness.

34. *sprang up* MT has simply *wyqm,* "arose," but 4QSam^b *wypḥz* (= LXX *anepēdēsen*) is to be preferred as *lectio difficilior.* The reading of MT is a case of the substitution of a familiar word for one that is rare (and in this case much more graphic, since *pḥz* carries a connotation of impudence or arro-

gance, as the evidence of Biblical and Postbiblical [Jastrow, 1152] Hebrew and of cognate Aramaic terms shows). See also the third *Textual Note* to 25:9.

because his father had humiliated him so This is preceded in MT by another clause (viz. *ky nʿṣb ʾl dwd,* "for he was grieved over David"), which changes the sense to make David the object of Saul's vituperation ("for he was grieved over David that his father had so humiliated him [David]"). The clause can be omitted as expansive with LXX. Note that LXX itself shows some corruption in the remaining clause under the influence of *klth,* etc., in the last verse (see above). Thus LXX^{B} has *hoti synetelesen ep' autou ho patēr autou,* reflecting *ky klh ʿlyw ʾbyw,* which can be translated only with difficulty ("because his father had plotted [i.e. resolved himself] against him"?), unless it might mean "because his father had finished (i.e. exterminated) him" (in view of which LXX^{L} seems to paraphrase: *hoti ebouleusato ho patēr autou syntelesai auton,* "because his father wanted to finish him off"). In any case MT is clearly superior: *ky hklmw ʾbyw,* "because his father had humiliated/insulted him (Jonathan)" (cf. Saul's speech in vv 30,31).

35. *for the appointment* Reading *lmwʿd* with MT, LXX (*eis to martyrion*), etc. In LXX this is preceded by *kathōs etaxato,* which suggests *kʾšr yʿd,* "as (David) had arranged . . ." but this may be a second rendering of *lmwʿd* (Budde, Stoebe).

36. *find* MT *mṣʾ* (so LXX, which adds *moi* = *lî,* "for me"; cf. v 21a). 4Sam^{b} has *qḥ,* "fetch" (cf. LXX^{L}, OL, Syr. in v 21a).

the arrow (1) Here as elsewhere reading *hḥṣy* for MT *hḥṣym.* Cf. the *Textual Notes* to vv 20,21 above.

And So LXX, Vulg., Targ. Omitted in MT.

causing it to fly toward the city So 4QSam^{b}: [*lhʿbyrh*] *hʿyrh.* In all other witnesses *hʿyrh* was lost by haplography caused by *homoioteleuton,* and *lhʿbyrh* (in the orthography of MT, *lhʿbyrw*) remains alone.

37. *after the youth* So LXX: *opisō tou neaniou* = *ʾḥry hʿlm.* MT *ʾḥry hnʿr,* "after *the lad,*" conforms to the usage elsewhere.

The arrow is on the far side of you, is it not? That is, MT *hlwʾ hḥṣy mmk whlʾh,* "Is not the arrow beyond you?" For *hlwʾ,* "Is not . . . ?" LXX has *ekei,* perhaps reflecting *hlʾh,* etc.—thus, "Farther on! The arrow is on the far side of you!"

38. *the lad* So MT (*hnʿr*). LXX = *nʿrw, "his* lad," 4QSam^{b}: *ʿlmh,* "his *youth.*"

the arrow So MT (*kĕtîb*). MT (*qĕrê*), LXX: "the arrows."

and brought it Revocalizing MT *wayyābōʾ* ("and he came") as *wayyābēʾ* with LXX^{AL}. The corresponding Greek word was omitted altogether in LXX^{B} but restored in the margin by later scribes.

39. *knew what was meant* That is, *ydʿw ʾt hdbr,* lit. "knew the thing." These words are unaccountably omitted from LXX^{B}, but they seem necessary to the sense.

40. *return* Here MT adds *hbyʾ,* "(and) take (them)" and LXX$^{B(\text{cf. A})}$ *eiselthe* = *bʾ,* "enter." Omit with LXX^{L} (Smith).

41. *the mound* So LXX (= *hʾrgb*); cf. the *Textual Note* to "beside that mound" at v 19 above. MT: *hngb,* "the Southland." Syr. = *ʾbn,* "a stone."

on his face So LXX^{BL}. MT adds "on the ground."

At the end of the verse MT has *'d dwd hgdyl,* "until David magnified (?)." The translation of LXX (*heōs synteleias megalēs,* probably reflecting *'d hgrl hgdl,* thus with two attempts to represent *hgdl*) suggests that *dwd* should be deleted (cf. Wellhausen). But no easy translation of what remains emerges. Perhaps the sense is *'d hgdyl lbkwt,* "unto weeping greatly," elliptically expressed (so BDB).

42. *and Jonathan said* So LXX^{B}. MT (cf. LXX^{AL}) adds "to David."

we two So 4QSam^{b} (cf. LXX): [*'nḥnw*] *šnynw.* MT reverses the order: *šnynw 'nḥnw,* "The two of us, we. . . ."

Yahweh will be LXX adds *martys* = *'d,* "witness." Omit with MT, Syr.

and between my seed and your seed So MT: *wbyn zr'y wbyn zr'k.* The *Vorlage* of LXX has lost *zr'y wbyn* by haplography caused by *homoioarkton.*

21 1. *David* So LXX and 4QSam^{b}. Though omitted in MT the name should probably be restored, since the verse is not simply ambiguous without it (as often happens) but quite unintelligible.

NOTES

20 3. *he has sworn a pact between me and Death.* Hebrew *kî nišba' bênî ûbên hammāwet* (see the *Textual Note*). If the reading is correct, the meaning must be that Saul has sworn to take David's life, though no parallel for such an expression exists in Biblical Hebrew (Judah's "treaty with Death" [*bĕrît 'et-hammāwet*] in Isa 28:15,18 is expected [by Judah] to be beneficial). Death is here personified as David's partner in a sworn agreement, a kind of grim parody of the covenant between David and Jonathan mentioned below (v 8).

5. *the New Moon.* In the liturgical calendar of ancient Israel the first day of the lunar month (*ḥōdeš,* "new moon") was a day of rest (cf. Amos 8:5) and feasting. Special sacrifices were prescribed (Num 28:11-15), for which the king in the monarchical period, like the "prince" in Ezekiel's restoration vision (Ezek 45:17), seems to have had particular responsibility. The details of our story suggest that the Feast of the New Moon continued at least a second and a third day.

6. *a seasonal sacrifice.* Hebrew *zebaḥ hayyāmîm;* cf. the NOTE at 1:21.

7. *he intends evil.* Hebrew *kālĕtâ hārā'â mē'immô,* lit. "evil is determined from him." The expression occurs only here in vv 7,9, and 33, in 25:17, and in Esther 7:7. For "evil" as the unfavorable treatment of a partner in a formal relationship, see the NOTE at 24:10. Cf. also 20:13; 23:9; 25:26.

8. David implores Jonathan to "deal loyally," that is, to act in accordance with *ḥesed* (fidelity to an agreement, as defined in the NOTE at 15:6). The basis for the loyalty is a "covenant of Yahweh" into which Jonathan has brought David. Our narrator has not mentioned this sacred agreement before, but it was an important part of the tradition and described in 18:1-5, part

of the additions to the story of David's early days at court (see § XXIV-B).

11-17. Jonathan's plea for his family is probably a secondary interpolation in the narrative (so also vv 23 and 40-42). The answer to David's question in v 10 is found in Jonathan's long speech that begins in v 18. Verses 11-17, with their emphasis on David's loyal treatment of Jonathan's descendants, are editorial anticipation of the Mephibosheth episode in II Samuel 9. See further the COMMENT.

13. On the oath formula in this verse see the NOTES at 3:17 and 14:44.

And may Yahweh be with you. This central theme (NOTE at 16:18) is expressed here on the lips of the eldest son of Saul and (evidently) the heir to the kingship of Israel, thus giving new clarity to the inevitability of David's succession to the throne. Jonathan wishes that Yahweh might be with David as he was with Saul, that is, that the divine favor that brought Saul to power might now be with David. This and what follows shows that Jonathan is quite content to acknowledge what his father still refuses to accept (cf. v 31 and the NOTE there), viz. that Saul will establish no dynasty and that instead Yahweh is going to replace him with "a man of his own choosing" (cf. 13:13-14). Note, however, that this is part of the additions to the story; the older narrative is nowhere this explicit. See the COMMENT.

14,15. *deal loyally . . . your loyalty.* Hebrew *ta'ăśeh ḥesed . . . ḥasdĕkā;* cf. the NOTE at v 8. In the interpolation (see the NOTE on 11-17 above) the relationship between Jonathan and David is reversed: it is the king's son who invokes the condescending loyalty of the fugitive servant, whom he acknowledges to be the future king; in v 8 it was David who implored Jonathan to "do *ḥesed*." Jonathan's appeal is to "the covenant of Yahweh" (v 8) that exists between him and David, and his hope is for treatment in accordance with that covenant, i.e., for *ḥesed.* As already noted, this anticipates II Samuel 9, where the responsibility laid on David here is discharged by the "loyalty" (*ḥesed;* see vv 1,3,7) shown there to Mephibosheth.

17. Jonathan's deep affection for David is a part of the close relationship that has developed between the two young men; also it is surely a sign of the irresistible charm of the man who has Yahweh's favor. J. A. Thompson has suggested further that the use of the verb *'āhēb,* "love," here and elsewhere is deliberately ambiguous, pointing at once to the personal aspect of the relationship and, at another level, to a political aspect at the same time (see the NOTE at 16:21). In other words the fact that Jonathan swore to David "out of his love for him" (*bĕ'ahăbātô 'ōtô*) hints of a political loyalty to David on Jonathan's part. To the statement that Jonathan "loved him as he loved himself" (*'ahăbat napšô 'ăhēbô*), compare the command of loyalty given to the future vassals of the Assyrian king Ashurbanipal: *ki-i nap-šat-ku-nu la tar-'a-ma-ni,* "You must love (him) as yourselves!" (cited by W. L. Moran, "The Ancient Near Eastern Background of the Love of God in Deuteronomy," *CBQ* 25 [1963] 80; M. Fishbane, "The Treaty Background of Amos 1:11 and Related Matters," *JBL* 89 [1970] 314). See also 18:1,3 (§ XXIV-B).

19. *on the day of the deed.* Hebrew *bĕyôm hamma'ăśeh,* evidently a reference to the time David hid in a "secret place" (19:2) while Jonathan spoke to

Saul on his behalf; but what exactly the "deed" here referred to was is unclear. Perhaps, since *ma'ăśeh* often comes close to meaning "crime, wrongdoing" (Gen 44:15; Neh 6:14; etc.), the reference is to Saul's announcement of his desire to have David's life (19:11).

23. The verse is secondary, having been inserted along with Jonathan's plea for his family, to which it refers (cf. the NOTE on 11-17 above).

26. *"By some mischance he is not clean."* Since the Feast of the New Moon is an official act of the cult (NOTE at v 5), the participants are required to be pure or "clean" (*ṭāhôr*). Ritual uncleanness might arise from any number of accidents in daily living—various bodily discharges (including emissions of semen), contact with the carcass of an animal, etc. (see the laws in Leviticus 11-15)—and a period of isolation and certain cleansing procedures would be necessary before the contaminated person could participate in a cultic ceremony. Saul assumes that something of this kind has kept David away from the feast.

30. *"You son of a rebellious servant girl!"* Cf. Judith 16:12 (Wellhausen). This insult is directed toward Jonathan, not his mother. "Son of" in such a case means "member of the class of," viz. in this instance, of people who forsake those to whom they properly owe allegiance.

your mother's nakedness. "Nakedness" (*'erwâ*) most often refers euphemistically to genitals. Jonathan, says Saul, has disgraced his mother's genitals, whence he came forth.

31. Saul betrays his own awareness of David's destiny. Jonathan's behavior, moreover, is incomprehensible to him: David stands in the way of the establishment of his (Jonathan's) kingship, and yet Jonathan is "in league" with him. See further the COMMENT.

36. *And as the lad ran, he shot the arrow.* Hebrew *hanna'ar rāṣ wĕhû' yārâ haḥēṣî*, a sequence of perfect verbs suggesting rapid succession: "As soon as the lad began to run, he shot the arrow. . . ." See the first NOTE at 9:5.

40-42. This is further expansion from the author of vv 11-17,23, renewing the theme of David's pledge to Jonathan and his descendants (42b). It has been clear all along that if Jonathan signaled bad news, David was to flee immediately (v 22). Indeed, if it was going to be possible for the two men to meet and talk as they do here, there would have been no need for the elaborately planned signals in the first place!

42. *For.* Hebrew *'ăšer*, on this use of which see the NOTE at 15:15.

COMMENT

After the narrow escape through his bedroom window David seeks out Jonathan, whose intervention reconciled him to Saul on a previous occasion (18:28-29a; 19:1-7); but this time Jonathan has heard nothing of his father's hostility and refuses to believe it. He is, however, as willing as ever to do what he can for David, and he agrees to David's request that he sound Saul out at the Feast of the New Moon, which begins on the following day. David is to hide and Jonathan—this part is his own contribution to the scheme—will signal him in a sham archery session as soon as he learns his father's mind. David's worst fear proves true: Saul avows his determination to have David's life and accuses Jonathan of conspiracy (v 30). The signal for bad news is given (v 37, cf. 22), and David departs, never to return to Saul's service.

In its present form this story serves as a vehicle for expressing a theme of little importance here but of considerable interest in the larger narrative in which our complex of stories about David's rise to power has been joined to those concerned with his reign as king. In II Samuel 9 we learn how Jonathan's lame son Mephibosheth, who has escaped the Gibeonite's massacre of the descendants of Saul (cf. II Sam 21:1-6,8-14, which is chronologically prior to II Samuel 9; see the commentaries), comes to live with David, who receives him warmly, we are told, because he wants to "deal loyally with him for Jonathan's sake" (II Sam 9:1). The language is directly reminiscent of that in vv 14-15a of the present passage, which may be said to anticipate the Mephibosheth incident editorially. As explained in the NOTES, vv 11-17 interrupt the flow of our narrative and seem to have been inserted, along with vv 23,40-42, by the hand that joined the history of David's rise to the subsequent material. The welfare of Mephibosheth was of special interest, since it was through him alone that the line of Saul was preserved and from him and his son Mica (II Sam 9:12) an important Israelite family was descended (cf. I Chron 8:35-40; 9:41-44). It was the purpose of the author of these verses, who was probably the Josianic historian himself (cf. the COMMENT on § XXIV-A and see LITERARY HISTORY in the Introduction, esp. pp 16-17), to show that the survival of the house of Saul was the direct consequence of an act of "loyalty" (*ḥesed*) by David, stemming from his old attachment to Jonathan.

But if, as we have implied, the theme of David's future loyalty to Jonathan's family was not an original part of the present story, what were the chief ideas the story carried in its unexpanded form? That is, what contribution did it make to the old narrative of David's rise to power? A number of things may be listed in answer to these questions. First of all, we should note that the previously developed theme of the attachment of Saul's own household to David is brought to maturity here as the king's son is presented as the agent of David's preservation. Seen in connection with the Michal episode and his own previous intervention on David's behalf, Jonathan's alignment with David against Saul here shows that the spontaneous allegiance David commands is stronger than the filial loyalty of Saul's own children; seen in connection with the Nob incident that follows, it shows how the leading citizens of Saul's own kingdom are involved in David's escape. To this first theme a second is related. David does not act alone in his decision not to return to Gibeah; rather he does so with the assistance and counsel of Jonathan. Moreover he does not go willingly but is forced to flee by Saul's animosity. This episode, in other words, falsifies any charge that David left Saul's service out of disloyalty or a desire for personal gain; see "The History of David's Rise" in the Introduction (LITERARY HISTORY).

Yet another theme to be mentioned in this context is that of Saul's fear of David, an old theme which takes on a new dimension here. Verse 31 shows that Saul is now aware not only that his own position is threatened by David's popularity but also that Jonathan's is; that is, Saul now knows that David stands in the way of his establishment of a dynasty. The implication of this awareness is important: it will not suffice for Saul to drive David away where he cannot be a rival to the throne during Saul's own lifetime, for as long as David is alive the danger will continue to exist that he might become king when Saul dies. This sets up the pattern of the stories that follow. David has left Gibeah, but his troubles with Saul are not at an end. The king believes he must pursue him and will do so relentlessly and obsessively. And in this unceasing pursuit a number of other lives will become inextricably involved, for better or, as we are about to see, for worse.

XXXI. DAVID AND THE PRIEST OF NOB
(21:2-10)

21 2 David went to Ahimelech, the priest, at Nob, and Ahimelech
came trembling out to meet [him]. "Why have you come alone?" he
said. "There is no one with you."
3 David said to the priest, "The king charged me with an errand
and said to me, 'Let no one know of the errand upon which I am
sending you, the one with which I have charged you.' So I have made
an appointment with [my] servants for a certain place. 4 Now then,
there are five loaves of bread in your possession. Give me whatever
can be found!"
5 "There is no common bread in my possession," said the priest in
reply to David. "There is only holy bread. If [your] servants have
kept themselves from women, you may eat of it."
6 "We have abstained from women!" David told him in reply. "In
the past whenever I have marched out, each of [my] servants has
been consecrated, even if it was an ordinary journey. How much more
so today when [our journey] is consecrated at arms!" 7 So the priest
gave him the holy [bread], for there was no bread there except the
Bread of the Presence that had been removed from before Yahweh to
be replaced with hot bread at the time it was taken away.
8 Now one of Saul's servants was there that day, detained before
Yahweh. His name was Doeg the Edomite, the chief of Saul's runners.

The Sword of Goliath

9 Then David said to Ahimelech, "Is there a spear or sword here in
your possession? I brought neither my sword nor my armor with me,
for the king's business was urgent."
10 "The sword of Goliath, the Philistine you slew in the Valley of
the Terebinth, is behind an ephod," said the priest. "If you want to
take that one, take it! For there is no other but it here."
"There is none like it!" said David. "Give it to me!"

TEXTUAL NOTES

21 2. *Ahimelech* So MT, LXX[L] (*'ḥymlk*). LXX[B] = *'bymlk*, "Abimelech."

3. *to the priest* So LXX[B], 4QSam[b]. MT (cf. LXX[AL]): "to Ahimelech the priest."

an errand So MT. LXX adds "today."

Let no one know of the errand So LXX[(BA)] (= *'yš 'l yd' 't hdbr*). MT: *'yš 'l yd' m'wmh 't hdbr*, "Let no one know *anything* about the errand."

I have made an appointment MT *ywd'ty* is unparalleled and offers no defensible translation (hardly, "I appointed"; GK §55b). Instead read *y'dty* with 4QSam[b] (cf. LXX).

a certain So MT: *plny 'lmwny*. LXX seems to render the rare (Ruth 4:1; II Kings 6:8) expression twice: 1. (*en tō topō*) *tō legomenō theou pistis*, as if *plny 'l 'mwnh*, "a certain place of God in faithfulness" (?); 2. *phellanei maemōnei*, a (slightly corrupt) transcription.

4. *there are* Read *yēš* with LXX[B]. MT: *mh yš*, "what is there (in your custody? Five loaves of bread?)" LXX[AL], Syr. = "*If* there are. . . ."

Give me whatever can be found! Reading *tnh bydy hnmṣ* with LXX[(B)]. MT: *tnh bydy 'w hnmṣ'*, "Give (them) to me, or whatever can be found!"

5. *common* That is, *ḥl*, which is followed in MT by *'l*, a corrupt dittograph which may be deleted with LXX, 4QSam[b].

For the last sentence MT has *'m nšmrw hn'rym 'k m'šh*, "If *only* (your) servants have kept themselves from women—" LXX[BL], 4QSam[b] omit *'k*, "*only*," and supply the missing apodosis. Thus 4QSam[b]: [ ] *ṁ'šh w'kltm mmṅẇ*, "[ ] from women, you may eat of it," to which *'k* (['\]*k*) has been added supralinearly above *w'kltm*. One might argue for the shorter text of MT, but *'k* seems to be a vestige of the longer reading. Perhaps the present shape of MT is the result of haplography (*m̱'šh . . . m̱mnw*) and secondary correction. See further Cross, "Oldest Manuscripts," 172.

6. *We have abstained from women!* Reading *ky* (GK §157b) *m'šh 'ṣrnw* on the basis of LXX[(B)], *alla apo gynaikos apeschēmetha*. MT: *ky 'm 'šh 'ṣrh lnw*, "But indeed women have been kept away from us," which has equal claim to originality.

In the past That is, *tmwl wšlšwm*; so LXX[B(cf. L)]. MT: *ktmwl wšlšwm*, "*as* in the past."

whenever I have marched out LXX adds *eis hodon* = *ldrk*, "on a journey." Omit with MT.

each of [*my*] *servants* Reading *kl hn'rym* with LXX[(B)]. MT *kly hn'rym*, "*the weapons* [a euphemism?] of (my) servants," is an anticipation of *bkly*, "at arms," below.

7. *So the priest gave him the holy* [*bread*] So MT: *wytn lw hkhn qdš*.

LXX(B) = *wytn lw 'bymlk hkhn 't hpnym,* "So Abimelech the priest gave him the showbread."

that had been removed Reading *hmwsr* with 4QSam[b] for MT *hmwsrym,* which has been cast into the plural by attraction to the preceding word (*pnym*).

8. *one of Saul's servants* MT (LXX[L]): *'yš m'bdy š'wl.* LXX[B] = *'ḥd mn'ry š'wl.*

detained MT *n'ṣr,* rendered twice in LXX(B) as *synechomenos,* "constrained," and *neessaran,* a transcription.

the Edomite MT *h'dmy* (so LXX[L]). LXX[B], OL = *h'rmy,* "the Aramean" (so Josephus *Ant.* 6.244). The similarity of *d* and *r* throughout the period of the transmission of the text renders the correct reading uncertain.

the chief of Saul's runners That is, "the mighty one of the runners that Saul had": *'byr hrṣym 'šr lš'wl.* This at least is the old suggestion of H. Graetz, which many critics have adopted (Budde, Smith); the reading *hrṣym* is derived from 22:17. But textual support is lacking. MT has *'byr hr'ym 'šr lš'wl,* "a mighty one of *the shepherds* that Saul had." LXX is obscure: *nemōn tas hēmionous saoul,* "keeper of Saul's mules" (so Josephus *Ant.* 6.244); as noted by Stoebe, the suggestion of P. A. de Lagarde to restore *'byl h'yrym* on the basis of *nemōn tas hēmionous* (adopted by Smith) ignores the likelihood that *nemōn* corresponds somehow to *r'h.* Evidently *nemōn* and *tas hemionous* reflect originally distinct, alternative readings, viz. *r'h š'wl* and *'yry š'wl* respectively, conflated in an ancestral text of LXX; *'byr* is thus not represented at all. Only a scrap of 4QSam[b] is extant ([ ]*ṁ 'šr*), but it is enough to show that in 4QSam[b] as in MT the possessive was indicated periphrastically (*'šr lš'wl*) and not by a simple genitive (*š'wl*). The primitive reading continues to elude us.

9. *Ahimelech* So MT, LXX[AL]. LXX[B]: "Abimelech."

Is there Reading *whn hyš* on the basis of LXX *ide ei estin* in preference to MT *w'yn yš* (vocalized *wĕ'în yēš*), which is unintelligible (cf. Driver).

urgent Reading *nḥrṣ* for MT *nḥwṣ,* which is without parallel; cf. also LXX. This suggestion seems first to have been made by A. Klostermann; it is supported by the fact that *w* and *r* were almost interchangeable in scripts of the third century B.C.

10. *behind an ephod* So 4QSam[b]: *'ḥr 'pd;* cf. MT: *'ḥry h'pwd* (so LXX[AL], Syr.); omitted in LXX[B]. There follows in all witnesses (including LXX[B]) a reflection of the reading *lwṭh bśmlh,* "wrapped in a garment"; but this probably arose as a gloss on *'ḥr 'pd* (on the assumption that the ephod was a garment; see the NOTE), which it displaced in the ancestral text of LXX and with which it was combined in that of MT.

NOTES

21 2. *Ahimelech, the priest, at Nob.* "The priestly city of Nob," as it is called in 22:19, lay a very short distance N of Jerusalem in Benjamin, not far from Gibeah (Isa 10:32; Neh 11:31-32). Here the presiding priest who greets David is Ahimelech, son of Ahitub (22:9, etc.), the brother of Ahijah, Saul's chaplain, and great-grandson of Eli, the priest of Shiloh (cf. the NOTE at 14:3). Nob, then, seems to have inherited at least some of the authority of Shiloh after the fall of the latter (cf. the NOTE at 1:3 and the COMMENT on 4:1b-11). See further below and the COMMENT on 22:6-23.

came trembling out to meet [*him*]. Hebrew *wayyeḥĕrad . . . liqrā't dāwīd* (cf. 16:4). The reason for Ahimelech's apprehension is that David has come alone without his usual retinue of soldiers; perhaps he suspects that he comes as a fugitive. Although David quickly invents a fiction (v 3) to allay the priest's suspicion, the outcome of the episode in 22:6-23 will grimly vindicate Ahimelech's first reaction.

5. *common bread . . . holy bread.* Ahimelech has no common or "profane bread" (*leḥem ḥōl*) on hand, but there is always "holy bread" (*leḥem qōdeš*) in the sanctuary (cf. Exod 25:30). Verse 7 identifies this as the "showbread" or "Bread of the Presence" (*leḥem happānîm*), which according to Lev 24:5-9 consisted of twelve cakes of pure wheat flour arranged in rows (hence it is also called *leḥem hamma'ăreket*, "row bread"; I Chron 9:32; etc.) on a table in the sanctuary. The offering was renewed on the sabbath, and the old bread could be eaten only by the priests (Lev 24:8-9); so if David and his men are to eat it, they must at least be ritually pure. This, it seems, is the thinking of Ahimelech, who is especially concerned about ceremonial abstinence from sexual activity (cf. Exod 19:15). The incident is cited in the New Testament as an instance of an excusable violation of cultic regulation (cf. Matt 12:3-4; Mark 2:25-26; Luke 6:3-4).

6. David reminds the priest that no pious Israelite soldier will touch a woman while he is on active duty (cf. esp. II Sam 11:11). Fighting men are consecrated before battle (Josh 3:5), and the camp is kept ritually pure (Deut 23:10-15[English 23:9-14]).

the Bread of the Presence. See the NOTE at v 5.

8. Though hardly more than a parenthesis in the progress of the narrative, this verse has a crucial role to play. It gives a presentiment of what is to come. We are introduced to the skulking Edomite (probably a mercenary in Saul's employ; on Edom, cf. the NOTE at 14:47) who will serve Saul as informer (22:9-10) and executioner (22:18-19) in the dark days to come.

detained before Yahweh. Hebrew *ne'ṣār lipnê yahweh.* The detention is for some ceremonial purpose, no doubt, but the expression has no parallel in the

Old Testament (Jer 36:5 and Neh 6:10, compared by Driver, are both somewhat different), and whether Doeg is undergoing some kind of "act of penance," as Hertzberg surmises, is uncertain. The verb *neʿĕṣar* does occur in Postbiblical Hebrew with the meaning, "be detained (for religious reasons, at the temple or a festival)"; see Jastrow, 1103. Ernst Kutsch, in a general study of the verb ("Die Wurzel *ʿṣr* im Hebräischen," *VT* 2 [1952] 57-69), argues that in *Qal* it may mean "refrain from work" and in *Nipʿal*, "hold one's self back from work" = "take a holiday." Doeg, says Kutsch (65-67), was celebrating a holiday before Yahweh in the temple; it was thus a special day, as evidenced by the fact that the Bread of the Presence had been put out.

the chief of Saul's runners. Hebrew *'abbîr hārāṣîm 'ăšer lĕšā'ûl* (see the *Textual Note*). For *'abbîr*, "bull, stallion," hence, "leader, chief," see P. D. Miller, "Animal Names as Designations in Ugaritic and Hebrew," *UF* 2 (1970) 180-181; for the king's "runners" or palace guard, see the NOTE at 8:11.

10. The last we heard of Goliath's weapons was the notice in 17:54 to the effect that David kept them in his own tent after the duel in the Valley of the Terebinth (17:1*ff*).

behind an ephod. On the ephod as a priestly garment see the NOTE at 14:3. Here and in certain other passages, however, it seems unlikely that any kind of vestment is meant. In Judges 8, for example, it is said that Gideon fashioned out of reworked golden earrings and other jewelry (cf. Exod 32:2-4) an ephod that is condemned in the language of apostasy and idol worship, viz. "and all Israel played the harlot after it there, and it became a snare to Gideon and his house" (Judg 8:27; cf. Ps 106:36,39; etc.). Elsewhere, too, the ephod is often associated with teraphim (Judg 17:5; 18:14-20; Hosea 3:4), the household "gods" described in the NOTE at 19:13. It is possible, then, that the ephod that appears here in the temple at Nob is some kind of object of veneration, perhaps even a divine image.

COMMENT

David obtains food and arms from Ahimelech, the chief priest at the sanctuary of Nob. Thus the religious establishment of Saul's kingdom is also involved in the preservation of David's life, a further development of the theme already examined in the COMMENT to the last section. But there is an important difference here. Unlike Michal or Jonathan, Ahimelech does not *knowingly* abet David's escape from Saul;[1] rather he acts under deception, believing David's claim to be upon a royal errand. This state of affairs points ahead to the indebtedness that David, when he discovers

[1] Note, however, that Abiathar's later participation in David's affairs is willing and aware, so that the theme of the conscious contribution of the priesthood to David's rise is not really clouded by what we see here.

what hideous fruit his deception has borne, will acknowledge to the sole survivor of the Nob priesthood. But the grim sequel to this interview, which the frightened priest of the present passage seems to anticipate, is described in 22:6-23, and our commentary on the entire incident and its significance in the thematic development of the larger narrative may be reserved until then.

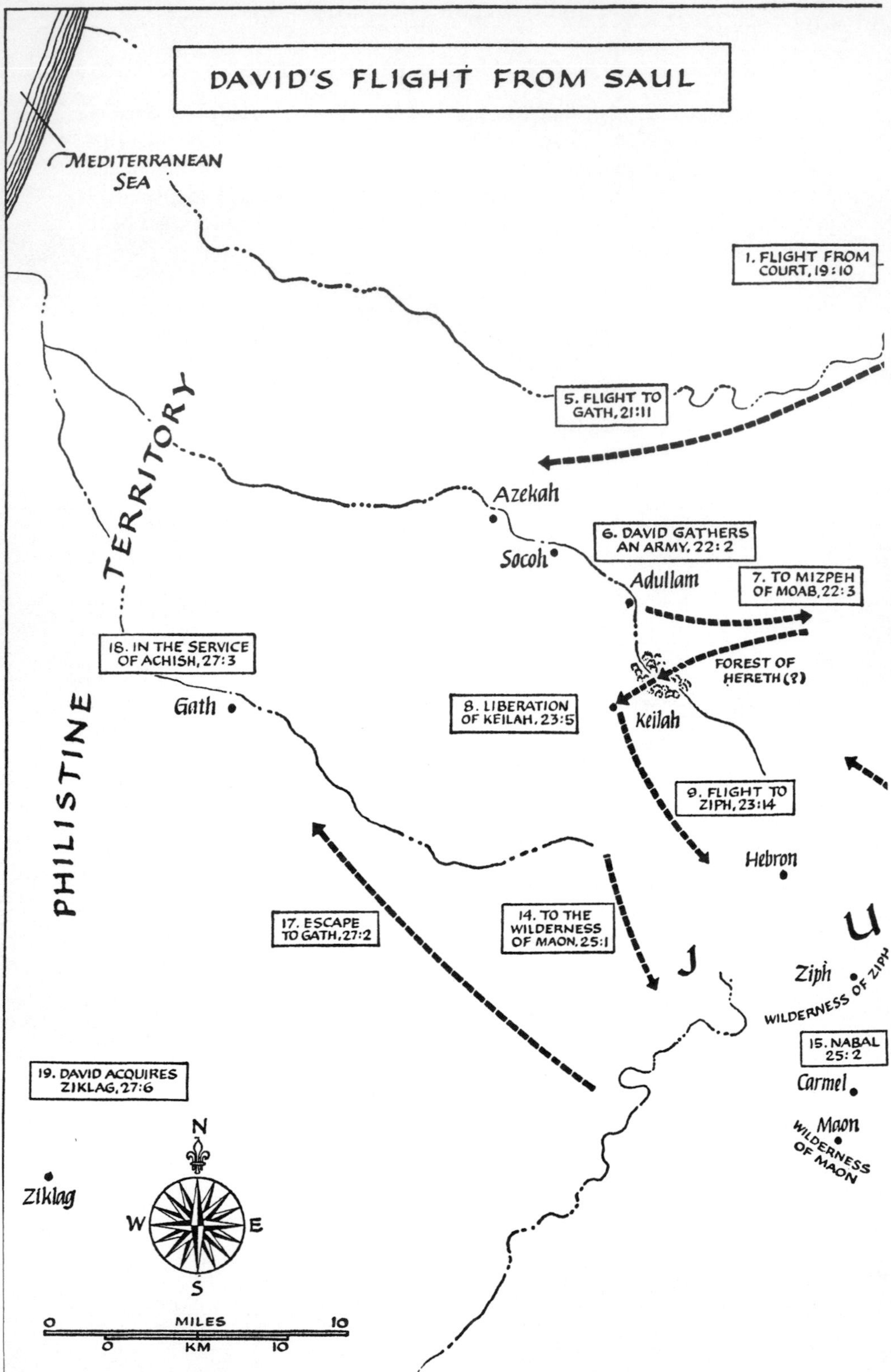
DAVID'S FLIGHT FROM SAUL
MEDITERRANEAN SEA
1. FLIGHT FROM COURT, 19:10
5. FLIGHT TO GATH, 21:11
PHILISTINE TERRITORY
Azekah
6. DAVID GATHERS AN ARMY, 22:2
Socoh
Adullam
7. TO MIZPEH OF MOAB, 22:3
16. IN THE SERVICE OF ACHISH, 27:3
FOREST OF HERETH (?)
Gath
8. LIBERATION OF KEILAH, 23:5
Keilah
9. FLIGHT TO ZIPH, 23:14
Hebron
17. ESCAPE TO GATH, 27:2
14. TO THE WILDERNESS OF MAON, 25:1
J
U
Ziph
WILDERNESS OF ZIPH
15. NABAL 25:2
19. DAVID ACQUIRES ZIKLAG, 27:6
Carmel
Maon
WILDERNESS OF MAON
Ziklag
N
W
E
S
0
MILES
10
0
KM
10

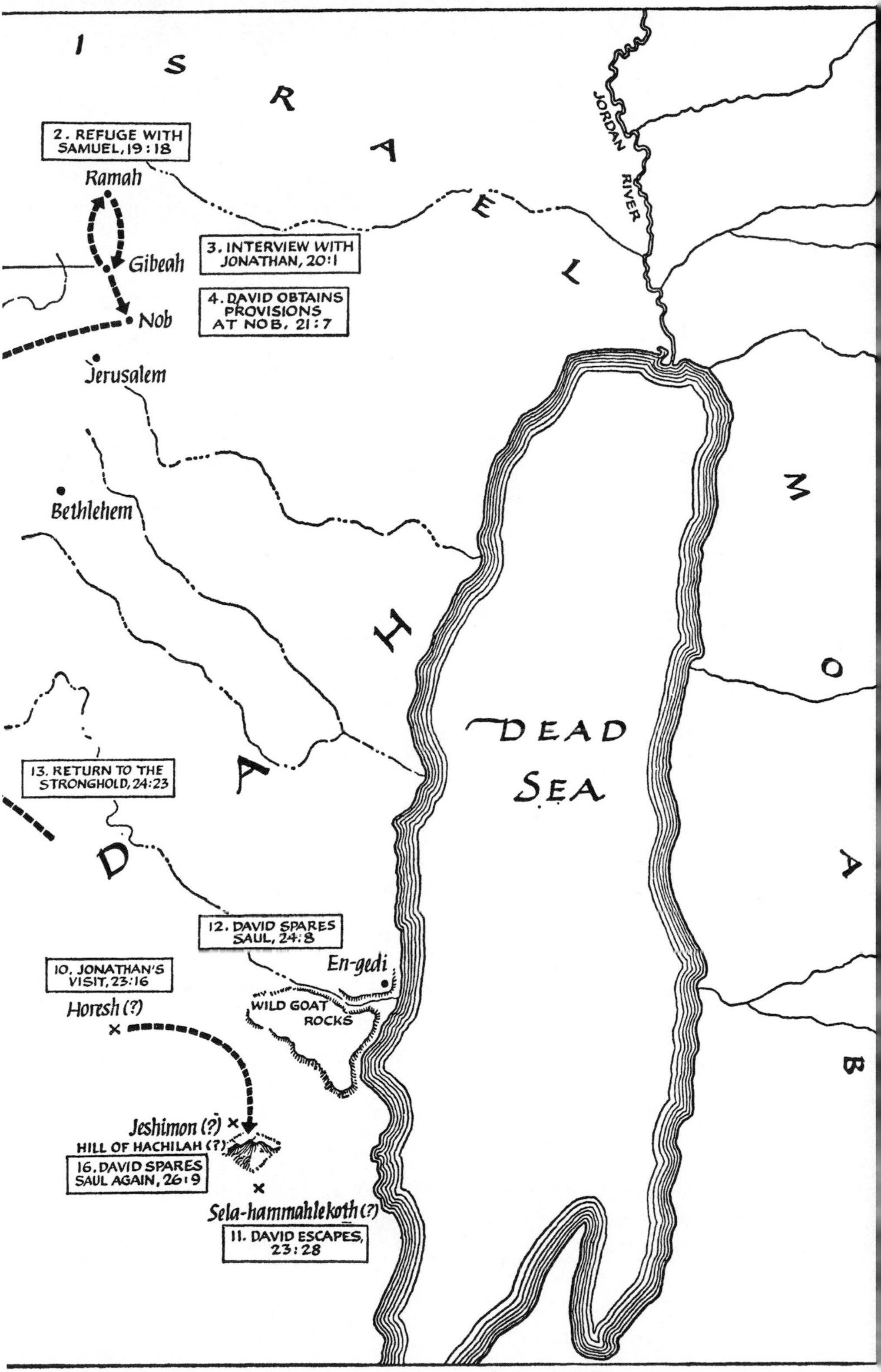

ISRAEL
2. REFUGE WITH SAMUEL, 19:18
Ramah
Gibeah
3. INTERVIEW WITH JONATHAN, 20:1
4. DAVID OBTAINS PROVISIONS AT NOB, 21:7
Nob
Jerusalem
JORDAN RIVER
Bethlehem
MOAB
DEAD SEA
JUDAH
13. RETURN TO THE STRONGHOLD, 24:23
12. DAVID SPARES SAUL, 24:8
En-gedi
10. JONATHAN'S VISIT, 23:16
Horesh (?)
WILD GOAT ROCKS
Jeshimon (?)
HILL OF HACHILAH (?)
16. DAVID SPARES SAUL AGAIN, 26:9
Sela-hammahlekoth (?)
11. DAVID ESCAPES, 23:28

XXXII. DAVID THE FUGITIVE: A MISCELLANY (21:11-22:5)

21 11 On that same day David arose and fled from Saul.

In Gath

He went to Achish, king of Gath. 12 But the servants of Achish
said, "Is this not David, the king of the land? Is it not of him that they
sing in their dances, saying:

Saul has slain his thousands,
And David his ten thousands?"

13 As David pondered these words, he became greatly afraid of
Achish, king of Gath. 14 So he disguised his judgment when in sight of
them and feigned madness while in their custody. He spat upon the
doors of the gate and let the slaver run down his beard.
15 Then Achish said to his servants, "You can see that he is a mad-
man, so why do you bring him to me? 16 Am I so in need of madmen
that you must bring this one to throw fits for me? Should this fellow
come into my house?"

At the Stronghold of Adullam

22 1 David departed from there and escaped to the stronghold of
Adullam. When his brothers and [the men of] his father's house
heard, they came down to him there. 2 To him gathered every man in
difficulties and every man sought by a creditor and every man with a
bitter spirit, and he became their commander. About four hundred
men were with him.

In Mizpeh of Moab

3 From there David went to Mizpeh of Moab and said to the king
of Moab, "Let my father and mother remain with you until I learn
what God is going to do with me." 4 So he left them with the king of

Moab, and they lived with him all the time that David was in [his] stronghold.

5 But Gad, the prophet, told David, "Do not remain in Mizpeh! Go! Make your way to the land of Judah!" So David left and went to the Forest of Hereth.

TEXTUAL NOTES

21 11. *He went* So MT. LXX: "*David* went. . . ."

Achish MT: *'ākîš*. LXX^B: *anchous*. LXX^L: *akchous*. See the NOTE.

14. *So he disguised* Reading *wyšnh*, lit. "And he altered," on the basis of LXX *kai ēlloiōsen*. MT has *wyšnw*, "And he altered *it/him*. . . ." Cf. Ps 34:1.

his judgment So MT: *'t ṭ'mw*. LXX (cf. Vulg.) *to prosōpon autou* seems to reflect *'t pnyw*, "his appearance."

in sight of them So MT: *b'ynyhm*, lit. "in their eyes." LXX is slightly different: *enōpion autou* = *lpnyw*, "in his (Achish's) presence."

and feigned madness That is, *wythll* (MT), evidently rendered twice by LXX^(B) (which provides two translations for the rest of the verse), as *kai prosepoiēsato*, "and pretended," and *kai parephereto*, "and misled."

in their custody So MT (*bydm*, lit. "in their hand"). LXX^(B): (1) *en tē hēmera ekeinē* = *bywm hhw'*, "on that day"; (2) *en tais chersin autou*, "in *his* (Achish's) hands."

He spat Reading *wayyāṭop*. MT has *wytw*, "and he scribbled (?)," but the correct reading is reflected by LXX *kai etympanizen*, "and he drummed," representing *wytp*, which however should probably be referred not to *tpp*, "beat the drum," but rather to *tpp*, "spit," which, though unattested in Biblical Hebrew (but cf. *tōpet*, "spitting," in Job 17:6), occurs in (Talmudic) Aramaic. The second rendering of LXX, *kai epipten*, seems to reflect *wypl*, "and he fell."

the gate So MT (*hš'r*) and LXX in its second rendering (the first reflects *h'yr*, "the city." Cf. the confusion of the same words in 9:14,18.).

22 1. *and escaped* So MT (*wymlṭ*). LXX: "and escaped and came (*wymlṭ wyb'*).

the stronghold MT (so LXX, etc.) has *m'rt*, "the cave," but in view of vv 4,5 Wellhausen is probably correct in suggesting an emendation to *mṣdt*, "the stronghold" (a correction to be made in II Sam 23:13 = I Chron 11:15 as well).

and [the men of] his father's house So LXX^B. MT, LXX^AL: "and *all* [the men of] his father's house."

3. *remain* MT has *yṣ'*, "let (them) go forth," which is inappropriate to the context. We might read *yhy*, "let (them) be" (cf. LXX) or *yšb*, "let (them) reside" (cf. Syr., Vulg.), but MT is then difficult to explain. A better solution is to restore *ynḥ*, "let (them) settle, remain," which Syr. and Vulg. might reflect

and from which MT is more easily derived. Cf. also *wynḥm* in the next verse (see below).

4. *So he left them* Vocalizing *wynḥm* (which is read by all versions) as *wayyannīḥēm* with Targ., Syr. (Wellhausen, Driver). MT understands it as *wayyanḥēm,* "so he *led* them," and LXX as *waynaḥēm,* "So he *consoled. . . .*"

in [his] stronghold So MT: *bmṣwdh.* LXX *en tē periochē,* "in the circumscribed place," represents *bmṣwrh,* "in (his) bulwark" (so also v 5). Syr. (here and in v 5) = *bmṣph,* "in Mizpeh."

5. *in Mizpeh* Reading *bmṣph* (cf. Syr. here and in the preceding verse) despite MT, LXX *bmṣwdh,* "in the stronghold"; Adullam was certainly a part of Judah (Josh 15:33-35). Here we follow the suggestion of Klostermann (so Budde, Smith).

and went So MT. LXX adds "and settled (in)."

the Forest So MT (*y'r*). LXX: "the City" (= *'yr*).

Hereth MT *ḥāret.* LXX$^{(B)}$: *sareik.* Josephus (*Ant.* 6.249): *sarin* (i.e. *saris*).

NOTES

21 11. *that same day.* Viz. the day of David's interview with Ahimelech, priest of Nob, described in 21:2-10. The material that follows in this section gives brief reports of three episodes in David's life as a fugitive from Saul's court.

Achish, king of Gath. The Philistine city of Gath (Tell eṣ-Ṣâfī?; see the NOTE at 5:8) lay some 23 miles WSW of Nob, as the crow flies. Why David should enter Philistine territory at this point is unclear, but as we shall see (cc 27; 29), he will later have much more extensive dealings with Achish, the local ruler. Like "Goliath" (cf. the NOTE at 17:4a) the name "Achish" (*'ākîš*) seems to be "Philistine" in origin; that is, it may belong to an originally Aegean-West Anatolian onomasticon. According to T. C. Mitchell (*AOTS,* 415) it "is found in a list of what are described as *kftiw* [Cretan] names on an Egyptian school writing-board probably of the Eighteenth Dynasty, and is probably cognate with Anchises, the name, according to Homer, of a Trojan, the father of Aeneas."

12. David is immediately recognized by the Gittites, who because of his exploits and popular acclaim (cf. 18:7) call him "king of the land." Hertzberg explains that "the title, chosen by non-Israelites and enemies, is once again meant to underline the fact that the divine plan is inviolably bound up with David." Nevertheless the title *melek hā'āreṣ,* "king of the land," is a surprise; perhaps it simply connotes "local chieftain" here—its only occurrence in the singular in Biblical Hebrew—as it does in plural form elsewhere (cf. esp. Josh 12:1,7). In other words the Philistines, though they do not mistake David for

"the king of the Hebrews" (as they might have described Saul), are unaware of his true status and assume on the basis of his reputation that he is a local ruler of some kind.

13,14. David realizes that once recognized he is in mortal danger from the Philistines, upon whom he has personally inflicted so much grief, and adopts the desperate stratagem of pretending to be insane.

22 1. *the stronghold of Adullam.* A 10-mile journey ESE from Gath, Adullam (modern Tell esh-Sheikh Madhkûr) was a Judahite fortress city that lay some 16 miles SW of Jerusalem in the Shephelah (Josh 15:33-35; cf. II Chron 11:7). The stronghold of Adullam (*mĕṣūdat ʿădullām;* cf. the *Textual Note*) was probably a well-fortified hilltop like the stronghold of Zion (II Sam 5:7 = I Chron 11:5; cf. II Sam 5:9); it served David as a base of operations later in his career as well (II Sam 23:13,14 = I Chron 11:15,16; also II Sam 5:7 [?]).

2. *every man with a bitter spirit.* Hebrew *kol ʾîš mar-nepeš.* The expression *mar-nepeš,* "bitter of spirit," suggests embitterment and discontent, especially as occasioned by some kind of deprivation. Thus Hannah on account of her barrenness is described as *mārat nāpeš* earlier in 1:10, and the men of Ziklag are said to be *mārâ nepeš* over the loss of their children later in 30:6; similarly the homeless Danites of Judg 18:25 are said to be "bitter of spirit," as are David and his followers in their flight from Absalom in II Sam 17:8 (n.b. the instructive simile in this last passage: ". . . and they are bitter of spirit, *like a bear bereft* [*of its cubs*] . . ."). The point of the present passage, then, is that David becomes the leader of all those men who have suffered some kind of loss or deprivation that has left them embittered; he is now champion of the discontented, the disenchanted, and the mistreated.

3. *Mizpeh of Moab.* On Moab, see the NOTE at 14:47. Mizpeh is mentioned nowhere else, and the site is unknown; presumably it was a Moabite royal city. The tradition that David sequestered his parents in Moab during his outlaw days is an odd one, but we should recall in this regard that tradition also attributed to his family Moabite blood through Ruth, David's great-grandmother (cf. Ruth 4:13-22). See further the COMMENT.

4. *in* [*his*] *stronghold.* That is, at Adullam (cf. v 1 above).

5. *Gad, the prophet.* An obscure seer associated with David's reign (cf. I Chron 29:29; II Chron 29:25), especially in the census episode (see II Sam 24:11-19 = I Chron 21:9-19); it is surprising to find Gad with David this early.

the Forest of Hereth. The area is mentioned nowhere else. Compare perhaps "Kharas," the name of a modern village near Khirbet Qîlā, which preserves the name of ancient Keilah (see the NOTE at 23:1).

COMMENT

The two parts of the Nob episode (21:2-10 and 22:6-23) were separated in the course of the compilation of the old narrative of David's rise to power by the insertion of the little medley of traditions that now stands as 21:11 - 22:5.[1] Of the three narrative scraps collected here only the notice (for it is hardly more than that) about David's recruitment of a band of followers at Adullam (22:1-2) can be said to have an important place in the development of the larger story. The two other pieces—one about an early encounter between David and Achish of Gath (21:11b-16), the other about a visit to Moab (22:3-5)—seem to reflect unrelated traditions about David's early career that were included at this point for want of a better occasion.

1) *21:11b-16.* David is said to have gone to Gath after his departure from Nob. What he intended to do there we are not told—perhaps he wanted to enter the service of Achish, as he does later (27:1*ff*)—but in any case he finds himself to be known in Gath as a Philistine slayer and so in danger of his life. The ruse by which he escapes is reminiscent of his trickery at Nob, and this provides at least some continuity between these two consecutive accounts.

But what is the relationship of the present episode to the longer account in 27:1*ff* of a sojourn in Gath during which David actually serves Achish and is rewarded for his efforts? An uncritical answer would be that this first visit simply anticipates the second, which David will undertake in hope of a better reception; but the narrative in c 27 gives no hint that any previous visit has taken place, and the subsequent account, therefore, seems in no way to be dependent upon this one. Indeed, this passage might even be said to *contradict* the story of David's sojourn in Philistia, insofar as it shows how he and Achish failed to strike an acquaintance. It was the last point that led the older source critics to conclude that 21:11b-16 reflected late, midrashic reinterpretation of 27:1*ff* (Budde) or simply "an attempt to explain away the facts of history" (Smith). That is, the passage is, according to many scholars, a secondarily introduced "corrective" to 27:1*ff*, where the future king of Israel is depicted in the embarrassing role of a Philistine-hired mercenary. More recently the tendency among scholars has been to suppose that the episode had some early

[1] Compare the similar treatment of the Michal episode (18:20-21a,22-27 + 19:8-17) and the (primary) story of David in the service of Achish (27:1 - 28:2 + 29:1 - 30:31).

traditional life of its own (Hertzberg)[2] from which it was co-opted into the sequence of events at this point by the compiler of the larger narrative.[3]

2) *22:1-2.* At a rallying point in Judah, which will also be important later in his career (see the NOTE at 22:1), David gathers a band of outlaws and malcontents. These men are fugitives and so can identify David's situation with their own; and insofar as they are all aggrieved in one way or another by the political system to which David seems to represent an alternative, they readily claim him as their leader. Note that two important things have now occurred: (1) David has returned to Judah, where he is among kinsmen; and (2) he has publicly assumed the identity of a fugitive or (from Saul's perspective) an outlaw. These developments prepare us for cc 23-26, which reports events from David's days as an outlaw leader in the countryside of Judah.

3) *22:3-5.* David takes his father and mother to Moab, apparently thinking they will be safer there until he knows what is going to become of him (". . . until I learn what God is going to do with me"). But why Moab? No doubt the Moabites would have been glad enough to assist any enemy of Saul, who according to 14:47 once defeated them in war; but subsequent materials suggest that they received no better from David when he became king (II Sam 8:2; I Chron 18:2). One clue to the solution of this problem, which seems impervious to a full solution, must be the Moabite connections in David's family (for what follows, cf. the NOTE on "Jesse" at 16:1). According to Ruth 4:17-22 (cf. I Chron 2:11-12), Ruth the Moabitess was David's great-grandmother. Presumably, then, Jesse and his wife could claim some kind of a right of protection in Moab on the grounds of kinship.

[2] The arguments of Bič ("La folie de David") for an early *cultic* background to the episode have received little support; cf. also Grønbaek (*Aufstieg Davids,* 143-147), who makes a more modest, but still unpersuasive, case for a myth-and-ritual interpretation of the passage.

[3] Another intriguing but essentially unprovable hypothesis is suggested by the rubric to Psalm 34, a psalm of thanksgiving for deliverance from personal danger which has been ascribed to David and editorially associated with the present episode. The rubric reads: "Concerning David, when he altered his judgment before Abimelech [= Ahimelech; cf. the *Textual Note* to 21:2], so that he drove him off, and he went away." The fact that Ahimelech appears here in place of Achish is generally assumed to be the consequence of a simple error on the part of the author of the rubric, and it may be. But suppose it is a reflection of authentic tradition. It is easy to imagine that in an early version of the story of David and Ahimelech, parts of which are known to have been lost (cf. the NOTE at 22:10), the interview concluded with David in danger. His lie may have been found out, so that feigning madness was the only way to escape. This part of the story may have been altered subsequently to preserve a bit of David's integrity vis-à-vis the priests of Yahweh.

XXXIII. THE SLAUGHTER OF THE PRIESTS OF NOB (22:6-23)

22 6 Saul heard that David and the men with him had been discovered. Saul was sitting under the tamarisk on the high place at Gibeah
with his spear in his hand and all his servants standing about him,
7 and he said to them, "Listen, Benjaminites! Is it to any of you that
the son of Jesse will give fields and vineyards; is it from any of you
that he will appoint captains of hundreds and captains of thousands;
8 that you should all conspire against me, that there should be no one
to tell me that my own son has been in league with the son of Jesse,
and that there should not be one of you who felt enough compassion
for me to tell me that my own son has raised up my servant against
me as a highwayman, as [he is] this very day?"

9 Then Doeg the Edomite, who was presiding over Saul's servants,
spoke up. "I saw the son of Jesse come to Nob, to Ahimelech, the son
of Ahitub," he said, 10 "who consulted God for him, gave him provisions, and gave him the sword of Goliath, the Philistine."

11 So the king had Ahimelech, son of Ahitub, summoned with all
his father's house, the priests who were in Nob, and they all came to
the king.

12 "Hear me, son of Ahitub!" said Saul.

"Here I am, my lord!" he replied.

13 And Saul said to him, "Why have you conspired against me with
the son of Jesse, giving him food and a sword and consulting God for
him, so he could rise up against me as a highwayman, as [he is]
today?"

14 In reply to the king [Ahimelech] said, "But who of all your servants is as trustworthy as David, the king's son-in-law and the commander of your bodyguard, who is honored in your house? 15 Was
that the first time I have consulted God for him? Far be it from me!
Let the king not accuse his servant or anyone in my father's house of
anything, for your servant knew nothing small or great of all this!"

16 But the king said, "You shall surely die, Ahimelech, you and all
your father's house!" 17 Then the king spoke to [his] runners, who
were standing about him, "Go around and kill the priests of Yahweh,
for their hand is with David! Though they knew he was a fugitive,
they did not inform me!" But the king's servants were unwilling to lift
a hand to sin against the priests of Yahweh. 18 So the king said to
Doeg, "You go around and strike down the priests!" And Doeg the
Edomite went around and killed the priests that day—eighty-five men
who wore the linen ephod. 19 The priestly city of Nob he also struck
with the edge of the sword, man and woman, child and infant, bull,
ass, and sheep!

The Escape of Abiathar

20 One son of Ahimelech, son of Ahitub, whose name was
Abiathar, escaped and fled after David. 21 When [he] told David that
Saul had slain the priests of Yahweh, 22 David said to [him], "I knew
that day that [Doeg] would surely inform Saul. I am the one responsible for the lives of your father's house! 23 Live with me! Do not be
afraid! He who seeks my life will seek yours as well! You are under
my protection!"

TEXTUAL NOTES

22 6. *on the high place* So LXX^{BL}(= *bbmh*). MT, LXX^{A}, OL: *brmh,* "on the height"(?).

7. *and he said to them* LXX presents a conflation of longer and shorter readings: (1) *kai eipen saoul pros tous paidas autou tous parestēkotas autō* = *wy'mr š'wl l'bdyw hnṣbym 'lyw,* "and Saul said to his servants who were standing about him," followed by (2) *kai eipen autois* = *wy'mr lhm,* "and he said to them." The first reading, which clumsily duplicates the last part of the preceding verse, appears alone in MT. The second, shorter reading is more likely to have been original and should be retained in the form given (with LXX$^{BA,\ cf.\ L}$).

is it from any of you So MT: *lklkm* (for the translation, see the NOTE). LXX *kai pantas hymas* = *wklkm,* ". . . and all of you (he will appoint, etc.)" may have developed because of confusion about the preposition. Alternatively, we might adopt the reading of LXX on the assumption that MT *lklkm* arose in reminiscence of the preceding *lklkm* (so Budde, Dhorme, Smith, Stoebe).

captains of hundreds and captains of thousands So LXX^B. In MT, LXX^AL the order is reversed.

8. *one* (2) . . . *who felt* . . . *compassion* MT has *ḥlh*, "one who was sick," which LXX *ponōn* seems at first glance to sustain; but *ḥmltm*, "you have felt compassion," in 23:21 and its treatment in LXX (*eponesate*) favor emending MT *ḥlh* to *ḥml* here (cf. Budde).

as a highwayman Here and in v 13 reading *l'rb* with MT (cf. Syr.), which is to be preferred as *lectio difficilior* to LXX *eis echthron* = *l'yb*, "as an enemy." The forms of *y* and *r* were easily confused in scripts of the fourth and early third centuries B.C.

9. *servants* So MT (*'bdy*). LXX has *tas hēmionous*, "asses" (*'yry*), perhaps under the influence of 21:8 (see the fourth *Textual Note* there).

the son of Ahitub LXX, Syr. add "the priest." Omit with MT.

10. *God* So LXX (cf. vv 13,15 below). MT has "Yahweh."

11. *Ahimelech, son of Ahitub* MT, LXX^AL add "the priest." Omit with LXX^B.

his father's house MT *byt 'byw*. LXX = *bny 'byw*, "the sons of his father."

Nob So (correctly) MT (*nōb*). LXX^B: *nomma* (cf. v 19: *nomba*).

12. *"Here I am, my lord!"* So MT. LXX reflects "Here I am! Speak, my lord!" a simple expansion.

13. *as a highwayman* See the second *Textual Note* to v 8 above.

14. [*Ahimelech*] The name is actually supplied by MT, LXX^AL, etc. Omit with LXX^B.

and the commander of Reading *wśr 'l*, "and commander over," in preference to MT *wsr 'l*, "and the one who turns aside to"; cf. LXX (*kai archōn pantos* = *wśr kl*, "and commander *of all*"). Syr., Targ. also reflect *śr*.

15. *or anyone in my father's house* Reading *wbkl byt 'by* (cf. LXX). MT omits the conjunction.

16. *the king* LXX^(B) adds "Saul." Omit with MT.

17. *for their hand* Reading *ky ydm* (LXX, Syr.). MT *ky gm ydm*, "for their hand, *too*," is preferred by Stoebe.

they did not inform me MT (*kĕtîb*) is different: *wl' glw 't 'znw*, "they did not inform *him*" (lit. "they did not uncover his ear"). But read *'zny*, "*my* ear," with LXX, MT (*qĕrê*).

to sin against the priests So LXX^BA: *hamartēsai eis tous hiereis kyriou* = *lhṭ' lkhny yhwh*. MT has *lpg' bkhny yhwh*, "to *strike down* the priests of Yahweh," which seems to anticipate v 18.

18. *Doeg* In this passage the name is spelled *dwyg* in MT; previously, *d'g*. Cf. the NOTE at 21:8.

the Edomite See the *Textual Note* at 21:8.

and killed Reading *wymt* on the basis of LXX^B *kai ethanatōsen*. MT has *wypg' hw'* . . . *wymt*, "and he struck down (the priests) and killed. . . ."

the priests Cf. MT. LXX: "the priests *of Yahweh*."

eighty-five So MT. LXX^BA: "three hundred and five." The smaller number is more likely to have been original.

who wore the linen ephod Reading *nś' 'pwd bd* (so MT). LXX^(B) reflects *kl nś' 'pwd,* "each wearing the ephod." LXX has lost *bd* by haplography after *'pwd; kl* is a simple expansion.

19. At the end of the verse MT repeats *lpy ḥrb,* "with the edge of the sword" (cf. LXX^{AL}). Omit with LXX^{B}.

21. *the priests* So MT. LXX: *"all* the priests."

22. *I knew that day that* [*Doeg*] *would surely inform* MT has *yd'ty bywm hhw' ky šm dwyg h'dmy ky hgd ygyd,* "I knew that day that Doeg the Edomite was there, that he would surely inform. . . ." LXX reflects *yd'ty ky bywm hhw' ky dwyg h'rmy ky hgd ygyd,* "I knew that on that day that Doeg the Aramean, that he would surely inform. . . ." The first *ky* of LXX$^{(B)}$ is clearly superfluous and can be omitted with MT (cf. LXX^{L}). The omission of *šm,* "(was) there," in LXX$^{(B)}$ shows it to be secondary, inserted to make a clause of *ky dwyg h'dmy;* LXX^{L} solves the same problem by omitting the second *ky.* In fact MT is a conflation of longer (*ky dwyg h'dmy hgd ygyd*) and shorter (*ky hgd ygyd*) readings, of which the latter must have been original. Thus we read *yd'ty hywm hhw' ky hgd ygyd,* "I knew that day that he would surely inform. . . ."

I am the one responsible for Reading *'nky ḥbty* on the basis of LXX *egō eimi aitios* (cf. Syr.) in preference to MT *'nky sbty,* "I have gone around . . . (?)." Cf. Driver.

the lives of your father's house Reading *bnpš(wt) byt 'byk* with LXX^{B}. MT: *bkl npš byt 'byk, "every life* in your father's house." LXX^{L} = *bnpš(wt) bkl byt 'byk,* "the lives of *all* your father's house."

NOTES

22 6. The curtain opens on the familiar scene of a ruler sitting in council under a sacred tree; as illustrated in the first NOTE at 14:2, this situation was a stock component of ancient Northwest Semitic narrative art. In the earlier episode Saul's seat was on a threshing floor shaded by a pomegranate tree; here he is on the high place, and the tree is a tamarisk; but the picture is much the same.

the tamarisk. A desert tree with small, flat leaves covering delicately plumed and sprawling branches. A tamarisk marked the shrine of 'El-'olam at Beersheba (Gen 21:33), and Saul himself will be buried under another (cf. 31:13).

high place. Hebrew *bāmâ* (see the *Textual Note*), the local place of worship; cf. the NOTE at 9:12.

Gibeah. Cf. the NOTE at 9:1. Saul has remained at his home and capital city while we have been following David's travels.

7,8. Saul's "servants," that is, the ranking members of his court (see the NOTE at 8:14), are Benjaminites and cannot, says Saul, expect to be treated with distinction in the court of David of Judah; specifically, they cannot hope to be enriched by feudal grants and appointments (cf. the NOTES at 8:11-17). Saul's point is that since these men have nothing to gain from David, they should not be abetting his rise to power, as it seems to him they are. On this passage in general, see also A. F. Rainey in Fisher, *Ras Shamra Parallels* 2. 100-101, and bibliography cited there.

7. *Is it to any of you . . . is it from any of you.* Hebrew *gam-lĕkullĕkem . . . lĕkullĕkem.* The subtleties of the grammar and syntax are quite important here: (1) as Stoebe points out, the force of *gam* is to stress the contrast between the Bejaminites, who cannot hope for feudal grants, and (though they are not mentioned) the Judahites, who can; this is difficult to represent in translation (Stoebe: ". . . *wohl auch* euch allen . . ."); (2) the meaning of Saul's words is enhanced syntactically by the emphatic first position of the repeated prepositional phrase *lĕkullĕkem,* the force of which our translation seeks to preserve in English syntax (contrast RSV: ". . . will the son of Jesse give every one of you, etc."); (3) *lĕ-* in the second *lĕkullĕkem* requires the translation "from," as often in Northwest Semitic (cf. Rainey in Fisher, *Ras Shamra Parallels* 2.100); cf. the *Textual Note.*

8. *has been in league with.* Saul seems to have learned more about the events described in 19:1-7. The verb used is *kārat,* "make a covenant" (here used without *bĕrît,* "covenant," as in 11:2; also I Kings 8:9 = II Chron 5:10), but Saul is referring to Jonathan's relationship with David in a general way—the formal covenant-making described in 18:3 (cf. 20:8) is not mentioned except in the late supplements to the text which are missing from LXX^{B}.

9,10. Cf. 21:2-10. We were notified of Doeg's presence in 21:8. Here he is "presiding over" (*niṣṣāb ʿal*) Saul's retinue; cf. the NOTE at 19:20,21.

10. *consulted God for him.* In the account in 21:2-10 we were not told of this part of David's interview with Ahimelech. For another interpretation, see Caird.

13. Compare the language to that of Saul's accusation of his courtiers in v 8 above. In his paranoia the deluded king sees conspiracy everywhere.

giving . . . and consulting. Hebrew *bĕtittĕkā . . . wĕšāʾôl,* an infinitive absolute in sequence after an infinitive construct, as in 25:26,33; see GK §113e.

14,15. Ahimelech's defense is that in the past he has always believed David to be Saul's trusted servant and treated him accordingly; nor was he aware of the recent developments in David's relationship with Saul. When he gave David assistance, therefore, he assumed that he was doing so in accordance with the king's wishes. We might add to this that David deliberately deceived Ahimelech and in so doing sealed the doom of the priests of Nob. Cf. vv 21-22 below.

14. *the commander of your bodyguard.* Hebrew *śar ʿal mišmaʿtekā.* In David's own court this position will be held by a certain Benaiah, son of Jehoiada (II Sam 23:20-23 = I Chron 11:22-25). The term *mišmaʿat* can refer to a city or state giving special allegiance to a king (as in the so-called "Moabite Stone," a royal inscription of Mesha, a ninth-century king of Moab: *KAI* 181:28; *ANET*^{3}, 320-321, tr. W. F. Albright; cf. also Isa 11:14) or to an intimate circle of royal retainers, i.e. a king's bodyguard.

17. *runners.* The palace guard; see the NOTES at 8:11 and 21:8.

their hand is with David. That is, they are assisting David (cf. Jer 26:24), are in collusion with him (cf. II Sam 14:19).

18. The Edomite proves useful again. Saul's Benjaminite servants shrink from their lord's command, but Doeg, as a foreigner and (presumably) a non-Yahwist, has no religious scruple to prevent him from slaying the priests of Nob.

the linen ephod. The uniform of priesthood; see the NOTE at 21:18.

20-23. Hertzberg: "Whereas Saul is in this way alienating the priests, David gains possession of one, a 'real' priest, of the house of Eli. We must regard this as the focal point of the chapter." See further the COMMENT.

20. *Abiathar.* See the COMMENT.

22-23. David now realizes the consequences of his selfishness and deceit and acknowledges a permanent responsibility to Abiathar.

COMMENT

The consequences of David's deception of Ahimelech are described here in the darkest passage in the story of David's rise to power. Saul, now totally possessed by his own fears and suspicions, commands not only the massacre of the entire priesthood of Nob but also a pogrom against the inhabitants of the sacred city itself. The demented king, then, is again the villain of the piece; but this time David is also implicated, and by way of acknowledging his responsibility in the bloody affair, he undertakes the protection of Abiathar, a son of Ahimelech who has somehow escaped the carnage.

The events recorded in this passage conclude the drama begun in 21:2-10 and editorially interrupted by the materials in 21:11-22:5. Viewed as a whole it divides naturally into three acts: (1) 21:2-10, David's visit to Ahimelech at Nob; (2) 22:6-10, Saul's consultation with his servants at Gibeah; and (3) 22:11-19, the interrogation and execution of the priests of Nob, also at Gibeah (with the slaughter of the citizens of Nob taking place offstage). The three acts are connected by the sinister figure of Doeg the Edomite, whom we saw lurking in the temple at the beginning of the story (21:8), and who serves as informer (22:9-10) and executioner (22:18) here in the conclusion. All of this is followed by an epilogue (22:20-23) describing Abiathar's escape and meeting with David.[1]

It is in the epilogue that scholars have discerned the focal point of the narrative (cf. Hertzberg's remarks quoted in the NOTE on vv 20-23). The story shows David acquiring a priest of Yahweh, who will be associated with him throughout the remainder of his fugitive days (23:6,9; 30:7). And at the same time that David is joined to a priest, Saul is left without

[1] The analysis above is essentially that of Grønbaek, *Aufstieg Davids,* 127.

one. His brutal act of reprisal, which is such a sacrilege that even the members of his own court shrink from it (v 17b), will alienate him from Yahweh's priesthood forever; and in fact the priests are all dead, except the one who is with David. Probably, then, we should press the comparison further. The narrative not only depicts David as one who will have the benefit of priestly counsel in contrast to Saul, who will not; it also depicts David as the protector and therefore preserver of the priesthood of Nob in contrast to Saul, who is its destroyer.

The priest David protects, Abiathar, will eventually share the position of high priest with Zadok during David's reign as king (II Sam 20:25; etc.), until finally, having sided with Adonijah over the succession issue (I Kings 1:7; etc.), he will be banished from court by Solomon after David's death (I Kings 2:26-27). This then is the "one man" spared at Yahweh's altar "to wear out his eyes and use up his strength," of whom the man of God foretold in the oracle in 2:27-36, and the slaughter described here is the fulfillment of the threat made there to Eli ("The days are coming when I shall cut off your descendants and the descendants of your father's house . . ." [v 31]), insofar as the priests of Nob are his (Eli's) descendants (see the NOTE on Ahimelech at 21:2). So we can see that this passage came to have an important function in the prophecy and fulfillment scheme of the Josianic history of the kingdom (cf. pp. 14-17 in the Introduction) with its emphasis on the election of Jerusalem and its priesthood and the corresponding rejection of Shiloh and the house of Eli (cf. the COMMENT on 2:27-36).

Viewed as a part of the older narrative of David's rise to power, however, the story displays a rather different emphasis. It is only in light of such passages as I Sam 2:27-36 and I Kings 2:26-27 that the theme of the rejection of the Shilonite priesthood can be detected here, and apart from the larger editorial framework, then, the passage is simply another part of the gradual exposition of the relationship between Saul and David. So to return to our earlier line of discussion, the account presents, as we have seen, Saul as the destroyer of the priesthood of Nob and David as its preserver, with final emphasis on the latter point. Since Nob is evidently to be thought of as the most sacred shrine of Saul's kingdom (or at least as a kind of official state sanctuary),[2] it would not be overstating the case to say that David is pictured here as saving the cult of Yahweh from formal

[2] See the interpretation of A. Alt, "The Formation of the Israelite State," in *Essays in Old Testament History and Religion* (Garden City, N.Y.: Doubleday, 1968) 251-253. Alt argues that whereas Shiloh had served all Israel in the days before the monarchy, "at the time of Saul the successors of the priests of Shiloh served a sanctuary at Nob, which not only lay in the territory of the king, who ruled in nearby Gibeah, but was actually controlled by him. Does this not also indicate an attempt to incorporate the remnants of the old institutions into the new organism [i.e. the monarchy]?"

extinction in Israel. In the coming episodes we shall see Saul chasing about furiously without priestly guidance—Yahweh hereafter will refuse to communicate his will to Saul in any accepted manner (cf. 28:6)—whereas David, with whom the remnant of Yahweh's priesthood is now living, will be presented to us as a man guided by the divine oracle at every turn. It is the purpose of the next section of our story to make this last point clear.

XXXIV. THE KEILAH EPISODE
(23:1-13)

23 1 David was told that Philistines were fighting against Keilah and
looting the threshing floors, 2 so [he] consulted Yahweh, "Shall I go
attack those Philistines?"
"Go!" said Yahweh. "Attack the Philistines and liberate Keilah!"
3 But David's men told him, "Even here in Judah we are afraid.
How much more so if we go to Keilah deep in the recesses of the Philistines!" 4 So David consulted Yahweh again.
"Arise!" said Yahweh in reply to him. "Go down to Keilah, for I
shall deliver the Philistines into your power!" 5 So David and his men
went to Keilah and fought against the Philistines. He drove off their
cattle and inflicted a great defeat on them. Thus David liberated the
inhabitants of Keilah.
6 (Now when Abiathar, son of Ahitub, fled to David, he had gone
down with David to Keilah, taking an ephod with him.)
7 When Saul was told that David had gone to Keilah, [he] thought,
"God has shut him up in my hand, for by going to a city with doors
and a bar he has shut himself in!" 8 So Saul summoned the entire
army to war, to go down to Keilah and besiege David and his men.
9 When David realized that Saul was devising evil against him, he
said to Abiathar, the priest, "Bring the ephod!" 10 Then David said,
"O Yahweh, god of Israel! Your servant has heard that Saul seeks to
come to Keilah and destroy the city on my account! 11 Now then, will
Saul come down as your servant has heard? O Yahweh, god of Israel!
Inform your servant!"
"He will come down," said Yahweh.
12 Then David asked, "Will the lords of Keilah hand me and my
men over to Saul?"
"They will hand you over," said Yahweh.
13 So David and his men (about six hundred men) arose and departed from Keilah to wander where they might. When Saul was told
that David had escaped, he gave up the march.

TEXTUAL NOTES

23 1. *looting* So MT: *šsym*. LXX has two corresponding words, viz. *diarpazousin*, "plundering," and *katapatousin*, "tramping down." Rather than rendering the same Hebrew original twice (Budde), these probably reflect the alternative readings *šsym* (so MT) and *špym*, "treading upon." See the *Textual Note* to 17:53.

2. *said Yahweh* MT, LXX^{AL}, Syr. add "to David." Omit with LXX^{B}.

the Philistines So MT, LXX^{L}. LXX^{B} has "those Philistines," as above.

and liberate So MT (*whwšʻt*). LXX$^{(BL)}$: *kai pataxeis* = *whkyt*, "and attack," as above.

3. *deep in the recesses* MT has *'l mʻrkwt*, "to/against the *ranks*" (cf. c 17 *passim*); but this is not corroborated by LXX, and we expect a geographical designation to contrast expressly with "here in Judah." The evidence of LXX is confusing: LXX^{B} *eis ta skyla*, "to the booty"; LXX^{L} *eis tas koiladas*, "to the hollow places"; LXX^{MSS} *tas koilias*, "to the cavities/bowels"; etc. Evidently all of these are inner-Greek corruptions of something like *eis tas koilas*, "to the hollow places/valleys." All of this may point to some such reading as *'l ʻmqy*, "to the valleys," or more likely (in view of MT) *'l yrkty*, "to the deep recesses/remote places," which is here adopted. (Contrast Wellhausen's more radical solution, which considers *eis ta skyla* a corrupt duplicate rendering of *qʻlh*, "to Keilah," from which the other LXX readings also arose.) In any case the LXX addition at the end of the verse is to be deleted with MT as secondary (*eisporeusometha* = *nbw'*, "we shall go in"; as if, "How much more so if we go to Keilah! *Shall we go into* the recesses of the Philistines?").

5. *and his men* So MT (*qěrê*). LXX: "and the men who were with him." Cf. the *Textual Note* at v 13.

against the Philistines At this point LXX adds *kai ephygon ek prosōpon autou*, reflecting *wynsw mlpnyw*, "and they fled before him," evidently a simple expansion.

6. *to David . . . with him* The original text can be restored on the basis of LXX^{B}: *pros daueid kai autos meta daueid eis keeila katebē echōn ephoud en tē cheiri autou*, which reflects *'l dwd whw' 't dwd qʻylh yrd 'pwd bydw*, lit. ". . . to David, and he with David to Keilah had gone down, an ephod in his hand." The tradition behind MT (cf. LXX^{L}) suffered a haplography of several words: *'l dwd whw' 't dwd qʻlh*, after which *yrd* and *'pwd* were transposed to allow for some such interpretation as ". . . to David at Keilah. An ephod went down in his hand" (cf. Targ.).

7. *shut him up* MT has *nkr* (*nikkar*), "treated him as a stranger," and LXX *pepraken* reflects *mkr*, "sold him" (cf. 12:9). The context suggests that the original was *skr*. The expression *sikkar běyad*, "shut up in the hand of," is a rare (only here and Isa 19:4) equivalent of *siggar běyad*, "enclose in the hand

of" (cf. 17:46; 24:19; 26:8). Confusion of *n* and *s* was possible especially in scripts of the second century B.C., and confusion of *m* and *s* was extremely easy in scripts of the third through the first centuries B.C.

9. *that Saul was devising evil against him* So MT: *ky ʿlyw šʾwl mḥryš hrʿh,* to which 4QSam^b has been corrected by erasure (see Cross, "Oldest Manuscripts," 173). LXX$^{B (cf. L)}$ reflects a differing interpretation and (perhaps) word order: *hoti ou parasiōpa saoul peri autou tēn kakian* (= *ky* [*lʾ*] *hḥryš šʾwl ʿlyw hrʿh*), "that Saul would not pass over the evil concerning him in silence" (the intrusive negative arising from misunderstanding of the uncommon word *mḥryš,* "devising," as "keeping silent about").

he said So MT. LXX (and probably 4QSam^b; see Cross, "Oldest Manuscripts," 173): "*David* said."

the ephod LXX (and probably 4QSam^b; see Cross, "Oldest Manuscripts," 173) adds "of Yahweh." Omit with MT.

11,12. These verses are corrupt in all witnesses except (apparently) 4QSam^b (see Cross, "Oldest Manuscripts," 173-175). We read: [11]*wʿth hyrd šʾwl kʾšr šmʿ ʿbdk yhwh ʾlhy yśrʾl hgydh lʿbdk wyʾmr yhwh yrd* [12]*wyʾmr dwd hysgrw bʿly qʿlh˙ty wʾt ʾnšy byd šʾwl wyʾmr yhwh ysgyrw.* (1) At the beginning of v 11 MT omits *wʿth* and has in its place *hysgrny bʿly qʿylh bydw,* "Will the lords of Keilah hand me over to him?" a dittograph from v 12 incorrectly inserted at this point. (2) LXX^B reflects a similar fragment at the beginning (*ei apokleisthēsetai* = *hysgr*), but in this case the intrusive words represent a "correction" made after the loss in LXX^B of everything from the first *wyʾmr yhwh* to the second in a long haplography (cf. Wellhausen). (3) The originality of *wʿth,* "Now then," supported by LXX^{BL} and the space requirements of 4QSam^b, was already recognized by Budde. (4) The reading *hgydh lʿbd*[*k*], "Inform your servant!" is that of 4QSam^b (cf. LXX). It varies slightly from MT (*hgd nʾ lʿbdk,* "Inform your servant!"), and there is no basis for choosing between them.

13. *and his men* So MT, LXX^L, OL. LXX^B: "and the men who were with him." Cf. the *Textual Note* to v 5.

six hundred So MT. LXX gives "*four* hundred" as the number, perhaps under the influence of 22:2 (Wellhausen), but there is uncertainty throughout the story (cf. 25:13; 27:2).

When Saul was told Represented variously by *wlšʾwl hgd* (MT, LXX^B) and *wygd lšʾwl* (4QSam^b, LXX^L); cf. Cross, "Oldest Manuscripts," 174.

NOTES

23 1. *Keilah.* The name is preserved in the name of the village of Khirbet Qîlā, some 8 miles NW of Hebron, and the ancient site is Tell Qîlā, just S of Tell esh-Sheikh Madhkûr, ancient Adullam (see the NOTE at 22:1). Keilah, though nominally a city of Judah (Josh 15:44), is here considered by David's men to be "deep in the recesses of the Philistines" (v 3), and the attitude of the lords of Keilah as described in v 12 suggests that the inhabitants were not Judahite at this time. Evidently we are to understand that Keilah was an independent city (like Jerusalem), which because of its location was important to both Philistine and Israelite interests.

5. *He drove off their cattle.* An odd detail. Why would the Philistines have cattle with them on such a raid? Why is the capture of the livestock mentioned before the defeat of the owners? Perhaps the cattle were brought along to forage for what was left on the threshing floors. David's first task would then have been to stop the destruction by driving the cattle away before proceeding to the battle itself.

6. This parenthetical verse prepares the reader for the appearance of Abiathar and the ephod in vv 9*ff* and also tightens the connection between the present episode and the foregoing material. Some commentators regard the verse as a redactional expansion. It is curious that no mention of priest or ephod is made in connection with David's consultations of Yahweh in vv 1-5 above, and Grønbaek (*Aufstieg Davids,* 153-154) takes this as evidence for a combination of originally discrete traditions, one of them (vv 1-5) concerned primarily with David's liberation of Keilah, the other (vv 7-13) interested in the Keilah affair only as a backdrop to the conflict between David and Saul. See further the COMMENT.

an ephod. That is, an instrument of divination (see the NOTE at 14:3). The answers received in vv 11b and 12b below are essentially of the "yes" or "no" type, and we may assume that the Urim and Thummim are employed (cf. the NOTE at 14:40-42).

9. *Saul was devising evil against him.* Cf. the NOTE at 24:10.

13. *to wander where they might.* Hebrew *wayyithallĕkû ba'ăšer yithallākû,* lit. "and they went about where they went about." Cf. esp. II Sam 15:20: *wa'ănî hôlēk 'al 'ăšer 'ănî hôlēk,* "and I am going where I am going," that is, "when I go wherever I may go." For further examples of the idiom in Biblical Hebrew and related languages, see Driver. J. A. Soggin has argued for a translation, "'And they went where they were to go' or something similar, thus presupposing plans and itineraries that had been established beforehand, just as the terrain required." See "*wayyithallᵉkû ba'ᵃšer yithallākû,* 1 Samuel 23,13a," in *Old Testament and Oriental Studies* (Rome: Pontifical Biblical Institute, 1975) 235-236; first published in *BeO* 14 (1972) 78.

COMMENT

The subtitle of this section might be "The Value of a Priest." It illustrates the immediate significance of the events just described in the Nob story: for all of Saul's dogged pursuit, David, with a priest of Yahweh at his side, will never come to harm. The divine oracle is now David's ally to guide him into safety, and Saul can do no more than chase blindly and hopelessly after him. So it is that David, finding himself in danger of being trapped inside the walls of Keilah after liberating it from a Philistine raiding party, is warned away in the nick of time by Yahweh's oracle under Abiathar's administration.

A certain tension exists within the narrative here. Verses 1-5 seem to represent a complete unit by themselves. They present David as a kind of unofficial protector of Israel, or at least of Judah, who is instructed by oracle to save Keilah. No mention is made of Abiathar. The unit ends with the concluding formula, "Thus David liberated the inhabitants of Keilah." Verses 7-13 describe subsequent events; the relationship of Saul and David, the overriding interest of the compiler of the larger narrative, is again at the center of attention. Abiathar now administers the oracle; indeed, the parenthesis in v 6 seems designed specifically to smooth over the transition from vv 1-5, where the oracle is operated anonymously, to vv 7-13, where Abiathar is in charge.

It seems clear, then, that this section was produced when the compiler of the history of David's rise enlarged upon an existing bit of narrative about the liberation of Keilah—a story in which the oracle already played a part—in order to make his point about the value of an oracle priest to David at this particular juncture in the larger story, immediately following the Nob episode and David's acquisition of Abiathar (for Grønbaek's somewhat different interpretation, see the NOTE at v 6). Apparently we are to assume that David's alliance with his priest of Yahweh continued to serve him well, though our narrator will mention the oracle only once more (30:7).

XXXV. JONATHAN'S VISIT (23:14-18)

23 14 David lived in strongholds in the wilderness; he lived in the
hill country in the wilderness of Ziph. And although Saul sought him
day after day, Yahweh did not give him up to him. 15 Still David was
afraid because Saul had marched out seeking his life.

Once, when David was in Horesh in the wilderness of Ziph,
16 Jonathan, Saul's son, arose and came to [him] at Horesh and encouraged him through Yahweh.

17 "Do not be afraid!" he told him. "For my father, Saul, will never
lay a hand on you! You will rule over Israel, and I shall be your
second-in-command. Even Saul, my father, knows this!" 18 Then
when the two of them had made a covenant before Yahweh, Jonathan
went home and David remained in Horesh.

TEXTUAL NOTES

23 14. *in strongholds* So MT: *bmṣdwt*. LXX here and in 23:19 conflates transliterated (LXX^{B} *en maserem*, LXX^{A} *en masereth*, OL *in masseret*) and translated (LXX *en tois stenois*, "in the narrow places"; cf. OL) forms, all reflecting *bmṣrt*. Cf. the second *Textual Note* at 22:4.

in the hill country in the wilderness of Ziph So MT: *bhr bmdbr zyp*. As Cross ("Oldest Manuscripts," 174, n. 49) has pointed out, "There is extensive conflation of transliterated and translated forms of the names [in LXX] leading to some subsequent corruption. [But] critical restoration of the Old Greek makes clear that LXX and MT do not diverge significantly here. . . ." MT's order "in the hill country in the wilderness" (cf. LXX^{AL}) is reversed in LXX^{B} (*en tē erēmō en tō orei*), which also appends after "Ziph" (*zeiph*) the phrase *en tē gē tē auchmōdei*, "in the parched land," shown by 23:19 and 26:1 (where *zpym*, "Ziphites," is rendered with a form of *auchmōdēs*, "drought-stricken"; cf. 23:15) to be another attempt to render all or part of the preceding words.

Yahweh So LXX, 4QSam^{b}. MT: "God."

15. *was afraid because* This is shown by v 17 to be the correct understanding of *wyr' ky* (thus *wayyīrā' kî*), which MT, LXX treat as *wayyar' kî*, "saw that."

in Horesh in the wilderness of Ziph We read *bmdbr zyp bḥršh*, "in the wilderness of Ziph, in Horesh," with MT, as corroborated by Syr. and LXX^{L} *en tē erēmō tē auchmōdei en tē kainē*, "in the wilderness of the parched land/Ziph [see above], in the newness [*bḥdšh*]." LXX^{B} is different: *en tō orei tō auchmōdei en tē kainē zeiph* = *bhr zyp bḥdš* [again for *bḥrš*] *zyp*, "in the hill country of Ziph, in the newness [Horesh] of Ziph."

16. *Yahweh* So LXX, 4QSam^{b}. MT: "God."

NOTES

23 14. *in the hill country in the wilderness of Ziph.* David has fled farther S into the Judean hills. The ancient town of Ziph (Josh 15:55) was perched high on the ridge of hills that overlooked the wilderness of Judah some 12 miles SE of Keilah; Tell Zîp is ca. 5 miles SSE of Hebron.

15. *in Horesh.* That is, in the Wood (*baḥōrĕšâ*). Most commentators point to modern Khirbet Khoreisa, ca. 2 miles from Tell Zîp.

16. *and encouraged him through Yahweh.* Hebrew *wayḥazzēq 'et-yādô bĕyahweh*, lit. "and strengthened his hand in Yahweh." The expression "strengthen the hand" (*ḥizzēq yād*) generally means "encourage," especially of the fearful (Neh 6:9; etc.), and it is used here to describe Jonathan's encouragement of his frightened (vv 15,17) friend; but as Judg 9:24 suggests, it also implies support in an undertaking. In this case the pledge of encouragement and support is formally sanctioned *bĕyahweh*, "in/through Yahweh" (cf. v 18).

17. *I shall be your second-in-command.* The tone of Jonathan's speech is reminiscent of his plea for his family in 20:11-17 (see the NOTE there), an interpolation in the story of Jonathan's contribution to David's escape from court. Here Saul's sons acknowledges the inevitability of David's succession (cf. the second NOTE at 20:13) and relegates himself to the position of "second-in-command" (*mišneh;* cf. Esther 10:3, where it is said that Mordecai was *mišneh* to King Xerxes). II Chron 28:7 suggests that *mišnê hammelek*, "the King's Second-in-Command" was a formal title; it is listed there with *ben-hammelek*, "the King's Son, the Crown Prince," and *nĕgîd habbayit*, "the Minister of the (Royal) Household."

18. Cf. 18:1-5 (§ XXIV-B); 20:8 and the NOTES there.

COMMENT

Jonathan visits David at his wilderness hideout, encourages him, and renews his pledge to him. As in 20:11-17 Jonathan fully acknowledges David's future greatness, now adding explicitly that he knows David will be king and that he expects nothing more for himself than the position of second-in-command (cf. the NOTE at v 17).

This passage should be read as a kind of preface to the first story of David's sparing Saul's life in 23:19 - 24:23. As we shall see, this first such story, when critically examined, proves to have been introduced secondarily and revised on the pattern of the second (26:1-25), which once stood alone in the larger history of David's rise to power. The first story shares the spirit of the tale of David's duel with the Philistine champion, as well as certain other passages, including 20:11-17,23,40-42 and 25:28-31 (cf. 18:1-4); it is introduced with this account of a secret conversation in the wilderness, which reasserts David's high destiny and Jonathan's willing complicity in the course of events, and in particular prepares the audience for Saul's climactic speech in 24:17-22, especially 20-21, where he accedes to the inevitability of David's succession. The present passage further provides that in the first story in which David spares Saul's life, David will be fully aware of his own future, thus heightening the piety and mercy of his self-restraint. The formal beginning of this story follows immediately.

XXXVI. ANOTHER NARROW ESCAPE (23:19-24:1)

23 19 Some Ziphites went up to Saul at Gibeah to tell him, "David is
hiding near us in the strongholds of Horesh on the hill of Hachilah,
which is south of Jeshimon. 20 Therefore whenever the king wishes to,
let him come down! It will be our task to hand him over to the king."
21 "May you be blessed by Yahweh," said Saul, "for feeling compassion for me! 22 Go investigate again, and learn the place where his
fleet foot is!" (For he thought, "Perhaps he is planning some trickery!") 23 "Watch and find out, and then I shall go with you. And if he
is in the area, I shall track him down out of all the thousands of
Judah!" 24 So they arose and went to Ziph ahead of Saul.

David and his men were in the wilderness of Maon, in the desert
south of Jeshimon, 25 when Saul and his men came looking for him;
and when David was told, he went down to a certain crag which was
in the wilderness of Maon. As soon as Saul heard of this, he pursued
David into the wilderness of Maon. 26 [He] made his way to the
slope of the mountain on one side, David and his men being on the
mountain's slope on the other side. As David was hurrying to get
away from Saul, and Saul and his men were circling in on David and
his men to capture them, 27 a messenger came to Saul to say, "Come
quickly, for the Philistines have made a raid on the land!"; 28 so Saul
turned back from his pursuit of David and went to oppose the Philistines. (It is for this reason that that place is called Sela-hammahlekoth.)

24 1 Then David went up from there and ensconced himself in the
strongholds of En-gedi.

TEXTUAL NOTES

23 19. *Some Ziphites* So MT: *zpym.* LXX *hoi zeiphaioi* suggests *hzpym,* "*The* Ziphites." This is followed in LXX by *ek tēs auchmōdous,* "from the parched land," which (as in 26:1) is a second attempt to render *hzpym* (cf. the *Textual Notes* to 23:14 and 23:15), as if "Those from the parched land went up to Saul, etc." The basis for the representation of *zyp* by *auchmōdēs* is unknown.

to tell him, "David . . ." LXX *legontes ouk idou daueid* reflects *l'mr l' hnh dwd,* lit. "saying, 'No! Behold, David . . .' " which should surely be *l'mr lw hnh dwd,* lit. "saying *to him,* 'Behold, David. . . .' " MT is somewhat different: *l'mr hlw' dwd,* lit. "saying, '*Is not* David . . . ?' "

the strongholds See the *Textual Note* to 23:14.

20. *whenever the king wishes* Reading *lkl npš hmlk,* lit. "according to all the desire of the king (to come down)," on the basis of LXX *pan to pros psychēn tou basileōs.* MT has *lkl 'wt npšk hmlk,* lit. "according to all the desire of your soul, O king!" But *'wt* and *npš,* both of which can mean "desire," represent a conflation of variants.

to, let him come down That is, "to come down, let him come down!" So 4QSam^b: *lrdh yrd.* Surely the rare form of the infinitive (cf. Gen 46:3) is original, despite MT *lrdt.* For *yrd,* MT has *rd,* "come down!"

It will be our task Reading *'lynw* with 4QSam^b (cf. Smith). Compare MT *wlnw,* "*And* it will be our task . . ." (but *l-* rarely has such force, for which we expect *'l* [Driver]); LXX *pros hymas* = *'lynw,* "to us" (read with the preceding words).

22. *investigate* Reading *hbynw* with Syr. and a few Hebrew MSS. MT has *hkynw,* "make firm" (cf. LXX *kai hetoimasate,* "and prepare"); but this nowhere else means "consider" (or even "make certain") in a sense appropriate to this passage.

and learn After which (*wd'w*) MT (cf. LXX^{AL}) adds *wr'w,* "and see," in anticipation of the next verse. Omit with LXX^B.

the place Literally, "*his* place" (*mqwmw*).

fleet MT has *my r'hw,* "Who saw him?" (thus MT: "and learn and see his place where his foot is! Who has seen him there?"), which though shared by Targ., Syr., is probably a corruption of *mhrh,* "quickly," as preserved in the *Vorlage* of LXX (*en tachei*), on the basis of which we may restore *hmhrh,* "swift, fleet," with Wellhausen, Budde, Hertzberg.

Perhaps Reading *'ūlay* (cf. LXX: *mē pote*), which is misvocalized in MT as *'ēlay,* "to me."

he is planning some trickery MT *'rwm y'rm hw';* LXX = *y'rm.* There is no reason to emend to the plural (*y'rmw,* "*they* [i.e. the Ziphites] are planning some trickery"); Saul is remembering how David evaded him at Keilah. See further the NOTE.

23. *Watch and find out* MT, followed by LXX^{AL}, Syr., here adds *mkl hmḥb'ym 'šr ytḥb' šm wšbtm 'ly 'l* [= *'l*] *nkwn*, "in which of all the hiding-places he is hiding, and return to me assuredly [that is, 'with sure information'; cf. Driver]. . . ." All of this was missing from the Old Greek, as shown by its absence in LXX^{B}, where there is no apparent motivation for its loss. It may be an old variant of v 22a, which found its way into the text at this point. In any case the shorter reading of LXX^{B} is to be preferred.

I shall go So MT, OL. LXX^{BA}, Syr.: "*we* shall go."

24. *So they arose and went to Ziph* So MT. LXX^{B} (cf. LXX^{A}, Syr.): "So *the Ziphites* arose and went."

Maon MT *m'wn* (*mā'ôn*); LXX^{A} *maōn* (= *m'wn*); LXX^{B} *maan* (= *m'n*). LXX^{L} (*tē epēkoō* = *šm'wn*) and Josephus (*Ant.* 6.280: *tē simōnos* =*šm'wn*) add *š* to read the more familiar name *šm'wn*, "Simeon," perhaps partly under the influence of *hyšmwn*, "Jeshimon," later in the verse.

south of MT *'l ymyn*. LXX *kath' hesperan ek dexiōn* seems to reflect a conflation of two slightly different readings, viz. *'l ym*, "*west* of," and *mymyn*, "south of" (cf. 23:19).

25. *looking for him* Reading *lbqšw*, lit. "to seek him," with LXX. MT omits *-w*, "him," before the following word (*wygdw*).

which Reading *'šr* on the basis of LXX in preference to MT *wyšb*, "and dwelt."

26. *hurrying* So MT: *nḥpz*. LXX: *skepazomenos*, "covered" (= *nḥph?*).

from Saul LXX and certain other MSS add "and his men." Omit with MT.

circling in So MT: *'ṭrym*, which has been questioned because of a misunderstanding of the situation depicted. Saul's men are circling around the mountain in an attempt to trap David, who is on the other side; see the NOTE. LXX has *parenebalon* (= *'ṭym*, "were dashing [at]"?); LXX^{L}: *pareplagiazon* (= *'brym*, "were crossing over [against]"?).

NOTES

23 19. *on the hill of Hachilah . . . south of Jeshimon.* Neither of these places, mentioned also in 26:1, can be located with certainty. The connection with Maon in v 24 below places the action somewhere S and E of Hebron (see the NOTE at v 24).

24. *the wilderness of Maon.* Maon, modern Tell Ma'în, ca. 8 miles S of Hebron, commanded the surrounding territory from atop a tall hill. David and his men were encamped to the E of the town in the desert.

26. The tactical situation described here requires some explanation. David and Saul are both at "the crag" (*hassela'*, v 25)—David and his men on one slope, Saul and his men on the other (*miṣṣad hāhār mizzeh . . . miṣṣad hāhār*

mizzeh). Saul's troops are "circling in on (*ʿōṭĕrîm ʾel*) David and his men"; that is, Saul is advancing toward David around the mountain from both directions in a kind of pincer movement. David, though "hurrying (*neḥpāz*) to get away," is trapped and cannot hold out for long.

27. The messenger arrives in the nick of time and David escapes.

28. *Sela-hammahlekoth.* That is, *selaʿ hammaḥlĕqôt.* This popular explanation of the name relates it to *maḥălōqet,* which elsewhere in Biblical Hebrew means "division," as a formal division of the people or course of the Levites, and, at least in Postbiblical Hebrew (cf. Jastrow, 762), could also mean "dissension, strife; faction." The point then is either *Crag of Divisions,* "Saul and David there parting from the neighborhood of one another" (Driver), or *Crag of Factions/Crag of Dissension,* that is, the place where dissenting parties struggled with one another. Popular explanations aside, however, it is likely that we should think not of *ḥālaq,* "divide," but of *ḥālaq,* "be slippery, smooth," and that something like "Slippery Rock" (see BDB) or "Bald Mountain" (cf. Mount Halak [*ḥālāq*] in Josh 11:17; 12:7) was originally meant.

COMMENT

Saul pursues his fugitive son-in-law to a remote mountain in the wilderness of Maon, which becomes the scene of another close call for David. Just as Saul's troops, circling round the mountain on both sides in an effort to surround David's smaller force, are ready for the final assault, a messenger arrives (as if by chance but presumably by providential intervention) and Saul is called away to war.

Viewed in broader perspective, this passage is to be read with 24:2-23; together they compose an account of how David spares Saul's life that is shaped on the pattern of another, older such account in 26:1-25. Verses 19-24a of the present story can be seen to be an expanded version of 26:1, the introduction to the story, and the continuation of 23:24a in 24:2 corresponds to 26:2. See further the COMMENT to 24:2-23.

However, 23:24b-24:1, in which the main action of the present section occurs, corresponds to nothing in 26:1-25. It is an etiological narrative that preserves a traditional explanation of the place name Sela-hammahlekoth (see the NOTE at v 28). It may have been inserted quite late into the larger narrative, after the later expansion of which 23:14-24a and 24:2-23 were a part; or on the other hand it may have already stood at this point in the older history of David's rise between the Keilah episode (23:1-13) and the (original) story of how David spared Saul's life (26:1-25), having been incorporated into the retelling of the story. In any case, it now serves to retard the story begun in 23:19-24a and continued in 24:2*ff* below.

XXXVII. DAVID SPARES SAUL'S LIFE
(24:2-23)

24 2 When Saul returned from his pursuit of the Philistines, he was
told that David was in the wilderness of En-gedi. 3 So he took three
thousands of men picked from all of Israel and went to search for
David and his men upon the Wild Goat Rocks. 4 When he reached the
sheepfolds beside the road, there was a cave there, and [he] went in
to relieve himself.

Now David and his men were sitting in the inner recesses of the
cave, 5 and David's men said to him, "This is the day of which Yahweh said to you, 'I am going to deliver your enemy into your power,
and you may do with him as seems good to you!'" So David arose and
stealthily cut off the skirt of Saul's robe.

6 Afterwards, however, David was conscience-stricken because he
had cut off the skirt of [Saul's] robe. 7 "Yahweh forbid," he told his
men, "that I should do such a thing to my lord, to Yahweh's anointed,
to raise my hand against him! For he is Yahweh's anointed!" 8 David
restrained his men with words and did not permit them to attack Saul,
and Saul got up and went on down the road.

9 Then David emerged from the cave behind [Saul] and called after
[him], "My lord, the king!" When Saul looked behind him, [David]
knelt down face to the ground and paid homage. 10 "Why do
you listen to the words of the people," [he] said to Saul, "when they
say, 'David is seeking to harm you'? 11 This very day you have
seen that although Yahweh delivered you into my power in the cave, I
refused to slay you and looked on you with compassion. I said, 'I shall
not raise my hand against my lord, for he is Yahweh's anointed!'
12 Look, the skirt of your robe is in my hand! I cut off the skirt but
did not slay you! Know this and see that there is no wickedness or
perfidy in me. I have not sinned against you, but you are hunting me
down to take my life. 13 May Yahweh judge between me and you! For
Yahweh will give me vengeance upon you, though I shall not touch
you. 14 As the proverb of the ancients says: 'From wicked men does
wickedness proceed.' So I shall not touch you!

15 "After whom has the king of Israel marched out? After whom
are you chasing? After a dead dog or even a single flea! 16 But Yahweh will be the arbiter and will judge between me and you. May he
take notice and uphold my case and set me free from your power!"
17 When David had finished saying these things to Saul, Saul said,
"Is that your voice, David my son?" and began to weep. 18 "You are
in the right rather than I," he told David, "for you have rendered me
goodness and I have rendered you evil. 19 And today you have demonstrated how you treat me with goodness, in that Yahweh handed
me over to you and you did not slay me. 20 For when a man finds his
enemy, does he send him on his way with goodness? So may Yahweh
repay you in kind for the goodness you have done today! 21 And now,
since I know that you will surely become king and that the kingship
of Israel will be established in your hand, 22 then swear to me by Yahweh that you will not cut off my descendants after me or blot out my
name from my father's house!"
23 So David swore to Saul, and then Saul went home while David
and his men went up to the stronghold.

TEXTUAL NOTES

24 3. *he took* MT: "*Saul* took"; LXX: "he took *with him.*" The original had neither expansion.

the Wild Goat Rocks So MT: *ṣwry hyʿlym.* The mistake in LXX[B] (*eddaiem/saddaiem,* "Saddaim"?) was corrected marginally to read *tēs thēras tōn elaphōn* (so LXX[L]), which agrees with MT.

6. *the skirt of* [*Saul's*] *robe* Reading *'t knp mʿylw* with LXX against MT *'t knp 'šr lš'wl,* "the skirt that Saul had."

7. *to my lord* So MT. Omitted by LXX, perhaps by haplography before "to Yahweh's anointed" (*l'dny lmšyḥ yhwh*).

8. *restrained* MT has *wyšsʿ,* which ought to mean "tore to pieces," and seems too strong even if taken figuratively. Can *šsʿ* mean "disperse" (KB)? Stoebe assumes a colloquialism in popular speech meaning to take away from someone the possibility of doing something. But *wyšsʿ* remains dubious. LXX *kai epeisen,* "and he persuaded/prevailed upon," is little help (a guess from context?). Budde proposed *wymnʿ,* "restrained"; this is the meaning we require, but can hardly have been the original reading. The formal similarity of *s* and *q* suggests *wyšqʿ,* "settled down, calmed," but the verb does not occur in Biblical Hebrew with exactly the sense required here.

to attack MT *lqwm 'l* (= *'l*), lit. "to arise against." LXX$^{L(cf. BA)}$: "to arise *and slaughter*."

and Saul got up and went on down the road Reading *wyqm š'wl wyrd bdrk* on the basis of LXX^{B} *kai anestē saoul kai katebē tēn hodon.* MT: *wš'wl qm mhm'rh wylk bdrk,* "and Saul arose from the cave and went on his way" (cf. LXX^{L}).

9. At the beginning of the verse we follow the text of LXX^{B}, which reflects *wyqm dwd 'ḥryw mhm'rh wyqr' 'ḥry š'wl l'mr,* lit. "and David emerged behind him from the cave, and he called after Saul, saying. . . ." MT has *wyqm dwd 'ḥry kn wyṣ' mn hm'rh wyqr' 'ḥry š'wl l'mr,* "and David arose *afterward and went out* of the cave, and he called after Saul, saying. . . ."

[*David*] *knelt down* LXX found it necessary in Greek (as it is in English) to make the subject explicit. Omit "David" with MT.

10. *the words of the people* So LXX (= *'t dbry h'm*). MT has *'t dbry 'dm,* "the words of *men*." There is no basis for a preference here.

to harm you So MT: *r'tk,* lit. "your evil." LXX = *npšk,* "your life."

11. *I refused* Reading *w'm'n* on the basis of LXX *kai ouk ēboulēthēn.* MT: *w'mr* (*wĕ'āmar*), "He will say" (?), in anticipation of *w'mr* (*wā'ōmar*), "I said," later on in the verse.

and looked on you with compassion Reading *wtḥs 'yny 'lyk,* lit. "and my eye looked compassionately upon you" (cf. Vulg.: *sed pepercit tibi oculus meus*). Extant MSS of MT and LXX reflect the loss of *'yny* before *'lyk* (*homoioarkton*), and LXX seems to have been adjusted to read *w'ḥs 'lyk,* "and I spared you" (*kai epheisamēn sou*).

12. *Look* The short, simple reading of LXX (*kai idou* = *whnh*) seems preferable, but how are we to account for MT *w'by r'h gm r'h,* "And, my father, see, yea, see!" Perhaps this a conflation of variants (*w'by r'h* and *gm r'h*) of which LXX *whnh* is a third.

I cut off the skirt So LXX$^{(B)}$ (*egō aphērēka to pterygion* = *'nky krty 't hknp*). MT is somewhat different: *ky bkrty 't knp m'ylk,* "For when I cut off the skirt of your robe. . . ."

Know this and see So MT: *d' wr'h.* LXX reflects *wd' wr'h hywm,* "*And* know (this) and see *today*."

perfidy MT *pš',* evidently rendered twice by LXX as *asebeia,* "ungodliness," and *athetēsis,* "lawlessness."

are hunting . . . down MT *ṣdh* (*ṣōdê*). The verb occurs elsewhere only in Exod 21:13, which requires the meaning, "lie in wait for" or "hunt down (with malicious intent)." LXX *desmeueis,* "you would put (me) in chains," suggests *ṣr* (or less likely *ṣrr*), a simple corruption of *ṣd* (*ṣād*), "hunting."

14. *the ancients* It has long been conjectured that MT *hqdmny,* "the ancient one," should be read as a plural, the final *-m* having been lost before the succeeding *mrš'ym,* and this is now supported by 4QSam^{a}: [*hqd*]*mnyym.*

15. At the beginning of the verse LXX inserts, "And now. . . ."

has the king of Israel marched out So MT. LXX: "have you marched out, O king of Israel!"

or So 4QSam^{a}: *'w* (cf. LXX). Omitted in MT before *'ḥry,* "after."

16. *May he take notice* So LXX (= *yr'*). MT *wyr'*, "and he will take notice."

19. *you have demonstrated* LXX adds *moi* = *lî*, "to me." Omit with MT.

in that 4QSam[a] (cf. LXX): *'šr*. MT *'t 'šr* is reminiscent of the preceding *'t 'šr*.

20. *when a man finds* MT's reading *ky ymṣ' 'yš*, which has been questioned (Budde, Smith, GK §112hh,N; cf. Stoebe), is now also represented by 4QSam[a]: *[ky' ymṣ' ']yš*.

his enemy Followed in LXX by *en thlipsei*, "in a tight place" (= *bṣr?*), perhaps reflecting a vestige of a variant of *'ybw*, "his enemy," viz. *ṣrw*, "his adversary"(?).

may Yahweh repay you in kind So MT: *wyšlmk*. LXX reflects *wyšlmw*, "may Yahweh repay *him* in kind," a reminiscence of the first part of the verse.

you have done today Reading *'šr 'śyth hywm* with LXX[B], as partly confirmed by 4QSam[a], which ends the verse with *hywm hzh*, "this day." MT: *tḥt hywm hzh 'šr 'śyth ly*, "in return for this day wherein thou has wrought for me" (Driver).

21. *and that the kingship . . . in your hand* Space considerations show that the word order of 4QSam[a] agrees with that of LXX[L] (*wqmh mmlkt yśr'l bydk*) against MT and LXX[B] (*wqmh bydk mmlkt yśr'l*).

23. *home* So MT: *'l bytw*, lit. "to his house." LXX reflects *'l mqwmw*, "to his *place*," a simple variant.

NOTES

24 2. *his pursuit of the Philistines*. See 23:27-28.

the wilderness of En-gedi. En-gedi was the most important and permanent of the several spring-fed oases that lay in antiquity below the cliffs of the wilderness of Judah on the W shore of the Dead Sea (cf. Josh 15:62). The name is preserved in that of the modern village 'Ain Jidi, ca. 18 miles ESE of Hebron and ca. 17 miles ENE of Ma'în, ancient Maon, near which David was encamped in the last episode.

three thousands. Three units or contingents; see the NOTE at 4:10.

the Wild Goat Rocks. Hebrew *ṣûrê hayyĕ'ēlîm*. "Although the site is not precisely known, it was in the limestone wilderness near En-gedi . . . where ibexes are still plentiful." So L. E. Toombs in *IDB*, 4.843.

4. *to relieve himself*. That is, "to defecate." MT's euphemism is "to cover his feet."

5. *the day of which Yahweh said to you. . . .* We have been told of no such promise.

5b-6. *So David arose . . . the skirt of* [*Saul's*] *robe*. Some commentators prefer to relocate these verses after v 8a. Accordingly David's speech in v 7 would be understood as a reply to the implied suggestion in v 5a that he slay Saul; then after having restrained his men he would proceed to cut off Saul's skirt. Other arrangements have also been proposed (for a full discussion, see Stoebe). It is difficult, however, to explain how such a displacement could have come into the text, and in the absence of textual evidence to the contrary we must reckon with the present arrangement. Nevertheless, Smith's suggestion that vv 5b-6 and 12 (or 12ab$_a$) are expansive (based on the spear incident in c 26) carries much conviction. See the COMMENT.

5b. *the skirt of Saul's robe.* Cf. 15:27-28 and the NOTE there. The situation here is not, however, the same. The piece of Saul's robe that David cuts away is to serve as proof of David's refused opportunity to strike down his king and thus of his loyalty to him (see v 12).

6. *David was conscience-stricken.* Hebrew *wayyak lēb-dāwīd 'ōtô,* lit. "David's heart smote him"; cf. II Sam 24:10.

7. Yahweh's anointed, by virtue of his endowment of divine spirit (see the NOTES at 9:16 and 10:6), was considered sacrosanct. To lay violent hands upon him was thus a sacrilege, indeed a capital offense (cf. I Sam 26:9,11,16,23; II Sam 1:14,16). "Behind this, of course, lie the common primitive ideas of the mana-filled chief and medicine man surrounded by tabus. But in Israel the tabus and sacred character of the king have a different basis. In ancient Israel, when a man was equipped with supernatural powers, it was thought that it was Yahweh's spirit that had 'come into him', had 'clothed itself with him', had been 'poured out into him', and the like" (so S. Mowinckel, *He That Cometh,* tr. G. W. Anderson [New York: Abingdon, n.d.] 65). Here and in c 26 David is presented as absolutely fastidious with respect to the sanctity of Yahweh's anointed, and in II Samuel 1 his outrage over the slaying of Saul is also absolute; the authors of the history of David's rise at every stage of its growth agree in admitting of no possibility that David was tainted by Saul's death.

10. *'David is seeking to harm you.'* Hebrew *dāwīd mĕbaqqēš rā'ātekā,* lit. "David is seeking your evil." The expression "seek (*biqqēš, dāraš*) good/evil" belongs to the formal language of relationships (see the NOTE at 19:4). Note for example Deut 23:7(English 23:6), where Israel is instructed concerning Ammonites and Moabites that "you must not seek their peace and their good (*lō tidrōš šĕlōmām wĕṭōbātām*) all your days, forever!" (cf. also Esth 9:12); that is, Israel is forbidden to enter into any treaty or other formal relationship that will promote the welfare of these old enemies. More generally, then, one who "seeks the good/evil" of someone else is formally and deliberately involved in the promotion or reduction of that person's welfare; thus in Neh 2:10 the enemies of the Jews are described as displeased that someone (viz. Nehemiah) has come "to seek good for the sons of Israel (*lĕbaqqēš ṭôbâ libnê yiśrā'ēl*)." So one who seeks another's evil is deliberately trying to endanger him (I Kings 20:7); he is his enemy (Num 35:23). Compare also 25:26 below.

15. *a dead dog.* Used elsewhere as a term of self-abasement (II Sam 9:8; cf. II Kings 8:13 [LXX]) or, when referring to someone other than oneself, of contempt (II Sam 16:9); the emphasis seems to be more on insignificance than anything else. "Dog" or "dead dog" as a term of self-disparagement is found also in Akkadian letters of the Neo-Assyrian Sargonid period and in the

Amarna archive (cf. *CAD* 8.72; note also the contemptuous expression *kalbu ḫalqu*, "stray dog," in *EA* 67:17); and "dog" is used the same way in the Lachish letters (see ostraca no. 2 [*KAI* 192], line 4; no. 5 [*KAI* 195], line 4; and no. 6 [*KAI* 196], line 3).

a single flea. That is, a single flea upon the dead dog! Hebrew *par'ōš 'eḥad* is obviously another term of self-disparagement. To this use of *'eḥad* compare *EA* 202:13 *miyami anāku kalbu ištēn*, "who am I, a single dog . . . ?"

18-20. In reading these verses one must keep in mind what is said about the terms "goodness" and "evil" in the NOTES at 19:4 and 24:10 above. David has rendered to Saul "goodness" (*haṭṭôbâ*), that is, favorable treatment consistent with their relationship, whereas Saul has rendered David "evil" (*hārā'â*), ill treatment. David is legally in the right, Saul in the wrong; and Saul himself acknowledges this. For the expression "render (*gāmal*) good/evil," cf. Gen 50:15,17; Isa 63:7; cf. 3:9; Prov 3:30; 31:12. For "treat with/do (*'āśâ*) goodness/evil," cf. the discussion in the NOTES at 19:4 and 25:30.

21-22. Cf. 20:13b-16 and the NOTES there where Jonathan acknowledges the inevitability of David's succession (also 23:17) and enters a plea for his family. Here and in the companion piece in c 26 Saul is finally willing to admit the same thing, and like his son he exacts from David an oath of protection for his descendants. Note that Saul seems to acknowledge not only that David will succeed him ("you will surely become king") but that David will also found a dynasty ("the kingship will be established in your hand"); and we must recall in this regard Samuel's words in 13:13-14 above.

23. *the stronghold.* That is, at Adullam (22:1; etc.).

COMMENT

Resuming his pursuit of David after the interruption mentioned in 23:28, Saul returns to the wilderness of Judah and, in obedience to a call of nature, happens alone into the very cave where the object of his search is hiding. David, whose presence "in the inner recesses of the cave" is completely unknown to Saul, piously restrains the impulse of his companions to attack Yahweh's anointed and contents himself instead with a piece of the skirt of the royal robe. When Saul leaves the cave, David follows him out and calls after him, protesting his loyalty and offering the swatch of cloth in evidence. Seeing that David has refused an opportunity to kill him and in fact has protected him from harm at the hands of others, Saul is moved to aver the younger man's innocence and his own culpability. Indeed he goes so far as to acknowledge in words reminiscent of those of Jonathan at Horesh (23:17) that David will become king one day and to exact from David an oath of protection for his descendants, again in words that recall those of his son (20:14-17).

This is the first of two stories in which David refuses an opportunity to take the life of his persecutor. Unlike the second, which is found in 26:1-25, this one is told in a highly tendentious way, recalling by its expansive and flowery speeches the extended insults and threats of the tale of David's single combat with the Philistine champion in c 17, or the earnest entreaty of Jonathan in 20:11-17, or (by way of anticipation) the prognostications of Abigail in 25:28-31. David is portrayed as innocent and pious in the extreme in his fastidious treatment of Saul and elaborate professions of reliance on Yahweh. In contrast, Saul's depiction is completely degrading. His role in the cave scene is ignoble, if not downright vulgar, and his own words in vv 18*ff* condemn his past behavior as unjust and indefensible. The certainty of David's succession is made explicit to a degree that the older narrative of David's rise consistently avoids, and the prediction of kingship is placed in the mouth of Saul himself. Saul's plea for his family in v 22, like the similar but longer plea made earlier by Jonathan (see the NOTE at 20:11-17 and especially the COMMENT on 20:1-21:1), not only looks ahead to subsequent events (esp. II Samuel 9) but also implies that the very survival of the house of Saul will be a result of the generosity and mercy of David.

This passage, then, belongs not to the older history of David's rise to power, but to the series of later expansions and elaborations that includes the overlay of the story of David and the Philistine champion (see the COMMENT on 17:11-11,32-40,42-48a,49,51-54 [§ XXIV-A]), as well as 20:11-17,23,40-42; 23:14-18,19-24a; and 25:28-31. The growth of this section and its incorporation into the larger context seem to have been rather complex processes. As we have already seen (cf. the COMMENTS on 23:14-18 and 23:19-24:1), 24:2-23 should be read together with materials that precede it as a single narrative unit extending from 23:14-24:23. Viewed in this larger perspective the story shows clear signs of revision toward the pattern of the second (older) account of how David spared Saul's life in 26:1-25.[1] An expanded version of the intro-

[1] The marked similarities between the stories in cc 23-24 (A) and c 26 (B) have been interpreted in several ways. The older source critics tended to regard one as derived from the other (usually A from B) in a purely literary way (cf. Smith; Wellhausen, *Prolegomena,* 264-265; etc.) or to explain the duplications in terms of redactional adjustment (cf. Budde, etc.). More recent scholars, working under the impact of the insights of form criticism, have preferred to think of a traditional source common to both accounts which developed in different ways in two locations (viz. En-gedi and Ziph); for a variety of reasons, especially the greater detail in parts of B, these scholars have often regarded A as an older, less developed version. The classic form-critical study is that of Klaus Koch (*The Growth of the Biblical Tradition,* tr. S. M. Cupitt [New York: Charles Scribner's Sons, 1969] 132-148). While admitting the possibility of traditional sources lying behind both accounts (see below), the interpretation given here and in the NOTES stands closer to that of the older literary critics, who seem more persuasive for several reasons. The basic stories are really quite different, sharing only the common theme of David's respect for Yahweh's anointed when given the opportunity to slay his enemy. Certain elements

ductory notice in 26:1 appears here in 23:19-24a, and the insertion of 24:5b-6,12 introduces an element into the story to correspond to the business of the spear and cruse of water in c 26 (see the NOTE at vv 5b-6 above). Where the two accounts have internal features in common, the treatment in c 24 regularly looks exaggerated or overstated in comparison with that in c 26. In the present story, for example, David takes no initiative whatever in getting his opportunity to kill Saul; rather he is an innocent, passive participant, into whose power Yahweh delivers his enemy (cf. v 5). In c 26, on the other hand, David creates his own opportunity by leading a secret expedition into Saul's camp, and the divine direction of the affair, though still an important theme (cf. 26:8), must be understood in a more subtle way. Similarly, there is nothing in the spear and cruse of water incident in c 26 to correspond to David's outburst of pious compunction in 24:6-7 after taking the skirt of Saul's robe.[2] Most pointed, however, is c 24's expanded version of Saul's blessing of David in 26:25; in 24:21-22 it has become an acknowledgment of David's future kingship and a plea for mercy on Saul's descendants. As we have already noted (the COMMENT on 3:14-18), these themes were introduced into the present account earlier by the prefaced report of Jonathan's visit at Horesh, an element to which there is no equivalent in 26:1-25.

If we must regard 23:14-24:23 as a tendentiously fashioned equivalent to 26:1-25, however, we are still entitled to wonder what traditional materials have gone into its production. As noted earlier (the COMMENT on 23:19-24:1), the Sela-hammahlekoth episode is probably an old etiological narrative that was absorbed into the whole. Was there a traditional account of an encounter between Saul and David on the Wild Goat Rocks near En-gedi? It seems quite possible that there was. If so, we may be sure that it included nothing about the cutting of Saul's robe and no explicit acknowledgment on Saul's part of David's future as king. Instead it illustrated in a subtle way David's respect for Yahweh's anointed and Saul's dim realization of the veracity of David's vows of loyalty. But the extreme degradation of Saul that we have found here seems inseparable from the story, and for this reason we cannot be confident about our ability to penetrate to an underlying account and discern its shape with certainty.[3]

---

of A, such as 23:19*ff*, have *direct* literary equivalents in B (26:1), and others, which tend to adjust A toward the pattern of B, can be shown to be intrusive in A (vv 5b-6). Finally, the tendentious elaborations of A strongly suggest that it reflects later speculation on the subtle themes of B.

[2] As noted already, the outburst in v 7 must be so interpreted in consequence of the editorial insertion of vv 5b-6. Originally it was a response to the suggestion of David's men in 5a that David should kill Saul. See the NOTE at 5b-6.

[3] Setting this difficulty aside, we might regard the following parts of c 24 as deriving from a narrative based on a traditional source: 24:2-5a,7-11,17-20,23b.

XXXVIII. NOTICE OF SAMUEL'S DEATH (25:1)

25 1 Now Samuel died, and all Israel gathered to mourn for him; and they buried him at his home in Ramah. Then David arose and went down to the wilderness of Maon.

TEXTUAL NOTE

25 1. *Maon* So LXX^B: *maan* = *m'n* (*m'wn*). Cf. LXX^L *tēn epēkoon* = *šm'wn*, "Simeon" (so Syr.), exactly as in 23:24 (see the *Textual Note* there). To be sure, MT has *p'rn*, "Paran," which might seem to command authority as *lectio difficilior;* but the wilderness of Paran, which cannot have extended farther N than the southern extreme of Canaan, is simply too far away to figure into the narrative at this point. In any case the material that follows presents David as resident in the wilderness of Maon.

COMMENT

The second part of the verse (if the reading is correct—see the *Textual Note*) is easy to understand. It is redactional, serving to join what precedes it to the story in 25:2*ff*, in which David will be in the vicinity of Maon. The first part, however, is more difficult. It is the obituary of Samuel, added presumably by the prophetic hand that shaped the earlier stories of Samuel and Saul. It anticipates the story of the seance at En-dor, where it is repeated (28:3). But why, especially since it *does* appear in c 28, has it been inserted here? Perhaps we are to assume that it was at this time that Samuel died and that the notice in 28:3 is not an independent announcement but merely a reminder, included as part of the preparations for the strange story that follows. Indeed, here it is said, *wayyāmot šĕmû'ēl,* "Now Samuel *died,*" and there, *ûšĕmû'ēl mēt,* "Now Samuel *was dead.*"

XXXIX. ABIGAIL AND NABAL
(25:2-25, 27-41, 26, 42-44)

25 2 There was a man of Maon, whose business was in Carmel. The
man was very rich: he had three thousand sheep and one thousand
goats. When he was shearing his sheep in Carmel— 3 (Now the man's
name was Nabal, and his wife's name was Abigail. The woman was of
good intelligence and a lovely appearance, but the man was coarse
and ill-behaved; he was a Calebite.) 4 David heard in the wilderness
that Nabal was shearing his sheep, 5 and [he] dispatched ten young
men.

"Go up to Carmel," he told the young men, "and when you come to
Nabal, hail him in my name 6 and say, 'Thus [. . .]: "May you have
peace! May your house have peace! May all that is yours have peace!
7 Now then, I have heard that you have sheepshearing. Well, some of
your shepherds were with us in the wilderness, and we did not abuse
them; nor did they lose anything all the days they were in Carmel.
8 Ask your young men and they will tell you! So look with favor on
these young men, since we have come at a special time. Give whatever you can find to your son, David!"' "

9 When the young men went and reported all these things to Nabal
in David's name, he behaved arrogantly. 10 [He] made this reply to
David's servants: "Who is David," he said, "and who is the son of
Jesse? Today there are many servants who break away from their
masters! 11 Shall I then take my bread and my wine and the meat I
have butchered for my sheepshearers and give them to men who
come from I know not where?" 12 So David's young men made their
way back and on their return went and reported all these things to
him.

13 "Let everyone strap on his sword!" said David to his men. So
each man strapped on his sword, and David too strapped on his
sword. And there went up behind David about four hundred men,
with two hundred remaining with the gear.

14 Abigail, Nabal's wife, was told by one of the young men, "David
sent messengers from the wilderness to salute our master, and he flew

at them. 15 Yet these men were very good to us: we were not abused,
and we lost nothing all the days we went about with them while we
were out in the field. 16 They were a wall beside us day and night, all
the time we were with them tending sheep. 17 Now then, know this
and consider what you should do, for misfortune is in store for our
master and for all his house. As for him, he is such a scoundrel that
no one can speak to him."

18 Quickly Abigail took two hundred loaves, two skins of wine, five
dressed sheep, five seahs of parched grain, one omer of raisins, and
two hundred fig cakes, and having loaded them on some asses 19 said
to her young men, "Go on ahead of me! I shall be coming along
behind you!" But to her husband she said nothing.

20 It happened that as she was riding her ass down under the cover
of the mountain, David and his men were coming down opposite her.
When she fell in with them— 21 (Now David was just saying, "It was
only in vain that I watched over everything this fellow had in the wilderness, so that nothing was lost of all that was his! For he has repaid
me with evil instead of goodness! 22 May God do thus and so to David
and thus again, if I spare till morning a single one of all he has who
piss against a wall!") 23 When she fell in with them and saw David,
Abigail quickly got down from the ass, fell down before David on her
face, and prostrated herself on the ground 24 at his feet.

"Let the guilt be mine, my lord!" she said. "Let your maidservant
speak to you! Hear what your maidservant has to say! 25 Let my lord
pay no attention to that scoundrel! For as his name is, so is he: his
name is "Foolish," and foolishness is with him. And as for me, your
handmaid, I never saw the young men you sent. 27 So now, let this
gift which your maidservant has brought to my lord be given to the
young men who go about at my lord's heels.

28 "Pardon your maidservant's offense! But Yahweh will surely
make my lord a secure house, for my lord fights the wars of Yahweh,
and through all your days no evil can be found in you. 29 Should a
man arise to pursue you and seek your life, my lord's life will be tied
up in the Document of the Living in the keeping of Yahweh, your
god; but the lives of your enemies he will sling away in the pocket of
a sling. 30 So when Yahweh does for my lord all the good he has
spoken of you and appoints you prince over Israel, 31 this must not be
an obstacle or stumbling block to my lord, that blood was shed in

vain and that my lord gained victory by his own hand. And when
Yahweh has done well by my lord, remember your maidservant!"
32 Then David said to Abigail, "Blessed be Yahweh, god of Israel,
who has sent you to meet me! 33 And blessed be your judgment! And
blessed be you yourself for preventing me this day from entering into
bloodguilt and gaining my victory by my own hand! 34 For as Yahweh, god of Israel, lives, who has restrained me from injuring you, if
you had not come so quickly to meet me, then by morning light Nabal
would have had remaining not one who pisses against a wall!"
35 Then taking from her what she had brought him, David told her,
"Go up to your home in peace! See, I have heard you out and granted
your request!"

36 When Abigail came to Nabal, he was having a banquet in his
house like a king's banquet. [His] heart was merry, for he was very
drunk; so she told him nothing, small or great, until the light of morning. 37 But in the morning when Nabal's wine had left him, his wife
told him these things and his heart died within him; he became a
stone. 38 Some ten days later Yahweh struck him, and he died.

39 When David heard, he said, "Blessed be Yahweh, who has
upheld the case of my insult at Nabal's hand, who has withheld his
servant from evil, and who has turned Nabal's evil back upon his own
head!" Then David sent word to Abigail that he would take her as his
own wife.

40 When David's servants came to Abigail at Carmel, they spoke to
her as follows: "David has sent us to you to take you to be his wife."
41 She arose and bowed down, face to the ground.

"Your maid would be a slave," she said, "to wash your servants'
feet! 26 And now, my lord, as Yahweh lives and as you yourself live—
since Yahweh has restrained you from entering into bloodguilt and
gaining your victory with your own hand, may your enemies and
those who seek my lord's harm be like Nabal!" 42 Then [she] arose in
haste, mounted her ass, and with five maidservants following her,
went after David's messengers and became his wife.

43 (Now David also took Ahinoam from Jezreel. So both of these
women also became his wives. 44 But Saul had given David's wife
Michal, [Saul's] daughter, to Palti, the son of Laish, who was from
Gallim.)

TEXTUAL NOTES

25 2. *Maon* So MT, LXX^B. LXX^L, Syr.: "the wilderness."

whose business So MT, LXX^L, Syr. (*wm'śhw*). LXX^B: "whose sheep" (= *wṣ'nw*).

3. *and a lovely appearance* So MT: *wypt t'r*. LXX (cf. OL): *kai agathē tō eidei sphodra* = *wṭwbwt t'r m'd*, "and a *very good* appearance."

he So MT. LXX, $4QSam^a$: "the man."

a Calebite So MT (*qĕrê*): *klby* (cf. Targ., Vulg.). LXX *kynikos*, "dog-like," probably reflects the same reading. MT (*kĕtîb*): *klbw*, "according to his heart" (?); cf. Smith.

4. *Nabal* So MT. LXX: "Nabal *the Carmelite*."

5. *he told the young men* $4QSam^a$ here reads: [*wy'*]*mr dwyd 'l hn'r*[*ym*], lit. "and David said to the young men." The expressed subject (so also MT) may be omitted with LXX^{BL}. Note that *'l hn'r*[*ym*], "to the young men," agrees in detail with LXX^L *pros ta paidaria* against MT *ln'rym* and LXX^B *tois paidariois*.

6. *Thus* In MT *kh*, "thus," is followed by the perplexing sequence *lḥy* (vocalized *leḥāy*). Does this, in the understanding of the Masoretes, mean "to the one who lives" (pausal form of *laḥay;* so Driver), or "to my brothers" (for *lĕ'eḥāy;* so Smith)? To LXX *eis hōras*, "unto the time," may be compared the LXX treatment of Gen 18:10,14; the understanding of LXX, then, is, "Thus may it be *next year:* may you have peace, etc.," and the renderings of OL (*multis annis*, "for many years") and Josephus (*ep' etē polla*, "for many years") may point to a common elaboration of the same interpretation. So all versions (cf. Syr., Targ.) seem to share the obscure reading of MT. The original may have been: (1) an expression of duration of the following blessing, as the versions suppose (this is least likely); (2) a reference to Nabal as recipient of the message (thus Wellhausen, *lĕ'āḥî*, "to my brother"; cf. Vulg.); or (3) a reference to David—"Thus (says). . . ? . . . ." Our translation assumes the last possibility.

7. *with us in the wilderness, and . . . not* Reading *'mnw bmdbr wl'* with LXX, Syr. MT has suffered a haplography from *w* to *w* and reads *'mnw l'*, "with us. (We did) not. . . ."

8. *these young men* MT *hn'rym*, lit. "the young men" (cf. LXX^{AL}). LXX^B reflects *n'ryk*, "*your* young men/servants," in reminiscence of the same reading earlier in the verse.

we have come MT *bnw* for *b'nw* (so many MSS of MT; cf. LXX *hēkomen*); see GK §§72o, 74k, 76g.

to your son Preceded in MT by "to your servants and," in LXX^A by "to your servants," and in LXX^L by "to the servants." The inconsistency of detail suggests that the expression is secondary and that LXX^B, which omits it entirely, is original.

9. *the young men* So LXX^BL^. MT has "*David's* young men."

all these things to Nabal So MT (cf. LXX^AL^): *'l nbl kkl hdbrym h'lh,* lit. "to Nabal according to all these words." LXX^B^ represents a conflation of slightly variant treatments of the same thought (= *'t hdbrym h'lh 'l nbl wkl hdbrym h'lh,* "all these words to Nabal and all these words").

he behaved arrogantly We read *wypḥz*. MT has *wynwḥw,* "and they (i.e. the young men) rested (waited for a reply?)," but the correct reading can be recovered from LXX with the help of the evidence of 4QSam^b^ for 20:34. In both places LXX has *kai anepēdēsen,* "and he sprang up," which corresponds to *wypḥz* in 4QSam^b^ in the earlier passage (see the *Textual Note* to 20:34). In the present passage it is easy to see how *wypḥz* became *wynḥw: p* and *n* on the one hand and *z* and *w* on the other are among the most easily confused letter-forms in the scripts in which the biblical manuscripts were transmitted.

11. *and my wine* So LXX: *kai ton oinon mou* = *w't yyny*. MT: *w't mymy,* "and my *water*." It is difficult to decide between these variants; but cf. Driver.

for my sheepshearers So LXX: *tois keirousin mou ta probata,* reflecting *lgzzy ṣ'ny,* as confirmed by 4QSam^a^ [*lgzzy ṣ'*]*ṅy*. MT has lost *ṣ'ny* by haplography after *lgzzy* (*homoioteleuton*) and thus reads "for my shearers."

13. *So each man . . . and David too strapped on his sword* So MT (cf. LXX^AL^): *wyḥgrw 'yš 't ḥrbw wyḥgr gm dwd 't ḥrbw* (following immediately upon the command, *ḥgrw 'yš 't ḥrbw,* "Let everyone strap on his sword!"). LXX^B^ omits this rather inelegant sequence, and many translators have welcomed the opportunity to exclude it. But it seems more likely that LXX has suffered a long haplography, a scribe's eye having skipped from the first *tēn rhomphaian autou,* "his sword" (or *'t ḥrbw* if the accident occurred in the *Vorlage* of the Old Greek) to the third.

14. *and he flew at them* MT *wy'ṭ bhm*. See Driver for the attempts of the versions to render this. LXX *kai exeklinen ap' autōn,* "and he fled from them," may represent *wyṭ mhm*.

15. *and we lost nothing* MT: *wl' pqdnw m'wmh*; LXX (somewhat differently): *wl' npqd lnw* (*oude eneteilanto hēmin;* cf. v 7).

while we were out in the field So MT. LXX, Syr. read, "*And* while we were out in the field," and associate the clause with what follows. MT seems preferable in view of 16b, which this stipulation of time, if attached to v 16, would duplicate.

16. *a wall* So MT: *ḥwmh* (see the NOTE). LXX, deeming the metaphor too strong, has softened it to a simile, as if *kḥwmh,* "*like* a wall." Cf. the *Textual Note* to v 37 below.

17. *that no one can speak to him* Represented in MT and the *Vorlage* of LXX by different constructions. MT: *mdbr 'lyw,* lit. "from speaking to him"; LXX *ouk estin lalēsai pros auton* = *'yn ldbr 'lyw,* lit. "it is not (possible) to speak to him" (GK §114).

18. *dressed* MT (*kĕtîb*) *'śwwt;* MT (*qĕrê*) *'ăśûyōt*. Cf. Driver; GK §75v.

one omer So LXX: *gomor hen* = *ḥmr 'ḥd*. MT: *m'h,* "a hundred."

19. *to her husband* MT, LXX^AL^ add "Nabal." Omit with LXX^B^.

20. *were coming down* So MT, LXX^BA^. LXX^L^: "were coming *up*."

22. *to David* So LXX^{BA}. MT, LXX^{L}: "to *the enemies of* David." This expansion is surely a deliberate attempt to distort the original meaning. The threat is never carried out, and a scribe has changed David's words to protect him (or his descendants!) from the consequences of the oath.

23. *before David on her face* Reading *lpny dwd ʿl ʾpyh* on the basis of LXX *enōpion daueid epi prosōpon autēs;* this has become curiously jumbled in MT to *lʾpy dwd ʿl pnyh* (Wellhausen).

and prostrated herself LXX adds "to him" (*autō* = *lô*); delete with MT.

23,24. *on the ground at his feet* Reading *ʾrṣh ʿl rglyw* with LXX$^{B (cf. L)}$. MT: *ʾrṣ wtpl ʿl rglyw,* "on the ground (?). *And she fell down* at his feet. . . ."

24. *the guilt* So MT: *hʿwn.* LXX = *ʿwny,* "*my* guilt."

mine, my lord Reading *by ʾdny* (cf. LXX); MT: *by ʾny ʾdny* (where *ʾny,* "I," is probably a corrupt dittograph of *ʾdny*).

25. *to that scoundrel* MT, LXX^{AL} add: "to Nabal." Omit with LXX^{B}.

the young men Or rather, "*your* young men" (so LXX; MT has "the young men *of my lord*").

26. Verse 26 is clearly out of place. It assumes (1) that David has already been restrained from assaulting Nabal personally, and (2) that Nabal has already met his downfall. It fits most comfortably between vv 41 and 42 below and is tentatively restored there. Perhaps it was displaced from there because Abigail is addressing David directly though he is not present; but such is already the case in v 41!

27. *let this gift . . . be given* MT: *hbrkh hzʾt . . . wntnh,* lit. "this gift . . . let it be given." LXX is different: *labe tēn eulogian . . . kai dōseis* = *qḥ ʾt hbrkh . . . wntth,* "take the gift . . . and give (it). . . ."

who go about at my lord's heels So MT: *hmthlkym lrgly ʾdny.* Again LXX is divergent: *tois parestēkosin tō kyriō mou,* "who are in the company of my lord"; but the Hebrew this reflects is uncertain.

28. *the wars* So MT (correctly): *mlḥmwt.* LXX^{B} reads a singular noun here, suggesting that the Old Greek was reading the word in "defective" orthography (*mlḥmt*). Note also that a different interpretation of the entire clause has arisen in LXX: *hoti polemon kyriou mou ho kyrios polemei,* "for my lord's war does the Lord fight." Comparison with 18:17 seems to exclude the possibility that this reading (which is appropriate enough to the context) arose other than by inner-Greek confusion.

29. *Should a man arise* Reading *wqm ʾdm* for MT *wyqm ʾdm.* See Wellhausen, Driver, Budde, etc.

your god So MT. LXX omits "your."

he will sling away So MT, LXX^{L}, OL. LXX^{B}: "*you* will sling away."

in the pocket of The *Vorlage* of LXX expressed this by *btwk,* "in the midst of," alone. MT shows an expansion: *btwk kp,* "in the midst of the hollow of."

31. *obstacle* 4QSam^{c} reads (with erasure of the second letter) *lṗnqm,* thus *lnqm,* "for vengeance," to which compare Josephus *Ant.* 6.303. But the unusual reading of MT, *lpwqh,* is to be preferred as *lectio difficilior.* The noun *pûqâ* is unique, but the verb *pwq,* "totter," shows its meaning to be similar to that of the following noun, *mkšwl,* "stumbling block" (from *kšl,*

"stumble"); it refers to a cause of tottering. Perhaps *mkšwl* (*lb*), "a stumbling block (of the heart)," arose originally as a gloss to this rare term.

stumbling block MT, LXX[AL] add "of the heart (conscience)." Omit with LXX[B] and 4QSam[c] (as required by space considerations).

that blood was shed in vain and that my lord gained victory by his own hand We read *lšpk dm ḥnm wlhwšy' yd 'dny lw*, lit. "to shed blood in vain and for my lord's hand to gain victory for him." We omit: (1) the conjunction (*w*), which appears at the beginning in MT (thus, "*and* to shed blood, etc."); so LXX, Syr.; and (2) the adjective *athōon* = *nqy*, "innocent," which appears modifying "blood" in LXX. We read *yd 'dny* with LXX; MT omits *yd*.

remember your maidservant LXX[(B)] adds *agathōsai autē* = *lhṭyb lh*, "to do well by her." Omit with MT.

32. *who has sent you* MT adds "this day." Omit with LXX[(B)].

34. *come* Represented in MT by *wtb'ty*, an apparent "mongrel form," combining *wb't* and *wtb'y* (Smith: cf. GK §76h), upon which Driver recognized the influence of the following *lqr'ty*. We read *wtb'y*. The form in MT has been discussed by C. R. Krahmalkov ("The Enclitic Particle TA/TI in Hebrew," *JBL* 89 [1970] 218-219), who contends that it ends with an enclitic particle known from Amorite and Amarna Akkadian texts.

35. *from her what she had brought* So MT. LXX[B]: "from her *everything* she had brought"; LXX[L]: "*everything* from her that she had brought."

36. *he was having . . . a king's banquet* MT *whnh lw mšth bbytw kmšth hmlk*. LXX[B] has suffered haplography, a scribe's eye having skipped from the first *mšth* to the second (thus, "he was having a king's banquet"); LXX[ABmg] (cf. LXX[L]) agree with MT. Note, however, that LXX[B] is probably correct in excluding the definite article from *mlk*, "king," which has arisen in MT by dittography (". . . like *the* king's banquet").

37. *a stone* So MT. LXX: "*like* a stone." Cf. the *Textual Note* on "a wall" at v 16 above.

39. *heard* MT (cf. LXX[AL]) add, "that Nabal was dead." Omit with LXX[B].

from evil So MT: *mr'h*, probably with the sense of "from *doing* evil." LXX: *ek cheiros kakōn* = *myd r'ym*, "from the hand of evildoers."

41. *your servants' feet* So LXX[B]. MT (cf. LXX[AL]): *rgly 'bdy 'dny*, "the feet of *my lord's* servants."

26. *since* So LXX: *kathōs* = *k'šr*. MT *'šr* has lost *k-* after the preceding word (*npšk*).

into bloodguilt So MT: *bdmym* (cf. v 33, MT, LXX). Here LXX has *eis haima athōon*, reflecting *bdm nqy* (cf. 19:5), "into innocent blood" (cf. also v 31 above).

42. *and with five maidservants following her* Reading *wḥmš n'rwt hlkwt lrglh* (cf. LXX[B]). MT has *wḥmš n'rtyh hhlkwt lrglh*, "and *her* five maidservants *who were* following her." So according to MT (1) the five maidservants were all she had (cf. Budde, who thinks this likely), and (2) all six women rode ("Abigail and her five maidservants . . . arose and mounted, etc."). But we prefer the shorter text of LXX[(B)]; the two superfluous *h*'s may have arisen from repeated dittography.

David's messengers So MT, LXX^{L}: *ml'ky dwd.* LXX^{B} *tōn paidiōn daueid* = *'bdy dwd,* "David's *servants,*" is reminiscent of v 40.

43. *Jezreel* So MT: *yzr"l* (cf. LXX^{L}). LXX^{B}: *israēl,* "Israel."

44. *Laish* So MT: *layiš* (LXX^{A}: *lais*). LXX^{B} has *annais,* which is a simple corruption of *lais* (or the like) written in Greek majuscules. LXX^{L}, OL: *iōas.*

Gallim So MT: *glym* (Isa 10:30). LXX$^{(B)}$: *rhomma* (again easily explained as a corruption in the Greek majuscules, where *r* and *g* on the one hand and *m* and *l* on the other are quite easily confused). LXX^{L}, OL: *goliath,* "Goliath"(!).

NOTES

25 2a. *Maon . . . Carmel.* For Maon see the NOTE at 23:24. Carmel was the nearby village (Josh 15:55) where Saul erected a monument after his victory over the Amalekites; see 15:12 and the NOTE there.

2b-4. *When he was shearing . . . David heard. . . .* For the syntax cf. the NOTE at 1:4-7. The temporal clause, "When he was shearing his sheep in Carmel" (v 2b) initiates a narrative sequence (*wayhî bigzōz,* etc.) which requires for its continuation an imperfect consecutive or its equivalent (cf. GK § 111f, g): the latter is found only in v 4, "David heard . . ." (*wayyišma' dāwīd . . .*). It follows that all of v 3 with its disjunctive syntax is parenthetical information inserted between the protasis (2b) and apodosis (4) of the main sequence.

2b. *shearing his sheep.* "Sheepshearing" (*gōzĕzîm;* v 7) was a time of work and also festivity (cf. II Sam 13:23*ff*).

3. *Nabal.* In Biblical Hebrew the adjective *nābāl* means "foolish, senseless, esp. of the man who has no perception of ethical and religious claims, and with collat. idea of *ignoble, disgraceful*" (BDB ad loc.). See further Levenson, "1 Samuel 25," 13-14, where he argues "that the historical figure's real name has been suppressed in order to give him a name indicative of his character."

The woman . . . the man. The contrast between Nabal and his wife is striking, and furthermore, as Levenson observes ("1 Samuel 25," 17-18), "Abigail's qualities, intelligence and beauty, are precisely those of the man who the audience may already suspect will become her new husband. . . . Abigail is as well matched with David as she is mismatched with Nabal."

a Calebite. Caleb, eponymous ancestor of the Calebites, is a prominent and heroic figure in the conquest traditions (cf. esp. Numbers 13, 14), where he is considered a Judahite (Num 13:6). Evidently, however, the Calebites were a people of non-Israelite origin (Num 32:12; Josh 14:6,14; cf. Gen 36:11,15,42) later incorporated into Judah (Josh 15:13); their territory included the region around Hebron (Josh 14:13-15; cf. Judg 1:10-20), where the present story takes place, and apparently certain tracts further S (cf. 30:14).

7. *some of your shepherds.* Hebrew *hārō'îm 'ăšer-lĕkā,* not simply *rō'ĕkā,* "your shepherds"; cf. the NOTE on "some asses that belonged to Kish" at 9:3.

8. *a special time.* Hebrew *yôm ṭôb,* lit. "a good day, i.e. a time of feasting, as in Esther 8:17; 9:19,22; cf. also Zech 8:19 (Smith). The expression has received a full study from Franz Rosenthal (*"yôm ṭôḇ," HUCA* 18 [1944] 157-176), who shows that although by Mishnaic times it had become a general designation for a legal holiday (as in subsequent Jewish usage), it had no such technical use in ancient (i.e. biblical) times. The "good day" was essentially "the day of well-being, plenty, and pleasure" (164). In the present passage, then, it refers not to some official holiday (so Rashi) but simply to an occasion of good eating and drinking, viz. the time of sheepshearers (so Kimchi); in other words, "David and his men seize the good opportunity of the *yôm ṭôḇ,* the day of plenty, to quasi-invite themselves. . . ."

to your son. David so characterizes himself out of deference to the wealthy and influential Nabal. Cf. the same usage in messages elsewhere: (1) II Kings 8:9, where Ben-hadad, king of Damascus, is described in a petition to the prophet Elisha as "your son"; (2) II Kings 16:7, where Ahaz in submitting to Tiglath-pileser refers to himself as "your servant and your son"; in this latter case the statement is in fact a formal gesture of fealty.

15. *these men were very good to us.* Cf. the NOTE at 19:4.

16. *a wall beside us.* Hebrew *ḥômâ . . . 'ālênû,* a perfectly intelligible bit of metaphor. Still it is quite tempting to read *ḥammâ* for *ḥômâ,* reckoning the *mater w* as late in any case, and translate: "They were *a sun above us* at night as well as in the day. . . ."

17. *misfortune is in store for our master.* Hebrew *kālĕtâ hārā'â 'el-'ădōnênû.* Cf. the NOTE at 20:7.

a scoundrel. Hebrew *ben-bĕlîya'al,* lit. "a son of worthlessness." Cf. 1:16; 2:12; etc. and the NOTE at 10:26,27.

18. The provisions Nabal has refused will be provided by his more prudent and courteous wife. Because her husband turned away the messengers sent by David "to salute, bless" (*lĕbārēk;* v 14) him, she now prepares for David what she will call *bĕrākâ,* "a gift, blessing," in v 27 below.

five seahs of parched grain. The seah (*sĕ'â*) was a dry measure of capacity probably equivalent to about a third of an ephah (on which see the NOTE at 1:24); thus five seahs would be about a bushel (cf. R. B. Y. Scott in *BAR*[3], 352). "Parched grain" (*qālî*) is also mentioned in 17:17 (§ XXIV-B); it seems to refer to wheat or barley, roasted and then stored in large quantities.

one omer of raisins. The omer (*'ōmer*) was equal to about a tenth of an ephah or about two dry quarts. See the NOTE at 16:20.

20b-23. *When she fell in with them . . . and saw David.* The syntax is the same as in 2b-4 above (see the NOTE there), except that here the parenthetical material (vv 21-22) is even more extensive. We must repeat the protasis in English ("When she fell in with them") to be sure that the translation is intelligible; but no such device was necessary in Hebrew, where the disjunctive syntax of vv 21-22 clearly sets off the parenthesis, and the resumption of the syntax of ordinary past narration in v 23 returns us smoothly to the main narrative line.

21. *he has repaid me with evil instead of goodness.* Cf. Prov 17:13: "As for him who repays with evil instead of goodness, evil shall not depart from his house!" For "evil" and "goodness" in the formal terminology of relationships, see the NOTES at 19:4 and 24:10. In the present instance David's point is that his own vigilant treatment of Nabal's men and property constituted "goodness," i.e. honorable and favorable behavior toward another, whereas the Calebite's contumelious response to the request for provisions was "evil."

22. On the oath formula in this verse, see the NOTES at 3:17 and 14:44; cf. 20:13.

of all he has who piss against a wall. That is, of all the men and boys of his family and household. The expressions occurs elsewhere in the same stereotyped formula, always with reference to the extermination of the male members of a family: v 34 below and I Kings 14:10; 16:11; 21:21; II Kings 9:8. It is well, then, that with David in this mood the intercessor from Nabal's household is a woman! The present translation, incidentally, is inspired by that of the *KJV:* ". . . any that pisseth against the wall . . ."; the verb has become vulgar in modern English, but perhaps a vulgarism is appropriate on David's lips in his present state of mind.

24. *"Let the guilt be mine, my lord!"* Hebrew *bî 'ădōnî he'āwōn.* Cf. II Sam 14:9, where a petition in a similar context is longer: "Let the guilt be upon me (*'ālay*), my lord the king, and upon my father's house! Let the king and his throne be innocent!" In both cases the meaning is simply, "Let any burden of blame that might arise from our conversation rest upon me and not you!" This is the polite way of initiating a conversation with a superior; the expression is most often used elliptically as *bî 'ădōnî,* "Let it (i.e. the possible burden of guilt) be mine, my lord!" (so correctly KB^3; for the older, fallacious interpretations of the expression, see BDB). Note especially that this reference to guilt has nothing to do with Nabal's misbehavior or David's danger of bloodguilt (v 26), as unanimously supposed by the commentaries; instead it is simply a part of the conventions of courteous and respectful behavior.

25. *his name is "Foolish," and foolishness is with him.* See the NOTE at v 3 above. The wordplay here is a simple one: "his name is *nābāl* (= 'Nabal' but also 'foolish'), and *nĕbālâ* (= 'foolishness') is with him." Taking Driver's clue, Levenson ("1 Samuel 25," 13-14) draws out the instructive parallel of Isa 32:6, where the same pun is made (*kî nābāl nĕbālâ yĕdabbēr,* "For a fool utters foolishness . . .") and where also it is said to be characteristic of a fool "to leave a hungry man's appetite unsatisfied and deny a thirsty man a drink."

27. *gift.* Hebrew *bĕrākâ;* cf. v 14 and the first NOTE at v 18 above.

28-31. Abigail's second speech is probably a secondary insertion. See the COMMENT.

28. *Pardon your maidservant's offense!* That is, forgive me for speaking further—another politeness (cf. the NOTE at 24 above). Abigail has delivered her gift, but she has more to say. Her purpose in looking ahead to David's career in vv 28b-30 is apparently to establish a further basis for dissuading him from wreaking vengeance on her husband.

a secure house. Hebrew *bêt ne'ĕmān,* as in 2:35 above, but used here of the

Davidic dynasty in accordance with the usage familiar from I Kings 11:38 and esp. II Sam 7:16. See the COMMENT.

the wars of Yahweh. That is, the wars of Israel, which David, not Saul, has directed since the alienation of the two men began (see 18:13,16). Cf. also 18:17 (§ XXIV-B), where the same expression is used.

through all your days. Hebrew *miyyāmêkā,* lit. "from your days," to which compare I Kings 1:6 (Driver); but a more instructive comparison is to Job 27:6: "My heart does not reproach me [present tense!] in all my days (*miyyāmay*)," that is, I now have no self-reproach for anything I have ever done (cf. also GK §119w, N). Similarly Abigail is saying to David that he has no evil in him now in consequence of anything he has ever done.

29. *a man.* The Hebrew is *'ādām,* the generic term for man, so that we should not seek in this verse a reference to any particular adversary of David, such as Saul or Absalom or still less of Goliath (because of the sling metaphor at the end).

tied up in the Document of the Living. Hebrew *ṣĕrûrâ biṣrôr haḥayyîm.* As shown by N. H. Tur-Sinai (*The Book of Job: A New Commentary,* rev. ed. [Jerusalem: Kiryath Sepher, 1967] 240-241) *ṣĕrôr* here and in Job 14:17 refers to a tied document (cf. *ṣārar,* "tie up (a document)," as in Isa 8:16), and the expression "Document of the Living" is thus the equivalent of "Book of the Living" (*sēper ḥayyîm*) in Ps 69:29(English 69:28; cf. Isa 4:3). This is the heavenly book in which all living people are recorded; exclusion from it means death (Exod 32:32,33). In later Jewish and early Christian thought it played a part in eschatological concepts of judgment and the afterlife (cf. Dan 12:1; Rev 3:5; 13:8; 17:8; 20:12; 21:17; etc.).

30. *when Yahweh does . . . all the good he has spoken of you.* The promising and doing of "good things" by a lord for his vassal belongs to the formal terminology of relationships described in the second NOTE at 19:4. With particular regard to the expression "speak/promise a good word/thing" (*dibbēr ṭôbâ*) compare the extrabiblical evidence cited by A. Malamat ("Organs of Statecraft in the Israelite Monarchy," in *BAR*[3], 195-198), as well as I Kings 12:7 and II Kings 25:28, to the effect that to speak a good word, said of a suzerain, suggests the initiation of a covenant relationship. Cf. especially David's prayer to Yahweh in II Sam 7:28 in which he says, ". . . and you have spoken of your servant this good thing (*haṭṭôbâ hazzō't*)." There the "good thing" is the dynastic promise (cf. v 27), and here it is evidently the same. On *dibbēr,* "speak," in the sense of "promise," see Cross, *CMHE,* 253-254, nos. (6) and (21).

prince over Israel. Hebrew *nāgîd 'al yiśrā'ēl,* as in 9:16; 10:1; and esp. 13:14. See the NOTE at 9:16.

31. *blood.* On the significance of bloodguilt and the importance of a king's (or a future king's!) avoidance of it, see the NOTE at 19:5. The danger in the present case is not that David might act in an unrighteous cause, but that he might usurp the prerogative of God by gaining "victory by his own hand."

33. *from entering . . . and gaining my victory by my own hand.* Hebrew *mibbô' . . . wĕhôšēa' yādî lî,* an infinitive absolute in continuation of an

infinitive construct, as in 22:13 (see the NOTE there). This sequence leads in the present case (and v 26) to the extraordinary circumstance that, as Driver points out, "The inf. abs. . . . [is] followed by a subst. standing to it in the relation of a subject." See also GK §113gg.

bloodguilt. Hebrew *dāmîm,* here and in v 26 below (!), as in Exod 22:1 (English 22:2); etc. See also the preceding NOTE.

35. *and granted your request.* Hebrew *wā'eśśā' pānāyik,* lit. "and raised up your face," to which compare Gen 19:21 and Job 42:8-9.

39. *who has turned Nabal's evil back upon his own head.* Exactly as in I Kings 2:44. See also the NOTE at v 21 above.

41,26 Abigail speaks as if David himself were present. On the syntax of v 26, see the NOTE at v 33 above.

26. *those who seek my lord's harm.* Or rather, those who seek his *evil;* cf. the NOTE at 24:10.

43-44. An editorial appendix enumerating David's wives up to this point after the fashion of 14:47-52.

43. *Ahinoam from Jezreel.* Cf. 27:3; 30:5; II Sam 2:2. This Ahinoam evidently had nothing to do with Saul's wife by the same name who is mentioned in 14:50 (but cf. Levenson, "1 Samuel 25," 27). Her home was evidently not the well-known northern Jezreel but a Judahite village of the same name in the vicinity of Maon, Ziph, and Carmel (cf. Josh 15:55,56). She was to become the mother of Amnon, David's eldest son (II Sam 3:2; I Chron 3:1). Abigail for her part became the mother of David's little-known second son, Chileab (so II Sam 3:3) or Daniel (so I Chron 3:1).

44. By taking Michal away Saul must have hoped to weaken David's claims to the throne of Israel. It is in light of this that we must understand David's later demand (II Sam 3:12-16) that she be returned to him before Israel and Judah could be joined firmly under his rule.

Palti, the son of Laish. In II Sam 3:15 a longer form of his name, viz. Paltiel, is used.

Gallim. An unknown town located—if it is the same as the Gallim of Isa 10:30—somewhere N of Jerusalem.

COMMENT

In the present shape of our text the account of David's dealings with Abigail and Nabal is embraced by two passages in which David, out of respect for Saul's status as the anointed of Yahweh, refuses an opportunity to lay violent hands on him. Here, too—thanks primarily to the good offices of Abigail—David refrains from violence against an enemy. So in contrast to the many places earlier in our story in which he was saved from some external danger, these chapters (24, 25, 26) show David being saved from himself, or rather from the consequences of deeds potentially disastrous to his own interests.

The present case, however, differs from those that precede and follow it in that David's first impulse is a violent one that must be curbed; he does not exhibit the necessary restraint spontaneously, as in the cave at En-gedi or the encampment on the hill of Hachilah, but *learns* it in the course of events. Indeed, it would not be overly precise to describe this as a story about the education of a future king. David is like the young man to whom so much of the Book of Proverbs is addressed, who finds himself in contact with both the proverbial "fool" (*nābāl;* cf. the NOTES at vv 3 and 25) and the proverbial "stalwart woman" (*'ēšet ḥayil;* see Prov 31:10), who "opens her mouth with wisdom" (Prov 31:26). From the latter he learns (or at least is reminded of) the importance of self-control and reliance upon Yahweh. Specifically, he is helped by Abigail's intervention to avoid "entering into bloodguilt" and "gaining [his] victory with [his] own hand" (vv 33,26; cf. 31). "Through Abigail," writes Hertzberg, "the Lord saves David from a danger different from that in the cave with Saul, but none the less great. It consists . . . in the possibility that David may take matters into his own hand and thus make himself master of his fate, instead of letting it be guided by the Lord." This lesson of final reliance on Yahweh, a lesson that poor Saul never really learned, is one fit for a king, as hinted by Abigail's words in vv 30-31 (words which, though secondary to the account [see below], make explicit a theme that is, in this case, already implicit in the story). It will stand David in good stead in the years to come.

The years to come are the particular focus of the second part of Abigail's speech (vv 28-31), where she asks mercy for her husband in the context of a prognostication about David's kingship. The future orientation of these verses, their flowery rhetoric, and their tendency to give explicit statement to implicit themes are reminiscent of the series of secondary elaborations previously identified in 20:11-17,23,40-42; 23:14-18, 19-24a, and the overlay of the story of the Philistine champion in c 17 and that of the cave incident in c 24. Most especially, they remind us of the speeches in which Jonathan (20:14-18) and Saul (24:21-22) ask mercy for their families, again with reference to David's future kingship. These similarities, when combined with the fact that David in vv 32*ff* responds only to the first part of Abigail's speech, assure us that vv 28-31 represent another such elaboration of the older narrative. In this case, however, the words look ahead specifically to the dynastic promise to David in phrases that seem to be drawn directly from Nathan's oracle in II Samuel 7,[1] the cornerstone passage in the Josianic history of the kingdom.[2] Key expressions are *bayit ne'ĕmān,* "(David's) secure house," to which compare II Sam 7:16 (see also the NOTE at I Sam 2:35), and *ṭôbâ,*

[1] See L. Schmidt, *Menschlicher Erfolg und Jahwes Initiative,* 122. Cf. Veijola, *Die ewige Dynastie,* 52-53; Mettinger, *King and Messiah,* 35-37.

[2] D. J. McCarthy, "II Samuel 7," 131-138; Cross, *CMHE,* 241-261.

"the good (which Yahweh has spoken of David)," that is, the dynastic promise (see the NOTE at v 30), to which compare II Sam 7:28. Such correspondences suggest that the Jerusalemite hand from which the several elaborations in the history of David's rise derive may have been that of the Josianic historian himself (see LITERARY HISTORY in the Introduction). In any case, the old story of David's meeting with Abigail, evidently an original part of the history of David's rise to power, has been employed as a vehicle for an early reference to the promise of dynasty to David.

We should not, however, focus all our attention on David here. The story is designed to illustrate the excellent qualities of one of David's wives and to show that she became his wife precisely because of her excellence (and Yahweh's help), not because of mere accident or (emphatically) any wrongdoing on David's part. The partnership of such a wife bodes well for David's future, not only because of her "good intelligence" (v 3) and counseling skills but also because she is the widow of a very rich Calebite landowner.

The last point is an important one. David has lost his newly acquired base of power in consequence not only of his exile from Gibeah, where he had become a popular hero, but also, as we learn in v 44, the loss of his royal-blooded wife, Michal. He has been required to return to his homeland. Now we find him marrying the widow of a high-ranking member of the clan that controlled Hebron (see the NOTE at v 3)[8] as well as another woman from nearby Jezreel (v 43). He is becoming a prominent figure in the heartland of Judah. To be sure, the narrative does not suggest that he is deliberately building a base of power—all of this is the working out of a divine plan in which he, too, is caught up—but when the time comes—that is, when Saul falls—David will be ready. And he will become king first at Hebron (II Sam 2:1-4).

But that time is yet to come. As the next episode shows, Saul is still alive and David still in danger.

[8] This point is stressed by Levenson ("1 Samuel 25," 26-27), who speculates that Nabal may have been the leader of the Calebite clan and that David thus laid claim to the position by marriage to Abigail.

XL. DAVID SPARES SAUL'S LIFE AGAIN (26:1-25)

26 1 Some Ziphites came to Saul at Gibeah to say, "David is hiding
on the hill of Hachilah, opposite Jeshimon." 2 So Saul arose and went
down to the wilderness of Ziph along with three thousands of the
picked men of Israel to search for David in the wilderness of Ziph.
3 [He] made camp beside the road on the hill of Hachilah, opposite Jeshimon.

When David, who was staying in the wilderness, saw that Saul had
come into the wilderness after him, 4 [he] sent out spies and learned
that Saul had come to Hachilah. 5 So David arose, and when he came
to the place where Saul had encamped, [he] saw the place where Saul
and Abiner, son of Ner, the commander of his army, were lying.
(Now Saul was lying within the encampment with the troops encamped all around him.)

6 David spoke up and said to Ahimelech the Hittite and to Abishai,
the son of Zeruiah, Joab's brother, "Who will go down with me to
Saul's camp?"

"I!" said Abishai. "I shall go down with you."

7 So David and Abishai made their way among the troops by night,
and there was Saul lying asleep within the encampment, his spear
thrust into the ground at his head, with Abiner and the troops lying
about him.

8 "God has delivered your enemy into your power today!" said
Abishai to David. "Now let me pin him to the ground with the spear!
One stroke, and I shall not touch him again!"

9 But David said to Abishai, "Do not destroy him! For who can
raise his hand against Yahweh's anointed and be innocent? 10 As
Yahweh lives," [he] went on, "it must be Yahweh himself who strikes
him down, whether his time comes and he dies or he goes down into
battle and is taken! 11 Yahweh forbid that I should raise my hand
against the anointed of Yahweh! Now then, take the spear that is at
his head and the cruse of water, and let us go!" 12 So David took the

spear and water juglet from their place at his head, and they left. No one saw, no one knew, no one awoke! All of them slept on, for the slumber of Yahweh had fallen over them.

13 David crossed over to the opposite slope and stood far away on
the mountain top. With this great distance between them, 14 [he]
called to the troops. To Abiner he said, "Will you not answer, Abiner?"

"Who is it that calls?" said Abiner in reply.

15 "Are you not a man?" said David to Abiner. "And who in Israel
is your equal? Then why were you not watching over your lord, the
king, when one of the soldiers went in to destroy [him]? 16 This thing
that you have done is not good! As Yahweh lives, you who should have kept watch over your lord, the anointed of Yahweh, are dead men! Now look! Where is the king's spear, and where is the cruse of water that was at his head?"

17 Recognizing David's voice Saul said, "Is that your voice, my son
David?"

"It is my voice, my lord the king!" said David. 18 "Why," he said,
"is my lord pursuing his servant? What have I done? What evil is
there in me? 19 Now then, let my lord the king hear the words of his
servant! If it is God who has incited you against me, may he accept an offering! But if men, let them be cursed before Yahweh! For they have driven me out today from sharing in Yahweh's estate, saying,
'Go serve other gods!' 20 Therefore let my blood not spill on the
ground away from Yahweh's presence! For the king of Israel has come out to seek my life just as though he were hunting the calling-bird in the mountains!"

21 Then Saul said, "I have sinned! Come back, my son David! I
shall not mistreat you, since you have regarded my life as precious today. I have acted foolishly and made a very great mistake."

22 "Here is the king's spear!" said David in reply. "Let one of the
young men come over and get it. 23 It is Yahweh who returns to each
man his righteousness and faithfulness: since Yahweh delivered you into my power today and I refused to raise my hand against Yahweh's
anointed, 24 then just as I valued your life today, so may Yahweh
value my life and rescue me from every danger!"

25 Then Saul said to David, "You are blessed, my son! In whatever
you undertake you will surely succeed!" And when David had gone on his way, Saul returned to his place.

TEXTUAL NOTES

26 1. *Some Ziphites* MT *hzpym,* corresponding to *hoi zeiphioi ek tēs auchmōdous,* "The Ziphites from the parched land . . ." in LXX. As in 23:14,15,19, and occurrences to follow, *hzpym* is rendered twice in LXX, once correctly as the designation of a group of people and once (inexplicably) as a term meaning "parched land." See the *Textual Note* to 23:19.

David So LXX$^{(BL)}$: *idou daueid* = *hnh dwyd.* MT has *hlw' dwd,* "Is not David . . . ?" as in 23:19.

is hiding LXX adds "with us" (cf. 23:19). Omit with MT.

2. *Ziph* (*bis*) MT: *zyp.* LXX^{B}: *zeip* = *zyp.* LXX^{L}: *tēn auchmōdē/tē auchmōdei,* "the parched land"; see the first *Textual Note* to v 1 above and references there.

4. *to Hachilah* MT has *'l nkwn,* "of a certainty"; but as Driver points out, we expect a place name. LXX^{L} has *eis sekelag,* "to Ziklag" (cf. Josephus *Ant.* 6.310), probably a corruption of *eis* (*h*)*echelath* = *'l ḥkylh,* "to Hachilah," and probably this was also the original of LXX^{B} *ek keeila* (as if *mq'ylh,* "from Keilah"; cf. 23:13, etc.), another inner-Greek corruption of [*eis*] (*h*)*echela*(*th*), or the like. In any case, "to Hachilah" is what we expect: David already knows "of a certainty" that Saul has come (cf. v 4), so what he needs are spies to tell him precisely where Saul is; and we know from v 3 that Saul's camp is at Hachilah. MT *'l nkwn* may be a corruption of *'l ḥkylh* (influenced by the MT plus in 23:23?); if so, it was secondarily added to LXX, which precedes *ek keeila* with *hetoimos,* "prepared" (= *nkwn*), in a double reading. For a full discussion, see Thornhill's article, "A Note on *'l-nkwn,*" where the same conclusion is reached.

5. *arose* LXX^{BL} add *lathra*(*iōs*) = "in secret, stealthily." Omit with MT.

to the place where . . . the place where So MT, which reads *'l hmqwm 'šr ḥnh šm š'wl wyr' dwd 't hmqwm 'šr.* The repetition caused haplography in the ancestral text of LXX (so LXX^{BA}, corrected in LXX^{L}), a scribe's eye having skipped from the first *hmqwm 'šr* to the second.

and Abiner So MT: *w'bnr.* LXX$^{(B, cf. L)}$ inserts *ekei* = *šm,* "there," producing a separate sentence: "And there was Abiner, etc."

6. *Ahimelech* So MT, LXX^{L}. LXX^{BA}, OL: "Abimelech."

8. *God* So MT. LXX: "Yahweh" (cf. 24:5).

to the ground with the spear So LXX^{B}: *tō dorati eis tēn gēn* = *bḥnyt b'rṣ.* MT *bḥnyt wb'rṣ,* "with the spear *and* to the ground," represents a misdivision of *bḥnytw b'rṣ,* "to the ground with *his* spear," and as LXX shows the suffixed pronoun was expansive in the first place.

9. *who can raise his hand* Reading *my yšlḥ ydw,* lit. "who extends his hand" (cf. LXX), in correction of MT *my šlḥ ydw,* "who *has extended* his hand," in which *y* has fallen out after *my.* But cf. GK §112h, which suggests

that the opposite case might be made, viz. that MT is better and LXX reflects dittography of *y*.

12. *at his head* Reading *mmr'štyw* with LXX in preference to MT *mr'šty š'wl*, where *m-* has fallen out after the preceding *hmym* and the *y* is (despite GK §87s) a vestige of the original reading. See Wellhausen, Driver.

13. *distance* So LXX: *hē hodos* = *hdrk*, lit. "(the) road" (thus lit. "Great was the road between them"). MT has *hmqwm*, "the place" (thus, "Great was the space between them"). There is no basis for a choice between these variants.

14. *To Abiner he said* Reading *w'l 'bnr dbr l'mr* with LXX. MT has *w'l 'bnr bn nr l'mr*, "and to Abiner, son of Ner. . . ."

"Who is it that calls?" Reading *my 'th hqwr'* with LXX^B^ (*tis ei su ho kalōn*). The other versions reflect one or both of two expansions: (1) *my 'th hqwr' 'ty*, "Who is it that calls *me?*" (cf. LXX^L^); (2) *my 'th hqwr' 'l hmlk*, "Who is it that calls *to the king?*" (cf. Syr.). LXX^A^ reflects *my 'th hqwr' 'ty 'l hmlk*, a conflation of the two expansive readings, and this also lies behind the text of MT, which has become further corrupt: *my 'th qr't 'l hmlk*, "Who are you? You have called to the king." See also the NOTE at v 20.

said Abiner in reply We read with MT: *hlw' t'nh 'bnr wy'n 'bnr wy'mr*, lit. "'Will you not answer, Abiner?' And Abiner answered and said. . . ." LXX^(B)^ has lost "And Abiner answered" as a result of haplography, a scribe's eye having skipped from the first *'bnr* to the second.

16. *you who should have kept watch* Reading *'tm 'šr šmrtm* with LXX^B^. MT, LXX^L^ add *l'* under the influence of v 15—thus, "you who have *not* kept watch."

over your lord So MT. LXX^(B, cf. L)^: "over the king, your lord," under the influence of v 15.

and where Reading *w'y* for MT *w't* (Budde, Driver, GK §117m,N). But contrast the fuller discussion of Stoebe.

17. *It is my voice* So MT (*qwly*). LXX has *doulos sou* = *'bdk*, "your servant," on which see Wellhausen.

18. *he said* So MT, LXX^B^. LXX^AL^: "*David* said."

my lord So MT. LXX^B^: "*the* lord." LXX^L^: "my lord *the king.*"

What have I done? So MT: *mh 'śyty*. LXX *ti hēmartēka* reflects *mh ḥṭ'ty*, "How have I sinned?" Cf. 20:1.

What evil is there in me? So MT: *wmh bydy r'h*, lit. "And what evil is in my hand?" LXX^B(cf. L)^: *kai ti heurethē en emoi adikēma* = *wmh nmṣ' by r'h*, "And what evil *is found in me?*"

19. *the words* So MT, LXX^L^. LXX^B^: "the word."

God So LXX. MT: "Yahweh."

20. *my life* So LXX^B^: *psychēn mou* = *npšy*. MT (cf. LXX^L^): *pr'š 'ḥd*, "a single flea," which arose under the influence of 24:15.

the calling-bird So MT: *hqr'*, "the partridge, calling-bird," which we expect LXX to represent as *ho perdix*. But in fact LXX (cf. OL) has *ho nyktikorax*, "the night-raven," which may reflect some alternative reading such as *h'rb*.

21. *mistreat you* MT, LXX^{AL} add "again." Omit with LXX^{B}.

precious today. I have acted foolishly So MT. Some MSS of LXX have: "precious. And today I have acted foolishly. . . ."

22. *"Here is the king's spear"* Reading *hnh ḥnyt hmlk* with LXX (*idou to doru tou basileōs*), 4QSam^{a} (*hnh ḥn*[*yt hmlk*]), and MT *qĕrê.* MT *kĕtîb* with dittography of *h* reads *hnh hḥnyt hmlk,* "Here is the spear, O king!"

23. *into my power* So LXX (= *bydy,* lit. "in my hand"). MT: *byd,* "into hand."

24. *and rescue me* MT *wyṣlny,* rendered twice in LXX$^{(B)}$ as *kai skepasai me,* "and shelter me" (as if from *ṣll*), and *kai exeleitai me,* "and rescue me" (as if from *nṣl;* so MT).

25. *my son* MT, LXX^{AL}, Syr. add "David." Omit with LXX^{B}.

his way . . . his place So MT (correctly). The order is reversed in LXX^{BL}.

NOTES

26 1. *Ziphites.* See the NOTE on the Wilderness of Ziph at 23:14.

on the hill of Hachilah, opposite Jeshimon. See the NOTE at 23:19.

2. *thousands.* That is, military units or contingents; see the NOTE at 4:10.

5. *Abiner, son of Ner.* Saul's kinsman and the commander of his army; see the NOTES at 14:50,51.

6. *Ahimelech the Hittite.* Mentioned nowhere else.

Abishai, the son of Zeruiah. According to I Chron 2:16, Zeruiah was David's sister and the mother of Abishai, Joab, and Asahel, who was later slain by Abiner (II Sam 2:18-23). Abishai was the commander of David's army and a prominent figure in the stories of his reign, in which he figures as a loyal and heroic supporter of the new Davidic kingdom and is intimately involved in the palace intrigue of his uncle's years as king.

9. *Do not destroy him.* Hebrew *'al tašḥîtēhû,* not simply, "Do not kill him!" Though to be sure Abishai's wish is to slay Saul, David's cry of intervention implies more. The verb *hišḥît,* "destroy," often carries with it a connotation of spoliation (cf. 13:17; 14:15), ruination (cf. 6:5), or corruption; its Phoenician equivalent can refer to the defacing of an inscription as well as the breaking of a head (e.g. *KAI* 24:14,15), and a related Syriac word means "mutilate" (cf. BDB). The sense of "mutilate, deface" (cf. Deut 20:19, "When you lay siege to a city for many days . . . you must not mutilate [*lō'-tašḥît*] its trees by wielding an ax against them . . .") is important here: Saul as king and anointed of Yahweh is sacrosanct and not to be physically defiled—a reflection of beliefs about the inviolability of the king's body. It is a capital offense to "destroy" the king even to administer the *coup de grace* when he is already dying, as clearly shown by II Sam 1:14-16 (where the form of *šḥt* used is not *Hip'il* but *Pi'el*). Saul, then, is protected from harm by taboos, which David is careful to respect.

It is true, however, that as the speech that follows shows, the main concern of our narrative is to demonstrate David's innocence with particular regard to Saul's death, and the issue, then, is not merely one of ritual purity but of legal blamelessness with regard to the succession (see the NOTE at 24:7).

10. *goes down into battle and is taken.* The anticipation of c 31 is rather explicit here, and some commentators have regarded this entire verse as secondary. In any case it is consistent with the sentiment David will express in II Sam 1:14-16.

12. *the slumber of Yahweh.* Hebrew *tardēmat yahweh.* A case could be made for translating this expression as "an awesome slumber" or something similar on the analogy of the intensifying use of *'ĕlōhîm* in such expressions as *ḥerdat 'ĕlōhîm,* "convulsion of God, awesome convulsion" in 14:15 (see the NOTE there). But even so we should have to grant that there is an implication here of divine involvement in the events that are transpiring. Yahweh is helping David's cause by casting over the camp of Saul a *tardēmâ,* a very deep sleep or even trance that elsewhere is most often divinely imposed (Gen 2:21; 15:12; Isa 29:10).

16. *you . . . are dead men.* That is, "You deserve to die!"

19. *may he accept an offering.* Or rather, "let him smell (*yāraḥ*) an offering." That is, let him smell the pleasing scent of an offering (exactly as in Gen 8:21) and assume a more favorable disposition toward me.

from sharing in Yahweh's estate. Hebrew *mēhistappēaḥ bĕnaḥălat yahweh.* "Yahweh's estate" is his personal plot of land, Israel, as explained in the NOTE at 10:1. The verb *spḥ,* though appearing in *Hitpa'el* only here, may be understood from its use in 2:36 (*Qal*), where it means "assign, attach (to a priestly order)," and especially in Isa 14:1 (*Nip'al*), where it is used of foreigners who "attach themselves to, join themselves to" the house of Jacob; the reference here, then, is to David's previous attachment to Israel. Exclusion from Israel, moreover, means exclusion from the worship of the Israelite national god, so that David, as he says, also feels barred from the service of Yahweh.

20. *the calling-bird.* That is, the partridge, Hebrew *haqqōrē',* lit. "the caller," as the various partridges of Palestine were dubbed in Hebrew. There is a bit of wordplay going on in this metaphor. David is standing on a mountain (v 13) calling (v 14), and he compares Saul's pursuit of him to the hunting of "the caller" in the mountains. Specifically the play revolves upon Abiner's question in v 14, *mî 'attâ haqqôrē'* (see the *Textual Note*), "Who is it that calls?" or more literally, "Who are you, O caller?" Thus in David's reply he wryly compares himself to "the caller" hunted in the mountains. (Cf. also the explanation of *'ên-haqqôrē',* "Partridge Spring," the name of a place near Lehi, given in Judg 15:18-19.) Wordplay aside, the metaphor is particularly apt, since the partridge seems to have been hunted by relentless chasing; see W. S. McCullough, *IDB* 3.661.

25. *In whatever you undertake you will surely succeed.* The thought is the same, though differently worded, as that expressed in 18:14 . . . but now on the lips of Saul himself!

COMMENT

Betrayed by fellow Judahites from Ziph, David finds himself again pursued by Saul. His spies quickly give him the advantage of the king, and with one companion he steals into the sleeping camp at night. At the center of the encampment he finds Saul asleep and unprotected but refuses to lay violent hands on him or to allow his nephew to do so. Instead he takes Saul's spear and a cruse of water and departs. Standing on a hill opposite the camp David calls aloud to awaken the soldiers. He chides Abiner, Saul's principal general, with a lack of vigilance in guarding his lord and then protests his own loyalty to Saul and Israel, offering the spear and cruse in evidence. Seeing that David has refused an opportunity to take his life, Saul is moved to acknowledge the rightness of the younger man's claim and to bless him in a fatherly manner.

The similarity of this story to that describing David's encounter with Saul in a cave near En-gedi may be judged from a comparison of the summary given above to that at the beginning of the COMMENT on 24:2-23, where the implications of the similarity are considered in detail. We concluded there that the present passage is the older of the two accounts and the one to which the other has been conformed. It shares with 24:2-23 the theme of the divine participation in the interplay between Saul and David —in both passages it is clear that Yahweh is directing events (see 24:5a and 26:8; cf. also the NOTE on "the slumber of Yahweh" at v 12 above)— but explicit statements about David's future and overt or extreme demonstrations of his innocence and piety and of Saul's abjection are avoided here, as they are in the rest of the older narrative about David's rise to power. David's respect for Yahweh's anointed one (cf. the NOTE at v 9) is amply demonstrated without the excesses of 24:6-7; and though Saul, in development of a theme introduced in 18:14, finally comes to the point of openly acknowledging David's uncanny knack for success, he is still far from ready to name David as his successor, and we are left with the feeling that he is not fully aware of the implications of his own words when he says to David, "In whatever you undertake you will surely succeed!"

A special literary device that animates the passage is discussed in the NOTE at v 20 (cf. the second *Textual Note* to v 14). David, calling from the mountain opposite Saul's camp, is addressed by Abiner as *haqqōrē'*, "the caller" (v 14), and finds in this a chance to drive home his point to Saul by describing himself as *haqqôrē'*, "the partridge, calling-bird," a creature whose fate was to be chased relentlessly by the fowler. "For the king of Israel," he says, "has come out to seek my life just as though he were hunting the calling-bird (*haqqôrē'*) in the mountains!"

When Saul and David part company at the end of this episode, it is for the last time. According to the story that follows David will leave Israel now to enlist in the service of a Philistine prince and will return only after his lord is dead.

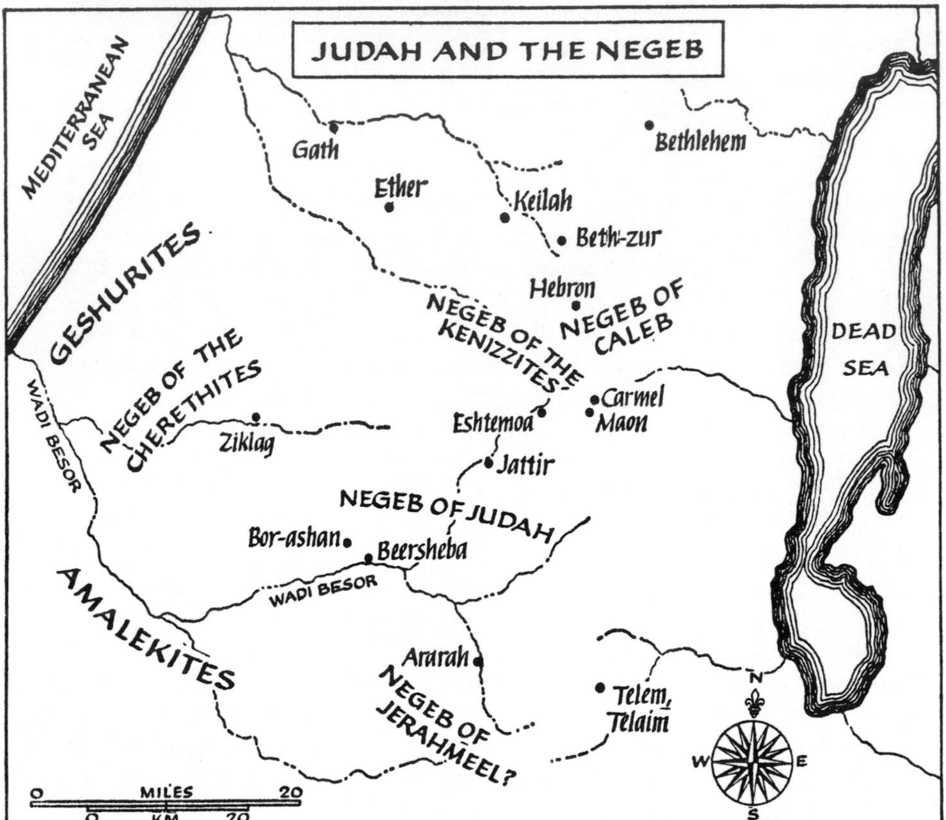

XLI. DAVID IN THE SERVICE OF ACHISH OF GATH (27:1-28:2)

27 1 David said to himself, "Any day now I might be taken by Saul.
There is nothing better for me than to escape to the land of the Philistines. Then Saul will give up on me and no longer seek me throughout
the territory of Israel, for I shall be safely out of his reach."
2 So David arose, and he and the six hundred men who were with
him crossed over to Achish, son of Maoch, the king of Gath. 3 David
and his men took up residence with Achish, each man and his household: with David were his two wives, Ahinoam of Jezreel and
Abigail, widow of Nabal, of Carmel. 4 When Saul was told that David
had fled to Gath, he sought him no longer.

Ziklag

5 Then David said to Achish, "If I have found favor with you, let
me be given a place in one of the outlying cities, so that I may live
there. Why should your servant live in the royal city with you?" 6 So
he gave him Ziklag at that time. (For this reason Ziklag has belonged
to the kings of Judah to this day.) 7 The amount of time David lived
in Philistine territory was a year and four months.
8 David and his men went up and made raids against the Geshurites
and the Amalekites— (Though the land was inhabited from Telem to
Shur and on toward Egypt, 9 David, when he would make a strike in
the land, would leave neither man nor woman alive; but he would
take sheep, cattle, asses, camels and articles of clothing.) When he returned and brought [the booty] to Achish, 10 Achish said, "Against
whom did you go raiding today?"
"Against the Negeb of Judah," said David, "and against the Negeb
of Jerahmeel, and against the Negeb of the Kenizzites." 11 (Not one
man or woman did he ever bring alive to Gath, for he thought, "They
might give information about us and say, 'David did thus and so'!"

Such was David's custom all the days he lived in Philistine territory.)

12 So Achish became confident of David, thinking, "Surely he has become loathsome to his own people, Israel! I shall have him for a servant always!"

28 1 When it happened in those days that the Philistines had called their forces to duty to do battle with Israel, Achish said to David, "You must understand that you and your men are to march out to battle with me."

2 "Then you will learn for yourself what your servant does!" said David to Achish.

"Then I shall appoint you as my permanent bodyguard!" said Achish to David.

TEXTUAL NOTES

27 1. *than to escape* Reading *ky 'm 'mlṭ*, lit. "except that I escape," on the basis of LXX^BL *ean mē (dia)sōthō*. In MT, after *'m* was lost by simple haplography, the verb was strengthened with the infinitive absolute; thus, *ky hmlṭ 'mlṭ*, "because I shall surely escape."

2. *six hundred* So MT, LXX^AL. LXX^B: "*four* hundred." Cf. the *Textual Note* to 23:13.

and he . . . crossed over That is, *wy'br hw'*; so MT, LXX^AL. LXX^B unaccountably omits this, but it seems indispensable. There is also some weak MS support (LXX^A, Syr.) for a third verb, *wyb'*, "and came," before "to Achish."

Maoch MT *mā'ôk*. LXX^B *ammach*. LXX^L *acheimaan*. OL *achimaac*. See the NOTE.

3. *with Achish* MT, LXX^A add "in Gath" (cf. LXX^L). Omit with LXX^B.

of Carmel Or rather, "the Carmelite" (*hkrmly*); cf. LXX. MT reflects *hkrmlyt*, "the Carmelitess," perhaps erroneously, under the influence of *hyzr''lyt*, "the Jezreelitess," earlier in the verse. Either reading is possible, but most critics prefer the masculine form, which in fact is used in 30:5 in the same context.

4. *he sought him no longer* MT (*kĕtîb*) points to *wĕlō' yôsīp 'ôd lĕbaqšô*, while MT (*qĕrê*) has *wĕlō' yāsap*, etc. The former, which is preferable, expresses habitual action in the past (cf. the NOTE at 1:4-7)—"and he no longer sought him"—and the latter is ordinary past narration—"and he did not seek him again." See also Driver, who compares Josh 15:63.

5. *I have found* So MT. LXX^B(cf. L): "*your servant has* found."

let me be given Literally, "let them give me": *ytnw ly* (so MT; LXX = *ytnw n' ly*).

6. *he gave him* So LXX^B^. MT, LXX^L^: "*Achish* gave him."

7. *a year and four months* So MT: *ymym w'rb'h ḥdšym* (for *ymym*, "a year," cf. Driver). LXX omits *ymym w-* (thus reading "four months"), perhaps as a result of the loss of *ymym* after the preceding *plštym, with* subsequent exclusion of the *w-*. Smith makes the opposite case, viz. that *ymym w-* arose from duplication of the preceding *-ym*, and prefers LXX.

8. *against the Geshurites* MT (cf. LXX^L^, OL) has *'l hgšwry whgrzy* (*qĕrê: haggizrî*), showing a conflation of variants; we must choose between the Geshurites and Gezerites. The Geshurites, not the Transjordanian people but the neighbors of the Philistines (see the NOTE), are entirely appropriate here; but the Gezerites lived much too far N. LXX^B^, though ambiguous, seems to approximate the original reading: *epi panta ton geseiri kai epi ton amalēkeitēn* = *'l kl hgšyry w'l h'mlqy*, "against all the Geshurites and against the Amalekites" (from which we may omit *kl* and the second *'l* with MT as simple expansions).

Though the land was inhabited Reading *whnh h'rṣ nwšbt* on the basis of LXX^(B)^ *kai idou hē gē katōkeito*. MT originally had *whnh nšbt h'rṣ*, the same reading with simple inversion, but the confusion of *n* for *y* led to reinterpretation and further confusion. Thus MT: *ky hnh yšbwt h'rṣ 'šr*, "For they (*hēnnâ*) were inhabiting the land which. . . ." Presumably *hnh* (though feminine!) refers to the Amalekites. But LXX is patently superior.

from Telem to Shur We read *mṭlm šwr(h)*. MT *m'wlm bw'k šwrh*, "from *ancient times as you go* to Shur," is the result of confusion of *ṭ* for ' and the intrusion of *bw'k* from 15:7 (see the *Textual Note* there). LXX^(B)^ conflates two interpretations of each term in rendering *apo anēkontōn hē apo gelampsour teteichismenōn*, viz. (1) *apo anēkontōn*, "from those coming up," and *apo gelam-*, "from Gelam-," both reflecting *m'lm*, and (2) *-(p)sour*, "-sour," and *teteichismenōn*, "walled," both reflecting *šwr(h)*. Some twelve MSS of LXX actually read *telam-* for *gelam-* (cf. Wellhausen, Driver), but in view of the evidence of MT this may be coincidental (note the similarity of the Greek majuscules *t* and *g*): the confusion of *ṭ* for ' seems already to have affected a common ancestral text of MT and LXX. There is no sure evidence for reading *mṭlm*, which must be listed as conjectural.

and on toward Egypt Reading *w'd mṣrym* with LXX. MT: *w'd 'rṣ mṣrym*, "and on toward *the land of* Egypt."

9. *and brought* [*the booty*] The object is not expressed, a fact that led MT to mispoint *wyb'*, properly *wayyābē'*, as *wayyābō'*, "and *came*." Cf. v 11.

10. *Achish said* LXX adds "to David." Omit with MT.

Against whom So LXX (*epi tina* = *'l my*) and apparently 4QSam^a^ (*'l* [*my*]). Only a vestige survives in MT: *'l* (= *'l*). Targ. suggests *'n* or *'nh*, "Where/Whither?"

said David LXX adds "to Achish." Omit with MT.

and against the Negeb of Jerahmeel 4QSam^a^ has *w'l ngb yr*[*ḥm'*]*l*, supporting MT (cf. LXX^AL^) *w'l ngb hyrḥm'ly*, "and against the Negeb of the Jerahmeelites" (showing a minor alteration under the influence of *hqyny*, "the Kenites"), against LXX^B^ *kai kata noton iesmega* = *w'l ngb yšm'y*, "and against the Negeb of . . . ? . . ."

the Kenizzites So LXX[(B)]: *tou kenezei* = *hqnzy*. MT: *hqyny*, "the Kenites." See the third *Textual Note* at 30:29.

11. *he* So LXX[B]. MT, LXX[L]: "David."

give information LXX adds "to Gath." Omit with MT.

12. *Achish . . . David* So MT. In LXX[(B)] the order has been reversed, thus "David became confident of/put his trust in Achish."

28 1. *their forces* MT *'t mḥnyhm*, lit. "their camps" (as in 17:1, etc.). LXX[(B)] = *bmḥnyhm*, *"in* their camps."

to duty MT *lṣb'*. LXX[(B)] reflects *lṣ't*, "to march out."

you and your men In both MT and LXX this stands at the end of the verse (". . . that with me will you march out to battle [so LXX; see below], you and your men"), but 4QSam[a] displays a substitution made in anticipation of 29:1,11. It reads *yzr"l[h]* "at Jezreel" (thus, ". . . that with me will you march out to battle *at Jezreel*"). F. M. Cross points out that Josephus (*Ant.* 6.325) has a corruption of the same reading (*eis rega/rella* < **iesraela*) and conflates the readings of MT and 4QSam[a] (cf. "History of the Biblical Text," 293).

to battle So LXX (*eis polemon*) and 4QSam[a] ([*lm*]*lḥmh*). MT has *bmḥnh*, "from the camp" (cf. M. Dahood in *Orientalia* 45 [1976] 334).

2. *you will learn for yourself* So MT: *'th td'*. LXX reflects *'th td'*, "you may *now* learn." It is difficult to choose between these variants.

NOTES

27 2. *Achish, son of Maoch, the king of Gath.* Achish, concerning whom see the NOTE at 21:11, is here given a patronymic for the first time, viz. *mā'ôk*, called *ma'ăkâ* in I Kings 2:39 (if the same Achish is meant there).

3. On David's two wives see 25:43-44 and the NOTES there.

5-6. The granting of landed properties to favored servants was a common part of the feudal economy of the city-states of the ancient Near Eastern Bronze Age. The practice seems to have been perpetuated in the Philistine principalities of the Iron Age, just as it was under the Israelite monarchy (see 18:14; cf. 22:7). In the present case the grant is evidently made in return for certain services at arms—a true military fief—as the materials that follow show. All such grants were permanent and inalienable, and the parenthesis at the end of v 6 traces the fact that Ziklag was in the writer's time a special crown property in Judah (a situation about which we have no other information) to the events here recorded.

6. *Ziklag.* Though formally assigned to Simeon (Josh 19:5; I Chron 4:30) Ziklag finds its place in the list of Judahite cities in Josh 15:20-63 (see v 31) as belonging to the Negeb province. The location is still uncertain. It was long identified as Tell el-Khuweilfeh, ca. 14 miles N of Beersheba, but Tell esh-Sherî'ah, ca. 15 miles SE of Gaza on the N bank of the Valley of Gerar

(Wadi esh-Sherî'ah) and thus some 35-40 miles SW of Tell eṣ-Ṣâfī (Gath?), seems now preferred. Cf. A. F. Rainey, *IDBSup*, 984-985.

7. This notice seems to refer to all the time David was in the service of Achish, whether in Gath or Ziklag. See also the NOTE at 29:3.

8-12. By a raid on the Geshurites and Amalekites, which he cunningly represents to Achish as having been against Judahite territory, David wins the confidence of his Philistine overlord. The description of the episode is laced with parenthetical information about David's customary raiding procedures, and the mixture is somewhat confusing; but close attention to the Hebrew syntax, in which the main narrative is expressed by prefixed verbs joined to the conjunction ([8]*wayya'al . . . wayyipšĕṭû* . . . [9]. . . *wayyāšob wayyābē'* . . . [10]*wayyō'mer . . . wayyō'mer* . . . [12]*wayya'ămēn* . . .) and the parentheses by the so-called "frequentative" tenses, i.e. by independent prefixed verbs and suffixed verbs joined to the conjunction (. . . [9]*wĕhikkâ . . . wĕlō' yĕḥayyeh* . . . *wĕlāqaḥ* . . . [11]*lō' yĕḥayyeh*), will sort out the problems. Cf. the NOTE at 1:4-7; also GK §112e,dd.

8. *the Geshurites.* A little known people, geographically associated in Josh 13:2-3 with the Philistines and the Avvim, who were ancient inhabitants of the Gaza area (Deut 2:23); they are not to be confused with the people of the Transjordanian state of Geshur (Deut 3:14; Josh 12:5; 13:11,13), though some historical connection unknown to us may have existed.

the Amalekites. See the NOTES at 14:48 and 15:7.

from Telem to Shur and on toward Egypt. That is, from the Negebite city of Telem or Telaim (on which see the NOTE at 15:4) to the Wilderness of Shur in the direction of Egypt; see also the NOTE at 15:7.

10. *the Negeb of Judah . . . of Jerahmeel . . . of the Kenizzites.* The arid *negeb* or "Southland" of Palestine was traditionally divided into districts by population. The Negeb of Judah seems to have centered upon Beersheba (cf. II Sam 24:7; II Chron 28:18), though it eventually encompassed all the cities listed in Josh 15:21-32. Jerahmeel (cf. 30:29) was evidently an independent tribe, later incorporated into Judah (I Chron 2:9,25-27, etc.); its precise territory cannot be located with certainty but may have lain to the S of Beersheba. The Kenizzites, of whom the Calebites (see the NOTE at 25:3) were a subdivision (cf. Num 32:12; Josh 14:6,14), must have lived in the vicinity of the Calebite city Hebron and of Debir (Tell Beit Mirsim), the town occupied by Othniel, a second Kenizzite subdivision (Josh 15:15-17; etc.). In the present passage all of this is to be understood as Judahite and thus Israelite territory.

12. *a servant always.* Hebrew *'ebed 'ôlām*, lit. "a slave of eternity," a category of bondsman which seems to have involved some kind of formal and voluntary acceptance of status by a servant, who thereby surrendered his chances of freedom forever; see Deut 15:17; Job 40:28(English 41:4; cf. also *CTCA* 5 [= 67].2.19-20; 14 [= Krt].127).

COMMENT

In the desperate knowledge that Saul will sooner or later overtake him David decides to leave Judah, just as he once left Israel. He and his men enlist in the service of the king of Philistine Gath, who gives David the city of Ziklag as a kind of feudal grant. In this way the future king of Israel becomes a soldier in the army of Israel's enemies! Yet his true loyalty has not changed, and all his cunning is required to avoid having either to disclose to Achish his abiding love for Judah or to shed Judahite blood.

This section is part of a larger narrative subdivision in the history of David's rise to power that also includes 29:1-30:31. All of this concerns the sojourn at Ziklag—it is interrupted only by the insertion of the account of Saul's visit to the ghostwife at En-dor in 28:3-25—and should be viewed as a whole, so that at this point not only the present episode comes into our purview but also the report of David's dismissal from the northern campaign in 29:1-11 and the story of his victory over the Amalekites in c 30.

No writer as sympathetic to David as the narrator of this material was would have invented the notion that the primogenitor of the kings of Judah once served as a Philistine vassal, and we cannot doubt that it was an ineradicable element of the story. If so, it was also an *embarrassing* element of the story.[1] For this reason the Ziklag pericope has a markedly apologetic tone. It allows that although David *did* defect to Philistia, he did so only when driven to it by Saul's persecutions, and although he *did* enter the service of a Philistine king, he was merely using the opportunity to acquire a base of operations from which to fight other enemies of Israel (the Geshurites and the Amalekites, for example [27:8]). Never did he make a raid on a Judahite city or in any way violate Judahite territory, though he led Achish to believe that he did, just as he outwitted him in a number of other ways. In the end, in fact, he found a way to use his sojourn as an occasion for enriching the people of Judah (30:26-31).

Apologetics aside, however, the Ziklag pericope functions in the larger narrative as a further example of David's ingenuity and ability to succeed in the most hostile circumstances, and as the story continues in 29:1-11 below, we shall see that Achish is another of those like Michal and Jonathan who, despite the suspicions of others, give their whole-hearted loyalty to David and seem always willing to help his cause.

[1] Cf. the earlier account of a visit by David to the court of Achish in 21:11b-16 and the COMMENT there, where the possibility is considered that that passage was introduced to "correct" the impression made by this one.

XLII. THE SEANCE AT EN-DOR
(28:3-25)

28 3 Now Samuel was dead. All Israel had mourned for him and
buried him in Ramah, his city. And Saul had banished necromancers
and mediums from the land.

4 After the Philistines were assembled, they came up and encamped
at Shunem; so Saul assembled all Israel, and they encamped on Gilboa. 5 When Saul saw the Philistine camp, he became so frightened
that his heart beat violently. 6 [He] inquired of Yahweh, but Yahweh
did not answer him, not by dreams or by lots or by prophets. 7 So Saul
said to his servants, "Find me a ghostwife, so that I may go make my
inquiry through her!" and his servants told him that there was a
ghostwife in En-dor.

8 Saul disguised himself, putting on different clothes, and set out
with two companions. They came to the woman at night, and [Saul]
said, "Divine for me by a ghost! Bring up the man I declare to you!"

9 "You must know what Saul has done," the woman told him, "how
he has cut off necromancers and mediums from the land! Then why
are you laying snares for my life to get me killed?"

10 But Saul swore to her, "As Yahweh lives, no guilt will fall upon
you in this matter!"

11 Then the woman said, "Whom shall I bring up for you?"

"Bring up Samuel for me!" he said.

12 When the woman saw Samuel, she cried out in a loud voice.
"Why have you deceived me?" she said to Saul. "You are Saul!"

13 "Do not be afraid!" the king said to her. "What do you see?"

"I see a god," she told him, "coming up from the earth!"

14 "What is his appearance?" he asked her.

"An erect man is coming up," she said, "and he is wrapped in a
robe." Then Saul knew that it was Samuel, and he fell down face to
the ground and paid homage.

15 Then Samuel said, "Why have you disturbed me by bringing me
up?"

"I am in great distress!" said Saul. "The Philistines are fighting against me, and God has turned away from me, answering me no more, either through prophets or by dreams. So I have called upon you to tell me what I should do."

16 "Why do you inquire of me," said Samuel, "when Yahweh has turned away from you to be with your neighbor? 17 For Yahweh has dealt with you just as he declared through me: [he] has torn the kingship from your hand and given it to your neighbor David! 18 It is because you disobeyed Yahweh and did not execute his hot anger against Amalek that [he] has dealt with you this way today. 19 And tomorrow you are going to fall along with your sons—indeed Yahweh will deliver the camp of Israel into the hand of the Philistines!"

20 Saul immediately fell down full-length upon the ground, for he was greatly frightened by Samuel's words. Indeed he had no strength left, since he had eaten nothing all that day and night. 21 Then the woman came to Saul and, seeing that he was badly shocked, said to him, "Your maidservant listened to you: I put my life in your hands and heeded the instructions you gave me. 22 Now then, you listen to your maidservant! Let me set a bit of food before you; eat it, and you will have strength when you go on your way." 23 He would not eat; but when his servants and the woman together pressed him, he complied with their request, got up from the ground, and sat upon a couch. 24 Now the woman had a stall-fed calf in the house; so she quickly slaughtered it and taking some meal, kneaded it and baked unleavened bread; 25 then she served Saul and his servants. When they had eaten, they arose and departed that night.

TEXTUAL NOTES

28 3. *in Ramah, his city* Reading *brmh b'yrw* with LXX (cf. GK §154a,N). MT: *brmh wb'yrw*, "in Ramah *and* in his city."

4. *Shunem* MT *šûnēm*. LXX^{B} *sōman* shows metathesis, but the correct form, *sōnam*, is attested in several Greek MSS.

7. *ghostwife* In both occurrences MT conflates two terms referring to a (female) necromancer, viz. *'št 'wb*, "ghostwife," and *b'lt 'wb*, "ghostmistress"; thus, *'št b'lt 'wb . . . 'št b'lt 'wb*. LXX *gynaika engastrimython . . . gynē engastrimythos* suggests that *'št 'wb* was original.

8. *and [Saul] said* Reading *wy'mr*, "and he said," with MT. LXX^{B}: "and he said *to her*." LXX^{L}: "and *Saul* said *to her*."

Divine MT (*qĕrê*): *qāsŏmî* (GK §10h). MT (*kĕtîb*): *qĕsômî* (GK §46e).

9. *and mediums* MT reads *hyd'ny,* the singular, having lost *-m* before the succeeding *mn,* "from." Read *hyd'nym* (cf. LXX).

10. *Saul swore to her* So LXX^B. MT, LXX^A add "by Yahweh." LXX^L adds "by God."

13. *"What do you see?"* Reading *mh r'yt,* before and after which LXX^B and LXX^L (respectively) add "Speak!" Omit with MT, which has an intrusive *ky* of its own before *mh.*

she told him So LXX^B. MT, LXX^L: *"the woman* told *Saul."*

14. *What is his appearance?* So MT: *mh t'rw.* LXX has *ti egnōs* = *mh yd't,* "What do you know?" on the pattern of *mh r'yt* in v 13.

erect So LXX: *orthion* = *zqp.* MT has *zqn,* "old," as a result of confusion of the quite similar letters *p* and *n* (cf., for example, the third *Textual Note* at 25:9), but LXX is surely to be preferred as *lectio difficilior.* The verb *zqp,* "stand upright, erect," though it occurs only once elsewhere in the Hebrew Bible (in Ps 145:14), is well attested in Postbiblical Hebrew (Jastrow, 409-410), as well as Aramaic and Akkadian.

she said LXX adds "to him." Omit with MT.

paid homage LXX adds "to him." Omit with MT.

15. *Samuel said* MT adds "to Saul." Omit with LXX^{BL}.

So I have called On MT's anomalous *w'qr'h,* see GK §48d and (for a fuller discussion) Stoebe. LXX *kai nyn keklēka* reflects *w'th qr'ty,* "And *now* I have called. . . ."

16. *Why* So LXX. MT: *"And* why. . . ."

with your neighbor So LXX: *meta tou plēsion sou* = *'m r'k* (cf. Syr.). MT has *'rk,* which some critics would render "your adversary" as a simple corruption of *ṣrk* (cf. Symmachus' *antizēlos sou,* "your rival, antagonist") or a transcriptional error for *ṣrk* "by a scribe to whom the Aramaic form [*'rk*] was familiar" (Smith). See further Driver.

17. *with you* So LXX^B: *soi* = *lk.* MT (cf. LXX^L) has *lw,* "with *him,*" probably in consequence of the loss of *k* before the following word (*k'šr,* "just as").

the kingship So MT, LXX^L. LXX^B: *"your* kingship."

19. This verse is corrupt in all witnesses, conflating two versions of one clause, viz. (1) *wytn yhwh gm 't yśr'l 'mk byd plštym* (MT v 19aα), "And Yahweh will give Israel, too, with you into the hand of the Philistines," and (2) *gm 't mḥnh yśr'l ytn yhwh byd plštym,* "Indeed the camp of Israel will Yahweh give into the hand of the Philistines" (v 19b). There is no reason to prefer the second variant, except that (since 19aβ is presupposed) we know that it is the first that is out of place (Wellhausen).

you are going to fall along with your sons Reading *'th wbnyk 'mk nplym* on the basis of LXX^B *su kai hoi huioi sou meta sou pesountai.* MT has a defective text: *'th wbnyk 'my,* "you and your sons (will be) with me."

23. *He would not eat* Reading *wl' 'bh l'kl* on the basis of LXX^B *kai ouk eboulēthē phagein.* MT expresses it somewhat differently: *wym'n wy'mr l' 'kl,* "But he refused and said, 'I shall not eat!' " LXX^L (= *wy'mn wl' 'bh l'kl*) shows the influence of both readings.

pressed him LXX *kai parebiazonto* points to *wypṣrw*. MT (as in II Sam 13:25,27; cf. II Kings 5:23) has *wyprṣw*, as if "broke out upon him," showing metathesis.

24. *kneaded it* MT *wtlš* = *wattālōš*. 4QSam[a] [*w*]*tlwš* = *wattālôš*, to which compare II Sam 13:8 (MT).

25. *that night* 4QSam[a] (cf. LXX): *hlylh h*[*hw'*]. MT: *blylh hhw'*, "*on* that night."

NOTES

28 3. This verse provides preliminary information necessary to the story that follows. For the notice of Samuel's death and burial, see 25:1 and the COMMENT there.

necromancers and mediums. Hebrew *'ōbôt* and *yiddĕ'ōnîm*, terms which, as J. Pedersen noted, are most often met with in conjunction: Lev 19:31; 20:6,27; II Kings 21:6; 23:24; etc. "They denote departed souls who speak to the living," wrote Pedersen (*Israel* 4.482), "Their whispering voices can be heard from the ground (Isa. 29,4), but most frequently they speak through a man or a woman who understands how to make them active. This spirit is said to *be in* the man or woman in question (Lev. 20,27). That means that it enters their soul and unites with it. Therefore the person through whose mouth the departed speaks can also be called *'ōbh* and *yidh'ōnī* (II Kings 23,24). . . ." Hence our translation, "necromancers and mediums." Priestly law forbade doing business with them (Lev 19:31; 20:6; etc.), and the present tradition records that such a prohibition was enforced by Saul himself.

4. *Shunem . . . Gilboa.* The battle camps are pitched far to the N of the southern desert where the last episodes have taken place. Mount Gilboa and the Nebī Daḥī (the so-called "Hill of Moreh"), on the southern slope of which lies Sôlem, ancient Shunem, loom opposite one another, overlooking the Valley of Jezreel.

6. Now that Saul's repudiation is complete he can no longer expect the guidance of Yahweh, who refuses even to reply to his inquiries. This verse offers us a brief catalogue of the (accepted) methods by which an Israelite might seek divine guidance: (1) "dreams," on which cf. Job 33:15*ff*; (2) "lots," or rather "Urim," as our text reads literally; see the NOTES at 14:40-42; and (3) "prophets," here used in the general sense of "seers, visionaries."

7. *a ghostwife.* Hebrew *'ēšet 'ôb*, a woman who communicates with spirits of the deceased. The accepted means of divining the answers to his questions having failed, Saul turns to a medium he himself has forbidden.

En-dor. Modern Khirbet eṣ-Ṣafṣafe; the ancient name is preserved in that of the modern village of Endôr, which lies nearby on the northern slope of the Nebī Daḥī. The old Manassite (Josh 17:11) city lay only 4 or 5 miles NE of the Philistine camp at Shunem.

8. *Divine for me by a ghost!* That is, get me answers for my questions by contacting a departed person: it is assumed that the deceased have access to information about the divine plans. The Hebrew verb used here is *qsm,* which elsewhere pertains to the practices of foreign diviners or false Israelite prophets, while "he who practices divinations" (*qōsēm qĕsāmîm*) is explicitly condemned by Deuteronomic law (Deut 18:10).

Bring up. That is, from the underworld (the "earth"; cf. the NOTE at v 13).

9-12. The confusion in these verses is a consequence of the incorporation of the figure of Samuel into the story of Saul's interview with an originally anonymous ghost (see the COMMENT). In the unamended version of the story the woman recognized Saul (v 12) because of his authoritative oath of reassurance (v 10): only the king himself could speak thus! The inclusion of vv 11-12a as part of the prophetic reworking of the episode obscures this connection, giving the impression that her visitor's imperious tone has aroused no suspicion in the woman and that seeing Samuel somehow alerts her to Saul's identity.

13. *a god.* That is, a supernatural being, in this case a shade. The use of *'ĕlōhîm,* the ordinary term for God or a god, in reference to a ghost is peculiar to this passage in the Old Testament; but see the NOTE at v 15 below.

the earth. Or rather "the underworld," which *hā'āreṣ* so often designates. See N. J. Tromp, *Primitive Conceptions of Death and the Nether World in the Old Testament* (Rome: Pontifical Biblical Institute, 1969) 23-46.

14. *wrapped in a robe.* The *mĕʿîl* or "robe," though here it seems to serve as a sort of shroud, was Samuel's characteristic garment (15:27; cf. 2:19), and it is perhaps on this basis that Saul recognizes his old nemesis.

15. *disturbed me.* For the use of *rgz* in reference to "disturbing, rousing up" the underworld, cf. Isa 14:9 (Driver). The Phoenician equivalent of the verb often refers to the violation of tombs in sepulchral inscriptions; cf., for example, its use in the fifth-century epitaph of King Tabnit of Sidon, *KAI* 13.4,6,7. It is also quite possible, in view of these things and the use of *'ĕlōhîm'* "god," to mean "shade" in v 13 above, that the expression *margîzê-'ēl,* "those who disturb a god," in Job 12:6, where it is parallel to *šōdĕdîm,* "robbers, looters," means in effect "grave robbers"; thus read:

> The tents of looters are prosperous!
> There is security for those who disturb a "god"
> For that which the "god" has brought with him!

17-18. These verses allude directly to the story of the rejection of Saul in 15:1-34. To v 17, cf. esp. 15:28, and for v 18, see the account of Saul's Amalekite campaign in c 15 *passim.*

20. *he had eaten nothing.* Saul had fasted to purify himself in preparation for the seance.

24. *a stall-fed calf.* Hebrew *'ēgel marbēq,* elsewhere only metaphorically (Jer 46:21; Mal 3:20[English 4:2]).

COMMENT

Events are moving swiftly now toward a major confrontation between the Israelite and Philistine armies. Saul anxiously calls upon Yahweh for instructions, but as we anticipated in the COMMENT on 22:6-23, the oracle is silent for him now. In desperation he turns to a "ghostwife" (*'ēšet 'ōb*) in violation of his own interdiction of traffic with "necromancers and mediums." Later tradition came to regard this as among the most heinous of Saul's crimes (cf. I Chron 10:13), but the present narrative lays less stress on the impropriety of the means of divination that on the somber character of the information thus received. The woman's efforts produce an apparition that turns out to be the shade of Samuel himself, and the old prophet in death offers no more hope to Saul than he did in life. His words are no less dour and no more comforting than at the last meeting of the two men at the altar in Gilgal. He repeats the condemnation of Saul for failing to carry out the ban against the Amalekites and foretells the death of the king and his sons in the coming battle.

The battle report appears in 31:1-13, and in the received text of the Bible it is separated from the present passage by the account of David's dismissal from the Philistine army and his punishment of the Amalekite plunderers of Ziklag (29:1 - 30:31). We have already noted that the latter material goes with the description of David's entry into the service of Achish in 27:1 - 28:2 to make up a single narrative subunit. So in light of all this the present passage, separated from its natural sequel and disruptive in its present location, looks out of place. Geographical considerations reinforce this impression. As Driver says, "In 28,4 the Philistines are at *Shunem* (in the plain of Jezreel); in 29,1 they are still at *Apheq* (in the Sharon, Jos. 12,18), and only reach Jezreel in 29,11. The narrative will be in its right order, if the section be read *after ch.* 29-30." But if Driver and most other commentators are correct in believing the narrative sequence to be out of order here, how is the received arrangement to be accounted for? Budde and others have supposed that the passage was once removed entirely from its original position before c 31 by a Deuteronomically oriented editor who was offended by its content (cf. Deut 18:10-12) and restored subsequently by another hand but at the wrong point in the story. It might, however, be fruitful to ask whether someone wanted Samuel's speech with its reminder of the failure of Saul's Amalekite campaign (v 18) to stand as a kind of *praeparatio* before the account of David's punishment of the Amalekites in cc 29-30. Accordingly, the relocation of the passage might be considered a part of its prophetic revision.

And there *is* evidence of prophetic reworking here, reworking of the sort so familiar from the first half of the book. As pointed out in the NOTE at vv 9-12, the introduction of Samuel in v 11 disrupts the natural flow of the narrative and leaves the ghostwife's recognition of Saul in v 12b without explanation. Originally it was Saul's imperious tone in v 10 that alerted the woman that her client was not an ordinary man but the king himself; vv 11-12a are secondary. Similarly the references in vv 17-18 to Saul's Amalekite campaign and the earlier oracle of Samuel, which point back to the thoroughly prophetic account of the rejection of Saul in 15:1-34, are entirely superfluous and out of place here; the original of this speech of the ghost included only the material in vv 16 and 19, the direct answer to Saul's inquiry about the battle. These things suggest that Samuel had no part in this story before it was revised to reflect the prophetic conviction that Saul's death was a direct consequence of his disobedience to the prophetically transmitted word of Yahweh (cf. 15:23,26 and the COMMENT on 15:1-34). In unrevised and unrelocated form, though, the somber account of the seance at En-dor served first of all to set the tone for the report of the death of Saul and Jonathan in c 31. It showed Saul completely severed from Yahweh; the illegal divination symbolized his extremity. As Ward has noted,[1] this situation was thrown into relief by the contrasting picture, still fresh in the mind of the audience, of Yahweh's oracular guidance of David in his punishment of the Amalekites. The prophetic reworking of the passage has left most of this intact while adding the new themes of its own.

[1] See "Story of David's Rise," 101.

XLIII. ACHISH DISMISSES DAVID
(29:1-11)

29 1 The Philistines assembled all their forces at Aphek, Israel having encamped at the spring at Jezreel.
2 As the lords of the Philistines were advancing with their hundreds
and thousands, David and his men were advancing in the rear with
Achish; 3 and the Philistine commanders said, "What are those Hebrews [doing here]?"
"Is this not David, the servant of Saul, king of Israel?" said Achish
to the Philistine commanders. "He has been with us now for some
time, and I have found no fault with him from the day he defected to
me until this day."
4 But the Philistine commanders grew angry with [Achish]. "Send
the man back to the place you assigned him," they told him, "so that
he will not go down into battle with us and be an adversary in [our
own] camp! For how can this fellow regain the favor of his master,
if not with the heads of these men? 5 Is he not the David of whom
they sing in the dances, saying:

Saul has slain his thousands,
And David his ten thousands?"

6 So Achish summoned David. "As Yahweh lives," he told him,
"you are an honest man, and the way you have marched in and out of
camp with me seems good to me; indeed I have found no fault with
you from the day you came to me until now. And also in the opinion
of the Philistine lords you are a good man. 7 Therefore, go back! Return in peace, so that you will do nothing wrong in the opinion of the
Philistine lords!"
8 Then David said to Achish, "What have I done? What fault have
you found with your servant from the day I entered your service until
this day that I should not go out and fight against the enemies of my
lord, the king?"
9 "I acknowledge," replied Achish to David, "that in my opinion

you are a good man. But the Philistine commanders have said, 'He
shall not go up with us into battle!' 10 Therefore, start early in the
morning—you and the servants of your master who have come with
you—and go to the place I assigned you. As for base remarks, take
none to heart; for you have done well in my service! So be on the
road early; and when you have light enough, go!"

11 So David and his men set out early to return to the land of the
Philistines, while the Philistines themselves went on up toward
Jezreel.

TEXTUAL NOTES

29 1. *at the spring* So MT (*b'yn*), LXX^{L} (*en ain*). LXX$^{A (cf. B)}$ *en aendōr*, "at En-dor," shows the influence of 28:7.

Jezreel So MT, LXX^{AL}. LXX^{B}: "Israel."

3. *commanders* (*bis*) Hebrew *śry* (MT), rendered by LXX *stratēgoi*. In its first occurrence in the verse it is wrongly rendered *satrapai*, as if *srny*, "lords," by LXX^{B} in reminiscence of v 2, and LXX^{L} conflates this reading with the correct one of MT (thus *satrapai kai hoi stratēgoi*, as if *srnym wśry*).

Hebrews So MT: *h'brym*. LXX, Syr. render the same reading as "(those) who cross over, advance," under the influence of v 2.

He has been Cf. LXX. MT connects this more closely with the foregoing by inserting *'šr*—thus, "Is this not David . . . *who* has been, etc.?"

with us So LXX^{B} (*meth' hēmōn* = *'tnw*), Syr., against MT *'ty*, "with me." There is no basis for preference between these variants.

now for some time We read *zh ymym*, lit. "now for days." MT (cf. LXX) has *zh ymym 'w zh šnym*, lit. "now for days or now for years," thus displaying a conflate text preserving two synonymous expressions, viz. *zh ymym* and *zh šnym*, artificially joined by the copulative *'w* (which is not represented in LXX). See S. Talmon, "Double Readings in the Massoretic Text," in *Textus* 1 (Jerusalem: Magnes, 1960) 171.

from the day he defected to me until this day Reading *mywm nplw 'ly* (*w*)*'d hywm hzh* with LXX$^{(B)}$; cf. v 6. MT has suffered a haplography triggered by the similar sequences *-lw* and *-ly* and reads *mywm nplw 'd hywm hzh*, "from the day he defected until this day."

4. *Send the man back to the place* So LXX^{B}. MT, LXX^{A}, Syr.: "Send the man back *and let him go back* to the place. . . ."

they told So LXX. MT: "*the Philistine commanders* told."

and be an adversary in [*our own*] *camp* Cf. OL: . . . *consiliarius in castris nostris*. We read *wl' yhyh śṭn bmḥnh* on the basis of LXX$^{(B)}$ *kai mē ginesthō epiboulos tēs parembolēs*. MT has *wl' yhyh lnw lśṭn bmlḥmh*, "and (he will not) *become* an adversary *to us* in the *battle*."

6. *you are a good man* So LXX$^{(B)}$: *agathos su* = *ṭwb 'th*. MT confuses the conversation thoroughly by inserting *l'* (thus, *l' ṭwb 'th*, "you are *not* a good man"), so that David's questions in v 8 are pointless in MT. Both Achish and the Philistine lords (*srnym*) have found David worthy; it is the Philistine commanders (*śrym*) who object to his participation (cf. v 9).

8. *What have I done?* LXX adds "to you." Omit with MT.

9. *replied* So LXX^{B}. MT, LXX^{AL}: "replied *and said*."

that in my opinion you are a good man MT (cf. LXX^{AL}) has *ky twb 'th b'yny kml'k 'lhym*, "that you are as good in my opinion as a messenger of God." This comparison is inappropriate here; it elsewhere applies to David as having the judicial insight of a divine being (II Sam 14:17; 19:28). We omit *kml'k 'lhym* with LXX^{B}.

10. MT has suffered a long haplography in this verse, and we read the text of LXX$^{(B)}$: *kai nyn orthrison to prōi su kai hoi paides tou kyriou sou hoi hēkontes meta sou kai poreuesthe eis ton topon hou katestēsa hymas ekei kai logon loimon mē thēs en kardia sou hoti agathos su enōpion mou kai orthrisate en tē hodō kai phōtisatō hymin kai poreuthēte* = *w'th hškm bbqr 'th w'bdy 'dnyk 'šr b'w 'tk whlktm 'l hmqwm 'šr hpqdty 'tkm šm wdbr bly'l 'l tśm blbbk ky ṭwb 'th lpny whškmtm bdrk w'wr lkm wlkw*. MT has *w'th hškm bbqr w'bdy 'dnyk 'šr b'w 'tk whškmtm bbqr w'wr lkm wlkw*, "Therefore, start early in the morning . . . and the servants of your master who have come with you. . . . So start early in the morning; and when you have light enough, go!" The history of the corruption in MT may be reconstructed as follows: (1) *bdrk* became *bbqr* under the influence of the earlier *bbqr;* (2) a long haplography occurred from *hškm bbqr* to *whškmtm bbqr*, which may have appeared immediately beneath it in the succeeding line; (3) the lost material was partially restored, *w'bdy 'dnyk 'šr b'w 'tk* being added from another MS. Other explanations are possible, but this one at least has the advantage of identifying a mechanism for the long omission and accounting for the loss of *'th*.

11. *set out early* MT, LXX^{AL}, Syr. add "in the morning." Omit with LXX^{B}.

to return to So MT: *lšwb 'l*. LXX, which has *kai phylassein*, evidently reads *wlšmr ('t)*, "to watch over."

NOTES

29 1. *Aphek*. See the NOTE at 4:1. The notice in 28:4 to the effect that the Philistines were already encamped far to the N of Aphek at Shunem is difficult to reconcile with the present statement. Unless, as we have suggested, the episode recorded in 28:3-25 is out of place (see the COMMENT there), we must suppose that the Philistines here mentioned are gathering at Aphek on their way up to join the main army at Shunem.

the spring at Jezreel. The city of Jezreel, modern Zer'în, lay on the NW slope of Mount Gilboa, fully 35–40 miles NE of Aphek. The spring is "probably . . . the source of the Harod (the modern *'ēn jālūd*), south-east of the city of Jezreel at the foot of Mount Gilboa where Gideon undertook his famous attack on the Midianite camp" (so Noth, *History*, 177-178).

2. *their hundreds and thousands.* Their military units of smaller and larger size; see the NOTE at 4:10.

3. *Hebrews.* As Israelites are usually called in foreign speech; see the NOTES at 4:6 and 14:21.

now for some time. Hebrew *zeh yāmîm;* cf. II Sam 14:2; etc.

defected. For *nāpal,* "fall," in the sense of "fall away, defect," cf. II Kings 7:4; 25:11(*bis*) = Jer 52:15(*bis*); Jer 21:9; 37:13,14; 38:19; 39:9(*bis*); I Chron 12:20(*bis*),21(English 12:19,20).

4. *the place you assigned him.* That is, Ziklag. Cf. 27:6 and 29:10; 30:1.

go down. In v 9 "go up" is used instead (cf. v 11) and seems better, since in fact the Philistines are on their way up from the coastal plain into the hills of Samaria (cf. Driver).

5. Exactly as in 21:12 (cf. 18:7).

6-7. Achish reluctantly agrees to send David back to Ziklag, but he chooses his words carefully so as not to alienate his loyal (as he supposes) servant by seeming not to have his best interest at heart. David, he says, has the good opinion of the Philistine lords (cf. the NOTE at 5:8) and should return home in order to avoid doing anything that might jeopardize that desirable situation.

6. *"As Yahweh lives."* The oath formula itself is not unusual (cf. 14:39; etc.) . . . but surely Achish is no Yahwist! We must assume either that the Philistine king swears by David's god as a matter of courtesy or, more likely, that this is a slip on the part of our Yahwistic narrator.

marched in and out. See the NOTE at 18:13.

8. *from the day I entered your service.* Hebrew *miyyôm* (so! cf. GK §130c) *'ăšer hāyîtî lĕpānêkā,* lit. "from the day on which I was (first) before you." To be before someone is to be in full view and eligible for critical appraisal; as in 3:1, for example, it also suggests a position of service (cf. also the NOTES on *hithallēk lipnê,* "walk before," at 2:30 and 12:2).

the enemies of my lord, the king. The courteous phrases permit David a wry ambiguity of meaning. Achish assumes that he himself is the king referred to, but in David's own mind he is still loyal to Saul. It seems likely that the fears of the Philistine commanders (v 4) were well founded and that David is truly reluctant to quit the march and lose a chance to be "an adversary in [the Philistine] camp."

10. *base remarks.* Hebrew *dĕbar bĕliyya'al,* lit. "word(s) of worthlessness," which occurs elsewhere only in Ps 41:9(English 41:8) where, though the immediate context is obscure, the surrounding verses deal with slander and insult.

you have done well in my service. Hebrew *ṭôb 'attâ lĕpānay,* lit. "you have been good before me," to which compare vv 6,9 and the NOTE at v 8 above.

COMMENT

Achish is fully persuaded of the loyalty of his Israelite vassal and so is perfectly willing to have David at his side as he takes the field against Saul. But "the Philistine commanders," the ranking generals, are not of the same opinion. They have been free of the spell of David's charm and are mindful of his old reputation as a Philistine killer (cf. I Chron 12:20 [English 12:19]). So David finds himself excused from duty in the northern campaign and on the road back to Ziklag.

This episode continues the story of David's Ziklag sojourn that was begun in 27:1-28:2. It makes it even more clear how thoroughly he has outwitted his Philistine host, who considers him loyal to Gath and completely estranged from Israel (cf. 27:12). His particular predicament here is posed by the coming battle with Saul: how can he participate without either fighting against his own countrymen or exposing to Achish his true loyalty? We cannot doubt what he had intended to do, for the sly irony in his expressed wish to "go out and fight against the enemies of my lord, the king," though it eludes Achish, is not lost on the audience (see the NOTE at v 8), and its import vindicates the suspicions of the Philistine generals. But fate, or rather Providence, intervenes, and David is set free from the predicament and sent back to Ziklag. What he finds there is the subject of the next section.

XLIV. ZIKLAG AVENGED
(30:1-31)

30 1 On the third day, when David and his men reached Ziklag,
some Amalekites, who had made a raid on the Negeb including
Ziklag, had attacked Ziklag and set it aflame. 2 Of the women and everyone else who was there, from the youngest to the oldest, they had
killed no one; rather they had taken them prisoner and gone their
way. 3 So when David and his men entered the city, it had been set
aflame and their wives, sons, and daughters taken prisoner.

4 David and the soldiers with him wept aloud until there was no
strength for weeping left in them. 5 (Now David's two wives, Ahinoam of Jezreel and Abigail, widow of Nabal of Carmel, had also
been taken prisoner.) 6 David was in desperate straits, for the soldiers,
each of whom was bitter on account of his sons and daughters, spoke
of stoning him; but David strengthened himself in Yahweh, his god.

7 "Bring me the ephod!" [he] said to Abiathar, the priest, Ahimelech's son. 8 Then David inquired of Yahweh as follows: "Should I
pursue this raiding party? Can I overtake them?"

"Pursue!" he was told. "For you *shall* overtake them and you *shall* make the rescue!"

9 So David and the six hundred men who were with him set out and
came to the Wadi Besor. 10 Then as David and four hundred men
continued the pursuit, two hundred men, who were too exhausted to
cross the Wadi Besor, stayed behind.

11 They found an Egyptian in the open country and took him to
David. They gave him food, and he ate; and they gave him water to
drink. 12 They gave him a slice of fig cake; and as he ate his vitality
returned, for he had neither eaten food nor drunk water for three
days and three nights.

13 Then David said to him, "To whom do you belong? Where are
you from?"

"I am an Egyptian lad," he said, "the slave of an Amalekite. My
master left me behind three days ago, because I was ill. 14 We had

made a raid against the Negeb of the Cherethites and against that of
Judah and against the Negeb of Caleb. Ziklag we had set aflame."

15 Then David said to him, "Will you lead me to this raiding
party?"

"Swear to me by God," he said, "that you will not kill me or hand
me over to my master, and I shall lead you to this raiding party!"

16 So he led him down, and there they were, lounging about all over
the ground, eating, drinking, and celebrating amid all the vast plunder they had taken from the land of the Philistines and the land of
Judah. 17 David battered them from the first light of dawn until the
evening of the next day. He put them to death, and none escaped except four hundred young men, who mounted camels and fled.
18 David rescued all that the Amalekites had taken; his own two wives
he also rescued. 19 None of them was missing from the youngest to the
oldest, including both sons and daughters; and of the plunder and all
that they had taken, David recovered everything. 20 He also took all
the sheep and the cattle and drove them before him, and [his men]
said, "This is David's plunder!"

21 When David came to the two hundred men he had posted in the
Wadi Besor because they had been too exhausted to follow [him],
they came out to meet [him] and the soldiers that were with him and,
as David approached with the soldiers, greeted them. 22 But in reply
every evil and worthless one of the men who had gone with David
said, "Since they did not join us in the chase, we shall not give them
any of the plunder we recovered—except for each man's own wife
and children: let them lead these away and go!"

23 But David said, "Do not behave this way after what Yahweh has
given us! Why, he has watched over us and delivered the raiding
party that came against us into our power! 24 So who would listen to
this proposal of yours? For the share of the man who stays by the gear
will be the same as the share of the man who goes down into battle:
they will share alike!" 25 And from that day on, he made it a statute
and custom for Israel, [as it is] to this day.

The Division of the Spoils

26 After his return to Ziklag David dispatched portions of the plunder to the elders of Judah city by city, saying, "This is from the plunder of the enemies of Yahweh!" 27 [There were portions] for those in

Beth-zur, for those in Ramath-negeb, for those in Jattir, 28 for those in Ararah, for those in Siphmoth, for those in Eshtemoa, 29 for those in Carmel, for those in the cities of the Jerahmeelites, for those in the cities of the Kenizzites, 30 for those in Hormah, for those in Borashan, for those in Ether, 31 for those in Hebron, and all the places that David and his men had frequented.

TEXTUAL NOTES

30 1. *Ziklag* (1) So MT. LXX$^{(B)}$: *keeila,* "Keilah."

on the Negeb. So LXX (*epi ton noton* = *'l hngb*). MT: *'l ngb,* "southward."

2. MT and LXX$^{(B)}$ are somewhat different, and our translation follows the latter. MT has, "And they had taken prisoner the women who were there; from the youngest to the oldest they had killed no one. Then they had led [them] off and gone their way."

4. *and the soldiers with him* So MT: *wh'm 'šr 'tw.* LXX = *w'nšyw,* "and his men" (cf. vv 1,3).

strength for weeping MT *kḥ lbkwt.* LXX^{L} (cf. LXX^{B}) = *kḥ lbkwt 'wd,* "strength for weeping *any longer.*"

7. At the end of the verse MT (cf. LXX^{AL}) adds *wygš 'bytr 't h'pd 'l dwd,* "And Abiathar brought the ephod to David." Omit with LXX^{B}.

8. *Should I pursue* Reading *h'rdp* on the basis of LXX$^{(B)}$ *ei katadiōxō* (cf. Driver). MT: *'rdp,* "I shall pursue."

9. *six hundred* So MT. LXX^{B}: "four hundred." Cf. the *Textual Note* to 23:13.

At the end of the verse MT has *whnwtrym 'mdw,* "and those who remained stayed behind" (so also all versions). This is out of place at this point, anticipating 10b. On the problems of these two verses see further Wellhausen, Stoebe. The extensive confusion exhibited by LXX in vv 9 and 10 must have developed partly out of uncertainty about the size of David's force (see the preceding *Textual Note*) and partly out of the intrusion of these words.

10. *Then as David and four hundred men continued the pursuit* So MT: *wyrdp dwd hw' w'rb' m'wt 'yš.* LXX$^{(B)}$ *kai hoi perissoi ediōxan en tetrakosiois andrasin* seems to reflect *whnwtrym rdpw b'rb' m'wt 'yš,* "And those who remained pursued with four hundred men."

who were too exhausted to cross the Wadi MT *'šr pgrw m'br* (*mē'ăbōr*) *'t nḥl. . . .* LXX$^{(B)}$ has *hoitines ekathisan peran tou cheimarrou,* apparently reflecting *'šr yšbw m'br* (*mē'ēber*) *nḥl . . . ,* "who sat down on the other side of the Wadi . . ." (preceded in LXX^{L} by *tou phylassein* = *lšmr;* thus, "*to guard* those who lived on the other side of the Wadi . . .").

11. *and took him* MT *wyqḥw 'tw.* LXX has *kai lambanousen auton kai*

agousin auton, "and seized him and led him," which seems to be a conflation of two translations of *wyqḥw 'tw.*

to David LXX here adds *en agrō* = *bśdh,* "in the open country," a second time. Omit with MT.

12. *a slice of fig cake* MT adds *wšny ṣmqym,* "and two (bunches of) raisins" (so LXX^{L}, Syr.; cf. LXX^{A}). Omit with LXX^{B}.

14. *against* Reading *'l* (LXX *epi*), which is omitted in MT. Cf. Driver.

the Cherethites So MT: *hkrty* (LXX^{A} *tou cherēthei*). LXX^{B} *tou cholthei* may show the influence of *hplty,* often associated with *hkrty* (II Sam 8:18; etc.). To LXX^{L} *tou chorrei,* compare II Sam 20:23 (MT).

Caleb MT *klb* (cf. LXX^{AL}, Syr.). LXX^{B} *gelboue* (as if "Gilboa") is an inner-Greek corruption.

15. At the end of the verse LXX^{L} adds "and he swore to him." Omit with LXX^{B}, MT.

16. *So he led him down* LXX^{B} adds "there." Omit with MT, LXX^{L}.

and there they were, lounging about LXX$^{B(cf.\ L)}$ has *kai idou houtoi diakechymenoi* = *whnh hm nṭšym,* perhaps correctly. MT: *whnh nṭšym.*

17. *David battered them* So MT: *wykm dwd.* LXX: *kai ēlthen ep' autous daueid kai epataxen autous* = *wyb' 'lyhm dwd wykm,* "David *went against them and* battered them."

of the next day. He put them to death Reading (*w*)*lmḥrt wymytm* on the basis of LXX^{L} *kai tē*(*s*) *epaurion kai ethanatōse*(*n*). MT (cf. LXX^{B}) has the anomalous reading *lmḥrtm,* "of *their* (?) next day," evidently a corrupt condensation of the reading of LXX^{L}, perhaps by haplography from *t* to *t.*

18. *he . . . rescued* So LXX^{B}. MT: "*David* . . . rescued."

19. This is the word order of MT. In LXX$^{B(cf.\ L)}$ the words that appear as "including both sons and daughters; and of the plunder" here are transposed; thus, "None of them was missing from the youngest to the oldest and *from spoil to sons and daughters* and to all that they had taken: David recovered everything." There is little basis for choosing between these arrangements; but as Driver points out, if we retain that of MT, we must move the Masoretes' disjunctive accent (*zāqēp*) from *wmšll* to *wbnwt.*

20. *He also took* So LXX^{B}. MT: "*David* also took."

and drove them before him MT has *nhgw lpny hmqnh hhw'* "and they drove (them) before *that property,*" viz. before the recovered property referred to in the previous verse. LXX^{B} reflects *wynhg lpny hšll* (*emprosthen tōn skylōn*) *wlšll hhw'* (*kai tois skylois ekeinois*), that is (apart from the double reading), "and he drove them before *the spoil.*" The differing objects of the preposition in the two versions are evidently explicating expansions, explaining (incorrectly) an original pronominal object (*lpnyw,* "before it, him[!]"; so Vulg.). LXX^{B} has preserved the verbal form intact; in MT it has become plural by attraction to the following *wy'mrw,* "and they said" (see below). Thus read *wynhg lpnyw.* See also Wellhausen, Driver.

and [*his men*] *said* So MT: *wy'mrw,* lit. "and they said," which is almost an impersonal construction. Cf. LXX: *elegeto,* "it was said."

21. *he had posted* Reading *wayyōšîbēm* with five MSS of MT and LXX$^{(B)}$ *kai ekathisen autous* in preference to MT *wayyōšîbūm,* "*they* had posted."

as David approached with the soldiers So MT: *wygš dwd 't h'm* (though MT seems to misunderstand the *'t;* see below). LXX reflects *wygš dwd 'd* (*heōs*) *h'm,* "as David approached *toward* the soldiers"; but as the first part of the verse indicates David is with "the soldiers" (*h'm*) already, not approaching them.

greeted them That is, those who had stayed behind greeted David and the soldiers. Thus LXX^B: *kai ērōtēsan auton ta eis eirēnēn = wyš'lw lw lšlwm,* "(and they) greeted them." MT (cf. LXX^L) *wyš'l lhm lšlwm,* "(and [the soldiers]) greeted them," arose from a misunderstanding of *'t,* "with," in the preceding clause: assuming that David was approaching the soldiers, it has made the soldiers the subject of the verb here. On v 21b in general, see also Driver.

22. *evil and worthless* So MT, LXX^L, OL. LXX^B: "worthless and evil."

the men So MT. LXX: "the men, *the warriors."*

they did not join us in the chase So LXX: *ou katediōxan meth' hēmōn = l' rdpw 'mnw,* lit. "they did not chase with us." MT: *l' hlkw 'my,* "they did not *go* with *me."*

23. *after what Yahweh has given us* Comparison of the witnesses yields no fully satisfactory reading. MT has *'ḥy 't 'šr ntn yhwh lnw,* ". . . my brothers! That which Yahweh has given us. . . ." This leaves "That which Yahweh has given us" isolated, unless we understand it as the object of *l' t'św,* "Do not behave this way, do not do so" (Hertzberg); thus, "Do not do so, my brothers, with that which Yahweh has given us"; but good parallels for such a use of *'śh* do not exist. So if MT is retained, some kind of anacoluthon must be assumed (". . . my brothers! That which Yahweh has given us— Why, he has . . ."); cf. Stoebe. LXX has *meta to paradounai ton kyrion hēmin = 'ḥry 'šr ntn yhwh lnw,* which we have followed Wellhausen in translating, "after what Yahweh has given us"; but admittedly the more natural rendering of this is "after Yahweh has given us . . ." calling for an object for *ntn.* The latter is supplied by LXX^L as *tous hypenantious,* "the adversaries," and (alternatively) by some modern scholars as *hyšw'h,* "the victory"; but neither the ancient nor the modern addition inspires confidence.

24. *this proposal of yours* At this point LXX^B(cf. L) adds *hoti ouch hētton* (*hēttous*) *hymōn eisin,* "for they are not inferior to you" (perhaps, *ky l' ṣ'r[ym] mkm [hmh]*). We have omitted these words as expansive (so MT), though the possibility of haplography exists (from *hzh ky l'* to *hmh ky kḥlq*).

25. *he made it* So MT: *wyśmh.* LXX reflects *wyhy,* "it became," to which MT is to be preferred as *lectio difficilior.*

26. *city by city* Conjectural. MT has *lr'hw* (cf. GK §91k), "to his neighbors" (LXX *"and* to his neighbors"), which we assume to have been an early corruption of *l'ryw,* lit. "according to its (Judah's) cities" (**l'ryw > lr'yw* [cf. LXX] > *lr'hw*).

"This is from the plunder of the enemies of Yahweh" Reading *hnh mšll 'yby yhwh* with LXX^B. MT (cf. LXX^AL, OL): *hnh lkm brkh mšll 'yby yhwh,* "Here is a gift for you from the plunder of the enemies of Yahweh!" The originality of the longer reading could be argued on the assumption of haplography in the *Vorlage* of LXX^B from *hnh* to *brkh.*

27. *Beth-zur* So LXX^{B}: *baithsour* = *byt ṣwr*. MT (so LXX^{ALmss}) has *byt 'l*, "Bethel"; though it is not impossible that there was a town in Judah by this name, Beth-zur is quite at home in this list. See the NOTE.

Ramath-negeb Reading *rmt ngb* for MT *rmwt ngb*, "Ramoth-negeb"; cf. LXX and Josh 19:8 (MT).

Jattir So MT: *ytr*. LXX^{B}: *geththor*.

28. *Ararah* MT has *'ărō'ēr*, "Aroer," showing the influence of the name of the well-known Transjordanian city (Num 32:34; etc). The original of the name of the Judahite city is shown to have been *'r'rh* by (1) its identification as *'d'dh* (MT; LXX^{B} *arouēl*) in Josh 15:22, (2) the evidence of LXX^{B} in the present passage, where the reading of MT (*aroēr*) is conflated with *ammadei*, which Wellhausen has shown to be a corrupt reflection of *'r'rh*, and (3) the modern name, 'Ar'arah (see the NOTE).

Siphmoth . . . Eshtemoa MT: *śpmwt . . . 'štm'*. LXX^{B} in vv 28,29 + seems to have a triple rendering of these two names as (1) *saphei* and *estheie*, (2) *geth* and *keimath*, and (3) *saphek* and *theimath*. The expanded list is missing from LXX^{AL} and 4QSam^{a}.

29. *Carmel* So LXX: *karmēlō* = *krml*. MT: *rkl*.

the Jerahmeelites So MT: *hyrḥm'ly* (cf. LXX^{A} *ieramēlei*). LXX^{BL}: *tou israēl*, "Israel."

the Kenizzites As in 27:10 MT has *hqyny*, "the Kenites," while LXX$^{(B)}$ preserves the correct reading (*tou kenezei* = *hqnzy*), now confirmed by 4QSam^{a} *hqṅży*.

30. *Hormah* MT *ḥormâ*. LXX^{B}: *ieremouth*. LXX^{L}: *erma*.

Bor-ashan MT: *bwr 'šn*. In LXX this has been transformed into the familiar name "Beersheba."

Ether MT has *'tk;* but such a place name occurs only here, and *'tr* is associated with *'šn* in Josh 15:42 (where LXX^{B} has *ithak*) and 19:7. The representations of LXX at this point are perplexing: LXX^{B} *noo*; LXX^{L} *nageb*; LXX^{MSS} *nombe*.

NOTES

30 1. In the past Ziklag provided David with a base of operations against the Amalekites (27:8), the archetypal bandits of biblical tradition (see the NOTE at 14:48). Now the Amalekites have returned the favor, raiding in the Negeb (cf. the NOTE at 27:10) in David's absence and burning his unguarded city.

5. We were prepared for this by the notice in 27:3b. On Ahinoam and Abigail see also 25:43-44 and the NOTES there.

6. *David was in desperate straits*. Hebrew *wattēṣer lĕdāwīd mĕ'ōd*, lit. "And it was very narrow for David," exactly as in Judg 10:9; cf. Gen 32:8(English 32:7); Judg 2:15; II Sam 13:2; Job 20:22. Cf. GK §144b.

was bitter. Hebrew *mārâ nepeš*, on which see 1:10 and esp. 22:2 and the NOTE there.

David strengthened himself in Yahweh. That is, he met the crisis of confidence caused by the raid by enlisting the authority of the divine oracle, though Hertzberg is probably correct to insist that this "does not mean that his trust is merely in an inquiry of the holy oracle" but in the good offices of Yahweh in general. "Strengthen oneself" (*hitḥazzēq*) may carry implications both of taking courage (see the NOTE at 4:9) and of consolidating one's postion vis-à-vis some group of people (II Sam 3:6); cf. also the NOTE at 23:16.

7. *the ephod.* On the ephod as an instrument of divination, see the NOTE at 14:3.

Abiathar. The Elide priest who has been with David since the Nob massacre; see 22:20-23 (cf. 23:6).

9-10. *the Wadi Besor.* The first prominent wadi SW of Tell esh-Sherî'āh (ancient Ziklag) is the Wadi Ghazzeh, into which the Wadi esh-Sherî'āh itself drains. The former was identified with the Wadi Besor by those who took Tell el-Khuweilfeh to be the site of Ziklag (see the NOTE at 27:6), partly on the grounds that a hard journey of 25 miles—the distance between Tell el-Khuweilfeh and the Wadi Ghazzeh—would have certainly sufficed to exhaust a third of David's companions. Tell esh-Sherî'āh is much closer to the Wadi Ghazzeh, 12–15 miles at the most; but David's men were traveling fast and probably had not stopped to rest in Ziklag after the return journey from Aphek. Accordingly, the Wadi Ghazzeh remains a likely candidate for identification as the Wadi Besor.

14. *the Negeb of the Cherethites.* On the Negeb and its districts, including that of Judah, see the NOTE at 27:10. The Cherethites (*hakkĕrētî*) were identical to or at least closely associated with the Philistines (cf. Ezek 25:16; Zeph 2:5), and in view of the Aegean origins of the latter (see the NOTE at 4:1) we are justified in relating "Cherethite" to "Cretan." The Cretan Negeb, then, was that part of the southern desert controlled by the Philistines or, perhaps, a subdivision of it in the vicinity of Ziklag. The presence later on in King David's army of a contingent of Cherethites, who showed a particular loyalty that continued into Solomon's reign, suggests that David won their allegiance decisively in his days at Ziklag (cf. II Sam 8:18 [= I Chron 18:17]; 15:18; 20:7,23; I Kings 1:38,44).

the Negeb of Caleb. This must refer to the desert around Hebron, the Calebite capital (see the NOTE at 25:3), a subdivision presumably of the Negeb of the Kenizzites (see the NOTE at 27:10).

16. *celebrating.* Hebrew *ḥōgĕgîm,* which would ordinarily mean "making a pilgrimage" or "having a pilgrims' festival," which is out of the question here. Driver: "It is best to acquiesce in the cautious judgment of Nöldeke . . . who declares that he cannot with certainty get behind the idea of a *festal gathering* for the common Semitic *ḥāg*. Here then the meaning will be 'behaving as at a *ḥāg* or gathering of pilgrims,' i.e. enjoying themselves merrily."

17. *the first light of dawn.* Hebrew *hannešep,* usually "twilight," but with the present sense in Job 7:4 and Ps 119:147 (BDB) and commonly in Postbiblical Hebrew (Jastrow, 941).

21. *the two hundred men.* Cf. v 10 and the NOTE at 9-10 above.

23-25. A custom current in the writer's own day is traced back to the youth of David: "the share of the man who stays by the gear [is] the same as the share of the man who goes down into battle." The reasoning is characteristic of the Israelite ideology of warfare. Victory belongs to Yahweh alone. No man, therefore, whatever his contribution to the battle, has any claim over another; all share the spoils alike (cf. Deut 20:14).

26-31. David distributes the spoil among a number of larger and smaller cities in the vicinity around and to the S of Hebron. The gifts are of "plunder of the enemies of Yahweh," the god of Israel, and so will serve not only to bind this territory to the person of David but also to the political entity known as Israel. These events, therefore, look ahead to David's assumption of kingship at Hebron in II Sam 2:1-4 and finally to his unification of north and south into one nation with a common loyalty. See also the COMMENT.

27. *Beth-zur.* An old Calebite town (cf. I Chron 2:45) in the Judean hills (Josh 15:58). The name is preserved in that of the modern village of Beit Ṣûr, from which the site of the ancient city is a few hundred yards away at Khirbet et-Tubeiqah, ca. 4 miles N of Hebron.

Ramath-negeb. The site of the southern Ramah, also known as Baalath-beer (Josh 19:8), is unknown.

Jattir. A Levitical city (Josh 21:14; cf. I Chron 6:42[English 6:57]) in the Judean hills (Josh 15:48); the site is Khirbet 'Attir, ca. 12 miles SSW of Hebron.

28. *Ararah.* See the *Textual Note.* Ararah was a village in the Negeb of Judah (Josh 15:22, where *'r'rh* is to be read for *'d'dh*), ca. 12 miles SE of Beersheba. The modern town is called 'Ar'arah.

Siphmoth. The city is not mentioned elsewhere (cf. I Chron 27:27), and the site is unknown.

Eshtemoa. A Levitical city (Josh 21:14; cf. I Chron 6:42[English 6:57]) in the Judean hills (Josh 15:50); the modern site is es-Semū'a, ca 8 miles S of Hebron near Carmel and Maon.

29. *Carmel.* Modern Tell el-Kirmil, ca. 7 miles S of Hebron. See the NOTES at 15:12; 25:2a.

the cities of the Jerahmeelites. The region S of Beersheba? Cf. the NOTE at 27:10.

the cities of the Kenizzites. The vicinity of Hebron and Debir; see the NOTE at 27:10.

30. *Hormah.* Though formally assigned to Simeon (Josh 19:4) Hormah, like nearby Ziklag, finds its place in the Judean cities list as belonging to the Negeb province (Josh 15:30); the location of the site is uncertain.

Bor-ashan. Also known simply as "Ashan," modern Khirbet 'Asan, a few miles NW of Beersheba. Bor-ashan was a Levitical city of Judah (Josh 21:16 LXX^{B}) in the Shephelah (Josh 19:7; cf. 15:42).

Ether. See the *Textual Note.* Another village in the Shephelah (Josh 19:7; cf. 15:42), Ether lay ca. 15 miles NW of Hebron; the modern site is Khirbet el-'Ater.

31. *Hebron.* The major city of the region and the old Calebite capital (see the NOTE at 25:3), Hebron will be the place where David is first proclaimed king (II Sam 2:1-4) and his capital before the capture of Jerusalem.

COMMENT

A woeful sight awaits David and his men on their return from the northern march of the Philistines. Their city is in flames and their wives and children have been carried away by Amalekite raiders. The grief-stricken soldiers are at the point of putting David to death out of bitterness and despair, but he maintains control and organizes a forced march in pursuit of the plunderers. Gradually they overtake their quarry and guided by an Egyptian slave whom the Amalekites had left for dead, come upon them carousing amid the booty at the end of the day. The next evening, after a long and bloody fight, most of the enemy lie dead, and the plunder of Ziklag—wives, children and property—is recovered in full along with the rest of the Amalekites' ill-gotten property as a bonus. The latter is partly divided among David's men and partly dispatched to the elders of the various cities and regions of southern Judah.

Here as in the Keilah episode (23:1-13) David appears as a kind of unofficial policeman or protector of Judah. By punishing Amalek, Judah's old nemesis, he has avenged not only Ziklag but also the other towns of the Negebs of the Cherethites, of Judah, and of Caleb (v 14)—wherever the Amalekites were in the habit of making their raids. Moreover, he uses his successes to enrich the people of southern and southwestern Judah (vv 26-31). Indeed the entire Ziklag pericope may be said to demonstrate a historical basis for a bond between David and the people of the Judahite Negeb as surely as the preceding stories do for the Wilderness of Judah and specifically the area east of Hebron. Taken together these materials prepare us for II Sam 2:1-4, the proclamation of David as king of Judah in Hebron.

In the larger narrative this episode also provides further illustration of David's successes and further contrast of his career with that of Saul. For Saul the oracle of Yahweh, which guides David here (vv 7-8), has now become silent as illustrated by the account of the seance at En-dor, which seems originally to have followed the present episode (see the COMMENT on 28:3-25). According to the present, prophetically revised arrangement of the story, however, the report of Saul's death follows immediately.

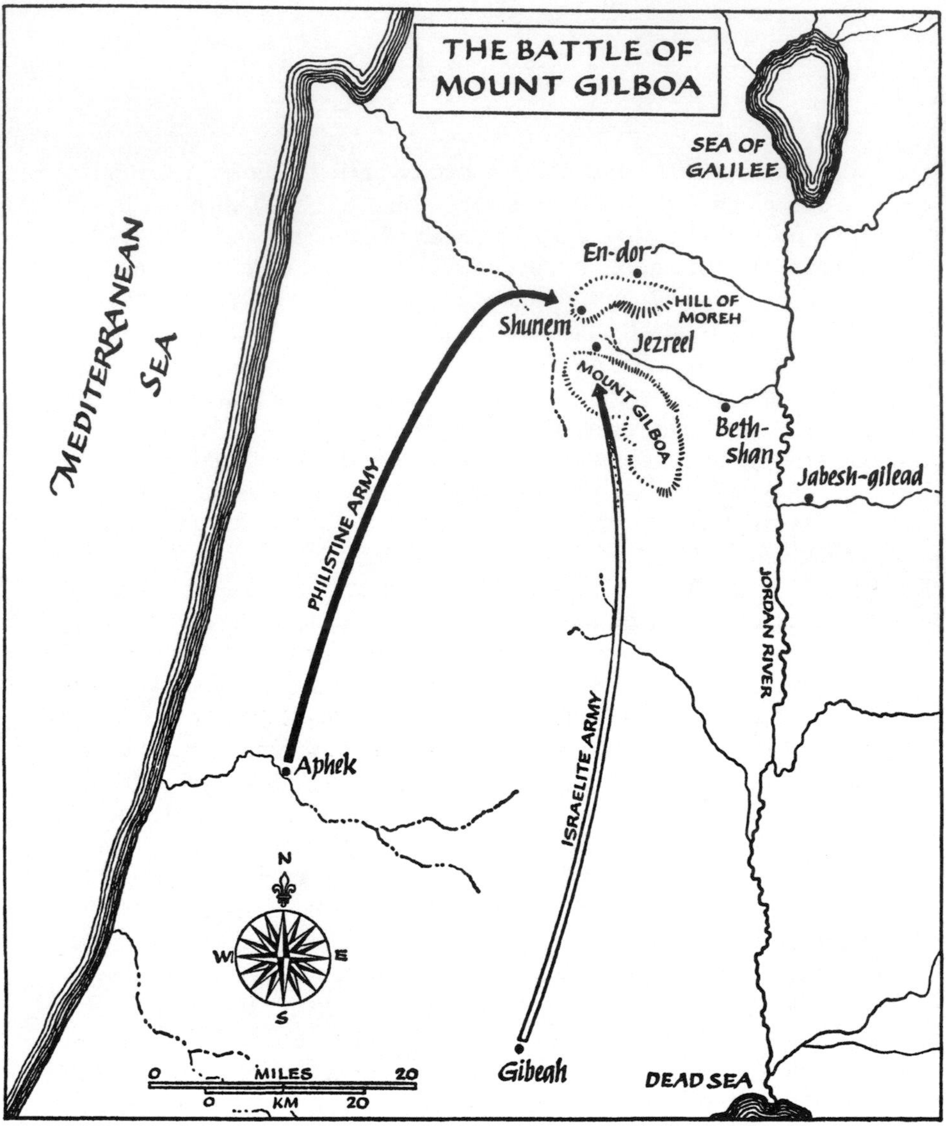
THE BATTLE OF
MOUNT GILBOA
SEA OF
GALILEE
MEDITERRANEAN
SEA
En-dor
HILL OF
MOREH
Shunem
Jezreel
MOUNT GILBOA
Beth-
shan
Jabesh-gilead
PHILISTINE ARMY
ISRAELITE ARMY
JORDAN RIVER
Aphek
N
W
E
S
0
MILES
20
0
KM
20
Gibeah
DEAD SEA

XLV. THE DEATH OF SAUL
(31:1-13)

31 1 The Philistines fought with Israel, and as the men of Israel fled
before [them], falling wounded on Mount Gilboa, 2 the Philistines
overtook Saul and his sons. [They] cut down Jonathan, Abinadab,
and Malchishua, Saul's sons.

3 The battle raged on against Saul. The archers found him with
their bows, and he was wounded in the belly. 4 So [he] said to his
weapon-bearer, "Draw your sword and run me through with it, lest
these uncircumcised come and have their way with me!" But his
weapon-bearer was unwilling, for he was greatly afraid; so Saul took
the sword himself and fell upon it. 5 When his weapon-bearer saw that
Saul was dead, he too fell upon his sword and died with him. 6 So
Saul, his three sons, and his weapon-bearer died together on that day.
7 When the men of Israel who were on the other side of the Valley
(and on the other side of the Jordan) saw that the men of Israel had
fled and that Saul and his sons were dead, they deserted their cities
and fled, and Philistines came and occupied them.

8 On the following day when the Philistines came to strip the slain,
they found Saul and his three sons fallen on Mount Gilboa. 9 They
stripped off his armor and had the good news carried throughout the
land of the Philistines to their idols and people. 10 They deposited his
armor in the house of Astarte; his corpse they nailed to the wall of
Beth-shan.

11 When the inhabitants of Jabesh-gilead heard what the Philistines
had done to Saul, 12 all their warriors arose, traveled all night long,
took Saul's corpse and the corpses of his sons from the wall of Beth-
shan, and brought them to Jabesh, where they burned them. 13 They
took their bones and buried them under the tamarisk in Jabesh and
fasted seven days.

TEXTUAL NOTES

31 1-13. The account of Saul's death that appears here is duplicated in I Chron 10:1-12. The present translation is based upon a text established by comparison of the direct witnesses to I Sam 31:1-13 only; but as the following *Textual Notes* show, the text of the synoptic passage in I Chronicles 10 seems to hark back to a shorter, more primitive version of the account at many points.

1. *fought* We read *nlḥmw* with LXX (*epolemoun*), as in I Chron 10:1 (MT). Here MT has *nlḥmym*. Contrast Hertzberg.

the men of Israel fled MT: *wynsw 'nšy yśr'l*. I Chron 10:1: *wyns 'yš yśr'l.*

Gilboa MT (cf. LXX^{B}): *hglb'*. I Chron 10:1: *glb'* (cf. LXX^{L} in the present passage). So also v 8.

2. *overtook Saul and his sons* So MT (cf. LXX): *wydbqw* (reading *wayyadbīqû* for MT *wayyadbĕqû* [cf. Judg 18:22]; but see GK §53n for parallels to the Masoretic vocalization) . . . *'t š'wl w't bnyw*. I Chron 10:2: *wydbqw . . . 'ḥry š'wl w'ḥry bnyw*, ". . . pursued Saul and his sons closely."

Abinadab So MT (*'byndb*). LXX^{B} has *iōnadab*, "Jonadab," which appears nowhere else as the name of a son of Saul. See also the first *Textual Note* to 14:49.

Saul's sons So MT, I Chron 10:2. LXX$^{(B)}$: "Saul's son."

3. *The archers . . . with their bows* Both MT and LXX have "the archers, *men* with the bow" (*hmwrym 'nšym bqšt*), a conflation of variants. We read *hmwrym bqšt* (as in I Chron 10:3). Cf. Stoebe.

and he was wounded in the belly So LXX^{B}, which reads *kai etraumatisthē eis ta hypochondria*, reflecting *wyḥl* (*wayyēḥel*) *bḥmš* (so Budde; the Hebrew correspondent seems impossible to determine with certainty). MT (cf. I Chron 10:3) has *wyḥl* (*wayyāḥel*) *mhmwrym*, "and he writhed in fear of the archers."

4. *come and have their way with me* MT, LXX^{B}: "come *and run me through* and have their way with me." The expression "and run me through" is out of place here and should be omitted; so I Chron 10:4.

5. *with him* Omitted in I Chron 10:5, probably reflecting an original reading.

6. This verse appears in the various witnesses as follows:

MT:	*wymt š'wl wšlšt bnyw wnš' klyw gm kl 'nšyw*	*bywm hhw' yḥdw*
LXX^{B}:	*wymt š'wl wšlšt bnyw wnš' klyw*	*bywm hhw' yḥdw*
I Chron 10:6:	*wymt š'wl wšlšt bnyw*	*wkl bytw yḥdw mtw.*

Our translation reflects the text of LXX^{B}, to which MT adds *gm kl 'nšyw*, "indeed, all his men," in its list of the slain (so LXX^{AL}). I Chron 10:6 points to an early reading which lacked the expansions *wnš' klyw*, "and his weapon-bearer," and *bywm hhw'*, "on that day"; but I Chron 10:6 itself expands *yhdw*, "together," into a clause reading *wkl bytw yḥdw mtw*, "and all his house together were dead." Thus a primitive form of the present verse, not reconstructible from the evidence of I Sam 31:6 alone, may have been: *wymt š'wl wšlšt bnyw yḥdw*, "So Saul and his three sons died together."

7. *the men of Israel* MT (cf. LXX): *'nšy yśr'l*. I Chron 10:7: *kl 'yš yśr'l*, "all the men of Israel."

who were on the other side of the Valley (and on the other side of the Jordan) I Chron 10:7 has only *'šr b'mq*, "who were in the Valley"; but I Sam 31:7 reads: *'šr b'br h'mq w'šr b'br hyrdn* (so MT; cf. LXX^B). It is possible that *'šr b'br h'mq*, "who were on the other side of the Valley," is original (from this *'šr b'mq* could plausibly arise), but *w'šr b'br hyrdn*, "and on the other side of the Jordan," is unquestionably expansive. The reading of LXX^A, "who were on the other side of the Jordan," is the result of haplography in a Greek MS tradition which originally had the longer reading of MT, LXX^B.

that the men of Israel had fled Though MT and LXX make the subject explicit (*'nšy yśr'l*; cf. I Chron 10:7 [LXX] = *yśr'l*), I Chron 10:7 (MT) has *ky nsw*, "that they had fled," probably a primitive reading.

their cities So LXX (*tas poleis autōn*), I Chron 10:7 (*'ryhm*). MT: *h'rym*, "*the* cities."

and occupied them So MT: *wyšbw bhn*. I Chron 10:7 has *wyšbw bhm*, which can only mean "and dwelt with them."

8. *and his three sons* I Chron 10:8 omits "three," but the expansion is present in all witnesses to I Sam 31:8.

9. *They stripped off his armor* We read *wypšyṭw 't klyw*. In all versions there is reference to Saul's beheading as well, but its variety of form and location show it to be secondary (under the influence of 17:51?). The verses that follow do not assume that Saul was beheaded (except I Chron 10:10; see below). MT: *wykrtw 't r'šw wypšyṭw 't klyw*, "They *cut off his head and* stripped off his armor"; I Chron 10:9: *wypšyṭwhw wyś'w 't r'šw w't klyw*, "They stripped *him and carried off his head and* his armor"; LXX^B: *kai apostrephousin auton kai exedysan ta skeuē autou*, "*And they brought him back and* stripped off his armor," which in LXX^L reads *kai apokephalizousin*, etc., "And they *beheaded* him, etc."

and had the good news carried That is, "and sent to gladden with the tidings": *wyšlḥw . . . lbśr*. This corresponds to the consonantal text of MT, the first part of which, however, should be vocalized *wayyišlĕḥû* in preference to MT *wayšallĕḥû* ("and sent [Saul's head and armor] . . ."). Cf. Driver.

their idols So LXX, I Chron 10:9. We read *'t 'ṣbyhm* as object of *lbśr* (thus lit. "to gladden their idols with the tidings"). MT has *byt 'ṣbyhm*, "*the house of* their idols."

10. *the house of Astarte* We read *byt 'štrt*, probably the original of LXX *to astarteion*, "the Astarteion." MT has *byt 'štrwt*, "the house of Astartes/(foreign) goddesses." I Chron 10:10: *byt 'lhyhm*, "the house of their gods."

his corpse So MT: *gwytw* (cf. LXX). I Chron 10:10: *glgltw*, "his skull/head."

they nailed All versions read *tq'w,* which refers to striking with sharp blows and often specifically to driving nails or pegs, where the object fastened in place is direct object (Gen 31:25, a tent). So there seems to be no need to perpetuate the old suggestion of P. A. de Lagarde (so Wellhausen, Driver) to read *hq'w* (cf. II Sam 21:6,13), "they exposed(?)/crucified(?)," without textual support (cf. Mendenhall, *Tenth Generation,* 117 and n. 50, who proposes a revocalization of *taqĕ'û* as *tōqī'û,* "an archaic 3 pl impf. form with preformative *t-* instead of *y-";* but this does not meet the tense requirements of the sentence and seems less likely still). The present reading accords perfectly with the notice in II Sam 21:12 that Saul's corpse was among those "hung" (*tl*[']*wm*) by the Philistines in Beth-shan plaza.

to the wall of Beth-shan So MT (cf. LXX): *bḥwmt byt šn;* cf. II Sam 21:12. Here (and below) I Chron 10 is different, reading *byt dgwn,* "in the house of Dagon."

11. *the inhabitants of Jabesh-gilead* So MT, LXX. I Chron 10:11: "all Jabesh-gilead."

heard MT, LXX^{AL} add *'lyw,* "of it(?)," or perhaps (= *'lyw*) "concerning it/him." Omit with LXX^{B} (cf. I Chron 10:11).

what MT (cf. LXX): *'t 'šr,* "that which." I Chron 10:11: *'t kl 'šr,* "everything which."

12. *took* MT (cf. LXX): *wyqḥw.* I Chron 10:12: *wyś'w,* "(and) carried off."

corpse . . . corpses MT has *gĕwiyyat . . . gĕwiyyōt,* but the word used in I Chron 10:12, viz. *gûpat . . . gûpōt,* appears nowhere else in the Hebrew Bible and is likely to have been original, replaced in I Sam 31:12 by a more familiar term (under the influence of v 10?) that was graphically quite similar.

of his sons So MT. LXX$^{(B)}$ "of Jonathan, his son" shows correction to II Sam 21:12.

from the wall of Beth-shan Lacking in I Chronicles 10.

and brought them Vocalizing *wyb'w* as *wayyābī'û* in preference to *wayyābō'û,* "and came," as in MT. The object is understood. I Chron 10:2 (cf. LXX^{B} in the present passage) has *wyby'wm,* which eliminates the ambiguity and renders the object explicit.

where they burned them MT: *wyśrpw 'tm šm,* lit. "and they burned them there." Lacking in I Chron 10:12, and the notice probably arose secondarily and late.

13. *They took their bones and buried them* The text reads *wyqḥw 't 'ṣmtyhm wyqbrw* (so MT, LXX). I Chron 10:12b preserves a shorter version: *wyqbrw 'ṣmtyhm,* "They buried their bones."

the tamarisk So MT (cf. LXX): *h'šl.* I Chr 10:12b has *h'lh,* "the terebinth," a far more frequently mentioned tree and therefore less likely to have been original to the account.

NOTES

31 1. *Mount Gilboa.* The site of the Israelite camp; see 28:4 and the NOTE there.

2. On Saul's sons, see the NOTE at 14:49.

4-5. Contrast this account of Saul's death to that given David by the Amalekite in II Sam 1:6-10. The easiest and most popular explanation of the discrepancy is that the Amalekite is lying in an attempt to gain favor with David.

4. *and have their way with me.* Hebrew *wĕhit'allĕlû bî,* on which see the NOTE at 6:6. Saul is afraid of being tortured before he dies.

7. *on the other side of the Valley.* That is, of the Valley of Jezreel. The notice refers to the Israelites who lived N of Jezreel in the southern reaches of the Galilean hills. The additional comment to the effect that Transjordanian people were also involved seems to be secondary (see the *Textual Note*).

10. *the house of Astarte . . . of Beth-shan.* Beth-shan was an old Canaanite city, here under Philistine control, guarding the E end of the Valley of Jezreel (cf. Josh 17:16); the modern site is Tell el-Ḥuṣn, and the name is preserved in that of a nearby village called Beisan. "The house of Astarte" mentioned here evidently refers to the temple of the principal goddess of Beth-shan (since "Astarte" might be used in reference to any foreign goddess, as pointed out in the NOTE at 7:4), whose name seems to have been "Antit" or perhaps "Anat" (cf. G. M. Fitzgerald, "Beth-shean," in *AOTS,* 184-196). To the deposit of Saul's armor in a temple, cf. 21:9-10.

11-13. The people of Jabesh-gilead now find their chance to render kindness for kindness to Saul, who rescued them from disgrace and slavery at the beginning of his career (10:27b - 11:15). But Jabesh will not be the final resting place for the bones of Saul and Jonathan: see the grim story of the Gibeonites' vengeance in II Sam 21:1-4, esp. 12-14.

11. *Jabesh-gilead.* See the NOTE at 10:27b.

13. *the tamarisk.* See the NOTE at 22:6.

COMMENT

The report of Saul's death is remarkable for its lack of finality. To be sure, Saul is gone now—and also Jonathan, his heir—and the Gibeah episode in the history of the Israelite monarchy is over forever. But the new king is not yet on the throne, and an atmosphere of incompleteness surrounds the account of the battle of Mount Gilboa and its aftermath. The larger narrative to which this passage belongs has, as we have seen, two major themes, viz. the demise of Saul and the rise of David. Only the former is completed now. Several more chapters (II Samuel 1-5[7]) will be required to finish the whole (see LITERARY HISTORY in the Introduction).

The details of the present episode contribute to the atmosphere of incompleteness. The political consequences of the Philistine victory are such that northern Israel is left in an intolerable condition of military occupation (v 7). We are forced to look ahead for consolation to the successful and liberating Philistine wars of David described in II Sam 5:17-25. The kindness of the Jabeshites recorded here in vv 11-13 looks back to Saul's liberation of Jabesh in 10:27b-11:15 but also specifically ahead to the account of the Gibeonites' revenge in II Sam 21 (see the NOTE at 11-13 above). But most especially the report made here leaves entirely untouched the question of the succession to the throne of Israel. It is not the answer to this question that is in doubt—David will become king—but the particular way in which the issue will be resolved. This resolution begins when the news of Saul's death is brought to Ziklag in the episode that follows.

INDEX OF AUTHORS

INDEX OF BIBLICAL REFERENCES, INCLUDING APOCRYPHA AND RABBINIC LITERATURE

Versification of English Bibles, where it differs from that of the received Hebrew Text (MT), is indicated in parentheses.

KEY TO THE TEXT

Chapter	*Verses*	*Section* (§)
1	1-28	I
2	1-10	II
2	11-26	III
2	27-36	IV
3	1-21	V
4	1a	V
4	1b-11	VI
4	12-22	VII
5	1-12	VIII
6	1-21	IX
7	1	IX
7	2-17	X
8	1-22	XI
9	1-8	XII
9	9	XII
9	10	XII
9	11-27	XII
10	1-16	XII
10	17-27a	XIII
10	27b	XIV
11	1-15	XIV
12	1-25	XV
13	1	XVI
13	2-15	XVII
13	16-23	XVIII
14	1-23a	XVIII
14	23b-46	XIX
14	47-52	XX
15	1-34	XXI
15	35	XXII
16	1-13	XXII
16	14-23	XXIII
17	1-11	XXIV-A
17	12-31	XXIV-B
17	32-40	XXIV-A
17	41	XXIV-B
17	42-48a	XXIV-A
17	48b	XXIV-B
17	49	XXIV-A
17	50	XXIV-B
17	51-54	XXIV-A
17	55-58	XXIV-B
18	1-5	XXIV-B
18	6-8a	XXV
18	9	XXV
18	10-11	XXIV-B
18	12a	XXV
18	13-16	XXV
18	17-19	XXIV-B
18	20-21a	XXVI
18	22-27	XXVI
18	28-29a	XXVII
18	29b-30	XXIV-B
19	1-7	XXVII
19	8-17	XXVIII
19	18-24	XXIX
20	1-42	XXX
21	1	XXX
21	2-10	XXXI
21	11-16	XXXII
22	1-5	XXXII
22	6-23	XXXIII
23	1-13	XXXIV
23	14-18	XXXV
23	19-28	XXXVI
24	1	XXXVI
24	2-23	XXXVII
25	1	XXXVIII
25	2-25	XXXIX
25	26	XXXIX
25	27-41	XXXIX
25	42-44	XXXIX
26	1-25	XL
27	1-12	XLI
28	1-2	XLI
28	3-25	XLII
29	1-11	XLIII
30	1-31	XLIV
31	1-13	XLV